Afro-Latino Voices

Narratives from the Early Modern Ibero-Atlantic World, 1550–1812

To Lynn Mostoller, companion in life and love
—K.J.M.

To Natalia Sisa Garofalo-Iberico, my dear daughter
—L.J.G.

Afro-Latino Voices

Narratives from the
Early Modern Ibero-Atlantic World, 1550–1812

Edited by
Kathryn Joy McKnight
and
Leo J. Garofalo

Hackett Publishing Company, Inc.
Indianapolis/Cambridge

Printed in the United States of America
14 13 12 11 10 09 1 2 3 4 5 6 7

For further information, please address:
Hackett Publishing Company, Inc.
P.O. Box 44937
Indianapolis, IN 46244-0937
www.hackettpublishing.com

Cover design by Abigail Coyle
Text design by Meera Dash
Composition by Agnew's, Inc.
Printed at Sheridan Books

Maps 1–6, 8, 12, 14, and 15 by David E. Chandler. Map 7: From "Caught between Rivals: The Spanish-African Maroon Competition for Captive Labor in the Region of Esmeraldas during the Late Sixteenth and Early Seventeenth Centuries" by Charles Beatty-Medina in *The Americas* 63.1 (2006): 113–36. Courtesy of Charles Beatty-Medina. Map 9: Courtesy of the University of Texas Libraries, The University of Texas at Austin. Map 11: From María Elena Díaz, *The Virgin, the King, and the Royal Slaves of El Cobre: Negotiating Freedom in Colonial Cuba, 1670–1780.* Copyright © 2000 by the Board of Trustees of the Leland Stanford Jr. University. All rights reserved. Used with the permission of Stanford University Press, www.sup.org. Map 13: Reprinted with permission from *Planting Rice and Harvesting Slaves* by Walter Hawthorne. Copyright © 2003 by Walter Hawthorne. Published by Heinemann, Portsmouth, NH. All rights reserved.

Library of Congress Cataloging-in-Publication Data

Afro-Latino voices : narratives from the early modern Ibero-Atlantic world, 1550–1812 / edited by Kathryn Joy McKnight and Leo J. Garofalo.
p. cm.
Includes bibliographical references and index.
ISBN 978-0-87220-993-0 (pbk.) — ISBN 978-0-87220-994-7 (cloth)
1. African diaspora—History—sources. 2. Africans—Latin America—History—Sources. 3. Africans—Latin America—Social life and customs—Sources. 4. Spain—Colonies—America—History—Sources. 5. Portugal—Colonies—America—History—Sources. I. McKnight, Kathryn Joy, 1961– II. Garofalo, Leo.
DT16.5.A37 2009
305.897'080903—dc22 2009029474

The paper used in this publication meets the minimum requirements of American National Standard for Information Sciences—Permanence of Paper for Printed Library Materials, ANSI Z39.48-1984

∞

Contents

Part III: Religious Beliefs and Practices

Part IV: Claiming and Defending Rights

List of Maps

Acknowledgments

Many people contributed to this collaborative project. We express our thanks here knowing that we will forget someone. Most importantly, we thank the contributors whose names appear in the table of contents for their excitement and passion for this project, their words of encouragement, their dedication to carrying this through despite many individual setbacks and even tragedies, and their patience with our endless emails, multiple edits, and periods of silence as the sometimes sorrowful challenges of our own lives put the book on a back burner. We thank Joseph P. Sánchez, Angelica Sánchez-Clark, Larry D. Miller, and Luis Madureira for their careful translations of some of the documents. And we recognize with great appreciation the ways in which our own many conversations have enriched our vision of the project and enhanced the final version of the book.

This project would not have gotten off the ground without the generous and inspiring guidance of Joseph C. Miller in his 2003 National Endowment for the Humanities (NEH) summer seminar at the University of Virginia, "Roots: African Dimensions of the History and Culture of the Americas (through the Transatlantic Slave Trade)." All the members of "Roots" 2003 led Kathryn McKnight to believe that this project was possible and that there were readers and, especially, teachers waiting for it.

Students at the University of New Mexico (UNM) test-drove some of the materials and helped shape their eventual presentation in this volume. Several colleagues read our proposal and made insightful recommendations, including Diana Rebolledo, James Sweet, and members of the Colonial Studies Working Group at UNM, especially Celia López-Chávez and Cynthia Radding. The enthusiasm and suggestions of the manuscript readers selected by Hackett also buoyed and guided us. The long hours of hard work that Andrés Sabogal put into the project in its final months were indispensable, especially in pulling together the glossary, maps, and suggestions for films and music to teach alongside the texts. It has been a pleasure working with everyone at Hackett, especially Rick Todhunter, who was willing to take a leap of faith on our proposal for a trilingual edition, when other presses were not, and Meera Dash, who was so helpful and flexible at every step of the process.

No book is written without financial support. We thank the NEH for the summer seminar stipend, UNM for sabbatical support, the Latin American and Iberian Institute at UNM for funding a graduate assistant who worked on the project, the UNM Research Allocation Committee, the Feminist Research Institute, and Connecticut College for grants that supported some of the translations in the volume.

Finally, we thank our families and friends who gave us support throughout, especially during those times when the book came before almost everything else. Thanks especially to Lynn Mostoller for her patience and for always seeing another possibility and to Yony for laughing when it mattered. Natalia Sisa brought joy and humor to both editing and parenting.

Introduction

Recovering Afro-Latino Voices from the Early Modern Ibero-Atlantic World

African and African-descent peoples played central roles in building Spanish and Portuguese empires and their American colonies from the 1500s through the 1800s. They sailed ships, built infrastructure, produced crops and material goods, provided services, shaped societies, and molded cultural attitudes, beliefs, and expressions; yet their voices have been largely barred from the published record. We know of their lives from recent historical scholarship and through historical and literary works of the period in which primarily European authors represent them, more often than not distorting their voices and experiences.

During the past fifteen years, scholars made greater efforts to unearth and publish Afro-Latino voices as recorded more directly in documentary narratives, but the sources are still scattered and few.[1] *Afro-Latino Voices* offers for the first time a book-length collection of narratives of people of African descent in the early modern Ibero-Atlantic world.

Although some Afro-Latinos in the early modern world did read and write and many engaged with literate culture, almost none composed texts that were considered publishable at the time. Consequently, the written sources in which their voices survive are primarily juridical, ecclesiastical, and administrative documents located in the archives of Europe and Latin America. This collection includes judicial inquiries, letters, last wills and testaments, petitions, trial proceedings, written dialogue, and as-told-to biography. In these texts, people of African descent speak about war and politics; they define and support their families and communities; they reveal a broad gamut of spiritual beliefs and practices; and they claim and defend their rights against the cruelties of enslavement and the discrimination of a racialized society.

The Afro-Latino stories in this collection help break down assumptions, stereotypes, and overgeneralizations that continue to limit our understanding of the lives of people of African descent and how they themselves imagined their lives. These narratives counteract the still prevalent myth of Ibero-Atlantic blacks as primarily enslaved, working on plantations in Brazil and the Caribbean, and excluded from determining the course of their own lives.

These stories highlight the complexity of experiences and identities of a population that was enslaved, free, and slave owning, both urban and rural, and highly resourceful in its interactions with people of all ethnic, racial, and social types. They show that African-descent peoples were often divided by national origin, slave vs. free status, occupation, and political and familial relationships but that they also banded together for mutual support, for collective action, and to build communities.

[1] The section Additional Publications of Afro-Latino Voices at the end of the Bibliography is indicative of the lack of such sources.

The Afro-Latinos in this volume formed and exercised control within religious societies, autonomous communities, and states. They used the languages, institutions, and literate practices of the Ibero-colonial enterprise to improve their own situations. Their stories reveal how they transformed their lives as they moved between places, cultures, and historical moments. They help dispel that "absolute sense of ethnic difference" about which Paul Gilroy writes in *The Black Atlantic* (3) by showing how, in their daily lives, people of African descent participated in racially diverse social circles and often adopted and adapted European and indigenous American beliefs, practices, and elements of identity. Although these stories cannot represent the full range of black experiences and voices in the Ibero-Atlantic, they speak strongly to its diversity.

This book supports the reintegration of a black Ibero-Atlantic world broken apart by institutional structures that separate history, literatures, and cultures into distinct national frameworks and divide Africa from Europe and from the Americas. With Paul Gilroy, we see a black Atlantic as a space across which people moved back and forth, taking with them ideas, beliefs, practices, and artifacts in a rich international and transcultural exchange.

This volume brings together narratives from Kongo and Ndongo in Central Africa, Spain and Portugal in Europe, and Cuba, Puerto Rico, Brazil, Río de la Plata, Peru, Ecuador, Panama, the New Kingdom of Granada, and New Spain in the Ibero-American colonies. By gathering voices from around the Ibero-Atlantic, we ask readers to stretch beyond the national boundaries with which they are familiar to see cultural and historical connections that the academy's national divisions have dimmed or erased.

The list of places above shows, however, that the book does not achieve a full integration of the black Atlantic. The restriction of sources to the Ibero-Atlantic world is motivated by the uncomfortable tension we experience working and teaching within institutional parameters and the very real considerations of current academic curricula and readerships. We hope that by stretching readers past some traditional national and geographic boundaries, this book will invite them to take up texts from the Francophone Caribbean and Anglo-America, among others. The other limitation in the book's parameters that requires explanation is that of the time frame we have chosen: the mid-sixteenth to the early nineteenth centuries. These years roughly correspond to the Iberian colonial control of the Americas and to the historical period that suffers perhaps the greatest need for published source texts of Afro-Latino voices.[2]

We have envisioned this book for the needs of our own students, both undergraduate and graduate. Although the sources are valuable to scholars as an introduction to this area of study, our presentation is aimed at novice readers of early modern texts. Rather than offer paleographic transcriptions more appropriate for scholarly inquiry, we have edited the documents for inexperienced readers, as we explain below.

We have designed the anthology as a coming together of two disciplinary perspectives—literary and historical studies—though the book fills a void in a much broader range of fields, including Latin American studies, African diaspora studies, black stud-

[2] In the Additional Publications section of the Bibliography, we provide a list of those late-eighteenth- and early-nineteenth-century sources available in published form.

ies, cultural studies, ethnic and race studies, gender and women studies, and anthropology. The editors and contributors teach and research in the fields of Latin American and African history, Spanish-American and *Luso-Brazilian* literature, African American studies, and gender studies. All these perspectives are evident in the introductions to the documents, where contributors contextualize the narratives and invite a variety of approaches to their reading.

We present the documents in the original languages of Spanish and Portuguese because so much is lost in any translation; but to make them accessible to a broader audience, we provide English translations. Although the presentation of original languages most obviously responds to the need for teaching materials in departments of Spanish and Portuguese, it also supports the study of languages across the curriculum.

The bilingual facing-page publication allows students specializing in history and other disciplinary approaches to the Ibero-Atlantic world the opportunity to explore the challenges of primary text research and obtain some preparatory training for carrying out archival research. For students of literature, the anthology responds to the Modern Language Association's recent call for departments of languages and literatures to develop interdisciplinary curricula that focus not only on literature but also, more broadly, on cultural narratives.

The Book's Thematic Organization

The narratives are grouped thematically in four parts titled "Politics and War," "Families and Communities," "Religious Beliefs and Practices," and "Claiming and Defending Rights." Within each part, the narratives are in chronological order. These groupings express a sense of the different stages and aspects of the African experience in the Ibero-Atlantic world, even though they do not represent a strict chronological evolution.

Part I begins the volume with autonomous African political organizations and moves through Central African slave wars to the early armed conflicts between *Maroons* and European colonizers in the Americas. Parts II and III look at the rebuilding of social organizations and belief systems in the Americas by African-descent communities after the calamities of the *Middle Passage.* Part IV shows experiences of cultural integration in which Afro-Latino subjects draw on their knowledge of Iberian law to claim and defend their rights. These four themes are only a few of the many that enrich a consideration of both the common experiences and worldviews of these African diasporic groups and individuals and their great diversity. Other thematic groupings might include the following:

Afro-Latino responses to European expansion, imperialism, and colonization: Chapters 1, 2, 3, 5, 8, 12, 18
Gendered relationships and their representation: Chapters 3, 5, 6, 7, 9, 11, 13, 14, 16
Inheritance: Chapters 6, 7, 9, 14
Maroon communities: Chapters 2, 5
Racial, ethnic, and national identity: all chapters
Self-governance: Chapters 1, 2, 3, 5, 8, 10, 14
Slavery, slave ownership, *manumission,* and *coartación:* Chapters 3, 5, 7, 8, 9, 13, 15, 16, 17

Travel and movement: Chapters 4, 9, 11, 12, 13, 15, 18
Violence: Chapters 2, 3, 5, 8, 15, 16, 17

African Demographics in the Ibero-Atlantic World

The Atlantic slave trade began to take shape in the early fifteenth century with Portuguese traders and raiders seeking new trade routes and claiming territories for Portugal south along the West African coast. During this first century, the Portuguese merchants used their seafaring strength to establish sea routes along the coast and to insert themselves into land-based West African trade networks. They acted primarily as intermediaries and bought and sold kola nuts, cattle, salt, ivory, gold, and enslaved people, depending on African traders for goods and people.

The first European sales of enslaved people captured or purchased by Iberians in sub-Saharan Africa took place after a Portuguese raid in 1444 and established important precedents for all subsequent European participation in the Atlantic slave trade: Traders operated with royal license; they paid a significant portion of the profit as a tax to the state (one fifth in Portugal and Spain); and they deployed a series of justifications for enslavement and sale, ranging from opportunity and economic need for commerce and labor to religious and moral motives such as eradicating paganism and winning converts to Christianity before people could be converted to Islam. In Iberia, peasants farmed the land; so people brought to Europe as slaves worked primarily in domestic and urban labor as they would initially in Spanish America.

In the sixteenth century, Portuguese, Italian, and Spanish merchants began to produce sugar on Madeira, the Canaries, Cape Verde, *São Tomé,* and Príncipe using enslaved islanders and then, increasingly, slaves from Africa, thus establishing the association of coerced labor and the production of sugar and other plantation crops that would be extended to the Americas. In this process and in the era of booming trade that it ushered in, Iberian merchants transported an estimated 5.7 million people to Europe and the Americas (mostly to the Americas) out of an estimated total of 12 million people forced into slavery in the African diaspora. These basic elements characterized the slave trade until the middle of the nineteenth century.

The African people sold as slaves in 1444 before the gates of the Portuguese port of Lagos were from many ethnic groups, some having already lived as slaves in Africa and others having been captured in Iberian raids and through trade. Edging out their Castilian competitors, the Portuguese built diplomatic and trading relationships with West and Central Africans, especially with the Kgola and Kongo peoples. Africans initially sold criminals and prisoners captured in war to the Europeans, but droughts in the 1570s created new demographic pressures and opportunities for Europeans to force more people into bondage.

Economic and political gain pushed this destructive dynamic of enslavement into Africa's interior. People were frequently sold and resold during the long and dangerous march to the sea, where African merchants organized them into warehouses for purchase and transportation overseas by the Europeans. Many perished before reaching European vessels waiting at ports arrayed along the coast. To buy and embark these

slaves, the Portuguese built fortified bases at Arguim and *Elmina* (Ghana). The Dutch captured *Elmina* in the seventeenth century.

The Portuguese also established a trading center and holding pens in Central Africa at Luanda (*Angola*). In the nineteenth century, Brazilian traders developed a port further south at *Benguela* (*Angola*). In these and many other coastal enclaves and trading centers, mixed Euro-African communities (complete with blended families, languages, and religions) developed from the late 1400s on, both as a product of the diaspora and to facilitate the expansion of the traffic in human beings.

The greatest motors driving the enslavement and sale of Africans were the demand for workers on tropical plantations and lowland gold and diamond mines in the Americas and the profits that could be made supplying coerced laborers. Small numbers of Africans and Afro-Iberians accompanied Spanish explorers and conquistadors to the Caribbean, Mexico, and Peru in the 1490s and early 1500s. Spanish and Italian entrepreneurs brought larger numbers when they introduced sugar plantations on the island of Hispaniola and then in Mexico, Venezuela, and Peru in the 1520s and 1530s.

Between this time and 1600, the Portuguese and Italians replicated in northeastern Brazil the Atlantic island sugar industry based on slave labor. In both the Caribbean and Brazil, planters depended on indigenous peoples as laborers until disease, abuse, and flight decimated this native workforce. Starting in the 1560s, the Portuguese began importing Africans to Bahia and Pernambuco. Brazil received half a million Africans during the 1600s and 1.7 million during the 1700s; in all, approximately 2.5 million Africans were imported by 1800.

Approximately one million Africans arrived in Spanish America during the same period. In both regions, enslaved Africans and their descendants grew sugar, coffee, tobacco, cacao, and cotton for export and extracted precious metals and stones from rainforest regions. Amerindians dominated the highland silver and gold mines of Mexico and Peru, but gold rushes in hot lowlands in the Pacific coastal regions of Colombia and Minas Gerais and Goiás in Brazil (where diamonds were also found) relied almost exclusively on African slave labor organized into work gangs (Klein, 1–46).

As Ibero-American economies developed, slaves and free blacks participated alongside other workers in a wide variety of economic activities. They worked in transportation as muleteers, porters, and stevedores. They labored in urban occupations such as construction and manufacturing, producing furniture, clothing, glass, iron, and ships. They also worked in artisans' workshops to make leather goods, shoes, clothing, metal items, and so forth. Some even rose through the ranks of apprentices and journeymen to become master artisans in the skilled trades and to exercise influence in guilds and even own slaves themselves. Bakeries also utilized many black slaves in the cities.

From the very beginning of the colonial period, and even before that in Europe, Portuguese and Spanish elites and even more middling sectors of artisans, professionals, and traders valued the domestic service of black slaves and the status owning slaves bestowed. In the Americas, slave servants became ubiquitous in major slave ports such as Bahia, Rio de Janeiro, Havana, Cartagena, and Buenos Aires and in major cities from Mexico in North America to Quito, Lima, and La Paz in South America. Black

servants—enslaved and free—went to market, cooked and cleaned, nursed and raised children, and cared for horses and their masters in a thousand different ways.

Beyond the household, black men, women, and children in urban areas engaged extensively in street vending of all sorts as well as the production and public sale of food and drink. Their importance and successes in these urban occupations and in domestic service meant that slaves and their descendants often constituted a visible and significant presence in the cities and mining centers in regions of Mesoamerica and the Andes, which were populated primarily by indigenous peoples. Even in specific rural areas dedicated primarily to plantation agriculture or food production for local consumption in otherwise indigenous zones, black people could dominate the labor force, as in the subregions of Guerrero in Mexico and Ica in coastal Peru.

Mortality was high among slaves, and the importation of slaves declined in nonplantation regions after the mid-1700s, so it is easy to forget that more Africans than Europeans arrived to places like the Andes and created vibrant and diverse communities during the colonial era. In fact, cities such as Lima, the capital of the Peruvian viceroyalty, had an African and African-descent majority or near majority from at least 1614 until 1800. An export orientation and insufficient indigenous labor transformed Brazil, Venezuela, and—in the second half of the 1700s—Cuba and Puerto Rico into the most important centers of slavery and the heartlands of colonial Afro-Latin America.

The lack of indigenous workers and the inability of the enslaved population to reproduce itself guaranteed a steady flow of people from Africa. Harsh and brutal work and living conditions, malnourishment, and a sexual imbalance created by planters favoring the importation of men all militated against enslaved people bearing and raising children past infancy and childhood to adulthood. Despite considerable hardships, Africans and Afro-Latin Americans formed free and slave families; in some communities, they developed African-based cultures, and in others they became part of neighborhoods, guilds, religious brotherhoods, and the other institutions and activities that characterized life for all colonial subjects.

In some parishes and towns, blacks came to run their own artisan associations, confraternities, local town councils, and marketplaces. In others, blacks participated alongside others in the workplace, local governance, negotiation with authorities, and forms of worship. The appearance of free individuals and their growth into the majority of the black population in many areas was possible because Spanish and, to a lesser extent, Portuguese law permitted slaves to buy their own freedom or that of family members and to use the courts to secure freedom in the case of extreme abuse or notorious sexual impropriety by masters.

People saved from their earnings and worked on the side to purchase freedom. If owners resisted, they could sometimes be compelled in Spanish courts to accept a fair price for freedom. Likewise, especially abusive slave owners might be legally compelled to free a slave they had savaged or raped. More rarely, owners freed slaves as a gift, a negotiated reward, or in recognition of paternity. In short, despite the difficulties, Afro-Latino communities formed and included quite a few free members who built up their numbers over time.

Free communities in Afro-Latin America also appeared because slaves resisted slavery through flight and force of arms. Runaway or *cimarrón* communities were usually quite small, numbering a few dozens of escapees. Typically they replenished their numbers with other runaways or by seizing people to bring them to freedom. Hiding in inaccessible locations like marshes, mountainsides, or tropical forests, these groups usually found it hard to last for more than a few years or to form self-sustaining communities. They usually survived by trading with and raiding the farms, haciendas (landed estates), Indian villages, and fishing communities nearby. In a few cases, larger and long-lasting *palenques* or *quilombos* formed, which brought together people from different ethnic groups who reconstituted aspects of African life and culture or invented new ones and subsisted through their own agricultural activities as well as trade with outsiders.

These larger *Maroon* communities tended to be located farther from colonial centers and excited considerable anxiety and hostility among colonial authorities, even though they proved impossible to completely eradicate and occasionally secured from the colonial state a right to exist as free towns. A few such communities endure to the present day in Mexico, Panama, Colombia, Suriname, Ecuador, and Brazil. Free and enslaved blacks also banded together in urban mutual aid societies, often within the structure of lay Catholic religious confraternities. These societies often organized along lines of ethnic identity, whether those bonds were formed in the African communities of origin or after enslavement.

Historical Protagonists and Questions of Identity

This book offers an opportunity to meet a few of the individual protagonists who participated in creating the history and the cultures of the diverse African communities in the Ibero-Atlantic world. The focus of the collection is on slave and free black agency understood as the actions people took against the structural and circumstantial forces arrayed against them. Actions ranged from flight and rebellion to more subtle forms of response such as negotiation with owners, altering the speed of work, or appealing to royal courts or Church authorities. At times the protagonists succeeded, at other times they failed. Most often, they created complicated and contradictory results that affected how slavery and colonial society functioned in small ways.

To capture some sense of the variety of these actions and their articulation by the protagonists themselves, this collection ranges over four continents—Africa, Europe, North America, and South America—highlighting the transatlantic nature of the legacy of the diaspora and its wide-ranging impact beyond the Americas. The documents also represent three standard historical periods that characterize the Iberian enterprise of colonialism: exploration and conquest, mid-colonial or mature colonial society, and the late colonial age of reform and revolution.

Happily, several monographs extensively treat some of the areas that fall outside this volume's selective sampling. Within the Americas, the range of documents offers an overview of the kinds of places Africans and Afro-Americans lived and worked. To this end, colonial societies in the Caribbean, Mexico, and South America are included,

along with accounts from runaway (*Maroon*) communities and the views from both the rural and urban environments these protagonists inhabited. Likewise, both enslaved and free blacks find a place in the volume.

The interaction of these two legal statuses is particularly significant for Ibero-America and in many of the cases presented. Children appear infrequently in this collection, in part because of the difficulties youth adds to finding ways to articulate and record a voice. The collection draws together a broad sampling of young, middle-aged, and older adults and of men and women. A number of the occupations typical of Africans in the Iberian world can be viewed in these chapters; especially significant is the attention to religious, ritual, or spiritual expression and to economic activity. Again, the richness of African life in the Americas means that many occupations receive less attention, such as militiamen, surgeons/barbers, and midwives.

To understand the protagonists in this book, it is important to recognize and problematize the ethnic and racial naming and labeling employed inside and outside Africa in the diaspora. During the 1600s, enslaved Africans came primarily from the Atlantic coast of West Africa, Congo, and *Angola.* As demand intensified, trade routes reached farther into Central Africa but still remained closer to the coast in West Africa, with Biafra (Nigeria) leading the way in numbers. By 1800, Mozambique saw Portuguese and African slave traders linked to the Atlantic, where none had operated before. This regional scope of the trade created great diversity among Africans in the Americas. Although ethnic homogeneity was never achieved, some concentrations were discernable. For example, Rio de Janeiro connected to Congo and *Angola* held more speakers of Bantu languages than any other region; but West Africans and Mozambicans were also present. Bahia traded more with West Africa (three quarters of its slaves) than with Congo and *Angola* (one quarter). Between 1790 and 1806, Buenos Aires held 4,800 slaves from Mozambique, 4,000 from West Africa, and 2,700 from Congo and West Africa (Andrews, 20).

The point of embarkation proved notoriously unreliable for establishing accurate ethnic identification. In addition, many of the ethnic categories employed by traders and later scholars working with their records are in reality slave trade labels that provided a convenient, if inaccurate, shorthand for recording origin. These labels might suggest an affinity that did not exist, even if people were from the same region or the same linguistic group or boarded a ship in the same port.

African ethnicities did exist, however, as did complex histories of interaction and shifting organization among African polities. Both created bonds, but also divisions; and these divisions proved key to the success and longevity of the slave trade and explain many of the obstacles to creating African solidarity against the European slave trade and bondage in the Americas. In the Americas, people of African descent also divided themselves into *naciones* (nations). The word *nación* could refer to a place of birth or African origin, but it could also be a name imposed by European slave traders determined by the place of enslavement.

At times, an individual or a small group might adopt or choose to associate with a new ethnicity in order to fit in with a locally dominant group or create the links that allowed a person to survive the *Middle Passage* and life in the Americas. So, although a person's *nación* is a problematic marker of identity, *naciones* did function in important

ways to organize black communities in Ibero-America and foster the preservation and re-creation of African cultural and social practices. Thus, all use of *ethnonyms* or names that apparently refer to ethnic identity must be interpreted with care.

Europeans used other important racial labels to categorize Afro-Latinos. One important distinction for both slaves and owners was that between *bozal,* or African-born, and *criollo,* or American-born. Generally speaking, *bozales* possessed little or no knowledge of European or local indigenous languages, often were not baptized, and had little understanding of Catholicism. Not surprisingly, they usually suffered lower colonial status, worse work assignments, and poorer treatment.

The term *ladino* could be used to highlight Christian status and a person's knowledge of Spanish and/or Portuguese even when that individual was not born in the Americas. Furthermore, in the Americas, individuals were identified as belonging to a certain *casta* or caste.[3] Such identities were constructed partly through racial markers or phenotype such as facial features, skin color, and hair characteristics. But they also depended on perceptions of family history, language, economic success, occupation, religious practice, dress, cultural practices, residence, and marriage partnership to determine a person's legal status or local reputation.

The most common color terms used were *mulato, zambo,* and *mestizo,* suggesting mixed African and European, indigenous and African, and European and indigenous parentage, respectively. In each case, these identity labels were combined with other markers and sometimes replaced with labels that suggested a finer distinction of the lineage. In other words, race and ethnicity operated as social constructions rooted in a particular place at a particular historical moment.

Voice and Mediation

This book claims to present "voices," but what is voice and how is it manifested in these narratives? The word "voice" appears to be deceptively straightforward, but the circumstances within which these narratives were produced make the voices they contain challenging to hear. Nevertheless, by using this term, we claim to offer the reader access to Afro-Latinos' words and thoughts. We even assert that these stories undo some of the inherent distortion of their representation in the chronicles and histories of European, *mestizo,* and Amerindian authors.

And yet, in almost all the narratives in this book, European scribes have recorded the Afro-Latino voices, not with the word-for-word transcription enabled by modern recording devices, but as colonial officials intent on interpreting the speaker's words from within their own European ideological and discursive worldview. These are not stories that Afro-Latinos told within their own communities, not oral traditions that pass on cultural values and foster group identity. Such oral traditions have survived, but they, too, present complex issues of immediacy, as they have undergone the transformations of oral transmission across centuries (see, for example, Lienhard, "Padrões"). Rather, the voices in this anthology are mostly narratives told within the

[3] José Ramón Jouve-Martín contributed to the discussions of *nación* and *casta* in this Introduction.

bureaucratic systems of a European colonial world, recorded by European-educated scribes, often under circumstances of duress in which the recorded narrative contributed to life-changing decisions exercised against the speaker. That is, they are molded and transformed by layers of mediation and circumstance often outside the ordinary context of daily life.

How is it, then, that Afro-Latino voices speak in these texts? To hear these voices through the static of circumstance and mediation, we invite you to bear in mind two sets of issues. First, consider conceptions of voice, speech, and utterance that will help you identify those ways in which speakers have exercised control over their narratives, despite the molding of their exact words into bureaucratic formulas. Second, seek to understand the types of mediation that have affected the voice in these narratives, to better identify the lines between which you might read the voices. By giving attention to what constitutes voice and narrative perspective, and with a knowledge of the social relationships and circumstances in which each narrative was spoken, we argue that these highly mediated documents allow modern readers to approach the voices of these distant speakers and glimpse the ways in which Afro-Latinos saw, understood, and presented themselves and their worldviews in the early modern Ibero-Atlantic world.

We ask you to read these documents as rhetorical and symbolic texts rather than as straightforward sources of historical information. Some students of history or social sciences may find it uncomfortable to move from a search for what "really happened" and what people "really believed" to an examination of how historical actors presented that reality, but history as a discipline has already made that move with the New Philology (see Restall) and an appreciation for the "content of the form" (see White).

Some students of literature may feel at a loss as to where to begin and what tools to use to analyze such "nonliterary" texts, but as cultural studies' approaches have become more established in the literary corner of the academy, this discipline, too, has brought together literary texts with other cultural representations. For all readers, the introductions to each document provide some clues for how to proceed in reading these documents as rhetorical and symbolic texts.

The nineteenth-century Romantic understanding of voice as the individual's expression to the world of an inner vision still informs the way many readers understand voice in a text. But, although the narratives of this collection do express a vision or worldview, contemporary critical theory sees such a vision as informed by both individual and social experiences. By studying the experiences and symbolic worlds of the communities into which the speakers were born and in which they lived, as well as the symbolic worlds of those to whom they speak, you will be better able to sort out the worldviews they express.

In the black Atlantic, in the age of the slave trade and Iberian empire building, voice had a particular quality. Afro-Latinos spoke with a "double consciousness," that is, they saw themselves from within their own cultural worldview as well as from the perspective of the European colonizer and slave society (Gilroy, 1). So, you will find that even those perspectives that can be identified with the Afro-Latino speakers and their communities do not separate them absolutely or essentially from their European or Euro-American interlocutors. Here, several theoretical paradigms can be useful for

understanding the relationship of these voices to their diverse contexts, including *transculturation,* hybridity, and cultural diglossia.[4]

Finally, it is important to understand that any voice and the identity it constructs are not essential or fixed qualities of a person or culture, but rather performances that are fluid and changing, as they respond to social structures, relationships, and circumstances (Butler, 177). Every voice that speaks in this book does so under particular circumstances among individuals whose relationships are molded by relative access to power and by specific interests and aims.[5] As you read the narratives, consider how the speakers mold their voices and stories in response to their audience and circumstances. You will find help in building this contextual understanding in both the introductions to each document and the bibliographies of suggested contextual materials that correspond to each chapter.

So far, we have considered how the Afro-Latino speakers shaped their own words. These words have also been modified after they were spoken by at least three processes of writing. First, the European scribe transcribed the speaker's utterance into an early modern (often bureaucratic) genre. Second, the contributors to this volume prepared that transcription for publication. Third, the contributors translated the transcription from Spanish or Portuguese to English. Just as the conventions of poetry, narrative, drama, or theater affect the meaning that a literary text produces, so too, the conventions of Ibero-Atlantic documentary genres shape the narratives in this volume. Understanding those genres will help you as a reader interpret their meanings and distinguish the speakers' voices from the forms and worldviews of these bureaucratic genres.

The genres in this volume include the following:

Official inquests in both criminal and civil causes: Chapters 1, 5, 6, 10, 12, 17
Petitions: Chapters 2, 8 16, 18
Personal and official letters, including denunciations, negotiation, and diplomacy: Chapters 2, 3, 8
Last wills and testaments: Chapters 6, 7, 9
Records of inquisition trials: Chapters 11, 15
One as-told-to hagiographic biography: Chapter 13
One formal dialogue: Chapter 14

These genres were produced by scribes, notaries, monks, and priests—men trained in the writing of bureaucratic or ecclesiastic forms and discourses. As they recorded the voices of the Afro-Latino speakers, they melded their words and narrative forms with bureaucratic conventions, which carry their own cultural and ideological content. In documents such as court and inquisition testimonies, the scribes transformed the speaker's first-person testimony into a third-person—he said or she said—narrative.

In wills and petitions, the dominant "I" represents a partial fiction as a scribe molds the testator or petitioner's wishes into conventional ecclesiastical or bureaucratic discourses. Some narratives underwent another layer of transformation as the speakers

[4] See Ortiz (86), Rama, García Canclini, and Lienhard ("De mestizajes"), respectively.

[5] Martin Lienhard sets out a framework for studying the forces that mold witness testimony by captured *Maroons* in "Una tierra sin amos."

used an African language that was translated by a *ladino* translator. The chapter introductions offer clues to interpreting the ways in which each documentary genre mediates the speaker's voice.[6]

Finally, the contributors to these volumes have interpreted these documents as they have sought to make them more readable for you. They have modernized spelling and added punctuation in ways that sometimes require fixing one interpretation in preference over another. They have often omitted repetitive bureaucratic language, particularly the "saids" and "aforesaids" (*dichos*); they have resolved abbreviations—for example, replacing the standard *dhos* with *dichos;* and they have replaced spelled-out numbers with numerals, as in "1634" for "mil y seiscientos y treinta y cuatro." They have added explanatory headings and clarifications in brackets [ ]. In their translations, they have sought a conservative rather than fluid rendition of the original; yet no linguistic utterance in one language has an exact equivalent in another, and thus every translation is an interpretation.

Given these numerous layers of mediation, you may wonder whether these documents do provide access to Afro-Latino voices; yet we insist that they can. As you read, think of how the symbolic systems and genres of speaker and addressee shape the voice and narrative, and consider the ways in which worldview and agency might survive the mediation of the scribes and editors. Although original words are mostly lost, the speakers' choice of what they relate and in what order they present it often survives. At times speakers offer an "excess" of information, recounting something that is not required by interrogation or genre; these excesses give clues to voice and agency.

Particular ways of naming and describing other people or specific uses of symbolic language stand out as more likely to be those of the speaker than of the scribe. When more than one witness speaks about the same event, the similarities and differences among their testimonies provide clues to what belongs to bureaucratic mediation and what belongs to a speaker's worldview. Occasionally, an abrupt shift from a formulaic quality of language to evident orality signals the eruption of the original voice. Although hearing the Afro-Latino voices in this text presents many challenges, and although as readers we must hold any interpretation as tentative, these challenges make the reading more exciting as we seek to move across time and space to hear voices so different from our own and so vital in their own time.

Reading and Teaching from This Book

When reading and teaching from this book, it is useful to understand its organization and the resources it contains. Following this Introduction, each of the book's four parts is introduced by a short description of the chapters it includes and how they relate to themes or trends in the field. The first part covers politics and wars and ranges from Africa to Europe to the Americas. The second part highlights how Afro-Latinos

[6] Pedro Luis Lorenzo Cadarso's study titled *La documentación judicial en la época de los Austrias* offers detailed help in understanding the documentary genres related to judicial cases, and, because other courts often modeled their documentary production on these, the study can be helpful for understanding a broader range of document genres.

created families, communities, and relationships. The third part describes religious beliefs and practices. The fourth part presents cases of people defending themselves and claiming rights.

The chapters in each of these parts begin with a scholarly introduction to reading and interpreting the document or document excerpt(s). Following this introduction is the document, in its original language on left-hand pages, and the English translation on the right-hand pages.

Footnotes throughout the book provide additional help to contextualize and interpret the texts. They define a specific meaning or term in the context of that narrative, place, or period. They give historical, biographical, and geographical information. They point out possible errors in the manuscript as well as difficulties in translation. They also point to other helpful resources.

A few unfamiliar words are italicized and defined only at their first appearance. But most italicized words in the chapter introductions, the original source texts, and the translations are defined and discussed in the book's Glossary. The Glossary brings out some of the regional and temporal variation in word use.

In the Bibliography, for each chapter you will find a list of sources that combines both the works cited in the text and recommended readings for further exploring the chapter's themes. Following the chapter bibliographies, you will find a separate listing of "Resources for Teaching Early Modern Afro-Latino Experiences and Their Legacies," which includes other published voices from the black Ibero-Atlantic, films that re-create or document both early modern Afro-Latino experiences and their legacies today, a sample of music that has developed within Afro-Latino communities in the regions represented, and sources for the study of African and Afro-Latino arts.

The Index offers a way to track themes, issues, and location throughout the volume and may help to reveal unexpected parallels and trends. Together the scholarly introductions, notes, Glossary, Bibliography, and Index are included as "readers' tools" in order to allow readers as much freedom as possible in deriving their own interpretations and insights from working with this new corpus of voices from the African diaspora.

Students in particular can apply their own critical reading skills when working with these chapters and the primary sources in English translation and in the original Spanish or Portuguese. We suggest the following specific strategies when reading the documents:

1. Define specific words by comparing their use within a document and between documents.
2. Consider the interaction between questions and answers in interrogatories:
    a. How do questions structure narrative?
    b. Where do speakers go beyond the question (agency)?
3. When there is more than one testimony regarding the same event,
    a. What can readers learn from the similarities?
    b. What can readers learn from the differences?
4. What type of document is this? Who created this document, for whom, and for what purpose?

5. What does this document tell readers? What questions does this document answer?
6. Can one read "between the lines" of what is discussed to determine what issues motivated the participants in a document's creation and the events it recorded?
7. What does the record leave silent?
   a. What questions does it pose that one needs other sources to answer?
   b. How can readers use other documents in this collection to address these silences?
8. As you work through individual sources and through the book's parts, consider how these sources fit into or challenge a wider historical narrative or the established understanding of a period.

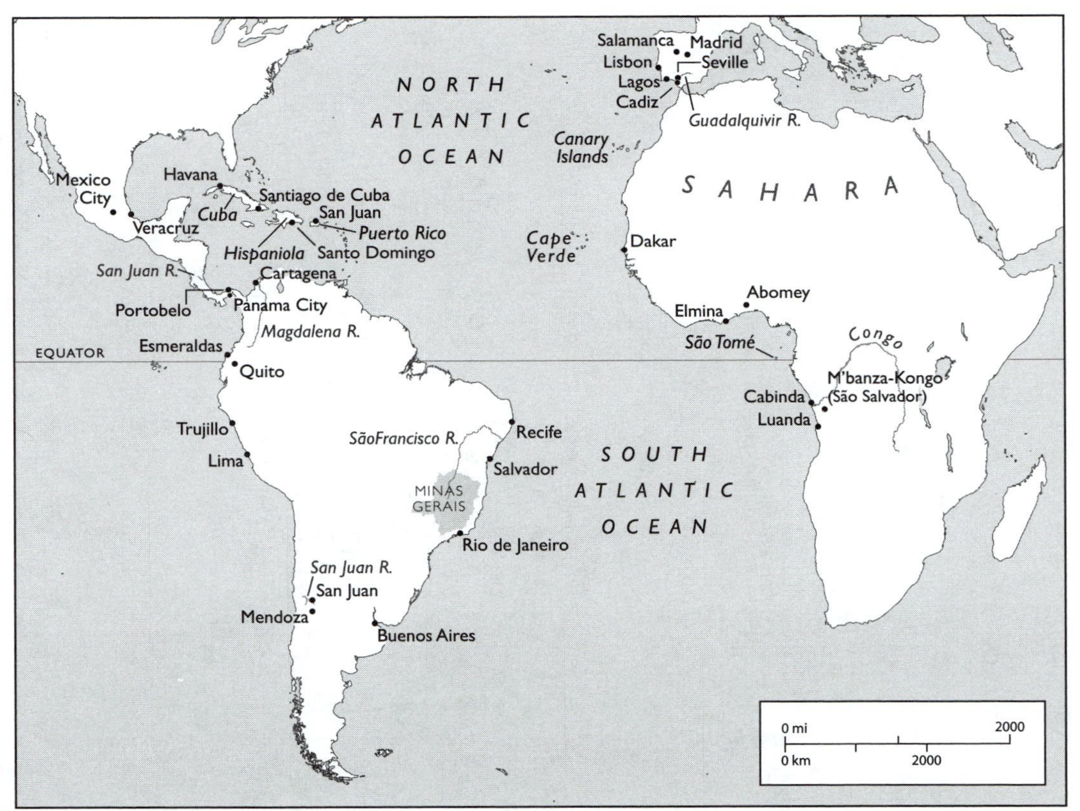

Map 1 The Ibero-Atlantic World

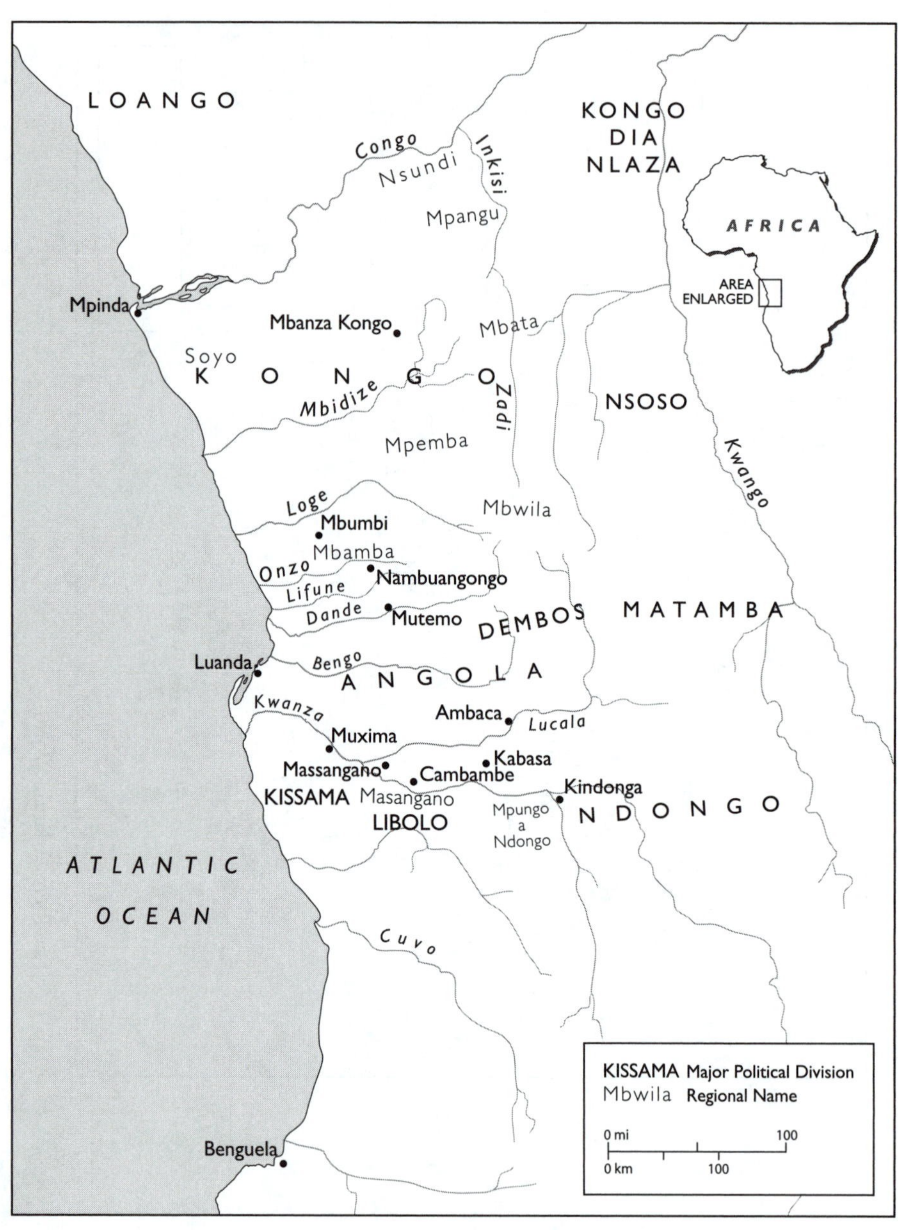

Map 2 Central Africa: Kongo, Angola, and Ndongo

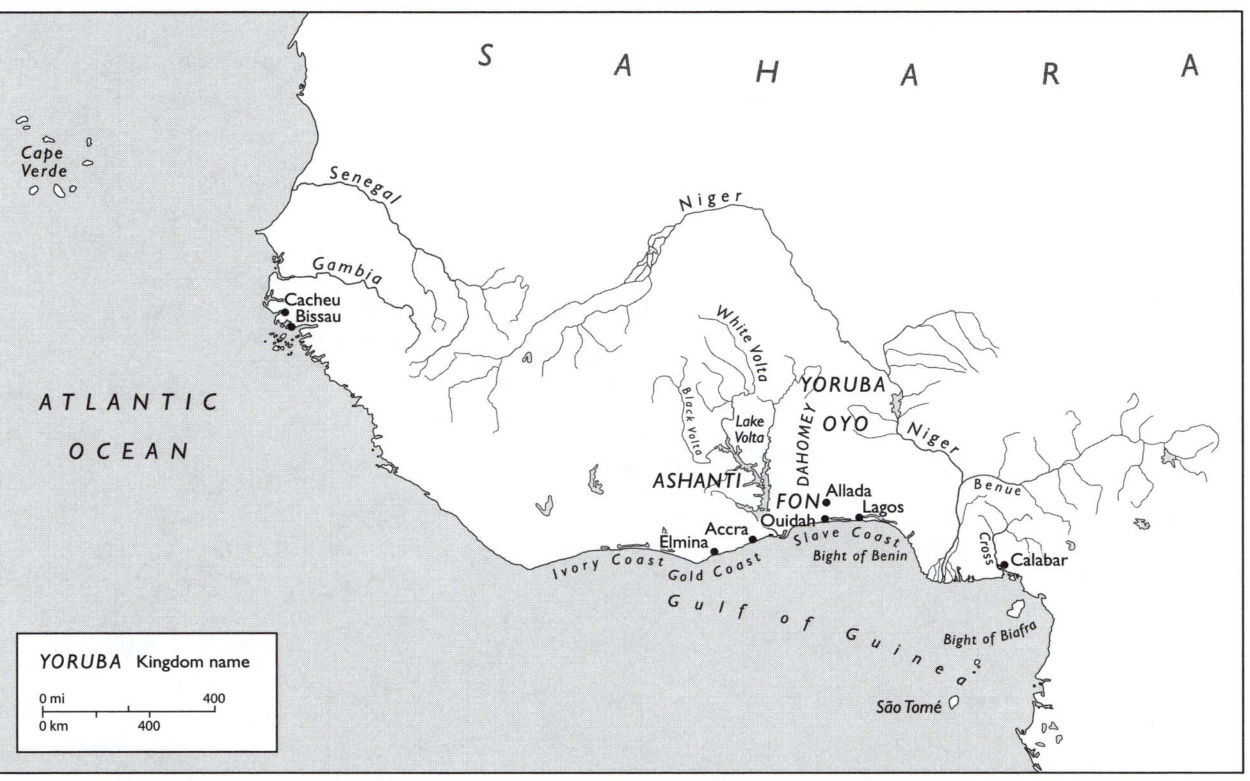

Map 3 West Africa

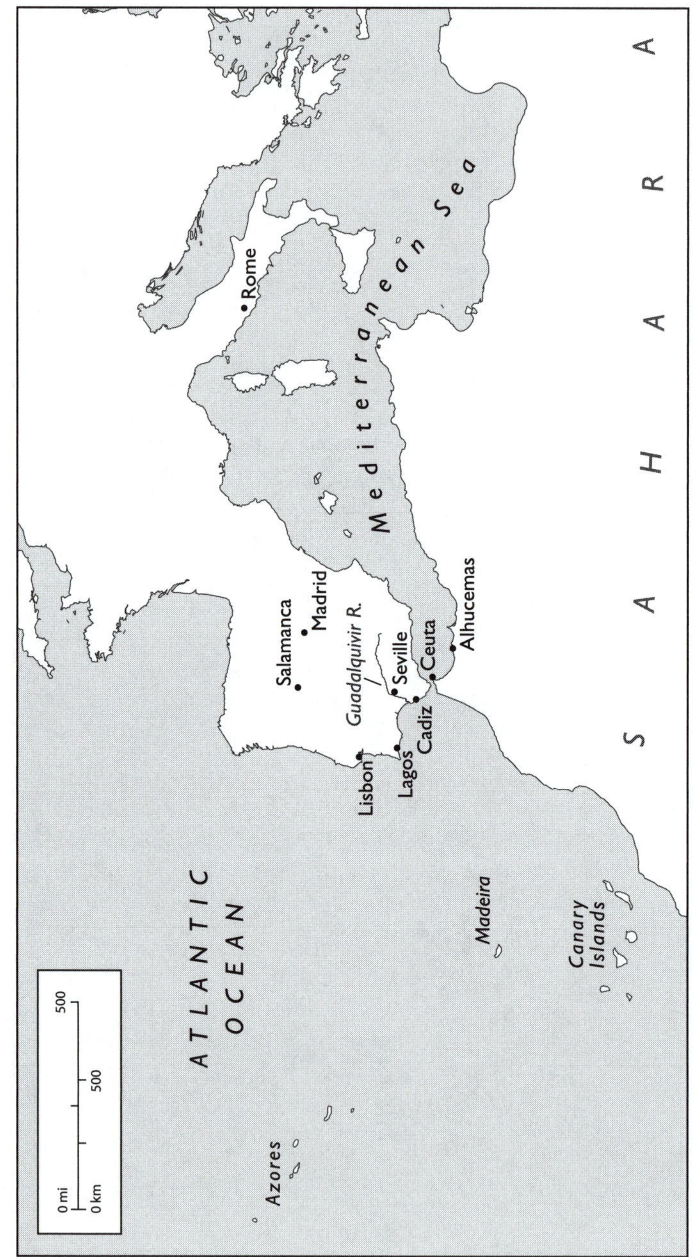

Map 4 Europe and North Africa

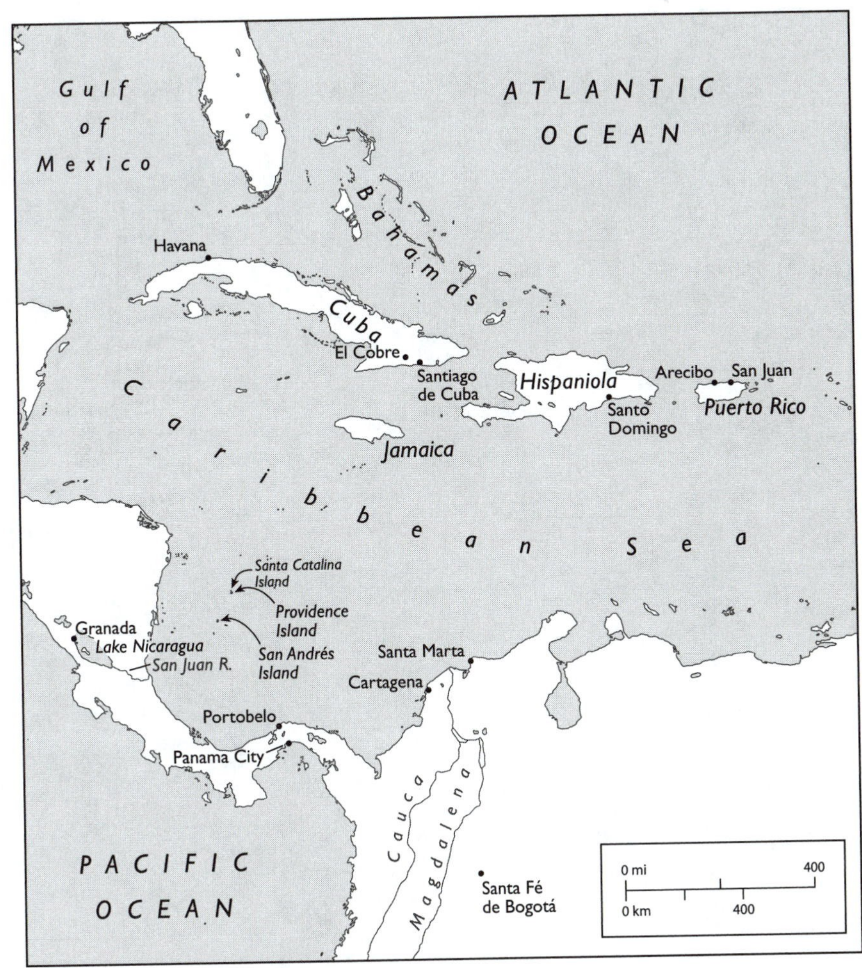

Map 5 Caribbean and Central America

Map 6 South America

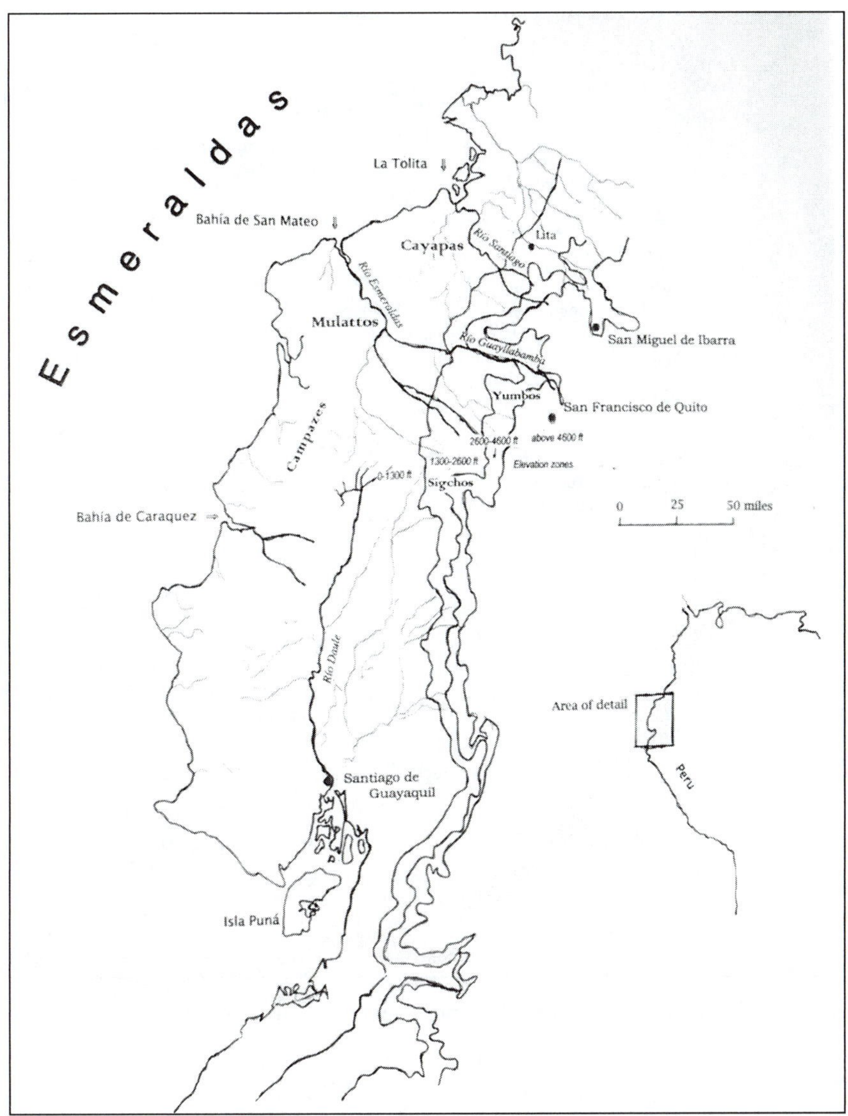

Map 7 Esmeraldas (Ecuador)

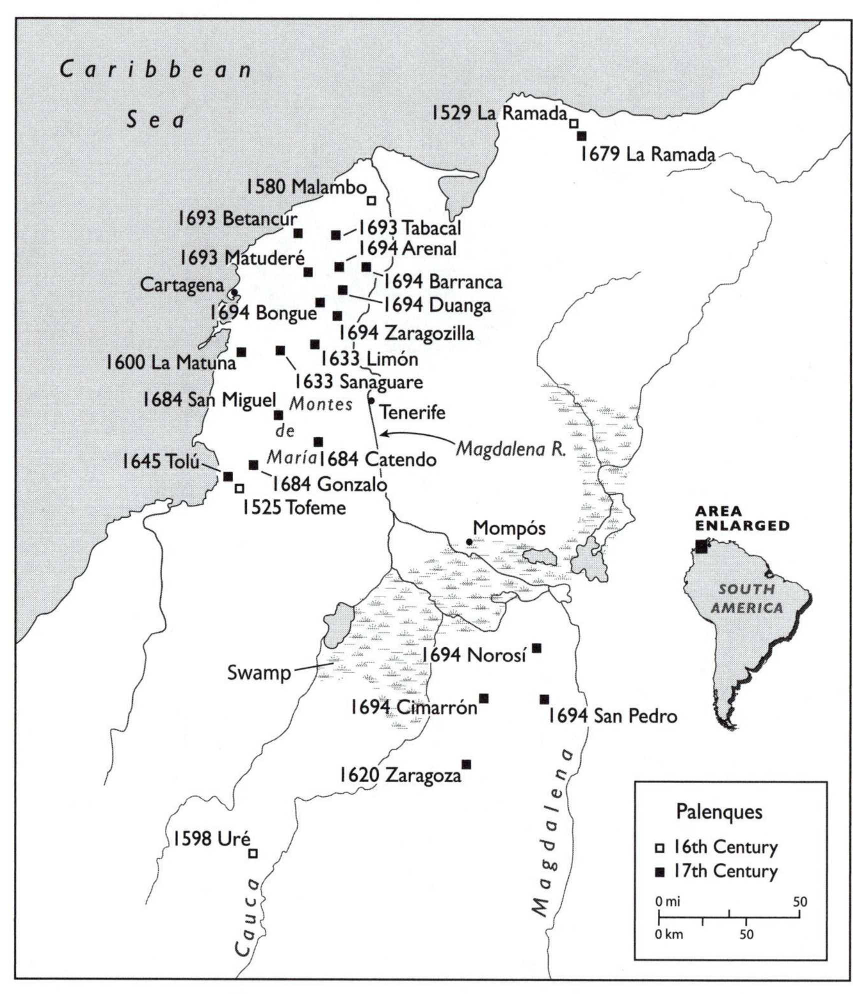

Map 8 Palenques (Maroon Settlements) in the Government of Cartagena

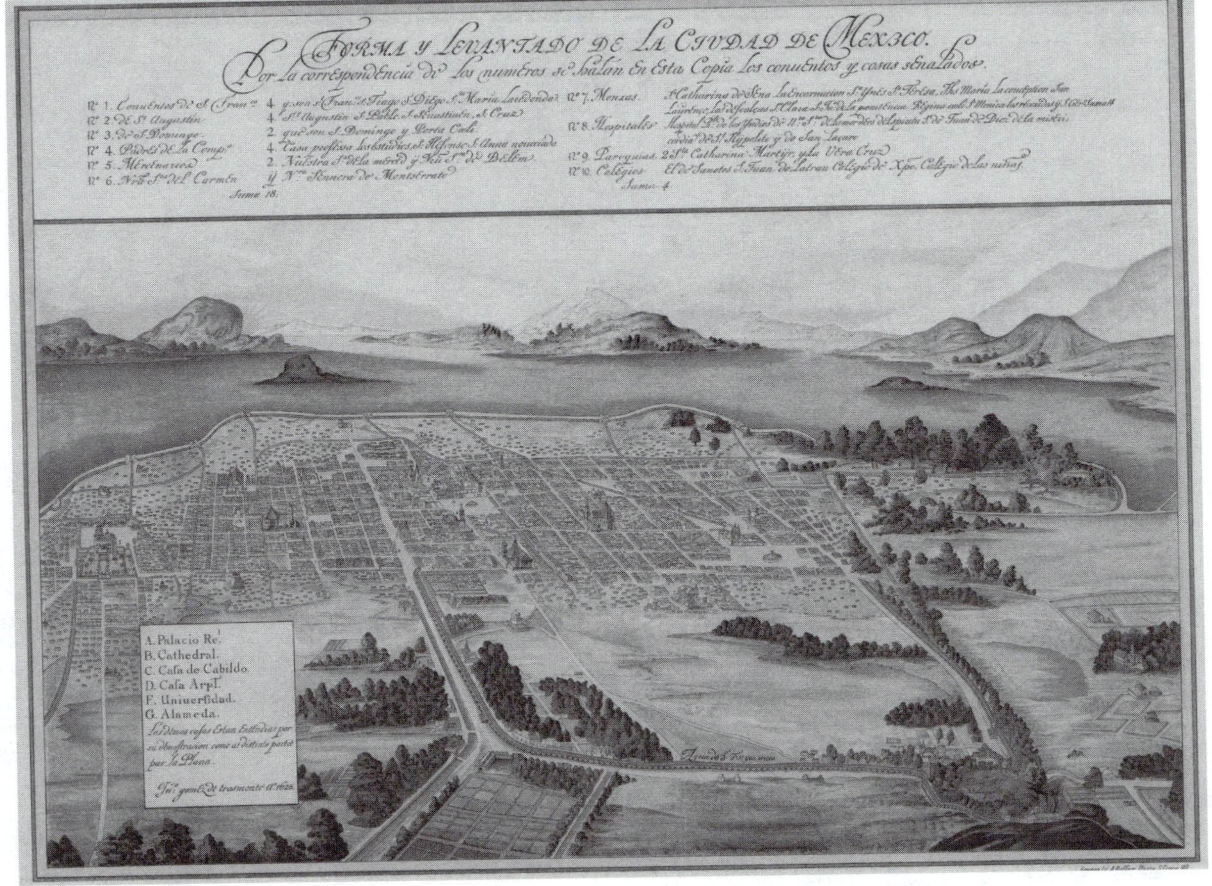

Map 9 Mexico City, chromolithograph (1907) based on a map by cartographer Juan Gómez de Trasmonte (1628)

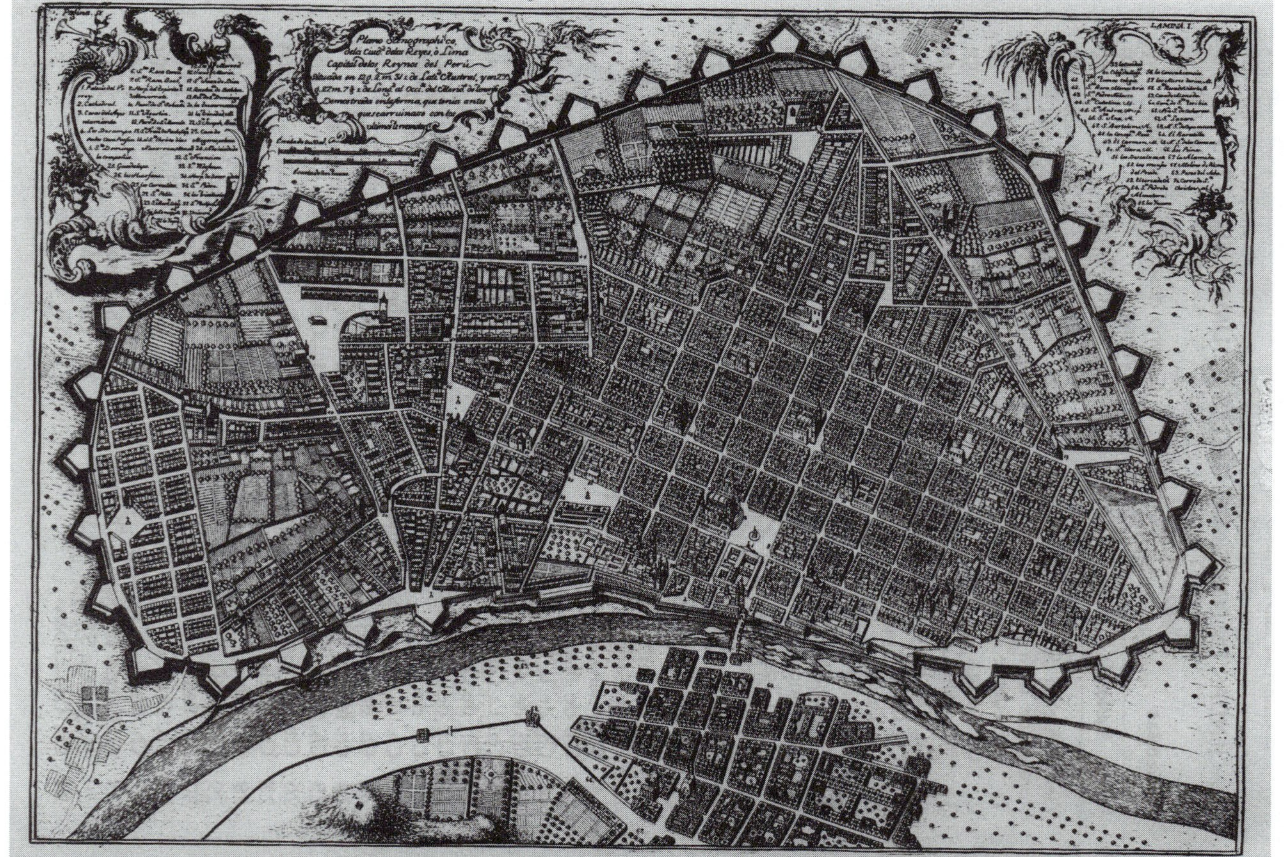

Map 10 Lima (Ciudad de los Reyes, 1685) by the cartographer Pedro Nolasco Mere

Map 11 Cuba: The Oriente Region

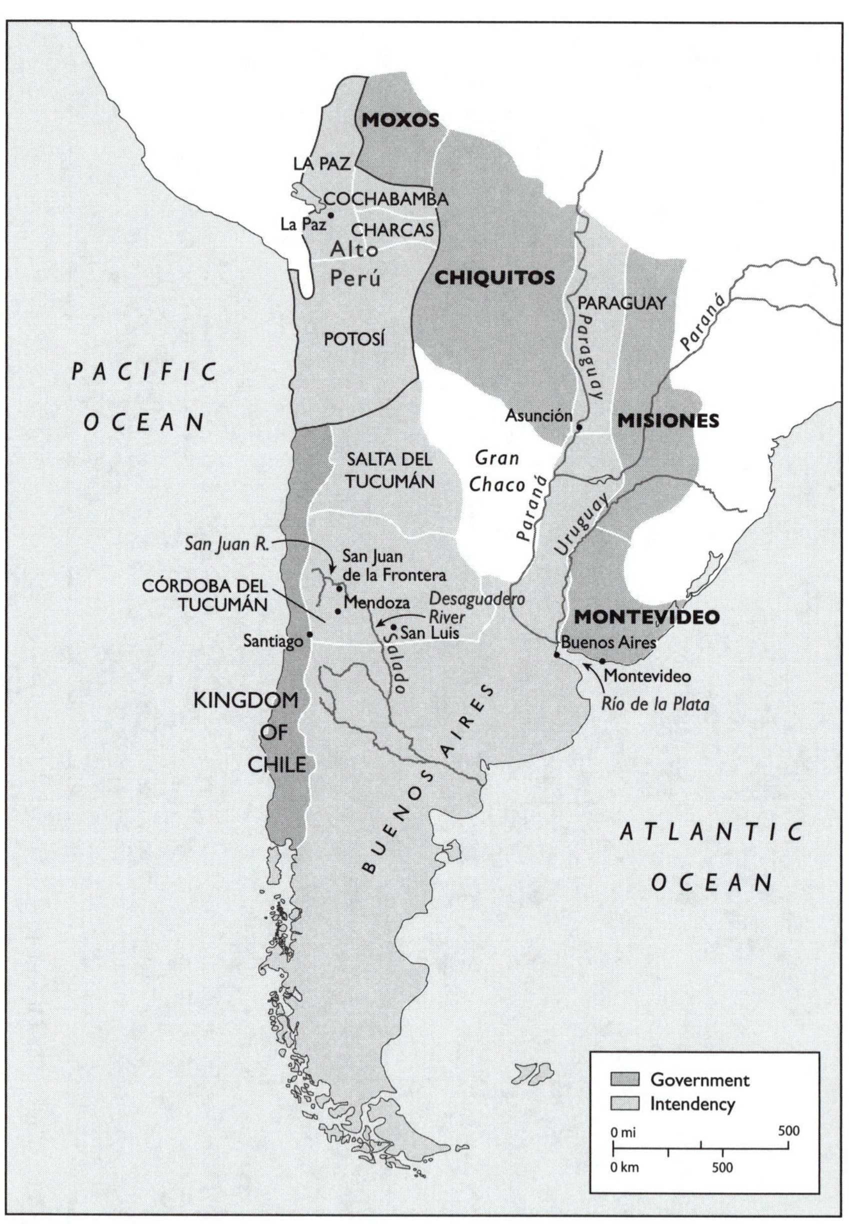

Map 12 Viceroyalty of Río de la Plata

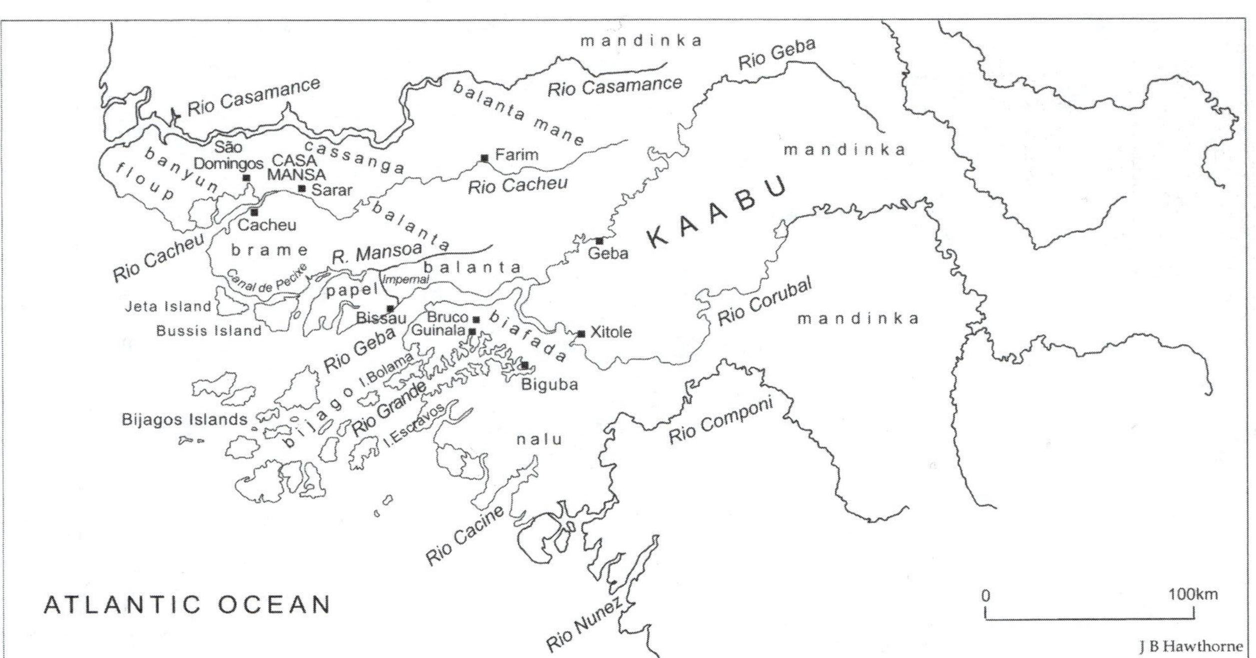

Map 13 Guinea-Bissau Region and Its People

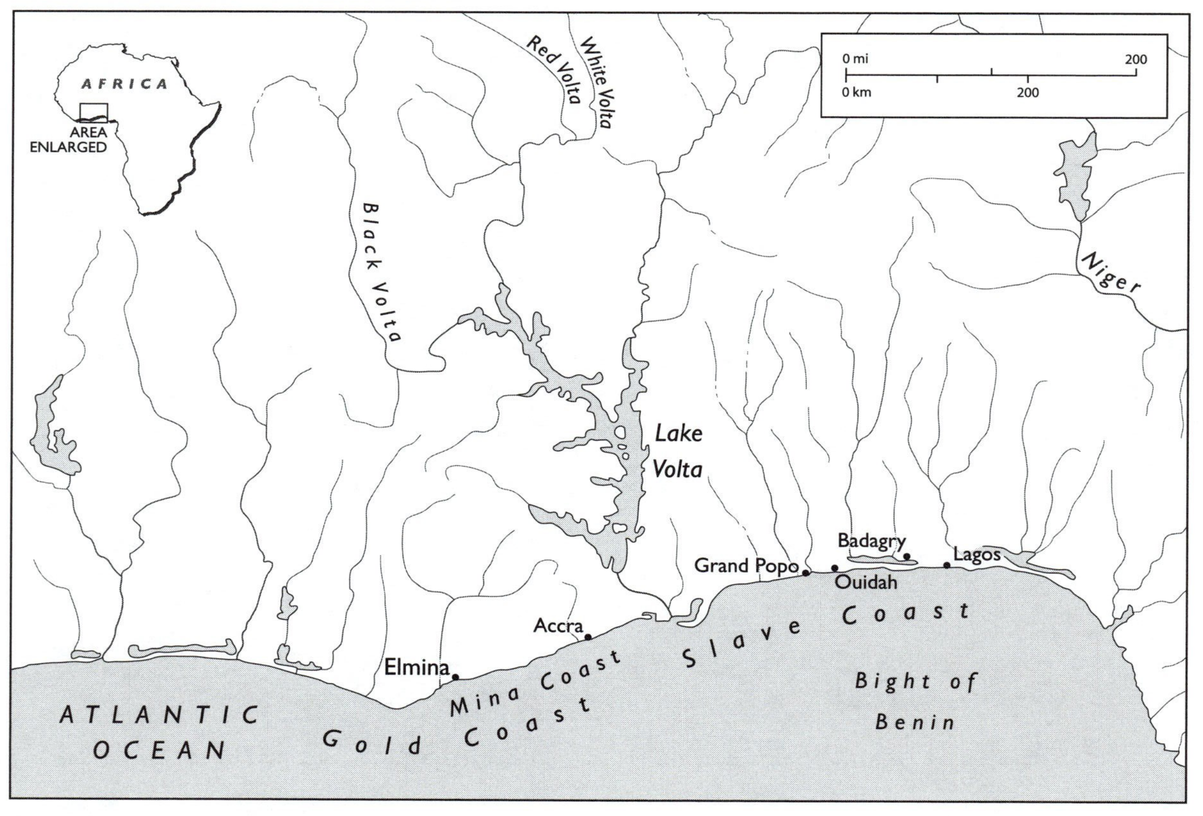

Map 14 Mina Coast: Slave Ports

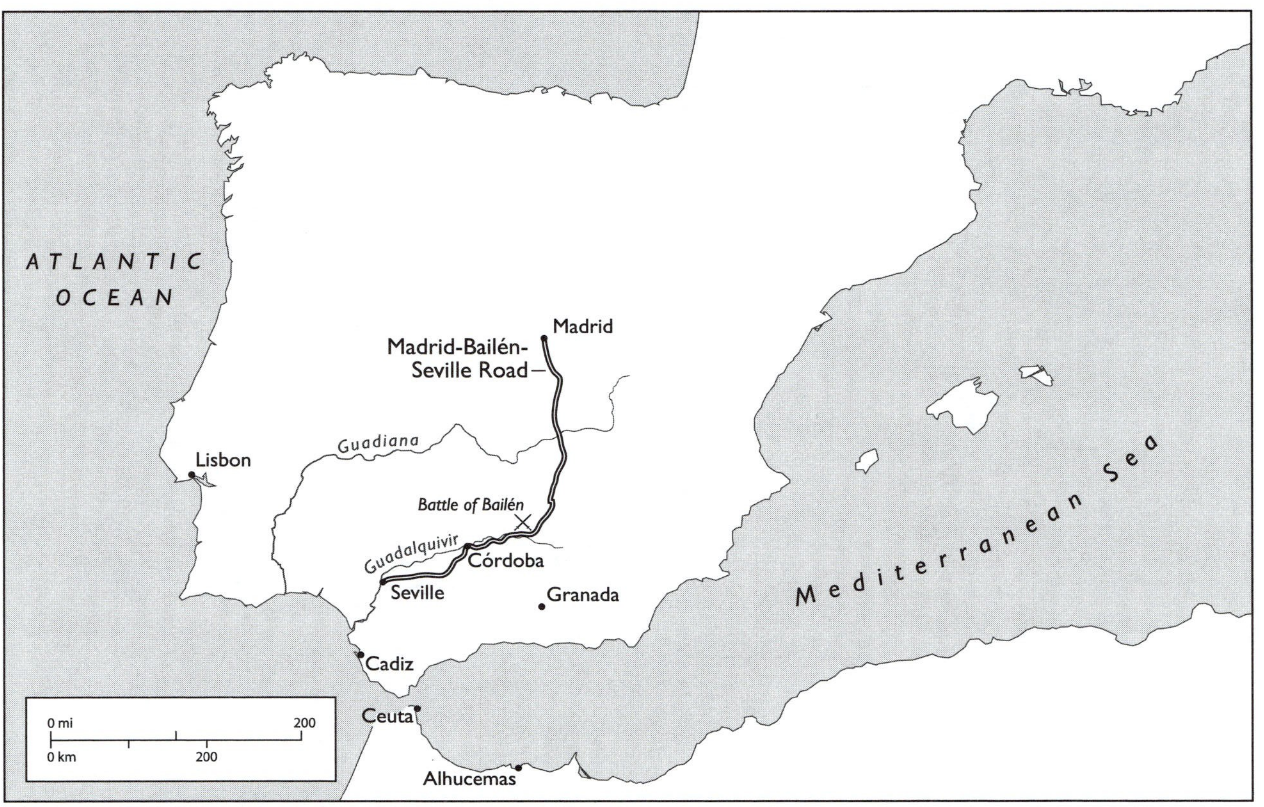

Map 15 Spain, North Africa, and the Battle of Bailén

Part I
Politics and Wars

"Politics and Wars" highlights African communities and states in conflict with European or internal entities. This section represents an early stage in the struggles between African communities and European colonizing powers in Africa and Ibero-America. When the Portuguese first arrived in Central Africa in 1483, the Kingdom of Kongo controlled an area as large as Portugal itself. In the early sixteenth century, the kings of Kongo converted to Catholicism but remained politically independent. The 1550 inquest into a case of treason (Chapter 1) shows powerful Central African leaders engaging European modes of discourse and political action to work out internal divisions.

The chapter informs a reading of Afro-Latinos in Ibero-America as often having had prior experience with complex political organizations and an Africanized Catholicism. Brought forcibly to the Americas, many Africans escaped and formed clandestine communities called *palenques.* In numerous cases, leaders negotiated with Spanish authorities, promising loyalty to the Crown in exchange for a peaceful coexistence. Sometimes these negotiations were successful. Although Alonso de Illescas' 1586 petition was rejected (Chapter 2), the Spanish government granted his community its freedom less than two decades later. Illescas' community settled in Ecuador before the first large boom in the Atlantic slave trade.

This boom occurred during the reign of Queen Njinga of Ndongo (*Angola*) in the early to mid-sixteenth century (Chapter 3). In letters spanning three decades, Njinga negotiated her relationship with Portuguese governors and showed her development of an African style of leadership while Portuguese slaving interests promoted local wars to feed the trade. Although most Africans came to the Americas via the traumatic *Middle Passage,* some who shaped the Ibero-Atlantic world came from the Afro-Iberian communities in southern Spain and Portugal and crossed the Atlantic as soldiers and sailors in the service of the Crown. In the petitions excerpted in Chapter 4, their female relatives at home defended their rights before the Crown as loyal subjects, with corresponding social status.

Contemporary to Queen Njinga and near the slave port of Cartagena de Indias (Colombia), the autonomous *Palenque* del Limón thrived with about two hundred inhabitants, many of them Central Africans or their descendants. In 1633, Spanish soldiers captured many residents and took them to Cartagena. The testimony of three residents (Chapter 5) reveals the everyday functioning of this clandestine community and the varying attitudes residents held toward Spanish masters and the colonial government. It also reveals the role *palenques* played in the creative reconstruction and preservation of African spirituality and spiritually based military leadership in the New World.

1

The Treason of Dom Pedro Nkanga a Mvemba against Dom Diogo, King of Kongo, 1550[1]

John K. Thornton and Linda Heywood

A Document of Inquiry: Its Origins and Historical Value

On April 10, 1550, Dom Diogo I, King of Kongo, ordered his magistrate and purveyor, Jorge Afonso, to conduct an inquiry into a treasonous plot raised against him by Dom Pedro Nkanga a Mvemba, a former king of Kongo whom Diogo had recently unseated. A number of declarants were interrogated by the magistrate, and their comments were set in writing by the royal scribe, Belchior Dias. Some two years later, a copy of the inquest was sent to Portugal so that "in the Kingdom of Portugal, his brother the king will be informed of the truth" and to support the Kongolese throne's request that one of the culprits—a Kongolese noble named Dom Rodrigo who had fled to *São Tomé*—be extradited.[2]

The document found its way into the Portuguese archives, where it is today, the Kongolese original having been destroyed along with the Kongolese archives. It was first published in Portugal in 1877, and a revised edition was published by the Portuguese scholar-priest António Brásio in 1953.[3] The first was a somewhat defective transcription made by Paiva Manso and published in 1877. António Brásio published a better version in his magnificent collection of sources on Central African history in 1953.

The document, which gives a fascinating "insider's view" into the intrigues of the Kingdom of Kongo in the middle of the sixteenth century, has been used by several historians. Both Jan Vansina (*Kingdoms*) and Georges Balandier used it to illustrate points concerning Kongo's history. It is indeed a document of central importance for understanding Kongo's history and political structure in the mid-sixteenth century and is the earliest source to shed real light on these questions.

But (King) Diogo's inquiry has the added advantage of being, first, a completely internal source, made by Kongolese witnesses for a matter of Kongolese domestic affairs and, second, a document not intended for public consumption in Europe.

[1] See Map 2.

[2] Arquivo Nacional de Torre do Tombo, Corpo Chronologico, Lisbon, Parte II, maço 242, doc. no. 121. Henceforth citations to this document will be cited as, for example, "fol. 1." On its use to support the extradition of Dom Rodrigo, see Brásio (II:325), "Demands of D Diogo to King of Portugal," 1553.

[3] The document is now in the Corpo Cronologico section of the Arquivo Nacional de Torre do Tombo in Lisbon (Brásio II:248–62).

Although these two strengths make it an important source, they also make it a difficult one: It discusses Kongo from an insider's point of view, with vague references to structures and events known too well by the makers of the document to merit description but understood imperfectly by historians three centuries later.

The Kingdom of Kongo and Its Political Structure

The Kingdom of Kongo was probably founded toward the end of the fourteenth century and expanded from a nucleus just south of the Congo River to include its capital Mbanza Kongo in modern-day northern *Angola* and the Democratic Republic of Congo and then to the east to the Kwango River and south as far as modern-day Luanda (Thornton, "Origins"). When the Portuguese arrived in the area in 1483, the Kingdom of Kongo was probably larger than Portugal, though the population was smaller. Portuguese visitors regarded it as the most powerful kingdom south of the equator. Almost from the beginning of their interaction, Portugal and Kongo formed an alliance in which Portuguese soldiers assisted the kings of Kongo in their wars and obtained the captives taken in by them as slaves.

The kings of Kongo converted to Christianity, and a Kongo noble was named a bishop in 1518. Although Portuguese culture deeply influenced at least the elite's customs, from very early in the encounter, the Portuguese did not conquer or dominate in Kongo as the Spanish did in the Americas or as the Portuguese themselves eventually did in Kongo's southern neighbor Ndongo after they founded the colony of *Angola* in 1575.

As a Christian kingdom, Kongo built schools and started literacy in Portuguese. The kings of Kongo and Portugal corresponded regularly, and these letters are a vital source of information, not just about the relations between the two countries but also about the internal affairs of Kongo. The correspondence of King Afonso of Kongo (1509–1542) included more than twenty letters, some of them very long. These letters in fact are our most important source of information about Kongo. Written sources composed by Africans document the history of the Angolan kingdom for the first half of the sixteenth century—a unique situation for the lands that Europeans encountered along the Atlantic seaboard of Africa.

We learn from Afonso's correspondence that the relationship between Kongo and Portugal was not always smooth. Afonso complained that the Portuguese soldiers who helped him were cowardly and incompetent, that some of the priests were not paragons of Christian morality, and that Portuguese merchants sometimes promoted disobedience among his vassals, primarily in order to obtain slaves. In 1526, Afonso brought the situation under control by creating a board to supervise the slave trade.

Kongo's ruling class was often divided, and plots were common. These plots typically involved factions of the royal family maneuvering to determine succession, and, thus, they were particularly strong after the death of a king (Thornton, "Early Kongo-Portuguese Relations"). The document in question gives the fullest details we have for such a plot, in this case involving the relatively long crisis from the death of Afonso in 1542 to the final succession of Diogo I in 1545.

The Plot to Overthrow Dom Diogo, King of Kongo

It is clear from the testimony of witnesses that Dom Pedro "Cangua Mobemba"[4] (Nkanga a Mvemba in modern Kikongo) was deeply engaged (from his base in a church) in gathering a group of supporters to overthrow the king, but the document says little more about it. The comings and goings are quite mysterious, and it is difficult to place this plot in historical context by using contemporary or near contemporary documents. Dom Pedro Nkanga a Mvemba was, in fact, the son of King Afonso I (1509–1542) and handpicked by him to be his successor.

In a letter to the king of Portugal in 1549, Captain Francisco Barros da Paiva of the Portuguese island colony of *São Tomé* mentioned his problems with King Diogo of Kongo and then went on to refer to "King Dom Pedro who is in the church and Dom Rodrigo who is on this island."[5] From da Paiva's remarks, we can have no doubt that the Pedro who plotted in a church and involved a certain Dom Rodrigo on *São Tomé* in his plots was the main figure of the inquest and was a former king of Kongo.

This information allows us to establish a sequence of events with some certainty. When Afonso I died in 1543,[6] he was indeed succeeded by his son Pedro. But formal election as king of Kongo was never enough to ensure that the Crown would pass smoothly to anyone. The election was frequently followed by further jockeying as the newly crowned king rewarded his followers and supporters with offices, titles, and promotions and overcame the opposition of those whose futures were inevitably harmed by his actions. These latter would be the source, sometimes for many years, of friction, plots, and—as apparently happened in the case of Dom Diogo and his supporters—active attempts at usurpation of the Crown.

Pedro's rule lasted about two years, for it seems that Diogo ascended to the throne in 1545.[7] Pedro apparently sought asylum in a church, and from that safe, if constricted, location he fomented his plot. Five years later, Diogo was still dealing in delicate manipulations and still meeting opposition as he replaced Pedro's appointees with his own.

The real stake for most of the participants in the plot, and even those who wavered, was the granting or revocation of *rendas,* a Portuguese feudal term meaning, generally, any sort of income-bearing property. In Kongo, however, unlike in Portugal, the king closely controlled this rent-bearing property and no one held real property rights.

[4] The writer spells this name "Camgua mo bemba" (or Cangua mo bemba), which probably is quite close to how it was pronounced in sixteenth-century Kikongo, which would be roughly Nkanga Mubemba. Since that time, Kikongo has changed, and words that once began with "mu" have become shortened to just "n," whereas the "b" of the older documents is often now a "v." Thus a modern spelling and one that is widely accepted by specialists is Nkanga a Mvemba.

[5] Francisco Barros da Paiva to el-Rei Joao III, January 28, 1549 (Brásio II:236).

[6] This date is established by the correspondence of his brother Manuel in Lisbon—Manuel to the Queen of Portugal, July 15, 1543 (Brásio II:124–25).

[7] The date of Diogo's accession is established by testimony in an inquiry conducted by Diogo, November 21, 1548. A witness, Manuel Varela, indicated that Diogo had been king for three years, "more or less," at the time of the inquest.

During the inquest, Pedro reminded his nephew Dom Afonso that Diogo had not given him the *renda* of Nsundi, Kongo's northeastern province, which carried considerable income and prestige (fol. 3v).

Likewise, when Pedro's close associate Dom Bastião visited *Mani* (governor) Mpemba (a large province south of the capital), he played on what must have been *Mani* Mpemba's real fears that Dom Diogo would eventually take his *renda* back. If the governor was able to retain his office, supporting the king would probably allow him to keep his *renda* or even move up to a better one. Opposing him would obviously mean deprivation of income, if not of life. On the other hand, simple support might not have been enough.

Apparently this is what Dom Pedro was banking on in his negotiations with *Mani* Mpemba, for Diogo, with friends, family, and supporters to reward, might easily take the *rendas* of those he judged less worthy and give them to his family or close friends. In his desperate letter to his cousin and ally Dom Rodrigo in *São Tomé* (which follows the document of inquest, below), Pedro makes this plight clear—Diogo had already taken his *renda* and was apparently taking those of Pedro's immediate family and giving them to his family and supporters—Pedro's own *renda* went to Diogo's son (fols. 7v and 10v).

Family ties were obviously important, perhaps critical, in the delicate game of *renda* distribution. As indicated in his letter to Dom Rodrigo, Pedro clearly saw the threat of Diogo's rule not just as a personal one but also as one against his whole family and line—"*nossa geração de Quybala.*"[8] That perception could scarcely have been a vain one if Diogo had indeed sent out letters to the provincial governors demanding that in case of Diogo's death they must not support anyone of Pedro's lineage (*geração*), neither "son nor daughter nor male nor female relative even if they are slaves" (fol. 10v).[9]

The inquest clearly shows that the struggle for the throne of Kongo was never a personal one between rival kings but was, rather, a family one (often among rival branches of the same family), in which large groups of relatives, clients (like Dom Bastião, Pedro's frequent go-between), and even slaves stood in contention with each other. To the winning family group went prestigious and wealthy *rendas,* according to such criteria as loyalty, seniority, and degree of relationship; to the losers went imprisonment, poverty, or even death.

Diogo apparently moved rather slowly in consolidating his power. Five years after his accession to office, he was still allowing Pedro's followers considerable power; indeed, some of Pedro's group still held power in a variety of places. No doubt the king had to proceed slowly, first replacing a few top officials and then gradually working the others out. He needed to do this fast enough to satisfy his followers yet slowly

[8] *Quybala* probably means the faction formed at court, as *mbala* means "court" in Kikongo (Thornton, "Elite Women," 445).

[9] The Portuguese term *geração* is probably a translation of the Kikongo word *kanda* (plural *makanda*), which is often translated as "lineage" or "clan." In Kongo, however, *makanda* were complex sets of alliances including clients, allies, and slaves. It has a secondary meaning of "faction," so that brothers and their followers might form two separate *makanda* if they became rivals (Thornton, "Elite Women," 439–41).

enough to maintain the loyalty of those he had not yet forced out—and perhaps give the most loyal time to join his group.

Mani Mpemba was, it seems, one who hoped to gain Diogo's favor in spite of his position. The fact that Pedro's agents worked hard to convince *Mani* Mpemba that he would not be able to keep his position indicated that his position was a marginal one. On the other hand, *Mani* Mpangala (the lord of the market town that lay near the capital) was removed once the king was secure enough after five years in office to begin a general replacement of Pedro's group (fol. 9).[10] That all the lesser nobles of Vunda, Kondongo, and Lumbo (fols. 3v and 4r) were loyal to Pedro is an indication that Diogo had allowed them to stay in place for many years because he was afraid to move against them. Preserving the balance between removing potentially hostile but powerful people and continuing to keep the loyalty of one's closest supporters was no doubt the mark of a successful king in Kongo.

Essentially, Pedro was banking on the residual support left to him all over Kongo, both in the capital and in the provinces. His main striking action was to arrange the simultaneous murders of Diogo's top-level officials by lower ranking subordinates of Pedro's group. He had, in fact, even made some of these grants out; for example, *Mani* Mbampa (probably a subordinate of *Mani* Lumbo) was to cut off *Mani* Lumbo's head and get his *renda* (fol. 4). Pedro's nephew Dom Afonso and Dom Afonso's brother were to raise armies in Nsundi and Nkola (an unknown location), and after killing Diogo's appointments in Nsundi, they were to join Pedro in attacking the capital.

Pedro himself would leave the church where he had been closely watched for years and go to Mbata, probably to request the blessings of *Mani* Mbata, who held a traditionally neutral position controlled by its own line of hereditary nobility and attached to a *renda* that was not granted by the throne (fol. 3).[11] Although he did not say it, Pedro no doubt hoped to have both hereditary posts and *Mani* Vunda (apparently a nonhereditary post) as those holding these posts were the electors of Kongo.[12] The final acts needed to legitimize Pedro's reaccession to the throne were to obtain a papal bull recognizing Pedro's claim and to communicate this to all those who did not follow him—these tasks being left to Dom Rodrigo, who obviously had considerable international connections (fols. 10v–11r).[13]

Another point not made clear in the inquiry but visible in other documents of the era is the amount of support that Pedro could obtain outside of Africa. In addition to

[10] This interpretation rests on the reading of *tambuquado* as meaning "removed from office," as the term was defined by Lopes and Filippo Pigafetta (36), noting that if an appointed official failed to pay the tribute required of him he was said to be *Tambocado* or "deprived of his revenue and government."

[11] On the role of *Mani* Mbata, see the later tradition reported by Cavazzi da Montecuccolo (II:89); Cardoso (47–48); and João III to Afonso I, c. 1531 (Brásio I:535). Brásio dates the letter 1529; on the correct date, see Bontinck (166). Here Dom Jorge *Mani* Mbata is called the "first voice of Kongo and it is not possible to make a king without him, according to the custom of the land."

[12] On the electoral system and its early history, see Thornton ("Origins," 113–14).

[13] On Rodrigo's connections, see Thornton ("Early Kongo-Portuguese Relations," 192, 197).

Dom Rodrigo, who apparently had land and influence in *São Tomé* (fols. 10v–11r), Pedro had connections in Portugal. Most significant was the Jesuit Order; for as late as 1552, Jesuit correspondence was still speaking of the overthrow of Diogo (who had thwarted the Jesuits' claims to authority) and the installation of a king who was "completely ours," that is, one who would favor the Jesuits.[14]

The Portuguese in Diogo's court were greatly favored, including those who were secular clergy and long-term residents of Kongo. However, those who had recently come from the *metropole* itself found it difficult to be established, even those who were high ranking and favored by the king of Portugal, including officials from *São Tomé,*[15] the bishop of *São Tomé,*[16] and those of the Jesuit Order.

All these groups met opposition from locally entrenched factions of Portuguese who were consistently favored by Diogo.[17] Not surprisingly, they entered into alliances with Pedro, who could promise them favors in Kongo once he was king. Pedro thought this alliance with high-status Portuguese in the *metropole* might work to his advantage. It is quite possible that it was they who succeeded in blocking Diogo's attempts to send a diplomatic mission to Rome (the first of was sent in 1547; each failed).[18] In any case, Diogo succeeded in crushing the plot and began a long campaign to have Dom Pedro's ally Dom Rodrigo extradited from *São Tomé* to Kongo. A royal *alvara* was finally granted to this end in 1561, at the very end of Diogo's life,[19] but we do not know if Dom Rodrigo was ever delivered to his enemy. We have no information about Dom Pedro either, except that apparently he no longer threatened Diogo once his plot was discovered.

The Inquiry as a Source of Kongolese Political Culture

In addition to the light that it sheds on the political history of Kongo in the mid-sixteenth century, the inquiry gives us some interesting secondary information. The very existence of the document, for example, shows that in Kongo certain Portuguese legal forms were well established and in general use. We know of two other inquests similar to this one: one conducted by Afonso I in 1517 and the other by Diogo I in

14 Cornelio Gomes to Ignatius Loyola, July 18, 1552 (Brásio II:275).

15 Francisco Barros da Paiva to João III, February 18, 1549 (Brásio II:231–37).

16 Pigafetta (54–56); Cristovao Ribeiro to Francisco Barros da Paiva, January 25, 1549 (Brásio II:222); Diogo I to João III, August 15, 1546 (Brásio II:151–52).

17 Minute on demands of Diogo I, c. 1553 (Brásio II:327–30). On the general interpretation of this correspondence, see Thornton, "Early Kongo-Portuguese Relations." It is obvious that neither Pedro nor Diogo could be considered either "pro-Portuguese" or "anti-Portuguese," as both used the services of the Portuguese extensively.

18 Diogo to Diogo Gomes, August 15, 1546 (Brásio II:147); Cornelio Gomes to a father of Portugal, October 29, 1553 (Brásio II:302). Also see fol. 11. Pedro's letter to Rodrigo that is cited in the text is undated, and the reference to a white man being sent by Diogo to Rome may refer to Gomes' mission of 1546, or more likely to Jacome da Fonseca's of 1552–1553.

19 Apontamentos sobre Paulo Dias de Novais, 1560–1561 (Brásio II). Also see minutes on dispatches of João III to Kongo, c. 1556 (Brásio II:396).

1548. Both of these inquests, however, concerned Kongo's relations with Portugal and were conducted to inform the Portuguese king of matters relevant to that relationship.[20]

But only the Inquest of Diogo of 1550 concerned a purely internal affair and thus must indicate that the practice of a judicial inquest was established in Kongo, the copy that went to Portugal being only an "information copy" to support the request for extradition. It should be noted, however, that all the officials concerned were Portuguese. It would thus appear that Diogo had imported both the legal forms and the experts to conduct them. Because of a great lack of subsequent documentation, we cannot know if, in fact, the Kongolese later conducted the inquiries or even if the inquiry as a legal form survived the sixteenth century in Kongo.

In addition to the light it sheds on legal systems in Kongo, the inquest attests to the existence of archives in Kongo. That the document was created, filed, and then retrieved two years later for transmission to Portugal shows this as well as the fact that writing had obviously become an important system of information storage and transmission.

The writing of letters from one Kongolese actor to another is mentioned several times in the inquest. Dom Matias, when in Mpangu, wrote a letter to Dom Pedro that Dom Afonso testified to having seen. It was an intercepted letter from Pedro to Rodrigo that was attached to the inquest and gave the most damning evidence: that letter mentions five more letters sent from Dom Diogo to others in the kingdom.[21] The custom of writing was fixed enough that the custom of storing the correspondence must have been well established. A half century after the Luso-Kongolese contacts, Kongo was fully literate—at least, its upper classes were. In the sixteenth century, literacy was an upper-class phenomenon everywhere.

A final piece of incidental information concerns the presence of Christianity. Although it is sometimes believed that Christianity did not survive the reign of Afonso, an impression created in part by the slanderous correspondence of Jesuit missionaries and *São Tomé* officials written against Diogo,[22] in fact, all the actors appear as fairly solid Christians. For example, when he first broke the plan to Afonso, Dom Pedro asked him first to swear on a Holy Bible to keep it secret (fol. 2v). Furthermore, Diogo apparently observed the right of Christian asylum in a church enough to allow Pedro to operate from a church for years after his deposition, even though officials from that same church were important witnesses in the trial and obviously played a significant part in revealing the plot (fols. 2r–2v; 4v; 5r–5v; 8). Both Pedro and Diogo respected the decisions of the Pope in the question of succession, and both sought to obtain the requisite bulls recognizing them as rulers of Kongo.[23]

[20] Brásio published both (I:393–97 and II:197–206).

[21] Fol. 3v, letter of Dom Matias, and fols. 10v–11v, other letters.

[22] Cristovão Riberio to Captain of *São Tomé,* January 25, 1549 (Brásio II:222); Francisco Barres da Paiva to João III (Brásio II:231–36); Cornelio Gomes to Ignatius Loyola, July 18, 1552 (Brásio II:275); Jesuit Chronicle of Afonso Polanco, extract in Brásio II:227–28.

[23] See note 18, above, fol. 11.

The Document

The text that follows is the complete inquest, made from a photocopy of the original found in the Arquivo Nacional de Torre do Tombo in Lisbon.[24] We have followed Paiva Manso's text, emending it from the original document and modernizing it. The text, like many from this period, uses little punctuation; therefore, the translation supplies enough to make sense of the text. We have also altered the reading of Kikongo words and titles in one or two places to change the division into words.

Lords Loyal to Dom Diogo

Mani Kandongo
Mani Kwanzila
Mani Lumbo
Mani Nsunda
Mani Vunda

Lords Whose Loyalty is in Flux

Mani Mpangala Dom Francisco (official of Dom Pedro's rule, eventually replaced by Dom Diogo)
Mani Mpemba (official of Dom Pedro's rule, trying to gain Dom Diogo's favor, reportedly godson of Diogo)

Lords Reportedly Loyal to Dom Pedro

Dom Matias Mani Mitombe (appointed by Dom Diogo)
Mani Mbampa (subordinate to Mani Lumbo)
Mani Wembo
Nsungo a Mala Mani Mpemba
Tambuke Mpemba (ex-Mani Mpemba)[25]
Nsala a Kibela

Lords of Vunda, Left in Place by Dom Diogo, Reportedly Loyal to Dom Pedro

Dom António Mani Nsimsa
Dom Francisco Mani Mpangala
Dom Francisco Mani Zalita
Dom João Mani Katila
Mani Tenga

Figure 1. Factions and loyalties as reported by witnesses in the "Judicial Inquiry Concerning the Treason which Dom Pedro Nkanga a Mvemba Mounted against Dom Diogo, King of Kongo" (1550)

[24] We are grateful to D. Maria Teresa Geraldes Barbosa Acabado of the archive for transmitting the copy to us.

[25] See note 5 in the document.

Traslado de uma *devassa* que Sua *Real Senhoria* [Dom Diogo] mandou tirar ao *ouvidor* e *provedor* Jorge Afonso, sobre a traição que lhe armava Dom Pedro Cangua Mobemba[1]

Saibam quantos este público instrumento, dado por mandado e autoridade de justiça ao muito poderoso e cristianíssimo Rei Dom Diogo, de Deus por Sua Santa Graça, virem: que no ano do nascimento de Nosso Senhor Jesus Cristo de 1552, aos dez dias do mês de Janeiro do presente ano, nesta cidade de Comguo, nos paços de Sua *Real Senhoria,* logo pelo dito Senhor foi[2] mandado ao *ouvidor* e *provedor* Jorge Afonso, em presença de mim, *escrivão,* lhe mandasse passar o presente instrumento, com o traslado da *devassa* e *inquirição* que se tirou, sobre a traição que lhe armava Dom Pedro Cangua Mobemba. E porque Sua *Real Senhoria* quer que no Reino de Portugal El-Rei seu irmão seja informado da verdade, mandou ao dito *ouvidor* lhe mandasse passar o presente instrumento, com o traslado da *[de]vassa,* a qual eu *escrivão* ao diante do [nome]ado trasladei toda de verbo a verbo . . . a que ao diante [se] segue.

Eu, Belchior Dias, *escrivão* e público *tabelião* neste Reino e [nos] senhorios d[o] Comguo, trasladei: e é o seguinte.

Auto e *inquirição* que Sua *Real Senhoria* mandou tirar ao *ouvidor* e *provedor* Jorge Afonso sobre a traição que lhe armava Dom Pedro Cangua Mobemba.

Ano do nascimento de Nosso Senhor Jesus Cristo de 1550, aos dez dias do mês d[e] Abril do presente ano, nesta cidade de Comguo, [nos paços] de Sua *Real Senhoria,* logo por Sua *Real Senhoria* foi dito ao dito *ouvidor* e *provedor* Jorge Afonso, em presença de mim *escrivão,* abaixo nomeado, lhe perguntassem certas testemunhas e devassasse em como Dom Pedro Cangua Mobemba armava traição contra Sua *Real Senhoria,* para se [ilegível]tar com o reino e se apossar dele, [ilegível]. [O] qual o dito *ouvidor* mandou a mim, *escrivão,* fizesse este *Auto* e se perguntassem [a] todas as testemunhas que Sua *Real Senhoria* mandasse apresentar, ao que tudo foi satisfeito.

Eu, Belchior Dias, público *tabelião* e *escrivão* do judicial e orfãos neste reino e senhorios d[o] Comguo, por El-Rei Nosso Senhor e por Sua *Real Senhoria,* que isto escrevi.

[1] Arquivo Nacional de Torre do Tombo, Lisbon, Corpo Cronológico, parte II, maço 242, doc. no. 121. Also published by Brásio (II:248–62) and by Paiva Manso (101–10). All Portuguese names have been modernized, consistent with the rest of the volume. However, Kikongo names in the original have been given their original Portuguese spelling. In the translation, they have been modernized according to current Kikongo usage. The reason for this difference would take too much space to explain here; it involves a complicated linguistic history, including historical changes in both spelling and phonetics.

[2] Paiva Manso has *foi foi.*

Copy of a Judicial Inquiry That His Royal Lordship [Dom Diogo] Ordered the Magistrate and Purveyor Jorge Afonso to Carry Out, Concerning the Treason That Dom Pedro Nkanga a Mvemba Mounted against Him

May it be known by all those who see this public instrument, given by order and authority of justice, by the most powerful and Christian King Dom Diogo, by God through His Holy Grace: that in the year of our Lord Jesus Christ 1552, on the tenth day of January of this same year, in the city of Kongo in the palaces of His Royal Lordship, this same lord ordered the magistrate and purveyor, Jorge Afonso, in the presence of me, the clerk, to complete the present instrument, with a copy of the inquest and inquiry which were gathered concerning the treason that Dom Pedro Nkanga a Mvemba raised against him. And as His Royal Lord [Dom Diogo] wishes that in the Kingdom of Portugal, his brother the king should be informed of the truth, he ordered the magistrate to have the present instrument completed for him with a copy of the inquest, which I, the clerk, copied before the above-named [*ouvidor* Jorge Afonso] completely word for word . . . which is what follows.

I, Belchior Dias, clerk and notary public of the Kingdom and Dominions of Kongo, transcribed it. And here it follows:

Act and Inquiry That His Royal Lordship Ordered the Magistrate and Purveyor Jorge Afonso to Gather, Concerning the Treason Raised against Him by Dom Pedro Nkanga a Mvemba.

In the year of Our Lord Jesus Christ 1550, on the tenth day of April of this same year, in this city of Kongo, in the palaces of His Royal Lordship [Dom Diogo, King of Kongo], after His Royal Lordship ordered the magistrate and purveyor Jorge Afonso, in my presence—the clerk named below—to question certain witnesses and inquire into how Dom Pedro Nkanga a Mvemba had mounted treason against His Royal Lordship, so that he [illegible][1] the kingdom and take possession of it himself [illegible]. Thereupon the magistrate ordered me, the clerk, to make this act of inquiry and to question all the witnesses whom His Royal Lordship ordered to appear, all of which was completed.

I, Belchior Dias, notary public and clerk of the judiciary and orphans in this Kingdom and Dominions of Kongo, wrote this for the King [of Portugal], Our Lord, and for His Lordship [Dom Diogo, King of Kongo].

[1] Probably "so that he might usurp."

[Testemunha de João Ane, *moço de capela*]

Item, João Ane, *moço de capela,* e testemunha jurada aos Santos Evangelhos, em que pôs a mão direita, que lhe pelo *ouvidor* e *provedor* Jorge Afonso foi dado. E prometeu de dizer verdade do que lhe perguntassem. Disse ele testemunha que é verdade que ele viu estar falando por muitas vezes Dom Bastião e Dom Pedro Cangua Mobemba, e que sabe terem muita conversação e amizade. E que isto viu ele testemunha por muitas vezes por estarem ambos. E que outra coisa não sabe. E mais declarou ele testemunha pelo juramento que tinha recebido, que era verdade, que viu com seus olhos muitas vezes entrar Pedro Álvares na igreja a falar com Dom Pedro. E, tanto que lá era, entravam na sacristia e fechavam as portas e falavam ambos de dois. E porém que não sabia o que, nem o que não.

E mais não disse do dito caso. E por verdade assinou aqui com o di[to] *ouvidor,* e do costume disse nada.

[Bel]chior Dias, *escrivão,* que isto escrevi.

[Testemunha de Dom Afonso]

Item, Dom Afonso, testemunha jurada aos Santos Evangelhos, que lhe foram dados pelo *ouvidor* e *provedor* Jorge Afonso, em que pôs a mão direita. E prometeu de dizer a verdade do que lhe perguntassem. Disse ele testemunha que é verdade que o dito Dom Pedro Cangua Mobemba o chamara um dia, estando ele testemunha um dia na igreja. E lhe dissera a ele testemunha que lhe queria falar em segredo. E que lhe disse o dito Dom Pedro que jurasse num livro dos Santos Evangelhos porque lhe queria dizer um segredo muito grande. E ele testemunha a porfiara com ele que não havia de jurar, que o dissesse, que não havia de dizer nada do que lhe[3] dissesse. E o dito Dom Pedro lhe tornara a dizer que jurasse ele testemunha; então jurou de o não dizer. Então lhe dissera o dito Dom Pedro que ele tinha determinado de se ir, que se queria ele testemunha ir com ele e assim seu irmão dele testemunha, porque se ele Dom Pedro Cangua Mobemba fosse e eles ficassem, que Sua *Real Senhoria* os mandaria matar. E assim lhe dissera o dito Dom Pedro Cangua Mobemba, que não houvessem medo de ir com ele, que não eram eles sós os que haviam de ir com ele, que a maior parte da gente do reino havia de ir com ele. E disse ele testemunha que não respondera ao dito Dom Pedro Cangua Mobemba nada ao que lhe dissera.

E como o dito Dom Pedro viu que ele testemunha lhe não respondia nada, o remeteu a um seu privado dele, dito Dom Pedro, por nome Dom Bastião, que lhe daria o

[3] Paiva Manso has *lha;* it could be *lá.*

[Testimony of João Ane, Chapel Boy]

Item. João Ane, chapel boy,[2] a witness sworn on the Holy Gospels, on which he placed his right hand, which were given to him by the magistrate and purveyor Jorge Afonso, and promised to tell the truth regarding all that was asked him. He, the witness,[3] said that it is true that on several occasions he saw Dom Bastião and Dom Pedro Nkanga a Mvemba speaking together, and he knew that they had conversed considerably and were friendly. And [João Ane] saw this because they were frequently both [at the church]. And that he knew nothing else. And [João Ane] further declared under oath that it was true that with his own eyes he saw Pedro Álvares enter the church many times and speak with Dom Pedro. And when [Pedro Álvares] was there, [Dom Pedro and Pedro Álvares] entered the vestry and closed the doors, and they both spoke with each other. And nevertheless, [João Ane] did not know what they did and did not say.

And he said no more of this case. And to certify, he signed in the presence of the magistrate, and regarding the customary [questions], he said nothing.

[Bel]chior Dias, clerk, who set this down in writing.

[Testimony of Dom Afonso]

Item. Dom Afonso, witness sworn on the Holy Gospels, which were given to him by the magistrate and purveyor Jorge Afonso, on which he placed his right hand, and promised to tell the truth regarding all that was asked him. The witness [Dom Afonso] said that it was true that the said Dom Pedro Nkanga a Mvemba called him one day when [Dom Afonso] was in church, and that [Dom Pedro] said to [Dom Afonso] that he wanted to speak with him in secret, and that Dom Pedro told him to swear on the book of the Holy Gospels because he wanted to tell him a very important secret. And [Dom Afonso] contended that he would not swear, that [Dom Pedro] should tell him [the secret], that he would not tell anything that Dom Pedro told him. And Dom Pedro told him again to swear an oath, and [Dom Afonso] then swore to say nothing. Then Dom Pedro said to him that he had determined to leave [the church stronghold] and that he wanted [Dom Afonso] to go with him and so, too, [Dom Afonso's] brother, because if Dom Pedro Nkanga a Mvemba left and they remained, His Royal Lordship [Dom Diogo] would order them killed. And Dom Pedro Nkanga a Mvemba also told [Dom Afonso] that they should not be afraid to go with him, that they were not the only ones who would go with him, that a majority of the people of the kingdom would go with him. And [Dom Afonso] said that he did not respond to anything that Pedro Nkanga a Mvemba said to him.

And as Dom Pedro saw that [Dom Afonso] did not answer him at all, he sent him to his steward, named Dom Bastião, who gave him details on how he should proceed.

[2] Although "chapel boy" implies a youth, it is quite possible that in Kongo these chapel boys were adults, as we know that Diogo sent them on diplomatic missions and to evangelize foreign countries. They were in fact as much lay evangelists as simply youths who helped around the church.

[3] This repetitive bureaucratic language is retained in the Portuguese but hereafter is replaced in the English translation with the names of the witnesses in brackets in order to facilitate comprehension.

aviso e maneira como havia de fazer. E ele testemunha se saiu fora da igreja. E logo ao outro dia pela manhã, o dito Dom Bastião, privado do dito Dom Pedro, que seus negócios negociava, mandou chamar a ele testemunha e a seu irmão. E lhe disse que seu senhor Dom Pedro lhe mandava que o irmão dele testemunha se fosse para Su[n]de e para Nocolla e que fizesse duas guerras, então que ele fugiria da igreja donde estava, e veria se Sua *Real Senhoria* tinha tanto poder que acudisse à guerra de Su[n]de ou a ele Dom Pedro.

E logo o dito Dom Bastião, que suas coisas fazia, deu o recado a ele testemunha. E logo naquele próprio dia o tornou a chamar a ele testemunha o dito Dom Pedro. E logo[4] o dito Dom Pedro lhe perguntara se Dom Bastião lhe dera o seu recado, e disse ele testemunha que sim. E lhe tornara a dizer que esforçase e não temesse nada, que muitos eram da sua parte, a saber, Manymytombe, Dom Matias, e Nusu[n]guo Amaalla, Manypemba e assim todos os *fidalgos* da Vu[n]da e Manue[m]bo, e Tambuque Penba Asalla Aquibella. E o dito Dom Pedro lhe dissera a ele testemunha outras vezes que não temesse nada, que Dom Matias lhe fora pedir perdão das coisas passadas.

E dizendo-lhe que Sua *Real Senhoria* lhe prometera a *renda* de Su[n]de e que lha não dera. E assim lhe dissera o dito Dom Pedro a ele testemunha que quando ele Dom Matias estava em Pamguo lhe esperava uma carta, e que dizia que ele Dom Matias iria matar Manysu[n]de e se levantaria com a terra. E que ele dito Dom Pedro fugiria para Bata então que ambos ajuntariam suas guerras e viriam sobre [o] Comguo. E que ele Dom Pedro seria rei d[o] Comguo. E que quando ele vira a carta do dito Dom Matias, tomara conselho com suas irmãs se fugiria da igreja. E que elas lhe disseram que não, que aquilo era engano que já lhe tinham mortos seus filhos, que assim queriam fazer a ele. E que agora vê que é tudo verdade pelas desculpas e cumprimentos que o dito Dom Matias tivera com ele. E com isto esforçara a testemunha para que fizesse o que lhe ele mandava. E que ele Dom Pedro tem por certo [e] certeza todos estes *fidalgos* aqui nomeados serem de sua banda e se irem com ele. E que ele testemunha lhe dissera que lhe não dava resposta de nada, que tudo estava nas mãos de Deus.

E mais não disse do dito caso. E do costume disse que era sobrinho do dito Dom Pedro.

Item, mais disse e declarou Dom Afonso, pelo juramento que tomou, que [a] ele lhe dissera um *fidalgo* de Vu[n]da, por nome Manychallyta e por nome de cristão Dom Francisco, e lhe dera conta a ele testemunha em como Dom Pedro tinha assentado em não sair fora deste outeiro, senão aqui fazer sua guerra, porque ele tinha mais gente

[4] This is an apparent error in Paiva Manso or in the manuscript: *e logo lhe.*

And [Dom Afonso] left the church. And then on the morning of the next day, Dom Bastião, confidante of Dom Pedro, who took care of his affairs, had [Dom Afonso] and his brother called. And [Dom Bastião] said that his lord, Dom Pedro, had ordered that the brother [of Dom Afonso] should go to Nsundi and Nkola and raise two armies. Then [Dom Bastião] would abandon the church where he was, and he would see if His Royal Lordship had enough power to stop the army of Nsundi or Dom Pedro.

And not long afterward, Dom Bastião, who looked after [Dom Pedro's] affairs, gave a message to [Dom Afonso]. And later that same day Dom Pedro called on [Dom Afonso] again. And then Dom Pedro asked him if Dom Bastião had given him his message; and [Dom Afonso] said yes. And [Dom Pedro] said again to [Dom Afonso] that he should be strong and have no fear, as there were many on his side, namely *Mani*[4] Mitombe, Dom Matias and Nsungo a Mala, *Mani* Mpemba, and also all the *fidalgos* of Vunda and *Mani* Wembo and Tambuke Mpemba Nsala a Kibela.[5] And Dom Pedro told [Dom Afonso] on other occasions he should not fear anything, that Dom Matias would beg his forgiveness for things past.

And saying to him that His Royal Lordship [Dom Diogo] had promised him [Dom Afonso] the *renda* of Nsundi and that he had given him nothing, Dom Pedro said to [Dom Afonso] that when Dom Matias was in Mpangu there was a letter waiting for [Dom Pedro]; and it said that Dom Matias would go and kill *Mani* Nsunda and would rise up and revolt with the [people of the] land and that Dom Pedro should flee to Mbata; whereupon both would join their armies and attack Kongo, and Dom Pedro would be King of Kongo. And when he saw the letter from Dom Matias, he took counsel with his sisters as to whether he should abandon the church. And they told him no, [fleeing] was a mistake,[6] they had already killed his sons, and they wished to do the same to him. And now he sees that [Dom Matias' letter] is all true, because of excuses and compromises that Dom Matias had made to him. And with this [Dom Pedro] gave him, the witness [Dom Afonso], courage to do as he ordered him, [telling him] that Dom Pedro believes it to be true that all these above-named *fidalgos* are on his side and that they will follow him and that [Dom Afonso] said to [Dom Pedro] that he would not give him any response, that everything was in God's hands.

And [Dom Afonso] said no more of the case. And regarding the customary [questions], he said that he was a nephew of Dom Pedro.

Item. Dom Afonso said, and moreover declared under oath, that a *fidalgo* of Vunda by the name of *Mani* Zalita, and by the Christian name of Dom Francisco, spoke to him and gave him, the witness, an account of how Dom Pedro had decided not to leave this hill but to raise his army here, because he had more supporters than were

[4] *Mani* is a form that is frequently encountered in documents from Kongo meaning "lord of." Though its correct orthography in modern Kikongo is probably *mwene,* its use is sufficiently widespread in modern literature on Kongo that we will retain this spelling here.

[5] This name is interesting; it suggests that Nsala a Kibela (a personal name) was a former *Mani* Mpemba who had been removed from power (*tambuquado*).

[6] The word *engano* is ambiguous, and the sentence may be saying that the letter was a trick.

por si do que ficava a Sua *Real Senhoria.* E que Sua *Real Senhoria* não tinha mais por si que Manycomdomgo e Manyllu[m]bo e Manyvu[n]da, sem gente nenhuma, senão ele só em pessoa. E que já tinha dado a *renda* de Manyllu[m]bo a Manybanpa, que havia de cortar a cabeça a Manyllu[m]bo sem mais causa[5] nenhuma, e que a gente de Manyvu[n]da havia de cortar a cabeça ao dito Manyvu[n]da e a Manycomdomgo.

E assim disse mais ele testemunha que um dia fora à casa do dito Dom Bastião, e lhe contou como ele—Dom Bastião—estivera falando com o dito Dom Pedro sobre a maneira que haviam de ter na sua guerra. E, como soube que Manypemba vinha fugindo para cá, lhe dissera que folgava com a sua vinda. E que seria para esforçar sua guerra. E que com sua vinda acabaria seus negócios e não haveria mais que fazer. E disse ele testemunha que se confessara, e que o padre que o confessara lhe mandara que descubrisse tudo a Sua *Real Senhoria,* porquanto era caso de traição e tocava à sua *real* pessoa. De maneira que ele testemunha o descobriu assim da maneira que dito tem. E disse mais ele testemunha que como o dito Dom Pedro soube que isto era descoberto, lhe mandara dizer a ele testemunha e a seu irmão que não o[6] descubrissem a ninguém, porque o que ele trabalhava não era senão para proveito deles.

E disse mais ele testemunha que o dito Dom Pedro lhe dissera que ele tinha esperança duma *bula* que lhe havia de vir do Santo Padre para que lhe tornassem o reino. E que por isso trabalhava de se sair dali, porque se ali estivesse Sua *Real Senhoria,* mandá-lo-ia matar quando a *bula* viesse.

E mais não disse do dito caso. E do costume disse que era sobrinho do dito Dom Pedro. E, por verdade, assinou com o dito *ouvidor,* eu Belchior Dias, *escrivão* que isto escrevi.

Dom Afonso
Jorge Afonso

[Testemunha de Pedro Afonso Milando, *moço da capela*]

Item, Pedro Afonso Milando, *moço da capela,* estante desta cidade de Comguo, testemunha jurado aos Santos Evangelhos, em que pôs a mão direita, que lhe pelo *ouvidor* e *provedor* Jorge Afonso foram dados, que disse[sse] a verdade do que lhe perguntassem, a qual ele prometeu de dizer. Disse ele testemunha que é verdade que ele foi língua na confissão de Dom Afonso, testemunha atrás perguntada, e que o padre lhe deu em

[5] Paiva Manso transcribes this word as *cosa.* It may be *coisa,* though *causa* makes more sense.

[6] Transcribed as *no* in Paiva Manso.

with His Royal Lordship [Dom Diogo]; and that His Royal Lordship did not have any followers other than *Mani* Kandongo and *Mani* Lumbo and *Mani* Vunda, who had no people[7] except for him alone; and that [Dom Diogo] had already given *Mani* Lumbo's *renda* to *Mani* Mbampa, who would behead *Mani* Lumbo without any other cause; and that *Mani* Vunda's people would behead *Mani* Vunda and *Mani* Kandongo.

And [Dom Afonso] said, moreover, that one day he went to the house of Dom Bastião and he, Dom Bastião, spoke to him about how [Dom Bastião] had spoken with Dom Pedro, about how they ought to conduct their war. And as he knew that *Mani* Mpemba was fleeing in this direction, [Dom Bastião] said to [Dom Afonso] that he was glad that he was coming, and that [his coming] was to support [Bastião's] army, and that with his coming, his negotiations would end, and there would be no more to be done. And [Dom Afonso] said that he made confession and that the father to whom he confessed ordered him to disclose all to His Royal Lordship [Dom Diogo], as this was a case of treason and concerned the Royal Person. Thus [Dom Afonso] disclosed [the matter] in the way he has declared. And [Dom Afonso] also said that since Dom Pedro knew that this was disclosed, he ordered that [Dom Afonso] and his brother be told that they should reveal nothing of what they knew to anyone, because what [Dom Pedro] was planning was only for their benefit.

And moreover [Dom Afonso] said that Dom Pedro told him that he was hoping for a [papal] bull, which would be sent to him by the Holy Father, so that they would return the kingdom to [Dom Pedro], and that for this reason he was thinking of leaving there [the church], because if he stayed, His Royal Lordship would order him killed when the bull arrived.[8]

And [Dom Afonso] said no more of this case. And regarding the customary [questions], he said that he was a nephew of Dom Pedro. And to certify, he signed in the presence of the magistrate. I, Belchior Dias, clerk, who set it down in writing.

Dom Afonso
Jorge Afonso

[Testimony of Pedro Afonso Milando, Chapel Boy]

Item. Pedro Afonso Milando, chapel boy, being from this city of Kongo, witness sworn on the Holy Gospels, on which he placed his right hand, which were given to him by the magistrate and purveyor, Jorge Afonso, that he was to tell the truth regarding what was asked him, and he promised to tell [the truth]. [Milando] said that it was true that he was interpreter at the confession of Dom Afonso, the witness previously questioned,[9] and that the father ordered that as penance [Milando] should reveal to His

[7] Supporters.

[8] The plotters apparently believed that the law of sanctuary could be superseded by a papal bull, and Pedro could be seized by Diogo if he got a bull to that effect. For his own part, Pedro believed that a papal bull could declare him king.

[9] The use of an interpreter suggests that the priest in question was Portuguese, as, presumably, a Kongo priest would not need an interpreter. However, the use of interpreters was also considered a part of confession in Kongo at later periods regardless of the linguistic skills of the priest.

penitência que ele testemunha que descubrisse tudo o que o dito Dom Afonso dizia a Sua *Real Senhoria,* porquanto era traição e tocava o seu real estado, o qual ele veio dizer. E é tudo o que atrás está escrito.

E mais não disse. E, por verdade de tudo, assinou aqui, com o dito *ouvidor.* Eu, Belchior Dias, *escrivão* que isto escrevi.

Pedro Afonso Milando
Jorge Afonso

[Testemunha de Dom Pedro Afonso]

Item, Dom Pedro Afonso, testemunha jurada aos Santos Evangelhos, em que pôs a mão direita, que lhe pelo *ouvidor* e *provedor* Jorge Afonso foram dados. E prometeu de dizer a verdade do que lhe perguntassem. Disse ele testemunha que ele estava presente quando Dom Pedro Cangua Mobemba dera conta a Dom Afonso, e que é verdade tudo o que o dito Dom Afonso testemunhou e disse em seu juramento.

E, por verdade assinou aqui, com o dito *ouvidor,* e do costume disse nada. Eu, Belchior Dias, *escrivão* que isto escrevi.

Dom Pedro Afonso
Jorge Afonso

[Testemunha de Dom Bastião]

Item, Dom Bastião, *fidalgo* de Sua *Real Senhoria,* testemunha jurado aos Santos Evangelhos, em que pôs a mão direita, que lhe pelo *ouvidor* e *provedor* Jorge Afonso foi dado, o qual estava preso num *leba[m]ba.* E prometeu de dizer a verdade do que [lhe] perguntassem. Disse ele testemunha que é verdade que antes que partisse Dom Rodrigo para a ilha de *São Tomé,* ele testemunha não tinha amizade nem conversação com Dom Pedro Cangua Mobemba, senão o dito Dom Rodrigo disse a ele testemunha e lhe encomendou muito que lhe rogava que disesse a Dom Pedro que se não saísse da igreja até lhe ele não mandar seu recado, que, ainda que Sua *Real Senhoria* mandasse que se saísse fora da igreja, que se não saísse até não ver seu recado. E que lhe dissera a ele testemunha o dito Dom Rodrigo que pois ele ia corrido deste reino, que ele buscaria maneira, por onde houvesse uma dispensação do Papa, por onde tornasse a mandar dar o reino ao dito Dom Pedro. E que se Sua *Real Senhoria* não usasse com ele de piedade e lhe não quisesse perdoar, que havia de trabalhar por destruir este reino, não lhe mandando perdão, e mandando-lho, que não faria coisa nenhuma do que determinava.

Royal Lordship [Dom Diogo] everything that Dom Afonso had said, as it was treason and touched upon his royal state. This is what [Milando] has come to state. And [what he heard] is everything that has been written above.

And he said no more. And to certify, he signed in the presence of the magistrate. I, Belchior Dias, clerk, who set it down in writing.

Pedro Afonso Milando
Jorge Afonso

[Testimony of Dom Pedro Afonso]

Item. Dom Pedro Afonso, witness sworn on the Holy Gospels, on which he placed his right hand, which were given to him by the magistrate and purveyor, and promised to tell the truth regarding all that was asked him. [Dom Pedro Afonso] said that he was present when Dom Pedro Nkanga a Mvemba gave an account [of the plots] to Dom Afonso and that all that Dom Afonso testified and said in his sworn [testimony] was true.

And to certify, he signed in the presence of the magistrate. And regarding the customary [questions], he said nothing. I, Belchior Dias, clerk, who set it down in writing.

Dom Pedro Afonso
Jorge Afonso

[Testimony of Dom Bastião]

Item. Dom Bastião, *fidalgo* of His Royal Lordship, witness sworn on the Holy Gospels, on which he placed his right hand, which were given to him by the magistrate and purveyor Jorge Afonso, who was imprisoned in a *lebamba,*[10] and he promised to tell the truth regarding all that was asked him. [Dom Bastião] said that it is true that before Dom Rodrigo left for the Island of *São Tomé,* [Dom Bastião] had no friendship or conversation with Dom Pedro Nkanga a Bemba, rather Dom Rodrigo told him [Dom Bastião] and encouraged him greatly and entreated him[11] to tell Dom Pedro to not leave the church until he had sent him his message that even if His Royal Lordship [Dom Diogo] ordered that he leave the church, he should not leave until he had seen his [Dom Rodrigo's] message. And [Dom Bastião said] that Dom Rodrigo told him that he was being run out of this kingdom, that he would look for a way whereby to obtain a dispensation from the Pope, which would mandate the return of the kingdom to Dom Pedro, and that if His Royal Lordship did not treat him with mercy and did not wish to pardon him, he would work to destroy this kingdom, not ordering a pardon for him and ordering that nothing be done according to his [Dom Diogo's] orders.

10 *Lebamba* or *libambo,* "a device," often a forked wooden object used to secure prisoners. Some included chains.

11 The Portuguese is unclear here, stating *e lhe encomendou muito que lhe rogava que dissesse.* If this meant that Dom Rodrigo begged Dom Bastião to entreat Dom Pedro, the verb *rogar* should be conjugated in the subjunctive *rogasse.*

E disse ele testemunha que o dito Dom Rodrigo dissera a Francisco de Almada que dissesse a ele testemunha que tudo o que ele fizesse na ilha, que Francisco de Almada lhe traria o recado. E que ele sabe o dito Francisco de Almada estar em Pinda com o recado do dito Dom Rodrigo para ele testemunha.

E declarou mais ele testemunha que é verdade que Dom Rodrigo dizia que confiava mais dele que de nenhum parente seu, nem irmão, porque quando lhe o dito Dom Rodrigo aquilo dissera, estava no presente sua mãe e irmãs e todos seus parentes. E disse que dele o havia de confiar, e de ninguém outrem não.

E disse mais ele testemunha que é verdade que todos os *fidalgos* de Manyvu[n]da, ao tempo que ele entrou na igreja e teve amizade com Dom Pedro, já todos os *fidalgos* de Vu[n]da estavam concertados com o dito Dom Pedro que saísse da igreja. E todos se iriam para ele, a saber, Dom António Manysimsa e Dom Francisco Manypamgallas, e Dom João Manycatila.

E disse ele testemunha que tudo o que Dom Afonso e seu irmão testemunharam é verdade, porque ele esteve presente e o sabe certo. E declarou mais ele testemunha que Dom António Manysimsa se foi despedir de Dom Pedro na igreja, que ele ia por mandado de Sua *Real Senhoria* e de Manyvu[n]da. E posto que fosse por mandado de Sua *Real Senhoria,* que ele saberia lá de todos os *fidalgos* de Vu[n]da, se estavam certos e prestes para o ajudarem.

E assim declarou ele testemunha que ele foi além do E[m]brize. E primeiro que se partisse ele testemunha se foi despedir do dito Dom Pedro, e Dom Pedro lhe dissera que perguntasse lá a um seu *criado,* que lá estava com Manypemba, se vendera uma espada que ele lá mandara que vendesse. E que se era vendida, que lhe trouxesse o dinheiro. E lhe disse mais o dito Dom Pedro que chegasse a Temgua a falar com Manytemgua, *fidalgo* de Manyvu[n]da, e que lhe dissesse que lhe mandasse alguma coisa para comer.

E disse ele testemunha que ele fizera tudo o que lhe o dito Dom Pedro mandara e fora ter com Manytemgua e lhe dera o recado do dito Dom Pedro. E o dito Manytemgua lhe dera cinco mil zi[m]bos que desse a Dom Pedro, ou que os comesse ou fize[sse] o que quisesse deles.

E declarou mais ele testemunha que é verdade que Manypemba e o dito Dom Pedro se ajuntaram em casa dele testemunha uma noite. E disse o dito Dom Pedro a Manypemba que lhe desse conselho como sairia daquela igreja, que havia tanto tempo que ali estava. E que lhe respondeu Manypemba que não tinha remédio nenhum porque ainda estava fazendo mocano da sua terra, onde estava *tambuquado,* e estava sem gente, que a que tinha era de Sua *Real Senhoria.* E que isso faria ele se Sua *Real Senhoria*

And [Dom Bastião] said that Dom Rodrigo told Francisco de Almada to tell him [Dom Bastião] that he would send him word concerning everything that he did on the island, and that Francisco de Almada would bring him a report, and that he knew that Francisco de Almada was in Mpinda with the report from Dom Rodrigo for him.

And moreover [Dom Bastião] declared that it is true that Dom Rodrigo said that he trusted him more than any of his own relatives, even brothers, because when Dom Rodrigo said this to him, his mother was present and sisters and all his relatives. And [Dom Bastião] said that he could trust in him and in no one else.

And moreover [Dom Bastião] said that it is true that at the time that he entered the church and took up friendship with Dom Pedro, all the *fidalgos* of *Mani* Vunda were already in agreement with Dom Pedro that he should leave the church. And all of them would follow him, namely Dom António *Mani* Nsimsa and Dom Francisco *Mani* Mpangala and Dom João *Mani* Katila.

And [Dom Bastião] said that everything that Dom Afonso and his brother testified to is true, because he was present and knows it to be sure. And [Dom Bastião] declared moreover that Dom António *Mani* Nsimsa went in the church to say good-bye to Dom Pedro, that he went by order of His Royal Lordship [Dom Diogo] and of *Mani* Vunda. And although it was by order of His Royal Lordship, he would know about all the *fidalgos* of Vunda, whether they were ready and disposed to help him.

And [Dom Bastião] also declared that he went across the [River] Ambrize.[12] And before leaving, he went to say good-bye to Dom Pedro, and Dom Pedro told him that he should ask one of his clients, who was there with *Mani* Mpemba, if he had sold a sword which he sent there to be sold. And if it was sold, that he should bring the money back. And moreover Dom Pedro said to him [Dom Bastião] that he should go to Tenga to speak with *Mani* Tenga, a *fidalgo* of *Mani* Vunda, and tell him to send him something to eat.

And [Dom Bastião] said that he did all that Dom Pedro ordered him to do. And having met with *Mani* Tenga, he gave him the message from Dom Pedro. And *Mani* Tenga gave him five thousand *nzimbu,*[13] which he gave to Dom Pedro so that he could eat them or do whatever he wanted with them.

And moreover [Dom Bastião] declared that it is true that *Mani* Mpemba and Dom Pedro met together in the witness' house one night. And Dom Pedro asked *Mani* Mpemba to advise him how he should leave that church, where he had been for so long; and that *Mani* Mpemba responded that he had no solution, because there was still a *mocano*[14] taking place in his land where he was *tambuquado,*[15] and he was without supporters; and that those that he had were those of His Royal Lordship; and that he

[12] Kikongo speakers call the river "*Mbidizi.*"

[13] *Nzimbu* is the Kikongo name for the seashells drawn from Luanda Island that were used in Kongo as money. Earlier documents suggest that several *lifuku* (a unit of ten thousand) would be the price of a single slave or wages for a mason for a long period. This would therefore be a relatively small amount of money.

[14] A judicial process, *nkanu* in modern Kikongo.

[15] See note 10 in the chapter introduction.

lhe tornasse a *renda,* e faria e saberia a vontade de sua gente. E lhe dissera o dito Dom Pedro ao dito Manypemba—Vêdes quão pouco tempo há que vos Sua *Real Senhoria* deu a *renda,* e já vo-la tornou a tirar, e, pois vo-la tiraram agora, é tempo de me ajudardes.

E disse e declarou o dito Dom Bastião, pelo juramento que tinha recebido, que é verdade que Manue[m]bo, irmão de Manynoquaquate, também era em ajuda do dito Dom Pedro.

E mais não disse do dito caso. E, por verdade, assinou aqui com o dito *ouvidor* e d[e] costume disse que era amigo do dito Dom Pedro. E eu Belchior Dias, *escrivão* que esta escrevi.

Dom Bastião
Jorge Afonso

[Testemunha de Pedro Afonso]

Item, Pedro Afonso, estante nesta cidade de Comguo, testemunha jur[ada] aos Santos Evangelhos, em que pôs a mão direita, que lhe pelo *ouvidor* e *provedor* Jorge Afonso foi dado, o qual prometeu de dizer a verdade do que soubesse. Disse ele testemunha que sabe certo, que Manypemba lhe contou em confissão, que ele era convidado de Dom Matias que se levantassem contra Sua Senhoria. E Manypemba lhe dissera que tal nem faria nem havia de fazer porque Sua *Real Senhoria* era seu compadre. E que isto sabe ele testemunha por o dito Manypemba lho dizer em sua confissão, e que o dissesse a Sua *Real Senhoria,* o qual ele testemunha nunca disse, senão o dia de sexta-feira de Endoenças, foi ele testemunha com o dito Manypemba a confessá-lo a Sua *Real Senhoria.*

E mais não sabe do dito caso, e, por verdade, assinou com o dito *ouvidor* e do costume disse nada. Eu, Belchior Dias *escrivão,* que isto escrevi.

Pedro Afonso
Jorge Afonso

[Testemunha de Francisco Fernandes]

Item, Francisco Fernandes, testemunha jurado aos Santos Evangelhos, em que pôs a mão direita, que lhe pelo *ouvidor* e *provedor* Jorge Afonso foi dado, o qual prometeu de dizer a verdade do que lhe perguntassem e soubesse. Disse ele testemunha que é verdade que um dia estava na *casa dos atabaques.* E, como acabou de tanger, se foi para o *terreiro* e aí chegou a ele Dom Bastião. E ele testemunha lhe perguntou acerca dos navios que haviam de vir da ilha e lhe disse que eram vindos, porém que não sabia quantos nem quantos nem quantos não [sic]. E o dito Dom Bastião disse a ele testemunha

[*Mani* Mpemba] would do this if His Royal Lordship returned to him the *renda,* and he would do and would know the will of his people. And Dom Pedro said to *Mani* Mpemba, "See how short a time it has been since His Royal Lord gave you the *renda,* and already he wants to take it back, and since he wishes to take it back, now is the time to help me."

And Dom Bastião said and declared, under the oath that he had sworn, that it is true that *Mani* Wembo, the brother of *Mani* Nkakate,[16] also went to the aid of Dom Pedro.

And he said no more of this case. And to certify, he signed here in the presence of the magistrate. And regarding the customary [questions], he said that he was the friend of Dom Pedro. And, I, Belchior Dias, clerk, who set this down in writing.

Dom Bastião
Jorge Afonso

[Testimony of Pedro Afonso]

Item. Pedro Afonso, being in this city of Kongo, witness sworn on the Holy Gospels on which he placed his right hand, which were given to him by the magistrate and purveyor Jorge Afonso, and he promised to tell the truth regarding what he knew. [Pedro Afonso] said that he knew for certain, as *Mani* Mpemba had told him in confidence, that [*Mani* Mpemba] was invited by Dom Matias to rise up against His Royal Lordship. And *Mani* Mpemba told [Pedro Afonso] that he would not and was not going to do that, since His Royal Lordship was his godfather. And [Pedro Afonso] knew this because *Mani* Mpemba told him in confession, telling him to tell His Royal Lordship, but [Pedro Afonso] never did so, except on Maundy Thursday, when he went with *Mani* Mpemba to confess it to His Royal Lordship.

And he knows no more about this case. And to verify it, he signed with the magistrate. And regarding the customary [questions], he said nothing. I, Belchior Dias, clerk, who set it down in writing.

Pedro Afonso
Jorge Afonso

[Testimony of Francisco Fernandes]

Item. Francisco Fernandes, witness sworn on the Holy Gospels, on which he placed his right hand, which were given to him by the magistrate and purveyor Jorge Afonso. And he promised to tell the truth regarding all that was asked and what he knew. [Fernandes] said that it is true that one day he was in the *casa dos Atabaques.*[17] And since he had just stopped playing, he went toward the *plaza* and there he met Dom Bastião. And [Fernandes] questioned him about the ships that were coming from the island, and he said that they had arrived; however, he did not know how many there were or

[16] Modernization of *Manynoquaquate* is problematic. The position to which the title refers is unknown.

[17] The "house of drums."

que Dom Pedro lhe queria falar, e ele testemunha lhe dissera que não queria lá ir, e isto aporfiando com ele testemunha três vezes que fosse.

E de se ver importunado do dito Dom Bastião, se foi à igreja a falar com o dito Dom Pedro. E tanto que se viu com o dito Dom Pedro, lhe rogou o dito Dom Pedro a ele testemunha que fosse falar a Manypemba, que viesse a falar com ele aqui a Comguo. E ele testemunha lhe respondeu que não podia lá ir, que era homem conhecido e que o saberia Sua *Real Senhoria,* e que em nenhuma maneira podia lá ir porque Sua *Real Senhoria* tinha tomados todos os portos e caminhos, e que havia medo de ir e de o prenderem, que portanto que não havia de ir lá.

E mais não disse do dito caso e, por verdade, assinaram, e do costume disse nada. E eu, Belchior Dias, *escrivão* que isto escrevi.

Francisco Fernandes
Jorge Afonso

[Testemunha de Dom Pedro Afonso]

Item, Dom Pedro Afonso, testemunha jurado aos Santos Evangelhos, em que pôs a mão direita, que lhe pelo *ouvidor* e *provedor* Jorge Afonso foi dado, o qual prometeu de dizer a verdade do que soubesse. Disse ele testemunha e declarou que era verdade que ele ouviu dizer a Dom Bastião que [ele] se espantava das coisas que haviam de passar neste reino. E nomeou um homem que foi Manypamgallas, *fidalgo* de Sua *Real Senhoria,* que ele era um dos que iam sempre com Sua *Real Senhoria* às guerras, e que agora pois o *tambuquara* que havia de ver quem ia com ele. E isto lhe contara a ele testemunha Dom Bastião, que Manychallyta lh[e] contara que ele e Manypamgallas passaram estas razões.

E que mais não sabia do dito caso. E, por verdade, assinaram, e do costume disse nada. E eu, Belchior Dias, *escrivão* que isto escrevi.

Dom Pedro Afonso
Jorge Afonso

[Testemunha de Dom João de Melo]

Item, Dom João de Melo, porteiro-mor de Sua *Real Senhoria,* testemunha jurado aos Santos Evangelhos, em que pôs a mão direita, que lhe pelo *ouvidor* e *provedor* Jorge Afonso foi dado. E prometeu de dizer a verdade do que soubesse. Disse ele testemunha que é verdade que Dom Pedro Cangua Mobemba lhe dissera que ao tempo [em] que

anything.[18] And Dom Bastião said to [Fernandes] that Dom Pedro wanted to speak with him, and [Fernandes] told him that he did not want to go there, and [Dom Bastião] argued with him, three times insisting that he go.

And seeing himself constantly pressed by Dom Bastião, [Fernandes] went to the church to speak with Dom Pedro. And as soon as he met with Dom Pedro, Dom Pedro begged him to go speak with *Mani* Mpemba and ask him to come to speak with him here in Kongo. [Fernandes] responded that he could not go there; that he was a well-known man; and that he was known to His Royal Lordship, and he could in no way go there, because His Royal Lordship had closed all the ports and roads, and he was afraid to go; and that they might capture him, and for that reason he would not go there.

And he said no more of the case. And to certify they signed, and regarding the customary [questions], he said nothing. And, I, Belchior Dias, clerk, who set it down in writing.

Francisco Fernandes
Jorge Afonso

[Testimony of Dom Pedro Afonso]

Item. Dom Pedro Afonso, witness sworn on the Holy Gospels, on which he placed his right hand, which were given to him by the magistrate. And he promised to tell the truth regarding what he knew. [Dom Pedro Afonso] said and declared that it was true that he had heard Dom Bastião say that he was frightened of the things that were to happen in this kingdom. And he named a man who was *Mani* Mpangala, *fidalgo* of His Royal Lordship, who was one of those who always went to war with His Royal Lordship, and that now, since he had been *tambuquado* [removed from office], he would see who would go with him [to war?]. And Dom Bastião told [Dom Pedro Afonso] that *Mani* Zalita told him that he and *Mani* Mpangala had related these things.[19]

And he did not know anything more of the case. And to certify he signed. And regarding the customary [questions], he said nothing. I, Belchior Dias, clerk, who set this down in writing.

Dom Pedro Afonso
Jorge Afonso

[Testimony of Dom João de Melo]

Item. Dom João de Melo, principal porter of His Royal Lordship, witness sworn on the Holy Gospels, on which he placed his right hand, which were given to him by the magistrate and purveyor, Jorge Afonso. And he promised to tell the truth regarding what he knew. [Dom João de Melo] said that it was true that Dom Pedro Nkanga a

[18] The original reads, *não sabia quantos nem quantos nem quantos não,* which either is a copyist's error or perhaps means "how many, how many, how many" or "how many were and were not there."

[19] The Portuguese is confusing and might also mean, "he and *Mani* Mpangala had overlooked these reasons."

ele estava em prisão numa casa, onde Sua *Real Senhoria* o tinha, e mandava guardar por a sua gente, ele Dom Pedro não fugira da dita casa donde estava, senão por conselho de Dom Rodrigo, e depois de ele Dom Pedro estar na igreja. Daí [a] algum tempo o dito Dom Rodrigo o cometera que fugissem e se fossem por esse reino. E o dito Dom Pedro lhe dera em resposta que se não havia de sair da igreja nem ir por nenhuma parte que antes ali queria estar.

E assim declarou mais ele testemunha que, estando um dia em sua casa, Sua *Real Senhoria* o mandara chamar à igreja onde estava, e lhe dissera Sua *Real Senhoria* a ele testemunha [ide] lá onde está Dom Pedro Cangua Mobemba que diz que vos quer dizer não sei [o] quê. E ele testemunha fora e desse dissera que era o que queria. E o dito Dom Pedro lhe dissera que dissesse a Sua *Real Senhoria* como Dom Rodrigo o cometera que fugissem da igreja e ele que não quisera.

E disse ele testemunha que isto era o que sabia do dito caso. E mais não disse e do costume disse nada. E, por verdade, assinaram. Eu, Belchior Dias, *escrivão* que isto escrevi.

Dom João de Melo
Jorge Afonso

[O *escrivão* faz cópias das testemunhas]

E depois disto, aos treze dias do dito mês de Abril do presente ano de 1550, o *ouvidor* e *provedor* Jorge Afonso mandou[-me] a mim *escrivão,* abaixo nomeado, [dar] o[s] traslados a Sua *Real Senhoria,* quantos ele quisesse e necessários lhe fossem, com o instrumento que pede, ao que tudo foi satisfeito. Eu, Belchior Dias, *escrivão* que isto escrevi.

[Uma carta de Dom Pedro Cangua Mobemba a Dom Rodrigo]

E depois disto, aos onze dias do mês de Janeiro do presente ano, nesta cidade de Comguo, por Sua *Real Senhoria* foi dado a mim, *escrivão,* uma carta assinada por Dom Pedro Cangua Mobemba, que mandou à ilha de *São Tomé* a Dom Rodrigo, a qual carta é a que se ao diante segue.

Eu, Belchior Dias, *escrivão* que esta escrevi.

Senhor, muito amado irmão,

Eu saúdo Vossa Senhoria. Não vos posso contar as coisas que passámos com este traidor [D. Diogo] que ainda não acaba de se vingar na nossa *geração.* E jura sempre em seu *terreiro* que não há de descansar até não acabar de matar toda nossa *geração.* E ele diz que me há de matar, e que há de ficar seu filho na minha *renda.* E se[7] ele não há de vingar como me eu vinguei, [s]erá[8] maldito. E nunca lhe sai da boca a nossa *geração* de Quybala. Ele, Manyvu[n]da tem feito cinco cartas para seu filho as outorgar, a saber, uma a Manysu[n]de, e outra a Manyllu[m]bo, e outra a Manycomdomgo, e outra a Manyvu[n]da, e outra a Manynoquoagylla, para a mostrarem a seu filho, e assim o

[7] Transcribed as *se se* in Paiva Manso.

[8] Transcribed as *pera* in Paiva Manso.

Mvemba told him that at the time when he was in prison, in a house where His Royal Lordship kept him and ordered him guarded by his people, Dom Pedro did not abandon the house where he was, except by the advice of Dom Rodrigo and after he, Dom Pedro, had been in the church for some time. Sometime later, Dom Rodrigo encouraged him, that they should flee to go to this kingdom. And Dom Pedro told him in response that he would not leave the church nor go anywhere, because above all else he wished to remain there.

And [Dom João de Melo] declared further that one day while he was in his house, His Royal Lordship ordered him called to the church where he was, and His Royal Lordship said to [Dom João de Melo], "Go there where Dom Pedro Nkanga a Mvemba is, who says he wants to speak with you about I don't know what." And [Dom João de Melo] went and said that he asked what he wanted. And Dom Pedro told him to tell His Royal Lord that Dom Rodrigo had proposed that he leave the church and that he did not want to.

And [Dom João de Melo] said that this is what he knew about the case and he said no more. And regarding the customary [questions], he said nothing. And to certify, they signed. I, Belchior Dias, clerk, who set this down in writing.

Dom João de Melo
Jorge Afonso

[The Clerk Made Copies of the Declarations]

And after this, on the thirteenth day of the month of April of this year 1550, the magistrate and purveyor Jorge Afonso ordered me, the below-named clerk, to make copies for His Royal Lordship, as many as he wanted and needed as an instrument that he requested, and all was done according to instructions. I, Belchior Dias, clerk, who set this down in writing.

[A Letter from Dom Pedro Nkanga a Mvemba to Dom Rodrigo]

And after this, on the eleventh day of January of the present year [1552], in this city of Kongo, a letter was given to me, the clerk, by His Royal Lordship, [and it was] signed by Dom Pedro Nkanga a Mvemba, which he sent to the island of *São Tomé* to Dom Rodrigo, and the letter is the following.

I, Belchior Dias, clerk, set this down in writing.

My dearly beloved brother,

I greet Your Lordship. I can hardly tell you the things that we have suffered with this traitor who still does not cease to take his revenge against our lineage. And he is always sitting in judgment at the *plaza* and will not rest until he has killed our whole lineage. And he says that he will kill me and that he will put his son in my *renda,* and that if he does not take vengeance on me, I will take it on him, and nothing but curses will come from his mouth concerning our lineage of Kibala. And he, *Mani* Vunda, has written five letters for his son to grant, namely one to *Mani* Nsunda, and another to *Mani* Lumbo, and another to *Mani* Kandongo, and another to *Mani* Vunda, and another to *Mani* Kwanzila, to show to his son and also to leave him in his will when

deixar em seu testamento quando ele morrer. E diz que não há de estar com pessoa de nossa *geração,* nem filho nem filha, nem parente nem parenta, senão hão de ser escravos. Louvores a Deus para todo [o] sempre. E diz que os que estão por parir, não estarão com seu filho, nem vós mesmo Dom Rodrigo, nem nenhum rogasse a seu filho por vós, senão que há de ser degradado para todo sempre, jamais.

Irmão, eu vos encomendo não vos esqueçais de nós. Vós há muito tempo que estais lá, e em vós está toda ajuda para nós, p[or] vós serdes um tão mau homem. Já não atentemos à perda d[a] nossa *geração,* pois ainda vós estais assim, e não temos outra esperança senão em vós porque vós estais da parte da verdade. Nós cuidamos que vós mandásseis já a El-Rei de Portugal que mandasse a Roma para nos socorrer com uma santa *bula* para tirar aquele traidor, porque este traidor não tem outro medo senão da *bula,* e se ele ouvir novas da *bula,* não há de fazer nenhuma dúvida d[e que] a *bula* há de vir secretamente, que o não saiba ninguém, porque se o souber alguém, logo há de matar a todos geralmente. E a *bula* há de contar desta maneira, que não perca ninguém, nem matem ninguém, nem leve ninguém, senão tornasse com a sua gente, e também ele que há de obedecer a seu rei, com excomunhão para todo o sempre, jamais. Agora ele tem mandado a Roma um homem branco a buscar uma *bula* para quando vier a *bula* matar-nos a todos geralmente. Agora começa, prendeu vossa irmã Manynabua, e mandou a guardá-la em Su[n]de com Dona Catarina, minha irmã, Manyluqueyne. Lá em Nzinga perdeu vossa irmã, mãe de Dom Bastião, que Deus tem. Vós não tenhais paixão [disto] porque nós temos cercado este traidor para o matarmos, nem vós não tomeis paixão, senão sempre trabalhai p[ara o] perdão d[as] nossas almas no mais, senão que Nosso Senhor acrescente à Vossa Majestade muitos dias de vida.

A qual carta, eu, *escrivão* ao diante nomeado, dou minha fé estar assinada com um sinal que dizia "Dom Pedro," e o sobrescrito dizia, "ao muito prezado Senhor, o Senhor Dom Rodrigo na Ilha de *São Tomé* seja dada, meu irmão".

O qual instrumento de *devassa* e *inquirição* eu, Belchior Dias, *escrivão* e público *tabelião* neste reino e senhorios d[o] Comguo, por El-Rei Nosso Senhor e por Sua *Real Senhoria,* trasladei do próprio original que fica na minha mão, bem e fielmente assim e da maneira que está, e ao pé da letra, sem outra linha nem coisa que dúvida faça, e aqui meu público sinal fiz, que tal é—lugar do sinal público—concertada comigo, Jorge Afonso, *ouvidor* neste reino de Comguo.

Jorge Afonso

he dies. And he said that he is not to associate with anyone of our lineage, neither son nor daughter nor male nor female relative, even if they are slaves. Praise to God for all time. And he said that if anyone reveals one who does not follow his son, nor will you Dom Rodrigo, neither should anyone plead to his son on your behalf, lest he be disgraced for all time.

Brother, I entreat you not to forget us. You have been there a long time, and all our help rests with you, for you to be such a bad person. Now we are not expecting the loss of our lineage, for you are still there, and we have no other hope except for you, because you are on the side of truth. We take care that you have now sent [word] to the king of Portugal [requesting that he] send to Rome to aid us with a Holy bull that will dismiss this traitor, because this traitor fears nothing but a bull, and if he hears news of the bull, he will not have any doubt.[20] The bull should come secretly, so that no one knows of it, because if anyone were to find out about it, he would carry out a general killing of everyone at once. And the bull should read in such a way that no one is condemned nor killed, nor rebel, but rather they should go back to their people, and also that he should obey his king, with a perpetual excommunication. Now he has sent a white man to Rome to seek a bull by which he will have us all generally killed. He is starting now; he has arrested your sister *Mani* Nambwa and sent her to be guarded in Nsundi with Dona Caterina my sister, *Mani* Lukeni. There in Singa he has arrested your sister, the mother of Dom Bastião, who is with God. Do not be upset about this, because we have encircled this traitor in order to kill him, neither should you be upset, but rather work for the pardon of our souls or anything else, except that our Lord in His Grace give you many more days of life.

This letter which I, the below-named clerk, certify is signed with a signature which says "Dom Pedro," and on the outside says, "To be given to the most esteemed Lord Dom Rodrigo, on the island of *São Tomé,* my brother."

This instrument of inquiry, I, Belchior Dias, clerk and notary public of this kingdom and Dominion of Kongo, for the King our Lord and for His Royal Lordship, copied from the original, which is in my hand, well and faithfully, thus and in the manner in which it is found, letter for letter, without altering a line or anything which would create any doubt, and here I place my public seal, such as it is. [public seal] Approved by me, Jorge Afonso, magistrate of this Kingdom of Kongo.

Jorge Afonso

[20] The lack of punctuation creates ambiguity here. The sense may be that there should be no doubt that the bull must come secretly.

2

Maroon Chief Alonso de Illescas' Letter to the Crown, 1586[1]

Charles Beatty-Medina

The Esmeraldas *Maroons* in the Age of Spanish Conquest

In Spanish America, enslaved Africans employed strategies of escape, or marronage, in order to gain their freedom. Even while Amerindians suffered the convulsive shocks of European invasion, fugitive Africans carved out independent enclaves on the scarred landscape of the conquest. This happened in colonial Ecuador's northern coast region, Esmeraldas, during the second half of the sixteenth century. The letter presented here is the work of Alonso de Illescas, an African *Maroon* leader in Esmeraldas, and it reflects the roles that fugitive slaves acquired as Spain worked to subjugate and consolidate its empire.

Contrary to scholarship proposing that escaped slaves attempted to "resurrect an archaic social order," Illescas' letter suggests that African *Maroons* involved themselves in dynamic relationships with their environment, native societies, and colonial authorities, and that their social order developed out of contingencies largely beyond their control (Genovese, 3). It illustrates some of the ways that escaped Africans became critical agents in the colonial process. In his missive, Illescas acknowledged Spain's power in the Americas. However, his purpose was to subvert colonial authorities' plans to establish Spanish settlements in the *Maroons'* homeland.

Not unlike the many native leaders who petitioned the Crown for redress from Spanish abuses, Illescas pled with authorities to reverse their policies. Far from archaic, the *Maroons'* project grew out of the interstitial spaces that fugitives claimed for themselves—spaces that they created and nurtured as they interacted with distinct cultures, peoples, and colonial practices.

The themes in Illescas' letter, in many ways, are shaped by the methods that marked the creation of Spain's colonial world. As Mathew Restall has shown, the "age of conquest" imagery, of well-armed Spaniards handily defeating indigenous armies, is a myth on many counts (*Seven Myths*). Indeed, Spanish success at subduing indigenous civilizations was limited to certain places, at certain times, and under certain conditions. In many areas of Ibero-America, where circumstances were less than ideal for European methods, the Spanish dominated the people they encountered only gradually and incorporated new territories piecemeal and over time (Elliot, 40, 41; Williams, 3). Such was the case in coastal Esmeraldas.

Between 1526 and 1603, the Spanish made more than fifty failed attempts—military, religious, and diplomatic—to subjugate the area (Alcina Franch, 80–99); their repeated failed efforts demonstrating that Esmeraldas, along with much of the Pacific coast of northern South America, was a nearly impenetrable frontier to Spanish settlers (Calero,

[1] See Maps 6 and 7.

50, 51; Williams, chapter 1). By contrast, Alonso de Illescas, and twenty-three fellow fugitives, succeeded in making Esmeraldas their home following a shipwreck in the early 1550s (Cabello Balboa, 18). Although they faced different challenges and arrived with different aims than the Spanish, Illescas and his small band of African renegades established a community that would thrive for generations; their survival resulted from factors that included the region's remote geography and its prolonged indigenous resistance to Spanish rule.

The Spanish named Esmeraldas for the precious green stones that they gained in trade during early encounters with the region's indigenous inhabitants. The dense forests and mangroves that covered the landscape added much to the region's mystery. Although the Bay of San Mateo became popular with ships plying the waters between Panama and Guayaquil (see Maps 1, 6, and 7), the area was of only marginal interest to Peru's viceroy and the Spanish Crown. In the highland city of Quito, however, merchants and Spanish authorities coveted Esmeraldas for its proximity and its potential as a port.

As John Leddy Phelan (5) notes, during the second half of the sixteenth century, Quiteños came to see securing Esmeraldas and San Mateo as critical to increasing trade with their neighboring colonies: Peru and Panama. After 1563 and the establishment of the Crown Court (the *Real Audiencia*) in Quito, creating a port in Esmeraldas became a priority of local government. In 1577 they sent an official mission to offer the rebel Alonso de Illescas authority over the region, in exchange for which he was to resettle his people near San Mateo. On the evening that the *Maroons* were to arrive, warfare broke out in Esmeraldas and the project was abandoned. Though a failure, the mission opened what would be a sporadic line of communication between authorities and the *Maroons* for decades to come.

By 1586 when Illescas wrote to crown authorities in Quito and Madrid, European pathogens and Spanish raids had destroyed much of Esmeraldas' precontact population (Newson, 68). However, the Spanish did not bring enslaved Africans in great numbers to replace the dwindling native population of Quito's coastal regions. During the sixteenth century, the small number of Africans taken to Quito, like those who traveled to Peru with the conquistadors, became servants.

After the conquest, Africans were employed and exploited in many urban occupations, such as bakers, ironsmiths, textile producers, marketplace peddlers, prostitutes, and muleteers. By the seventeenth century, as colonization expanded, Africans formed an important labor source for mining and sugar plantations (Bryant, 86; Lane, chapter 2). In addition, a population of free people of color came into existence, often competing for resources with native peoples and Spanish commoners. As a fringe territory, however, Esmeraldas remained less integrated into the patterns developing in and around highland cities like Quito, Ibarra, and Cuenca.

It was within this geographical and historical context that Alonso de Illescas and his companions rejected their status as slaves, risking their lives under dangerous circumstances to make Esmeraldas their new homeland. As rebels, they would learn to live side by side (and at times in conflictive relationships) with native societies. Some indigenous groups allied themselves with the *Maroons,* whereas others (like the Campaces mentioned in Illescas' letter) remained the *Maroons'* bitter enemies. Two *Maroon*

communities emerged in Esmeraldas and continually faced these competitive conditions. Each in turn gave birth to a first generation of mixed-race progeny, called *mulatos* (and later *zambos*) by Spanish observers and authorities. By the 1590s, the children of these intermarriages were old enough to assume command of their communities.

Don Alonso de Illescas' Letter of Negotiation (1586)

The letter of Alonso de Illescas is an unusual document, primarily because it was produced by an unlikely author: an African slave with little formal education. The person most responsible for penning the missive was probably a young Trinitarian friar named Alonso de Espinosa, sent to aid in the colonization of the *Maroons* in 1583. At the time, Espinosa was supposed to serve on the military expedition of conquistador Diego López de Zúñiga. However, soon after arriving in the lowlands, the young friar became a vocal advocate for the *Maroons.* He roundly condemned López de Zúñiga's conquest and denounced the excesses of his soldiers, their greed, and their desire to find gold (Beatty-Medina, "Caught," 123–24).

Although Espinosa may have been the one to put pen to paper, much of the letter's content reflects the experience and knowledge gained by Illescas from years steeped in Hispanic culture. Unlike the Africans captured and brought directly from their homelands, called *bozales,* Illescas was repeatedly described as *muy ladino;* that is, he was well-versed in Spanish language, customs, and culture. He was raised on the island of Tenerife, a Spanish possession since the 1400s, and later was taken to Seville, Spain's jumping-off point for the conquest and colonization of the Indies. His owners were members of Seville's merchant elite, and Spain trained Illescas in the Hispanic way of life (Cabello Balboa, 43). In his early twenties, he was uprooted once more, this time to travel to the Spanish Indies.

The time that Illescas spent in slavery influenced his actions as a *Maroon* leader. In captivity, he was a personal servant. Like many of the Africans who operated as agents for their Spanish masters, Illescas—would have experienced "considerable responsibility and relative freedom of movement" (Restall, "Black Conquistadors," 175). Illescas' letter reflects his years of exposure to the workings of Spanish authority. Rather than emitting raw defiance, the letter demonstrates a keen awareness of what was important to Spanish authorities and to the Crown. Instead of refusing to submit, Illescas supplicates the Crown and denounces its proposed conquest of Esmeraldas, calling it a disservice to the moral interests of Spain and the Catholic Faith.

Importantly, the letter was not a solitary interaction. It may be considered one piece of an ongoing dialogue between authorities in Quito and the *Maroon* leaders. That conversation began nine years earlier, in 1577, when the *Audiencia* offered Illescas the governorship of Esmeraldas in exchange for resettling his community near the Bay of San Mateo (Beatty-Medina, "Rebels," chapter 2). The failure of that project promoted Spanish attempts to have López de Zúñiga subjugate the *Maroons* militarily in 1583. By 1585, a wealthy merchant named Rodrigo de Ribadeneyra received full rights from the Crown to establish settlements in Esmeraldas. In response, Illescas petitioned the king to rescind Ribadeneyra's grant and allow the *Maroons* to pacify Esmeraldas' native inhabitants.

There are numerous ways in which this petition attempts to influence the court's policies, and Friar Espinosa may have proposed much of the rhetorical phrasing. First, there is a clear emphasis on religion and God—matters not taken lightly by the Spanish Crown as the defender of the Roman Catholic Church throughout Europe and the Americas. Second, Illescas carefully couches his defiance in the language of service. He states that the Crown's plan will only bring chaos, whereas his own solution will save souls. Finally, he presents his actions as being in the royal interest, when in fact they were more important to the *Maroons'* autonomy and independence.

Illescas' letter was a final attempt to stave off Ribadeneyra and other Spanish attempts to colonize the region. But with Ribadeneyra's reputation, wealth, and connections at court working against them, the letter was received in Quito as little more than a bothersome attempt by Espinosa to manage events that Quito's *Audiencia* saw as within its purview. Upon receiving it, the *Audiencia* trumped up charges of murder against Espinosa and placed him in chains to be sent off to Spain. Ribadeneyra never gained the alliance of the *Maroons,* and his settlers failed to establish themselves in Esmeraldas: without the aid of the African rebels, neither could achieve their ends in Esmeraldas.

Fourteen years later, in 1600, the *Audiencia,* under new leadership, recognized the *Maroons'* dominance in the region, granted them their freedoms and liberties, and began a process of pacifying all of Esmeraldas' native societies (Lane, 48). Illescas did not survive long enough to witness this victory of *Maroon* diplomacy, but his sons and daughters lived to receive their legally recognized freedom from slavery.

Carta de Don Alonso de Illescas, *negro* que está en las Esmeraldas [1586][1]

Muy poderoso señor,

Habiendo el devoto padre Fray Alonso de Espinosa de la orden de la Santísima Trinidad, por mí y en mi nombre, por una carta que de mí llevó a vuestra *Real Audiencia,* pidió que tenía deseo de reducirme al servicio de Dios Nuestro Señor y de vuestra Real Corona, con que de vuestra parte se me enviase remisión y perdón general, por razón de haber estado fuera de vuestro servicio, y que enviándonos sacerdote que nos predicase el Santo Evangelio y enseñase [a] nuestros hijos y mujeres, haría todo cuanto en mí fuese y procuraría traer de paz todos los naturales de aquesta provincia.

Y habiendo Vuestra Señoría concedido lo que por mí fue pedido y suplicado, doy a Dios Nuestro Señor muchas gracias por tantas mercedes como he recibido de la mano liberalísima de Dios y de Vuestra Señoría.

Y así el dicho padre me dio noticia cómo Vuestra Real Persona en España tiene proveída esta gobernación en Rodrigo de Ribadeneyra, al cual le viene cantidad de gente para proseguir en el allanamiento y población de esta tierra; y así mandé que todos nos juntásemos para ver y comunicar lo que más conviniese a Vuestro Real Servicio.

Y si Vuestra Real Persona encomendó esta gobernación en Rodrigo de Ribadeneyra, no habiéndole sido hecha *relación* [de] la voluntad que yo tenía de reducirme al *gremio* de la Iglesia y de su Real Corona.

Y así lo que se puede conquistar con la doctrina del Santo Evangelio no será servicio de Dios ni de Vuestra Real Persona entrar con fuerza de armas a costa de tantas almas de la una parte y de la otra, y para domeñar a los campaces y hacerlos venir en conocimiento de mi Dios.

Quiero por haber estado fuera de vuestro servicio, animarme con la gente que tengo debajo de mi dominio dándome Vuestra Alteza licencia [para] entrar en Campaz, y requerirles que vengan de paz a vuestro servicio y poblarlos junto a la mar en la parte que mejor fuere. Y también pediré a su tiempo socorro a Vuestra *Real Audiencia* para poblar otra provincia donde se poblarán dos *pueblos* a Vuestra Real Corona y de ello se servirá Dios Nuestro Señor.

Y así pido y suplico a Vuestra Alteza que no se entienda gobernación lo que yo me ofrezco poblar. Y así suplico a Vuestra Alteza se suspenda la entrada de los soldados porque será alborotar lo que el devoto padre ha pacificado con la doctrina del Santo Evangelio.

Y si hubiera de entrar gente, sea en el Valle Vicioso y Barbacoas, porque realmente estoy temeroso porque vuestros capitanes siempre me han quebrado la palabra que en

[1] Ministerio de Cultura, Archivo General de Indias, Sevilla, Sección Escribanía 922b, fols. 192v–193v.

Letter from Don Alonso de Illescas, a Black Man in Esmeraldas [1586]

Most powerful sir,

Having the devout Fray Alonso de Espinosa of the Holy Order of Trinitarians, by me and on my behalf, in a letter that he carried from me to your *Real Audiencia,* requested that I desire to submit to God Our Father and to Your Royal Crown and that on your part I be sent a general pardon and remission, because I have not been in your service,[1] and that you send a priest to preach to us the Holy Gospel and teach our women and children, I will do everything in my power and I will try to pacify all the natives of this province.

And Your Highness having conceded what I have requested and entreated, I give thanks to God Our Father for the many mercies I have received from His most liberal hands and from Your Lordship.

And so Father Espinosa brought me news that Your Royal Highness in Spain has granted the government of this land to Rodrigo de Ribadeneyra, who will bring many people to pacify and populate this land. And so I ordered that we should all gather to discuss and communicate [to His Royal Highness] what will best serve your royal interest.

And if Your Royal Highness granted Rodrigo de Ribadeneyra this government, it was before, without our report expressing our desire and willingness to join in union with the Church and Your Royal Crown.

And so what can be conquered with the indoctrination of the Holy Gospel would only be of disservice to God and Your Majesty to conquer by force of arms and at the cost of many souls on the one hand, and on the other in order to dominate the Campaces and have them recognize and know of my God.

Therefore, because I have not been in your service, I will encourage the people under my command, and receiving your license to enter the territory of the Campaces and require them to surrender peacefully to your service. And I will settle them near the sea in the best place possible. And in time I will ask your *Real Audiencia* for aid in order to form two towns in another province for Your Royal Crown that will be in the service of Our Lord.

Thus I beseech and supplicate Your Highness: do not form another government of the areas I offer to settle. Likewise, I ask Your Highness to suspend the expedition of soldiers; it will only bring chaos to the peace the devoted father [Espinosa] has brought with the Holy Gospel.

If you must allow a [Spanish] settlement, let it be in the Valle Vicioso and Barbacoas,[2] as I am truly afraid because your captains have always broken their promises

[1] Here, Illescas refers to his recent illegitimate status as a *Maroon,* when he was not acting as an obedient subject of the Crown.

[2] The Valle Vicioso and region of Barbacoas were both located to the north of Esmeraldas in modern-day Colombia. For more on the history of Spanish conquest in these regions, see Calero.

vuestro nombre me han dado; y del devoto padre hemos hecho confianza por haber entendido de su pecho la mucha voluntad que tiene de reducirnos al *gremio* de la Iglesia y al de Vuestra Real Corona.

Y así para la certificación y creencia de lo en ésta contenido, envío a Juan Mangacho con el dicho padre a vuestra *Real Audiencia,* para que a Vuestra Señoría bese los pies. Y confiado como de cristianísimo rey en todo, Vuestra Señoría nos hará mercedes no más sino que Nuestro Señor dé a Vuestra Señoría larga vida con aumento de *mayores* reinos y señoríos.

De esta provincia de las Esmeraldas 24 de febrero de [15]86, muy poderoso señor, bese a Vuestra Señoría los pies vuestro humilde vasallo, Don Alonso de Illescas.

Y el sobre escrito de esta carta dice: Al muy poderoso señor el rey don Felipe, nuestro señor en la *Real Audiencia* de Quito en su acuerdo real.

given in Your Majesty's name. The devoted father has gained our confidence, and we know it is from his heart that he comes to bring us into union with the Church and Your Royal Crown.

To prove and make credible what is contained herein, I am sending Juan Mangacho with the said father [Espinosa] to the *Real Audiencia* [in Quito] to kiss the feet of Your Highness. And with the same trust as a most Christian king in all things, Your Highness will give us mercies, and [we desire] that Our Lord provide Your Highness with long life and the growth of many kingdoms and lands.

From the Province of Esmeraldas, the twenty-fourth of February [15]86, most powerful Lord, your humble vassal, Don Alonso de Illescas, kisses the feet of Your Highness.

And the letterhead of this letter says, "To the most powerful Lord, King Don Felipe, our Lord and his royal agreement in the *Real Audiencia* of Quito."

3

Queen Njinga Mbandi Ana de Sousa of Ndongo/Matamba: African Leadership, Diplomacy, and Ideology, 1620s–1650s[1]

Linda Heywood
Document translation by Luis Madureira

Portuguese *Angola* and Queen Njinga's Leadership in the Seventeenth Century

Queen Njinga of Ndongo/Matamba (1582–1663) lived during a tumultuous period in the history of Central Africa. Njinga's birth in 1582 occurred just two years after the unification of Spain and Portugal (1580–1640) and a mere seven years after the Portuguese had planted their first colony on the coast of modern-day *Angola* (1575). Between 1575 and Njinga's death in 1663, the Portuguese made relentless attacks against the Kingdom of Ndongo and neighboring Central African kingdoms and had conquered large sections of Ndongo.[2]

Ndongo was a kingdom that measured about forty thousand square kilometers. Its population of about one hundred thousand people lived under local rulers called *sobas.* These *sobas* owed allegiance to the king who lived in the capital city of Kabasa. In their wars against Ndongo, the Portuguese had as allies *Imbangala* (*Jaga*) guerrillas, widely feared among non-*Imbangala* Central Africans because of their cannibalism, their disregard for settled life, their wanton destruction of settled communities, and their propensity for capturing and forcibly integrating young children into the *Imbangala* bands through horrific initiation rituals.

Njinga first came into direct contact with the Portuguese in 1622 when she traveled to Luanda, the capital of the Portuguese kingdom of *Angola,* to negotiate a peace treaty on behalf of her brother Ngola Mbandi, who was king of Ndongo. Njinga remained several months in Luanda, during which time she agreed to be baptized and received the baptismal name of Ana de Sousa. Before her baptism. Njinga followed the practices connected with Kimbundu religious beliefs, which included rituals connected to the ancestors (past kings) as well as others dealing with the seasons.

In Luanda, Njinga also succeeded in negotiating a treaty with the Portuguese. The treaty did not last long. With the death of Ngola Mbandi in 1624 and her election as queen by a faction of the eligible electors from Ngola's court, Njinga's rivals refused to regard her as the legitimate ruler of Ndongo, and they joined with the Portuguese in an attempt to remove her from the throne. Njinga's efforts to be accepted as queen of Ndongo developed into a thirty-year struggle against the Portuguese and her Ndongo

[1] See Map 2.

[2] For an in-depth treatment of this period, see Heywood and Thornton (chapter 3).

rivals. Like the Portuguese, Njinga sought *Imbangala* alliance and eventually became head of a band. Between 1626 and 1655, Njinga personally commanded her army in many of the wars that the Ndongos fought against the Portuguese.

Moreover, Njinga's life included the period when an armada sent by the Dutch West India Company attacked and conquered Luanda (1641), bringing the wars of the Protestant Revolution into Central Africa. Indeed, during the Dutch occupation (1641–1648), Njinga joined in an Afro-Dutch alliance that also included the neighboring Kingdom of Kongo and set up a siege of all the Portuguese forts in *Angola.* This action almost brought Portuguese rule in the region to an end.

The tide turned against Njinga and her Kongo and Dutch allies when an armada sent from Brazil under Salvador de Sá in 1648 rescued the embattled Portuguese, who had been pinned down at their fort in Massangano, some 160 kilometers from Luanda. Instead of continuing the alliance, the Dutch quickly capitulated, and Njinga retreated to Matamba, a state she had conquered in the early 1630s. Njinga continued her resistance against the Portuguese and their Ndongo allies until 1654.

In 1654 Njinga decided to give up the military life that had consumed so much of her time and turned again to diplomacy. Using *Capuchin* missionaries who arrived in her court as part of the negotiations to end the war between her and the Portuguese, she began a rapprochement with her former enemies and even wrote directly to the Vatican.

Between 1655 and 1663, Njinga signed a peace treaty with the Portuguese, welcomed the return of her sister Dona Barbara (Funji Mbandi) from Portuguese captivity, reconciled with the Church by giving up her many male consorts and marrying one according to Catholic rites, and built a chapel in Matamba. Moreover, Njinga set an example for the rest of the population who had followed her through her years of resistance: they, too, gave up their *Imbangala* ways, married according to Catholic rites, and began rearing children instead of following the *Imbangala* policy, which prohibited the birth of children in the camps.

The most important consequence of the Portuguese (and Dutch) presence in Central Africa during Njinga's lifetime was the expansion of the slave trade. *Angola* became a major center for slaves imported into the Spanish and Portuguese colonies in the Americas. In fact, during the period 1580–1640 when Portugal held the *Asiento,* the wars that the governors of *Angola* carried out against Ndongo were actually slave-raiding forays. Central Africa often annually accounted for more than 80 percent (and for some years 100 percent) of all the slaves transported to the plantations, mines, fisheries, and urban centers of Ibero-America.

Many of the slaves were also war refugees captured as Njinga and her supporters fled Portuguese advances. Others were purchased in the network of slave markets that developed throughout the region. Moreover, Njinga also engaged in slave trading, and some of the Africans exported through Luanda came from the regular slave trading that had developed between African rulers like Queen Njinga and the Europeans.

Njinga's Letters of Diplomacy

Njinga's letters are relevant to the history of Afro-Latin populations in Ibero-America because the majority of the enslaved Africans whom the Portuguese (and Dutch)

exported between the 1620s and 1663 came from *Angola,* Ndongo, and Kongo and went to Spanish America and Brazil. Many of these Central Africans came from communities that had long been integrated into the *Creole* culture, including the mixed Portuguese-Kimbundu vocabulary, and religious, dietary, and other cultural practices that had developed in Portuguese *Angola.*

In fact, some of the slaves would have been familiar with the Portuguese language, would have been baptized as a result of the religious activities of parish priests and missionaries of regular orders such as the *Capuchin* and Jesuits, and may even have adapted other elements of the *Creole* culture such as dress, food, and music. Notably, some of the African leaders in the *Maroon* communities in both Palmares in Brazil and Limón in Colombia conducted wars of resistance against the Portuguese, Dutch, and Spanish that resembled Njinga's wars against the Portuguese in *Angola.*

Njinga was the head of an independent African kingdom with its own army and the ability to engage in diplomacy, wage wars, or do business with Europeans. The states she ruled—Ndongo and later Matamba—had subjects loyal to her but also contained various groups of dependents, some of whom were slaves. Njinga was an independent monarch fighting to uphold her right to be the queen of Ndongo. Most of the peoples of African descent in the Ibero-Atlantic world never found ways to sustain years of wars against Europeans or live in autonomous communities,

In order to interpret Njinga's engagement with European writing as an instrument of negotiation, one needs familiarity with the history of European literacy in Central Africa. Exposure to Catholic Christianity and Portuguese customs made rulers like Njinga more familiar with European forms of governance and lifestyle than their counterparts in other areas of Atlantic Africa, whose states supplied slaves to the Portuguese or with whom they conducted diplomatic relations. The earliest European-style school for Kongos was established in 1491 by a literate member of the Kongo elite who had returned to the kingdom with the first Portuguese cultural mission.

From 1491 onward, the Kongo elite had access to European-style education. In 1625, for example, Jesuits in the capital of Kongo, São Salvador, had established a college for children of the Kongo nobility. Literate Kongos went as ambassadors to Portugal, the Vatican, the Portuguese in the Kingdom of *Angola,* and Njinga's court. Furthermore, some Kimbundus who had been integrated into Portuguese *Angola* were also educated by Jesuit missionaries in Luanda, and many joined Njinga's cause.

Njinga herself was not literate in Portuguese; in 1656 when she signed the peace treaty with the Portuguese, she placed her mark on the document. Nevertheless, she had Kimbundus and Kongos in her court who were. Njinga most likely dictated the 1626 letter to one of these individuals, although she might have dictated the letters of 1651, 1655, and 1660 to her secretary "Dom João" who she mentioned in a letter of 1657 (Njinga of Ndongo, Letter to Serafino, 131–32).

Starting in 1648, Njinga had a literate Kongo-born priest, Don Calisto Zelotes dos Reis Magros, who served as her confessor and secretary. Njinga had captured the priest in a war she made against the Kongo region of Wandu in 1648. When the *Capuchin* missionary Gaeta arrived in her court in 1656, Zelotes dos Reis Magros was turned over to the priest to serve as his translator. Zelotes informed Gaeta that he had been "a slave of the queen for many years" (Napoli, fol. 252).

The use of some Kimbundu terms (*muenho,* for example) suggests that the writers of the letters were Kimbundu or were familiar with Kimbundu, the language of Ndongo. The letters that Njinga wrote represented just one aspect of the strategies she adopted to deal with the Portuguese, because she also sent numerous emissaries to the Portuguese governors and other officials. These emissaries were famous for their skill in transmitting long complex messages from Njinga in the oral prose that the people valued and that astounded the Portuguese who heard them.

Njinga dictated a wide range of letters and sent them to various Portuguese governors and officials in *Angola, Capuchin* missionaries, Propaganda Fide (the Vatican agency responsible for overseas missionary work), and even the Pope. The letters that Njinga wrote in 1654 represent the period when she decided to pay less attention to the military life that had consumed so much of her time and to concentrate instead on diplomacy. Njinga's diplomatic skill and deep distrust of the Portuguese was based on more than thirty years of negotiating and having the Portuguese break the terms of the treaties they had signed. Her skill and skepticism are clear in her 1655 letter.

Although Njinga had agreed to make peace, she retained her voice as an independent African ruler, as is evident in her attempts to obtain the release of her sister Dona Barbara from the Portuguese. Despite several years of negotiations and large numbers of slaves sent as presents, the Portuguese continued to hold Njinga's sister prisoner. At the same time, the governor requested that Njinga turn over the *Jaga* Cabuco (an *Imbangala* leader), as the Portuguese wished to eliminate the *Jaga* influence in the region. Njinga insisted she would release Cabuco only after her sister arrived in her court.

These letters as well as others in the corpus that she wrote, vividly illustrate Njinga's belief that she was fighting for a just cause and her skill at combining war, diplomacy, and religion to achieve her aims. Njinga employs the conventions of European diplomacy in her greetings to the various Portuguese governors and religions officials, but the African oral tradition stands out when she refers to her history of contact with the Portuguese, as she does in her long letter of 1655.

Perhaps the most intriguing aspect of these letters is that they also touch on Njinga's gender. In her letter of 1625 when she was forty-three years old, Njinga asked the governor to send her several items of personal adornment. Missionaries who knew Njinga personally all noted that she paid a lot of attention to her appearance. The way Njinga used her gender to achieve her goals is another intriguing dimension of this phenomenal African leader.

[Carta da Rainha Njinga de Ndongo a Bento Banha Cardoso, 3 de março de 1626][1]

Na alma estimo o vir *Vossa Mercê* a essa fortaleza da Ambaca para que, como a pai, dar-lhe conta e, como mandando eu umas *peças* à feira de Bumba Aquiçanzo, saiu Aires com guerra e me salteou umas trinta *peças,* das quais, mandando eu tomar satisfação como a meu vassalo, acertou a minha guerra encontrar[-se] com uns nove homens que estavam com o Tigre na terra. E botando estes nove a vir encontrar-se com a minha guerra fora da pedra [de Pungo Andongo], quis Deus que dos meus fossem vencidos, donde me trouxeram seis vivos, de que me pesou muito de que na Pedra de Aires estivessem portugueses com guerra de socorro a Aires, aos quais faço muito bom agasalhado por serem vassalos d'El-Rey de Espanha, a quem reconheço obediência como cristã que sou. Ao sábado chegou aqui um *criado* meu *muenho,* o qual me disse que na Ambaca estava muita guerra junta, e que esperavam por *Vossa Mercê* pera a mover contra mim a libertar os portugueses cativos. Sendo que nenhuma cousa se quer levado por força, e isso é fazer-me mal a mim e a eles porque sem isso se pode fazer tudo por bem e, se alguns senhores moradores, [por] estarem endividados, metam ao Senhor Governador e a *Vossa Mercê* em cabeça que faça guerras pera se desendividarem, podem fazê-lo, que eu não quero nenhuma contra o capitão. Não se oferece outro. Nosso Senhor, etc. Hoje, três de março de 1625 anos.

Mande-me *Vossa Mercê* uma rede, e quatro côvados de grã para um cobertor, e uma colcha de montaria, e vinho bom, e uma *arroba* de cera de velas e meia dúzia de canequins, e duas, ou três toalhas de mesa de *rendas,* e umas granadas roxas, e vinhadas, e azuis, e um chapéu de sol grande de veludo azul, ou o que *Vossa Mercê* traz, e quatro mãos de papel.

Ana Rainha de Ndongo

[1] Heintze, *Fontes para a história de Angola do século XVII,* vol. 1, 244–45.

[Letter from Queen Njinga of Ndongo to Bento Banha Cardoso, March 3, 1626][1]

It gladdens my soul that Your Honor has come to the Fortress of Ambaca[2] so that I may recount to you, as to my own father, how a war party led by Aires[3] attacked the men I sent [to escort] some slaves to the market of Bumba a Kissanzo, and stole about thirty slaves from me. When I dispatched a party to seek redress, as I would against any vassal of mine, it happened that my army encountered about nine of the men who were stationed inland with Tigre.[4] Having decided to face my army outside the [Pungo Andongo] fortress, these nine men, by God's will, were defeated by my men, six of whom were brought to me alive. It caused me great grief that at Aires' fortress there were Portuguese forces that I have received with great kindness because they are vassals of the king of Spain,[5] to whom I recognize obeisance as a Christian. On Saturday, one of my *muenho* servants arrived here and told me that in Ambaca a large force had gathered, waiting for Your Honor to move against me to free the Portuguese held in captivity. Nothing is accomplished by force and to do so would bring both me and them harm because everything can be done peacefully and without force. And if some of the lords who have settled here have incurred heavy debts and have put it in the minds of Your Honor and the governor that you should wage war in order to get out of debt, they are welcome to do so, but I do not want to make war with the captain. No one else presents himself at this time. Our Lord, etc. On this, the third day of March in the year 1625.[6]

I ask that Your Honor send me a hammock, and four ells of red wool for a cover, a horse blanket, and good wine, and an *arroba*[7] of wax for candles, and half a dozen lengths of muslin, and two or three lace tablecloths, and some purple, wine-colored, and blue garnets, and a large broad-brim hat made of blue velvet, or the one Your Honor wears, and four measures of paper.

Ana Queen of the Ndongo

[1] Cardoso was military commander under Governor Fernão de Sousa (1624–1630) during the latter's campaign against Queen Njinga.

[2] *Ambaca* was an Mbundu trading center located near the western edge of *Angola*'s eastern plateau region.

[3] Hari a Kiluanji or Aquiloange Aire, ruler imposed on Ndongo by the Portuguese after the death of Ngola Mbandi (Heywood and Thornton, 129).

[4] Estêvão de Seixas Tigre, captain of forces sent by the Portuguese to reinforce Hari a Kiluanje against Njinga.

[5] At this time, Portugal was under Spanish rule.

[6] Should be 1626.

[7] A measure of weight equivalent to about thirty-three pounds.

[Carta da Rainha Ana Njinga à Propaganda Fide, 15 de agosto de 1651][2]

O santo zelo que as Vossas Eminências tinha[m] da saúde[3] da minha alma e da minha gente em mandar-nos o Padre Sacerdote *Capucho* Frei António Romano a pregar-nos o Santo Evangelho de nosso Senhor Jesus Cristo, verdadeiro Deus, me aperta de sorte, que lhes rendo as graças que devo. E confesso ser muito obrigada às Senhorias Vossas por este favor; porque agora temos conhecimento do verdadeiro Deus que antes não havíamos, por isso ficávamos enganados na nossa idolatria, em poder do demónio. A piedade de Deus é grande para connosco, que, não merecendo a sua divina misericórdia por nossos graves pecados, contudo isso, Ele nos está oferecendo por meio da vinda do Padre *Capucho,* que agora vivo com paz na alma e quietação do corpo. Nosso Senhor Jesus Cristo seja servido, que nós outros correspondamos à graça que nos está fazendo, para que não mereçamos castigo maior pelos nossos pecados. Se as Senhorias Vossas mandarem outros Religiosos *Capuchos,* os receberemos com boa vontade, que no nosso reino há muita gente para tomar o Santo Baptismo. Deus conceda às Vossas [Eminências] muitos anos de vida para bem de nossas almas.

Do nosso Reino de Matamba a 15 de Agosto de 1651.

Ana
Rainha Njinga D. Ana

[Carta da Rainha D. Ana Njinga ao governador geral de *Angola,* 13 de dezembro de 1655][4]

Senhor,

Recebi a carta de Vossa Senhoria, a qual me entregou o Capitão Manuel Frois Peixoto, embaixador de Vossa Senhoria, e por ela vejo gozar Vossa Senhoria saúde, a qual nosso Senhor aumente por largos anos, com muita paz e quietação, como para mim desejo. Eu tenho saúde para servir a Vossa Senhoria em nome de Sua Majestade, que Deus guarde, com tanta autoridade, e [Vossa Senhoria] propôs com tanto valor, que logo vi me fala verdade em tudo o que diz, porque estou tão queixosa dos governadores passados, que sempre me prometeram entregarem minha irmã, pela qual tenho dado infinitas *peças* e feito milhares de *banzos,* e nunca ma entregaram, mas antes moviam logo guerras, com que me inquietaram e fizeram sempre andar feita *jaga,* usando tiranias, como é não deixar criar crianças, por ser estilo de *quilombo,* e outras cerimónias. E todas deixarei. E dou a Vossa Senhoria minha real palavra, tanto que tiver religiosos, que me dêm bom exemplo a meus grandes, para que os ensinem a viver na Santa Fé

[2] Brásio, *Monumenta missionaria africana. África Ocidental (1651–1655),* 1971, XI:70–71.

[3] In this case, the meaning is "salvation."

[4] Brásio, *Monumenta missionaria africana. África Ocidental (1651–1655),* 1971, XI:524–28.

[Letter from Queen Ana Njinga to the Propaganda Fide (the Sacred Congregation for the Propagation of the Faith), August 15, 1651][8]

The holy zeal Your Eminences have shown concerning the salvation of my soul and that of my people, by sending us the *capuchin* friar Father Antonio Romano to preach to us the Holy Gospel of our Lord Jesus Christ, the one true God, has so filled me with good fortune that I must render my thanks to you. I confess I am very obliged to Your Lordships for this kindness, for now we have knowledge of the one true God that we did not have before. For this reason we had remained deceived by our idolatrous beliefs, possessed by the devil. God's compassion toward us is great, even though we are undeserving of his divine mercy on account of our grave sins. Nevertheless, mercy is what He is offering us through the arrival of the *capuchin* father, and now I live with my body and soul at peace. May our Lord Jesus Christ be served by allowing us to reciprocate the benevolence you confer upon us, so that we may not deserve greater punishment for our sins. If Your Lordships send us other *capuchin* friars, we will welcome them with open arms, for there are many people in our kingdom ready to receive the Holy Baptism. May God grant Your [Eminences] many years of life for the good of our souls.

From our Kingdom of Matamba on the fifteenth of August 1651.

Ana
Queen Ana Njinga

[Letter from Queen Ana Njinga to the Governor General of *Angola,* December 13, 1655][9]

My Lord,

I received Your Lordship's letter, which was brought to me by Your Lordship's envoy Captain Manuel Frois Peixoto, where I read that Your Lordship is enjoying good health, which I hope Our Lord will increase for many long years, along with as much peace and tranquility as I desire for myself. I possess the health to serve Your Lordship in the name of His Majesty, may God preserve him, with all due authority. You stated your purposes with so much merit that I saw directly that you speak the truth in all you say. For I have many complaints about past governors, who always promised to return my sister to me. [To secure her return,] I have given an infinite number of slaves and created thousands of *banzos*, but they never returned her to me. Rather, they waged war against my person and harried me, and constantly forced me to live like a *Jaga* and resort to tyrannical edicts, such as prohibiting the raising of children and other ceremonies because this is what life in a *quilombo* entails. I give Your Lordship my royal word that I will give up these warlike [practices], as long as I have clergymen among us who will provide me and my grandees with good examples and teach them

8 The Propaganda Fide was the Vatican congregation responsible for missionary work. In 1982, Pope John Paul II changed its name to the Congregation for the Evangelization of the Peoples. Its basic mission has remained unchanged.

9 The letter is addressed to Governor Luís Mendes de Sousa Chicorro.

Católica, assim que espero que Vossa Senhoria me faça [a] mercê [de] mandar o padre Frei Serafim e o padre Frei João da Ordem do Carmo, por ser hábito, que desejo ver e também me dizem ser bom pregador, e saber a língua de Ndongo.

Com estes dois religiosos pode Vossa Senhoria fazer-me mercê [de] mandar-me minha irmã, que com eles vem bem acompanhada e autorizada. E quando Vossa Senhoria fôr servido que venha mais alguma pessoa, seja um soldado que faz foguetes para com eles festejar minha irmã, querendo Deus. Também pode vir um soldado para que sirva de sacristão aos Reverendos Padres. E tanto que tiver notícia que está minha irmã na Ambaca, partirá desta minha Corte o Capitão Manuel Frois Peixoto a buscá-la, que a ele compete, pois teve o trabalho de reduzir meus grandes, que tão desconfiados estão de enganos passados, e não pareça a Vossa Senhoria que merece o capitão Manuel Frois Peixoto pouco louvor, pois chegou a acabar[5] com eles e comigo ser esta embaixada verdadeira, e não como as passadas, que tenho dito. E de quem estou mais queixosa é do Governador Salvador Correia [de Sá], a quem dei as *peças* que Vossa Senhoria lá saberá, e fiz duzentos *banzos* por ver [se] me mandava pessoa, como foi o Capitão Mor Rui Pegado por embaixador em nome de Sua Majestade, que Deus guarde, que me entregariam minha irmã e haveria muita paz. Entendi que não podia faltar à palavra real. E por estes enganos e outros, ando pelos matos, fora de minhas terras, sem ter quem informe a Sua Majestade, que Deus guarde, de meu pouco sossêgo, tendo eu tantos desejos de estar em paz com o dito senhor e seus governadores. Mas todos os passados vieram tratar do seu proveito, e não do serviço real, de que estou informada que tanto lhes encomenda Sua Majestade, pois tanto lhe importa este reino a seus reais direitos e mais importava estando eu sossegada em paz, fazendo feiras mais perto para [aos] *pombeiros* lhes não custar tanto trabalho trazer as fazendas tão longe e eu gozá-las mais baratas. Enfim, espero em Deus que só Vossa Senhoria há de ter louvor com Sua Majestade, que Deus guarde, de me deixar em paz e sossegada, e a Quissama conquistada, cousa que nenhum Governador fez, nem mereceu tal gloria.

Eu me ofereço para ajudar a Vossa Senhoria na conquista dela, quando não queira dar obediência, mandarei um dos meus grandes com o maior poder que ser possa, quando Vossa Senhoria levar gosto. Isto farei em sinal de obediência que dou a Sua Majestade, que Deus guarde, e também dou a minha palavra que, tanto que chegarem

[5] To convince.

to live in the Holy Catholic Faith. I am therefore hoping Your Lordship will grant me the favor of sending forth Friar Serafim[10] and Friar João from the Carmelite Order, whom I wish to see because he belongs to a religious order and also because I am told that he is a good preacher and knows the language of Ndongo.

Your Lordship would do me a great favor to send my sister back to me along with these two clergymen, for with them she would come in good and accredited company. And if it please Your Lordship to allow someone else to come, let it be a soldier with knowledge in fireworks so I can celebrate my sister's arrival with them, God willing. A soldier can also come who may serve as sacristan to the reverend fathers. As soon as I get news that my sister has arrived in Ambaca, I will dispatch Captain Manuel Frois Peixoto from my court to get her. This task falls to him, since he made the effort of appeasing my grandees, who are quite suspicious of past treacheries. Your Lordship ought not to suppose that Captain Manuel Frois Peixoto is undeserving of high praise, for he succeeded in convincing them and me that this delegation was in good faith and not like the previous ones I mentioned. The one against whom I have the most grievances is Governor Salvador Correia [de Sá],[11] to whom I gave the slaves Your Lordship knows about and made two hundred *banzos* to get him to send someone like Commander Rui Pegado,[12] who arrived as an envoy of His Majesty, may God protect him, and assured me that my sister would be brought back to me and that there would be complete peace. I decided I could not break my royal word [and accepted his assurances]. Because of this and other treacheries, I roam the forests, far from my own lands, with no one to inform His Majesty, may God protect him, of my unease, when to be at peace with the said commander and His Majesty's governors is what I most desire. Yet all His Majesty's past [agents and governors] acted out of personal gain and not in the king's service, as I have been informed His Majesty bids them do, for this kingdom is of the utmost importance to his royal privilege. It would be worth even more if I were allowed to live in peace and quiet, bringing my markets closer [to the coast], so the *pombeiros* need not go through so much trouble to bring their wares so far, and I could enjoy them at a cheaper price. Finally, I trust with God that Your Lordship will be in His Majesty's good graces only if you leave me in peace and tranquillity and conquer Quissama,[13] a thing that no governor has earned the glory of accomplishing.

I offer Your Lordship my assistance in the conquest of Quissama. If it refuses to pay obeisance to you, and if it pleases Your Lordship, I will dispatch one of my grandees with as large a force as can be mustered. This I will do as a sign of obeisance to His Majesty, may God protect him. I also give my word that as soon as the reverend

10 Frei Serafim de Cortona, Italian *Capuchin* missionary.

11 He was the military officer who was sent from Brazil at the head of the Portuguese forces that recaptured *Angola* from the Dutch in 1648 and served as governor of *Angola* until 1651.

12 Rui Pegado was an ambassador sent by the Portuguese to Njinga.

13 Quissama (or Kissama) was the name of a region on the southern bank of the Cuanza (or Kwanza) River inhabited by various small independent states that were the traditional enemies of the Bakongo and the Ndongo. At the time the letter was written, some of these states had joined Njinga's coalition.

os Reverendos Padres com minha irmã, tratarei logo de deixar parir e criar as mulheres seus filhos, cousa que até agora não consenti por ser estilo de *quilombo,* que anda em campo, o que não haverá, havendo paz firme e perpétua. E em poucos anos, se tornarão minhas terras a povoar como dantes, porque até agora me não sirvo senão com gente de outras províncias e *nações* que tenho conquistado e me obedecem como sua senhora natural com muito amor e outros por temor.

Não podia Vossa Senhoria mandarme embaixador que mais me alegrasse que o Capitão Manuel Frois Peixoto, por saber bem declarar-me tudo pela língua deste meu Reino [Kimbundu]. Todos [os] meus grandes estão tão contentes que dizem que só ele me traz paz verdadeira e fala verdade e [faz] tudo o que Vossa Senhoria lhe ordena por seu regimento. E já me considero com a prenda que desejo e com muita paz e quietação esses dias que viver, que já sou velha e não quero deixar minhas terras senão a minha irmã, e não a meus escravos, que haverá muita ruína e não saberão obedecer a S. Majestade, que Deus guarde, como minha irmã o saberá fazer, pois há tantos anos que assiste com os brancos e é tão boa cristã como me dizem. E não se leve Vossa Senhoria de ditos de moradores que sempre trataram de me inimistarem com os governadores passados. E Vossa Senhoria, como parente do senhor governador João Correia de Sousa, meu Padrinho que Deus tem em glória, me há de fazer mercê [de] alcançar esta paz por carta firmada da mão de Sua Majestade, para mais firmeza minha e de meus grandes, para que sosseguem e tratem de cultivar as terras como dantes.

O Capitão Manuel Frois Peixoto me pediu, da parte de Sua Majestade, o *jaga* Cabuco, por tão bom estilo, que lho não pude negar, posto que tenha tido de Cabuco muita queixa, por me haver destruído minhas terras, razão fora que andasse em meu serviço alguns anos para me satisfazer parte de tanta perda, como me deu. Contudo são tão grandes os desejos que tenho de ver minha irmã, que tanto que ela chegar a esta minha Corte, darei logo licença ao dito *jaga* para que ele se vá com o Capitão Manuel Frois Peixoto quando partir e que logo esteja às suas ordens. Isto pode Vossa Senhoria ter por certo, como o socorro que digo darei para a Quissama, se a Vossa Senhoria lhe fôr necessário, e tudo o mais que me fôr mandado, amigos de amigos, inimigos de inimigos.

No que toca às duzentas *peças* que Vossa Senhoria me pede pelo resgate de minha irmã, D. Bárbara, é um preço muito rigoroso, havendo eu dado as *peças* que Vossa Senhoria já deve saber aos governadores passados e embaixadores, fora mimos a secretários e *criados* de sua casa, e a muitos moradores, que ainda hoje sinto enganos. O que me atrevo a dar a Vossa Senhoria serão cento e trinta *peças,* o cento mandarei tanto que estiver minha irmã em Ambaca, e para isso há de ficar como refém o embaixador até que a dita minha irmã entre nesta minha Corte, que veja eu a verdade, porque me não suceda o que me tem sucedido e usaram comigo os governadores passados. E não

fathers arrive with my sister, I will immediately endeavor to allow women to give birth to and raise their children, which I have not permitted until now because we have been living in the countryside, in *quilombos.* This would not happen if we had a firm and lasting peace. It would take only a few years for my lands to be repopulated as they once were, for up to now I have taken as servants only people from other provinces and *nations* that I have conquered, and they have obeyed me as if I were their native queen, some out of love and others out of fear.

Your Lordship could not send me an envoy that would please me more than Captain Manuel Frois Peixoto, for he would well know how to convey everything to me in the language of this kingdom of mine [Kimbundu]. All my grandees are so happy that they say only he speaks the truth and reports everything that Your Lordship orders him to and in accordance with your instructions. I already consider myself in possession of the gift of peace and serenity that I desire for these few days I [have left] to live, for I am an old woman. I wish to bequeath my lands only to my sister, not to my slaves. Otherwise, great ruin will befall it, for they will not know how to obey His Majesty (may God protect him) and my sister, who has dwelled for so many years among the whites and is such a good Christian as they tell me. Your Lordship should not lend credence to what the settlers say; they have always tried to turn past governors into my enemies. As a relative of my godfather João Correia de Sousa [the governor of Portuguese *Angola* in 1622 when Njinga was baptized], who is in God's glory, [I know] Your Lordship will do me the kindness of attaining this peace, [and confirm it] in a letter signed by His Majesty's hand as greater assurance to me and my grandees, so they may rest at ease and turn to sowing their fields, as they once did.

Captain Manuel Frois Peixoto requested on His Majesty's behalf that I [hand over to him] the *Jaga* Cabuco.[14] [He asked me] with such fine manners that I could not refuse him, even though I have had many grievances against Cabuco for having devastated my lands. The satisfaction of so many losses as he caused me should be good enough reason for him to remain in my service a few years longer. Nevertheless, so great is my desire to see my sister again that as soon as Captain Manuel Frois Peixoto arrives in my court, I will give the said *Jaga* permission to leave with him and place himself at his orders. Of this Your Lordship can be certain, as well as of the aid I promised to give you in [subduing] Quissama, should Your Honor need it. This I will do and everything else you may instruct me to do. My friends' friends are my friends, and my enemies' enemies my own enemies.

With respect to the two hundred slaves Your Lordship requests as ransom for my sister Dona Barbara, that is a very exacting price, particularly since I have already given the slaves Your Honor must know of to past governors and envoys, to say nothing of my gifts to secretaries and servants from your noble house and to many settlers whose treachery I still endure to this day. What I am so bold as to offer Your Honor is one hundred and thirty slaves, a hundred of whom I will send as soon as my sister reaches Ambaca. I will keep your envoy hostage until I can see with my own eyes my sister arriving in my court to make sure that I will not be wrongly used again as I have been by past governors. Your Lordship should not regard it as strange that I want to take

14 *Imbangala* leader (see chapter introduction).

estranhe Vossa Senhoria querer-me segurar, é escusar desgostos, suposto que entendo ser esta embaixada muito verdadeira, mas os meus grandes estão duvidosos por lhes lembrar o passado.

Vossa Senhoria perdoe ser esta carta tão larga,[6] porque importa assim. O embaixador me entregou o mimo[7] que Vossa Senhoria me enviou, pelo qual lhe rendo as graças. Estimei muito o copo de madrepérola. Vossa Senhoria se não canse comigo porque tudo me sobra nesta minha corte, só de minha irmã a careço [sic]. E com a sua vinda, hei-de servir a Vossa Senhoria muito a seu gosto, como Vossa Senhoria verá. Este portador vai pela posta dar a Vossa Senhoria aviso do que assentei com o embaixador, e por ir depressa leva doze *peças,* não mais, que são para doces de Vossa Senhoria.

Matamba, minha Corte, treze de Dezembro de 1655 anos.

Rainha D. Ana de Sousa

[Carta da Rainha Njinga a António de Oliveira de Cadornega, 15 de junho de 1660][8]

Senhor Juiz,

A Carta que *Vossa Mercê* me escreveu sobre [a] sua gente fugida, [dizendo] que a minha gente os vend[e]m e os furtam, isso deve de dizer quem me quer mal [por] estas pazes e Cristandade, porque se pode *Vossa Mercê* perguntar a todos os *pombeiros* dos brancos, que nesta minha Corte vêm com fato de seus Senhores a negociar. Pois saiba *Vossa Mercê* que os *negros* de *Vossa Mercê* são tão atrevidos, sendo [que] quando vendemos com eles as *peças,* lhe[s] damos aviso que as *peças* sejam bem vigiadas, e presas. Eles, os ditos, como são velhacos mandam as *peças* soltas a fazer o seu serviço para dizer a *Vossa Mercê* que nesta minha *banza* me fogem muitas damas soltas antigas, como os ditos dirão. Quanto mais gente nova. Se estivessem aqui, poderiam fazer diligência como fez [o] *Negro* de João Pilato ao cabo de tantos anos e do Reverendo Padre Vigário, como dirão os Reverendos Padres que levam esta. Não [me] alargo mais. Guarde Deus [a *Vossa Mercê*] muitos anos com o poder, etc. Minha Corte de Matamba, hoje, 15 de Junho de 1660 anos.

R. D. Ana

[6] Long.

[7] Present, offering.

[8] Cadornega, *História geral das guerras angolanas. 1680,* 1972, 2:172–73.

these precautions. Even though I understand that this delegation is a very honest one, I will avoid further grief, for, because they remember the deceits of the past, my grandees remain suspicious.

May Your Lordship forgive so long a letter as this, but it needed to be thus. The offering Your Lordship sent me, and for which I render you my thanks, was delivered to me by your envoy. I appreciated the mother-of-pearl goblet very much. Do not be weary of me, Your Lordship, but I want for nothing in my court. What I miss the most is my sister. Once she returns to me, Your Lordship will see that I will serve Your Lordship much to your liking. The bearer of this letter will relay to you by post what I have agreed upon with your envoy. Because he leaves in haste, he takes no more than twelve slaves. [Accept them as] my offering to mollify Your Lordship.

My Court at Matamba, on the thirteenth of December of the year 1655.

Queen Dona Ana de Sousa

[Letter from Queen Njinga to António de Oliveira de Cadornega, June 15, 1660][15]

Your Honor,

The letter Your Honor wrote me concerning your runaway slaves, claiming that my people abduct and sell them must be based on charges made by those who wish me ill for being a Christian who lives in peace. Your Honor can make inquiries with all the *pombeiros* who work for the whites and travel to my court to trade their masters' wares. Your Honor ought to know that your black servants are such bold-faced [thieves] that when we sell slaves with them, we take caution to keep our slaves under close guard and in chains. Because they are such villains, the aforementioned [black servants] get their freed slaves to do their [dirty] work for them[16] and then inform Your Honor that many ladies who have resided for a long time at my *mbanza* have run away. It is all the more so with recent residents. Had these [courtiers] remained here, they would have been able to carry out official duties as the slave of the captain and of the Reverend Vigário [Vicar] did for so many years, and as the reverend fathers who bear the present letter will tell you. I will digress no more. May God keep you in power for many years, etc. The Court at Matamba, on this day, the fifteenth of June of the year 1660.

Queen D. Ana

[15] Cadornega was a Portuguese soldier and chronicler who participated in the wars against Njinga and wrote two volumes on the wars.

[16] Though the passage is somewhat obscure, it appears to suggest that Portuguese agents and tradesmen were in the habit of abducting members of Njinga's royal court and selling them into slavery.

4

Afro-Iberian Subjects: Petitioning the Crown at Home, Serving the Crown Abroad, 1590s–1630s[1]

Leo J. Garofalo

History of Southern Iberia's Black Communities

Afro-Iberians made up a small, but well-integrated, segment of southern Castilian and Portuguese society. The men and women who traced their roots or part of their heritage to the regions of West and Central Africa settled or grew up in a European world oriented toward artisanal work, local and transatlantic commerce, and seafaring. Many people of African descent who arrived in the early Americas began their transatlantic journey from the black communities of Spain and Portugal, and not from the African continent. And not all of the people who became Afro-Latin Americans crossed the Atlantic Ocean as slaves. In fact, free Afro-Iberian individuals and families, such as the ones highlighted in this chapter, became part of a rapidly changing region within Europe and part of the European expansion abroad.

An examination of the records that constituted the Spanish Crown's attempt to regulate the flow of people to the Americas reveals hundreds of petitions to officials in Seville from, or on behalf of, people of African heritage living in southern Spain and Portugal. These Afro-Iberian petitioners were members of local communities, and some of their families had lived in Europe for generations by 1600. Others were newer arrivals to the Iberian Peninsula from Africa or the Americas, or were the children of recent arrivals. In general, they were Christian, spoke European languages, and considered themselves subjects of the Spanish or Portuguese monarchies.[2]

The three cases in this chapter demonstrate how Afro-Iberians could resist marginalization and serve to strengthen the imperial system as soldiers and sailors, and as adherents to an ethnic and religious ideology valuing European identity and Catholicism over others. The documents represent the voices of Afro-Iberian women in the form of petitions and testimonies directed to royal authorities. In Spain, these women and other Afro-Iberians like them wrote to the Crown or appeared in royal courts to request permission to travel, reunite families, recover property or inheritances, prove their eligibility to sail or serve the Spanish Empire, return to homelands in the Americas or Europe, and defend their status as free from slavery.

The narratives in this chapter describe individuals from Andalusia's black population involved in the transatlantic movement of Iberians. They also mention Afro-Iberians' involvement in defending the Spanish empire from attack or religious heresy.

[1] See Maps 1, 4, and 6.

[2] Employing the Iberian term in use in the fifteenth and sixteenth centuries, scholars label this process of Christianization and the use of European languages "ladinoization."

In each case, the women addressed the judges of Seville's royal court that oversaw all trade, travel, and transactions with the Americas.

In the first case, the Afro-Iberian wife of a soldier stationed in Mexico asks to be allowed to join him as a way to remedy economic hardship. The second case shows an Afro-Iberian woman attempting to collect wages owed to a male family member who died while serving the Crown. The third case documents the successful efforts of an Afro-Iberian woman to follow her grown daughter to the Americas in order to escape poverty in Iberia while emphasizing her status as a Spanish subject and her family's freedom from the "taint" of other religions or investigation by the Spanish Inquisition.

The selections provide a view of key ways black Europeans in southern Iberia explained their position in society and their rights as subjects and militant servants of the Crown and Church. Afro-Iberians played a part in creating this early Spanish Atlantic world of networks, new kinds of people, and new cultures.

By the sixteenth and seventeenth centuries, Africans and Afro-Iberians were not necessarily newcomers to Europe or the Americas (Franco Silva, 73–84). Europe's first sales of slaves or people captured or purchased from African intermediaries in West Africa took place at Lagos in southern Portugal. Lisbon and the southern Portuguese Algarve region became home to numerous people of mixed African and European heritage. Many of them worked in shipping and all aspects of Atlantic commerce; they even took part in slave trading operations or relocated to European enclaves in Africa.

Overland routes, and eventually direct shipments, brought Portuguese slave traders to Spain. Castilian merchants and ship owners also engaged in raiding and slaving operations in West Africa, but they were soon eclipsed by the Portuguese. The Spanish Crown preferred to sell the rights to monopolize the trade in human beings to Portuguese merchants, leaving the Spanish sea captains and sailors to enlist with the Portuguese expeditions (see Stella, 23–37). Even without the monopoly, first southern Spain and then, after 1520, the Spanish colonies in the Americas constituted the principal markets for slaves until 1600 when Brazil's sugar plantations dwarfed all other enterprises in its insatiable demand for laborers.

In southern Spain, enslaved West and Central Africans labored in every economic sector, ranging from domestic service and small crafts shops to agricultural work and transportation on boats and mules (González Díaz, 23). African men and women entered southern Iberian society in roughly equal numbers, and they acquired freedom primarily by buying their freedom from their owners, although a few were freed by owners or as a legal remedy for abuse.

As both free and enslaved individuals, they intermarried and integrated into parishes, religious life (especially religious brotherhoods), artisanal professions, and petty commerce. Not surprisingly, Afro-Iberians became a permanent part of southern Iberian life (Pike, 345–60) and played a role in the enterprise to conquer and colonize the Americas (see Restall, 44–63).

The Afro-Iberian soldiers and sailors who perished while serving the Crown on ships and in garrisons and ports commonly left behind family members in the home communities of southern Iberia. More often than not, these relatives were Afro-Iberian women who petitioned to recover the deceased person's property and uncollected wages and rations.

Petitioning on Behalf of Servants of the Crown and the Faith

Witnesses, authorities, and members of local communities considered the black soldiers and sailors moving back and forth across the Atlantic to be servants of the Crown who served a royal purpose.[3] Black women living in the sailing and trading communities of Andalusia understood the implications and benefits of this service. They dictated the petitions excerpted in this chapter.

Felipa de Santiago, an Afro-Iberian woman[4] and former slave, appeared in Seville's royal court in 1594 to present a petition requesting permission to travel to Mexico with her children to be reunited with her husband, a soldier stationed there. She bolstered her request with affidavits from the priests who married the couple and baptized each of their children in Seville's San Vicente Parish and from neighbors who attested to their life together as a legitimately married couple with children. She also included sworn statements sent by her husband's commanders that he was indeed a soldier and stationed in Mexico. A month later she secured a royal order that allowed her and her *mulatto* children to travel to Mexico and also warned officials not to impede their passage because they were free from the restrictions placed upon slaves' movement.

The familial bonds and benefits of royal service extended beyond spouses to encompass other relatives, as shown in the second case. Clara Rodríguez, a free *morena* never subjected to enslavement, lost her young nephew Cristóbal López, described as a free *mulatto,* while he was serving in the fleet that sailed for New Spain in 1634 commanded by General Martín de Vallesilla. As was the custom at the time, the Spanish legal document offered a physical description of the nineteen-year-old Cristóbal taken from the ship's crew list: he was strong of body with a scar under his beard. The document noted that his birthplace was Ayamonte and his father's name was Antonio. Another sailor from his hometown, higher ranking and not an Afro-Iberian, testified that he knew the family well. Clara Rodríguez and Juana López, *de color negras* and free of slavery, were his full sisters and born of married parents.

After his mother's death, Cristóbal enlisted in the fleet as a *grumete,* the lowest rank of sailor and just above cabin boy or *paje.* He appeared for muster (roll call) seven times during the voyage and the port calls in the Caribbean before failing to appear in the muster taken in Veracruz on June 21, 1635.[5] The older sailor, aged thirty-four and from Cristóbal's hometown, explained how he crossed the Atlantic on the same royal ship with the young man and took him to the hospital in Mexico where he died. After her initial petition offered here and the first round of witnesses that she called, Clara Rodríguez signed a power of attorney, allowing another to press her suit and act in her name. The royal judges in Seville eventually ordered that she be paid the nephew's uncollected wages.

[3] Garofalo, "The Case of Diego Suárez."

[4] In the documents, she referred to herself as of *color negra.* Witnesses also used this label or called her *de color prieta.* In every case, they carefully emphasized her free status, and some mentioned the letter giving her freedom from Doña Beatriz de León, who owned de Santiago before she was married.

[5] He still remained missing at the muster on September 11, 1635.

Felipa de Santiago's case mentioned above illustrates how an impoverished condition together with respectable Christian conduct and royal service could persuade officials in the *Casa de Contratación* to issue a royal license allowing legal travel to the Americas.[6] Some petitioners who did not have sailors or soldiers in their immediate families made successful arguments for their eligibility to travel based solely on economic need and good Christian standing. In fact, they even claimed old Christian status free from past or present association with Islam or Judaism. In theory, law prohibited *new Christians* from traveling to the Americas. If proven in court, violations led to the confiscation of property, which was given as a reward to the prosecuting judges and those who detected violators. Therefore, it is perfectly understandable why some Iberians with sub-Saharan heritage claimed old Christian status and piety in court and used it to legitimize emigration to the Americas.[7]

One of these successful claimants was Francisca de Figueroa. The documents from her case include her relatively short, almost terse petitions as well as more extensive testimony by several people she brought before the court or notaries to explain who she and her daughters were and to defend her *limpieza de sangre.* She played an important and active role in shaping her image in court and in pushing her case forward before the Crown.

At no point did she employ an attorney, and she apparently never authorized another person to speak for her. During the first stage of her case in 1600, she obtained a royal decree that allowed her and her daughter to travel to the Americas. In 1601, she returned to Seville's royal court to definitively establish her legal right to join her daughter in Cartagena de Indias. During this second stage, the court copied the royal decree into the records of the *Casa de Contratación,* and the judges agreed to give her the licenses and permissions she sought.

In each of these cases, the goal has been to select the portion of the larger documents in which the Afro-Iberian petitioner speaks most directly. In the case of Francisca de Figueroa, she both dictated portions of the document herself and directed others she knew well to provide exactly the kind of testimony she knew the judges needed to hear in order to approve her travel. Therefore, in the Figueroa case, this chapter includes both her own words and a representative example of the witnesses she coached.

The three cases selected are quite short (totaling fourteen to sixteen pages each). The number of documents for each case remained small because third parties did not intervene and royal authorities quickly approved each petition. The excerpts include all or almost all the words attributed to each woman in the respective document. Not included are additional witnesses' statements and notes from the notaries on the progress of the cases and the final decisions (except in the Figueroa case). These Afro-Iberian women's petitions speak both to how they constructed an identity as subjects and how their lives intersected with the imperial efforts to secure and hold territory and enforce a strict religious conformity as an equally important strategic goal.

[6] Certainly many traveled without such licenses and without the added protection they offered against bureaucratic hassles, bribes, jail, or being forced into slavery.

[7] See Garofalo, "The Shape of a Diaspora."

Información de Felipa de Santiago, *negra,* 1594[1]

Yo, Pedro de Barahona, *escribano* del Rey Nuestro Señor, que sirvo [en] el oficio de *escribano* de la *Casa de Contratación* de las Indias de esta ciudad de Sevilla. . . . Doy fe que en la dicha casa a veinte y cinco de mayo de este presente año de 1594 ante los señores presidente y jueces oficiales del reino . . . parecía Felipa de Santiago de color *negra.* Y presentó una petición con tres testimonios, el tenor de la cual y del *auto* a ello proveído y de cierta información que dio es esto que sigue.

Felipa de Santiago, *negra* tesada, *vecina* de esta ciudad de Sevilla, mujer legítima que soy de Pedro Hernández de Rivera, artillero que al presente está sirviendo el dicho oficio en los fuertes de la Isla de San Juan de Ulúa. Digo que yo y el dicho Pedro Hernández somos marido y mujer legítimos. Y nuestro casamiento velamos en esta ciudad en la Iglesia de Señor Santo Vincente de ella como parece por esta fe y certificación que presento. Y como tales hemos hecho vida maridable en la dicha ciudad hasta que podía haber tres años que el dicho mi marido pasó a las Indias. Y reside sirviendo a su Magestad en los fuertes de la isla de San Juan de Ulúa como parece por esta fe que presento. Y de nuestro matrimonio hemos habido tres hijos: una hembra y dos varones. Y yo soy mujer libre y no sujeta a ningún captiverio ni los dichos mis hijos. Y el dicho mi marido me ha enviado a llamar para hacer vida conmigo. Y me favorece ir por ser pobre y estar él en servicio de Su Majestad como así mismo parezca por carta y misivas que tengo en mi poder, y porque yo quiero acudir a su Magestad a pedir licencia para pasar a hacer vida con el dicho mi marido y llevar conmigo mis hijos.

Proceso sobre bienes de Cristóbal López, grumete, natural de Ayamonte y difunto en Veracruz sin testamento, 1637[2]

En la Villa de Ayamonte a nueve días del mes de enero de 1637 años ante el *licenciado* Francisco Galves de Castro corregidor y *justicia mayor* en esta dicha *villa* y su marquesado y por ante mí Juan de Caliz, *escribano* del Rey Nuestro Señor y público del número de esta dicha *villa* pareció presente Clara Rodríguez, *morena vecina* de ella y presentó la petición siguiente.

Clara Rodríguez *morena* de color libre persona de esta *villa,* como tía y heredera, abintestado de Cristóbal López Riquel de color *mulato* mi sobrino hijo de Juana González mi hermana difunta *mulata* libre como lo era el dicho Cristóbal López mi sobrino cuyos bienes y herencia del dicho acepto con beneficio de *inventario,* como más lugar haya. Digo que a mi derecho conviene probar y averiguar de cómo el dicho mi sobrino fue sirviendo *plaza* de *grumete* en la capitana de Nueva España, de la flota

[1] Archivo General de Indias, Contratación, 5248, N. 1, R. 1, *Información de Felipa de Santiago, negra,* 1594, fols. 1r–7v.

[2] Archivo General de Indias, Contratación, 963, N. 2, R. 11, Proceso sobre bienes de Cristóbal López grumete natural de Ayamonte y difunto en Veracruz, 1637, fols. 1r–8r.

Inquiries Regarding Felipa de Santiago, *Negra,* 1594

I, Pedro de Barahona, Our Lord the King's notary, who serves in the capacity of scribe in the *Casa de Contratación* of the Indies in Seville. . . . I certify that Felipa de Santiago, of black color, appeared in the said house on the twenty-fifth of May of the present year of 1594, before the president and royal judges. . . . She presented a petition with three sworn testimonials, whose content and that of the decree she provided and of a certain account that she gave is as follows.

I, Felipa de Santiago, swarthy black, resident householder in the city of Seville, the legitimately married wife of Pedro Hernández de Rivera, a gunner who at present is serving in that occupation in the forts of the Island of San Juan de Ulúa,[1] declare that the said Pedro Hernández and I are legitimately married husband and wife. We celebrated our marriage in this city in the Church of Saint Vincent, as appears in the sworn certification that I present. We have lived as husband and wife in the said city until about three years ago, when my husband went to the Indies. He resides [there] serving Your Majesty in the forts of the Island of San Juan de Ulúa as appears in this certificate that I present. In our marriage we have had three children: one girl and two boys. I am a free woman not subject to any captivity, nor are my children. My husband wrote to send for me to live with him. It is to my advantage to go because I am poor and he is in the service of Your Majesty, just as it appears in the letter and missives that I have in my possession, and I want to appeal to Your Majesty for a license to travel [to the Indies] in order to live with my husband and to take my children with me.[2]

Suit over the Property of Cristóbal López, *Grumete,* Native of Ayamonte and Deceased in Veracruz without a Will, 1637

In the town of Ayamonte on the ninth day of January 1637, Clara Rodríguez, *morena* and a resident householder in town, appeared before the *licentiate* Francisco Galves de Castro, magistrate and justice of the peace in this said town and its marquisate, and before me, Juan de Caliz, one of the Lord King's notaries in this town, and she presented the following petition.

Clara Rodríguez, *morena* of color, a free person of this town, as aunt and heiress *ab intestate*[3] of the *mulatto* Cristóbal López Riquel, my nephew and son of Juana González, my deceased sister, a free *mulatta* as was the said Cristóbal López, my nephew, whose property and inheritance I claim with the benefit of an inventory as soon as possible. I state that it is fitting to my rights that it be proven and shown that my said

[1] Veracruz, New Spain.

[2] The notary then entered the letters from Mexico attesting to Pedro Hernández de Rivera's employment as a gunner and his request for her to sail in the next fleet to join him with their children and the letters from Seville's clergymen certifying the petitioner's married status and the dates of her children's baptisms.

[3] Died without making a will.

que pasó a las Indias de la dicha Nueva España el año pasado de que fue general Martín de Vallesilla. La cual dicha plaza sirvió hasta el Puerto de San Juan de Ulúa de las dichas Indias hasta que falleció en las dichas Indias. Y de cómo el dicho mi sobrino falleció mozo y soltero y que no dejó hijos ni padres ni otro heredero ni pariente más cercano que yo y que cómo a tal me pertenece la soldada que ganó en el dicho viaje y otros cualesquier bienes que hayan quedado por su fin y muerte.

A Vuestra Merced pido y suplico mande recebir la información que [a]cerca del dicho diere, y los testigos que presentare se examinen por esta petición. Y de sus dichos y declaraciones me mande dar un traslado autorizado en pública forma y de manera que haga fe para lo presentar ante quien me convenga, interponiendo Vuestra Merced en ello su autoridad y judicial decreto. Y pido justicia y para ello etcétera.

Clara Rodríguez

Expediente de información y licencia de Francisca de Figueroa, *mulata,* a Cartagena, 1600[3]

Francisca de Figueroa, Junio de 1600 años

Francisca de Figueroa de color *mulata,* digo que yo tengo en la ciudad de Cartagena una hija mía nombrada Juana de Figueroa. Y me ha enviado a llamar para me hacer bien. Y he de llevar conmigo en mi compañía una hija mía, hermana suya, nombrada María de la dicha color. Y por él he de enviar al Rey Nuestro Señor para que me haga merced de darme licencia para que yo y la dicha mi hija podamos ir a residir en la dicha ciudad de Cartagena. Y de ello tengo de dar información de lo asentado en esta relación. Y de cómo yo la dicha Francisca de Figueroa soy una mujer de buen cuerpo de color *mulata* . . . Y la dicha mi hija María de veinte años de la dicha color mediana de cuerpo. Y dada, se me dé por testigo para el dicho efecto.

A Vuestra Señoría suplico ansí lo probar y mande. Sobre que pido justicia.

En veinte y un días del mes de junio de 1600 años, los señores presidentes y jueces oficiales de Su Majestad de esta casa mandamos que se reciba la información que ofrece y se lo dé el testimonio de ella para el efecto que lo pide.

[Francisca de Figueroa presentó por testigo a Francisca de Mendoza, cuarenta y cuatro años]

En la ciudad de Sevilla en la *Casa de Contratación* de las Indias, a veinte y nueve días del mes de agosto de 1600, la dicha Francisca de Figueroa para la información que ha ofrecido y le está mandada dar, presentó por testigo a Francisca de Mendoza mujer de Sebastián de Sayavedra, correo de a caballo del reino, *vecina* de Sevilla, en la Collación de la Magdalena. De la cual fue tomado y recibido juramiento. . . .

Y siendo preguntada por el tenor de el pedimiento presentado por [Francisca de Figueroa]. Dijo que conoce a la dicha Francisca de Figueroa y a María su hija y a Juana de Figueroa otra hija suya, que ha oído decir que está en la ciudad de Cartagena de las

[3] Archivo General de Indias, Contratación, 5261, N. 2, R. 33, Expediente de información y licencia de Francisca de Figueroa, mulata, a Cartagena, Seville, 1600, fols. 1r–2v.

nephew was serving as a *grumete* in the fleet that sailed to New Spain in the Indies last year, and of which Martín de Vallesilla was admiral. He served in that post, traveling to the port of San Juan de Ulúa of the Indies, until he died in the said Indies. My nephew died young and unmarried and he left no children or parents or other heir or closer relative than I and as such the wage he earned in the said voyage and whatever other belongings he left behind upon his death belong to me.

I beg and beseech Your Mercy to order that the information I will give be received, and the witnesses that I present be examined regarding this petition. And that you order that I be given an authorized copy of his declarations in a public form and manner so that I can present it before whom it suits me, placing in it Your Mercy's authority and judicial decree. I ask for justice etcetera.

Clara Rodríguez

Proceedings of the Inquiry and License for Francisca de Figueroa, *Mulatta,* to Sail for Cartagena, 1600

Francisca de Figueroa, June 1600

Francisca de Figueroa, *mulatta* in color, declare that I have in the city of Cartagena a daughter named Juana de Figueroa. And she has written to call for me in order to help me. I will take with me in my company a daughter of mine, her sister, named María, of the said color. And for this I must write to Our Lord the King to petition that he favor me with a license so that I and my said daughter can go and reside in the said city of Cartagena. For this I will give an account of what is put down in this report. And of how I Francisca de Figueroa am a woman of sound body and *mulatta* in color . . . And my daughter María is twenty years old and of the said color and of medium size. Once given, I attest to this.

I beg Your Lordship to approve and order it done. I ask for justice in this.

On the twenty-first day of the month of June 1600, Your Majesty's lords presidents and official judges of this house [*Casa de Contratación*] order that the account she offers be received and that testimony for the purpose she requests be given.

[Francisca de Figueroa Presented as a Witness Francisca de Mendoza, Forty-Four Years Old]

In the city of Seville in the *Casa de Contratación* of the Indies, on the twenty-ninth day of the month of August 1600, the said Francisca de Figueroa for the account she has offered and that she is ordered to give, presented as a witness Francisca de Mendoza, wife of Sebastián de Sayavedra, mounted courier in this kingdom, resident householder in Seville, in the neighborhood of Magdalena. She was sworn in. . . .

Questioned about the petition presented by [Francisca de Figueroa]. She said that she knows Francisca de Figueroa and her daughter María and Juana de Figueroa, another daughter of hers, who she has heard is in the city of Cartagena in the Indies. She

Indias. Y sabe que ha enviado a la María la dicha Francisca de Figueroa su madre para remediar de sus necesidades, que por ser pobre padece con la dicha María su hija en estos reinos. Y sabe [Francisca de Mendoza] por haber *visto* cartas de la dicha Juana de Figueroa en que le envía a decir se vaya, ofreciéndole dineros para el costo del viaje. Y que la socorría como dicho tiene en [Cartagena] donde la dicha Juana de Figueroa vive. Y sabe que [Francisca de Figueroa] es mujer de color *mulata* de buen cuerpo de cuarenta y cuatro años. Y [María] será de edad de veinte años, mediana de cuerpo y de la dicha color. Y que todo lo susodicho es público y notorio y pública voz y fama entre todas las personas que las conocieron como este testigo. . . . No firmó porque no sabía escribir. . . .

Francisca de Figueroa, de color *mulata*, petición para Cartagena, Sevilla, 1601[4]

En 23 de enero de 1601, Francisca de Figueroa de color *mulata* digo que el Rey Nuestro Señor me hizo merced de darme licencia para pasar a la Provincia de Cartagena y porque yo soy natural de esta ciudad.

Ante Vuestra Señoría pido y suplico mande que se reciba información de la limpieza de mi persona y que en la contaduría de esta Casa se despache mi licencia. . . .

[Francisca de Figueroa presentó por testigo a Elvira de Medina, cincuenta años]

En Sevilla en la *Casa de Contratación* de las Indias a diez y nueve días del mes de enero de 1601, [Francisca de Figueroa] para la información, presentó por testigo a una mujer que se dijo llamar Elvira de Medina, viuda mujer que fue de Pedro García Benítez, cordonero, *vecina* de esta ciudad de Sevilla en la Collación de la Magdalena. . . . Dijo que conoce a la dicha Francisca Figueroa que está presente por testigo de más de treinta seis años a esta parte. Y conoció a Pedro de Figueroa su padre y María de León su mujer, *negra* atesada[.] Sabe que fueron marido y mujer legítimos casados e velados según orden de la Santa Madre Iglesia de Roma. . . . Les vido hacer vida maridable en una casa y compañía. Y vido que durante su matrimonio hubieron y procrearon por su hija legítima a la dicha Francisca de Figueroa[.] [E]ste testigo sabe que ella y sus padres y abuelos han sido y son cristianos viejos y de limpia *casta* y generación. Y no de *casta* de moros ni de judíos ni de los nuevamente convertidos a Nuestra Santa Fe Católica. Y que no han sido presos ni penitenciados por el Santo Oficio de la Inquisición. Ni tienen otras tachas ni defectos por donde no puedan pasar a las Indias, porque esta testigo como cristianos conoció a los dichos sus padres. Y tiene noticia de sus abuelos ansí de partes de padre como de madre por haber oído decir y tratar de ellos a sus

[4] Archivo General de Indias, Contratación, 5268, N. 2, R. 68, Expediente de información y licencia de Francisca de Figueroa, mulata, a Cartagena, Seville, 1601, fols. 1r–4v.

knows that she sent to call for the said Francisca de Figueroa her mother to remedy her need, which she and her daughter María suffer in these realms because of their poverty. [Francisca de Mendoza] knows this because she has seen letters from Juana de Figueroa in which she wrote to say that [her mother] should go, offering money for the cost of the trip. And that she will help her as she has said in [Cartagena] where Juana de Figueroa lives. And she knows that [Francisca de Figueroa] is a woman, *mulatta* in color, of sound body, and forty-four years old. [María] is about twenty years old, medium sized and of the said color. All of this is publicly known and spoken of among all the people who know them as does this witness. . . . She did not sign because she does not know how to write.[4] . . .

Francisca de Figueroa, *Mulatta,* Petition for Cartagena, Seville, 1601[5]

On January 23, 1601, [I], Francisca de Figueroa, *mulatta* in color, do state that Our Lord the King conferred on me the favor of a license to sail to the Province of Cartagena and because I am a native of this city [Seville].

Before Your Lordship, I beg and implore you to order that the account of the *limpieza*[6] of my person be received and that the accountancy of this *Casa* dispatch my license. . . .

[Francisca de Figueroa Presented as a Witness Elvira de Medina, Fifty Years Old]

In Seville in the *Casa de Contratación* of the Indies on the nineteenth of January 1601, [Francisca de Figueroa] for the inquiry, presented as a witness a woman who said she was named Elvira de Medina, widow of Pedro García Benítez, rope-maker,[7] resident householder in this city of Seville in the neighborhood of Magdalena. . . . She said that she has known the said Francisca Figueroa, who is present as a witness, for more than thirty-six years to date. And she knew her father Pedro de Figueroa and María de León his wife, a swarthy black. She knows that they were husband and wife legitimately married according to the laws of the Holy Mother Church of Rome. . . . She saw them live as a married couple together in the same house. And she saw that during their marriage they procreated as their legitimate daughter the said Francisca de Figueroa. This witness knows that she and her parents and her grandparents have been and are Old Christians and of unsullied caste and lineage. They are not of Moorish or Jewish caste or of those recently converted to Our Holy Catholic Faith. They have not been prisoners or penanced by the Holy Office of the Inquisition. Nor do they have other blemishes or defects that prevent them from going to the Indies, because this witness knew her parents to be Christians. And she has knowledge of her grandparents on both her father's and her mother's side from hearing them spoken of by her

[4] Two additional witnesses provide essentially the same information.

[5] Dossier of the report and license granted to Francisca de Figueroa, *mulatta,* to travel to Cartagena, presented in Seville, 1601.

[6] *Limpieza de sangre,* "purity of blood."

[7] Cordonero.

mayores. . . . Y esta testigo sabe que [Francisca de Figueroa] es natural de esta ciudad que nació en ella. Y que es soltera y no casada, ni sujeta a orden o religión alguna. . . . Y que ésta es la verdad para el juramento que tiene [hecho]. Y no firmó porque dijo que no sabía escribir. Y que es de edad de cincuenta años. . . .

Traslado de una cédula de Su Majestad que presentó Francisca de Figueroa, 1601

EL REY

Mis presidentes y jueces oficiales de la *Casa de Contratación* de Sevilla. Yo os mando dejéis pasar a la Provincia de Cartagena a Francisca de Figueroa *vecina* de esa ciudad, de color *mulata,* de buen cuerpo, de edad de cuarenta y cinco años, que va a estar en compañía de una hija suya. Y que pueda llevar a María su hija, de color *mulata,* de mediana estatura y de edad de veinte años. Presentando ante vos informaciones hechas en sus tierras ante las *justicias* de ellas. Y con aprobación de las mismas *justicias* de cómo no son casadas ni de las prohibidas a pasar [a] aquellas partes. Fecha en el Prado a veinte y siete de noviembre de 1600 años, yo el Rey. . . . Traslado fue corregido y concertado con la cédula de Su Majestad. Fecho a veinte y tres de enero de 1601 años.

elders. . . . This witness knows that [Francisca de Figueroa] is a native of this city and was born in it. She is single and unmarried, and not subject to any religious orders. . . . This is the truth according to the oath she has [made]. She did not sign because she said that she cannot write. She is fifty years old.[8] . . .

Copy of a Decree from His Majesty Presented by Francisca de Figueroa, 1601

THE KING

My presidents and official judges of the *Casa de Contratación* of Seville. I order you to allow passage to the Province of Cartagena for Francisca de Figueroa resident householder of that city, *mulatta* in color, of sound body, forty-five years old, who will be in the company of a daughter of hers. She can take with her the daughter María, *mulatta* in color, of medium stature, and twenty years old. Presenting before you accounts given in her jurisdiction before those justices, and with the approval of the same justices, that [the two women] are not married nor do they belong to those [groups] that are prohibited to travel to those lands. Dated in the Prado on the twenty-seventh of November 1600, I, the King. . . . The copy was corrected and certified with His Majesty's decree. Dated the twenty-third of January 1601.

[8] Two additional witnesses testified in a similar fashion.

5

Elder, Slave, and Soldier: *Maroon* Voices from the *Palenque* del Limón, 1634[1]

Kathryn Joy McKnight

Historical Background

Early in 1634, Francisco *Angola,* Sebastián *Anchico,* and Juan de la Mar testified about the recent violence in which their community of Limón had engaged. They were prisoners called before Don Francisco de Llano Velasco, lieutenant general of the city of Cartagena de Indias, on the northwestern coast of what is now Colombia. In the documents to follow, the name Cartagena refers variously to the province and its principal port city. Limón was a *palenque,* a clandestine settlement of people of African descent who had escaped slavery, also known as *cimarrones* or *Maroons.* Africans founded the hidden village around 1580 in the Sierra de María, near Cartagena, in the early days of the city's boom as a slave port. In 1633, their *criollo* descendants—those born in the New World—dominated the community's population and leadership.

Palenque soldiers had recently attacked surrounding ranches and carried off Indians and slaves. They stole livestock, burned buildings, killed Spaniards, and attacked and killed many of the residents of the Indian town of Chambacú. On December 9, 1633, Spanish soldiers responded with an assault on the *palenque* and eventually captured eighty or more community members whom they put on trial and punished.

Under interrogation, Limón residents told fascinating stories of *palenque* life and colonial society as the Spaniards sought information from them about the violence. After testifying, thirteen men were publicly executed, their bodies quartered and displayed to instill terror in the thousands of enslaved people of African descent in Cartagena. The remaining residents were sentenced to be sold by their owners into exile from the province. In these punishments, Cartagena officials acted out of fear that more enslaved people would escape to *palenques,* attack colonial properties, or, worse, rise up en masse against the Spaniards. Francisco *Angola,* Sebastián *Anchico,* and Juan de la Mar were among the nineteen residents whose testimony was recorded in these trials.[2] All three men were executed.

Maroon communities like Limón persisted throughout the Americas for as long as colonials enslaved people of African descent.[3] Their soldiers raided ranches, attacked

[1] See Maps 6 and 8. I wish to thank the helpful staff at the Archivo General de Indias, the University of New Mexico for a research grant to travel to Seville, and Jan Ankerson and Anne Benscoter for their careful reading and insightful suggestions on the presentation of these documents.

[2] To read the published testimony of three women residents, see McKnight, "Gendered Declarations."

[3] See Price for an overview of *Maroon* societies.

mule trains loaded with precious metals bound for Spain, and aided pirates who raided the Caribbean coasts. Their settlements attracted others who wanted to escape slavery. Some *Maroon* leaders became legendary, including Bayano in Panama, Yanga in New Spain (Mexico), Domingo Biohó in Cartagena, Ganga Zumba and Zumbi in Palmares, Brazil, and Nanny in Jamaica.

Colonial governments negotiated treaties with *Maroons* in Brazil, Colombia, Cuba, Ecuador, Hispaniola, Jamaica, and Surinam, establishing free black towns in exchange for promises of the cessation of anticolonial violence (Price, 3).[4] The letter from Alonso de Illescas in Chapter 2 of this volume represents an overture for such a negotiation. At least eight *palenques* existed in the seventeenth century in the province of Cartagena alone (Borrego Plá, 7, 26). Peace negotiations were underway between Governor Francisco de Murga of Cartagena and the *Palenque* del Limón in the months before the Spanish attack. However, it was not until 1714 that the province of Cartagena established the first free black town of San Basilio, which still exists today, as do black towns founded by *Maroons* throughout Latin America.

Palenques—elsewhere known as *quilombos,* mocambos, cumbes, ladeiras, and mambises (Price, 1)—provided important spaces where African-descent people preserved and created new cultural and social practices that had their roots in Africa. Such processes were dynamic, historically specific, and varied from one *Maroon* settlement to another.[5] A *palenque's* demographics, the birthplaces of its members, and the historical events through which these residents had lived all molded the community's social relationships and cultural expressions. *Palenques* did not exist in isolation, and thus these processes were also affected by the community's engagement with their European and Amerindian neighbors, the politics of nearby urban centers, and their interactions with free and enslaved Afro-Latinos outside the *palenque.* All these factors can be glimpsed in the Limón testimonies.

For years, Limón residents coexisted peacefully and exchanged labor and goods with neighboring Spanish ranchers and their slaves. Community members give conflicting explanations for the turn to violence. Some blame new arrivals for instigating attacks on ranches as revenge against cruel overseers, but others see the violence as part of a more global plan for the *palenque's* future. A group of new residents brought to power the *criolla* woman Leonor as *palenque* queen and stirred in her a new and violent vision of antagonism against Spaniards.

In this explanation, the attacks are seen as a way to grow the *palenque's* population by kidnapping slaves from surrounding ranches in an adaptation of an African form of slavery to a new American context. Before the advent of the European slave trade to Atlantic Africa, both West and Central African societies practiced forms of slavery

[4] See Navarrete; Rodríguez; and Ruiz Rivera for overviews of peace settlements in the Americas.

[5] In "Identifying Enslaved Africans," Paul Lovejoy presents a framework for studying the historically specific dynamics of cultural preservation and change in the African diaspora. In *Central Africans, Atlantic Creoles, and the Foundation of the Americas, 1585–1660,* Linda Heywood and John Thornton provide an invaluable resource for such an analysis in a series of maps showing the areas in Central Africa from which people were taken for the Atlantic slave trade, organized in five-year periods from 1615 to 1660 (227–35).

in which social elites accumulated their wealth, not in land but in people. Such slaves could act as personal servants, or as administrators or soldiers (Thornton, 101). In the new American context, Limón leaders sought to accumulate such slave wealth to increase the size of their fighting force and to provide Limón men with wives from outside the community.

As Spaniards planned their responses to the violence, *palenque* actions took on a more warlike character: for some the *palenque's* attack on the Indian town of Chambacú represented a preemptive strike. Chambacú's *encomendero,* Francisco Martín Garruchena, was planning to pay the Indians to attack Limón. The violence itself also took on Central African forms. According to one resident, the *palenque's* ritualized killing of a Spaniard "*era a uso de Guinea*" (was done in an African manner). He might have been referring to the practices of human sacrifice engaged in by the *Imbangalas,* mobile military groups that wreaked havoc on the Mbundu region in the early 1600s and provided slaves to the Portuguese in *Angola* (Heywood and Thornton, 93–95). Another resident suggests that the attacks emulated the violence with which the legendary African Domingo Biohó pressured Spanish colonials in Cartagena thirty years earlier.

Juan de la Mar's testimony provides a glimpse into the dynamic creation and recreation of Afro-Latino cultural beliefs and practices when he tells how *palenque*-born Leonor Criolla became queen and chief military leader. Queen Leonor's leadership style exemplifies the African models of monarchical leadership that dominated American *Maroon* life before a general shift to *criollo* leadership around 1700 (Price, 20).

Juan de la Mar speaks of newly arrived slaves putting "some devil into the black woman Leonor's head," after which everyone obeyed her. He identifies these men as *Malembas,* an *ethnonym* that suggests they were first-generation immigrants from the interior of *Angola.* These men brought with them Central African beliefs about spiritual–military leadership, which they may have formed through knowledge or experience of the *Angola*–Ndongo wars and of the legendary Queen Njinga, whose letters are presented in Chapter 3 of this volume.[6]

Interpreting the Narratives

The Limón testimonies form part of a 990-page dossier sent to Felipe IV, the king of Spain. The document title translates as "Testimony of the Trials and Punishments Carried out by Field Marshall Francisco de Murga, Governor and Captain General of Cartagena, against the Rebel Black *Maroons* of the *Palenques* of Limón, Polín, and Zanaguare." The dossier also includes petitions, *cabildo* minutes, decrees, the testimonies of Spanish officials, military men, and colonists, letters, and trial records.

The trial declarations represent a kind of coproduction under fire, rather than stories that speakers shape within their own oral traditions. The residents respond to the questions of Spanish interrogators who seek information that will help them quell the

[6] There is no concrete evidence of when these men were enslaved and transported, but the spiritual–military rituals that Juan de la Mar described suggest this Angolan connection; see McKnight, "Confronted Rituals."

rebellion. To sift out the narrative strategies and worldviews of Francisco *Angola,* Sebastián *Anchico,* and Juan de la Mar, readers must assess the effects on their stories of a context of interrogation in which they faced possible execution.

At some points, the interrogator exercised control through his questions; at others, Spaniards and Limón residents negotiated the presentation of information. The Spanish scribe imposed a bureaucratic language over the speaker's own expressions. An African-language interpreter filtered the words of Sebastián *Anchico,* who spoke in a Central African language. Taking into account these thick layers of mediation, readers can hypothesize about those moments in which the *palenque* residents' voices broke through and expressed their own perceptions and truths.[7]

To hypothesize about the speakers' own narratives and agency, readers can look for narrative "excesses," pay attention to ways in which speakers identify themselves and others, examine how speakers link these identities to their narration of violence, and seek out symbolic images.

1. "Narrative excesses" are those utterances that offer more information than is requested, such as when Francisco *Angola* is asked about his arrival and time in the *palenque,* and he responds by criticizing the whites' deceitful actions.
2. The ways in which speakers identify themselves and each other involve distinctions that both they and the interrogator make among community members. For the modern reader, thinking about identity can transform long lists of names with brief identifiers into challenging but vital sources of *palenque* thought. How does Juan de la Mar organize and describe Limón members in his list of names, and what does this list suggest about oral traditions, or about his and his interrogators' perceptions of *palenque* social order and group identity?
3. Differences can also be seen between how older residents, such as Francisco *Angola,* do not discuss the violence, perhaps to protect their own kin; while newer arrivals, represented by Juan de la Mar, express abhorrence at the violence, painting themselves at times—perhaps deceptively—as helpless observers.
4. Finally, potent symbols emerge from the narratives, as when Francisco *Angola* recalls his homeland in the word "*Guinea*" and evokes the forest as a sacred burial place for a friend, when he places a cross on his grave.[8]

Readers of this anthology should keep in mind that the testimonies excerpted in this chapter comprise only a small portion of the Limón residents' testimonies and, therefore, only hint at their full content and complexity. Missing from the entire dossier are the voices of the top *palenque* leaders, who escaped capture. Although perceiving the *palenque* residents' *narrative agency* and voice is challenging and problematic, their stories offer rare and invaluable glimpses into *palenque* members' worldviews and the ways in which they molded their thoughts and expression out of African histories, ancestry, and cultures, as well as their experience of the American world.

[7] Martín Lienhard ("Una tierra sin amos") discusses methods of reading highly mediated *Maroon* texts such as these.

[8] Lienhard (*O mar e o mato,* 20) analyzes the memory of the forest as a spiritual place in Afro-Brazilian and Afro-Caribbean oral traditions.

Testimonio de los procesos y castigos que se hicieron por el Maestro de Campo Francisco de Murga, gobernador y *capitán* general de Cartagena, contra los *negros cimarrones* y alzados, de los *palenques* del Limón, Polín, y Zanaguare[1]

[Declaración de Francisco *Angola,* sesenta años, antiguo residente del *palenque,* nacido en África]

En el Castillo de Manga del puerto de la ciudad de *Cartagena de Indias* en 18 días del mes de enero de 1634 años, el señor *licenciado* don Francisco de Llano Velasco, *teniente general* de la dicha ciuda[d], y en esta causa como *auditor general,* hizo parecer ante sí a uno de los *negros cimarrones* alzados del *Palenque* del Limón, de los que ayer trujeron presos del dicho *palenque;* que dijo llamarse Francisco *Angola,* del cual se recibió juramento en forma de derecho. Y habiéndolo hecho [el juramento] y prometido de decir verdad, se le tomó su declaración en la manera siguiente:

Preguntado si este declarante[2] ha estado en el *palenque* de los *negros cimarrones* del Limón, y qué tanto tiempo ha questá en él, y en qué se ha ejercitado, y si es libre o esclavo, dijo queste declarante vino muchacho pequeño de *Angola* en la armazón de *negros* que trujo[3] a [Cartagena] el *capitán* Antonio Cutiño. Y estando en esta ciudad, Juan *Angola,* compañero de Francisco *Angola* le dijo que los blancos los traían engañados. Y mostrándole el sol le dijo que aquel sol venía de *Guinea.*—Ahí está el camino. Vámonos— Y [Juan] y Francisco se fueron por el monte. Y estuvieron en él algún tiempo, que no sabe qué tanto sería, más de que pasó una luna. Y luego caminando fueron a dar al *Palenque* del Limón, adonde al cabo de tres años murió el dicho Juan *Angola* en el dicho *palenque.* Y lo enterraron en un hoyo del monte, y le pusieron una cruz. Y Francisco *Angola* [ha] asistido en el dicho *palenque* hasta que fueron los blancos y lo prendieron. Y que Francisco *Angola* se ejercitaba en hacer rozas[4] de los *negros* y en limpiarlas y en coger el maíz. Y esto responde. . . .

[Declaración de Sebastián *Anchico, bozal* de veinte y dos años de edad, siervo en el *palenque* por dos años]

En la ciudad de Cartagena en 23 días del mes de enero de 1634, el dicho señor teniente y *auditor general* mandó parecer a uno de los *negros cimarrones* que trujeron, que pareció ser medio *bozal,* por lo cual se le tomó su declaración y confesión por

[1] Ministerio de Cultura, Archivo General de Indias, Sevilla, Patronato 234, ramo 7, no. 2 (Digital images 283–84; 319–24; 533–42; 549–54; 556).

[2] Some of the most repetitive language that is confusing for readers unfamiliar with colonial documents has been suppressed in the transcription. For instance, the witness will be referred to as "Francisco *Angola*" or "Francisco" rather than the document's expression "this declarant" (*este declarante*). The same has been done in Juan de la Mar's testimony. This transcription also omits the frequent repetition of the term *dicho* or "abovementioned."

[3] *Trajo.*

[4] Food gardens.

Testimony of the Trials and Punishments Carried out by Field Marshall Francisco de Murga, Governor and Captain General of Cartagena, against the Rebel Black *Maroons* of the *Palenques* of Limón, Polín, and Zanaguare

[Statement of African-Born Francisco *Angola,* Sixty Years Old, Long-Time *Palenque* Resident]

In the Manga Castle of the port of Cartagena de Indias, on the eighteenth day of January 1634, Señor *Licenciado* Don Francisco de Llano Velasco, *teniente general* of the said city, and *auditor general* in this case, called before him one of the rebel black *Maroons* from the *Palenque* del Limón, of those whom they brought as prisoners yesterday from the *palenque,* who said his name was Francisco *Angola,* from whom an oath was taken as required by law. And having made the oath and promised to tell the truth, his statement was taken in the following manner: Asked if this declarant has been in the *palenque* of the black *Maroons* of Limón, and how long he has been there, and what his activities have been, and if he is free or a slave, he said that he came as a small boy from *Angola* in the slave ship that Captain Antonio Cutiño brought to [Cartagena]. And while in this city, Juan *Angola,* Francisco *Angola*'s friend, told him that the whites had them fooled. And pointing to the sun, he told Francisco that the sun came from *Guinea.* "There is the road. Let's go." And [Juan *Angola*] and Francisco *Angola* walked into the forest and were there for some time; he does not know how long, except that one moon passed. And later, as they were walking, they came on the *Palenque* del Limón, where, after three years Juan *Angola* died in the *palenque.* And they buried him in a hole in the forest, and they gave him a cross [on his grave]. And Francisco *Angola* was present in the *palenque* until the whites came and captured him. And he worked clearing and hoeing the blacks' fields and harvesting corn. And that is what he answered.[1] . . .

[Statement of Sebastián *Anchico,* Twenty-Two-Year-Old *Bozal,* Servant (or Slave) in the *Palenque* for the Past Two Years]

In the city of Cartagena, on the twenty-third day of January 1634, the said señor *teniente* and *auditor general* called before him one of the black *Maroons* whom they had brought [to Cartagena], who appeared to be a *bozal,* because of which his statement and confession were taken with the assistance of Andrés *Angola,* a black *ladino* slave—

[1] The Spanish reads, "And this he responds."

Andrés *Angola negro ladino,* esclavo de los padres de la Compañía de Jesús, a quien fue nombrado por intérprete, por ser *ladino* y entender la lengua de *anchicos.* Y debajo de juramento prometió de decir y declarar con verdad lo que respondiere el dicho *negro.* Y se le hicieron las preguntas siguientes:

Preguntado cómo se llama y de qué *casta* es y quién es su amo, y el intérprete dijo que se dice llamar Sebastián, de *nación anchico,* y ser esclavo de doña María de Viloria, *vecina* desta ciudad de Cartagena.

Preguntado cuánto tiempo ha que se huyó y con quién y adónde y en qué *palenque* y compañía ha estado, y el intérprete dijo que responde el dicho *negro anchico* que, yendo por leña por el camino grande, dieron con él tres *negros cimarrones*—Manuel *Quisama,* Simón *Angola,* y Sebastián *Congo*—y lo cogieron y [lo] amarraron el mismo día que cogieron a Domingo *Anchico.* Y que va para dos años que lo cogieron. Y los llevaron a la *estancia* de Saragosilla y allí estuvieron dos días. Y de noche caminaban hasta que llegaron a[l distrito de] María. Y siempre fueron por el monte. Y los llevaron al *palenque* de Polín adonde estaba Manuel *Malemba* y un *negro bran* que se llama Miguel. Y de allí a pocos días fue Juan *Criollo* de la Margarita y Juan *Angola* de Andrés Ortiz,[5] a quien[es] llevaron Sebastián [*Congo*] *capitán* y Manuel *Quisama.* Y también había cuatro *negras* que halló cuando fue al *palenque.*

Y allí se estaban de miedo de los blancos, y comían plant[a]s y yucas que tenían, y hicoteas y carne de monte, y no salían a hacer mal a naide. Y estándose allí quieto[s] fue la gente del *Palenque* del Limón. Los cogieron durmiendo para llevarlos a su *palenque.* Y porque no querían ir, les quitaban flechas, y los hirieron, y [los] amarraron, y los llevaron al Limón para que trabajaran. Y en el mismo *Palenque* de Polín mataron al *capitán* Sebastián *Congo,* diciéndole la gente del Limón que para qué cogía él todas las *negras* y ellos no las tenían, y que por envidia lo mataron. Les decían a los del Limón que cómo peleaban *cimarrones* con *cimarrones.* Y a todos los *negros* y *negras* que había en Polín los llevaron amarrados para que le[s] sirvieran. Y el dicho Sebastián *Anchico* servía a su amo Juan *Angola Criollo,* y pilaba, y traía agua y leña, y iba a la roza a trabajar. . . .

Y no firmó por no saber, ni supo decir su edad. Pareció por su aspecto de hasta veinte y dos años. Ante mí Francisco López Nieto.

[Declaración de Juan de la Mar, *negro criollo,* residente de dos años y, según algunos residentes, líder dentro del *palenque*]

En la ciudad de Cartagena, en 13 días del mes de febrero de 1634 años, Su Merced el señor *licenciado* don Francisco de Llano Velasco, *teniente* y *auditor general,* mandó parecer ante sí a Juan de la Mar, *negro criollo* desta ciudad y esclavo que se dice del *capitán* Agustín de Barahona, que trujeron del *palenque* y estaba según es notorio con

[5] Many *palenque* residents are identified by adding to their names the name of their owner; here, Juan *Angola* belongs to Andrés Ortiz. Juan *Criollo* de la Margarita's name, however, might be a nickname he has acquired or might refer to a geographic origin, such as Isla Margarita, an island off the Venezuelan coast.

who belongs to the Jesuits—who was named as interpreter because he was *ladino* and understood the *Anchico* language. And under oath he promised to tell and state truthfully what the aforementioned black man responded. And the following questions were asked of him:

Asked what his name is and to what caste he belongs and who his master is, the interpreter stated that he says his name is Sebastián, he is *Anchico* by birth, and is the slave of Doña María de Viloria, resident of this city of Cartagena.

Asked how long it has been since he ran away, and with whom, and where, and in what *palenque* and in whose company he has been, the interpreter said that the *Anchico* black man responded that, while he was fetching firewood along the big road, three black *Maroons*—Manuel *Quisama,* Simón *Angola,* and Sebastián *Congo*—came upon him and tied him up on the same day that they captured Domingo *Anchico.* And it has been almost two years since they caught him. And they took him to the Saragosilla ranch and were there two days. And they walked at night until they arrived in [the district of] María. And while walking, they stayed in the forest. And [the three *Maroons*] took them to the *palenque* of Polín, where Manuel *Malemba* was as well as a *Bran* black man named Miguel. And a few days later Juan *Criollo* de la Margarita and Juan *Angola*—who belongs to Andrés Ortiz—arrived, both brought by Captain Sebastián and Manuel *Quisama.* And there were also four black women whom [Sebastián *Anchico*] encountered when he arrived at the *palenque.*

And they waited there out of fear of the whites, and they ate plants and cassava that they had, and turtles, and game, and they did not leave the *palenque* to do harm to anyone. And while they were hiding there, the people from the *Palenque* del Limón arrived and caught them while they were sleeping in order to take them to their *palenque.* And because [those from Polín] did not want to go, [the people from Limón] took away their arrows, and wounded them, and tied them up and carried them off to Limón to make them work. In the *Palenque* de Polín, they killed Captain Sebastián *Congo,* asking him why he kept all the black women for himself and they did not have any [in Limón], and they killed him out of envy. And [the people from Polín] asked those from Limón why they were fighting, *Maroon* against *Maroon.* And they tied up all the black men and women that were in Polín and carried them off to work for them. And Sebastián *Anchico* served his master Juan *Angola Criollo,* and shelled corn, and carried water and firewood, and went to the fields to work. . . .

And [Sebastián *Anchico*] did not sign [his statement] because he did not know how to, neither did he know his age. He appeared from his looks to be about twenty-two years old. Before me, Francisco López Nieto.

[Statement of Juan de la Mar, Black *Criollo,* Two-Year Resident of Limón, Identified by Some Residents as a Leader]

In the city of Cartagena, on the thirteenth day of February 1634, his mercy Señor *Licenciado* Don Francisco de Llano Velasco, *teniente* and *auditor general,* called before him to take his statement Juan de la Mar, black *criollo* of this city whom they brought from the *palenque* and who, by his own account,[2] is the slave of Captain Agustín de

[2] Or "who is reputed to be"; the syntax is ambiguous.

los *negros cimarrones* y alzados, para tomarle su declaración. Y habiendo jurado a Dios y a la cruz en forma de derecho, prometió de decir verdad. Y se le hicieron las preguntas siguientes:

[Juan de la Mar cuenta cómo llegó a Limón]

Preguntado cuánto tiempo ha que se huyó y de dónde y por qué causa y quién lo llevó al *palenque* y qué tiempo estuvo en él, dijo que habrá dos años y medio que se huyó desta ciudad [Cartagena] y del servicio de su amo, a quien servía de arráez en el barco que tenía. Y por faltarle del maíz que le entregaba el *mayordomo,* y no tener con qué pagarlo a su amo, se huyó. Y se fue desde esta ciudad con un *negro* Francisco *Criollo* Corcovado, esclavo de don Juan de Sotomayor, el cual habiéndole dicho este declarante cómo andaba ausente de su amo por faltalle del maíz que le traía del diezmo, le dijo se fuese con él a[l distrito de] María, quel sabía adonde había un *palenque,* y que a la *estancia* de su amo vendrían los *cimarrones* por él.

Y así de miedo de su amo, Juan de la Mar se determinó a huirse, y se fue con el dicho *negro* Francisco *Criollo* a María a la *estancia* de su amo. Y allí estuvo siete meses sin que el dicho don Juan lo viese, más quel *negro* Francisco y los demás sus compañeros. Y acudía a la roza del dicho Francisco *Criollo,* trabajando en ella. Y al cabo destos siete meses fueron a la dicha *estancia* cinco *negros* de los del *Palenque* del Limón, que son Chale, y Simón, y Juan *Angola,* y Nicolás, *criollos* del *palenque,* y Tumba *criollo* de los Trejos. Y el dicho Francisco *Criollo* Corcovado entregó a Juan de la Mar a los dichos *negros,* diciéndoles cómo estaba huido de su amo, y ellos lo recibieron. Y al cabo de dos días questuvieron allí [en la *estancia* de Don Juan] lo llevaron al dicho *palenque,* donde ha estado hasta que lo cogieron.

Preguntado si el dicho don Juan de Sotomayor u otras personas o *negros* vieron y comunicaron a los dichos *cimarrones* [del *Palenque* del Limón] en la ocasión que . . . [los *negros* de Limón] [se] lo llevaron, y supieron que se lo entregaba el dicho Francisco *Criollo:* Dijo quel dicho Don Juan no estaba en la *estancia* en aquella ocasión, y que sólo el dicho Francisco *Criollo* Corcovado y sus compañeros y los *indios* del Alférez Piña fueron los que vieron entonces a los dichos *cimarrones* y hablaron con ellos, los dos días questuvieron en la *estancia* del dicho Don Juan, y no otra persona. Y esto responde.

[Juan de la Mar nombra a los residentes de Limón y dice cómo llegaron al *palenque*]

Preguntado qué *negros* había en el *palenque* cuando este declarante entró en él, así *criollos* como forasteros, y qué *negras* y chusma, dijo que había quince *negros criollos* de allí

Barahona and, according to public knowledge, was with the black rebel *Maroons* [of Limón]. And having sworn by God and on the cross, as required by law, he promised to tell the truth. And the following questions were asked of him:

[Juan de la Mar Tells How He Arrived in Limón]

Asked how long it has been since he ran away, and from where, and for what reason, and who took him to the *palenque,* and how long he was there, he said that it has been about two and a half years since he ran away from this city [Cartagena] and from the service of his master, whom he served as captain of his boat.[3] And because he was short some of the corn that the steward gave him, and was unable to pay his master for it, he ran away. And he left this city with a black man, Francisco *Criollo* Corcovado[4]—slave of Don Juan de Sotomayor. After Juan de la Mar told him how he was hiding from his master because he was missing some of the corn he was to deliver to him for the port tax, [Francisco *Criollo*] told him to go with him to [the district of] María, that he knew where there was a *palenque,* and that the *Maroons* would come for him at his master's ranch.

And so Juan de la Mar determined to run away because he was afraid of his master, and he went with the black man Francisco *Criollo* to his master's ranch in María. And he was there seven months, during which time he was seen only by this black man Francisco and his other companions, and not by Don Juan. And he worked in Francisco *Criollo*'s fields. And at the end of the seven months, five blacks from the *Palenque* del Limón went to the ranch, including the *palenque criollos* Chale and Simón, and Juan *Angola,* and Nicolás, and the *criollo* Tumba—who belongs to the Trejos. And Francisco *Criollo* Corcovado handed [Juan] over to the blacks, telling them how he was a fugitive from his master. And they received him, and after two days of being [on Don Juan de Sotomayor's ranch], they took him to the *palenque,* where he has been until [the whites] captured him.

Asked if Don Juan de Sotomayor or other people or blacks saw and communicated with the *Maroons* [from Limón] on the occasion that . . . they took him, and knew that Francisco *Criollo* handed him over [to them], he said that Don Juan was not at the ranch on that occasion, and that only Francisco *Criollo* Corcovado, and his companions, and Alférez Piña's Indians saw the *Maroons* and spoke with them the two days that they were at Don Juan's ranch, and no other person did so. And that is what he answered.

[Juan de la Mar Names the Limón Residents and Tells How They Came to the *Palenque*]

Asked what blacks—*criollos* or outsiders—were in the *palenque* when he joined, and what black women and rabble,[5] he said that there were fifteen *palenque*-born black

3 The word *arráez* might alternatively indicate the galley master or pilot.

4 *Corcovado* means "hunchback." This man is sometimes referred to in the testimonies as *el corcovado.*

5 Here, the interrogator divides up the *palenque* population in four groups. The terms he uses carry various meaning depending on who uses them and in what context. *Criollo* can refer to

nacidos: Francisco *capitán*[6] y su padre Domingo, Simón *mandador,* Nicolás, Juan *Angola,* otro Juan, Manuel, otro que llamaban Roldán, Sebastián, otro Manuel, otro Juanillo *Criollo,* Luis, Pablo, Domingo Chale, y Gonzalo Chale su hermano, y otro, Gaspar Pemba, de manera que eran dieciséis los *negros criollos* ya hombres; y doce *negras* mujeres nombradas Leonor, ques la reina, Gracia, Andrea hermana de Chale que la mataron, Madalena, Maquesu, Susaña, Antonia, Damiana, Vitoria, Juana, Inés, María, y la *negra* Antonia *Criolla* era mujer de Juan de la Mar, y más otra *negra* María que se murió en la *estancia* de Márquez. Y todas éstas eran *criollas* del *palenque.*

Y había otros muchos *criollos* y *criollas* hijos destas *negras,* que los que se acuerda son: dos hijos de Leonor llamados Marcos y Cristóbal; y Gracia tenía tres hijos nombrados Mateo, Felipa, y Antonico; y Madalena tenía dos hijos llamados Francisco y Lázaro; y Lucrecia tiene una hija que se llama Beatriz y dos nietas pequeñas llamadas María y Blanca; Vitoria tiene cuatro hijos llamados Pedro, y otro Pedro, y Mariquita, y Francisco; y la *negra* Antonia tiene un hijo que se llama Diego y éste es hijo de Juan de la Mar; y la *negra* Damiana tiene una hija llamada Juana; y Juana tiene cinco hijos: Esperanza y María y Colobi y Pedro, y otra hija que no se acuerda del nombre; y destos cinco hijos tres tiene consigo y los dos quedaron en el monte; y la *negra* Andrea tiene tres hijos: Antonio y Jusepa y otro hijo que no se acuerda del nombre, y más tiene otro hijo llamado Antonio questá en el monte; y otra *negra* Marta, que no está nombrada ques la mujer de Gonzalo Chale tiene tres hijos: Guiomar y Magdalena y Juan; y también estaba otra *negra* que se le olvidaba y se llama Isabel *Criolla.* Y otras seis *negras angolas* llamadas la una vieja que decían Mohongo, madre del *capitán* Francisco, Ángela, Felipa, Lucrecia, Catalina, y otra, chica de cuerpo y vieja, que llaman Gonga. Y no se acuerda de que hubiese más *negras* en el *palenque* cuando entró en él. Y esto responde.

Y demás de los dichos *negros* y *negras* halló otros cinco *negros* forasteros, que son el *Criollo* Tumba, Sebastián Cachorro de Duarte de León, Manuel *Angola,* y Antón *Angola,* y otro Manuel *Angola* que decían era del río.

Preguntado qué *negros criollos* y de *Guinea* y *negras* fueron al dicho *palenque* después que Juan de la Mar estuvo en él, y quién los llevó, dijo que fueron el *negro* Francisco

[6] The titles of *capitán* and *mandador* sometimes precede and sometimes follow the titleholder's name.

criollos: Captain Francisco, and his father Domingo, Commander Simón, Nicolás, Juan *Angola,* another Juan, Manuel, another they called Roldán, Sebastián, another Manuel, another Juanillo *Criollo,* Luis, Pablo, Domingo Chale, and his brother Gonzalo Chale, and another—Gaspar Pemba—so there were sixteen adult male *criollos;* and twelve black women: Leonor, who is the queen, Gracia, Chale's sister Andrea, whom they killed,[6] Madalena, Maquesu, Susaña, Antonia, Damiana, Vitoria, Juana, Inés, María, and the black woman Antonia *Criolla* was this witness's wife, and another black woman, María, who died at the Márquez ranch. And all these were *criollas* [born in] the *palenque.*

And there were many other *criollos,* male and female, children of these black women, and the ones he remembers are Leonor's two children named Marcos and Cristóbal; and Gracia had three children named Mateo, Felipa, and Antonico; and Madalena had two children named Francisco and Lázaro; and Lucrecia has a daughter named Beatriz and two small granddaughters named María and Blanca; Vitoria has four children named Pedro, and another Pedro, and Mariquita, and Francisco; and the black woman Antonia has a son named Diego and he is Juan de la Mar's son; and the black woman Damiana has a daughter named Juana; and Juana has five children: Esperanza and María and Colobi and Pedro, and another daughter whose name he does not remember; and of these five children, [Juana] has three who are with her, and two are still in the forest; and the black woman Andrea has three children: Antonio and Jusepa and another son whose name he does not remember, and she has another son named Antonio who is in the forest; and another black woman, Marta, not mentioned above, who is Gonzalo Chale's wife, has three children: Guiomar and Madalena and Juan; and there was another black woman Isabel *Criolla,* whom he forgot to name. And another six black *Angolan* women: an old woman they called Mohongo—Captain Francisco's mother—Ángela, Felipa, Lucrecia, Catalina, and another they call Gonga, who is small of body and old. And he does not remember any other black women being in the *palenque* when he entered. And that is what he answered.

And in addition to the aforementioned black men and women, he encountered another five—outsider black men—who are the *criollo* Tumba, Sebastián Cachorro—who belongs to Duarte de León—Manuel *Angola,* and Antón *Angola,* and another Manual *Angola,* who they said was from the river.[7]

Asked what black *criollos* and blacks from *Guinea*[8] and black women came to the *palenque* after he arrived, and who brought them, he said that the black painter

---

American-born vs. the foreign-born "forastero," but Juan de la Mar interprets the terms to mean those born in the *palenque* and those who have escaped their masters and joined later in life. The remaining categories the interrogator names are black women and masses; the word *chusma* has a negative connotation, meaning "galley slaves" or "rabble."

[6] This appears to be a reference to a casualty of the Spanish attack.

[7] Probably the Magdalena River, a vital artery for trade and travel, also referred to as *el río grande* and *el río grande de la Magdalena.*

[8] Here the interrogator more clearly distinguishes between American-born and African-born (*de Guinea*).

Criollo pintor del señor *Inquisidor fiscal,* y tres *negros* de Juan Ramos el uno llamado Sebastián *Congo,* y Cristóbal, y Antón, *malembaes,*[7] y otro, Francisco *Malemba,* que fue con ellos, y oyó decir Juan de la Mar que [él] era de un ollero que vive junto al hospital del Espíritu Santo. Y luego entró un *negro* Felipe *Angola* del *capitán* Blanquesel, y después otros dos *negros* del *depositario* uno llamado Andrés, y el otro Antonio, *angolas,* un *negro* Juan *Car[a]balí* del *alférez* Márquez, otro Jacinto *Angola,* y Manuel *Angola,* y Manuel Bran del mismo *alférez* Márquez. De manera que todos estos *negros* del *depositario* y de Márquez ellos mismos se fueron al *palenque* y en el camino los encontraron Juan de la Mar y otros *negros* del *palenque.* Y le dijeron cómo se huían porque tenían malos amos, y querían estarse en el *palenque.* Y ansí los llevaron.

Y al *negro* Francisco *Criollo* del señor *Inquisidor fiscal* lo entregó a la gente del *palenque* y a Juan de la Mar que venía con ellos el *negro* corcovado de don Juan en el *pueblo* de los *indios* [Chambacú].[8] Y después dello entregó al *Morisco* Francisco. Y también entregó el *negro* Francisco *Bañón* de don Andrés Hortensio a otro *negro* que decían era de[l] [*Capitán* Alonso] Cuadrado. Y el *criollo* Francisco Corcovado de don Juan también entregó al *negro* Juan *Criollo* de Francisco López Nieto. Y también se fue otro *negro* García *Angola* de Pedro Destrada y lo hallaron los *cimarrones* en las sabanas de Francisco Martín y de allí se lo llevaron. Y también se fueron a las sabanas Lorenzo *Criollo,* y Gaspar *Angola,* y Gonga, y Juan *Angola,* y Lázaro esclavo de Alonso Martín, y con ellos fue Jorge *Angola* de Diego Márquez, y otro *negrito angola* llamado Manuel, que no sabe quién es su amo. Y todos éstos se fueron ellos mismos a las sabanas de Francisco Martín ques camino del Limonar. Y de allí los llevaron los *negros* del *palenque* porque ellos se venían huidos. Y también un *negro* viejo con su mujer, que dijo venía de la *estancia* de Juan de Uriarte. Y a estos dos encontraron que se iban al *palenque* cuando la gente fue a Chambacú.

Y éstos son los *negros* que se fueron. Y los demás son los que llevaban de las *estancias.* Y también se fue al *palenque* sin que lo llevasen otro *negro* llamado Lázaro *Angola* de Márquez. Y esto responde.

[7] The original reads *balembaes,* but the slaves who belong to Juan Ramos are repeatedly referred to as "*Malembas.*"

[8] El *negro* Corcovado handed over Francisco *Criollo* and Juan de la Mar to the Limón soldiers when they were in Chambacú.

Francisco *Criollo*—who belongs to the Señor *Inquisidor Fiscal*—and three *Malemba* black men who belong to Juan Ramos, one named Sebastián *Congo,* Cristóbal, and Antón, and another Francisco *Malemba* who arrived with them—and Juan de la Mar heard that he belonged to a potter who lives next to the Hospital of Espíritu Santo. And later a black man, Felipe *Angola*—who belongs to Captain Blanquesel—came, and then another two black *Angolan* men who belong to the *depositario,* one named Andrés, the other Antonio, a black man Juan *Carabalí*—who belongs to the *alférez* Márquez—another, Jacinto *Angola,* and Manuel *Angola,* and Manuel Bran—who belong to the same *alférez* Márquez. So all these black men who belong to the *depositario* and to Márquez went to the *palenque* on their own, and Juan de la Mar and the other *palenque* blacks found them as they were on their way there. And they told him how they were running away because they had cruel masters, and they wanted to be in the *palenque.* And so they took them there.

And in the Indian town [of Chambacú], the black hunchback [Corcovado] who belongs to Don Juan handed over to the people of the *palenque* the black man Francisco *Criollo* who belongs to the Señor *Inquisidor Fiscal* and [Juan de la Mar], who came with them. And after that he handed over Francisco El *Morisco.* And the black man Francisco *Bañón*—who belongs to Don Andrés Hortensio—also handed over another black man they said belonged to [Captain Alonso] Cuadrado. And the *criollo* Francisco Corcovado—who belongs to Don Juan—also delivered the black man Juan *Criollo*—who belongs to Francisco López Nieto. And another black man García *Angola*—who belongs to Pedro Destrada—also went to the *palenque,* and the *Maroons* found him on Francisco Martín's savannas, and they took him from there. Lorenzo *Criollo,* and Gaspar *Angola,* and Gonga, and Juan *Angola,* and Lázaro, Alonso Martín's slave, also went to the savannas and with them went Jorge *Angola*—who belongs to Diego Márquez—and another young *Angolan* black man named Manuel, and Juan de la Mar does not know who his master is. And all of these went of their own volition to Francisco Martín's savannas, which are on the way to the lemon grove. And the blacks from the *palenque* took them from there, because they were running away from their owners. They also took an old black man with his wife, who said he came from Juan de Uriarte's ranch. And they found these two on their way to the *palenque* when the people went to Chambacú.

And [all] these were the blacks who came on their own [to the *palenque*]. And the others are the ones that [the *palenque* soldiers] carried off from the ranches. And another black man called Lázaro *Angola* who belongs to Márquez also went to the *palenque* without being taken there. And that is what he answered.[9]

[9] Juan de la Mar has been asked to name those who joined the *palenque* after he did and to divulge who took them there. The interrogators are seeking to identify those guilty of either running away from their owners, facilitating such escape, or kidnapping others. Here, Juan de la Mar notes that there are two men still living as slaves on neighboring farms who have brought a number of the new residents to Limón; these men are Francisco Corcovado (the *Creole* hunchback) and Francisco *Bañón.*

[La organización político–militar del *palenque*]

Preguntado declare las armas que traían los *negros* del dicho *palenque* y en qué se ocupaban y quién[es] eran los capitanes y *mandadores,* dijo quel *Morisco* y el *negro* Francisco *Criollo* del señor *Inquisidor fiscal* traían escopetas y tenían para ellas balas y pólvora. Y los demás *negros* traían arcos y flechas todos. Y era *capitán* el *negro* Francisco *Criollo* y el *mandador* era Simón. Y que cuando este declarante fue al *palenque* no había otros *mandadores.* Y después que entraron los *negros* de Juan Ramos le metieron a la *negra* Leonor algún diablo en la cabeza, porque desde entonces empezó a mandar. Y todos le obedecían, hasta el *capitán* y [el] *mandador* porque le daba una cosa en la cabeza que le hacía andar como loca, dando caídas y golpes primero que hablase, y cuando volvía en sí decía mil disparates. Y en efecto la temían todos y [le] obedecían por reina. Y que él vivía con la gente *criolla* de la banda del Chale. Y esto responde. . . .

[El ataque a la porquera de Diego Márquez y el sacrificio humano]

Preguntado quién fue a la porquera del dicho Diego Márquez, questá [a] media legua de la dicha *estancia,* y [quién] llevó al *mayordomo* y a un niño hijo suyo y a un *[i]ndio* y [a] una *india* que en ella estaban, dijo queste declarante no fue a la dicha porquera, pero que sabe que fueron por mandado de la reina Leonor el *capitán* Francisco, y dos *criollos,* Juan y Domingo, y Francisco El *Morisco,* y otros cuatro *negros* de *Guinea* que son Gaspar de Alonso Martín, *Camangala,* y Manuel *Quisama,* y Lázaro el de Márquez. Y no se acuerda que otros *negros* fuesen.

Y lo que hicieron fue traer al dicho *palenque* al dicho *mayordomo,* y a su hijo, y al *indio,* y a la *india* que tiene declarados. Y antes que entrasen en el *palenque* los amarraron y [los] trujeron delante de la reina, y los metieron en un *buhío.* Y a la tarde del dicho día los mandó sacar del dicho *buhío* y los llevaron al plantanal del dicho *palenque.* Y allí la dicha reina Leonor los tendió[9] en el suelo de un lado, y ella misma los degolló con una hachuela y bebió la sangre con otras *negras* nombradas Susaña, Inés, Maquesu, y otros *negros.* Y Felipe del *capitán* Banquesel y los de Juan Ramos nombrados *Male*[*mba*] bebieron también.

Y al tiempo que los sacaron del dicho *buhío* para matarlos iban atados con unas sogas. Y el dicho español [el *mayordomo*] decía que por amor de Dios no le matasen. Y a Juan de la Mar le dijo que le parecía que le conocía, y que rogase por él a los demás *negros,* quel los serviría. Y Juan de la Mar le dijo quel no podía [hacer] nada con ellos, porque eran más de veinte *negros,* y cualquiera que se les opusiese lo habían de flechar y matar. Y al tiempo que iba atado con el dicho *indio,* les iban ayudando a morir y

[9] In the manuscript: *tendieron.*

[The *Palenque*'s Political and Military Organization]

Asked to state what arms the blacks from the *palenque* carried and what their activities were and who their captains and commanders were, Juan de la Mar said that El *Morisco* and the black man Francisco *Criollo* who belongs to the Señor *Inquisidor Fiscal* carried shotguns and had bullets and powder for them and the other blacks all carried bows and arrows. And the black man Francisco *Criollo* was captain, and the commander was Simón. And that when Juan de la Mar arrived at the *palenque,* there were no other commanders. And after the blacks who belong to Juan Ramos came, they put some devil into the black woman Leonor's head, because from then on she began to command. And everyone obeyed her, even the captain and commander, because something happened to her in her head that made her walk like a crazy woman, falling down and beating about her before she spoke, and when she came to, she uttered a great deal of nonsense. And in effect everyone feared her and obeyed her as queen. And this declarant lived with the *criollos* in the Chale band. And that is what he answered. . . .

[The Attack on Diego Márquez's Farm and the Ensuing Human Sacrifice]

Asked who went to Diego Márquez's hog farm, which is a half league distant from the ranch, and carried off the steward and a boy who was his son and an Indian man and woman who were there, he said that this declarant did not go to the hog farm, but that he knows that Captain Francisco, and two *criollos,* Juan and Domingo, and Francisco El *Morisco,* and another four blacks from *Guinea* went under the orders of Queen Leonor: these are Gaspar—who belongs to Alonso Martín—*Camangala,* and Manuel *Quisama,* and Lázaro—the one who belongs to Márquez. And he does not remember that other blacks went.

And what they did was to bring to the *palenque* the steward and his son, and the Indian man and woman. And before they entered the *palenque,* they tied them up and brought them before the queen, and they put them in a hut. And that afternoon, the queen had them taken out of the hut and they took them to the banana grove in the *palenque.* And there Queen Leonor placed them on their side on the ground, and she cut their throats herself with a hatchet and she drank their blood, together with other black women named Susaña, Inés, Maquesu, and other black men, and Felipe, who belongs to Captain Banquesel, and the black men called Male[mba]—who belong to Juan Ramos—also drank.

And when they took them out of the hut to kill them, [the victims] walked along tied up with ropes. And the Spaniard asked that for the love of God they not kill him. And he said to Juan de la Mar that he thought he knew him, and asked him to plead with the other blacks on his behalf, and that he would serve them.[10] And Juan de la Mar said that there was nothing he could do, because they were more than twenty black men, and whoever opposed them, they would shoot and kill with arrows. And as he and the Indian walked along, tied up, the black man Tumba, slave of the Trejos,

[10] He offers to become their slave.

rezando con ellos el *negro* Tumba esclavo de los Trejos, y Francisco *Criollo* esclavo del señor *Inquisidor fiscal* y Juan de la Mar.

Y después que la dicha *negra* Leonor había herido a los dichos español e *indio* con la hachuela referida, les[10] acabaron de cortar las cabezas y abrir por el pecho un *negro* de un ollero que vive junto al Espíritu Santo, y el dicho *negro* se llama Francisco *Malemba.* Y le ayudaron los *negros* del dicho Juan Ramos. Y Juan de la Mar y otros *negros* los quisieron enterrar y no se lo consintieron todos los *negros angolas.* Y los dejaron en el campo y los comieron gallinazos. Y esto es lo que en él pasó.[11]

[Los blancos traicionan las negociaciones de paz]

Preguntado declare si fue a la *estancia* del *capitán* Francisco Julián de Piña y lo que robaron y saquearon, y por qué orden y causa lo hicieron, dijo queste declarante fue a la *estancia* del dicho Francisco Julián de Piña por mandado de la reina Leonor, junto con Francisco El *Morisco,* Francisco *Criollo* del señor Inquisidor, el *capitán* Francisco, y Juan *Criollo,* Sebastián, Cristóbal, y Pablo, y Niculás, y Luis Manuel, otro Juan *Criollo,* Rolán, Domingo, y Gonzalo Chale, y otro Juan *Criollo,* y Simón *mandador,* y la dicha reina, y toda la gente del *alférez* Márquez, y todos los demás *negros* que había en el dicho *palenque.*

Y cuando salieron fue con resolución[12] de que el *capitán* Francisco con los demás *criollos* viniesen a Cartagena a tratar de paces con el Señor gobernador y *maese de campo,* conforme lo que estaba determinado con el *capitán* don Juan de Sotomayor. Y estando ansí un *negro* de don Andrés Hortensio Paravecino, llamado Francisco *Bañón,* les dijo juntando a todos los *criollos* que mirasen lo que hacían porque lo que con ellos se trataba era sólo tratar de engañarlos. Y que [los españoles] los habían de prender, porque en Cartagena se estaba armando gente para enviar contra ellos. Y los dichos *criollos,* oyendo lo referido, y . . . [además] que Francisco Martín Garruchena había recibido plata del rey para pagar los soldados, con otras muchas razones quel dicho Francisco *Bañón* les dijo, mudaron de parecer y se resolvieron a no venir a esta ciudad.

Y quedaron entre los dichos *criollos* diciendo, ¡qué bien les pagaba Francisco Martín Garruchena lo que por él habían hecho [los de Limón]! Pues siendo [Garruchena] un hombre pobre, le habían hecho rico, trabajando en sus haciendas y haciéndole los *buhíos* y rozas, sembrándole la yuca y el maíz, y cogiéndoles. Teniéndoles ofrecido el dicho Francisco Martín Garruchena que los defendería, y siempre que [algún enemigo] se ofreciese [a] venir contra ellos los avisaría. De suerte que, viendo lo que el dicho Francisco *Bañón* les afirmaba no llevó efecto nada de lo que tenían determinado que era la venida a esta dicha ciudad.

[Juan de la Mar cuenta que, enfurecidos, los líderes deciden atacar a dos estancias vecinas. Aunque las tropas españolas terminan ganando la confrontación de 1633, muchos de los cimarrones *se escapan y siguen viviendo una vida libre en el monte.]*

[10] In the manuscript: *los.*

[11] In the manuscript: *esto es lo que en el passo passo.*

[12] In the manuscript: *resulucion.*

and Francisco *Criollo,* slave of the Señor *Inquisidor Fiscal,* and Juan de la Mar helped them in their dying and prayed with them.[11]

And after the black woman Leonor had wounded the Spaniard and Indian with the hatchet, a black man who belongs to a potter who lives next to the [Hospital of] the Holy Spirit finished cutting off their heads and opening up their chests; and the black man is named Francisco *Malemba,* and the black men who belong to Juan Ramos helped him. And Juan de la Mar and other blacks wanted to bury them, and the *Angolan* blacks did not allow them to do so. And they left them on the ground and the buzzards ate them. And this is what happened there.

[The Whites Betray the Peace Negotiations]

Asked to state whether he went to Captain Francisco Julián de Piña's ranch and what they stole and looted and by whose order and for what reason they did so, Juan de la Mar said that he went to Francisco Julián de Piña's ranch by order of Queen Leonor, together with Francisco El *Morisco,* Francisco *Criollo* who belongs to Señor Inquisidor, Captain Francisco, and Juan *Criollo,* Sebastián, Cristóbal, and Pablo, and Niculás, and Luis Manuel, another Juan *Criollo,* Rolán, Domingo, and Gonzalo Chale, and another Juan *Criollo,* and Commander Simón, and the queen, and all the people who belong to the *alférez* Márquez, and all the other black men that were in the *palenque.*

And when they left, they had resolved that Captain Francisco and the other *criollos* would come to Cartagena to negotiate a peace agreement with the Lord Governor and *maese de campo,* according to what had been decided with Captain Don Juan de Sotomayor. And while all the *criollos* were thus disposed, a black man named Francisco *Bañón,* who belongs to Don Andrés Hortensio Paravecino, gathered them and told them to examine what they were doing, because what was being planned for them was only an attempt to deceive them. And that [the Spaniards] were going to capture them, because in Cartagena people were being armed to be sent against them. And hearing this and also that Francisco Martín Garruchena had received royal monies to pay soldiers, and with many other explanations that Francisco *Bañón* gave them, the *criollos* changed their minds, and they resolved not to come to this city.

And the *criollos* talked among themselves saying how well Francisco Martín Garruchena was repaying what they had done for him! Seeing that he was a poor man, they had made him rich, working on his properties and building his huts and clearing fields, sowing cassava and corn and harvesting them. And Francisco Martín Garruchena having offered to defend them and saying that he would warn them anytime an attack was being planned against them. Having thus considered what Francisco *Bañón* averred, they did not carry out their earlier plan, which was to come to this city; rather, they exploded in rage.

[Juan de la Mar tells that in their rage, the leaders decide to mount attacks on two neighboring ranches. Although the Spaniards ultimately win this battle, many of the Maroons *escape capture and continue creating their own lives in the forest.]*

[11] They helped him prepare his soul to face death with a Christian attitude and thus to "die well."

Part II
Families and Communities

"Families and Communities" shows Afro-Latinos integrating into Ibero-American society in ways that supported their efforts to construct and defend families and communities and reshape African identities. Whether a re-uniting of African groupings or the re-creation of "fictive kinship," family and community allowed Africans in the Americas to sustain and transform their systems of cultural beliefs and practices after the calamitous interruption of the *Middle Passage.*

Juan Roque's donation of a house in his will to the *Zape* Confraternity in Mexico City (1623) shows Africans using Catholic religious organizations for mutual support and to foster group identity (Chapter 6). In seventeenth-century Lima, women of African origin helped mold their social organization through their material legacies, by engaging the lettered culture of Spanish legal documentation and doing so more frequently than did black men (Chapter 7). Their wills reveal stratification among African-descent populations as they list possessions that include not only goods but also slaves.

A unique case of community development occurred in El Cobre, Cuba, where the Crown confiscated the copper mines and transformed the mine's private slaves into *royal slaves.* These slaves founded a *pueblo* identity, speaking through a series of documents about their struggles to defend their *pueblo* against the former mine owners (Chapter 8). Another will and testament made by a black Peruvian woman allows a glimpse into the variety of attitudes toward identity construction among people of African descent (Chapter 9). The West African–born Ana de la Calle calls herself *Lucumí* to distinguish her superior status from that of other local blacks. A careful reading of her will shows how she uses this document of orthodox Catholicism to bequeath to her heirs the profits of a business based on African ritual specialization. Her will also speaks to the ways in which social identity changed from one generation to the next through marriage and colonial integration.

Finally, the judicial inquiry into events surrounding the coronation of Pedro Duarte as king of the *Congos* in Buenos Aires (1787; Chapter 10) shows the struggles African organizations had when they did preserve old-world practices that Catholic colonials saw as threatening. All these documents reveal individuals who gained vital knowledge of the Spanish colonial system in order to exercise a measure of self-determination over the vibrant lives of their communities.

6

Juan Roque's Donation of a House to the *Zape* Confraternity, Mexico City, 1623[1]

Nicole von Germeten

Zapes and Other Africans in New Spain

Africans living in colonial Mexico negotiated a place in their lives for an ongoing connection to their African ethnic identity, despite the desire to embrace some aspects of Catholicism and often the challenges of compromising to non-African spouses. From the time of the military conquest of Tenochtitlan, men and women of African descent inhabited the viceroyalty of New Spain. Some of these individuals were descended from Africans living in Spain for generations, but the majority, at least one hundred thousand Africans, arrived in New Spain on board Portuguese slave ships before 1640.

Although the descendants of indigenous peoples dominated population numbers for the entire colonial period, before 1640 more Africans than Spaniards came to New Spain. In urban areas, especially the viceregal capital of Mexico City, Africans and their descendants were a significant percentage of the population. Historians estimate that around sixty-two thousand people of African descent lived in and around Mexico City. Although many Africans in New Spain came from Central African regions under Portuguese influence, the participants in this case demonstrate that Mexico City inhabitants represented a much broader range of African ethnicities (Bristol, 4–5).

This reading is selected from a case disputing the rent of a house owned by the African Juan Roque, who died in Mexico City in 1623. Roque belonged to a religious brotherhood that, after the death of Roque's daughter Ana María, argued that they owned the property in question and its income. In 1634, the houses and their income had been under the control of a priest for the four years since Ana María's death. The first part of the document is Roque's last will and testament, dated 1623, and the second is testimony from several witnesses who gave evidence about what they knew about Roque's bequests. In these documents, Roque and his family and friends reveal fragments of their life stories, which subtly highlight the deep tensions Africans felt as they strove to incorporate into their lives the ideals of Spanish Catholicism, tried to maintain ties to the African community, and struggled to live up to familial duties.

Roque refers to himself as from the *Zape nation. Zape* is a word used in early modern Spanish and Portuguese to refer to Africans from coastal Sierra Leone.[2] The *Zapes* did not have a kingdom or empire but instead were organized in smaller political units. The term *Zape* was well-known as a specific African ethnicity in the Iberian world of the 1500s—*Zape* slaves were characters in Spanish dramas from the 1500s—but this

[1] See Maps 1 and 9.

[2] *Zape* is also spelled *Çape* and *Sape.*

ethnicity was rarely mentioned in documents from colonial Mexico. *Zapes* became embroiled in the slave trade due to mid-sixteenth century struggles with *Mande* speakers from the interior (Gomez, 89). The Portuguese took advantage of these hostilities and its prisoners of war to buy slaves in Sierra Leone before they had a consistent source of slaves from Central Africa.

Roque left the houses under dispute to his *cofradía* or Catholic brotherhood, founded by him and other *Zapes* living in Mexico City sometime in the late 1500s. The *Zape* brotherhood maintained an altar with an image of Our Lady of the Immaculate Conception in the Hospital of the Immaculate Conception. It is the only known brotherhood in New Spain based on an African ethnicity. Unlike in Cuba or Brazil, slaves were not shipped directly from Africa to New Spain after 1640. Therefore, New Spain did not see the same development of religious brotherhoods with membership from specific regions and language groups in Africa that other parts of the Ibero-American world did. By the 1700s, Afro-Mexicans formed brotherhoods based on their *mulatto* race label (von Germeten, *Black Blood Brothers*). The document excerpted here shows how difficult it was to maintain an African ethnic identity even in the 1630s.

During his lifetime Roque married a *Zape* woman with whom he had a daughter. His entire family was free by the time of his death, and his daughter married a non-African, a man named Juan Fraile, described as a *mulatto* tailor. If Ana María had borne children, they would have been members of the free working classes of Mexico City. Even if they had been poor, they would not have had to fear the abuses of slavery. However, they might have found it challenging to retain ties to their *Zape* identity, because by the 1630s, no *Zapes* were shipped to New Spain for at least a generation. Most Africans transported to New Spain as slaves in the 1600s were from Central Africa. Most *Zapes* already in Mexico City, including the ones who testify in this document, were relatively elderly, especially considering the shorter life spans experienced by the seventeenth-century poor.

Juan Roque's Bequest and the Dynamics of Maintaining the *Zape* Community

Roque's last will and testament is a unique document because few Africans in seventeenth-century New Spain left evidence of their final bequests. Although it seems likely that Juan Roque came to New Spain from Africa on a slave ship sometime during the late sixteenth century, he accumulated enough money and real estate to make a will and to make several pious bequests and arrange a moderately lavish baroque Catholic funeral. When he died in 1626, Juan's funeral cost fifty-four *pesos*.[3] Although his will emphasizes the Masses he wants to be said for the sake of his soul, it also shows how Roque valued community as he passed from this world to the next. The statements made by witnesses also reveal the strong *Zape* community that existed in seventeenth-

[3] In colonial New Spain, a laborer's daily wage was often under four *reales*, with one *peso* worth eight *reales*. As can be noted in this document, Roque's house rented for six *pesos* a month. Although some funerals at this time cost hundreds of *pesos*, fifty-four *pesos* would be a significant sum for the average worker in colonial Mexico City.

century Mexico City, forged through lifelong friendships (possibly made onboard the slave ship) and surrogate family ties.

When Ana María's husband tried to force her to sell Roque's houses, she turned to *Zape* elders and brotherhood members for help. Although a close friend of her father advised her to submit to her husband's authority, the rest of the *Zape* brothers gathered together to strengthen their position and defend what they believed was their property. The *Zapes* living in Mexico City might have wanted to do more than protect the income of a Catholic brotherhood or guarantee that they had the funds to pay for Roque's pious bequests. Even though the *Zape* political organization in Sierra Leone was based on villages, societies or religious organizations of both men and women were a fundamental part of *Zape* life (Gomez, 94–100). According to European observers going back to the 1600s, these societies helped regulate diplomacy, culture, and education and even provided charity. Women were deeply involved in these societies and in some special cases could join the male societies.

Both the male and female societies functioned to "prepare each [person] for full participation in community affairs" (Gomez, 97). Rank was based on age grades. In the stressful situation of enslavement far from Sierra Leone, it is likely that the *Zapes* turned to these organizations to govern their lives according to their traditional values. Europeans highlighted the secrecy of these societies, perhaps to make them seem more exotic and strange. However, the fact that the societies were known to be exclusive and secretive, especially to Europeans, lends weight to the conclusion that Juan Roque and the several other *Zape* men who testified in this case were protecting a brotherhood probably tied as strongly to their African identity as to their immersion in New Spain's Catholicism.

Later documents relating to this case reveal the *Zapes'* desire to retain the exclusivity of their organization and the ultimate futility of these efforts. In 1644, a free black man called Juan *Jolofo*[4] had taken over the brotherhood and the houses' income for ten years. Other *Zapes* determined that the houses had earned over a thousand *pesos* of rent in this period. Although other members had allowed this non-*Zape* takeover, in 1644 they wanted to revoke it, demanding that only *Zapes* enjoy membership in the brotherhood. In response, the defendant proclaimed that not only were many of the other leaders of the brotherhood not *Zapes* but one had even had his ears clipped for being a thief![5]

Two decades later, this brotherhood continued to experience conflicts within its leadership. In 1668, a petitioner mentioned that only three Africans remained among the original founders of the Immaculate Conception confraternity. He did not specify that they were *Zapes*.[6]

[4] Or *Xolofo*.

[5] The source for this document is the same file as the testament: Archivo General de la Nación, Mexico City, Bienes Nacionales, vol. 1175, exp. 11. These statements are made on fol. 71r.

[6] Autos hechos entre los morenos de la Cofradía de Nuestra Señora de la Limpia Concepción, Archivo General de la Nación, Mexico City, Cofradías y Archicofradías, vol. 6407, exp. 51, fol. 2r.

Testamento de Juan Roque, *negro* libre[1]

En el nombre de Dios, amén. Sepan cuantos esta carta vieren cómo yo Juan Roque de color *moreno* libre, de *tierra zape, ladino* en la lengua castellana, y cristiano por la gracia de Dios, creyendo como firmemente creo el misterio de la Santísima Trinidad, Padre e Hijo y Espíritu Santo, tres personas y un solo Dios verdadero, y todo lo demás que nos predica y enseña la Santa Madre Iglesia Católica Romana, en cuya fe y creencia me huelgo haber vivido y protesto de vivir y morir, tomando como tomo por mi abogada a la gloriosa siempre Virgen María Madre de Dios y Señora Nuestra con los demás santos y santas de la corte celestial, para que intercedan ante Nuestro Señor Jesucristo me perdone mis culpas y pecados. Estando enfermo en cama de la enfermedad que ha sido dar me,[2] y en mi seso y entendimiento natural, otorgo por esta carta que hago y ordeno mi testamento en la manera siguiente.

Primeramente encomiendo mi ánima a Dios Nuestro Señor que la crió y redimió con su preciosa sangre, y el cuerpo mando a la tierra de que fue formado.

Ídem. Mando que si Dios fuere servido de me llevar desta enfermedad mi cuerpo sea sepultado en la iglesia del Hospital de Nuestra Señora de la Concepción desta ciudad, que administra el marqués del Valle. Y no habiendo comodidad de enterrarme en la iglesia del dicho hospital m[e] entierre en la Iglesia de la Santísima Veracruz desta ciudad donde soy parroquiano. Y acompañen mi cuerpo doce acompañados y las *cofradías* de donde soy cofrade. Y se pague la limosna de mis bienes.

Ídem. Mando se diga el día de mi entierro siendo hora, y si no otro siguiente, una misa cantada de cuerpo presente con diácono y subdiácono y ofrendada. Y se pague la limosna de mis bienes.

Ídem. Mando se digan por mi ánima en la Iglesia de la Veracruz en altar de *indulgencia* diez misas rezadas. Y se pague la limosna acostumbrada.

Ídem. Mando se digan por mi ánima veinte misas rezadas en el Convento de Nuestra Señora del Carmen. Y se pague de mis bienes.

Ídem. Mando se digan en el Hospital de Nuestra Señora de la Concepción desta ciudad diez misas rezadas por mi ánima. Y se pague la limosna de mis bienes.

Ídem. Mando se digan por mi ánima en el Hospital del Espíritu Santo de esta ciudad cuatro misas rezadas. Y se pague la limosna de mis bienes.

Ídem. Mando se digan por mi ánima en el Hospital Real de los Indios diez misas rezadas. Y se pague la limosna de mis bienes.

Ídem. Mando se digan por el ánima de Isabel de Herrera *morena* libre, mi mujer difunta, y personas a quien sea algún cargo e obligación, y por las ánimas de purgatorio, veinte misas rezadas. Y se pague la limosna de mis bienes.

[1] Testamento de Juan Roque, *negro* libre, Archivo General de la Nación, Mexico City, Bienes Nacionales, vol. 1175, exp. 11, fols. 6r–7r and 17r–29r.

[2] The usual wording in wills is *que Dios Nuestro Señor ha sido servido de darme* or similar.

Last Will and Testament of Juan Roque, Free Black

In the name of God, amen. This document testifies that I, Juan Roque, free black from the *Zape* land, fluent in the Castilian language, and Christian by the grace of God, believe in the mystery of the Most Holy Trinity, Father, Son, and Holy Spirit, three persons and only one true God, and in all the rest that the Holy Mother Roman Catholic Church preaches and teaches, in whose faith and belief I have lived and continue to live and will die. I take as my advocate the forever glorious Virgin, Mother of God and Our Lady, with all the other male and female saints of the celestial court so that they intercede with Our Lord Jesus Christ and that he might pardon my sins. Being sick in bed with the sickness given to me, but being myself and having my natural understanding, I offer this last will and testament.

First, I entrust my soul to God, Our Lord, who cared for it and redeemed it with his precious blood, and my body I return to the earth from which it was formed.

Item. I order that if God wishes to take me with this illness, my body be buried in the church of the Hospital of Our Lady of the Immaculate Conception of this city, administered by the marquis of the Valley. If this is not convenient, I wish to be buried in the Santísima Veracruz Church in this city, where I am a parishioner. I order that twelve people accompany my body, along with the brotherhoods that I belong to, to be paid for by my property.

Item. I order that on the day of my burial, if time allows and, if not, on the following day, a sung Mass be said for me in the presence of my body with a deacon, subdeacon, and offering, to be paid for by my property.

Item. I order that ten spoken Masses be said for my soul in the Veracruz Church, at the altars of indulgence, paid for with the customary donation.

Item. I order that twenty spoken Masses be said for my soul in the Convent of Our Lady of Mt. Carmel, to be paid for by my property.

Item. I order that ten spoken Masses be said for my soul in the Hospital of Our Lady of the Immaculate Conception in this city, to be paid for by my property.

Item. I order that four Masses be said for my soul at the Hospital of the Holy Spirit in this city, to be paid for by my property.

Item. I order that ten Masses be said for my soul at the Royal Indian Hospital, to be paid for by my property.

Item. I order that twenty Masses be said for the soul of my deceased wife Isabel de Herrera, free black woman, and for others I may be indebted to and for the souls in purgatory, to be paid for by my property.

Ídem. Mando a la *Cofradía* del Santísimo Sacramento, fundada en la Iglesia de la Veracruz desta ciudad, porque acompañe con su cera el entierro de mi cuerpo, veinte *pesos* de oro común de limosna. Y se dé de mis bienes.

Ídem. Mando se tomen dos *bulas* de composición [por] lo que debiere o fuere a cargo de algo que no me acuerdo. Y se pague tres *pesos* por la limosna dellas de mis bienes.

Ídem. Mando a las mandas forzosas y acostumbradas, a cada una un *real,* con que las aparto de mis bienes.

Ídem. Declaro que no me acuerdo deber a persona alguna cosa ninguna. Declárolo por descargo de mi conciencia.

Declaro que me debe el *licenciado* Benavides, clérigo presbítero que asiste en la Iglesia de la Veracruz, cien *pesos* de oro común, de resto de ciento y ochenta que le di en *reales* con otros bienes en guarda, y los dichos bienes me volvió y me restó debiendo los dichos cien *pesos.* Mando se cobren por mis bienes.

Declaro que me debe María de Sosa, española que vive hacia el Alameda, veinte y ocho *pesos* que le presté en *reales.* Mando se cobren por mis bienes.

Ídem. Que me debe Pedro *indio,* sastre, cantidad de *pesos* de oro del arrendamiento de una casa mía en que vivió, de que tengo razón en una memoria por donde constará la cantidad. Mando se cobren por mis bienes.

Ídem.[3] Declaro que yo fui casado y velado según orden de la Santísima Iglesia con Isabel de Herrera de color *morena,* libre, de *tierra zape.* Y durante nuestro matrimonio hubimos por nuestra hija legítima a Ana María de color *morena,* libre. Declárola por mi hija legítima, que está casada con Juan Fraile de color *mulato,* libre, sastre.

Declaro tengo por mis bienes las casas de mi morada, que son del *barrio* de San Hipólito en el callejón questá detrás del Colegio de San Juan de Letrán, que sale al tianguis de San Hipólito, linde con casas del mariscal y con casas de don Ángel de Villasaña, con todo lo que le pertenece, cuyos títulos entrego al presente [suso].

Ídem. Declaro tengo otros bienes de poco valor que se inventariarán.

Y nombro por mis *albaceas* testamentarias a Francisco de León, *alguacil* de vagabundos desta ciudad, y Ana María, mi hija, a los cuales y a cada uno por sí *in sólidum* doy poder cumplido de derecho, bastante para que tomen de mis bienes la parte que bastare e cumplan e paguen este mi testamento, mandas, y legados, y deduce todo el tiempo necesario aunque sea pasado el año del albaceazgo.

Cumplido y pagado este mi testamento, mandas, y legados de él, dejo y nombro por mi heredera a la dicha Ana María, mi hija legítima, de color *morena,* mujer de Juan Fraile de color *mulato,* la cual quiero los haya y herede con la bendición de Dios y la mía.

Y revoco anulo y doy por ningunos y de ningún efecto otros qualesquier testamentos, mandos, o codicilos que haya hecho por escrito u de palabra, para que no valgan salvo este testamento que ahora hago y otorgo, que quiero valga por tal en la mejor vía y forma que haya lugar de derecho. En testimonio de lo cual lo otorgué en la Ciudad de México, veinte y seis de julio de 1623.

[3] There appears to be an "M" before the word *Ídem,* in the top left-hand corner of the folio.

Item. I order that the Brotherhood of the Most Holy Sacrament, founded in the Veracruz Church in this city, accompany my body to its burial, carrying candles. Twenty gold *pesos* from my property will be donated to them.

Item. I order that three *pesos* be given from my property for two bulls of composition[1] for that which I may have forgotten I owed or with whose care I was charged.

Item. I order that a *real* from my property be paid to each of the obligatory donations.

Item. I declare that I do not remember that I owe any person anything, and I declare this to relieve my conscience.

I declare that the *licentiate* Benavides, cleric from the Veracruz Church, owes me 100 *pesos* of gold, which is the remainder of the 180 that I gave him in *reales* with other goods held. The said goods were returned to me, and 100 *pesos* are still owed to me. I order that they be collected as my property.

I declare that the Spanish woman María de Sosa who lives near the Alameda owes me twenty-eight *pesos* that I loaned her in *reales*. I order that they be collected as my property.

Item. Pedro *Indio,* tailor, owes me a quantity of gold *pesos* for the rent of my house, where he lived, for which I have proof in a written document, which records the amount. I order that this be collected as my property.

Item. I declare that I was married according to the Most Holy Church to Isabel de Herrera, a free black woman from the *Zape* land, and during our marriage she gave birth to my legitimate daughter, Ana María, free black woman. I declare that she is my legitimate daughter, and she is married to Juan Fraile, a free *mulatto* tailor.

I declare that I own the houses where I dwell in the neighborhood of San Hipólito in the lane next to the College of San Juan where it meets the open air market of San Hipólito, bordering the houses of the marshal and those of Don Ángel de Villasaña, along with everything inside them, and I include their titles here.

Item. I declare that I have other possessions of slight value that will be inventoried.

I name for the executors of my testament Francisco de León, *alguacil* for vagabonds in this city, and Ana María, my daughter. To each one separately and jointly, I give legal power sufficient to take from my property what is necessary and to carry out and pay for this, my testament, its orders, and inheritance, for as long as is necessary even if it exceeds the year of executorship.

Once my legacies and wishes as stated in my testament are carried out and paid, I leave everything to my heir Ana María, my legitimate daughter, a free black woman and wife of Juan Fraile, *mulatto.* I wish her to be my heir with God's blessing and my own.

I revoke, annul, and declare null any other testaments, bequests, or codicils that I have made in writing or have spoken, such that they are worthless; and only this testament that I currently make and grant, do I wish to be valid, in the best way and form allowed by the law. I make this statement on July 26, 1623.

[1] A bull that gave permission to someone to keep property belonging to another.

Y el otorgante, que doy fe que conozco, no firmó [por]que dijo no sabe escribir. Por él firmó un testigo, siendo testigos Felipe de Herrera Ibáñez, Juan Fernández, Gregorio de Loayza, Juan Giles, Jacinto González, y Antonio Márquez *vecino* y [ilegible] en México. E lo firmaron: testigo Felipe de Herrera Ibáñez, testigo Juan Fernández, testigo Gregorio de Loayza, testigo Juan Giles, testigo Jacinto González, por testigo Antonio Márquez. Ante mí, Juan de León Figueroa, *escribano* de Su Majestad.

Hago mi signo [rúbrica] en testimonio de verdad,

Juan de León Figueroa, *Escribano* de Su Majestad
Sin derechos doy fe. . . .

[Interrogatorio para la litigación sobre las casas de Juan Roque, *negro de nación zape*]

Once de julio 1634 años
[ilegible]

Por las preguntas siguientes se examinen los testigos que fueren presentados por parte del *mayoral* y diputados de la *cofradía* de los *morenos* de la *nación zape,* fundada en el Hospital de Nuestra Señora de la Concepción de esta ciudad, en el pleito con el *licenciado* José de Peñafiel, presbítero, en cuyo poder están unas casas que fueron de Juan Roque, *negro zape,* y de Ana María, *negra criolla,* su hija, sobre que se declara pertenecer a la dicha *cofradía* con los arrendamientos de éstas.

1. Primeramente si conocen a las partes, y conocieron al dicho Juan Roque *negro* y a Ana María *negra,* su hija, y si tienen noticia de esta causa y de las casas sobre que se litiga, digan, etcétera.
2. Si saben y vieron que las casas en esta ciudad en el callejón que está detrás del Colegio de San Juan de Letrán, que quedaron por fin y muerte del dicho Juan Roque *negro,* las diera[4] a la dicha Ana María, su hija, mujer de Juan Fraile *mulato,* y saben que la dicha Ana María murió y pasó de esta presente vida sin dejar hijos legítimos ni naturales, ni heredero forzoso, ascendiente ni descendiente, y falleció sin hijos ni otorgar testamento, digan, etcétera.
3. Si saben y vieron que la dicha Ana María públicamente manifestó y dijo que el dicho su padre le había ordenado que si muriese sin hijos ni herederos forzosos, su voluntad era que las dichas casas quedasen como las dejaba a la dicha *cofradía,* para obras pías a su distribución en los arrendamientos de ellas. Y la dicha Ana María en su vida y poco antes que muriese y al tiempo de su muerte, estando enferma y en su juicio natural, con palabras articuladas que muchas personas le oyeron, dijo que su última y postrimera voluntad era dejar como dejaba a la dicha *cofradía* las dichas casas, en conformidad de la voluntad y disposición del dicho su padre, y para el mismo efecto de obras pías, por lo cual saben que las dichas casas pertenecen a la dicha *cofradía,* digan, etcétera.
4. Si saben y vieron que de las dichas casas se apo[deró] el dicho *licenciado* José de Peñafiel desde que murió la dicha Ana María, [y] las ha arrendado tiempo de cuatro

[4] Unclear; might be *den.*

And the grantor, whom I give my word that I know, did not sign, saying he does not know how to write. A witness signed for him, with the following witnesses: Felipe de Herrera Ibáñez, Juan Fernández, Gregorio de Loayza, Juan Giles, Jacinto González, and Antonio Márquez, citizen and [illegible]. Done in my presence, Juan de León Figueroa, notary of His Majesty.

Certified as authentic testimony,

Juan de León Figueroa, Notary of His Majesty
I give faith. . . .

[Interrogatory in the Litigation of the Houses That Belonged to the Black Man Juan Roque, of the *Zape Nation*]

July 11, 1634
[illegible]

The following questions are to be used to examine the witnesses presented by the foreman and deputies of the black brotherhood of the *Zape nation,* founded in the Hospital of Our Lady of the Immaculate Conception of this city, in the suit against the *licentiate* José de Peñafiel, presbyter, who has in his possession some houses that belonged to the black *Zape* man Juan Roque and his daughter Ana María, a black *Creole* woman, regarding which it is declared that they belong to the said confraternity together with the income from their lease.

1. First, if they know the litigants and if they knew the black man Juan Roque and his daughter, the black woman Ana María, and if they know about this case and the disputed houses, they should state what they know, etc.
2. If they know and saw whether the black man Juan Roque gave to his daughter Ana María, wife of Juan Fraile, *mulatto,* houses in this city in the lane behind the College of San Juan de Letrán, that remained on his death, and if they know that Ana María died and passed from this life without legitimate or illegitimate children or any other heirs, and that she passed away childless and intestate, they should state what they know, etc.
3. If they know and saw that Ana María publicly demonstrated and said that her father had ordered that if she died without children or heirs, that his will was that the houses would be left to the aforementioned brotherhood to use their rent for pious works. And Ana María, during her life and just before she died, and at the time of her death, when she was ill but of clear mind, said publicly so that many people heard that her final and deathbed wish was to leave to the brotherhood the aforementioned houses, in conformity with the will and disposition of her father, and for the same purpose of pious works, whereby they know that the houses belong to the confraternity, they should state what they know, etc.
4. If they know or saw that the said houses have been rented for six *pesos* a month, which is the rent they have always earned, under the control of the *licentiate* José de

años y medio a razón de seis *pesos* cada mes, que es lo que siempre han ganado y de los dichos arrendamientos, no ha dado cuenta a la dicha *cofradía,* digan, etcétera.

5. *Ídem.* De público y notorio, pública voz y fama, digan etcétera.

Don Agustín Guerrero

En la Ciudad de México, a once días del mes de julio de 1634 años, ante el señor doctor Andrés Fernández, *juez ordinario* de testamentos, *capellanías,* y obras pías en esta ciudad y su arzobispado, se presentó este interrogatorio de preguntas.

Su merced lo hubo por presentado y mandó que por su tenor se examinen los testigos que se presentaren en lo pertinente a él, y así lo proveyó.

Ante mí

Pedro de Becerro, Notario

Probanza hecha por parte de los *morenos* de la *Cofradía* de Nuestra Señora de la Limpia Concepción

[Testimonio de Juan, *negro ladino* de *nación zape,* esclavo, conocido de Ana María]

Testigo En la Ciudad de México, a trece días del mes de julio de 1634 años, Andrés de Galvez, procurador de la *Audiencia* Arzobispal, en nombre del *mayoral* y demás oficiales *negros* de *nación zape* de la *Cofradía* de Nuestra Señora de la Limpia Concepción desta ciudad, en el pleito sobre que se declare ser y pertenecer a la dicha *cofradía* unas casas en esta ciudad, que fueron de Juan Roque y [sic] *negro* libre, y después de Ana María *negra,* su hija, ambos difuntos, y lo demás que es el pleito, presentó por testigo a un *negro ladino* en lengua castellana que se dijo llamar Juan, y ser de tierra y *nación zape,* y que es esclavo de Juan Días, *alguacil, vecino* de esta ciudad. Del cual yo el notario recibí juramento. Y lo hizo por Dios Nuestro Señor y la señal de la cruz, en forma debida. Y habiendo jurado, prometió de decir verdad. Y siendo preguntado por el tenor de las preguntas del dicho interrogatorio, presentado por el dicho Andrés de Gálvez en esta causa, dijo lo siguiente:

1. A la primera pregunta, dijo que conoce a las partes que litigan y que conoció a Juan Roque y a Ana María su hija, *negros* difuntos, *vecinos* que fueron de esta ciudad. Y esto responde.

Generales: De las preguntas generales de la ley,[5] dijo que es de edad de 46 años y que no le tocan ninguna dellas. Y esto responde.

2. De la segunda pregunta, dijo que lo que della sabe, es que las casas contenidas en la pregunta, que son en un callejón detrás del Colegio de San Juan de Letrán,

Peñafiel since Ana María died four and a half years previously, and that he has not notified the brotherhood of these earnings, they should state what they know, etc.

5. Item. Let them state whether this is publicly known by all.

Don Agustín Guerrero

In Mexico City, July 11, 1634, in the presence of the *Señor* Doctor Andrés Fernández, judge for testaments, chaplaincies, and pious works in this city and archdiocese, the following interrogatory and its questions were presented.

His Mercy recognized the interrogatory as presented and ordered that the witnesses presented be examined accordingly and the pertinent facts be presented and examined.

Before me,

Pedro de Becerro, Notary

Examination by the Blacks of the Brotherhood of Our Lady of the Immaculate Conception

[Testimony of the Black Man Juan, of the *Zape Nation,* Slave, an Acquaintance of Ana María]

Witness In Mexico City on July 13, 1634, Andrés de Galvez, procurator of the archdiocese court, in the name of the foreman and other officers of the *Zape nation* of the Brotherhood of Our Lady of the Immaculate Conception of this city, in the case to determine if they own some houses in this city that were owned by Juan Roque, free black, and later by his daughter, the black woman Ana María, both now deceased, and the other aspects of the case, presented as a witness a black man, *ladino* in the Castilian language, who says his name is Juan and that he comes from the *Zape* land and *nation* and that he is a slave of Juan Días, *alguacil,* resident of this city. I, the notary, received his oath. And he swore by the Lord Our God and made the sign of the cross, as required. And having sworn, he promised to tell the truth. And being asked these questions presented by Andrés de Gálvez in this case, he said the following:

1. To the first question he said that he knows the litigants and he knew Juan Roque and Ana María his daughter, deceased black residents of this city. And this is his response.[2]

General questions: Regarding the general questions of law,[3] he stated that he is forty-six years old and that they do not apply to him.

2. For the second question, he said that he knows that the houses in this suit are on the street by the College of San Juan del Letrán and that Juan Roque, free black,

[2] The answer of every witness to every question contains this repetitive phrase, *Y esto responde,* and occasionally, *Es lo que sabe y responde,* both of which are omitted from here on in the English translation. The initial instance in each testimony is maintained to communicate some of the feel of the bureaucratic language.

[3] These are questions asked to ascertain the relationship of the witness to the parties and thus to assess the witness' partiality.

quedaron por muerte de Juan Roque, *negro* libre, que las heredó Ana María *negra,* su hija asimismo difunta. Y este testigo se las vio tener gozar y pose[e]r muchos años. Y sabe este testigo como persona que trató y comunicó familiarmente a la dicha Ana María *negra,* que no tuvo hijos del matrimonio que contrajo con Juan Fraile *mulato,* que ya es difunto. Y antes que contrajese el dicho matrimonio, la dicha Ana María no tuvo ningún hijo, ni después que murió el dicho su marido. De manera que la susodicha murió sin tener hijos ni herederos forzosos, ascendientes ni descendientes. Y no testó porque murió aprisa de un *cocoliste* en el Hospital de los *Desamparados.* Y este testigo la vio morir y enterrar en la dicha iglesia del dicho hospital, por lo cual sabe que no hizo testamento. Y esto responde.

3. De la *tercera* pregunta, dijo que lo que della sabe y pasa es que quince días antes que muriese la dicha Ana María *negra,* llamó al *mayoral* y oficiales de la *Cofradía* de la Limpia Concepción de Nuestra Señora, fundada en el hospital del señor Marqués del Valle por los *morenos* de la *[na]ción zape,* y los llevó a la casa sobre que es este pleito. Y estando en ella, presente este testigo como persona de la dicha *nación,* la dicha Ana María manifestó cómo el dicho Juan Roque *negro,* su padre, le había encargado mucho cuando murió que, si no tuviese hijos, dejase la dicha casa a la dicha *cofradía,* para que los *morenos* de la *nación zape,* de donde asimismo era el dicho Juan Roque, las administrasen y de su procedido hiciesen bien por su alma y de la dicha Ana María. Y que en la dicha conformidad los llamaba para que lo supiesen y que, supuesto questaba viuda del dicho Juan Fraile su marido, y no tenía hijos ni herederos, su voluntad expresa era hacer la voluntad de su padre, y que se apoderasen de las dichas casas para el dicho efecto. Y el dicho *mayoral* y oficiales estuvieron confiriendo el caso y resolvieron que aceptaban lo referido. Y que mientras viviese la dicha Ana María *negra* la poseyese y gozase, que después de muerta ellos las administrarían. Y de los alquileres harían bien por su alma y la del dicho su padre, pues que así lo quería. Mediante lo cual sabe este testigo que la dicha casa es y pertenece a la dicha *cofradía* mediante la última voluntad de la dicha Ana María. Y esto responde y es lo que sabe de lo contenido en la pregunta.

4. A la cuarta pregunta, dijo que lo en ella contenido lo ha oído decir públicamente a muchas personas, de cuyos nombres no se acuerda, que es y pasa como la pregunta lo refiere. Y esto responde.

5. De la quinta pregunta, dijo que lo que ha dicho es público y notorio, y la verdad para el juramento que hecho tiene, en que se afirmó y ratificó. Y no lo firmó, que dijo no saber escribir.

Ante mí

Pedro de Becerro, Notario

[Testimonio de Diego, de *nación zape,* esclavo, amigo de la familia Roque]

Testigo En la Ciudad de México, a trece días del mes de julio en 1634 años, Andrés de Gálvez procurador de la *Audiencia* Arzobispal, en nombre de sus partes para su probanza, presentó por testigo a un *negro ladino* en la lengua castellana, que dijo llamarse Diego de *nación zape* y que es esclavo de Juan de Santillán, *vecino* desta ciudad,

being deceased, left the houses to the black woman Ana María, his daughter, also deceased. This witness saw her enjoy the houses in her possession for many years. And this witness, communicating familiarly with Ana María, knew that no children came from her marriage with the *mulatto* Juan Fraile, now deceased, and that before her marriage Ana María had no children, nor did she have any children after her husband died, nor did she have any other heirs. She did not make a testament because she died quickly of a *cocoliste* [typhoid] in the Hospital de los *Desamparados.* This witness saw her die and saw her burial in the church of this hospital, so he knows that she did not make a last will and testament.

3. To the third question, he responded that he knows that fifteen days before she died, the black woman Ana María called on the foreman and officers of the Brotherhood of the Immaculate Conception of Our Lady, founded in the hospital of the Marquis de Valle by the blacks of the *Zape nation,* and she took them to the house about which these claims are made, and this witness being present there, as a person of the aforementioned *nation,* Ana María declared that the black man Juan Roque, her father, had urged her strongly when he died that if she did not have children, she was to leave the house to the brotherhood, so that the blacks of the *Zape nation,* of which Juan Roque himself was, would administer the houses and use their income to do good for his soul and the soul of Ana María. In conformity with this, she called together the members to inform them and, given that she was the widow of Juan Fraile her husband and that she did not have children or heirs, it was her express will to carry out the wishes of her father, and that they should take possession of the houses for this purpose. The foreman and officials discussed the case, and they resolved to accept this decision. And that as long as the black woman Ana María was alive, she was to own and enjoy the house. After her death, they would administer it and its rental income in order to do good for her soul and the soul of her father. It was thus that this witness knows that this house belongs to the brotherhood according to the last will of Ana María.

4. To the fourth question, he also said that all of this information has been discussed publicly by many different people whose names he cannot remember.

5. To the fifth question, he said that what he has said is known publicly and he swears on his oath it is true, and he affirmed and ratified it. He does not sign because he says he does not know how to write.

Before me,

Pedro de Becerro. Notary

[Testimony of Diego, of the *Zape Nation,* Slave, Friend of the Roque Family]

Witness In Mexico City on July 13, 1634, Andrés de Gálvez, procurator of the archdiocesan court, presented for the purpose of giving evidence on behalf of his parties, as a witness, a black man, fluent in the Castilian language, who said his name is Diego, of the *Zape nation.* He is a slave of Juan de Santillán, resident of this city. I, the notary, receive his oath by God and the sign of the cross, made in the correct form.

del cual yo el notario recibí juramento por Dios y la señal de la cruz, en forma de derecho. Y habiendo jurado, prometió de decir la verdad. Y siendo preguntado por las preguntas del interrogatorio en esta causa presentado, dijo lo siguiente:

1. A la primera pregunta, dijo que conoce las partes que litigan y tiene noticia deste pleito, y que conoció a Juan Roque y a Ana María *negra,* su hija, ambos libres de cautiverio, ya difuntos. Y esto responde.

Generales: De las preguntas generales de la ley, dijo que es de edad de 60 años poco más o menos, y que no le tocan ninguna de ellas. Y esto responde.

2. De la segunda pregunta, dijo que las casas sobre que es este pleito, y son en un callejón detrás del Colegio de San Juan de Letrán, son y fueron de Juan Roque *negro* libre y de Ana María *negra,* su hija, que ambos son ya difuntos. Y este testigo se las vio tener, gozar, y poseer como cosa suya propia muchos años hasta que murió el dicho Juan Roque. Y por su muerte las heredó la dicha Ana María, su hija, mujer que fue de Juan Fraile *mulato,* ya difunto, de cuyo matrimonio no tuvieron hijos ningunos. Ni la susodicha parió antes ni después que se case, ni después de viuda. Y murió sin herederos ascendientes ni descendientes. Y lo sabe este testigo como persona que trató y comunicó a la dicha Ana María desde que era muchacha y hasta que murió. Y esto sabe de lo contenido en la pregunta y responde a ella.

3. De la *tercera* pregunta, dijo que después que murió el dicho Juan Roque *negro,* la dicha Ana María tuvo a este testigo en lugar de su padre, y como tal le trataba y manifestaba sus causas y negocios, pidiéndole consejo. Y le comunicó cómo Juan Fraile *mulato,* su marido, quería vender las dichas casas y que para ello le pedía el testamento de su padre. Y que ella no podía dar permiso para la dicha venta, porque su padre le había dicho que, si no tuviese hijos, dejase la dicha casa a la *Cofradía* de Nuestra Señora de la Concepción para que los *morenos* de la *nación zape* las [sic] administrasen y de los arrendamientos hiciesen bien por el alma de su padre y de la Ana María. Y este testigo le dio por consejo que llamase al *mayoral* y oficiales de la dicha *cofradía* y que les diese noticia de lo que le había dicho. Y por entonces no supo el testigo si lo hizo. Y dentro de pocos días de como pasó lo que lleva dicho, murió el dicho Juan Fraile. Y como quince días poco más o menos a lo que se quiere acordar, antes que muriese la dicha Ana María, estando buena y con entera salud, llamó al dicho *mayoral* y cofrades a su casa, que es la misma sobre que es este pleito. Y estando en ella, y este testigo presente, manifestó lo mismo que había dicho a este testigo. Y que ya las había defendido de su marido y que así tenía voluntad y gusto que el dicho *mayoral* y oficiales se apoderasen de las dichas casas. Y en esta razón estuvieron confiriendo y vinieron a resolver que aceptaban el administrar las dichas casas, pero que sería después de los días de la vida de la dicha Ana María, porque antes no era justo que dejase de vivir en ellas. Y esto dejaron asentado. Y luego que pasó, le dio a la dicha Ana María un *cocoliste,* que murió dentro de tres días de como le dio, sin hacer testamento, por lo cual sabe este testigo con evidencia que las dichas casas son y pertenecen a la dicha *cofradía,* en conformidad de la voluntad y disposición última de la dicha Ana María. Y esto sabe desta pregunta y responde a ella.

4. De la cuarta pregunta, dijo que no la sabe. Y esto responde.

And having sworn, he promised to tell the truth. And being asked the questions of interrogation in this case, he answered with the following:

1. To the first question, he said that he knows the litigants and he knows about the case, and he knew Juan Roque and Ana María, the black woman, his daughter, both of them free from captivity and now deceased. This is his response.

General questions: To the general questions, he said that he is more or less sixty years old and that they do not apply to him.

2. To the second question, he said that the houses involved in this case are in the lane behind the College of San Juan de Letrán, and they belonged to Juan Roque, a free black man, and Ana María, a black woman, his daughter, both now deceased. This witness saw Juan Roque enjoy and possess them as his own for many years until he died. And by his death, his daughter Ana María inherited them. She was the wife of Juan Fraile, *mulatto,* now deceased. And their marriage did not produce any children nor did she give birth before marrying nor after she became a widow, and she died without heirs. This witness knows this as one who dealt with and communicated with Ana María from her girlhood to her death.

3. To the third question, he said that after the black man Juan Roque died, Ana María took on this witness in place of her father and treated him as such, discussing her concerns and business with him and asking his advice. She told him how Juan Fraile *mulatto,* her husband, wanted to sell the houses and because of this he asked her for her father's testament. And that she could not allow this sale, because her father said that if she did not have children she must leave the house to the Brotherhood of Our Lady of the Immaculate Conception, so that the blacks of the *Zape nation* would administer it and its income, to do good for her father's and her soul. This witness advised her to call the foreman and the officials of the aforementioned brotherhood to tell them what she had told him. And he does not know whether she did so then. Within a few days, the aforementioned Juan Fraile died. And around fifteen days before she died, according to his memory, and while she was still entirely healthy, Ana María called the foreman and brothers to her house, which is the same one referred to in this case. This witness was there, and she declared what she had told this witness. And that she had already defended [the houses] from her husband, and so she wished and desired that the foreman and officials take possession of the houses. They conferred and resolved to accept the administration of the houses, but only after Ana María's lifetime, because while she lived it was not right for her to cease living in them. They made this arrangement. And after this happened, Ana María suffered a *cocoliste* that killed her within three days, leaving her with no time to make a testament, by which evidence this witness knows that the houses belong to the aforementioned brotherhood in conformity with Ana María's last will.

4. To the fourth question, he responded that he does not know.

5. De la quinta pregunta, dijo que lo que ha dicho es la verdad, público y notorio, so cargo del juramento que hecho tiene, en que se afirmó y ratificó después de escrito y leído. Y no firmó, que dijo no saber escribir.

Ante mí

Pedro de Becerro, Notario

[Testimonio de Simón, de *nación zape,* esclavo]

Testigo En la Ciudad de México, a catorce días del mes de julio de 1634 años, el dicho Andrés de Gálvez, en nombre de su parte para la dicha probanza, presentó por testigo a un *negro ladino* en la lengua castellana, que se dijo llamar Simón y ser de *nación zape,* y que es esclavo del *capitán* Rodolfo, del cual yo, el notario, recibí juramento. Y lo hizo por Dios Nuestro Señor y la señal de la cruz, en forma de derecho. Y habiendo jurado, prometió de decir verdad. Y siendo preguntado por las preguntas del dicho interrogatorio, dijo lo siguiente:

1. A la primera pregunta, dijo que conoce a las partes que litigan, y conoció a Juan Roque y a Ana María su hija, ambos *morenos,* y que tiene noticia desta causa y de las casas sobre que es este pleito. Y esto responde.

Generales: De las preguntas generales de la ley, dijo que es de edad de más de cincuenta años y que no le tocan ninguna dellas. Y esto responde.

2. De la segunda pregunta, dijo que este testigo supo y tuvo noticia cierta cómo el dicho Juan Roque *negro* libre cuando murió, dejó unas casas que tenía en un callejón detrás del Colegio de San Juan de Letrán a Ana María, *negra* libre, su hija, mujer que fue de un *mulato* sastre llamado Juan Fraile, que ya es difunto. Y este testigo vio muerta naturalmente a la dicha Ana María, habrá cuatro años poco más o menos. Y se halló a su entierro, que fue en el Hospital de los *Desamparados.* Y no dejó hijos ni herederos forzosos ascendientes ni descendientes porque no los tuvo. Y murió sin hacer testa, de enfermedad de *cocoliste,* que no duró tres días, lo cual sabe porque desde que estuvo mala hasta que murió le acudió a visitar este testigo, por ser conocida de este testigo. Y quel dicho su padre era de la *nación* deste testigo y su amigo. Y esto responde.

3. De la *tercera* pregunta, dijo que lo que della sabe y puede testificar es que, siendo la dicha Ana María viuda por fin y muerte del dicho Juan Fraile su marido, como quince días antes que la susodicha muriese, estando en buena salud, llamó al *mayoral* de la *Cofradía* de Nuestra Señora de la Concepción de esta ciudad, fundada por los *negros* de *nación zape* y a los oficiales. Y los llevó a las casas donde vivía, que son las que la pregunta refiere. Y este testigo, como oficial que era de la dicha *cofradía* en la dicha ocasión, fue y se halló en la junta porque le avisaron. Y estando en la dicha casa, dijo la dicha Ana María que cuando el dicho su marido era vivo, la traía perseguida sobre que quería vender las casas. Y que lo había defendido respe[c]to de quel dicho Juan Roque su padre la había encargado mucho que, si muriese sin hijos, las dejase a la dicha *cofradía,* para que los *morenos* de la *nación zape* las administrasen y cuidasen y que lo que ganasen se hiciese bien por su alma y de la dicha Ana María. Y que en esa conformidad su voluntad era que el dicho *mayoral* y oficiales se entregasen desde luego de las dichas casas. Y se las entregó y el dicho *mayoral* y los *morenos* viejos y oficiales

5. To the fifth question, he said that what he said is publicly known to be true, by the oath he has taken, which he signed and ratified. He did not sign because he said he does not know how to write.

Before me,

Pedro de Becerro, Notary

[Testimony of Simón, of the *Zape Nation,* Slave]

Witness In Mexico City on July 14, 1634, the aforementioned Andrés de Gálvez presented as a witness in his case on behalf of his party a black man fluent in the Castilian language, who said his name is Simón, of the *Zape nation* and a slave of Captain Rodolfo, from whom I, the notary, received his oath, made by God Our Lord and the sign of the cross. And having sworn to tell the truth, being asked the questions of the interrogation, he said the following:

1. To the first question, he said that he knows the litigants and he knew Juan Roque and Ana María his daughter, both blacks, and that he knows about this case and the houses in question. And this is his response.

General questions: In response to the general questions he said that he is over fifty years old.

2. To the second question this witness said that he knew for certain that Juan Roque, free black man, when he died left some houses that he had in the lane behind the College of San Juan de Letrán to his daughter Ana María, a free black woman, who was the wife of a *mulatto* tailor named Juan Fraile, who is now dead. This witness saw the aforementioned Ana María die a natural death about four years ago. And he was present at her funeral, which was in the Hospital de los *Desamparados.* She left no children or heirs and, without making a testament, she died of the *cocoliste* disease that did not last three days. He knows this because he knew her and visited her when she was sick, until she died. And her father was of the same *nation* to which this witness belongs.

3. To the third question, he says that he knows and can testify that when Ana María was widowed by the death of Juan Fraile her husband, fifteen days before she herself died, being in good health, she called the foreman of the Brotherhood of Our Lady of the Immaculate Conception of this city, founded by the blacks of the *Zape nation.* The officials went to the houses where she lived, the ones mentioned in this question. This witness was an official of the aforementioned brotherhood and he joined this meeting because they notified him. In her house, Ana María said that when her husband was alive, he pressured her because he wanted to sell the houses, and she defended what her father Juan Roque had entrusted to her: that if she died without children she must leave the houses to the brotherhood, so that the blacks of the *Zape nation* would administer them and care for them, and what they earned would be used for the good of his soul and that of Ana María. Ana María said that she wanted the foreman and the officials to be entrusted with the houses, which she conveyed to them.

aceptaron y estuvieron confiriendo sobre el negocio. Y resolvieron que la dicha Ana María se estuviese como hasta allí en las dichas casas, que después que ella muriese, ellos las administrarían y harían lo que les pedía. Y esto quedó asentado según que lleva dicho. Y mediante ello y haber la susodicha muerto sin herederos, porque nunca los tuvo, y sin testar el año que se anegó México, sabe este testigo con certidumbre que las dichas casas son de la dicha *cofradía* y le pertenecen. Y esto responde.

4. De la cuarta pregunta dijo que no la sabe.

5. De la quinta pregunta dijo que lo que ha dicho es la verdad, público y notorio, so cargo del dicho juramento en que se ratificó. No firmó, que dijo que no saber.

Ante mí

Pedro de Becerro, Notario

[Testimonio de Juan, de *nación zape*, libre, amigo de Juan Roque]

Testigo En la Ciudad de México, a trece días del mes de julio de 1634 años, Andrés de Gálvez procurador, en nombre de su parte para su probanza, presentó por testigo a un *negro ladino* en lengua castellana que se dijo llamar Juan y ser de *nación zape* y libre de cautiverio, que vive en el *barrio* de Santo Domingo, del cual yo el notario recibí juramento por Dios, Nuestro Señor y a una señal de cruz, en forma de derecho. Y habiendo jurado, prometió de decir la verdad. Y preguntado por las preguntas del dicho su interrogatorio, dijo lo siguiente:

1. A la primera pregunta, dijo que conoce a las partes que litigan y conoció a Juan Roque *negro* y a Ana María *negra,* su hija, y que tiene noticia de esta causa y de las casas sobre que se litiga.

Generales: De las preguntas generales de la ley, dijo que no le tocan ninguna dellas y que es de edad de setenta años, poco más o menos. Y esto responde.

2. De la segunda pregunta, dijo que este testigo fue muy conocido y amigo del dicho Juan Roque *negro.* Y como tales estaban casi todos los días juntos, hasta que el dicho Juan Roque murió y dejó a Ana María, su hija, que no tuvo otra, las casas de su morada en el *barrio* del Alameda, en un callejón detrás del Colegio de San Juan, la cual las heredó y gozó en compañía de Juan Fraile *mulato,* su marido, hasta que el susodicho murió y después hasta que murió la dicha Ana María, la cual no tuvo hijos ni parió. Y no hizo testamento al tiempo que murió respe[c]to de que dentro de tres días cayó mala y murió de un gran *cocoliste* que le dio. Y no tuvo ni dejó herederos forzosos, ascendientes ni descendientes. Sábelo este testigo porque trató y comunicó a la dicha Ana María desde que nació hasta el día que murió, entrando y saliendo en casa de sus padres y después que murieron, en la de la susodicha y el dicho su marido. Y esto responde.

3. De la tercera pregunta, dijo que lo que della sabe es que antes que muriese el dicho Juan Fraile, marido de la dicha Ana María, intentó vender las casas que la dicha su mujer había heredado de su padre. Y la dicha Ana María no lo quería consentir. Y sobre ello tenían algunas disensiones. Y este testigo, deseando el bien y paz de la dicha

And the foreman and the black elders and officials accepted and conferred regarding this business, resolving that Ana María would remain in the houses, but after she died they would administer them and do what she asked. This was the agreement. Thus this witness knows for certain that the houses belong to the brotherhood, because she died without heirs and without making a testament the year that Mexico City flooded.

4. To the fourth question, he said that he does not know.

5. To the fifth question, he said that what he said is publicly known to be true, under the obligation of his oath, which he ratified. He did not sign because he says he does not know how.

Before me,

Pedro de Becerro, Notary

[Testimony of Juan, of the *Zape Nation,* Free Man, Acquaintance of the Roque Family]

Witness In Mexico City on July 13, 1634, Andrés de Gálvez, procurator, presented on behalf of his party for his case as witness a black man fluent in the Castilian language, who said his name is Juan and that he is of the *Zape nation* and is free from captivity and lives in the Santo Domingo neighborhood. I, the notary, received his oath by God our Lord and the sign of the cross. And having made his oath, he swore to tell the truth. And he said the following in response to the questions of the interrogation:

1. To the first question, he said that he knows the litigants and he knew the black man Juan Roque and the black woman Ana María, his daughter, and he knows about this case and the houses under litigation.

General questions: Regarding the general questions of law, he said that none of them applies to him, and that he is around seventy years old. And this is his response.

2. To the second question, this witness said that he was a good friend to Juan Roque because they were together almost every day until the day that Juan Roque died and that he left Ana María, his only daughter, the houses she lived in, in the Alameda neighborhood in a lane behind the College of San Juan. She inherited and enjoyed these houses in the company of Juan Fraile, *mulatto,* her husband until he died and then until her own death. Ana María did not have children nor did she give birth. And she did not make a testament, because she died only three days after falling sick with a terrible *cocoliste.* She did not have any heirs, and this witness knows this because he interacted and communicated with Ana María from her birth until the day she died, entering and leaving her parents' house and the house belonging to her and her husband after her parents died.

3. To the third question, he said that he knows that before he died, Juan Fraile tried to sell the houses that she had inherited from her father and that Ana María did not want to consent to this. This led to some arguments between them. This witness wanted peace and the best for Ana María, whom he thought of as a daughter. One day she complained of her husband's aspersions regarding the sale of the houses, and this witness advised her to do what her husband asked in order to conserve the peace, to

Ana María que la tenía en lugar de su hija, un día que se le quejó a este testigo de las asperezas del dicho su marido sobre la venta de las dichas casas, le aconsejó este testigo que hiciese lo que su marido le pedía y que con eso conservarían la paz. A lo cual dijo la dicha Ana María que ella no lo podía hacer, porque aunque las dichas casas eran suyas, el dicho su padre de quien las heredó le había dicho y dejado encargado que, si no tuviera hijos, no dispusiese de las dichas casas, sino que las diese a la *Cofradía* de Nuestra Señora de la Concepción, donde era cofrade y fundador, para que los *morenos* de la *nación zape* las administrasen y cuidasen y de los arrendamientos se hiciese bien por su alma y de la dicha Ana María. Y que así ella estaba con firme propósito de hacer la voluntad del dicho su padre. Y este testigo dio noticia de lo susodicho al *mayoral* y demás cofrades de la dicha *cofradía* para que estuviesen con cuidado. Y habiendo pasado algún tiempo de como sucedió lo que lleva dicho, murió el dicho Juan Fraile. Y en la ocasión que murió, este testigo era *mayordomo* de la dicha *cofradía.* Y avisaron a este testigo cómo el *mayoral* y demás oficiales de ella se juntaban en casa de la dicha Ana María. Y este testigo se halló en la junta. Y la dicha Ana María manifestó al dicho *mayoral,* que entonces lo era Antón de Medina, y a los demás oficiales que allí estaban, cómo la voluntad del dicho Juan Roque su padre había sido que aquellas casa[s] fuesen para la *cofradía* y que las había defendido de su marido, que muchas veces las había querido vender. Y que supuesto que estaba viuda y sin hijos, deudas, ni parientes, ella tenía voluntad de que se hiciese la de su padre. Y entregó las dichas casas al dicho *mayoral,* el cual y los demás oficiales las recibieron y estuvieron tratando y confiriendo el negocio. Y vinieron a resolverse en que la dicha Ana María se estuviese como hasta allí en las dichas casas y las gozase. Que después que ella muriese entraría el *mayoral* y oficiales de la dicha *cofradía* a poseerlas y administrarlas, en conformidad de la voluntad de la dicha Ana María, la cual lo tuvo por bien. Y como quince días después que pasó lo que lleva dicho en la dicha junta murió y pasó de esta presente vida la dicha Ana María, de un *cocoliste* que no duró tres días. Y este testigo la vio muerta y enterrar en la iglesia del Hospital de los *Desamparados,* mediante lo cual sabe que las dichas casas son y pertenecen a la dicha *cofradía.* Y esto dijo [que] sabe de lo contenido en la pregunta y responde a ella.

4. A la cuarta pregunta, dijo que habrá tiempo de cuatro años poco más que murió la dicha Ana María. No sabe este testigo con evidencia quién pose[e] las dichas casas ni quién las arrienda y cobra. Y esto responde.

5. A la quinta pregunta, dijo que lo que ha dicho es la verdad, público y notorio, pública voz y fama, para el juramento que hecho tiene en que se ratificó. Y no lo firmó, que dijo no saber escribir.

Ante mí

Pedro de Becerro, Notario

[Los] desta probanza fuera del [fisco] dos *pesos* y medio doy fe.

which Ana María replied that she could not do that because although the houses were hers, her father, from whom she had inherited them, had entrusted them to her and charged her that if she did not have children she should not dispose of the houses but give them to the Brotherhood of the Immaculate Conception, of which he was a brother and founder, so that the blacks of the *Zape nation* would administer them and take care of their earnings for the benefit of his soul and that of Ana María. And that thus she was firm in her intention to comply with her father's will. This witness told this to the foreman and the other members of the brotherhood so they would take care of it. Time passed, and Juan Fraile died, and when he died this witness was the majordomo of the brotherhood. And they notified this witness that the foreman, who was then Antón de Medina, and the other officials were meeting in Ana María's house. This witness attended the meeting, where Ana María told the foreman that the will of her father Juan Roque had been that these houses go to the brotherhood. She said that she had defended the houses against her husband many times because he had wanted to sell them. As she was a widow without heirs, debts, or relatives, she wanted to do what her father wished. And she entrusted the houses to the foreman and the other officials, who received them. This business was discussed and confirmed, and they came to resolve that Ana María should continue to enjoy the houses as she had up to that point and that after her death, the foreman and the officials of the brotherhood would take possession of them and administer them, in compliance with Ana María's will, to which she agreed. She died fifteen days after this meeting, passing from this life from a *cocoliste* that lasted less than three days. This witness saw her dead and buried in the church of the Hospital de los *Desamparados,* and therefore he knows that the houses now belong to the brotherhood.

4. To the fourth question, he said that it had been around four years since Ana María died. He does not know with certainty who possesses the houses nor who rents them or enjoys their rent.

5. To the fifth question, he said that what he said is known to be true, public, and notorious, and according to his oath, which he ratified. And he did not sign, because he says he does not know how to write.

Before me,

Pedro de Becerro, Notary
For this examination, two and a half *pesos,* I certify.

7

Death, Gender, and Writing: Testaments of Women of African Origin in Seventeenth-Century Lima, 1651–1666[1]

José R. Jouve-Martín

In 1651, Juana Barba, a free black woman, went to the office of Marcelo Antonio de Figueroa, a public notary in the city of Lima, in order to have him write her last will and testament. She was ill, feared that her death was imminent, and wanted to put her soul on the path to salvation. She also wanted to leave a detailed account of her belongings, which included clothes, money, jewelry, and no fewer than four slaves. She dictated clear instructions for how her property should be divided and used after her death.

In 1666, María de Huancavelica, another free black woman, carried out the very same ritual. Believing her end to be near, she went to a public notary to draw up a written document to guarantee that her religious obligations would be met and that she would have the final say over distributing the property she had accumulated in her lifetime. Her property included clothes, jewelry, money, and five slaves.

During most of the seventeenth century, a great number of women of African descent, some poor, others relatively rich, ordered their testaments to be written by colonial officials in a proportion that greatly surpassed that of men. These women testators left us with extremely rich documentation about their life and death in colonial Lima. Their actions underline the important role that writing and gender played in the structure of this urban slave society.

The Racial Demographics of Seventeenth-Century Lima

When Juana Barba approached Marcelo Antonio de Figueroa in 1651, Lima had become a predominantly black city, a feature accentuated by the forced relocation of most of its indigenous population to the nearby parish of Santiago del Cercado in 1590. The black population peaked as a proportion of the total probably around 1636, when a census ordered by the Marquis of Chichón showed that the capital of the Viceroyalty of Peru had a total of 10,758 Spaniards compared to 13,620 individuals classified as *negros* and 861 as *mulattoes* (Bowser, 341).[2]

In the second half of the seventeenth century, the city's black population began a slow decline in both absolute and relative terms. This decline was due partially to the emergence of new and more profitable markets for slaves in the Atlantic and the

[1] See Maps 6 and 10.

[2] For the usage of *negro, mulatto,* and other terms associated with individuals of African origin, see the Glossary.

Caribbean and partially to the problems that the Spanish slave trade experienced after the collapse of the dynastic union with Portugal in 1640, when the colonies were left without access to their main supplier of slaves (Vila Vilar, 557–64; Torres 117–18).

The reintegration of the Indian town of Santiago del Cercado into the city of Lima in the 1680s further modified the numeric and racial composition of the city. Although in 1700 peoples of African descent still constituted an important part of Lima's population, their numbers were only slightly above 10,000 of a total population of 37,234, according to the *Numeración general* (General Enumeration) commissioned by Viceroy Melchor Antonio Portocarrero Lazo de la Vega and completed by the Conde de la Monclova in 1700.

Gender and *Manumission* in Lima

Colonial censuses also show that, unlike the situation in the plantation setting, slightly more women of African descent than men of African descent lived in Lima. Of the 14,481 individuals classified as either black or *mulatto* in the 1636 census, 6,820 were listed as men and 7,661 as women. Similarly, in the *Numeración general* completed by the Conde de la Monclova in 1700, 4,012 were men and 5,323 were women. However, the gender imbalance reflected by these documents was much more marked when it came to freedom.

According to this latter census, 3,120 individuals of African descent were considered free, 1,762 of them women and only 553 of them men. The rest were children for whom no gender information is provided. This imbalance is also widely reflected in the *Protocolos notariales* stored in the Archivo General de la Nación in Lima, in which women appear as the main beneficiaries of *cartas de libertad* (deeds of *manumission*). Women were much more likely than men to be manumitted, partially due to their role as house servants. Working as servants allowed women to have a closer relationship with their masters and even to participate in the household economy by freely selling and buying in the market. Men were allowed into the house less frequently and were usually employed in more strenuous physical tasks or were "hired out" to others (Aguirre, 65). The decision to free slaves often took place at the end of their owners' life, and women slaves proved more likely than men to be granted their freedom in these testaments or to receive conditions that better enabled them to purchase it themselves. In addition to this, Spanish legislation established that bondage was transmitted matrilineally. Women were the child bearers; therefore, it made more economic sense for the families of African descent to try to put together their scant resources to free women first to ensure the freedom of their children (Hünefeldt, 32–36).

The fact that women were manumitted more often than men had a major effect on the position of women of African descent in colonial society vis-à-vis their male counterparts and members of other *castas.* Freedom allowed them to participate more fully in the social and economic life of the cities. Many remained in a position of servitude, barely making a living doing small household jobs such as cleaning, sewing, or cooking; others were able to buy land and trade in the city markets or set up small food shops, known as *chicherías,* or other businesses.

The most resourceful of these women, such as Juana Barba and María de Huancavelica, ended up amassing a small fortune. As their testaments indicate, they were able to participate in the informal but more lucrative trade of lending money to others. This lending sometimes had freedom as the object of negotiation. Given the difficulty slaves had raising the large sums needed to free themselves or their families (at the same time keeping their masters away from their earnings), borrowing money from other members of the black community was important for buying their own freedom.

Gender and money also allowed free women of African descent to interact with members of other *castas,* particularly other women, in a way that men could only dream of. In fact, most communication with women classified as Spaniards was all but closed to black and *mulatto* men but remained mostly open to black and *mulatta* women. Their testaments show that this communication took place and that it frequently involved social and economic exchanges. Freedom and trade also allowed women to establish extensive interactions with colonial lettered culture; and although many did not even know how to write their name, they knew full well the power of the written word and carefully guarded notarized documents in their possession.

Literacy, Orality, and the Preparation of a Last Will and Testament

Not surprisingly, the combination of social, economic, and spiritual concerns led many women of African descent to interact with colonial officials and write their testaments. Perhaps more than any other document in the life of an individual, a testament was a compendium of material and religious negotiations. Testaments were used to decide who inherited the possessions of the deceased, what moral and economic obligations needed to be satisfied, where the corpse was to be buried, which confraternities, if any, should be present at the funeral, how many Masses would be celebrated for the salvation of the soul, etc.

The Church strongly recommended that the faithful, rich or poor, write their testament before leaving this world for the next; the Church also benefited from this practice—both spiritually and economically (Le Goff, 289–333; Van Deusen, 32–37). Even though colonial notaries kept testaments within the boundaries of orthodoxy, testaments offer a wealth of information about the religious beliefs and concerns of peoples of African descent in colonial times.

They are also key documents in our effort to reconstruct the material culture of the members of this community and the myriad social interactions built upon it; they allow us to observe the processes of social stratification and racial negotiation that took place within this population. In fact, testaments are one of the few large bodies of documentation that permit us to analyze in depth the social and cultural life of this group from the perspective of both gender and literacy.

The writing of a testament was one of the most important occasions in which men and women of African descent had the opportunity to interact with colonial lettered culture. Even if the colonial legislation permitted the testator to write his or her own testament, it still favored mediation by those who had the capacity for legal representation: the *escribanos* or notaries (Eire, 34). Of course, most people of African descent

were illiterate, and, even though a few were able to write and read, a testament was a complex and important enough document that it required the mediation of colonial officials.

The place where a testament was written could vary according to necessity and the moment in which it was written. Usually it was redacted in the *escribanías,* but, in more exceptional cases, and in particular if the person was gravely ill and unable to stand up, the notary could write the testament at the bedside. Other people were present with the individual making the will and the notary; these were either companions of the testator or other individuals from the notary's office, who served as witnesses and helped to ratify the validity of the document (Jouve-Martín, 78–82). Access to the services of the *escribanos* was facilitated by the fact that most *escribanías* were located in Lima's central square or close to it, which made them highly visible to all members of colonial society, including blacks.

The language in which a testament was written was highly formulaic, particularly in the initial and concluding parts of the document. These formulas could change from one notary to another, but in general terms they were fairly standard (Herzog, 33). This standardization was a response to the fact that, since the thirteenth century, Spanish law had produced models on which these documents were based. From a linguistic point of view, they were texts written in the first-person singular, which created the autobiographical fiction that the person named in the document was also its author.

Only at the end of the testament is the identity of the colonial notary and his role in the creation of the document established. His signature, along with the signatures of the testator and witnesses, gave the document legal validity. In case the testator did not know how to write his or her name, a witness was called to do it in the testator's place. Despite the decisive role of the notary in the writing of the testament, its creation frequently bridged the oral/written divide in several ways. Apart from the clearly formulaic sections and the beginning and end of the document, the testator basically dictated to the notary his or her final dispositions concerning the funeral and possessions.

This fact frequently allows us to find elements of orality in the document. Once finished, the document was read aloud before being signed. Translating silent signs into oral ones, reading aloud was of fundamental importance for the effective participation of illiterate people in the colonial legal culture. Perhaps more importantly, black women might not have been able to read these documents by themselves, but they were acutely aware of documents' role in colonial society and usually knew how to use them. They might not have known how to write or read them, but they were familiar with the language of the law. The existing documentation demonstrates that the writing of a testament was not exclusive to women of a determined *casta* (*negro, mulato, zambo, pardo, cuarterón,* etc.) or a specific *nación* or ethnic group (*Folupa, Caboverde, Terranova, Bran,* etc.). Not even the condition of being an *horro* or *horra* (a free man or woman) was necessarily fundamental to be able to commission a will or a testament, and there are examples of slaves who gave their last wills under the supervision of their masters. Furthermore, although those with more material possessions were more likely to write a testament, there is also ample evidence in the Archivo Arzobispal de Lima of women of African descent who lived and died in poverty but

still wanted to make sure that their scant resources were sent to close relatives or used for the salvation of their souls (Jouve-Martín, 155–79).

The testaments of Juana Barba and María de Huancavelica, which follow, are remarkable as examples of economically successful black women. It is not remarkable, however, that black women made testaments. Both women were categorized as *negras,* which means that their socioeconomic position was not due to any genealogical relation with a Spaniard. In fact, María de Huancavelica was born in Africa and was probably brought to Peru as a slave. At the end of her life, like Juana Barba before her, she had become a slave owner herself. Both were relatively affluent and, although Juana Barba's list of possessions is longer and reveals her involvement in the cloth trade, María de Huancavelica did not lag behind and had the means necessary to establish a *capellanía* (chaplaincy) for her confessor.

Their testaments have left us with a testimony of power, stratification, and spirituality in colonial Lima and of the important role played by gender in its black community. Both documents come from the Archivo Arzobispal de Lima (Archiepiscopal Archive of Lima) that houses the ecclesiastical records for Lima, including court cases, divorces and separations, charges against priests, and many wills. They arrived at this repository through the *Tribunal de bienes de difuntos* (Colonial Tribunal of Property of the Deceased), which had authority over all mortuary dispositions registered in the testaments.

Due to the importance given to the testament in canon law (Church law), they were supervised by the ecclesiastical authorities even though they were written by civil officials. The wills themselves are a small but fundamental portion of the documents that make up each testator's full legal dossier. As is true with most testaments, they are accompanied by subsequent judicial proceedings and decrees (inventories, records of sale, provisions and reprimands to the executors, challenges, etc.).

In some cases, these *autos* (deeds) number twenty, thirty, or forty pages and, therefore, exceed the limitations of this anthology. A complete evaluation of the role of testaments in the life of this community would require taking into account the other documents and accompanying litigation. Although heavily mediated, wills constitute an important way through which people of African heritage expressed themselves and found a voice that endures to our day. They occupy a privileged position in the historical record for those interested in exploring not only the changing nature of religious beliefs, but also the role of gender, literacy, and freedom in shaping the life of a black community in colonial times.

Testamento de Juana Barba, *morena* libre [Lima, 1651][1]

En el nombre de Dios, Nuestro Señor, y de la gloriosa siempre Virgen María, Su preciosa madre, Señora Nuestra, concebida sin pecado original: Sepan cuantos esta carta de testamento vieren cómo yo, Juana Barba, *morena* libre, *vecina* desta ciudad de los Reyes [Lima] y natural della, hija de Domingo Hernández y Simona Barba, difuntos, estando enferma aunque levantada y en todo mi acuerdo y entendimiento natural como Dios, Nuestro Señor, ha sido servido dármele y creyendo como firmemente creo en el misterio de la Santísima Trinidad, Padre, Hijo y Espíritu Santo, tres personas distintas y un solo Dios verdadero, y en todo lo demás que tiene, cree, confiesa, y enseña nuestra Santa Madre Iglesia Católica Romana como católica romana y cristiana, y temiéndome de la muerte que es cosa natural a toda criatura humana, y deseando salvar mi alma, otorgo que hago y ordeno mi testamento [y] última voluntad en la manera siguiente:

Primeramente, encomiendo mi alma a Dios, Nuestro Señor, que la creó y redimió con su preciosa sangre, muerte y pasión, [y] el cuerpo a la tierra de que fue formado.

Ídem. Mando que, cuando la voluntad de Dios, Nuestro Señor, fuere servida de llevarme desta presente vida, mi cuerpo sea enterrado en el Convento del Señor Santo Domingo en la capilla de San Juan de Letrán, en la parte y lugar que pareciere a mis *albaceas,* y se amortaje mi cuerpo con el hábito del Señor San Francisco.

Ídem. Mando que acompañen mi cuerpo el día de mi entierro la cruz [una "+" encima de la palabra "cruz"] alta, cura y sacristán de mi parroquia, que es la Santa Iglesia Catedral desta ciudad, y el demás acompañamiento que pareciere a mis *albaceas* a cuya elección dejo toda la forma de mi funeral y entierro.

Ídem. Mando que el día de mi entierro siendo hora o, si no, el siguiente se diga por mi alma una misa cantada de cuerpo presente con su vigilia y ofrenda y el día de mis honras se diga otra en la misma forma y se pague la limosna acostumbrada de mis bienes.

Ídem. Mando que, luego que yo fallezca, con la *mayor* brevedad que ser pudiere, se digan por mi alma cincuenta misas rezadas en la parte y por los sacerdotes que pareciere a mis *albaceas.*

Ídem. Declaro que por la misericordia de Dios al presente no debo nada a nadie.

Ídem. Declaro que tengo en mi poder unos estribos de plata maciza empeñados en cincuenta *pesos* por mano de don Fernando de Castañeda. Mando que dando los dichos cincuenta *pesos* el dicho don Fernando o don Francisco Barba se le vuelvan los dichos estribos.

Ídem. Mando a los Santos Lugares de Jerusalén diez *pesos* de a ocho *reales* de limosna.

Ídem. Mando cien *pesos* de a ocho *reales* para que con ellos se haga un manto a la Virgen, Nuestra Señora, que está en el altar *mayor* de la Iglesia Catedral desta dicha ciudad por ser mi [sic] devota.

[1] Testamento de Juana Barba, morena libre, Archivo Arzobispal de Lima, Tribunal de Bienes de Difuntos 31:39, 1651, fifty-seven folios.

Last Will and Testament of Juana Barba, Free Black Woman [Lima, 1651]

In the name of God, Our Lord, and of the glorious Virgin Mary His precious mother, Our Lady, who was born free of original sin, know those who read this last will and testament that my name is Juana Barba, a free black woman, born and resident in this city of Lima, daughter of Domingo Hernández and Simona Barba, both deceased; and that I am ill, although able to stand and in possession of all the judgment and natural understanding that God, Our Lord, has seen fit to give me; and believing as I firmly believe in the mystery of the Holy Trinity of the Father, the Son, and the Holy Spirit, three persons in one true God, as well as in all that our Holy Roman Catholic Church believes, confesses, and teaches, as a faithful Roman Catholic and as a Christian; and fearful of death, which is consubstantial to all human creatures, and wishing to set my soul on the path to salvation, I hereby declare that I give and arrange my last will and testament in the following way:

First of all, I entrust my soul to God, Our Lord, who created it and redeemed it through his precious blood, death, and passion; and my body shall return to the dust from which it was formed.

Item. I order that, when God, our Lord, wishes to take me from this present life, my body be buried in the Chapel of Saint John of Letrán in the Convent of Saint Dominic in the place that my executors deem most appropriate and that my body be shrouded with the habit of Saint Francis.

Item. I order that on the day of my burial my body be accompanied by a presiding cross [a "+" above the word "cross"], a priest and a sacristan from my parish, which is the Holy Cathedral of this city and that the rest of the retinue be decided on by my executors to whom I leave all other details of my funeral and burial.

Item. I order that at some time during the day of my funeral or the next one, a Mass be sung for the salvation of my soul, with my body present, followed by a vigil and a pious offering, and that another Mass be celebrated on the day of my commemoration in the same way and the customary alms be paid from my estate.

Item. I order that as soon as possible after I die my executors pay and arrange fifty Masses for the salvation of my soul, and they shall be celebrated in the church and by the priest of their choosing.

Item. I declare that, by God's Mercy, I do not owe anything to anyone.

Item. I declare that I have in my power some stirrups of solid silver pawned at fifty *pesos* by Don Fernando de Castañeda. I order that, if Don Fernando or Don Francisco Barba pay the said fifty *pesos,* the said stirrups be returned to him.

Item. I order that ten *pesos* of eight *reales* be sent as alms to the Holy Sites in Jerusalem.

Item. I order that one hundred *pesos* of eight *reales* be used to make a cloak for the figure of the Virgin, Our Lady, found in the main altar of the Cathedral Church of this city as an expression of my devotion to Her.

Ídem. Mando a las mandas forzosas y acostumbradas, a todas ellas, ocho *pesos* con que los aparto de mis bienes.

Ídem. Mando a mi hermana Agustina de Ampuero y Barba quinientos *pesos* de a ocho *reales* para que haga lo que le pareciere de ellos y se le entreguen luego que yo fallezca.

Ídem. Mando a la dicha mi hermana dos gargantillas de perlas que tienen poco más de seis onzas, un par de zarcillos de oro con piedras verdes—y dos basquiñas, la una de [ilegible] de oro y seda y la otra verde y morada, y dos jubones blancos—asimismo mando que se le dé a la susodicha toda la loza que tengo en mi escaparate en lo alto del y algunos vidrios que allí hubiese.

Ídem. Mando a la dicha mi hermana Agustina de Ampuero y Barba una negrita, mi esclava, que nació en mi casa, nombrada María de la Cruz, *criolla,* que será de edad de diez años, poco más o menos, para que le sirva a la dicha mi hermana todos los días de su vida y después de ellos se hubiere *horra* de toda sujeción y cautiverio, y con sólo esta cláusula consiga su libertad.

Ídem. Mando a Juana Barrezo, mi amiga, treinta *pesos* de a ocho *reales* por ser pobre.

Ídem. Mando a doña Bernarda de Morales y a sus dos hijas cincuenta *pesos* de a ocho *reales,* los cuales se le han de dar de lo procedido de los estribos de plata cuando los desempeñasen, por lo mucho que las quiero.

Ídem. Mando a María Santoja, donada en el Monasterio de la Concepción desta ciudad cincuenta *pesos* de a ocho *reales* por ser pobre.

Ídem. Mando diez *pesos* de a ocho de limosna a la *Cofradía* de Nuestra Señora de la Presentación fundada en el Convento de Señor Santo Domingo de esta ciudad, los cuales le den a la priora que lo fuere de dicha *cofradía* de donde soy esclava.

Ídem. Mando para criar los niños huérfanos diez *pesos* de a ocho *reales* de limosna.

Ídem. Mando que de mis bienes se le entreguen al *licenciado* Diego de Ocampo, presbítero, un mil *pesos* de a ocho *reales* para que con consulta del Padre Francisco de Soria, mi *confesor,* los distribuyan en la forma que lo dejé comunicado a los susodichos en razón del descargo de mi conciencia y bien de mi alma sin que ninguna *justicia* eclesiástica ni secular se entremeta a pedirles cuenta dello porque yo la relevo dello por la mucha satisfacción que de los susodichos tengo.

Ídem. Es mi voluntad que, dando cincuenta *pesos* de a ocho *reales,* Laura *Carabalí,* mi esclava, casada con Alejandro *Carabalí,* sea libre de toda sujeción y cautiverio, y mis *albaceas* le den *carta de libertad,* y estos dichos cincuenta *pesos* los ha de ir dando la susodicha a mis *albaceas* a ocho *pesos* cada mes desde el día de mi muerte en adelante hasta que se *ajuste* la dicha cantidad.

Ídem. Declaro que tengo por mi esclava una *negra* nombrada Clara, de *casta bran,* casada, la cual es mi voluntad que dando cien *pesos* de a ocho *reales* se libre de toda sujeción y cautiverio y mis *albaceas* le den *carta de libertad* en forma.

Ídem. Declaro que tengo por mi esclava una *negra* nombrada Juana, de *casta bran,* que será de edad de treinta años, la cual es mi voluntad que sirva a mi hermana

Item. I set aside eight *pesos* to pay for the customary and obligatory alms.

Item. I bequeath to my sister, Agustina de Ampuero y Barba, five hundred *pesos* of eight *reales* so that she may do as she sees fit with the money after I die.

Item. I also bequeath to my sister two pearl necklaces weighing around six ounces, a pair of gold earrings with green stones, and two petticoats, one with its [illegible] of gold and silk and the other green and purple, and two white bodices. I also order that [my sister] be given all the chinaware and glass found in the top part of my glass cabinet.

Item. I bequeath to my sister, Agustina de Ampuero y Barba, a young black girl, my slave, who was born in my house and is named María de la Cruz, and who is more or less about ten years of age, so that she may serve my sister until she dies, and after that, I order that she be free of all subjection and captivity, and that this clause act as her deed of *manumission.*

Item. I bequeath to my friend, Juana Barrezo, thirty *pesos* of eight *reales* to alleviate her poverty.

Item. I bequeath to *Doña* Bernarda de Morales and to her two daughters fifty *pesos* of eight *reales* that are to be taken from the money collected once the silver stirrups are redeemed, and I do so out of the love I have for them.

Item. I bequeath to María Santoja, lay sister in the Convent of the Immaculate Conception of this city, fifty *pesos* of eight *reales* to alleviate her poverty.

Item. I bequeath ten *pesos* of eight *reales* as alms to the Brotherhood of Our Lady of the Presentation founded in the monastery of Saint Dominic of this city. I order that they be given to the prioress of the said brotherhood, of which I am a slave.[1]

Item. I bequeath ten *pesos* of eight *reales* as alms to help raise orphan children.

Item. I order that a thousand *pesos* of eight *reales* be given from my estate to the licenciate Diego de Ocampo, priest, so that, in consultation with Father Francisco de Soria, my confessor, they be distributed in the way that I have communicated to them for the unburdening of my conscience and my soul, and I exempt the ecclesiastical and secular justice of their obligation to oversee them based on the high esteem in which I hold them.

Item. It is my will that Laura *Carabalí,* my slave, who is married to Alejandro *Carabalí,* be freed from all subjection and captivity upon paying fifty *pesos* of eight *reales* and that my executors grant her the deed of *manumission.* She will give to my executors these fifty *pesos* at a rate of eight *pesos* each month, from the day of my death forward, until she pays the total amount.

Item. I declare that I own as my slave a married black woman named Clara, of the *Bran nation,* and it is my will that she be allowed to pay a hundred *pesos* of eight *reales* to be freed of all subjection and captivity, and once she does so, I order my executors to give her the deed of *manumission.*

Item. I declare that I own as my slave a black woman named Juana, of the *Bran nation,* thirty years of age. It is my will that she serve my sister Agustina de Ampuero

[1] Members of certain brotherhoods, particularly those devoted to the Virgin Mary or to the Sacred Heart of Jesus Christ, are frequently referred as "slaves" (devotees of the Virgin or of Jesus), but they are not slaves in the usual sense of being the possession of another individual.

Agustina de Ampuero y que, a tiempo de cuatro años después que yo fallezca, que después dellos sea libre y *horra* de toda sujeción y cautiverio, y con sólo esta cláusula consiga su libertad. Si la dicha *negra* quisiere entrar en el Convento de la Concepción donde ha de entrar la dicha mi hermana, entre, y, si no, le sirva desde fuera.

Ídem. Declaro por mis bienes los siguientes:

Primeramente dos mil y doscientos *pesos* de a ocho *reales* que me deben Mateo de Samacola y Martín de Larrinbe por escritura otorgada ante Sebastián Ortiz, *escribano* público desta ciudad, por el año pasado de 1650, cuyo plazo es cumplido, mando se cobren.
Ídem. Una gargantilla de perlas a trozos que tiene trece hilos con una imagen de la Limpia Concepción y cuentas de oro
Ídem. Unos brazaletes de perlas menudas
Ídem. Unos zarcillos de perlas y oro
Ídem. Una sortija de oro con un zafiro morado
Ídem. Unos brazaletes de granates azules con cuentas de oro
Ídem. Una gargantilla de cuentas de oro
Ídem. Dos tembladeras de plata medianas, y siete cucharas de plata ordinarias, un tenedor de plata, tres rebanadores de plata, y cuatro dedales de plata
Ídem. Las cuatro esclavas que tengo declaradas en este mi testamento
Ídem. Unos zarcillos de piedras verdes y las seis onzas de perlas en otro brazalete—y una gargantilla que dejo declarada en este mi testamento que son los que mando a la dicha mi hermana
Ídem. Un escaparate grande con la loza de china y barros que están en él
Ídem. Una caja grande de Panamá
Ídem. Otra caja mediana de Panamá
Ídem. Otra pequeña de costura
Ídem. Once camisas de mujer nuevas, unas hechas y otras por hacer
Ídem. Cuatro fustanes labrados nuevos
Ídem. Tres gorgueras nuevas con puntas
Ídem. Tres paños de cabeza nuevos de cambray y puntas finas
Ídem. Tres pañuelos de cambray de narices, nuevos con puntas finas
Ídem. Un par de medias de seda verde sin estrenar
Ídem. Dos o tres pares de calcetas nuevas y sus escarpines
Ídem. Seis almohadas blancas nuevas de ruan de cofre, las cuatro dellas con sus alamares y botones y otras cuatro almohadas tienen sus fundas de tafetán azul
Ídem. Ocho sábanas de ruan florete nuevas sin estrenar
Ídem. Un par de almohadas de ruan labradas con seda carmesí y otras de la misma forma, y un par destas dichas almohadas las dejo y mando a mi hermana Agustina de Ampuero y Barba
Ídem. Siete paños de manos de ruan de cofre y lienzo casero unos de la [ilegible] y otros labrados y otros llanos
Ídem. Tres tablas de manteles, las dos nuevas y otra usada
Ídem. Doce servilletas usadas
Ídem. Un [ilegible] de matices carmesí y verde fino
Ídem. Dos sobrecamas azules de lana de Quito y una delantera azul

for four years after my death, after which I order that she be freed from all subjection and captivity and that this clause act as her deed of *manumission.* If the said black woman would like to enter in the Convent of the Immaculate Conception in which my sister will take vows, then so be it. If not, then she may serve her from the outside.

Item. I declare the following as part of my estate:

First, two thousand two hundred *pesos* of eight *reales* that Mateo de Samacola and Martin de Larrinbe owe me according to a deed given before Sebastián Ortiz, public notary of this city, and that I lent them for the term of one year starting in 1650. Since the term is passed, I order that they be collected.

Item. A necklace of bits of pearls that has thirteen strings and is decorated with an image of the Immaculate Conception and beads of gold

Item. A bracelet of small pearls

Item. A pair of earrings of pearls and gold

Item. A ring of gold with a purple sapphire

Item. A bracelet of blue garnets with beads of gold

Item. A choker of gold beads

Item. Two medium-sized, double-handled bowls [or cups] of silver, and seven ordinary silver spoons, a silver fork, three knives of silver, and four silver thimbles

Item. The four slaves that I have declared in this testament

Item. A pair of earrings of green stones, and six ounces of pearls in another bracelet, and a necklace that I have already declared in this testament, which is the one that I ordered to be given to my sister

Item. A large glass-fronted cabinet and the chinaware and earthenware in it

Item. A large trunk from Panama

Item. A medium trunk from Panama

Item. Another small one for sewing items

Item. Eleven new shirts for women, some already made and others to be made

Item. Four new embroidered petticoats

Item. Three new ruffs with needlepoint stitching

Item. Three new chambray head kerchiefs and fine needlework

Item. Three new handkerchiefs of chambray with fine needlework

Item. A pair of green silk stockings, never worn

Item. Two or three pairs of new stockings and their slippers

Item. Six new white pillows of fine Rouen cloth,[2] four of which have their loops and buttons, and another four pillows [that] have their cases of blue taffeta

Item. Eight new sheets of fine flowered Rouen cloth, never used

Item. A pair of embroidered pillows made of fine Rouen cloth with crimson silk and others of the same form, and two of these pillows I bequeath to my sister Agustina de Ampuero y Barba

Item. Seven handkerchiefs of fine Rouen cloth and homespun linen, some of [illegible] and others embroidered and others plain

Item. Three tablecloths, two new and another used

Item. Twelve used napkins

Item. A fine crimson and green [illegible]

Item. Two blue woolen bedspreads from Quito and a blue blanket

[2] Probably fine linen.

Ídem. Dos pabellones buenos, el uno que está en mi cama y el otro que está en la caja, el cual mando a la dicha mi hermana Agustina de Ampuero y Barba

Ídem. Dos sobrecamas blancas una nueva y otra usada

Ídem. Otra delantera de cama labrada de hilo [ilegible] usada

Ídem. Una cuja de madera ordinaria

Ídem. Una tarima de delante de la cama

Ídem. Otro estrado grande en dos pedazos

Ídem. Una cajonera grande y otra pequeña, usadas, y otra pequeña nueva

Ídem. Un espaldar usado

Ídem. Cuatro petates ordinarios nuevos

Ídem. Cuatro bufetes dos grandes y dos pequeños, y un cancel, y dos escaños y nueve o diez sillas grandes y una pequeña de sentar ordinarias

Ídem. Un bufete pequeño de los arriba dichos mando a la dicha mi hermana Agustina de Ampuero Barba

Ídem. Una tinajera de madera con su alacena y con muchos platos grandes y pequeños

Ídem. Una piedra de estilar con su armazón

Ídem. Una artesa para amasar—y una puerta grande—y unas tablas de madera

Ídem. Cinco sayas de diferentes colores

Ídem. Dos mantellinas negras, la una nueva con cinco ribetes de terciopelo y la otra usada

Ídem. Una mantellina de color azul con tres sevillanetas de oro nueva y tres jubones de tela el uno verde y el otro morado y otro azul; los dos del luto pasado y otro jubón de tafetán negro doble y una pollera de tela verde—y un faldequín de damasco mandarín—y otro de [ilegible] azul

Ídem. Tres bateas, las dos grandes y la otra mediana y otra más pequeña

Ídem. Los demás trastes y menaje de casa que se declaren por mis bienes después de mi fallecimiento mando le hagan *inventario* dellos después de mi fallecimiento por mi *tenedor de bienes*

Ídem. Mando que una caja mediana y la batea mediana se le dé a la dicha mi hermana Agustina de Ampuero porque así es mi voluntad

Ídem. Mando que a todas mis esclavas [tachado: hermanas] se les dé lutos de bayeta de la tienda y a mi hermana, de Castilla, las azules y mantilla

Ídem. Un sillón usado

Ídem. Dos mesitas pequeñas y dos bancos de asentar

Ídem. Un almirez grande y una sartén, y un cacito nuevo, y otro usado, dos asadores una paila de regar y tres candeleros de azófar.

Y, para cumplir y pagar este mi testamento y lo en él contenido, dejo y nombro por mis *albaceas* y ejecutores del al *licenciado* Diego de Ocampo, presbítero, y a mi hermana Agustina de Ampuero y Barba, y por tenedor de mis bienes nombro al dicho *licenciado* Diego de Ocampo y les doy poder cumplido *in sólidum* para el uso y ejercicio del dicho albaceazgo, y para [a]parecer en juicio y haber y pedir todo cuanto convenga y fuere necesario, y para dar cartas de pago, cancelación y finiquitos y gastos y los demás recaudos necesarios que hubiesen del dicho albaceazgo, en todas las cosas y casos que convengan y fueren necesarios, todo el tiempo que convengan aunque sea pasado el año y día que la ley de suyo dispone.

Y cumplido y pagado este mi testamento y lo en él contenido, en todo el remanente que quedare de mis bienes, deudas, derechos y acciones, dejo y nombro por mi universal heredera a mi alma, para que lo que así fuere mis *albaceas* lo distribuyan según

Item. Two good canopies, one that is on my bed and the other that is in the box, and I bequeath the latter to my sister, Agustina de Ampuero y Barba
Item. Two white bedspreads, one new and the other used
Item. Another used blanket embroidered with [illegible] thread
Item. An ordinary wooden bed frame
Item. A wooden stand from in front of the bed
Item. And another large platform in two parts
Item. A large chest of drawers and another small, both used, and another new small one
Item. A used wall cushion
Item. Four ordinary, new mats
Item. Four tables, two large and two small, and a screen, and two benches and nine or ten large ordinary chairs and one small one for sitting
Item. I bequeath to my sister Agustina de Ampuero Barba one of the small tables I have just mentioned
Item. A wooden stand for earthenware jars with its cabinet and many plates, large and small
Item. A round whetstone with its mechanism
Item. A trough for kneading, and a large door, and some wooden boards
Item. Five skirts of different colors
Item. Two black shawls, the new one with five trimmings of velvet and the other used
Item. One new blue shawl with three bands of gold sevillaneta cloth, and three cloth bodices, one green, one purple, and the other blue; two from the last period of mourning and the other one of double black taffeta, and a skirt of green cloth, and one of Mandarin damask, and another of blue [illegible]
Item. Three basins, two large, the other medium, and the other smaller
Item. As to the rest of my household furniture and wares found to be part of my estate after my death, I order my trustee to make an inventory.
Item. I order that a medium-sized box and the medium-sized basin be given to my sister Agustina de Ampuero, and so it is my will.
Item. I order that all of my slaves [the word "sisters" has been crossed out] receive thick flannel for their mourning clothes, and my sister receive flannel from Castile, of the blue kind, and a veil.
Item. A used chair
Item. Two small tables and two benches for sitting
Item. A large mortar and a skillet, and a new pot, and another used one, two grills, a large, shallow pan for watering, and three brass candlesticks

And, in order to carry out this testament and its contents and pay for its dispositions, I name as my executors the *licentiate* Diego de Ocampo, priest, and my sister Agustina de Ampuero y Barba, and as trustee of my estate, I name the above-mentioned *licentiate* Diego de Ocampo. I give them complete power *in solidum* for the use and exercise of the said execution. I authorize them to appear in court and claim what they may deem necessary, and I allow them to issue deeds of payment and to cover all expenses that may arise and make all the decisions that may be required in the execution of this will, in all ways and cases, for as long as they may need even if it exceeds the period of one year and one day established by law to carry out this execution.

Once this testament and its dispositions have been carried out and paid, I leave and name my soul as the universal heir of whatever might remain of my estate, debts,

y en la forma que se lo dejo tratado y comunicado con intervención del dicho padre Francisco de Soria, de la Compañía de Jesús, mi *confesor,* sin que ninguna *justicia* eclesiástica ni secular les pidan cuentas dello porque yo les relevo de ello por la mucha satisfacción que de los susodichos tengo, atento a que no tengo herederos forzosos ascendientes ni descendientes, y ésta es mi última voluntad.

Y por la presente revoco y anulo y doy por ningunos y de ningún valor ni efecto otros cualesquiera testamentos, codicilos, poderes para testar y otras últimas *disposiciones* que antes de ésta haya hecho y otorgado, por escrito o de palabra o en otra manera, que quiero que no valgan ni hagan fe en juicio ni fuera del salvo este presente testamento que ahora hago y otorgo, que quiero que se guarde, cumpla y ejecute por mi última voluntad en aquella vía y forma que mejor haya lugar de derecho. En testimonio de lo cual otorgué el presente, que es hecho en la ciudad de los Reyes [Lima] en 28 de febrero de 1651. Y la dicha otorgante, a quien yo el presente *escribano* doy fe [que] conozco, no firmó porque dijo no saber firmar. A su ruego, lo firmó un testigo siendo llamados y rogados por testigos Gregorio de Herrera, *escribano real,* José Lozano de Esquivel y Bartolomé Canelas y don Álvaro de Lereceda y Agustín de Barragán, presentes a ruego de la otorgante y por testigo Gregorio de Herrera, ante mí, Marcelo Antonio de Figueroa, *escribano* publico.

[Firmas]

[Testamento de María de Huancavelica, *morena* libre, de *casta folupa,* Lima, 1666][2]

En el nombre de Dios, amén, con cuyo principio todas las cosas tienen buen medio, loable y dichoso fin: Sepan cuantos esta carta de mi testamento, última y postrimera voluntad vieren cómo yo, María de Huancavelica, *morena* libre, de *casta folupa,* natural de *Etiopía* en *Guinea,* residente en esta ciudad de los Reyes [Lima] del Perú, hija de padres no conocidos, estando enferma en la cama de la enfermedad que Dios Nuestro Señor ha sido servido de me dar, y creyendo, como firme y verdaderamente creo, el misterio de la Santísima Trinidad, Padre e Hijo y Espíritu Santo, tres personas distintas y un solo Dios verdadero, y en todo lo demás que tiene, cree y confiesa la Santa Madre Iglesia Católica Romana, debajo de cuya fe y creencia he vivido y protesto vivir y morir como católica cristiana, y temiéndome de la muerte que es cosa natural a toda criatura humana, otorgo que hago y ordeno mi testamento en la forma y manera siguiente:

Primeramente, encomiendo mi alma a Dios Nuestro Señor que la creó y redimió con el precio infinito de su sangre y el cuerpo a la tierra de que fue formado.

Ídem. Quiero y es mi voluntad que, siendo Nuestro Señor servido de llevarme de esta presente vida, mi cuerpo sea sepultado en el Convento del Señor San Francisco de esta ciudad o a donde mis *albaceas* les pareciere, y se amortaje mi cuerpo con el

[2] Testamento e inventario de bienes de María de Huancavelica, morena libre, de casta folupa, Albacea: Gracia de la Paz, *negra folupa* libre, Archivo Arzobispal de Lima, Tribunal de Bienes de Difuntos 69:6, 1666, 70 folios.

rights, and actions. My executors together with the Jesuit Father Francisco de Soria will ensure that this is done in the way and form that I have expressed and communicated with them, and they will not be held accountable by any ecclesiastical or secular justice, because I relieve them of such, due to the high esteem in which I hold these persons and to the fact that I do not have any heirs, and this is my last will.

And through this document, I hereby revoke all former wills, codicils, powers to make a will, and testamentary dispositions of every nature and kind heretofore made by me in word or writing or in any other way, and I do not want them to be valid nor can they be used in or outside court, except for this one that I now declare as my testament, and I want it to be carried out and executed as my last will in the way that follows best what is prescribed by law, in faith of which I granted this testament in the City of Kings [Lima] on the twenty-eighth of February of 1651. And the said testator, whom I, the notary, testify that I know, did not sign it because she stated that she did not know how to, and at her request, a witness signed on her behalf, being called and requested as witnesses Gregorio de Herrera, royal notary, José Lozano de Esquivel, Bartolomé Canelas, Don Álvaro de Lereceda, Agustín de Barragán, all of whom were present at the request of the testator, and Gregorio de Herrera served as witness. In witness thereof, I, Marcelo Antonio de Figueroa, public notary.

[Signatures]

[Last Will and Testament of María de Huancavelica, Free Black Woman of the *Folupa Nation,* Lima, 1666]

In the name of God, amen, in whose beginning all things have their just, praiseworthy, and fortunate end: Know, those who read this last will and testament, that I, María de Huancavelica, a free black woman of the *Folupa nation,* native of Ethiopia in *Guinea,* resident of the City of Kings [Lima] in Peru, daughter of unknown parents, being sick in bed of an illness that Our Lord God has seen fit to give me and believing as I firmly and truly believe in the mystery of the most Holy Trinity, the Father, the Son, and the Holy Spirit, three distinct persons in one true God, and in all the rest that the Holy Mother Roman Catholic Church believes, confesses, and teaches, under whose faith and belief I have lived and I profess to live and die as a Catholic Christian, and fearful of death, which is consubstantial to all human creatures, I hereby make and declare my last will and testament in the following way and form:

First of all, I entrust my soul to Our Lord God, who created it and redeemed it with the infinite price of his blood, and my body shall return to the dust from which it was formed.

Item. I want and it is my will that, once Our Lord sees fit to take me from this present life, my body be buried in the Convent of Saint Francis in this city or in the place that my executors deem most appropriate, and that my body be shrouded with the habit of Saint Francis to earn the graces and indulgences that it brings, and a

hábito del Señor San Francisco para ganar las gracias e *indulgencias* que están concedidas, y acompañe a mi entierro la cruz alta, cura y sacristán de la parroquia y en cuanto al demás acompañamiento y forma de mi entierro [lo] dejo a disposición de mis *albaceas,* y el día de mi entierro, si fuere hora, o, si no, el día que pareciera a mis *albaceas* se diga la misa cantada de cuerpo presente ofrendada de pan vino, y será como es costumbre, y se pague todo ello de mis bienes.

Ídem. Mando a las mandas forzosas y acostumbradas, a todas ellas, dos *pesos* con que los aparto de mis bienes.

Ídem. Mando para redimir niños *cautivos* que están en tierras de moros diez *pesos* de ocho *reales,* y se entregue una parte legítima.

Ídem. Mando a los Lugares Santos de Jerusalén donde se obró nuestra redención otros diez *pesos,* los cuales se entreguen al padre que pide esta limosna.

Ídem. Declaro que no debo cosa alguna. Declárolo para que conste.

Ídem. Declaro por mis bienes los siguientes:

Ídem. Declaro que me debe Juan de Villegas Álvarez, labrador, dos mil *pesos* de a ocho *reales* por escritura que en mi favor otorgó el susodicho ante *escribano,* que tengo entre mis papeles. Declárolo para que conste.

Ídem. Declaro que me debe Antonio *Carabalí* trescientos y cincuenta *pesos* de a ocho *reales* que le presté en *reales* para su libertad, los cuales le remito y perdono al susodicho para que no se le pida cosa alguna, y así suplico a mis *albaceas* no le pidan nada porque ésta es mi voluntad.

Ídem. Declaro que me debe Jacinta, de *casta folupa,* cuatrocientos *pesos* de a ocho *reales* de resto de ochocientos *pesos* que presté para su libertad. Mando se cobre de la susodicha los dichos *pesos,* y no más.

Ídem. Declaro por mis esclavas a María, de *casta folupa,* la cual quiero y es mi voluntad luego que yo fallezca sea libre la susodicha, y con sólo testimonio de esta cláusula y fallecimiento goce de su libertad sin otro recaudo ni instrumento alguno por ser así mi voluntad, por lo bien que me ha servido la susodicha.

María, de *casta* mandinga, la cual quiero y es mi voluntad que dando la susodicha u otra persona por ella trescientos *pesos* de a ocho *reales* sea libre y se le otorgue por mis *albaceas carta de libertad,* y no pueda ser vendida en más cantidad y, mientas no diere los dichos trescientos *pesos* para su libertad, quiero que la susodicha pague de *jornal* tan solamente a los dichos mis *albaceas* cuatro *pesos* de a ocho *reales* cada mes, y así lo declaro.

Ambrosio *Folupo,* quiero y es mi voluntad que dando el susodicho trescientos *pesos* de a ocho *reales* sea libre y se le otorgue libertad por mis *albaceas* y, si diere alguna [persona] por el susodicho los dichos *pesos,* no ha de ser vendido por más cantidad que los dichos trescientos *pesos,* y que, en el entretanto que da los dichos *pesos,* haya de dar a los dichos mis *albaceas* cuatro *pesos* cada mes, y ésta es mi voluntad.

Antón *Folupo,* quiero y es mi voluntad que dando el susodicho doscientos y cincuenta *pesos* de a ocho *reales* sea libre y se le otorgue libertad por mis *albaceas* y no ha de poder ser vendido en más cantidad que los dichos doscientos y cincuenta *pesos,* y, en el ínterin que no diese los dichos *pesos,* ha de ser obligado de pagar a los dichos mis *albaceas* cuatro *pesos* de a ocho *reales* de *jornal* cada mes;

presiding cross, priest, and sacristan from my parish accompany my burial. And with regard to the rest of the retinue and details of my burial, I leave them to the discretion of my executors, and I order that the day of my burial, or if not, the day deemed appropriate by my executors, a funeral Mass be celebrated with my body present that includes offerings of bread and wine, and it must be done as is customary and paid for from my estate.

Item. I set aside from my estate two *pesos* to pay for the customary and obligatory alms.

Item. I order ten *pesos* of eight *reales* to pay the ransom of captive children in Moorish lands, and it must come from a legitimate part of my estate.

Item. I order another ten *pesos* to be sent to the Holy Sites of Jerusalem where our Holy Redemption took place and to be given to the priest who asks for these alms.

Item. I declare that I do not owe anything. I declare it so that there is no doubt.

Item. I declare as my assets the following:

Item. I declare that the laborer Juan de Villegas Álvarez owes me two thousand *pesos* of eight *reales* according to a notarized document that I have among my papers. I declare it so that there may be no doubt.

Item. I declare that Antonio *Carabalí* owes me 350 *pesos* of eight *reales* that I lent him for his *manumission.* I pardon and forgive what I lent him for his freedom so that nothing more is asked of him, and in the same way, I implore my executors not to ask anything more of him because such is my will.

Item. I declare that Jacinta of the *Folupa nation* owes me four hundred *pesos* of eight *reales* of the eight hundred *pesos* that I lent her for her *manumission.* I order that the four hundred still owed be collected, and nothing additional.

Item. I declare as my slave María, of the *Folupa nation,* and I order and it is my will that after my death she be manumitted, and she needs only this clause and my death to obtain her freedom, without collection of any payment nor the writing of any other document, and this is my will because of how well she has served me.

[I declare as my slave] María, of the Mandinga *nation,* and I order and it is my will that she be freed and my executors give her the deed of *manumission* upon payment by her or by any other person of three hundred *pesos* of eight *reales,* and that she must not be sold for more than the said amount and, in the meantime until she can pay the full amount of three hundred *pesos* for her freedom, I want her to pay only four *pesos* of eight *reales* of wages each month to my executors, and this I order.

[I declare as my slave] Ambrosio *Folupo,* and I order and it is my will that upon his payment of three hundred *pesos* of eight *reales,* he be freed and my executors give him the deed of *manumission* and that he must not be sold for more than the said amount, and, in the meantime, until he can pay the full amount, he will be obligated to pay to my executors four *pesos* of eight *reales* of wages each month.

[I declare as my slave] Antón *Folupo,* and I order and it is my will that upon his payment of two hundred fifty *pesos* of eight *reales,* he be freed and my executors give him the deed of *manumission,* and he cannot be sold for an amount above the stated two hundred fifty *pesos,* and, in the meantime until he can pay the full amount, he will be obligated to pay four *pesos* of eight *reales* of wages each month.

Susana *Folupa,* quiero y es mi voluntad que dando la susodicha doscientos *pesos* de a ocho *reales* para mi entierro sea libre y se le otorgue *carta de libertad* en su favor por mi *albacea* y no ha de ser vendida en mas cantidad.

Ídem. Declaro dos tembladeras pequeñas de plata, una caja de Panamá y un baúl y la ropa de vestir que constara por *inventario.*

Ídem. Declaro que [tengo] una saya y una mantilla de bayeta negra y la saya de picote y un jubón de [ilegible] de Rafaela Zapata y asimismo tengo en mi poder, de la susodicha, ciento y cinco *pesos* de a ocho *reales* todo lo cual quiero que se le entregue por mis *albaceas* dando recibo o ante *escribano.*

Ídem. Declaro que me es deudora María, de *casta* conga, de cantidad de *pesos.* Mando que se le cobren tan solamente a la susodicha cincuenta *pesos* de a ocho *reales* y lo demás se lo remito y perdono a la susodicha porque me encomiende a Dios.

Ídem. Declaro que debo a Manuel Espadero, *negro,* de resto de unos *reales* que me entregó María *Folupa,* su mujer difunta, treinta y cinco *pesos* de a ocho *reales.* Mando se le paguen al susodicho y asimismo se le entregue unos brazaletes de corales y una cajita pequeña dando recibo dello.

Y para cumplir y pagar este mi testamento y las mandas y legados del, dejo y nombro por mis *albaceas* al *licenciado* Juan [¿Zapata de Henao?], presbítero, mi *confesor,* y a Gracia de la Paz, *Folupa,* [y] por tenedora de bienes a la dicha Gracia *Folupa,* para que los susodichos entren en los dichos mis bienes y los vendan y rematen en *almoneda* o fuera della y de su procedido cumplan y paguen este mi testamento y las mandas del, para lo cual les doy poder de *albaceas* y en bastante forma y les prorrogo todo el tiempo que hubieren menester demás del año que el derecho concede.

Ídem. Declaro que me dio a guardar Miguel *Folupo* treinta y tres *pesos.* Mando se le paguen de mis bienes.

Ídem. Declaro que me dio a guardar Simón *Folupa* veinte *pesos* mando que se le paguen de mis bienes.

Ídem. Declaro que compré de una *parda* que asiste en el hospital de San Bartolomé, llamada María de Bilbao, una *negra,* María *Folupa,* en precio de trescientos y cincuenta *pesos* por escritura ante Francisco de Acuña, *escribano* de Su Majestad, declaro que pertenece la dicha esclava a Juliana *Folupa* por cuanto la susodicha me dio los dichos *pesos* para el dicho efecto, y así lo declaro para el descargo de mi conciencia.

Ídem. Declaro que tengo en mi poder una tembladera y una cuchara de plata de Susana *Folupa* que me la dio a guardar. Mando se le entregue.

Y en el remanente que quedare de todos mis bienes, deudas, derechos y acciones dejo y nombro por heredera mi alma para que lo que así quedare líquido se imponga una *capellanía* de misas y patronazgo de legos, la cual ha de fundar el dicho *licenciado* Juan [¿Zapata de Henao?], mi *albacea* y *confesor,* a quien dejo por patrón y *capellán* della para que el susodicho haga los nombramientos de patrones que le pareciere para después de sus días, y ha de dotar la limosna de cada misa en la cantidad que le pareciere y según y como se lo tengo comunicado, la cual dicha fundación [se haga] para luego que yo fallezca, y no se ha de pedir ni tomar cuenta por ningún juez por ser así mi voluntad, y en la dicha fundación pondrá todas las cláusulas necesarias atento a que no tengo herederos forzosos ascendientes ni descendientes que me puedan [heredar].

[I declare as my slave] Susana *Folupa,* and I order and it is my will that upon her payment of two hundred *pesos* of eight *reales* for my burial she be freed and that my executors give her the deed of *manumission* and that she should not be sold for more.

Item. I declare two small double-handled bowls [or cups] of silver, a box from Panamá, a trunk, and the clothing that will be made clear in the inventory.

Item. I declare that [I have] a skirt and a shawl of black flannel, a skirt of silk, and a bodice of [illegible] that belongs to Rafaela Zapata and one hundred and five *pesos* of eight *reales* that also belong to her. I want my executors to return all these things to her and that she give them either a written receipt or that the transaction be done in front of a notary.

Item. I declare that María of the Congo *nation* is indebted to me in a certain amount of *pesos.* I order that only fifty *pesos* of eight *reales* be collected from her, and I forgive her the rest on the condition that she pray for me to God.

Item. I declare that I owe Manuel Espadero, a black man, a total of thirty-five *pesos* of eight *reales,* the remainder of some *reales* that his deceased wife, María *Folupa,* gave to me. I order that he be paid this amount and also that he be given some bracelets made of coral and a small box, and he must give a receipt for it.

And to fulfill and pay for this testament and the bequests and legacies in it, I leave and name as my executors my confessor, the *licentiate* Juan [Zapata de Henao?], presbyter, and Gracia de la Paz, of the *Folupa nation,* [and] as the trustee, the said Gracia *Folupa.* And I grant them power as executors to organize, sell, and resolve my estate at public auction or otherwise, in order to fulfill and pay for this last will and testament and its bequests, and I also grant them all the time they may require to do so even if it exceeds the year that the law concedes.

Item. I declare that Miguel *Folupo* gave to me thirty-three *pesos* to safeguard. I order that it be paid back to him from by assets.

Item. I declare that Simón *Folupa* gave me twenty *pesos* to safeguard, and I order that it be paid back to him from my assets.

Item. I declare that I bought a black woman, María *Folupa,* at a price of 350 *pesos* as certified in writing by Francisco de Acuña, royal notary, from a *parda* woman named María de Bilbao who assists at the hospital of Saint Bartholomew, and I declare that the said slave belongs to Juliana *Folupa,* who gave me the money for this transaction, and I declare it for the unburdening of my conscience.

Item. I declare that I have in my possession a double-handled bowl [or cup] and a silver spoon belonging to Susana *Folupa* that she gave me to safeguard. I order that it be returned to her.

And I leave and name my soul as heir of whatever assets, debts, rights, and actions might remain from the liquidation of my estate, and it is my wish that this money be used to establish a chaplaincy, which should be founded by the *licentiate* Juan [Zapata de Henao?], my executor and confessor, whom I leave as its patron and chaplain. And he is allowed to name his successor after he dies, and he can establish the alms to be given for each Mass according to what I have communicated to him, and this chaplaincy must be established after I die, and no judge should interfere because this is my will, and he can establish all the necessary clauses according to his judgment because I do not have any heirs who can inherit my estate.

Ídem. Mando al hospital del señor San Bartolomé doce *pesos* de a ocho *reales.*

Ídem. Mando al dulce nombre de Jesús contra los juramentos seis *pesos* de a ocho *reales.*

Ídem. Mando para la crianza de los niños huérfanos doce *pesos* de a ocho *reales* con cargo de que acompañen mi cuerpo el día de mi entierro.

Ídem. Declaro que tengo en *reales* novecientos *pesos* de a ocho *reales,* poco más o menos, los que pareciere de que se hará *inventario.*

Y con esto revoco y anulo y doy por ninguno y de ninguna voz ni efecto todos y cualesquiera testamentos, codicilos, poderes para testar y otras últimas *disposiciones* que antes de éste haya hecho y otorgado por escrito o de palabra, que quiero que no valgan ni hagan fe en juicio ni fuera del salvo este testamento que ahora otorgo que quiero que valga por tal o por aquella escritura que más y mejor haya lugar en derecho, en cuyo testimonio lo otorgue, que es hecho en la ciudad de los Reyes [Lima] del Perú en seis días del mes de enero de 1666. Y la otorgante que yo el *escribano* doy fe [que] conozco y que a lo que pareció, según las preguntas que le hice, estaba en su entero juicio y memoria natural, y así lo otorgó, y no firmó porque dijo no saber, y a su ruego lo firmó un testigo. . . .

Item. I order that twelve *pesos* of eight *reales* be sent to the Hospital of Saint Bartholomew.

Item. I order that six *pesos* of eight *reales* be sent to the Sweet Name of Jesus against Blasphemies.

Item. I order that twelve *pesos* of eight *reales* be sent for the rearing of the orphan children on the condition that they accompany my body the day of my burial.

Item. I declare that I have in *reales* a total of nine hundred *pesos* of eight *reales,* more or less, and the exact amount will be determined in the inventory.

I hereby revoke all former wills and testamentary dispositions of every nature and kind heretofore made by me in word or in writing or in any other way and I do not want them to be valid nor can they be used in or outside court, except for this one that I now declare as my testament, and I want it to be carried out and executed as my last will in the way that best follows the law. And I testify that this testament is done in the City of Kings [Lima] of Peru, the sixth day of the month of January of the year 1666. And the testator, whom, I, the notary, certify that I know, seemed to be in complete possession of her judgment and natural memory, judging from her answer to the questions that I asked her, and this is what she ordered, and she did not sign it because she said that she did not know how to write, and at her request a witness signed it. . . .

8

To Live as a *Pueblo:* A Contentious Endeavor, El Cobre, Cuba, 1670s–1790s[1]

María Elena Díaz

A *Pueblo* Founded by *Royal Slaves*

Spanning a long period of some 120 years, the four document excerpts in this chapter provide a rare composite view through time of an "unusual" community of people of African ancestry in colonial Latin America. The community was founded by "*royal slaves,*" that is, slaves belonging to the king of Spain. After the Spanish Crown confiscated the copper mines of Santiago del Prado (also known as El Cobre) in the 1670s, the slaves who had worked in the previously private mining settlement became the king's slaves.The transformation from "private" mining slaves to *royal slaves* produced a number of significant—even radical—changes in these enslaved subjects' identity and in their living and working arrangements. Foremost among these was the opportunity to found a *pueblo* in the newly deprivatized mining jurisdiction.[2]

The various direct and mediated voices represented in these documents evoke the difficulties that this controversial community faced after its inception in the 1670s. The texts also reflect the range of social categories, self-representations, and identities that these bonded subjects deployed in their lives and dealings with the state throughout the period in question. Of particular interest is the way they initially negotiated the discursive and practical meaning of the abstract category of *royal slavery* and combined it with a *pueblo* affiliation. In fact, one of the most fascinating aspects of the present case is precisely the communal identification as a *pueblo* that these subjects conjured and endeavored to make good despite their racial and ambiguous enslaved status.

Communities can take many formal and informal shapes, and not all communities can be considered *pueblos.* In the Spanish empire, *pueblos* were communal corporations with some land rights and limited self-governance, and they constituted political units within the broader imperial polity. Various legal, political, social, and cultural presuppositions underwrote these entities. For instance, only free people could constitute a corporate *pueblo* (enslaved subjects could not). Free family households were the basic building blocks of such communities. Local citizenship (*vecindad*) entailed rights to land and to local self-government by way of a municipal council (*cabildo*). In many localities local citizenship may have been constrained by "purity of blood"

[1] See Maps 5 and 11.

[2] For a quasi-ethnographic study of the transformations that took place in various spheres of life and work, see Díaz, *The Virgin.* For an examination of changes in specific areas, see Díaz, "Conjuring Identities" and "Mining Women."

(that is, racial) considerations. In the New World, however, *indios* constituted autonomous corporate *pueblos* of their own based on a separate jurisdiction known as the Republics of Indians (Díaz, "Conjuring Identities"). Given some of these legal and political criteria, a *pueblo* of *royal slaves* represented an anomalous formation in the Spanish colonial world.

Other criteria of affiliation to *pueblos* included territorial origin by birth (although marriage and long-term residence could also serve as bases of inclusion). Christian identification was paramount for membership, and at the center of every duly constituted *pueblo* there was a parish church. *Pueblo* identities were linked to the performance of local traditions and festivities, most of which had a religious character at the time (for example, celebrations of local patron saints). In the case of El Cobre, there was even a Marian shrine that may have helped legitimize this unusual community of *royal slaves* as a *pueblo.* Although *Maroon* communities of escaped slaves emerged on the margins of the colonial world (see Chapters 2 and 5), black corporate *pueblos* within the colonial body polity seem to have been rarer, even in the case of free people of African ancestry. Historians are beginning to find them scattered throughout the vast peripheries and frontiers of empire partly incorporated into the Crown's broader defense projects (see, for example, Granda; Landers; Taylor).

More generally, however, free and enslaved subjects of African descent lived in Spanish towns and cities or in plantations and other production locations and did not tend to constitute autonomous corporate *pueblos* of their own, particularly if they were bonded subjects.[3]

Enslaved status in the colonial context constituted virtual "social death" and exclusion from the body polity (Patterson, 1–14). Although no longer private slaves, most of the former mining slaves of El Cobre remained juridically enslaved to the king (or the state) and, in principle, they remained "socially dead" subjects with few, if any, rights and a legal condition in many ways analogous to that of chattel. Notwithstanding their bonded status, the *royal slaves* of El Cobre were able to capitalize on what they deemed to be their special status and relation to the king, linking it, with some success, to a number of prerogatives, including the option to live as a *pueblo.* Part of this case's interest lies in how the collective identity and the prerogatives of this anomalous community of enslaved people were negotiated and justified.

To be sure, *royal slaves* did not abound in the Spanish empire. Most bonded subjects throughout the Americas were private slaves subject to private masters. But the state did have some slaves at its disposal who were employed in public works and fortification projects. The strategic frontier location of this mining jurisdiction in a multinational Caribbean contributed to the concessions the community was able to obtain as the *royal slaves* took on an important role in the Crown's defensive system.[4]

[3] The most recent overview of African slavery in colonial Latin America can be found in chapter 1 of Andrews, *Afro-Latin America.*

[4] For the role of blacks in the Spanish Crown's imperial defense system, see Deschamps Chapeaux; Klein; and Vinson. For the Caribbean as a frontier region, see Pérez (39–45). See also the map section in Díaz, *El Cobre.*

No less surprising is how far these *royal slaves* mobilized to defend their right to live as a *pueblo* against the attacks of various sectors of colonial society, including some governors, royal officials, and, especially, the heirs of the former private owners of the mines. By the end of the eighteenth century the community had taken the extraordinary step of sending one of their own local leaders to Madrid to directly oversee a litigation process that dragged on for fifteen years over the community's collective freedom and the legality of the heirs' rights to the mining jurisdiction.

There are no cases on record to date of enslaved people in colonial Latin America, or for that matter of free people of African ancestry, who have litigated collectively so far up in the judicial system.[5]

This community's strong engagement with the colonial state throughout the years resulted in the production of abundant documentation. Moreover, as a result of the above-mentioned litigation in Madrid, documentary material that would have normally been scattered throughout different local and state archives (if not altogether lost) was carefully compiled into a legal dossier and subsequently conserved as a unified record in the Archive of the Indies. That opportune intervention has led to a particularly strong preservation of Afro-Latino voices in the record for this case.

Although some of these voices were mediated by the hand of an amanuensis—or perhaps a scribe—and by the conventions of the various genres to which their texts subscribed, at least two documents were allegedly written directly by literate subjects in this community. The selections in this chapter include a petition to authorities and three letters with varying purposes. All four constitute rich and unusual documents for the narratives they display, the representations of collective self they invoke, the remarkable claims they put forth, the events and details of life they portray, and the uses of writing among free and enslaved subjects mostly associated with oral culture. All things considered, many factors conspire to make of El Cobre a truly remarkable case study, one that opens up unexpected vistas of the Afro-Latin experience in the Iberian black Atlantic world.

Historical Background

When the Spanish Crown deprivatized the copper mining jurisdiction of El Cobre (from the Spanish for "copper"), some 270 former private mining slaves then became the king's slaves. By 1773, the community had flourished into a hybrid *pueblo* of some 1,200 inhabitants, of which 65 percent were *royal slaves,* 33 percent were free people of color, mostly relatives of the *royal slaves,* and 2 percent were private slaves (belonging to the clergy and to other members of the community, both free and *royal slaves*).[6]

[5] Although it was not uncommon for slaves in Iberian colonial societies to access local courts to seek redress regarding a series of issues including individual *manumission,* ill treatment, and other matters, few, if any, are known to have made it to the highest court of appeal in Madrid. For slaves' use of the courts, see Aguirre (181–210); Chaves (108–26); Díaz, *The Virgin* (285–313).

[6] For an account of these personal or private slaves and of slaveholding in El Cobre, see Díaz, *The Virgin* (179–98).

The transformation into a *pueblo* came to entail among other things a collective land grant, four militia battalions, and even a local *cabildo* (or municipal self-government) of *royal slaves.* Other transformations included *royal slaves'* appropriation of some mining resources and their creation of a small, informal, and mostly female mining industry in the village.

An important shrine to the Virgin of Charity also flourished in this black *pueblo* after 1670. That local Marian tradition became so important that more than two and a half centuries later Our Lady of Charity of El Cobre became the symbol of the Cuban nation, although by then her memory as the local patroness of a black *pueblo* had faded away.[7]

Yet the juridical and political status of this community remained tenuous throughout subsequent years. In the 1770s, the Crown decided to reprivatize the mines and return them to the heirs of the private contractor Don Juan de Eguiluz. That decision resulted in the most serious challenge to the *royal slaves'* collective existence as a *pueblo* in a whole century. After the new generation of owners repossessed the mining jurisdiction, they removed, "re-enslaved," and even sold away the *royal slaves*—whom they considered their private slaves—and demanded rents for land from those who had become freemen and -women and could not be captured as repossessed slaves.

In the face of such an attack the besieged community sent Gregorio Cosme Osorio, a literate freedman from El Cobre, to Spain to contest the Crown's decision and to litigate their claims. Sponsored by the free *cobreros* (natives of El Cobre) remaining in the *pueblo,* Osorio represented his compatriots in the metropolitan tribunals and corresponded with them over different aspects of the case.

In 1800, the community's long endeavor culminated in a royal edict granting collective emancipation to all the *cobreros,* formal recognition as a corporate community, and land rights.[8] The community's legal victory, however, opened up a new period of local struggle to bring about the local implementation of some of the concessions obtained in Madrid. Yet, freedom and the right to live as local citizens of a corporate community had been legally secured—at least for the first three or four decades of the nineteenth century.

A Letter from a Slave to His Mistress, 1672

The first two documents belong to the initial transitional decade of the 1670s and point to the transformations that took place as the former private mining slaves became a community of *royal slaves.* The first document, a letter allegedly written by a literate slave to his mistress in Havana, is of enormous interest in all its apparent simplicity. It not only chronicles the transformations taking place in the mining settlement barely two years after the Crown's confiscation of the mines but exposes as well

[7] See Díaz, *The Virgin,* for the emergence and development of this local Marian shrine (95–145) and the local mining industry (199–223). For the present significance of the cult to the Virgin of Charity and other related Afro-Cuban traditions, see Díaz, *El Cobre.*

[8] The status of the community was also upgraded from *pueblo* (village) to *villa* (town). See Diaz, *The Virgin* (325–27).

a web of conflictive voices, stances, claims, and understandings colliding over what royal slavery entailed at that early crucial moment. Note in particular the oblique association made by these former private slaves between the practical meaning of royal slavery and having become *horros,* or free.

Nicolás de Montenegro's own critical voice betrays his alliance with the interests of the Eguiluz family, which until recently had owned the rights to the mines and their slaves. It is the voice of a privileged family slave betraying a conventional understanding of slavery and pining for a previous order of things now rapidly falling apart in front of his very own eyes. There is, however, a hidden history further layering Montenegro's stance in this document. Although not evident from the text, we know that he was related by blood to his mistress Doña Paula, and, in this sense, their bond also embodied the disavowed hidden genealogies that often linked master and slave classes in colonial slave regimes.

Whether aware of it or not, Nicolás de Montenegro was the slave son of Don Juan de Eguiluz, the long-deceased private contractor of the mines, and his slave Paula de Eguiluz, who was prosecuted for witchcraft by the Inquisition of Cartagena de Indias when Nicolás was only an infant (see Chapter 11). To complicate identities and genealogies even further (and to note a slight Freudian twist), Eguiluz's own daughter was, like his slave mistress, named Paula de Eguiluz. In short, Doña Paula, who shared a name with Nicolás' mother, was also his stepsister and owner and may have raised him as a house slave after his mother's banishment from El Cobre in 1622. Nicolás could have identified with his paternal family's house and property—even regarding it partly as his own—in an analogous move to that of the *royal slaves'* identification with the king and his property (Díaz, *The Virgin,* 54–73).

Reading this letter today, we might consider the following questions: What were the conventional understandings of slavery to which Montenegro seems to subscribe? What kind of arrangements and prerogatives did these slaves associate with their new status as *royal slaves?* Did Montenegro identify himself as one of them? In what ways was the old social order of the collapsing and a new one emerging as Montenegro writes?

Petition from Captain Juan Moreno to Judge Don Antonio Matienzo, Mines of Santiago del Prado, 1677

The second document constitutes a "foundational" text insofar as in it enslaved subjects, in this case *creole royal slaves,* display for the first time claims related to a *patria* and *pueblo* identity. The context for this petition was a royal order that came down in 1677, once the Crown decided how to dispose of its confiscated property in the recently deprivatized jurisdiction. The edict ordered the transfer of part of the male slave population to work in the fortification projects of Havana and others could be allowed to purchase their own freedom.

This order would have meant the dispersal of the enslaved population and in effect the breakup of the community. The *royal slaves* responded with a political act of flight to the mountains and from there negotiated their stay in El Cobre as a community, thereby demonstrating that petitions and discursive negotiations of identity

had to be backed up with political action to be effective. The document is the first on record in which these enslaved subjects make collective claims.

Many other petitions would follow in the following century. In this one, the petitioning subjects portrayed themselves in various ways, including as soldiers.[9] Given the frontier character of this location in eastern Cuba (see Map 11), military service had special significance (Pérez, 39–45).

The title of captain that Juan Moreno held, however, did not at this time refer as much to a military rank as to authority in the enslaved community, perhaps along the lines of a *mandador*, as in the case of Nicolás de Montenegro. Captain Juan Moreno coauthored another foundational text ten years later: a deposition of the "apparition" of the Virgin of Charity that he had witnessed when he was a boy.[10] Perhaps his authority was partly related to his participation in that holy event of the past and the Christian identification it evoked.

Note that Moreno offered to allow the slaves to pay for their own freedom at some point in the future, a well-established practice in Cuba and many locations of Spanish colonial society that was known as *coartación* (self-purchase). Although a few members of the community eventually purchased their freedom, most never did. Since it was unlikely that they could come up with the sums required to purchase the freedom of 270 slaves, the allusion to *coartación* may have been a formality to strengthen their case for the main requested concession.

Moreno was not literate, so an ally or protector in the nearby city of Santiago de Cuba may have redacted the coarse petition. Despite the formulaic opening and closing, the text invokes a wide range of affiliations that the slaves claimed—as soldiers, family heads, and members of a *pueblo* and a local homeland. These affiliations could presumably trump the sheer property-like or "socially dead" status of enslaved subjects and their absolute subservience to a master's will. Questions we might consider include the following: What loyalties and claims were implicitly associated with these identities? How would they override conventional understandings of slaves as chattel? What concessions did the petition request? How did it make its case? What practices among these enslaved people seem more striking to you? How do Moreno's voice and account compare with those of Montenegro?

A 1792 Letter from Martín de Salazar Denouncing Abuses

The third and fourth documents are set more than a century later, in the 1790s. They were produced in the context of fighting back the threat of reprivatization of the mining jurisdiction and the brutal dismantling of the community as it had existed for more than a century. The identities laid out in the first two documents were tested and even reworked at this point as the *cobreros* now claimed full freedom.

This set of documents provides a window into the development of the *pueblo* during the previous century and the identities that were currently deployed. They also

9 For a detailed analysis of this petition and its implications, see Díaz, *The Virgin* (74–94).

10 See period maps and Moreno's "apparition" document in Díaz, *El Cobre.*

show events unfolding locally and in Madrid, as Gregorio Cosme Osorio represented the community in the Council of Indies and the Supreme Council of Justice denouncing the heirs' attacks and violent repossession of the jurisdiction and claiming collective freedom. The communication network established through metropolitan and local correspondence shows how the community's transatlantic litigation efforts were coordinated.

Specifically, the third document constitutes a chronicle of the atrocities and violence perpetrated by the heirs of the Eguiluz family against the *cobreros,* and more specifically against free members of the *pueblo.* The heirs had staged a private expedition akin to those of slave hunters to reclaim "their" escaped slaves who had taken refuge with their families in El Cobre and to collect rents for the use of land and wages for the labor of enslaved *cobreros* living on their own in the *pueblo.* Note the author's portrayal of all the subjects as *cobreros* to highlight their status as native members of the *pueblo* of El Cobre and as "captives" to refer to (illegally) enslaved *cobreros.* Why is the choice of language important?

The document also provides a glimpse into the internal orderings of the community: living arrangements; kinds of property holding; internal class, race, and gender distinctions; honor-related criteria and claims; and the mix of free and enslaved individuals within families.[11] Through this document, the *cobreros* not only communicated local news to their man in Madrid but also filed a formal grievance that Cosme Osorio would incorporate into the community's dossier.

Although there were some literate *cobreros* in El Cobre, the redaction and writing of this text may have been in the hands of an attorney or *letrado.* In this sense it may be a mediated or coauthored text that also reveals the local networks, resources, and alliances of the *cobreros* in Cuba. A *cobrero* familiar with the narrated events would have had to describe them to the scribe.

How might a present-day reader construct a profile of the community from the bits and pieces of information provided in this text? For example, what kind of property did people in this community own? How may they have made a living? How significant do racial and color classifications seem to be? What other considerations seem important? Is gender significant in this narrative? What seem to be the assumptions on each side that feed the conflict between them?

Gregorio Cosme Osorio's 1795 Letter from Madrid

The fourth document was written directly by Gregorio Cosme Osorio and describes his role and travails as the community's *apoderado,* or legal representative, in Madrid. Although Cosme was a free *cobrero,* his wife and children had been among the *royal slaves* repossessed by the heirs. This letter reflects the kind of communication he maintained with his community back home during the more than twelve years he spent in the court of Madrid. Also important here is the significance attributed to litigation,

[11] For a study of some of these arrangements see Díaz, "Of Life and Freedom."

particularly given the enormous material and human resources required by such a community to pull off such a feat.

Readers may speculate on the significance of skills such as literacy in this community to sustain such an enterprise. Note Cosme's reference to El Cobre as a *villa* rather than as a *pueblo.* Of special interest here as well is Osorio's claim to have spoken to the king himself, a vague and uncompromising encounter that may well have happened, but that was also directed at enhancing his status in the community that sustained him.

What does this letter reveal about the work Osorio performed as the community's *apoderado* in the court of Madrid? What does the ability to send a representative to litigate in Madrid say about this community? How did Cosme portray himself and his work? How indispensable was literacy in this whole endeavor? Overall, what do these documents suggest about subordinate subjects' views and uses of legal venues for redress in the Spanish empire?

[Carta de Nicolás de Montenegro a doña Paula de Eguiluz, El Cobre, 1672][1]

Traslado de un capítulo de carta de Nicolás de Montenegro, esclavo *mulato* hijo de una esclava del contador Juan de Eguiluz, que es uno de los *mandadores* que el gobernador de [Santiago de] Cuba, don Andrés de Magaña tiene nombrados en la minas del cobre, en que trata de la materia de éstas, escrita de su letra y firma a la ciudad de la Habana, a doña Paula de Eguiluz y Montenegro. Su fecha en dichas minas, en siete de julio de 1672 años.

Dos tengo escritas y ésta tres y en éstas he avisado a mi Señora de lo que por acá ha pasado después que mi Señora falta de estas minas. Y ahora vuelvo a hacerlo en ésta de [las] muchas novedades que de hora a hora se ofrecen y suceden. . . . Mi Señora, en cuanto a los cobres del río ha sido y es sin *ajuste*. . . . el cobre es la moneda que corre hoy en día en las minas pues hombres y mujeres y niños no se ocupan de otra cosa desde que amanece hasta que anochece. . . . Queriendo yo estorbarlo me dijo Pedro Viojo que estas minas no las [re]conoce por de mi Señora doña Paula, sino por del rey. Y lo mismo todos los demás. . . . Antes eran [muchas las] soberbias de hombres y mujeres, como mi Señora sabe, pero hoy es cosa mucha pues dicen públicamente que son *horros*. . . . El *hato* de Barajagua lo arrendó el padre Ramos en doscientos *pesos*, sólo las yerbas, dejando libres las *monterías* para la gente de estas minas. Y no les pareció a su gusto porque dicen que Barajagua y las *monterías* es suyo todo, que el rey se los dio. . . . Miguel Congolo desde que mi Señora salió de estas minas se fue y plantó en la *covacha* y se ha aprovechado de todo el cacao de ambas cosechas de este año pasado. Y diciéndole yo cómo hacía eso, que aquellos cacaos son de mi Señora doña Paula, me respondió que son del rey y él también. Manuel del Río después que estuvo por su voluntad por allá en paseos vino a sólo acabar de ayudar [a] azotar estas minas de cobre.

[Petición de Juan Moreno al Juez don Antonio Matienzo, Minas de Santiago del Prado, 13 de julio de 1677][2]

El *capitán* Juan Moreno*, negro criollo* y natural de las minas de Santiago del Prado del Cobre de esta ciudad de [Santiago de] Cuba, por mí y en nombre de los demás *negros criollos* naturales de estas minas, esclavos que somos de Su Majestad, que Dios guarde, y particularmente los que fuéremos nombrados en la división y *alcance* . . . parecemos [ante *Vuestra Merced*] en la mejor vía y forma que haya lugar en derecho y decimos que por cuanto todos los más *negros* y *mulatos criollos* de estas minas somos casados y

[1] Copia con carta de don Antonio de Matta y Haro, 15 diciembre 1672, Ministerio de Cultura, Archivo General de Indias, Seville, Santo Domingo 104 [no folio numbering].

[2] Minas de Santiago del Prado, trece de julio de mil seiscientos setenta y siete, Ministerio de Cultura, Archivo General de Indias, Seville, Santo Domingo 1631, fols. 451, 424–52v, 425v.

[Letter from Nicolás de Montenegro to Doña Paula de Eguiluz, El Cobre, 1672][1]

Transcription of a chapter of the letter of Nicolás de Montenegro, *mulatto* slave son of a [female] slave of the accountant Juan de Eguiluz, who is one of the *mandadores* in the copper mines appointed by the governor of [Santiago de] Cuba, Don Andrés Magaña, where he deals with matters regarding the mines and written in his own hand and signature to Doña Paula de Eguiluz y Montenegro, who resides in the city of Havana. Dated in the said mines on July 7, 1672.

I have written two, and with this three, letters where I have given notice to my Lady of what has been happening since she left these mines and now I will again [write] in this one about the many new things that are taking place hour by hour. . . . My Lady, regarding the copper from the river, it has been [obtained] without [due] regulation [*ajuste*]. . . . Copper is the currency that nowadays moves around in the mines because men, women, and children occupy themselves in nothing else from sunrise to sunset. . . . And as I tried to stop him [from taking copper] Pedro Viojo said to me that he did not recognize these mines as belonging to my Lady Doña Paula but that they are the king's. All the others said the same. . . . Before there used to be too much arrogance among these men and women, as my Lady well knows, but today it is too much, for they say publicly that they are free [*horros*]. . . . Father Ramos rented the cattle ranch lands [*hato*] of Barajagua for two hundred *pesos,* but only the grass, leaving free the hunting grounds [*monterías*] for the people of these mines. And they did not like it because they say that Barajagua and the *monterías* are all theirs, that the king gave it to them. . . . Since my Lady left these mines, Miguel Congolo has set himself up in the shanty [*covacha*] and has taken advantage of all the cacao produced in both harvests this last year. And when I asked him how he could do that, that those cacaos belonged to my Lady Doña Paula, he answered me that they belonged to the king and so did he. Manuel del Río, after idling there on his own, came back only to help cause trouble in these copper mines.

[Juan Moreno's Petition to Judge Don Antonio Matienzo, Mines of Santiago del Prado, July 13, 1677]

Captain Juan Moreno, a *Creole* black/slave and native of the mines of Santiago del Prado of El Cobre in this city of [Santiago de] Cuba, in my name and on behalf of all the other *Creole* blacks/slaves natives of these mines, slaves that we are of His Majesty, may God bless him, and especially those who were named in the division and settlement . . . we approach [*Vuestra Merced,* Judge Matienzo] by way of the best means available by right and say that most of the *Creole* black and *mulatto* slaves of these

[1] Doña Paula de Eguiluz is the daughter of Juan de Eguiluz, who is the owner of the black slave woman of the same name (Paula de Eguiluz), protagonist of the documents in Chapter 11 of this volume.

tenemos nuestras familias que siempre hemos sustentado quieta y pacíficamente, estando ocupados cuando se ha ofrecido en el trabajo de las minas, [las] fábricas de la Santa Iglesia, y demás en que se nos ha ocupado en ocasiones de rebate. Y como leales vasallos de Su Majestad hemos acudido con toda prontitud a nuestra costa y mención, guardando y obedeciendo todas las órdenes de los superiores y demás *justicias* de la Ciudad de [Santiago de] Cuba en que nos han ocupado, así en esto como en *rancherías* y *palenques* de *negros* esclavos fugitivos de los *vecinos* de toda esta Isla [a quienes] hemos apresado. [Hemos estado] deseando siempre *mayores* ocasiones del Real Servicio [y] que nos ocuparan para conseguir acciones [militares] grandes. Que aunque no se nos premiaran sólo quedaremos contentos de haberlas conseguido. Y siendo como es esto tanta verdad, y se hallara entre nosotros estar con grande prevención para la ocasión y defensa de la *plaza* de [Santiago de] Cuba u otro cualquier lugar, que aunque es verdad que todos sus *vecinos* lo están también y que conseguirán cualquier acción, en todo, cuanto se ha ofrecido ocasión de alguna novedad, los Señores gobernadores nos han ocupado haciendo memoria de nosotros, aunque [seamos] *negros* humildes esclavos de Nuestro Rey y Señor, por haber reconocido quizá nuestro buen deseo.

Y ha venido a nuestra noticia que los que llegaremos a quedar en el *alcance* que dicen hará Nuestro Rey y Señor a nuestro amo don Francisco en muchos esclavos [que] se han de sacar por *Vuestra Merced* para llevarnos a la ciudad de la Habana. Y porque parece [que] el amor de nuestra *patria* y nuestros trabajos nos mueven a suplicar a *Vuestra Merced* que si es posible se nos conceda de merced que quedemos en nuestro *pueblo* pagando tributo, conforme el estilo que se dispusiere, mientras buscamos [los medios] para [comprar] nuestra libertad, o lo que más bien se dispusiere por derecho en que de equidad y piedad por *Vuestra Merced* debemos ser amparados en nombre de nuestro Rey y Señor [y] habiendo lugar para ello.

Por tanto, a *Vuestra Merced* pedimos y suplicamos nos haya por presentados mandando concedernos licencia, que será *justicia* y merced que pedimos y lo más [necesario? ilegible].

Juan Moreno

[Carta Martín de Salazar][3]

Cobre y Agosto 21 de 1792

Apuntamos los violentos estragos, atrocidades y maldades que hemos sufrido y actualmente estamos sufriendo y aguantando todos los libres del Cobre, en este cautiverio en estos once años y meses pasados con don Fernando Mancebo, uno de los herederos de dicho *pueblo.* Primeramente convocó y aprestó allá en [Santiago de] Cuba hombres y armó *cuadrilla* y sacó licencia para venir a cobrar lo que importaba el *jornal* de los *cobreros* que trabajaban en la población del territorio del Cobre que como les entregaron [a los herederos] los *cautivos* y todas las tierras con este pretexto vino al Cobre con la *mayor* autoridad y violencia. Llegó a la casa de la viuda Ignacia de los Reyes

[3] Ministerio de Cultura, Archivo General de Indias, Seville, Santo Domingo 1627, Havana y Cuba, Año de 1792, cuaderno no. 1, fols. 209r–10v.

mines are married, and we have our families, which we have always sustained in a calm and peaceful way, [that] we have been occupied in the mining works when needed, [in] the construction of the Holy Church, and other [tasks] in which we have been employed when there have been attacks, and we have responded promptly as loyal vassals of His Majesty at our own cost and expense, [always] complying with and obeying all the laws of our superiors and of other justices in the City of [Santiago de] Cuba, who have employed us in all this as well as in [the hunt for] hamlets and *Maroon* communities of fugitive black slaves of the citizens [*vecinos*] of all of this island whom we have captured. We have always desired greater opportunities to do royal service and to be employed in important [military] actions; even if they are not rewarded, we will merely be content to have performed them. All this is so true, and our readiness for the occasion and defense of the fortress of [Santiago de] Cuba[2] or any other place is so real, even if it is [also] true that all of its citizens are ready as well to engage in any action, that the lord governors have called on us whenever there has been an occasion of any novelty remembering us even though we are [only] humble slaves of our king and lord, acknowledging perhaps our strong desire [to carry out military actions].

And it has come to our attention that those of us who will remain in the settlement that they say our king and lord will make with our master Don Francisco, giving him many slaves, [we] will be removed by *Vuestra Merced* [Judge Matienzo] to send us to the city of Havana. And the love for our *patria* and our work move us to beg *Vuestra Merced,* if it is possible, to grant us the mercy that we stay in our *pueblo,* paying tribute in whatever manner it is decided, while we find [the means] to [purchase] our freedom, or whatever is disposed so that in equity and piety *Vuestra Merced* can protect us in the name of our king and lord in whatever lawful way it may be possible.

Therefore, we ask and plead of *Vuestra Merced* that you consider us presented and order that we be given license [to stay], for this is the justice and mercy that we ask for and the most [necessary? illegible].

Juan Moreno

[Letter from Martín de Salazar]

El Cobre, August 21, 1792

We call attention to the violent despoliation, atrocities, and mischief that all of us free people of El Cobre have suffered for the last eleven years and months and are currently suffering and enduring in this captivity with Don Fernando Mancebo, one of the heirs of the said *pueblo.* First he convened men there in [Santiago de] Cuba and prepared them to form an armed band, and he obtained a license to come by and collect the wages of the *cobreros* who worked in the population settlement of the territory of El Cobre. Because [the heirs] had received the [illegally enslaved] captives and all the land [comprised in the jurisdiction of El Cobre], he [Mancebo] came to El Cobre on that pretense with the greatest authority and violence. He went to the house of the widow Ignacia de los Reyes and collected what the woman owed him, settling the debt for

[2] See maps of the fortress and its location in Díaz, *El Cobre.*

cobrándole [lo que] le debía dicha mujer, por lo que ajustaron quince *pesos.* Entró dentro y se los sacó. Después que los recibió salió al patio y llamó a uno de los de su *cuadrilla* y mandó desatar una vaca que con sus leches se mantenía y de propia autoridad la remitió para su casa en [Santiago de] Cuba. De ahí pasó a la *estancia* y morada de Angolosongo, allí encontró a uno de los *cautivos* nombrado Diego Ortiz y este mozo huyó y le dio un balazo que le derribó en el suelo y se llegó a él y sacando el sable, le dio con el [con lo] que le llevó media nalga y lo dejó por muerto. Y se vino al *pueblo* loándose del hecho y entonces el señor cura se fue corriendo a ver si lo hallaba vivo para administrarlo. . . . De allí el memorado don Fernando se partió a la *vega* y casa de Jacinto González, también *pardo* blanco, mas que Don Fernando a éste no lo encontró en casa sino sólo a su mujer y sus hijos. Mandó a los de su *cuadrilla* que se la amarraran. La hizo desnudar a la vergüenza. Tumbada en tierra, le metió un palo por las rodillas, le amarraron las manos, y la mandó a azotar con tanto rigor que los gritos los ponía en el cielo. Y le dieron más de cien azotes con un *manatí* y después de castigada le estuvo metiendo la punta del zapato por sus partes para que su marido no tuviera cópula con ella. Todo lo referido y lo [de]más que pasó a exponer ha sido con gente libre. . . . Pasó luego a la casa y morada del cabo de *milicias urbanas* Buenaventura Cosme, también lo hizo amarrar. No le azotó. Después pasó a la casa y *vega* de Buenaventura Quiala y como éste tiene dos hijos *cautivos* le dio muchos azotes a los dos hijos. De allí salió y vino al *pueblo* y llegó a la *estancia* nombrada las Animas, *estancia* que es del cura Caraballo. Amarró a los que halló allí, se cogió dos cerdos que estaban allí del señor cura y se los llevó consigo. De allí pasó a la *estancia* de la viuda Marcela Sánchez, la que había salido a buscar el *remedio.* Allí encontró dos hijas doncellas mujeres libres, señoras de su casa, [que] estaban durmiendo. Les quitó la sábana con las que estaban abrigadas, metió mano a coger los trastitos que encontró, hasta los aretes de las orejas, cintas de sus moños, sortijas de oro, candados, pañuelos, hebillas de zapato, y ropa de su uso y todo lo demás que quiso. Salió al patio, llamó por las llaves, cogió las gallinas y *guanajos,* cargó un caballo de estas aves y se fue. Pasó a la casa de Sale Cuzata solicitando por un hijo *cautivo* de éste y no lo halló. Mandó amarrar al padre que es *pardo* de color blanco y libre y lo castigó dándole más de cien azotes. Después se fue con las cargas que indebidamente había quitado para su casa en [Santiago de] Cuba. . . .

Amigo, todos estos sucesos han sido con gentes libres, hombres y mujeres de honra, asegurando a *Vuestra Merced* que esto es un rasgo de lo que pasamos al presente pues de antemano han sido los insultos sin tamaño ni medida, que fuera menester para explicarlos una resma de papel. En fin, Amigo, Dios quiera librarnos de tanta persecución y a *Vuestra Merced* le dé mucha salud y vida para que haga de su parte cuanto fuere dable, empeñándose con los señores que nos favorecen manden con toda prontitud al caballero que los ha de reponer en su *pueblo* a los mencionados esclavos. Pues en esta ciudad [Santiago de Cuba] [que] no hacen caso de órdenes, ni *disposiciones* de las superiores mandates, antes que acaben con todos los *cobreros,* tantos enemigos [son los] que nos persiguen.

fifteen *pesos*. He went inside and got them from her. After receiving the [fifteen *pesos*], he went out to the patio and called a man from his band and ordered him to untie a cow with whose milk she supported herself and on his own authority sent it to his house in [Santiago de] Cuba. From there he moved on to the farm [*estancia*] and residence of Angolosongo, where he found one of the captives, named Diego Ortiz. And this young man fled, and he shot and felled him to the ground and went up to him and taking out his saber struck him, cutting away one half of a side of his buttocks, and left him for dead. He came to the *pueblo* boasting of his act and then the Lord priest left, running to see if he could find him alive to administer him [the last sacrament]. . . . From there, the mentioned Don Fernando left for the tobacco farm [*vega*] and house of Jacinto González, [who is] also white-brown [*blanco pardo*]. But Don Fernando did not find him at home; only his wife and children were there. He ordered the men of his band to tie her up for him, making her take her clothes off and fully bare herself. [She was] thrown on the ground, [and] he put a stick between her knees. They tied her hands and had her flogged so harshly that her screams could be heard in Heaven. They gave her more than one hundred lashes with a whip; and after having punished her, he began thrusting the tip of his shoe inside her parts so that her husband could not copulate with her. Everything that I have related and what I now turn to describe has happened to free people. . . . He then moved on to the house and residence of the corporal of the urban militias Buenaventura Cosme. He also had him tied up, [but] did not flog him. Then he moved on to the house and tobacco farm of Buenaventura Quiala, and because he has two captive sons he gave the two sons a heavy flogging. From there he came to the *pueblo,* arriving at the farm named Las Animas that is Priest Caraballo's farm. He tied up those he found there, and took with him two hogs that were there that belonged to the Señor priest. He then moved on to the farm of the widow Marcela Sánchez, who had gone out to look for food. He found there two maiden daughters, free women, mistresses of their home, who were sleeping. He took off the bed sheet that covered them and went on to take all the trinkets that he found, including their earrings, hair ribbons, gold rings, locks, scarves, shoe buckles, and clothing and all that he wanted. He went to the patio, asked for the keys, and took the chickens and turkeys, loading up a horse with them, and left. He went to the house of Sale Cuzata asking for a captive son of his but did not find him. He ordered the father, who is brown of white color and free, be tied up and gave him more than a hundred lashes. Afterward he left with the whole load that he had unduly taken for his home in [Santiago de] Cuba. . . .

Friend, all these events have happened to free people, men and women of honor, assuring *Vuestra Merced* that this is an instance of what we are currently enduring because the insults have been outright so enormous and boundless that a whole ream of paper would be needed to explain them. In sum, friend, God will that we be freed from all this persecution and may He grant much health and life to *Vuestra Merced* so that you may do everything that can be done on your part, insisting to the gentlemen who favor us that the man who will restore the above-mentioned slaves to their *pueblo* be sent promptly, before they destroy all the *cobreros* [because] so many enemies are persecuting us, and in this city [Santiago de Cuba] no one heeds orders or dispositions

Nuestro Señor felicite su vida de *Vuestra Merced* y le guarde muchos años, como lo deseamos sus más humildes *compatriotas* y en nombre de todos.

Martín de Salazar
Nuestro amigo Gregorio Cosme Osorio

[Carta de Gregorio Cosme Osorio][4]

Madrid, diez y seis de marzo de 1795

Amados Dueños míos:

Francisco Sales Cruzata. Aviso a Ud. que en este correo pasan órdenes del rey en persona para poner a los *cobreros* en la posesión de su libertad y se remiten las órdenes al gobernador de la Habana y el de [Santiago de] Cuba, para ver si hacen caso de sus mandatos encargándoles la *mayor* brevedad del asunto. . . . Ya les aviso a todos que son libres y que me ha costado muchas cantidades, pero no es nada, por que ellos no se salgan con su gusto diera yo la vida. Ya verán lo que he trabajado sin que nadie me haya ayudado más que el abogado, procurador, y prestamista, el Señor don Pedro Sedano. Amigo Sales Cruzata, si me vieran no me habían de conocer porque con estas batallas de papeles me he puesto muy flaco y con las enfermedades mucho más, y con las desazones y sinsabores, porque cinco veces he apelado de todo, de modo que me ha sido preciso haber buscado modo de hablarle al mismo rey en persona por un gran amigo. Me puso en donde yo no pensaba y le hablé y presenté el *memorial* que me mandaron y el Testimonio de la Iglesia donde tenían las generaciones de los esclavos, por donde vino a conocer todo lo incierto. Y me ofreció el rey que siendo cierto lo que yo decía a favor de aquellos que se me tendría presente a mí y a todos. Y según me lo ofreció así lo ha ejecutado, pero mucho nos cuesta. Aviso que a todos les escribo en este mismo correo: a Ventura Cosme, [otros siete nombres] y a todos de esa *villa* con brevedad les mando dos providencias que les he ganado. . . . Y en fin, no puedo ser más largo en este correo porque me hallo ocupado. No hay que obrar nada en esos tribunales, solo sí remitirme todo lo que se ofrezca, y de lo contrario no hacer nada, que me ha costado para anular todos los *autos* que me decían se habían obrado en esos tribunales, que son nulos. Y basta que estoy de prisa en el Consejo. Y mande Ud. a éste su seguro servidor que su mano besa,

Gregorio Cosme Osorio

[4] Ministerio de Cultura, Archivo General de Indias, Seville, Santo Domingo 1631, fols. 11v–14r.

of superior mandates. May Our Lord praise and guard your life for many years, as your most humble compatriots wish you and on behalf of all.

Martín de Salazar
Our Friend Gregorio Cosme Osorio

[Letter from Gregorio Cosme Osorio]

Madrid, March 16, 1795

My Dearest Owners,

Francisco Sales Cruzata, I inform you that in this mail are going out orders from the king in person to put the *cobreros* in possession of their freedom, and the orders are remitted to the governor of Havana and of [Santiago de] Cuba to see if they will heed his orders recommending a speedy resolution of the matter. . . . I am announcing to all of you that you are free, and that it has cost me great amounts, but it is really nothing because I would gladly give my life just so that they [the heirs] do not get away with their wishes. You will see how much I have worked by myself with only the help of the lawyer, attorney, and moneylender Señor Don Pedro Sedano. Friend Sales Cruzata, if you saw me you would not recognize me because I have become very thin with these paper battles and with the illnesses even more, and with the distress and troubles. Because I have had to appeal everything five times and therefore it has been necessary to find a way to speak to the king himself in person through a great friend [who] placed me where I would not have thought [possible]. And I talked to him [the king] and presented to him the report that you sent me, along with the Church testimonial, where all the generations [baptism records] of slaves were [recorded] whereby he came to know all that was untrue. And the king offered that if everything I said on their behalf was true, he would have me and all of them [the *cobreros*] present. And he has carried [everything] out exactly as he offered to me, but it has been so hard for us. I let you know that I write to all in this same mail: to Ventura Cosme [and seven other names], to all in that town [*villa*] I am sending soon two provisions that I have won for you. . . . And finally, I cannot go on any further in this letter, because I am busy. Do not do anything in those tribunals [on the island]; only send me everything that comes up, and otherwise do not do anything because it has been very hard to annul all the writs [*autos*] that you told me had been issued in those tribunals, which are null. And enough; I am in a hurry in the council. This, your true servant, who kisses your hand, is at your command.

Gregorio Cosme Osorio

9

The Making of a Free *Lucumí* Household: Ana de la Calle's Will and Goods, Northern Peruvian Coast, 1719[1]

Rachel Sarah O'Toole

Who was Ana de la Calle? At first the question appears to be easily answered from the historical sources that survive in the provincial archive of Trujillo, a small city on the northern Peruvian coast: she was a free woman of color, as indicated by her claim to be a *morena.* When she died (in or around 1719), she had a small but close-knit family consisting of a daughter and a granddaughter and both of their husbands. Her household also included an enslaved woman with her young daughter.

Among Ana de la Calle's goods were trays she used to sell bread; selling bread was a common business for women of color. The name she called herself in public documents—de la Calle ("of the Street")—also explained that she sold her goods in the public thoroughfares and *plazas* of Trujillo, center of a bustling regional economy. Merchants from the city purchased woolen cloth from the highlands, along with the locally produced sugar, molasses, alcohol, soap, and wheat, to sell along the Pacific coast stretching from Lima to Panama. Together with other free people of African descent, Ana de la Calle would have joined indigenous vendors, muleteers, and artisans who all sold their goods and labor to maintain their families.

Ana de la Calle: *Lucumí*

Yet, the will and the estate that Ana de la Calle left to her family present a more complicated picture of her identity. She also called herself *de casta lucumí* ("of the *Lucumí* caste") in the will that she paid a notary to record in his bound volumes of public documents. By calling herself *Lucumí,* Ana de la Calle employed a term used by transatlantic slave traders to identify men, women, and children who were sold by Yoruba states to Atlantic merchants (Law, *Kingdom,* 18).

Slave traders and slaveholders in Cartagena and Panama, along the Pacific coast, and in the Andean highlands also employed the term *Lucumí* to distinguish certain enslaved people from others they called *Angola* (those sold through the West Central African port of Luanda) or *Mina* (captives from the *Gold Coast*). Slave traders employed these terms to indicate the port or region of origin for African captives, but slaveholders used the labels to suggest characteristics that they projected onto enslaved men and women.

In seventeenth-century colonial Trujillo, slaveholders imagined that *Mina* slaves were more "haughty" than those of other *nations* ("Demanda," fol. 58v). Yet, the constructed

[1] See Maps 3 and 6. I thank Juan Castañeda Murga for his assistance with the transcription of the document.

nature of the qualities attributed to these terms can be seen in the fact that, in contrast to their Spanish counterparts, eighteenth-century British colonists in South Carolina preferred enslaved men and women from the *Gold Coast,* or *Mina,* because they thought these African women and men were from a barren place and therefore more "hardy" (Littlefield, 18). In both cases, slaveholders created meanings that assisted them in assigning value to their property, enslaved men and women.

Even though Ana de la Calle was also a slaveholder, she employed the term *Lucumí* to describe herself, suggesting that she was laying public claim to an African diaspora identity. She may have employed the term to underline that she was a Yoruba speaker. This West African language was associated with nobility and elites among the people who lived close to the rising states of *Dahomey* and *Oyo,* in the interior of the Atlantic coast stretching from southeast Ghana to southwestern Nigeria.

By the seventeenth century, coastal people had begun to adopt the hinterland Yoruba (of the *Lucumí*) deities, providing evidence of the prestige associated with *Lucumí* (Anguiano, 238–40). As historian Robin Law explains, *lukumi* also became synonymous with valuable trade goods such as salt, cotton cloth, and other exports of the Yoruba kingdoms.[2] Whether Ana de la Calle originated within these interior West African states or survived the horrifying transatlantic passage by naming herself a *Lucumí,* she claimed a superior status to that of the majority of Africans in colonial Trujillo who, in the early eighteenth century, were people from the Slave Coast on West Africa's Bight of Benin (see Map 3).

In doing so, she marked herself off from the majority of enslaved men and women who called themselves or were called *arará* and *popo,* or *chala.*[3] Her claim to be a *Lucumí* woman, in addition to a free woman of color, may explain how she supported her family by selling bread on the streets of Trujillo.

A Diverse Family and Household

Even though Ana de la Calle identified herself as a *Lucumí* free woman of color, she did not pass on this identifier to her daughter or granddaughter. Instead, she recorded each of her female descendants with surnames that reflected their distinct positions in colonial society. She called her daughter by the full name of Doña María de la Cruz Cavero to suggest that unlike herself, her offspring had achieved a title of honor and respect in the provincial town. De la Cruz was a common surname that lower-status people chose, including those who had been slaves. Lacking a Spanish family name, de la Cruz expressed their piety. Yet, María had gained the additional surname Cavero, that of a powerful family that owned sugar haciendas on Peru's northern coast; therefore, this household of free people of African descent was connected through patronage or kinship with these Spanish, slaveholding elites.

In the legal document that Ana created, her last will and testament, she named her daughter a *parda,* or a woman of color who had been born free, rather than a *morena,*

[2] *Slave Coast,* 46–47. Law uses a different historical spelling of *Lucumí.*

[3] *Chala* was an identity also associated with Yoruba kingdoms, but *Chala* did not imply the same superior social status of *Lucumí.*

a term that was more often associated with enslaved or freedwomen. By naming her daughter in this way, Ana de la Calle established a public record that created honor for herself and her family. Lastly, Ana de la Calle reserved a special place for her granddaughter to whom she gave no Spanish colonial or African diasporic identifier at all, naming her simply "Juana de Silva." Indeed, one possibility is that the *Lucumí* free woman passed her family out of any public categorization associated with enslavement or the transatlantic slave trade.

Ana de la Calle—Pasqual de Segama (first husband)—[Agustín de Saavedra (second husband)]

⬇

Doña María de la Cruz Cavero—*Alférez* Baltasar de los Reyes

⬇

Juana de Silva—*Alférez* Don Faustino de Vidaurre

Figure 2. Ana de la Calle's family

The goods that Ana de la Calle left to her daughter and granddaughter, in addition to the roles each played within the family, raise questions about how she sought to construct public identities for her family, including her own. Ana de la Calle did not ascribe the *casta Lucumí* to either her daughter or her granddaughter, although she did apply this elite Yoruba identifier to Isabel, the enslaved woman who served the household. Perhaps, although she clearly chose an enslaved *Lucumí* woman to serve her, she understood that the term signified a slave in colonial Peru—an identity she wished to shed for her descendants.

More interestingly, Isabel's young enslaved daughter, who had been born in Ana de la Calle's house, carried the unusual name of Eduvigia—perhaps the notary heard Eduvigis or Saint Hedwig (a thirteenth-century Bavarian convent reformer). Still, provincial scribes were notoriously creative orthographers, especially of unfamiliar names and words. Ana de la Calle could have also been suggesting Saint Efigenia, an African martyr associated with Saint John and worshipped in African-descent communities in Peru, Brazil, and Mexico (Karasch, 85; Obregón, 31–32; von Germeten, 18–19).

The free *Lucumí* woman then passed on this infant to another member of her household, suggesting on one level how a slaveholder controlled the lives of enslaved people and how she determined who would raise the saint's namesake. Could this stipulation in the will have been a way to keep the child with the unusual (and possibly spiritual) name within Ana de la Calle's household? Finally, Ana de la Calle may have guarded her own identity by entrusting certain members of her family with the separate accounts that she kept for what appear to be two businesses, one selling bread "in the street" and another that operated within a community of people who "commonly called her" Mama Anica.

Her name suggests that she may have been a ritual specialist, as "Mother" was a title of respect in Brazilian houses of *Candomblé,* an African diasporic religion, and may have been used in the same way among Afro-Peruvians. Given the clerical supervision of Catholic orthodoxy, Ana de la Calle would have been wise to keep her second occupation discreet, just as *Candomblé* followers celebrated public Catholic rites that paralleled private or near secret African rituals (Reis, 145).

She owned a number of Catholic religious images as well as a silver-covered gourd, suggesting that within the walls of her house, Ana de la Calle may have served as a spiritual leader who healed, divined, or conducted religious services as did other Yoruba women in African diasporic religions of the Americas. Ana de la Calle's intentions are difficult to discern, but clearly she carried more identities than that of a mere bread seller.

Ana de la Calle molded her identity and fit her wishes into the dry and formulaic language of a last will and testament. But her last will and testament is also a document that can reveal a rich world of relationships and identities. A common record throughout colonial Spanish America and most regions of the early modern Christian world, a will was understood as both privately confessional and publicly declarative. When people dictated these documents, either alone with the notary or surrounded by their families, they revealed deep secrets, forgotten sins, and intimate surprises.

At the same time, in these handwritten entries, later bound in large notarial ledgers, colonial Spanish-American people who could afford to pay for the privilege explained who their legitimate children were, who would inherit their possessions, and who their debtors and creditors were. Wills were serious legal texts that formed the basis for the distribution of goods, recognition of kin, and protracted judicial disputes. In fact, Ana de la Calle's children and grandchildren employed her will in a protracted legal dispute over the ownership of her house.

Thus the language attributed to Ana de la Calle in the document is correspondingly formal and formulaic. The notary she employed, like others, followed the standard conventions for the drawing up of a will and its accompanying documents. These papers exhibit the required language and convoluted terms that were necessary to proclaim oneself a practicing Catholic, including the order in which the declarations are made and the stipulations regarding who could sign as witnesses.

People counted on the information in the document to be taken as factual and its provisions to become reality. They intended the orders and the relationships that they recorded in their wills to become truth as much as they recorded what they knew to be true (Burns, 352–53). Even though a will, like any legal document, could be disputed with regard to these provisions, these written sources of a testator's wishes were powerful in a predominately oral culture where the literate and illiterate alike counted on recorded language to "fix" realities—for better or for worse. The documents that Ana de la Calle caused to be created in her name invite interrelated questions and explorations. First, how can we use the will and list of possessions, mediated by the Spanish judicial official's act of writing, to understand Ana de la Calle's intentions? Second, what do her wishes tell us about her family, her livelihoods, and her understanding of slavery? And third, how well does the colonial document capture her reality and what still remains unsaid in this verbal legacy of a free *Lucumí* woman who lived her life in a provincial Peruvian town?

[Testamento de Ana de la Calle][1]

En el nombre de Dios y con Su Santísima Gracia, amén:

Sepan cuantos esta carta de testamento vieren cómo yo Ana de la Calle, *morena* libre de *casta lucumí, vecina* que soy desta ciudad de Trujillo del Perú, estando enferma en la cama de la enfermedad que Dios Nuestro Señor se ha servido de darme, creyendo como firmemente creo en el misterio de la Santísima Trinidad, Padre y Hijo y Espíritu Santo, tres personas distintas y un solo Dios verdadero, debajo de cuya fe y creencia he vivido y protesto vivir y morir como católica y fiel cristiana y en todo lo demás [que] tiene, cree, y confiesa, y predica Nuestra Santa Madre Iglesia Católica de Roma. Y temiéndome de la muerte que es cosa natural a toda criatura viviente y porque ésta no me coja sin haber dispuesto las cosas tocantes al descargo de mi conciencia, hago y ordeno este mi testamento última y postrimera voluntad. Y para poderlo hacer con el acierto que deseo, elijo y escojo por mis abogados y intercesores a la siempre Virgen Madre de Dios y Señora Nuestra y a los Santos Apóstoles, San Pedro y San Pablo, y al Santo Ángel de mi guarda con cuya protección y amparo hago y ordeno a dicho mi testamento, última y postrimera voluntad en [la] forma y manera siguiente:

Primeramente, ofrezco y encomiendo mi alma a Dios Nuestro Señor. [Cuando] fuere servido de llevarme de esta presente vida, sea sepultada en la Iglesia y Convento de Nuestro Padre San Francisco de esta dicha ciudad donde está enterrado Pasqual de Segama, mi marido, o en otra cualquiera iglesia o convento de ella que a mis *albaceas* les pareciera. Y lo acompañarán el día de mi entierro la cruz alta, cura, y sacristán de mi parroquia. Y la limosna de mi funeral y entierro se pagarán de mis bienes.

Ídem. Mando se dé de limosna a los santos lugares de Jerusalén donde Cristo Nuestro Redentor obró la redención del género humano cuatro *reales* que se pagarán de mis bienes.

Ídem. Mando para ayuda de la reedificación del convento de San Francisco de Asís que está en Italia cuatro *reales* que se pagarán de mis bienes.

Y declaro que fui casada y velada según orden de la Santa Madre Iglesia con Pasqual de Segama, *moreno* libre que [está] difunto y durante nuestro matrimonio no tuvimos hijos ningunos. Declaralo [sic] así para que conste.

Ídem. Declaro que al presente fui casada y velada según orden de Nuestra Santa Madre Iglesia con Agustín de Saavedra, *moreno* libre, del cual asimismo no tenemos hijos ningunos. Declárolo así para que conste.

Ídem. Declaro que antes de que contrajese mi primer matrimonio con el dicho Pasqual de Segama, como mujer frágil tuve una hija que al presente vive, nombrada María de la Cruz, *parda.* Declárola por tal mi hija.

[1] Expediente seguido por don Ambrosio Girón de Estrada promotor fiscal del obispado de Trujillo, albacea de Ana de la Calle, morena libre difunta, contra don Faustino de Vidaurre albacea y tenedor de bienes de doña María de la Cruz Cavero, difunta, sobre pago de los corridos que estuviere debiendo del censo impuesto acerca de la casa que hubo y heredó de la dicha Ana de la Calle. Archivo Departamental de La Libertad, Cabildo, Causas Ordinarias, legajo 41, exp. 753 (1727), fols. 8v–14v.

[The Will of Ana de la Calle][1]

In God's name and with His Most Holy Grace, amen: Let it be known to all those who see this letter of testament that I, Ana de la Calle, free *morena* of *casta lucumí, vecina* that I am of this city of Trujillo of Peru, being sick in bed of an illness that God Our Lord has seen fit to give me, believing as I firmly believe in the mystery of the Holy Trinity, Father and Son and Holy Spirit, three distinct persons and one single, true God, in whose faith and belief I have lived, and I proclaim to live and to die as a Catholic and true Christian and in all the rest that Our Holy Mother Catholic Church in Rome holds, believes, confesses, and preaches. And fearing death, which is a natural thing for all living creatures and so that this [death] may not take me until I have arranged matters for the sake of my conscience, I make and order this my last will and testament. And to do so with the prudence [good judgment/wisdom] that I desire, I elect and choose for my petitioners and intercessors the eternally Virgin Mother of God and Our Lady and the Holy Apostles, Saint Peter and Saint Paul, and my Holy Guardian Angel, with whose protection and favor I make and order this my last will and testament in the following form and manner:

First, I offer and entrust my soul to Our Lord God. When he is served to take me from this present life, may I be buried in the Church and Monastery of Our Father Saint Francis of this city where Pasqual de Segama, my husband, is buried, or in any other church or monastery of the Church that my executors choose. And [that my body] be accompanied on the day of my burial by the high cross, priest, and sacristan of my parish. And the donation for my funeral and burial will be paid from my estate.

Item. I order that a charitable donation of four *reales* be given from my estate to the holy places of Jerusalem where Christ Our Redeemer performed the redemption of humankind.

Item. I order for the aid in the re-edification of the monastery of Saint Francis of Assisi that is in Italy four *reales* that will be paid from my estate.

And I declare that I was married and veiled according to the order of the Holy Mother Church with Pasqual de Segama, free *moreno* who is deceased, and during our matrimony we did not have any children. Thus, I declare it so that it is known.

Item. I declare that at present I was married and veiled according to the order of Our Holy Mother Church with Agustín de Saavedra, free *moreno,* of which [matrimony], we also do not have any children. Thus, I declare it so that it is known.

Item. I declare that before I contracted my first marriage with the said Pasqual de Segama, as a weak woman I bore a daughter who is alive today named María de la Cruz, *parda.* I declare her, as such, to be my daughter.

[1]Dossier filed by Don Ambrosio Girón de Estrada, public prosecutor of the bishopric of Trujillo, executor for the deceased Ana de la Calle, free *morena,* against Don Faustino de Vidaurre, executor and trustee for the deceased Doña María de la Cruz Cavero, regarding payment of the rents owed on the lease imposed on the house that she had and inherited from the said Ana de la Calle.

Ídem. Declaro por mis bienes esta casa en que al presente vivo [que] la hube y compré de Claudio Juárez, hijo y heredero de María de Lorito por escritura pública otorgada ante Miguel Cortijo Quero, *escribano* público y de *cabildo* que fue de esta dicha ciudad a los 11 días del mes de agosto del año pasado de 1692, la cual tomamos posesión por la *real justicia;* entrego [yo] y el dicho Pasqual de Segama. Declárola por mis bienes.

Ídem. Más declaro por mis bienes una *negrita criolla* nombrada Eduvigia que tendrá de edad poco más de un año. Declárola por mis bienes.

Ídem. Declaro que la dicha mi hija María de la Cruz en diferentes partidas que le he dado a ella y a sus acreedores 461 *pesos* de a ocho *reales.* Declárolo así para que conste y se le haga cargo de ellos.

Ídem. Quiero y es mi voluntad que al dicho Agustín de Saavedra, segundo marido, se le den de mis bienes 25 *pesos* de a ocho *reales* para su entierro. Que asimismo viva todos los días de su vida que mi heredera no lo eche de la casa hasta en tanto que haya fallecido, porque así es mi voluntad.

Ídem. Quiero y es mi voluntad que el quinto de mis bienes se convierta en el dicho mi funeral y misas que se mandarán decir por mi alma. Declárolo así para que conste.

Ídem. Declaro por mis bienes una caja grande de cedro de Panamá con su cerradura y llave.

Ídem. Una mesa con su cajón y los pies torneados.

Ídem. Un fondo de cobre, una batea grande y otra pequeña.

Ídem. Más una *negra* nombrada María Isabel de *casta lucumí.*

Y atento a que no tengo más heredera de la dicha María de la Cruz, la nombro por tal mi heredera universal para que después de mi fallecimiento, haya y herede los dichos mis bienes con la bendición de Dios y la mía, porque así es mi voluntad.

Y nombro por mi *albacea* y *tenedor de bienes* al *licenciado* don Ambrosio Girón de Estrada, clérigo y presbítero al cual le prorrogo y alargo el año y día de albaceazgo y todo tiempo que necesitare más por el cumplimiento de este mi testamento, al cual doy todo mi poder, el que de derecho se requiere para su ejecución. Que así es mi voluntad.

Y revoco y anulo y doy por ningunos y de ningún valor ni efectos otros y cualesquier testamentos, codicilos, y poderes para testar y otras últimas *disposiciones* y voluntades que antes de este testamento haya hecho y otorgado por escrito o de palabra. Que quiero que todo ello no valga ni haga fe ni prueba en juicio ni fuera dél salvo este mi testamento que ahora hago y otorgo ante el presente *escribano,* el cual se ha de guardar, cumplir, y ejecutar como mi última y postrimera voluntad, o por aquella escritura que haya mejor lugar en derecho, en testimonio de lo cual otorgo la presente carta ante el presente *escribano.*

Que conozco a la otorgante doy fe y la doy asimismo de que está en su entero juicio según las cosas que por [el]lo trató y comunicó conmigo.

No firmó porque dijo no saber escribir. Firmólo a su ruego un testigo, siendo testigos el *ayudante* Juan Nevado, Alonso Gómez, y Joseph Márquez, que es hecha en esta ciudad de Trujillo del Perú el 25 del mes de abril de 1719 años. Antes de firmar, dijo

Item. I declare as my property this house in which I live at the moment, which I had and purchased from Claudio Juárez, son and heir of María de Lorito, by public deed sworn before Miguel Cortijo Quero, public notary and who was of the municipal council of this city on the eleventh of the month of August of the past year of 1692. We took possession of it before the royal justice who delivered it to me and the said Pasqual de Segama. I declare it as my property.

Item. I also declare as my property a little black *criolla* girl named Eduvigia, who is a little more than a year old. I declare her as my property.

Item. I declare that I have given, in different allotments, to my said daughter María de la Cruz and her creditors, 461 *pesos* of 8 *reales*. I declare it thus so that it is on record and it is taken charge of.

Item. I wish and it is my will that to the said Agustín de Saavedra, second husband, be given from my property 25 *pesos* of 8 *reales* for his burial. That he also live all the days of his life, that my heir not throw him out of the house until he has died, because thus is my will.

Item. I desire and it is my will that a fifth of my property be used for my burial and Masses that are ordered said for my soul. I declare it thus, so that it is on record.

Item. I declare as my property a large trunk of Panamanian cedar with its lock and key.

Item. A table with its drawer and carved legs

Item. A copper pan, a large tray, and another, small one

Item. Also a black woman named María Isabel of *casta lucumí*

And heeding that I have no more heir than the said María de la Cruz, I name her as such my universal heir so that after my death, she may have and inherit my property with God's blessing and mine because this is my will.

And I name as the executor of my will and trustee the *licentiate* Don Ambrosio Girón de Estrada, cleric and priest, whose term of executorship I defer and extend the time needed for the completion of this, my will, to whom I give all my power that I rightly have, that is required for its execution. This is my will.

I revoke and annul and give as none and of no value or effect any other testaments, codicils, and powers to make a will and other last dispositions and wishes that I may have made and executed in writing or orally before this testament. I wish that any of the preceding have no value, nor serve as verification or proof in or out of court, except this my testament, which I now complete and execute before the present notary, which will be observed, fulfilled, and executed as my last will and testament, or by that document, in the best manner and form according to law, in testimony of which I execute this letter before the present notary.

I witness that I know the executor and I also witness that she is in her right mind according to the matters that she dealt with and communicated with me.[2]

She did not sign because she stated she did not know how to write. A witness signed at her request, which was witnessed by the aide-de-camp Juan Nevado, Alonso Gómez, and Joseph Márquez. Done in this city of Trujillo of Peru the twenty-fifth of this

[2] Here, the notary inserts his witnessing statements.

la dicha Ana de la Calle que quiere y es su voluntad que se pongan y arrimen al quinto de sus bienes para que con ellos se hagan bien por su alma por ser así su voluntad. Y testigos los dichos y supra a ruego de la otorgante y por testigo: Joseph Márquez, ante mi: Felipe de San Román, *escribano* público y de *cabildo.*

[Codicilo de Ana de la Calle][2]

En la ciudad de Trujillo del Perú en catorce días del mes de mayo de 1719 años, ante mí, el presente *escribano* público y testigos que de susos irán declarados, pareció Ana de la Calle, *morena* libre. Y dijo que por cuanto el día 25 del mes de abril pasado deste presente otorgó su testamento, última y postrimera voluntad, en el cual deja dispuestas las cosas tocantes al descargo de su conciencia, y porque ahora se ofrece quitar y suplir y enmendar algunas *disposiciones* del dicho su testamento y lo quiere hacer por vía de codicilo o por aquella escriptura que haya mejor en derecho. Y poniéndolo en efecto otorga y dice que quiere y es su voluntad que a su nieta se le dé y entregue una negrita, su esclava nombrada Teresa de Eduvigia que será de edad de un año y ocho meses, *criolla,* nacida en su casa de una esclava. La cual quiere y es su voluntad se le dé y entregue por su *albacea* a la dicha Juana de Silva, su nieta luego que haya fallecido y que sus herederos no perturben ni inquieten a la dicha Juana de Silva en la posesión de la negrita. Y esto se da a entender, cayéndose entre los límites del quinto. Y quiere asimismo se guarde cumpla y ejecute este codicilo y el dicho su testamento en lo que fuere contrario en él. Y la dicha otorgante a quien yo, el *escribano,* doy fe que conozco y la doy asimismo de que está en su entero juicio, no firmó porque dijo no saber escribir. Firmolo, a su ruego, un testigo, siendo testigos Felipe de los Reyes, Félix Nieto, y Alonso Gómez presentes.

Memoria de los bienes que quedaron por muerte de María de la Cruz Cavero, mi madre, que paran en poder de Baltasar de los Reyes[3]

Primeramente, un mate guarnecido de plata que valdrá cuatro *pesos* poco más o menos: 4 *pesos*

Ídem. Una lámina de plata con su vidriera de Nuestra Señora de la Soledad que valdrá: 4 *pesos*

Ídem. Un Santo Lignum Crucis guarnecido de metal de príncipe con su vidriera que valdrá: 8 *pesos*

[2] Expediente seguido por el Alférez don Faustino Vidaurre como marido legítimo de Juana de Silva, albacea, heredera, y teneder de bienes de María de la Cruz Cavero, su suegra difunta contra el Alférez Baltasar de los Reyes, pardo libre, vecino de Trujillo sobre que desocupe el cuarto de la casa situada en la calle del Postigo del Dean. Archivo Departamental de La Libertad, Cabildo, Causas Ordinarias, legajo 41, exp. 752 (1727), fols. 1–2.

[3] Document created by Ana de la Calle's granddaughter and her spouse, Juana de Dios y Silva and *Alférez* Don Faustino de Vidaurre.

month of April of 1719. Before signing, the said Ana de la Calle said that she wanted and it is her will that a fifth of her property be set aside to be used for the good of her soul, as this is her wish. And the above said were witnesses at the executor's request, and as witness Joseph Márquez. Before me, Felipe de San Román, public notary and [notary] of the municipal council.

[Codicil of Ana de la Calle][3]

In the city of Trujillo of Peru on [the] fourteenth day of the month of May of the year 1719, Ana de la Calle, free *morena*, appeared before me, the present public notary, and witnesses, who will be declared below. And she said that inasmuch as the twenty-fifth day of the past month of April, she executed her last will and testament, in which she disposed matters for the sake of her conscience. And because now she offers to remove and add and amend some dispositions of said will and she wishes to do so by means of a codicil or by such document as best conforms to the manner of the law, and putting it into effect, she executes and states that she wishes and it is her will that to her granddaughter be given and delivered a little black girl, her slave, named Teresa de Eduvigia, who is about a year and eight months old, who is a *criolla*, born of a slave in her household. Which child she wishes and it is her will that she be given and delivered by her executor to the said Juana de Silva, her granddaughter, once she has died, and that her heirs should not trouble or harass the said Juana de Silva in her possession of the little black girl. And this it is given to understand falls within the limits of the fifth [part of her possessions]. And she wishes also that this codicil and said testament be observed, fulfilled, and executed against any opposition. And the said executor, whom I, the notary, certify that I know and also attest that she is in her right mind, did not sign because she said she did not know how to write. At her request a witness signed it, which was witnessed by Felipe de los Reyes, Félix Nieto, and Alonso Gómez, all present.

Account of the Possessions That Were Left at the Death of María de la Cruz Cavero, My Mother, That Ended Up in the Hands of Baltasar de los Reyes

First, a gourd adorned in silver that is worth about four *pesos:* four *pesos*

Item. A silver plate painted with the figure of Our Lady of Solitude with its glass cover that is worth about: four *pesos*

Item. A piece of the True Cross adorned in Prince's metal with its glass cover that is worth about: eight *pesos*

[3] This is a legal document for additions or changes to a will. "Dossier filed by Alférez Don Faustino Vidaurre, legitimate husband of Juana de Silva, executor, heir, and trustee for María de la Cruz Cavero, his deceased mother-in-law, against Alférez Baltasar de los Reyes, free pardo, resident of Trujillo, seeking that he vacate the room in the house located on Calle del Postigo del Dean."

Ídem. Un espejo que valdrá dos *pesos* poco más o menos: 2 *pesos*

Ídem. Una sartén de cobre nueva que valdrá: 3 *pesos*

Ídem. Más un rebozo piche que valdrá 10 *pesos:* 10 *pesos*

Ídem. Más una saya tornasol ya traída que valdrá: 4 *pesos*

Ídem. Un corte de puntitas de faldellín que importan: 20 *reales*

Ídem. Más una joyita de metal falso engastada de piedra de amatista, rubí, y diamantes del alquimia que valdrá cuatro *reales* con otras cuatro piedras de alquimia que valdrán otros cuatro *reales* y uno y otro importan: 1 *peso*

Ídem. Más una cuja que vale 25 *pesos:* 25 *pesos*

Ídem. Más un pabellón que vale 14 *pesos:* 14 *pesos*

Ídem. Más un dosel con su Santo Cristo rodeado de estampas que valdrá: 3 *pesos*

Ídem. Un asador grande que era de mi abuela valiendo en un *peso:* 1 *peso*

Ídem. Una Purísima [Virgen] pequeña de bulto con su coronita de plata que ésta es mía que vale tres *pesos:* 3 *pesos*

Ídem. Paran en poder del dicho Baltasar de los Reyes una cajeta con su cerquillo de plata que valdrá tres *pesos:* 3 *pesos*

Ídem. Todos los papeles de cuentas, recibos, paga[s], y finiquitos que hizo la dicha María de la Cruz Cavero por Ana, que comúnmente llaman Mama Anica, madre que fue de la dicha María de la Cruz Cavero. Los cuales papeles estaban en una cajeta de madera.

Ídem. El papel de cuentas que tuvo la dicha Mama Anica con el señor *licenciado* don Ambrosio Girón de Estrada sobre el pan que le echaba para la mantención de su familia.

Item. A mirror that is worth about two *pesos:* two *pesos*

Item. A new copper frying pan that is worth about: three *pesos*

Item. A wheat-colored shawl that is worth about ten *pesos:* ten *pesos*

Item. And a worn, iridescent skirt that is worth about: four *pesos*

Item. A length of lace underskirting that amounts to: twenty *reales*

Item. Also a small piece of false gold jewelry mounted with stones of amethyst, ruby, and diamonds of alchemy that is worth about four *reales* with another four stones of alchemy, that is worth about another four *reales,* and the two together amount to: one *peso*

Item. Also a bedstead that is worth twenty-five *pesos:* twenty-five *pesos*

Item. Also a canopy that is worth fourteen *pesos:* fourteen *pesos*

Item. Also a dais with its Holy Christ surrounded by engravings that is worth about: three *pesos*

Item. A spit that was my grandmother's with the value of one *peso:* one *peso*

Item. A small statue of the Most Pure Virgin with its little silver crown, that is mine, that is worth three *pesos:* three *pesos*

Item. In the possession of the said Baltasar de los Reyes, a snuff box with its silver fringe that is worth about three *pesos:* three *pesos*

Item. All the papers of bills, receipts, payments, and settlements executed by the said María de la Cruz Cavero for Ana, who they commonly call Mama Anica, who was mother of the said María de la Cruz Cavero. These papers were in a little wooden box.

Item. Accounting papers that the said Mama Anica had with the *Señor Licenciado* Don Ambrosio Girón de Estrada regarding the bread that she made for the sustenance of his family.

10

"El rey de los *congos*": The Clandestine Coronation of Pedro Duarte in Buenos Aires, 1787[1]

Patricia Fogelman and Marta Goldberg
Document translation by Joseph P. Sánchez, Angelica Sánchez-Clark, and Larry D. Miller

The Population of African Descent in Eighteenth-Century Buenos Aires and Its Organizations

In the eighteenth century, Buenos Aires grew as a result of both increased transatlantic trade and its own integration into the Peruvian economy. The growth of Buenos Aires was also spurred by contraband activities, which included the traffic of leather goods from the port's hinterland and cloth from the interior, and the response to the growing desire for European products not regularly supplied by the small Spanish fleets. Bourbon liberalization of the trade further stimulated the commercial exchange that tied Buenos Aires more closely to Alto Peru (Bolivia), now under the Río de la Plata jurisdiction. It also strengthened the Buenos Aires to Lima trade route, promoting trade in slaves, mules, and other merchandise, while much of the Andean metals that permeated regional economies flowed into the port.

Responding to complex factors, Buenos Aires' population grew almost fivefold at the end of the colonial period, increasing from 11,200 inhabitants in the 1744 census to around 50,000 in 1810, for an estimated annual growth rate of 2.2 percent. To explain this growth, historians have tended to highlight external immigration and the forced immigration of enslaved Africans from the Portuguese Atlantic, but later studies also give importance to internal migrations that included indigenous and *mestizo* populations (Díaz).

It is difficult to calculate precisely the population of African origin in Buenos Aires, though period iconography, literature, documentation from commercial houses in which blacks provided labor, and even militia records show their very real presence. Demographic sources account for their existence but omit important data regarding their origins and make errors in identifying their ethnicities. In 1810, blacks and *pardos*—six of every ten of whom were enslaved—constituted about 29 percent of the total census numbers. The distribution of the enslaved population in the city of Buenos Aires was not homogenous: the greatest density was found in the central zone integrated with the free population by virtue of their occupations in domestic service, petty commerce, laundry services, and the crafts they exercised.

[1] See Maps 6 and 12. We wish to thank Marina Mansilla for her collaboration in composing the glossary for this chapter, which forms part of the Glossary for the volume.

Despite omissions and errors, the census lists (Goldberg, "La población" and "Los estudios") and parish registers (records of baptism, marriage, and death) are sources of enormous importance in helping us to understand the realities of the African-descent population of Buenos Aires during the colonial period, especially when the two are compared as synchronic and diachronic sources, that is, sources that provide both a demographic snapshot of a single moment and a picture of demographic change over time. Around 1778, when the census closest in time to the clandestine coronation presented in this chapter was taken, the population of Buenos Aires was around 24,754, about 30 percent of whom were *Afroporteños.*[2]

Doubtless, the idea that Buenos Aires lacked a population of African descent is a careless, often insidious, generalization in regard to their contributions to the sociocultural development of Buenos Aires. History of the Río de la Plata region counts those of African descent among its actors and documentary sources, which despite their limitations and lost information signal the evident influence of *Afromestizo*[3] social groups who participated in the city's growth. They also show the implantation of African cultural traditions through the mixing of religious and musical practices during the colonial period and well into the nineteenth century (see Goldberg, "Los africanos," "Los negros," and "Presencia").

This presence was wrought through, among others, the constitution of different social collectives. We can recognize three basic types of African communal groupings in Buenos Aires: confraternities, *nations,* and societies. Their existence and functioning from the final decades of the eighteenth through the end of the nineteenth centuries are relatively well documented, with sporadic later references.[4] Their history is one of a progressive search for autonomy, rarely realized until the end of this period.

The links between confraternities, societies, and *nations* at the end of the eighteenth century is not clear, but the *nations* were consolidated at a time when civil authorities assumed control of functions that had been in the Church's hands. The police replaced the Church in controlling these societies or *nations,* which began as simple associations and evolved into real organizations after independence. The societies took the names of the different African *nations* from which they were embarked or where their ancestors originated, such as *Angola, Banguela, Cambunda, Congo, Mina,* and Mozambique, among many others.

They began to acquire properties and establish headquarters. There they celebrated festivities and dances, during which they held collections and raffles. Among the aims of the societies were to help individuals of the same ethnicity to purchase their freedom and to organize festivities and processions, which at their height were attended

[2] We use the terms *Afroporteños* and *Afrorioplatenses* to refer to residents of African descent in Buenos Aires and the Viceroyalty of Río de la Plata, respectively, as the territory would not be called Argentina until after 1860.

[3] The term *Afromestizo* is preferred in some regions, including Argentina and Mexico, to refer to people of mixed African and European heritage.

[4] See works by Andrews, Cirio, Fogelman, Goldberg, González, Mallo, and Rosal in the Bibliography.

by the governor of Buenos Aires and his family. Later, the viceregal administration rejected and often prohibited these celebrations.

Afrorioplatense Confraternities

Religious brotherhoods and confraternities (*cofradías*) were corporations that served as instruments and vehicles of Christian consolidation in the colonial period. There were Marian[5] confraternities and confraternities dedicated to the Eucharist, the saints, or the souls of purgatory (Fogelman, "Coordenadas"). The confraternities played diverse social roles with two primary realms of activity, one material and the other strongly spiritual: They constructed and administered a confraternal patrimony, and they promoted religious practices and discourses. Clearly, they participated in the shared social space, creating alliances and defining group identities, offering support and collective solidarity to their members (Fogelman, "Una cofradía").

Scholars differ in their use and interpretation of the words "brotherhood" and "confraternity." In colonial Rioplatense sources, especially for Buenos Aires and its surroundings, both terms were generally used interchangeably (Fogelman, "Una cofradía," 179). Often their constitutions and minutes use both terms to refer to the same institution. Confraternities were among various institutions dedicated to promoting the Catholic religion. They were constituted by a body, or "association of the faithful," with religious aims, and they operated within the sphere of the Catholic Church, ordered by officially approved statutes (rules or constitutions). Often this approval was not obtained, or was delayed, and the confraternities functioned more or less informally.

To belong to a confraternity one paid a fee and, sometimes, fines. Each confraternity or brotherhood had an organizational, administrative, and functional structure presided over by the *mayordomo* (or *hermano mayor*, literally "elder brother"), accompanied by a representative council, often known as the "twenty-four brothers," independent of their real number (Fogelman, "Élite," 105–06).

Confraternities varied a great deal in their composition: they could be segregated by ethnicity, profession, or craft—the latter including an important number of black artisans; they could be reserved for members of the military or clergy; men or women; or they could be mixed. They could be more or less socially inclusive. There were also confraternities composed exclusively of whites and those made up of only enslaved or free blacks. In the eighteenth century, there existed confraternities in which members of both African and European descent came together in devotion to a single patron saint.

The African confraternities reached their height in the colonial period. They brought together the aims of both their African members and the official Church; the former sought to gather those of like condition, whereas the latter sought to exercise control over any expression that could threaten the established order. These confraternities organized within churches and convents, similar to but apart from the model of white (European) lay religious brotherhoods. The confraternities in colonial Buenos Aires

[5] Dedicated to the Virgin Mary.

composed of people of African descent included the *Creole* Blacks of Our Lady of Luján, the Brotherhood of the Rosary, and the Brotherhoods of Saint Balthasar, Saint Benedict, and Saint Gaspar.

The favorite patrons of Afrorioplatense brotherhoods were saints considered black: Saint Benedict of Palermo and Saint Balthasar of the Magi. The brotherhoods also included Marian cults, such as those to Our Lady of Succor, of the Rosary, and of the Assumption. Members of Afrorioplatense brotherhoods identified strongly with these saints because they were thought to be black, but the Marian options also supported the search for protection in the passage from this life to the next. Identity and security were central characteristics of the discourses and practices of all colonial brotherhoods, where inclusion and exclusion were key to building group identity and solidarity; the Afroporteño brotherhoods were no exception.

The confraternities supported their activities with contributions from their members and collections taken at public dances; these allowed them to pay for masses, funerals, and aid to the ill. The membership fee in black and *mulatto* confraternities was about two *pesos,* and, in the case of enslaved blacks, registrants also needed permission from their owners. The *luminaria,* or annual fee, was four *reales.* The confraternities met once or twice a week, when they received instruction in Christian doctrine.

One weekly mass cost about three *pesos* in alms for the priest, whereas the *capellán* (chaplain) charged two *reales* to pray a chaplet.[6] Confraternities paid the priest about five *pesos* for a parish burial, with sung mass and body present, and additional prayed masses (González). Clearly there was a regular flow of money from the confraternity to the Church for the liturgy, in addition to the improper diversions that priests often made of confraternity funds.

If authority was nominally given to confraternities to elect internal leaders, they were always subject to strong external control by church and royal authorities, and often the *capellán,* syndic, and *mayordomo* elected successors without participation of the majority. Designation of leaders in the later black societies was carried out by election by the membership in the presence of a police delegate, from whom authorization was requested. The authorities in each confraternity consisted of a parish *capellán,* a syndic, and a black "elder brother," who were elected by the membership. The *capellán*'s duties were to celebrate Masses and other liturgies for the members. The syndic was charged with supervising the collection of alms at dances and *candombes.* The elder brother's duties were practically nominal, as important decisions were made by the white *capellán.*

The leadership structure, the presence therein of white colonial authorities, and the resulting tensions regarding decision-making power over confraternity activities produced a rich documentary record. In the Archivo General de la Nación Argentina (AGN) are found numerous complaints by African confraternities whose requests for masses and funerals were not properly attended to by the chaplains; that is, the service was not carried out with proper decency. There were even complaints because they were required to ask the priest's permission before speaking in their own meetings.

[6] A series of prayers corresponding to prayer beads.

Dances and *Candombes* and Their Control by Colonial Authorities

In the eighteenth century, dances and *candombes* were held on Sundays and feast days with the viceroy's permission. These were large gatherings of Afrorioplatenses. The Buenos Aires town council authorities demonstrated a fierce opposition to these *candombes* and did not authorize them, considering them indecent. In their reports to the viceroy the councilors argued that these dances were lascivious and lewd and that, in attending them, slaves neglected their responsibilities. They also expressed fear of outbreaks of violence; some confrontations with authorities had been registered. Another concern frequently voiced by the councilors revolved around the origins of the monies that those of African descent collected to support their festivities. They argued that the money had to have been robbed from the slaves' owners.

As previously noted, the viceregal administration prohibited gatherings of Africans carried out without appropriate official supervision, for example in 1766, 1770, and 1790. Nevertheless, in two cases, the viceroy approved petitions to hold *candombes*. In 1795 he gave permission to the *Nación Congo* to hold dances on Sundays and feast days and, in 1799, he gave the same permission to the *Nación Cambunda*. What the viceroy did prohibit absolutely was the coronation of a participant, fearing that this might weaken his own authority. Such is the case of Pedro Duarte, an enslaved man bound to the *Nación Congo*, who apparently had been crowned king during a *candombe* in 1787 and was forced to resign (Goldberg, "Los negros," 6).

These dances undoubtedly preserved strong links to the original rituals of different African religious celebrations.[7] Their practices had to be secretive and reserved for the initiates, but from the eighteenth century on, Afroporteños began to break the concealment of their dances and bring them into Catholic celebrations. The earlier secrecy can probably be explained because the early stage of the *candombe* coincided with the first communal organization of Africans in confraternities, under the unchallenged influence of the Church.

The later participation in Catholic ceremonies is relatively well documented from the last decades of the eighteenth until the end of the nineteenth centuries (Cirio, "Antecedentes" and "¿Rezan o bailan?"), with some later references. On certain days and times of the year, especially around Christmas and Epiphany but also during Carnival, Easter, and for Saint John's Feast Day, sacred images surrounded by virtual gardens of artificial flowers were carried in processions through the streets to the sound and step of the *candombe*, among a multitude of Africans who danced their dances in public and before white onlookers.

The name *candombe* designated music, dance, and festivity. This last could be held behind closed doors, on the street, or at wakes; it could have a sacred or profane character. The principal moment was the enthroning of the statue of Saint Benedict or Saint Balthasar or another religious image, followed by the entrance of the "court" together with the king and queen. The brotherhoods held solemn processions through the streets, especially during Christmas festivities, accompanied by the image of the

[7] See Cirio ("¿Rezan o bailan?") and Rodríguez Molas.

Virgin of Monserrat, patroness par excellence of the black *barrio.* She was carried on floats with candles and *candombes* and often the government lent a troop escort.

The *Congo* Confraternity of Saint Balthasar Struggles for Autonomy in Choosing Its Leader

The Confraternity of Saint Balthasar in Buenos Aires achieved transcendence in historical memory in large part due to a conflict at the end of the eighteenth century regarding the selection of a king of the *Nación Congo.* The coronation occurred during a *candombe* that celebrated the Day of Our Lady of Assumption in an urban *hueco,* or open space, in 1787. Devotion to the Assumption of the Virgin was dear to the colonial confraternities, which were concerned with the passage from earthly existence to the Christian afterlife, signified by the moment of death.

The "good death," which one achieved by having carried out the sacraments and thus adequately prepared one's spirit, was a topic of special interest for the confraternities and brotherhoods. They dedicated themselves to providing services to ill members, aiding them in their suffering, and supplying the priest who would perform the last rites. The "spiritual economy of salvation" occupied an important place in the agenda of colonial confraternities (Fogelman, "Una 'economía'") and the inevitable entrance of the souls into purgatory—at least according to the imagination of the times—confronted faithful subjects with the weighing of their sins and good works (Fogelman, "Coordenadas" and "Una 'economía'").

The Virgin's "dormition" or "assumption"—terms that sought to elude the idea of death—was considered relevant to these beliefs and was commemorated according to the liturgical calendar. The Feast of Our Lady of Assumption must have been especially important for the confraternities of Saint Balthasar and the Souls of Purgatory, and it was one of these occasions, in 1787, that gave rise to the events that took the "king of the *Congos*" before the law. On this occasion, it was a black enslaved man named Pedro Duarte who was allegedly crowned king.[8]

The practice known as coronation appears to have been taken as a challenge to the viceregal authority, whose seat was in Buenos Aires. Beyond the personal tensions among the individual actors mentioned in the document, the colonial magistrate had motive to intervene, questioning witnesses, repressing the actions of the confraternity, and forcing Pedro Duarte to resign. The account, which is taken from the AGN, records the events reviewed by the colonial authorities. The document consists of various sections. The first is a report given to Viceroy Marqués de Loreto by the *sargento mayor* of the Company of Free Blacks Manual Farías (informer and party in the case against the free black Pablo Agüero for contempt). This report is followed by the testimonies of several witnesses of African origin (many of them identified as being from *Guinea* or African born), who report on conflicts between Farías and Agüero.

Among these appears the testimony taken from Pedro Duarte himself, black *mayordomo* of the Confraternity of Saint Balthasar and supposedly regarded as king of

[8] In addition to the document in this chapter, see also Bernand and Cirio ("¿Rezan o bailan?") in the Bibliography.

the *Congos.* Finally, the commissioner Francisco Rodríguez sought punishment for several of the parties in the cause. With some nuances, it seems that the colonial magistrate frowned on the Afroporteño parties, the informer, the man he has denounced, and several of the witnesses.

The people whose voices are recorded in the document are considered inclined to disorder and insubordination against Spanish rule in the city. The festive practices of the Africans, with their dances, elections, and rituals related to ethnic authorities were seen as symptoms of the conflicts that overflowed the boisterous disorder of the festival with its dance and drink. These were practices and voices dangerous to the control that the Spanish Crown's regime exercised over its colonial subjects. The survival of ethnic identities and solidarities and the strengthening of social and cultural bonds they represented—in a somewhat underhanded way in the Christian celebrations—were a potential threat to colonial control.

[Lo que expone Manuel Farías en su *memorial* contra Pablo Agüero][1]

Excelentísimo Señor Virrey,

Manuel Farías, *vecino* de esta ciudad y *sargento mayor* de las *Compañías de negros libres,* con el mayor respeto y veneración que a Vuestra Excelencia debe, le hace presente:

que Pablo Agüero comisionado para recoger los *negros* fugitivos y gobernar los *tambos* de ellos, llevado de este *fuero* y sin reconocer ser soldado de la compañía del exponente [Farías], le ha negado enteramente la subordinación, sin quererle obedecer como es de ordenanza, manteniéndose además sin concurrir a la compañía, ni pedirle al suplicante [Farías] como *sargento mayor* el auxilio que necesitase en los casos precisos para el cumplimiento de su comisión, sino que de autoridad propia recoge los *negros* y se los lleva cuando los necesita, mirando al exponente sin reconocimiento de ser su jefe inmediato, con un total desprecio y aún tratando mal de palabra. En tal disposición que el día 11 de agosto del año próximo pasado, habiéndole [Manuel Farías] encontrado [a Pablo Agüero] junto a la quinta de Don Manuel Warnes, y sin motivo que el de persuadirse,[2] había dado parte [Farías] de la *coronación* del *negro* Pedro Duarte en cierto *tambo,* por orden y disposición de Agüero, trató al exponente de pícaro, indigno, soplón y otros dicterios, como justificará si Vuestra Excelencia lo considerare preciso.

Llegando a tanto extremo la enemistad que le profesa, que cerciorados de [esta enemistad] y del valimiento con el referido [Agüero], los propios soldados que trae en su compañía, el uno de ellos llamado Manuel [de] Jesús, valido de dicha protección, tuvo valor en la Plaza Nueva para tratar de "puta" a la mujer [de Farías], sólo porque queriendo [ella] cobrar de un indio cuatro *reales* que le debía en la *pulpería* de la esquina, [la mujer de Farías] le suplicó [a Manuel Jesús] que lo dejase hasta que se los pagara. A lo que [Manuel de Jesús] le respondió con aquel dicterio o mala palabra. Como en caso necesario, [Farías] ofrece igualmente justificar con el mismo pulpero o dueño de la *pulpería* y algunos otros testigos que presenciaron el lance.

Y por último si fuese [Farías] a puntualizar los varios pasajes ocurridos con dicho Agüero, y las muchas ocasiones, y quisquillas que [Agüero] busca para provocar y ofenderlo, faltándole a toda subordinación, sería proceder en infinito, y lo que es más, molestar la atención de Vuestra Excelencia, ocupada en otros graves asuntos de su elevado carácter, dejándolo todo a su alta y sabia comprensión, más hallándose cerciorado de algunas cosas de las expuestas en este *memorial,* y otras, el *teniente [del] rey* de esta *plaza,* como el exponente tiene comprendido.

Para comprobación de ello, a Vuestra Excelencia rendidamente suplica se digne mandar informe sobre todo lo que le conste, y con su exposición, proceder a dar aque-

[1] Información hecha para esclarecer lo que expone Farías en su *memorial* contra Pablo Agüero, ambos dos *negros*, hecha en Buenos Aires a 23 de enero de mil setecientos ochenta y siete, Archivo de la Nación, Buenos Aires, Escribanía mayor de Gobierno, Sala IX, 36:4:3, legajo 75, exp. 10.

[2] *Persuadirse* here is used in the sense of "to inform himself."

[Report by Manuel Farías against Pablo Agüero][1]

Most Excellent Lord Viceroy,

Manuel Farías, citizen of this city and *sargento mayor* of the *Compañías de negros libres* [Companies of Free Blacks], with the greatest respect and veneration that is due Your Excellency, presents the following:

that Pablo Agüero, commissioned to round up fugitive blacks and regulate their *tambos,* based on this *fuero* and without acknowledging that he himself is a soldier of the declarant's company, has completely refused to subordinate himself, refusing to obey [Farías] as required by ordinance. He has not reported for duty to the company and has not asked the petitioner [Farías] as *sargento mayor* for the aid he might need in certain cases for the fulfillment of his commission. Rather, without proper authority, he rounds up the blacks and takes them when he needs them. Without recognizing [Farías] as his immediate superior, [Agüero] treats him with complete scorn. He has even abused him verbally. For instance, on August 11 of last year, having seen [Agüero] near Don Manuel Warnes' estate, [Farías], for no reason other than to verify [what he had heard], told him about the *coronation* of the black man Pedro Duarte at a certain *tambo* by order and disposition of Agüero, [whereupon Agüero] called [Farías] a scoundrel, worthless, traitor, and other names, as [Farías] can prove, if Your Excellency considers it necessary.

The antagonism that he professes is so extreme that even the soldiers from [Agüero's] company, and with his protection, one of them, Manuel Jesús, availing himself of that protection at the corner store [*pulpería*] in the Plaza Nueva, had the audacity to call the declarant's wife a whore, just because [she] was trying to collect four *reales* from an Indian who owed it to her. She begged [Manuel Jesús] to leave the Indian alone until she could collect from him, to which [Manuel Jesús] responded with said insult or profanity. If necessary, [Farías] also offers to verify this by way of the tavern keeper or owner of the tavern and some other witnesses who were present at this incident.

Lastly, if the declarant were to specify the various dealings he has had with Agüero and the many occasions and the trivialities [Agüero] seeks to provoke and offend, [aside from] failing to act as his subordinate, it would take forever. Moreover, it would serve as a distraction for Your Excellency who, given your high office, has other serious matters equal to your prominent nature to consider, as all is left to your superior and wise understanding, more so as the *teniente del rey* of this *plaza* has verified some of the things that have been presented in this report and others, as the declarant understands them.

So that they can be further certified, [the declarant] most humbly begs Your Excellency to consider it worthwhile to order an inquiry regarding all the foregoing and,

[1] Information taken to clarify what [Manuel] Farías presents in his *memorial* [report] against Pablo Agüero, both black men, officiated in Buenos Aires, January 23, 1787 (Chief Government Notary Office).

lla seria providencia que su justificación gradúe correspondiente a las circunstancias de los asuntos tocados, como lo espera el exponente de la notoria integridad de Vuestra Excelencia. Buenos Aires 16 de enero de 1787.

Manuel Farías

[El testimonio de José García, *negro* libre]

Preguntado si ha *visto* o oído decir que el tal Agüero haya querido coronar por rey algún *negro,* diga de qué *nación,* cómo se llama, en dónde, y cuándo, responde que la víspera de Nuestra Señora del Transito hallándose el que declara [García] en su casa de noche, pasaron por la inmediación de ella unos *negros,* los que dice no conoció. Y que entre sí iban hablando y diciendo que el Día del Tránsito, que era el día siguiente, el *negro* Pablo Agüero disponía el que se coronase por rey de los congos al *negro* Pedro Duarte.

Preguntado si sabe o ha oído decir que se verificase la *coronación* de dicho rey, en ese día o en otro, responde que no ha sabido que se haya verificado tal *coronación* en ése ni en otro.

Preguntado si sabe que Agüero le haya faltado el respeto y subordinación al mencionado *sargento mayor* [Farías] diga en qué términos, y cuándo, responde haber oído al mismo Farías, y otros soldados decir que [Agüero] nunca le ha querido obedecer en cosa alguna, diciendo que no lo obedecería de ningún modo porque los *capitanes* y *sargento mayor* [Farías] todos eran tan soldados como él. Cuyas expresiones, y la de decir que no había más *sargento mayor* que él [Agüero], son frecuentes como se verifica en el tratamiento que le dan [a Farías] todos los *morenos.*

Preguntado si sabe que el *negro* Farías, y Agüero se tengan odio o mala voluntad, responde que sí, porque saliendo de esta ciudad para su casa un día—el que no tiene presente—los encontró dos cuadras antes de llegar a la quinta de don Manuel Warnes, agarrados los dos de palabras. Y que oyó que el *negro* Agüero, le decía, a Farías, que la causa de que los *negros* estuviesen insolentes, desobedientes a la *justicia* y a él, era porque el mismo Farías así se lo aconsejaba, por lo que dice el que declara [García] que viéndolos tan enfervorizados, y en términos de poderse agarrar y lastimarse, procuró separarlos como así lo ejecutó haciendo que cada uno de los dos tomase distinto camino y no se pudiesen volver a agarrar, lo que ejecutaron inmediatamente, retirándose el que declara [García]. Y no volvió a verlos más.

Preguntado si sabe que el mencionado Agüero haya querido coronar algún *negro* por rey, de alguna *nación,* responde [que] ignora el todo de la pregunta.

[El testimonio de José González, natural de *Guinea*]

Preguntado si conoce al *sargento mayor* de *negros* Manuel Farías, y al *negro* Pablo Agüero, y qué comisión tiene, responde [que] conoce a Manuel Farías, *sargento mayor* del declarante, y que le obedece sus órdenes verbales o por escrito. Y que a Pablo Agüero,

with its documentation, proceed to give it [the] serious consideration that is justly commensurate with the circumstances of the related subjects, given Your Excellency's notable reputation for fairness. Buenos Aires, January 16, 1787.

Manuel Farías

[Testimony of José García, Free Black]

Asked whether he has seen or heard that Agüero wished to crown some black as king, [he should declare] from what *nation,* what his name is, where, and when, he responds that on the eve of the feast of *Nuestra Señora del Tránsito,* the witness [José García] was at his home that night when some blacks, whom he says he did not know, passed in the vicinity. They were talking among themselves and saying that on the day of the *Tránsito* celebration, which was the following day, the black Pablo Agüero had arranged for the black Pedro Duarte to be crowned as King of the Congos.

Asked whether he knows or has heard that the *coronation* of said king has been confirmed on that day or any other day, he responds that he does not know if such a *coronation* has been confirmed on that day or any other day.

Asked whether he knows whether Agüero has failed to respect or subordinate himself to the aforementioned *sargento mayor,* he is to state the circumstances and when it occurred, he responds that he has heard Farías himself and other soldiers say that [Agüero] has never wished to obey him in anything, [that Agüero has] said he would not obey him in any way because the captains and the *sargento mayor* [Farías] were soldiers just like him. These statements, and saying there was no other *sargento mayor* than he [Agüero], are frequent, as is verified by the manner in which all the *morenos* [*negros*] treat him [Farías].

Asked whether he knows that the black Farías and Agüero hate each other or harbor ill will toward each other, he responds that it is so, because, leaving this city for his home one day—he does not remember which day—he encountered them two blocks before arriving at the *quinta* [estate] of Don Manuel Warnes, verbally tearing into each other. He heard the black Agüero saying to Farías that the reason the blacks were insolent and disobedient to the law and him was because Farías himself advised them to be so. For this reason, [García] says that, seeing them so worked up, about to attack and hurt each other, he moved to separate them, which he managed to do, making each one leave in a different direction so that they would not continue to fight each other. They left immediately, as did the witness, and he did not see them again.

Asked whether he knows that the aforementioned Agüero had wanted to crown a black as king of some *nation,* he responds that he knows nothing about what is being asked.

[Testimony of José González, Native of *Guinea*]

Asked whether he knows the *sargento mayor de negros,* Manuel Farías, and the black Pablo Agüero, and what commission he has, he responds that he knows Manuel Farías, [his own] *sargento mayor* and obeys his verbal or written orders. He also knows Pablo

también conoce, y que sabe [que] está comisionado con soldados de la misma *casta* para prender *negros* y *negras* huidos de sus amos, y para la pacificación de ellos mismos, por el Señor *Teniente Gobernador.*

Preguntado si sabe que el *negro* Agüero haya dispuesto en algún tiempo el que se coronase por rey alguno de sus *castas,* responde que en uno de los días de fiesta que se juntan a bailar los *negros* en el *hueco* destinado, vio el declarante que llevaban, debajo de un quitasol grande, a un *negro* nombrado Pedro Duarte y que en la cabeza llevaba puesta una especie de corona. Pero que habiendo *visto* el mencionado Agüero aquel aparato, hizo inmediatamente que se lo quitaran, lo que así se verificó, advirtiendo el declarante [González] que todos los otros *negros* de la *nación conga* veneraban, y obedecían todas las órdenes que como rey les daba el tal Pedro Duarte.

Preguntado si sabe o ha oído decir que se mantiene como tal rey el mencionado Duarte, responde [que] sabe que el día que se hace la función de San Baltasar en la Iglesia de La Piedad lo respetan, y obedecen como a tal rey, de su *nación,* y no como a *mayordomo.*

[Testimonio de Pedro Duarte, natural de *nación conga*]

Preguntado si sabe que el *negro* Farías y Agüero hayan tenidos algunas palabras, quimeras o desafueros, responde que hace muchos años que están discordes, y que el uno al otro se tiran cuanto es posible, de resultas de haber dado parte el mencionado Farías al *señor teniente del rey* y *sargento mayor* de que había reyes en varias *naciones.*

Preguntado cómo le consta a ciencia cierta que el mencionado Farías dio parte al *teniente del rey* y *sargento mayor de la plaza,* responde que por hallarse el que declara [Pedro Duarte] en la capilla de La Piedad, con otros *negros* hermanos de la Cofradía de San Baltasar, al tiempo de ir a enterrar un hermano difunto, llegó Farías con tropa, prendiendo al que declara [Duarte] en las inmediaciones de la capilla. Y a Pablo Agüero, fue buscarlo a su casa y los arrestó en la *ranchería.* Y de ella pasaron a la real cárcel.

Preguntado si el año pasado lo han nombrado los *negros* de su *nación* por rey, y si ha ido al *hueco del tambo* para que lo reconociesen por tal, el Día de la Nuestra Señora del Tránsito, responde [que] no ha ido al *hueco* con insignias de rey. Y sólo fue con los de su *nación* con su capa y sombrero de una pollera, hecho un quitasol, para que lo reconociesen por *mayor* pero no por rey.

Preguntado quién dispuso que lo diesen reconocer al declarante por *mayor,* responde que varios *negros* de su *nación,* pero que Pablo Agüero, no se mezcló en esto. Y sólo sí se mezcló en lo que luego ha *visto* al declarante [Duarte] con quitasol, lo hizo quitar y que lo llevasen a su casa. Pero que el referido Agüero vio que al declarante [Duarte] le dieron [a] reconocer.

[Testimonio de Pablo Agüero, natural de *Guinea*]

. . . Responde [que] se llama Pablo Agüero, natural de *Guinea* y que está comisionado por el *señor gobernador intendente* para prender *negros* y *negras* fugitivos de sus amos,

Agüero and knows that he is commissioned with soldiers of the same *casta* by the *señor teniente del gobernador* to arrest black men and women who have fled their masters and to have them submit [to authority].

Asked whether he knows whether the black Agüero had made arrangements at one point for someone from the *castas* to be crowned as king, he responds that on one of the feast days when the blacks gather to dance at the *hueco,* the preselected site, the witness saw they were leading a black man named Pedro Duarte under a large parasol and that he was wearing a sort of crown. But once Agüero had seen the [crown], he immediately had them remove it. And that is what happened. The witness observed that all the other blacks of the *Congo nation* respected and obeyed all the orders that Pedro Duarte gave them as king.

Asked whether he knows or has heard that the aforementioned Duarte continues to act as such a king, he responds [that] he knows that on the day when the celebration of Saint Balthasar is held in the Church of La Piedad, they respect and obey him like a king of their *nation* and not as *mayordomo.*

[Testimony of Pedro Duarte, Native of the *Congo Nation*]

Asked whether he knows that the black Farías and Agüero have had words, have quarreled, or have fought, he responds that for many years they have been at odds, and they fight with one another whenever possible, because the aforementioned Farías had told the *señor teniente del rey* and the *sargento mayor* that [there continued to be] kings in the various *nations.*

Asked how he knows for certain that the aforementioned Farías informed the *teniente del rey* and the *sargento mayor de la plaza,* he responds that when the witness was in the chapel of the Church of La Piedad with other black brothers of the *Cofradía* de San Baltasar, ready to go bury a deceased brother, Farías arrived with troops and arrested the witness near the chapel. Concerning Pablo Agüero, [Farías] went to look for him at his house and arrested [the rest of] them in the settlement, and from there they went to the royal jail.

Asked whether the blacks of his *nation* named him king last year and if, on the Feast of the Assumption he went to the *hueco del tambo* so that they might recognize him as such, he responds that he has not gone to the *hueco* with insignias of a king. He went solely with the people of his *nation* with his cape, a hat, and a parasol made of a *pollera* [a rigid hoop wire], so that they might recognize him as *mayor,* but not as king.

Asked who arranged for the witness to be recognized as *mayor,* he responds that various blacks from his *nation* did so, but Pablo Agüero was not mixed up in this. Rather, he only became involved after he saw [Duarte] with the parasol, which he made him remove, and ordered that he be taken home. But the said Agüero did see that the witness had already been recognized [as *mayor*].

[Testimony of Pablo Agüero, Native of *Guinea*]

. . . He responds that his name is Pablo Agüero, a native of *Guinea,* and that he is commissioned by the *señor gobernador intendente* to arrest black men and women, fugitives

y para tenerlos sosegados y quietos en sus diversiones y bailes, y que vive en el *barrio* de Monserrat.

Preguntado qué palabras ha tenido con la mujer del *Sargento Mayor* Farías, diga adónde y cuándo, responde que jamás mientras la conoce ha tenido ninguna palabra ofensiva con semejante mujer.

Preguntado si reconoce a Manuel Farías por su *sargento mayor* y si obedece sus órdenes concernientes al servicio del rey, y del bien público, responde que siempre lo ha obedecido por su *sargento mayor* e igualmente sus órdenes hasta que se le dio la comisión, la que dice el declarante le hizo presente cuando se la comisionaron.[3]

Preguntado si cuando necesita tropa de su *nación* para arrestar algún fugitivo le pide a su *sargento mayor* la tropa necesaria para ejecutarlo, responde [que] se la pidió sólo una vez para prender los *negros* que se estaban vistiendo de *cambunda* el día de San Baltasar en la Capilla de La Piedad, y como no se la quiso dar nunca se ha querido valer más de él, y se ha valido de tropas veteranas, como lo tiene mandado el *gobernador intendente* con permiso del Señor *Virrey*.

Preguntado qué más palabras pasaron entre los dos mencionados *negros,* responde [que] le dijo a Farías que no [era] cierto lo que le decía y que si lo era el de que el mismo fue buscar al *negro* Juan [de Belén] para [que] viniese a la casa del *ayudante de la plaza* arriba mencionado, y le dijese, que el *negro* Pablo Agüero quería coronarlo [a Duarte] por rey; siendo incierto todo, agregándole Farías al declarante que si él quería, solicitaría con el gobierno la misma comisión, en virtud de ser la ciudad grande, la multitud de *negros* mucha, y que de ese modo podían estar más sosegados; a lo que le respondió el que declara [Agüero], que estaba muy bien, y que le solicitase.

[Testimonio de Manuel de Jesús, natural de *Guinea*]

. . . Responde [que] se llama Manuel de Jesús, natural de *Guinea,* y que es comisionado de ordenanza del *negro* Pablo Agüero, y que vive en casa del mismo.

Preguntado qué sueldo tiene por hallarse con el referido Agüero empleado, y quién se lo paga, responde [que] tiene de sueldo seis *pesos* mensuales, los mismos que le satisface Agüero.

Preguntado de dónde se los paga Agüero, responde [que] tiene en su casa faena de badanas la que hace trabajar con peones, y de eso, y de lo que le dan los dueños de los *negros* esclavos fugitivos conceptúa le pagará los seis *pesos.*

Preguntado si sabe que Agüero cuando necesita soldados de la misma *nación* para prender algunos *negros* y para la quietud de los mismos le pide el auxilio correspondiente a su *sargento mayor,* . . . responde [que] le consta que para prender seis *negros,* de distintos amos que se hallaban escondidos en el monte de la quinta de Valentín le pidió auxilio para prenderlos, y no se lo dio [el *sargento mayor*] diciendo que no tenían soldados las compañías, y que así él mismo los buscase como en efecto así lo ejecutó, y prendieron a los mencionados *negros,* y se los entregaron a sus amos dándole por cada uno de ellos tres y cuatro *pesos.*

[3] In the manuscript: *comicieron.*

from their masters, and to keep them calm and quiet in their diversions and dances and that he lives in the neighborhood of Monserrat.

Asked what words he had with the wife of *Sargento Mayor* Farías [and that he] explain where and when, he responds that while he has known her, he has never spoken any offensive words to that woman.

Asked whether he recognizes Manuel Farías as his *sargento mayor* and if he obeys his orders concerning service to the king's and the public good, he responds that he has always obeyed him as his *sargento mayor,* and equally his orders, until he was given the commission, the one that the declarant [Manuel de Jesús] says he made [Farías] aware of when he was commissioned.

Asked whether, when he needs troops from his *nation* to arrest some fugitive, he asks the *sargento mayor* for the necessary troops to carry this out, he responds that he asked for them only once to arrest blacks who were dressing in *Cambunda* [style clothing] in the chapel of La Piedad on the day of Saint Balthasar. Because the *sargento mayor* refused to give [him the troops], he has never again counted on him. [Instead,] he has relied on veteran troops, as the *gobernador intendente* has mandated with the permission of the *Señor Virrey.*

Asked what other words were exchanged between the two blacks mentioned, he responds that he told Farías that what he said to him [was] not true. If anything is true, then it is that [Farías] himself went to look for the black Juan [de Belén], so that he might go to the house of the abovementioned *ayudante de la plaza* and tell him that the black Pablo Agüero wanted to crown [Duarte] king. As everything was uncertain, Farías added to [Agüero] that if he wanted, he would seek the same commission from the government, given that the city was large, that there was a great multitude of blacks, and that, in this way, they could be even more placated. To that [Agüero] responded that it would be very good and that he should request it [of the government].

[Testimony of Manuel de Jesús, Native of *Guinea*]

. . . He responds that his name is Manuel de Jesús, a native of *Guinea,* and he is commissioned under ordinance by the black Pablo Agüero, and he lives in his house.

Asked what salary he receives as an employee of the aforementioned Agüero and who pays him, he responds that he receives a salary of six *pesos* per month, which are paid by Agüero.

Asked from what source Agüero pays him, he responds that [Agüero] has work done on sheepskins at his house by laborers and from that, and from whatever the owners of the black fugitive slaves give him, he assumes that Agüero pays the six *pesos.*

Asked if he knows whether Agüero, when he needs soldiers from the same *nation* in order to arrest some blacks, and in order to keep them orderly, asks for the appropriate assistance from his *sargento mayor,* he responds that he knows for a fact that, in order to arrest six blacks from different masters who were hiding in the woods of Valentín's estate, he asked for assistance to arrest them; but the [*sargento mayor*] did not give him any, saying that the companies did not have soldiers, and that he himself should look for them, which is, in fact, what he did. They arrested the aforementioned blacks and delivered them to their masters, who gave him three to four *pesos* for each of them.

Preguntado si sabe o ha oído decir que el *negro* Agüero, haya querido coronar por rey algún *negro,* responde [que] se hallaba en ese tiempo en la costa patagónica en el barco del *capitán* Bautista pero que no tiene noticias que el *negro* Agüero haya dispuesto semejante cosa.

Preguntado con qué mujer tuvo unas palabras en la Plaza Nueva y cuáles fueron estas palabras, responde [que] estando el declarante [Manuel de Jesús] en dicha *plaza* en busca de una *negra* fugitiva vio que a la puerta de una *pulpería* estaba un indio ebrio, desvergonzándose con palabras descompuestas con un hombre español. Se arrimó a él, diciéndole se retirase de allí, y no fuese desatento con los españoles, porque de lo contrario lo llevaría preso. Y hallándose presente una *negra* la que dice no conoce—vendiendo empanadas o pasteles—le dijo [la mujer] al que declara [Manuel de Jesús], que el mencionado indio le debía tres *reales,* y que no le había de llevar preso. A lo que dice el que declara [Manuel de Jesús] que contestó a dicha *negra* que si ella volvía por el indio y lo defendía, también la llevaría presa. Que a estas razones la mencionada *negra* [la mujer de Farías] trató al declarante de "mi [ilegible]", y otras razones descompuestas; que sofocado de oír semejantes expresiones a la *negra,* dice ser cierto [que] la trató de "puta".

[Testimonio de Juan de Belén, natural de *Guinea*]

. . . Responde [que] dice conocer a Pablo Agüero por la comisión que tiene, para prender *negros* y *negras* fugitivos de sus amos, y para el sosiego y celo de los de su color.

Preguntado qué día, mes, y año tuvo el *sargento mayor* Farías una conversación, diga cuál es, responde que el día de Nuestra Señora del Tránsito se fue [¿advertir?] al *hueco del tambo,* y al día siguiente encontró Farías a [Juan de Belén] y le dijo que había de venir con él a la casa del *ayudante* don Francisco Rodríguez a decirle que Pablo Agüero quería coronar por rey, al *negro* Pedro Duarte, y que dijera si había visto la corona. [Juan de Belén] dice [que] le respondió al mencionado Farías, que no quería ir a la casa del expresado *ayudante* a decirle semejante cosa, pues él no había visto corona alguna para coronar al dicho Duarte, ni tampoco era sabedor, ni había oído decir semejante cosa, y que no podía en cargo de su conciencia decirlo. Y que no obstante de todas estas razones lo hizo ir a la casa del mencionado *ayudante* diciéndole que le daría un papel para que las *justicias* no se metiesen con él. A lo que le contestó diciendo no necesitaba papel, porque no había cometido delito alguno por donde la *justicia* pudiese perseguirlo y castigarlo. Y sin embargo de todo lo arriba expuesto lo hizo al declarante ir acompañado con él a la morada del mencionado *ayudante* a las once de la noche. Y no habiéndolo encontrado en ella, le dijo al que declara Farías [que] fuesen a casa del *mayor* de la *plaza* y que le dijere lo que tenía que decirle. . . .

En vista de todo lo cual, y al no esclarecerse plenamente la verdad, entre todos los testigos, por no estar contextes éstos, ni confrontar ninguna de las declaraciones, y sí lo están en que el *negro* Pablo Agüero no le tiene el respeto debido a Manuel Farías como *sargento mayor,* ni menos le pide los auxilios para las *prisiones* que tiene que hacer

Asked whether he knows or has heard that the black, Agüero, has wanted to crown a particular black as king, he responds that at that time he was on Captain Bautista's ship on the Patagonian coast, but he has heard nothing about the black Agüero having arranged such a thing.

Asked with which woman he had words at Plaza Nueva and what words they were, he responds that when the witness [he, Manuel de Jesús] was in the said *plaza* looking for a fugitive black woman, he saw, at the door of a tavern, an inebriated Indian making a fool of himself, speaking impudently with a Spaniard. He approached him, telling him to get out of there and watch his rudeness with the Spaniards; otherwise he would arrest him. There, a black woman, whom he said he did not know, was selling turnovers or pastries. She told [him] that the aforementioned Indian owed her three *reales* and that he [Manuel de Jesús] should not arrest him. The witness stated that he replied to the black woman that if she returned for the Indian and defended him he would also arrest her. For that reason, the black woman called the witness "my [illegible]" and other rude words. Provoked at hearing such expressions from the black woman, he said it was true that he called her a "whore."

[Testimony of Juan de Belén, Native of *Guinea*]

. . . He responds that he knows Pablo Agüero through his commission to arrest black men and women who have fled their masters and to keep them calm as well as for the zeal he has for those of his color.

Asked what day, month, and year did *Sargento Mayor* Farías have a conversation [with him] and that he recount it, he responds that on the Feast of the Assumption, he went to the *hueco del tambo* to make an announcement. On the following day, Farías found the witness [Juan de Belén] and told him he should come with him to the house of *Ayudante* Don Francisco Rodríguez to tell him that Pablo Agüero wanted to crown the black Pedro Duarte as king and that the witness should affirm that he had seen the crown. [Juan de Belén] said that he responded to Farías that he did not want to go to the house of the *ayudante* to tell him such a thing because he had not seen any crown to coronate Duarte, neither did he know nor had he heard tell such a thing, and that he could not in good conscience say so. Despite all these explanations, [Farías] made him go to the *ayudante*'s house, telling him he would give him a document so that the authorities would not bother him. [Juan de Belén] responded to this [by] saying that he did not need any document, because he had not committed any crime for which the authorities could pursue and punish him. However, despite all that has been stated above, [Farías] made the witness accompany him to the dwelling of the *ayudante,* at eleven o'clock at night. Not finding him there, Farías told him that they should go to the house of the *mayor de la plaza* and that he should tell him what he should tell him. . . .

In light of all [the testimonies], as the statements have neither been corroborated nor challenged, the truth is not entirely evident among all the witnesses. But they are [clear] in that the black Pablo Agüero has shown lack of the proper respect owed to Manuel Farías as *sargento mayor,* neither, at the very least, does he ask for assistance in the arrests he must make as part of his commission, thus abusing his own authority.

en su comisión, abusando de autoridad propia, debe de ser reprendido, o lo que Vuestra Excelencia fuese servido. Farías debe de ser *amonestado* y castigado por la influencia que hizo al *negro* libre Juan Belén para que fuese a la casa del *ayudante mayor* a decirle que el *negro* Pablo Agüero quería coronar por rey a Pedro Duarte, *moreno* libre, siendo todo incierto, como se prueba en la declaración del mismo, y las demás.

El *negro* Manuel de Jesús, separado de la comisión, porque sin [ilegible] de Pablo Agüero, quiso prender al indio, no teniendo facultades para ello, y confesar al mismo en su declaración haber llamado "puta", a la mujer de Farías, y no haber dado parte Agüero de esto mismo: está probado.

Los *tambos,* Señor, son muy perjudiciales, pues yo mismo he *visto* los escándalos gravísimos que tienen en sus bailes, y tan deshonestos como son, como así mismo las malas consecuencias que de ello resulta. Y la primera es que muchos de los amos que tienen esclavos no pueden contar con ellos en los días de fiesta, pues les parece que no son tales esclavos en estos dichos días. La segunda es el de que roban a sus dichos amos cuanto pueden para la contribución y conservación de dichos bailes, y la última es de que en los días de fiesta se encuentran en dichos *tambos,* y en las calles muchos de ellos ebrios, por cuyas causas los señores virreyes, y gobernadores antecesores al Excelentísimo Señor Virrey Marqués de Loreto, privaron enteramente todas estas danzas, y *tambos.* Pues por estas funciones, y en particular por la fiesta del Rosario, y San Baltasar han sucedido varias muertes, y desgracias. Los mismos *alcaldes* don José Gainza y don Manuel Antonio de Warnes vieron lo mismo que yo el domingo pasado, los que movidos del buen celo y la buena administración de *justicia* quisieron informarse y encontraron lo mismo. De todo lo cual me parece dieron parte al *teniente gobernador* para que pusiese *remedio* el que no se ha verificado, pues en el día siguiente.

No obstante de todo lo expuesto, Vuestra Señoría determinará lo que fuese de su superior agrado.

Buenos Aires 25 de enero de 1787
Francisco Rodríguez

He should be reprimanded or [dealt with] as Your Excellency might see fit. Farías should be admonished and punished for the influence he brought to bear on the free black Juan Belén, by making him go to the house of the *ayudante mayor* to tell him that the black Pablo Agüero wanted to crown Pedro Duarte, a free *moreno,* as king. Thus, everything appears questionable, as is evident by his and the rest of the testimonies.

The black Manuel de Jesús [should be] relieved of the commission because, without Pablo Agüero's [illegible], he tried to arrest the Indian without proper authorization. He confessed in his statement that he called Farías' wife a whore and that Agüero did not have any part in this. This is proven.

The *tambos,* Sir, are very harmful, for I myself have seen the serious scandals that occur in their dances, as well as how shameful they are, along with the unfortunate consequences that result from them. The first [ill consequence] is that many of the masters who have slaves cannot count on them on feast days, because they do not feel they are slaves on those days. The second is that they steal as much as they can from their masters in order to support and preserve their dances. And the last is that on those feast days many of them are drunk in the *tambos* and in the streets. For these reasons, the viceroys and governors previous to His Most Excellent Lord Viceroy Marqués de Loreto widely prohibited all these dances and *tambos* because several deaths and terrible things have occurred during these celebrations and, in particular, on the feast days of the Rosary and Saint Balthasar. Even the *alcaldes* Don José Gainza and Don Manuel Antonio de Warnes saw the same things as I did last Sunday. Moved by well-intended zeal and the proper administration of justice, they sought to inform themselves and concluded the same things. It seems to me that they testified about all of this to the *teniente gobernador* so that he might resolve this, which has not been carried out, well, on the following day.

Notwithstanding what has been said here, Your Lordship will make a determination in accordance with your supreme pleasure.

Buenos Aires, January 25, 1787
Francisco Rodríguez

Part III
Religious Beliefs and Practices

Religion was perhaps the most contentious sphere of cultural difference between Africans and Iberians. By 1502, Muslims and Jews who had not converted to Christianity were expelled from Spain, and converts and heretics under suspicion were punished by an active Inquisition. Religion and nationality built the foundations for racial differentiation and the social subordination of non-Christians. Africans were considered pagans who could be evangelized and saved, a purpose used to justify their enslavement, but when they continued to practice pagan beliefs or mixed them with Christianity, the Church felt threatened and prosecuted them as sorcerers, witches, and idolaters.

In times of high tension, colonials leveled accusations of witchcraft against Afro-Latinos as a social group out of fear of this more populous racial "inferior"; such fear may have played into the prosecution of Paula de Eguiluz (Chapter 11). In the Caribbean, Afro-Latinos were often caught between Catholic and Protestant worlds or navigated this European conflict to their advantage, as did many *Maroons* who aided Protestant pirates in their attacks on Spanish cities and wealth. In a contrary move, two *Beafada* men, slaves of a Cartagena woman who had been captured by a Dutch citizen and taken to the English colony of Providence Island, sided with Catholicism and gave informative and condemnatory accounts of the island's Puritan life to the Spaniards in Portobelo (Chapter 12).

Not all Catholic clergy thought alike, and, in the tradition of Saint Thomas Aquinas, Dominicans often saw pagan religious experience as preparation for Christian salvation. Perhaps this attitude provides some explanation for the survival in Sor Teresa Chicaba's as-told-to biography of syncretic elements of African religious belief, including a vision of a Holy White Lady in her West African homeland (Chapter 13). Many African religious societies in the Americas secretly sustained *transculturated* religious practices, but they could also proclaim orthodox Christianity to elevate themselves above other African *nations,* as did the leaders of the Confraternity of Saints Elesbão and Iphigenia in Rio de Janeiro, claiming superiority over the heathen *Angolans* (Chapter 14). All these stories show Afro-Latinos who adopted Catholicism continuing to live between religious worlds. Their stories allow glimpses into the ways that religion was a cultural space of transformation and a means to personal and communal survival and social standing.

11

The Witchcraft Trials of Paula de Eguiluz, a Black Woman, in Cartagena de Indias, 1620–1636[1]

Sara Vicuña Guengerich

Between 1623 and 1636, Paula de Eguiluz, a woman of African descent whose mother was of the *Biáfara* caste, was tried three times for witchcraft by the Inquisition in Cartagena de Indias on the northern coast of what is now Colombia. Paula was born on the Caribbean island of Santo Domingo but grew up serving different masters in Puerto Rico and Cuba. Her final master was Juan de Eguiluz, the royal treasury's accountant (*contador de la Real Hacienda de Su Majestad*) of the mines of El Cobre in Santiago del Prado, Cuba.[2]

In 1620, Juan de Eguiluz took over the copper mines as a private contractor and settled there with his household. Arriving with him from Havana were his daughter Doña Paula de Eguiluz, his slave Paula de Eguiluz, and other servants. The enslaved black population of Santiago del Prado at that time consisted of 205 males and 110 females (Díaz, 33).[3] Unlike several other female slaves of El Cobre, Paula de Eguiluz was a slave who dressed well and who was given permission to visit her friends in Havana from whom she learned spells to entice potential lovers. During the years prior to her arrest in Santiago del Prado, she was publicly known as a sorceress. The key suspicion that led to her arrest was that she had killed an Indian woman's child by means of witchcraft.

In 1623, Paula was accused of witchcraft (*brujería*), divination, and apostasy (declarations contrary to Church doctrine). In September of that year, the Inquisition prosecutor in Cartagena de Indias, Domingo Vélez de Asas y Argos, requested that the Inquisition authorities arrest her in Cuba, seize her goods, and transport her to the secret jails of the Cartagena Inquisition.[4] Paula de Eguiluz arrived in Cartagena in 1624 not yet informed of the specific charges she faced, because of the secrecy with which the Holy Office conducted the inquisitorial proceedings. Eleven witnesses had accused Paula of numerous offenses, among them causing the death of an infant by sucking her navel,[5] transforming herself into a goat, appearing and vanishing in different places without leaving a trace, and selling love spells.

[1] See Map 5.

[2] These rich mines constituted one of the most important enterprises in the Caribbean in the early seventeenth century because they provided for the needs of the Crown's artillery.

[3] For a history of the ownership of this mine and the slaves who worked it, see Díaz and Chapter 8 of this volume.

[4] According to Medina (108), the Inquisition tribunal in Cartagena de Indias built nine new cells to imprison their new offenders; among them was Paula de Eguiluz.

[5] A common indictment in witchcraft trials in Europe as well as in Spanish America was infanticide by vampirism (Henningsen, 27).

Her alleged crimes fell into the categories of sorcery and witchcraft, which the Church condemned. According to Colombian historian Diana Luz Ceballos Gómez (86–90), the Cartagena Inquisition distinguished between the application of the terms *hechicería* (sorcery) and *brujería*. *Hechicería* was the label given to an individual who used spells and remedies for both good and evil purposes, often with the aid of natural materials. With its European, Amerindian, and African origins, *hechicería* often used magic to help a person attract a mate or resolve spousal conflicts. Conversely, *brujería* was a label that defamed an entire group or category of people. A witch —a *bruja*—was thought to reject God and the sacraments and instead worship the devil and observe the witches' Sabbath.[6] Consequently, *brujería* represented a much more serious charge.

Although Spanish inquisitors were much more concerned with maintaining religious orthodoxy than they were with prosecuting witches per se, the discourses of race and ethnicity were fused with those of witchcraft and thus brought the attention of the Inquisition to accusations of witchcraft among non-European racial groups. Africans and their descendants used a variety of charms, talismans, and rituals to bring themselves luck and to protect themselves from various maladies; hence, their practices were suspected of being the work of the devil (Sweet, 164–75). Charges of witchcraft and heresy were common among the African-descent communities.

From 1610 to 1660, more than four hundred people were tried by the Inquisition in Cartagena de Indias. Sixteen percent of the accused, imprisoned, and punished were classified as blacks and eleven percent as slaves. About thirty percent of the accused, including blacks transported from the Caribbean islands, were tried for witchcraft, sorcery, and divination (Splendiani, Sánchez Bohórquez, and Luque de Salazar). Paula de Eguiluz was counted among the fifteen black women enslaved and free accused of being a witch and having made a pact with the devil (Blázquez, 215).

The documents in this chapter belong to the dossier of Paula de Eguiluz's first trial, which in its entirety includes 111 folios. This documentation reveals the peculiarities of inquisitorial procedures such as the initial denunciation of the offender by the familiars and professional informers of the Inquisition, the confiscation of property, the refusal to divulge the reasons for arrest, the three warnings (*amonestaciones*), the formal accusation of the prosecutor, the permission to obtain legal help for the victim, and the conclusion of the case with the victim's sentence and punishment (Kamen, 164–97). Paula de Eguiluz's first trial was composed of a series of *audiencias* or hearings, at which the prosecution and defense made their respective depositions of witnesses, and a series of interrogations carried out by the inquisitors in the presence of a notary.

The victim's confessions, such as Eguiluz's, in witchcraft trials offer a unique, if partial window into the life, religious beliefs, and supposed crimes of women of African descent. Paula's narrative, for example, employs a discursive strategy that speaks of a *transculturated* notion of Catholicism and upholds African cultural religious beliefs and practices often punished by the Church. Her confessions reveal her limited knowledge

[6] The witches' Sabbaths or *aquelarres* were supposedly assemblies where witches gathered on the eve of the festivals of the Christian year to commit themselves to the devil (Henningsen, 71).

of Christian doctrine; yet, they expose her devotion to the Virgin. They disclose her herbal cures to heal the ill as well as her potions to attract men. Most interestingly, they bring to light the shared cultural practices and social and kin affiliations of the African-descendant communities in the colonial period.

When both prosecution and defense completed their duties, Paula's case concluded with her acknowledgment that the devil had persuaded her to follow him. However, she repented of her sins and pled to be reconciled with the Church, which was the fate of the majority of the penitents in the Spanish Inquisition (Kamen, 185). Following the basic inquisitorial procedure, Paula appeared in an *auto de fe*,[7] wearing the penitential robe or *sambenito*.[8] She abjured publicly while receiving two hundred lashes, and she was ordered to serve in the city hospitals for one year.

Once reconciled with the Church, Paula remained in Cartagena de Indias as a free woman (*negra horra*), having obtained her *manumission* during the period of her first trial. After completing her sentence in the city hospital, she continued practicing love-related magic (*arte de bien querer*), spells, and healing, from which she obtained an income. In 1632 and again in 1636, the Inquisition of Cartagena de Indias tried Paula under new witchcraft charges. Her second and third trials highlighted the offenses from the first, adding only a few new accusations. In these new trials, Paula was accused of having made an explicit pact with the devil, conjuring the souls of purgatory to attract men, and initiating several women—white, black, and of other *castas*—into the witches' sect (*la secta de las brujas*).

After repeatedly hearing in her trials the highly doctrinal discourse of the Church's accusations, Paula altered her testimony and explanations, which previously had been rooted in an oral popular culture. Understanding that the Inquisition classified her African beliefs and practices as heretical, Paula began to rework her narrative according to Catholic discourse. Her testimony shifted from a total denial of all the charges to the acknowledgment of her herbal healing, to which she gave Christian purposes. As this did not satisfy the inquisitors' demands, Paula provided further confessions about her pact with the devil in which she admitted having committed aberrant sins. By the end of her third trial, not excerpted here, she provided the most symbolic images of witchcraft. She redefined the biblical concepts of the devil to provide a *transculturated* vision of the Catholic beliefs. As Paula de Eguiluz spoke with her inquisitors, and as her oral expressions were filtered through the bureaucratic discourse of the Inquisition, she left a narrative in which it is possible to hear her voice as she exercises agency in her own defense.

[7] Literally an act of faith. It was a public expression of penance for sin and hatred for heresy (Kamen, 185).

[8] The *sambenito* was usually a yellow, penitential garment displaying one or two diagonal crosses; the penitent was condemned to wear it as a mark of infamy (Kamen, 186).

Primera causa de Paula de Eguiluz, *negra horra* reconciliada por bruja, 1624[1]

[Paula de Eguiluz aparece por primera vez frente al inquisidor: 25 de mayo de 1624]

En la *audiencia* de la tarde de la Santa Inquisición de Cartagena, a 25 días del mes de mayo de 1624 años, estando en ella el señor Inquisidor Doctor Agustín de Ugarte Saravia, por su mandado fue traída de las *cárceles secretas* una mujer *morena* de la cual fue recibido juramento en forma debida de derecho. Y so cargo de él prometió de decir verdad así en esta *audiencia,* como en todas las demás que con ella se tuvieren hasta la determinación de su causa. Y que guardará secreto de todo lo que viere y entendiere. Y habiéndole preguntado cómo se llama, de dónde es natural, qué edad y qué estado tiene, dijo que se llama Paula de Eguiluz, natural de la ciudad de Santo Domingo de la isla Española.[2] Que al presente es esclava de Juan de Eguiluz, *alcalde mayor* de las minas del cobre, que son junto a la ciudad de Santiago de Cuba donde habrá cuatro años que está. De edad que dijo ser de treinta y tres años—poco más o menos. Y habiéndosele dicho que el *alcalde* ha hecho *relación* que ha pedido *audiencia,* que pues está en ella diga para qué la ha pedido.

Dijo que la ha pedido para declarar lo en que se halla culpada. Y habiéndola mandado que lo declare dijo que se acusa de un pecado de incesto. Que le cometió habiendo conocido carnalmente a dos hombres que eran parientes el uno de otro; no sabe en qué grado. Y que así mesmo se acusa de haber dado crédito a algunos sueños como fue que habiendo soñado una noche que venía ganado del Báyamo al Cobre, donde [Paula] estaba. Vio a la mañana cómo venía ganado de Barajagua, y entonces dijo a los que estaban presentes:—Mira si el sueño que yo soñé si no salió verdad. Ya vino ganado de Barajagua.—Y representándosele que veía a una persona, le sucedió verle otro día. Y en otras ocasiones sin haberlo soñado decía lo que veía y se alababa de que lo soñó. . . .

Ídem. Dijo que estando [Juan de Eguiluz] su amo malo de calenturas y andando ésta preguntando por algún *remedio* para quitárselos, Juana Gerónima, mujer soltera y española que vive en el Juan aconsejó a ésta que tomase unas cascarillas de naranjas que se ponen en el monumento [el sepulcro] y que con un huesito de muerto y un poco de romero lo pusiese en el dicho monumento y otro día lo moliese todo junto. Y de aquellos polvos le diese en vino al dicho su amo y que con eso se le quitarían las calenturas. Y [Paula], con el deseo que tenía de que su amo alcanzase salud lo quiso hacer y el dicho su amo no se lo consintió.

Y por ser dada la hora cesó esta *audiencia.* Y *amonestada* la rea, fue mandada llevar a su cárcel. Y habiéndosele leído esto que ha dicho dijo estar bien escrito. Y por no

[1] Records of the three Paula de Eguiluz trials are preserved in the Archivo Histórico Nacional, Madrid. These documents are also available online through the Portal de Archivos Españoles (PARES). Procesos de fe de Paula de Eguiluz, Ministerio de Cultura, Archivo Histórico Nacional, Madrid, Inquisición 1620, exp. 10.

[2] In the margin, *Edad 33 años.*

First Trial of Paula de Eguiluz, Accused of Witchcraft and Reconciled with the Church, 1624

[Paula de Eguiluz Appears for the First Time before the Inquisitor: May 25, 1624]

In the afternoon hearing of the Holy Inquisition of Cartagena on May 25, 1624, the Lord Inquisitor Doctor Agustín de Ugarte Saravia being present, a dark-skinned woman was ordered to be brought from the secret jails. Her oath was taken as required by law, under which she swore to tell the truth and to keep in secret what was revealed in this hearing as well as in the rest of the hearings until the resolution of her case. The inquisitor asked her name, origin, age, and status, to which she answered that her name was Paula de Eguiluz and she was originally from Santo Domingo in Hispaniola.[1] She said that at the present she was the slave of Juan de Eguiluz, administrator of the mines of El Cobre near Santiago de Cuba where she had been living for four years. She said she was about thirty-three years old. She was told that the *alcalde* reported her request for a hearing and now that she has one she should state why she requested it.

She said she requested it to declare her guilt. And having been told to declare it, she admitted the sin of incest, which she committed by carnal knowledge of two men who were relatives, but she does not know how they are related. She also accused herself of believing some of her dreams, such as the one she dreamed about some livestock that came from Báyamo to El Cobre, where she was at that time. The next morning, she saw livestock coming from Barajagua. Then she told everyone, "See how my dream came true: the livestock did come from Barajagua." Also, whenever she dreamed about a person, she happened to see this person the next day. Many other times she talked about what she saw without having dreamed it but bragged that she had dreamt it. . . .

Item. She said that one time her master [Juan de Eguiluz] had a high fever and she was looking for a remedy to heal him. Juana Gerónima, a single Spanish woman who lives in Juan[2] advised her to take some of the orange peels, place them on a grave and mix them with a little bit of ground bones from a dead person, along with rosemary leaves, and put them on the grave. Then the next day mix all that with wine so her master would drink it and become well. Paula did as indicated because she wanted her master to feel better; however, her master did not allow it.

And because of the hour, the hearing ended. The inquisitor admonished Paula and sent her back to her prison. Before she left, the scribe read the content of this document, and she said it was recorded correctly. The inquisitor Agustín de Ugarte Saravia

[1] A note in the margin reads, "Age: thirty-three years."

[2] This might be the name of a street or a neighborhood in colonial Havana. There are references to other geographical locations throughout the document that have masculine given names.

saber escribir lo firmó el señor inquisidor, el Doctor Agustín de Ugarte Saravia. Ante mí Luís Blanco de Salcedo, secretario.

[La segunda *audiencia:* 4 de julio de 1624]

En la *audiencia* de la mañana de la Sancta Inquisición de Cartagena—a cuatro días del mes de julio de 1624 años—estando en ella el señor inquisidor Doctor Agustín de Ugarte Saravia . . . fuele dicho [a Paula] que dé su genealogía. Y haciéndola, dijo que —como dicho tiene—nació en la ciudad de Santo Domingo en casa de Diego de Leguízamo de quien era esclava su madre Guiomar, *negra* de *casta biafara.* Y que no sabe quién fue su padre ni tiene noticia de sus abuelos paternos ni maternos ni de los demás transversales y colaterales. Y sólo conoce a dos hermanas que tiene en la dicha ciudad de Santo Domingo llamadas Ana y Juana. Que la Ana es libre y la Juana esclava de Antonio de Jaques en la dicha ciudad de Santo Domingo, adonde ésta estuvo hasta edad de trece años. Que por deudas que el dicho su amo debía [a] Juan Nieto, *criollo* de la dicha ciudad, se hizo pagado en ésta y otras de la deuda que a él se le debía. El cual la vendió después a Iñigo de Otazo que la llevó a Puerto Rico adonde en su poder estuvo cuatro años, al cabo de los cuales su mujer no gustó de que [Paula] estuviese en casa por tener celos de ella. E hizo que el dicho su marido la enviase a la Habana adonde la compró Juan de Eguiluz, el amo que hoy tiene, en cuyo servicio ha estado todo el demás tiempo hasta que fue presa por este Santo Oficio.

Preguntada si es cristiana bautizada y confirmada, dijo que es cristiana bautizada y que ha oído la bautizaron en [la] ciudad de Santo Domingo—en la iglesia *mayor.* Y que la confirmó don Fray Agustín Dávila, arzobispo de aquella ciudad. Y que oye misa ordinariamente los domingos y fiestas y confiesa y comulga cuando lo manda la Santa Madre Iglesia. Y que cumplió con ella en la cuaresma pasada en las dichas minas del cobre y la confesó y comulgó el padre Góngora.

Signose y santigüose; dijo el Padre Nuestro y el Ave María y el Credo y la Salve Regina. Y dijo los mandamientos de la ley de Dios todo bien dicho. Dijo no saber los artículos de la fe. Preguntada si sabe leer y escribir etc., dijo que no sabe leer ni escribir y que no sabe quién tenga libros prohibidos.

Fuele dicho que se le hace saber que en este Santo Oficio no se acostumbra prender a nadie sin tener bastante información de que haya hecho, dicho, y cometido o haya visto hacer, decir, y cometer a otras personas alguna cosa que sea, o parezca ser, en ofensa de Dios, nuestro Señor, y de su bendita madre la Virgen Santa María, y contra su santa fe católica y ley evangélica que tiene, predica y enseña la Santa Madre Iglesia Católica Romana; o contra el libre y recto uso y ejercicio del Santo Oficio. Por tanto, pues [Paula] debe entender que con la dicha información está presa.

PRIMERA AMONESTACIÓN

Y así se le amonesta . . . y encarga recorra la memoria y diga enteramente la verdad de todo lo que se sintiere culpada o supiere que otros lo estén, sin encubrir de sí ni de ellos cosa alguna y sin levantarse a sí ni a otros falso testimonio, porque haciéndolo así, su causa será despachada con la brevedad y misericordia que haya lugar. Donde no, se ha de hacer *justicia.* Dijo que ella ha dicho la verdad y no tiene más que decir. Y con tanto siendo *amonestada* la rea fue mandada volver a su cárcel. . . .

signed Paula's name because she did not know how to write. All this was done in my presence. I, the secretary Luis Blanco de Salcedo.

[The Second Hearing: July 4, 1624]

In the morning hearing of the Holy Inquisition of Cartagena—on July 4, 1624—the Lord Inquisitor Doctor Agustín de Ugarte Saravia being present . . . [Paula] was told to relate her genealogy. And complying, she said that as she has stated, she was born in Santo Domingo in the house of Diego de Leguízamo, who was her mother Guiomar's master. Her mother was a black slave of the *Biáfara* caste. She never knew her father or her grandparents on either side. She only knew that she had two sisters, Ana and Juana, living in Santo Domingo and that Ana is free and Juana is Antonio de Jaques' slave in Santo Domingo, where Paula lived until the age of thirteen. Her master at that time gave her and other slaves to Juan Nieto, a *Creole* living in that city, as a payment for a debt. Juan Nieto, she said, sold her to Iñigo de Otazo, who took her to Puerto Rico, where she stayed as his slave for four years. After that, Otazo's wife, jealous of her, demanded that her husband send Paula to Havana, where her current master Juan de Eguiluz bought her, and she served him until the Holy Office arrested her.

Asked if she was baptized and confirmed in the Catholic faith, she responded that she is a baptized Christian, and she has heard she was baptized in the city of Santo Domingo, in the main church, and that the archbishop of Santo Domingo, Don Fray Agustín Dávila, confirmed her. She also that said she hears Mass on Sundays and feast days, and that she confesses and takes communion on the days the Holy Church commands, and that she did so this past Lent in the El Cobre mines, and that Padre Góngora received her confession and gave her communion.

She made the sign of the cross, correctly recited the Lord's Prayer, the Creed, the Salve Regina, and the Ten Commandments. She said she did not know the Articles of the Faith. Asked if she knows how to read and write, she responded she does not and she does not know who might possess prohibited books.

The inquisitors told her that the Holy Office does not arrest anybody without having enough information that this person has done, said, or committed or has seen someone else do, say, or commit acts that are or appear to be an offense against our Lord God or His blessed mother, the Holy Virgin Mary, or against the Holy Catholic Faith and the law of the Gospels, which is preached and taught by the Holy Mother Roman Catholic Church or against the free and right exercise of the Holy Office. Therefore, Paula should understand that she has been arrested because this Holy Office has received such information about her.

First Admonition

So she is admonished . . . and instructed to search her memory and to tell the whole truth of what she feels guilty for or what she knows of the guilt of others, without hiding anything and without giving false testimony. If she does so, her trial will be settled quickly and mercifully. Otherwise, justice will be done. She said she has told the truth and has nothing else to confess. And having been admonished, the defendant was sent back to her prison. . . .

[Acusaciones del fiscal del Santo Oficio: 11 de julio de 1624]

En la *audiencia* de la mañana de la Santa Inquisición de Cartagena, a 11 días del mes de julio de 1624 años, estando en ella el señor inquisidor Doctor Agustín de Ugarte Saravia. . . .

Fuele dicho que se le hace saber que el fiscal la quiere poner acusación. Que antes que se la ponga le estará bien decir la verdad. Donde no, se oirá al fiscal y se hará *justicia.* Dijo que ha dicho la verdad y no tiene más que decir. Y luego pareció presente el *licenciado* Domingo Vélez de Asas y Argos, fiscal de este Santo Oficio, y presentó esta acusación firmada de su nombre. Y juró en forma que no la ponía de malicia sino por ser verdad lo contenido en la dicha acusación, la cual es del tenor siguiente. . . .

Parezco ante Vuestra Señoría y criminalmente acuso a Paula *negra* de Eguiluz, natural de la ciudad de Santo Domingo de la isla Española y al presente esclava de Juan de Eguiluz, *alcalde mayor* en las minas del cobre que son junto a la ciudad de Santiago de Cuba, presa en las *cárceles secretas* de esta Inquisición. . . .

[Primera acusación]

1 Digo que siendo [Paula] cristiana bautizada y confirmada . . . usando de todas las gracias e inmunidades, privilegios y exenciones e *indulgencias* de tal cristiana; con poco temor de Dios y en gran daño de su consciencia, condenación de su alma, y menosprecio de la *justicia* de este Santo Oficio ingrata a tanto bien ha cometido delitos contra nuestra santa fe católica, haciendo muchos hechizos y supersticiones, mezclando cosas sagradas con profanas, invocaciones de demonios con quienes ha tenido *pacto* y seguido la secta de los brujos. Y [ha] procurado saber las cosas futuras y que dependen del *libre albedrío* del hombre; atribuyendo a la criatura lo que sólo se debe al Creador.

[Segunda acusación]

2 En prueba de lo cual, esta rea, el año pasado de 1623, por el mes de agosto con poco temor de Dios y de su conciencia, habiendo cierta persona parido una criatura—por el dicho tiempo estaría [Paula] en cumplimiento del *pacto* y alianza que tiene hecho con el demonio de hacer y cometer semejantes delitos—habiendo tomado la dicha criatura en los brazos y desenvuéltola, la chupó por el ombligo. Y le hizo todo el mal que pudo. De suerte que se conoció que [Paula] lo había hecho así por estar buena la criatura antes que esta rea la tomase, como por la pública voz y fama que tiene de bruja y hechicera, como esta rea lo es, de que vino a morir la dicha criatura luego. . . .

[Cuarta acusación]

4 En prueba de su mal vivir y proceder y poca cristiandad, esta rea se fue a una iglesia en compañía de cierta persona—habrá cuatro años poco más o menos—estando su amo Juan de Eguiluz malo. Y detrás del *coro* comenzó a escarbar con un palo en una sepultura. Y de ella sacó dos pedacitos de huesos de muerto y los llevó muy escondidos.

[Accusations of the Prosecutor of the Holy Office: July 11, 1624]

In the morning hearing of the Holy Inquisition of Cartagena on July 11, 1624, the Lord Inquisitor Doctor Agustín de Ugarte y Saravia being present. . . .

Paula was advised that the prosecutor of the Inquisition wishes to accuse her and that it behooves her, first, to tell the truth. Otherwise, the prosecutor will be heard and justice will be done. She said she has told the truth and has nothing else to say. Then Domingo de Vélez de Asas y Argos presented the following accusation, signed in his name, and he swore in due form that he did not have evil intent, but because it was the truth. His accusation is the following: . . .

I come before Your Lordship and criminally accuse the black woman Paula de Eguiluz, imprisoned in the secret jails of the Inquisition, who was born in Santo Domingo in Hispaniola . . . and is currently the slave of Juan de Eguiluz, the superior officer of the copper mines near Santiago de Cuba. . . .

[First Accusation]

1 I state that [Paula], being a baptized and confirmed Christian . . . enjoying the mercies and immunities, privileges, and exemptions and indulgences of this state, without fearing God, harming her conscience, condemning her soul, and with little regard for the justice of this Holy Office, ungrateful for such mercies, has committed crimes against our Holy Catholic Faith. She has used spells and believed superstitions, mixing sacred objects with profane ones, calling on the devil, with whom she has a pact, and joining the witches' sect. And she has tried to foretell things that depend on the free will of man, attributing to human beings what belongs solely to the Creator.

[Second Accusation]

2 [I offer] as proof, that last year in August of 1623, this defendant established a pact with the devil for whom she had to commit crimes, without fear of God or her own conscience. When a certain person[3] had given birth, Paula took the newborn in her arms and uncovered her belly to suck the life out of her through her navel,[4] and she did all the harm that she could. And it was known that Paula did so, because the child was well before she took her in her arms, and because it is public opinion and well known that she is a witch and sorcerer and the child ended up dying. . . .

[Fourth Accusation]

4 I offer as proof of her evil life and behavior and insincere Christianity that the accused went to a church with a certain person one day—about four years ago—because her master Juan de Eguiluz was ill. She started digging in a grave with a stick and took a couple of pieces of bone and carried them off secretly. And she said to the certain

[3] The words "a certain person" (*cierta persona*) are used to hide the identity of a witness, to maintain the secrecy demanded by the inquisitorial process.

[4] Witches were sometimes thought to kill their victims by sucking that person's nose, ears, eyes, mouth, or navel so he or she would bleed to death (Splendiani, Sánchez Bohórquez, and Luque de Salazar, 140).

Y dijo a la dicha persona que había ido con ella que aquello era para dar salud al dicho su amo. Los[3] molió con unas cáscaras de naranjas y romero y los hizo polvos. Y [los] amarró en un paño o papel con una cinta colorada de los cuales usó y hizo sus hechizos y embustes esta rea.

[SEXTA ACUSACIÓN]

12 Y ansí mesmo estando [Paula] en la dicha ciudad de la Habana en compañía del dicho Juan de Eguiluz, su amo—habiéndose [él] enojado con ella y queriéndola dar con una catana[4]—esta rea se le desapareció de delante. Y se arrojó por una ventana abajo donde había mucha cantidad de piedras que era fuerza se lastimase. De lo cual no recibió esta rea por entonces lesión alguna—de que se lo hizo con la alianza y *pacto* que tiene con el demonio—en esta ocasión le sirvió de librarla de que no le recibiese. . . .

[OCTAVA ACUSACIÓN]

8 Y así mismo fue público en las dichas minas que esta rea estuvo presa por la *justicia ordinaria* por la grande fama y publicidad que había que era bruja. Y estando presa en el cuerpo de guardia envió cierta persona por ella para castigarla. Y esta rea dijo a los soldados, que a su cargo la tenían, que no la dejasen llevar por cuanto ella estaba presa por un grave delito que había cometido de haber muerto a una niña, como se lo imputaban. . . .

[DOCEAVA ACUSACIÓN]

12 Y ansí mesmo esta rea ha usado de ciertos palillos y cabellos del hombre con quien ha tenido sus *deshonestidades.* Y usado de ciertas aguas sacadas de la yerba curia. Y todo ello lo ha traído metido en una bolsilla de tela blanca como si fueran reliquias, o a lo menos dando muestras de ello. Y así mesmo las ha puesto en la cama debajo de las almohadas. Y usando de la misma raíz de la yerba curia para sus embustes—con lo cual se ve clara y evidentemente que esta rea está dejada de la mano de Dios, Nuestro Señor, y apartada de su sancta fe católica y entregada a la servidumbre y esclavitud del demonio. Y aunque por Vuestra Señoría ha sido *amonestada* muchas y diversas veces diga y confiese enteramente la verdad, no lo ha querido hacer; antes callándola se ha perjurado. . . .

. . . Suplico a Vuestra Señoría que habida mi *relación* por verdadera. . . . y la dicha Paula de Eguiluz haber cometido los dichos delitos de que por mí es acusada, condenándola por ellos en las *mayores* y más graves penas que de derecho lugar haya. . . . Y que siendo necesario, la susodicha, sea puesta a cuestión de tormento en que esté y persevere. Y en su persona se repita hasta que enteramente diga la verdad, sobre [lo] que pido *justicia.* Y juro en forma y para ello el Santo Oficio de Vuestra Señoría imploro. El *licenciado* Domingo Vélez de Asas y Argos.

[3] *Los huesos.*

[4] A coarse, heavy object or heavy cavalry sword with a curved blade and a single cutting edge.

person who had gone with her that it was to cure her master. She ground [the bones] into a powder together with orange peels and rosemary leaves. Then she put this mixture in a piece of cloth or paper and tied it with a red ribbon to use them for her spells and deceits. . . .

[Sixth Accusation]

6 And likewise, when Paula was still living in Havana with her master Juan de Eguiluz, he got upset at something she did and wanted to hit her with a saber, but Paula disappeared before his eyes. She threw herself through the window and fell on a rocky spot, where she should have been injured, but she received no injuries—which indicates that she did this with the alliance and pact she had with the devil—on this occasion he kept her from harm. . . .

[Eighth Accusation]

8 And likewise it was public knowledge in the mines that this defendant was imprisoned by order of the trial court [*por la justicia ordinaria*] because it was commonly held that she was a witch. And while she was imprisoned at the guardhouse, a certain person sent for her to punish her. And this defendant told the soldiers who were charged with her keeping that they should not let her be taken away as she was imprisoned for a serious crime that she had committed, that of killing a child, as was imputed to her. . . .

[Twelfth Accusation]

12 And likewise, the accused used twigs and hairs from a man with whom she had committed indecent acts and has extracted liquid from the *yerba curia.*[5] Mixing all these things, she put them in a little white bag as if they were relics, or at least pretending they were. Then she put this mixture underneath his pillow. And using the root from the same *yerba curia* for her deceits, wherefrom it is evident this woman has departed from Our Lord God and our Holy Catholic Faith and has surrendered herself to the servitude and slavery of the devil. And although she has been admonished by Your Lordship many and various times to confess the whole truth, she has refused to do it and has silenced it, committing perjury. . . .

. . . Therefore, I humbly ask Your Highness to take my word as the truth and that Paula de Eguiluz be condemned to the greatest and most serious punishments that the law allows. . . . And that if it is necessary, she be tortured. And the torture be repeated until she confesses the whole truth regarding the matter for which I request justice. This I swear according to form and request from Your Lordship's Holy Office. Domingo Vélez de Asas y Argos, prosecutor of the Inquisition.

[5] Possibly an herb called *Justicia pectoralis* or carpenter bush.

Y así presentada y leída la dicha acusación, fue recibido juramento en forma de derecho de la dicha Paula de Eguiluz. Y so cargo de él prometió de decir y responder verdad a la dicha acusación, la cual siéndole vuelta a leer capítulo por capítulo, respondió a ellos [los capítulos] en la forma siguiente:

[RESPUESTA A LA PRIMERA ACUSACIÓN]

Capítulo 1° . . . Dijo que es la contenida en la dicha acusación y que ella no es bruja ni ha hecho hechizos ni tiene *pacto* con el demonio; que [las acusaciones] son [de] enemigos que la quieren mal.

[RESPUESTA A LA SEGUNDA ACUSACIÓN]

Capítulo 2° Dijo que es testimonio y que lo que pasó es que Leonor de Estrada, *vecina* de Ana María, [le] llamó cuando estaba parada en la calle y le dijo que entrase en casa de la dicha Ana María que estaba gritando porque se le moría una niña que tenía. Y habiendo entrado la quiso ésta dar el pecho. Y viendo que no podía mamar la mandó la dicha su madre que la desfajase [a la niña] y mirase el mal que tenía.[5] Y ésta [Paula] lo hizo y vio que tenía aumentada la barriga. Y por consolar a la madre la dijo que no sería nada. Y la enseñaron el ombligo que le tenía bueno. Y ésta dijo que lo mirase y calentándole un pañito con alhucema y romero se le aplicó a la barriga y tornó a fajar la dicha criatura. Y se le entregó a la dicha su madre. Y al punto se fue ésta a su casa y no vio más a la dicha criatura. Y todo lo demás contenido en el dicho capítulo es falsedad y se lo levantan todos [los que] la quieren mal de muerte porque su amo la quiere bien y la ven bien vestida. . . .

[RESPUESTA A LA CUARTA ACUSACIÓN]

Capítulo 4° . . . Dijo que se refiere a lo que dicho tiene. Y que Juana Gerónima la mandó que tomase un hueso de muerto y un poco de romero y una cáscara de naranja de las que hubiesen estado en el monumento. Y que hecho polvos lo diese a su señor a beber en un poco de vino para quitalle[6] las cuartanas. Y que en dándoselo se lo dijese para que con el asco de haber tomado cosa tal vomitase. Y es verdad que ésta lo quiso hacer, mas habiéndolo comunicado con su señor—como él la riñó y no quiso—lo dejó ésta. Y no fue por el hueso aunque con el dicho propósito había dicho al sacristán que aquello le habían dado por *remedio* para su señor, y diciendo el dicho sacristán que de la iglesia no se podía sacar hueso de muerto la mandó que la pidiese al ermitaño un pedacito, mas ésta no lo hizo. Y niega lo demás contenido en el dicho capítulo. . . .

[RESPUESTA A LA SEXTA ACUSACIÓN]

Capítulo 6° . . . Dijo que es verdad que su amo [la] quiso castigar . . . porque había salido de casa sin su licencia. Y temiendo el castigo, [Paula] se echó desde el corredor

[5] It appears that the mother, Ana María, asks Paula to help her ill child by removing her wrappings and looking at her abdomen.

[6] *Quitarle.*

After hearing the accusation, Paula de Eguiluz swore to respond and tell the whole truth. Each chapter was read to her again, to which she responded in the following way:

[Response to the First Accusation]

Chapter 1 . . . She said she has already responded to this one and that she is not a witch and has not used spells. She said she does not have a pact with the devil either and that these accusations were made by enemies who hate her.

[Response to the Second Accusation]

Chapter 2 She said that her testimony is that one day when she was standing on the street, Leonor de Estrada who was Ana María's[6] neighbor called her inside because Ana María's daughter was dying and she was crying desperately. When Paula entered that house, the mother wanted to breastfeed the baby, but the girl was unable to feed. So, Ana María told Paula to unwrap the swaddling cloth to find out what was going on. When Paula did so, she saw that the baby's belly was swollen, but in order to calm her, she told Ana María not to worry about it. [She and Leonor] showed the mother the baby's navel, which was fine. Then Paula told her to look at the navel, and, warming a cloth infused with lavender and rosemary,[7] she applied it to the baby's belly and wrapped her up again, and gave her back to her mother. And immediately after that, Paula went home and did not see the baby again. And everything else in this chapter of the accusation is false, and they are accusations of people who hate her because her master loves her and they see her well dressed. . . .

[Response to the Fourth Accusation]

Chapter 4 She said that the accusation refers to what she has already declared. Juana Gerónima told her to prepare a mixture made from a dead person's bones and a little rosemary and orange peels that have been on the grave and to give it to her master in a drink as a remedy for his fever. She was supposed to tell him what he was drinking so he would throw up. She said she had the intention to do so, but after she told her master about it, he told her off and did not allow her to do it. Though Paula did not get the bones, she still told the sacristan that she had been given these instructions as a remedy for her master and, telling her that she could not take a dead person's bone from the church, the sacristan said she should go to ask the hermit for a little piece. However, she decided not to go. She denies the rest of the charges in this chapter.

[Response to the Sixth Accusation]

Chapter 6 She said that her master did want to punish her . . . because she left the house without his permission. And fearing the punishment, she threw herself from the

[6] Elsewhere identified as "Ana María india."

[7] *Alhucema,* or lavender, as well as rosemary leaves were used as natural remedies to heal injuries.

de su casa que cae a la mar. Y no se hizo mal por caer en el agua; si bien tuvo el brazo del lado de que cayó entumecido por mucho tiempo. Y niega lo demás, que es falso. . . .

[Respuesta a la octava acusación]

Capítulo 8° Dijo que lo que pasa es que como la levantaron el testimonio de que ella había muerto la criatura y chupádola, y lo anduvieron diciendo por las dichas minas, enojado su señor y confiado de que era mentira dijo que no había de quedar así este negocio. Que si ella lo había hecho que lo pagase y que si no, que se lo había de pagar quien se lo había levantado. Y así él propio hizo prender a ésta y ponerla en el cuerpo de guardia. Y estando allí sucedió que el dicho su amo fue a Cuba a ver al gobernador. Y queriendo doña Paula, su hija [de su amo], en su ausencia castigar a [Paula] porque tenía amistad deshonesta con su padre—y queriendo que la sacasen del dicho cuerpo de guardia para esto—con temor de castigo al tiempo de querer sacarla, es verdad que dijo [Paula] a los soldados y al teniente que cómo querían hacer aquello, estando ésta presa por lo que estaba. Con lo cual la dejaron. Mas todavía la hizo castigar allí la dicha doña Paula. Y esto es la verdad y niega lo demás contenido en el dicho capítulo. . . .

[Respuesta a la doceava acusación]

Capítulo 12 . . . Dijo que se refiere a lo que dicho tiene y confiesa también que muchos días de fiesta dejaba de ir a la iglesia y oír misa, mas que no era por falta de fe porque es verdadera cristiana, sino porque estaba cocinando y ocupada en otras cosas de casa. Que como estaban todas a cargo de ésta no podía descuidar de ellas.

[Respuesta a la decimotercera acusación]

Capítulo 13° Y al remate de la acusación dijo que se haga lo que fuere de *justicia.* Y que no se ha perjurado sino dicho la verdad. Y habiéndosele leído lo que ha respondido a la acusación del fiscal, dijo estar bien escrito. . . .

[Nombramiento de un abogado para Paula]

El Señor inquisidor mandó dar traslado a la rea de esta acusación y sus respuestas para que la trate y comunique con uno de los *letrados* que dan a defender semejantes causas en este Santo Oficio que son los *licenciados* don Pedro de Silva y don Francisco de Betancur. Que vea a cuál de ellos nombra por su abogado. Y la dicha Paula *negra* nombró por su abogado al dicho don Francisco de Betancur. El Señor inquisidor le hubo por nombrado y dijo que lo mandara llamar. Y con tanto *amonestada* la rea fue llevada a su cárcel. Ante mí, Luís Blanco de Salcedo, secretario.

[Confesión que hace el 15 de julio de 1624]

En la *audiencia* de la mañana de la Santa Inquisición de Cartagena a 15 días del mes de julio de 1624 años . . . fue traída de su cárcel la dicha Paula *negra.* . . .

hallway of her house into the sea. And she was not hurt because she fell into the water, although her arm on the side she fell on was numb for a while. She denied the rest of the charges, saying everything was false.

[Response to the Eighth Accusation]

Chapter 8 . . . She said her master got upset because everybody in the mines was saying that she had killed a child and sucked the baby's belly. Certain that this was a lie, he said that things should not be left as they were. If she had done as she was accused, then she should pay for her deeds, and if not, those who raised the false testimony should pay. So it was her master who had her arrested and placed in the guardhouse. While Paula was incarcerated, her master had to go to [Santiago de] Cuba to talk to the governor. Taking advantage of his absence, Doña Paula de Eguiluz [his daughter] wanted to punish Paula because she was having indecent relations with her father. Doña Paula demanded Paula's release in order to punish her, but Paula, seeking her self-preservation, told the soldiers and the lieutenant that they should not release her because of the nature of the crimes for which she was imprisoned, and they let her stay. However, Doña Paula still ordered them to punish her inside the jail. She said all this was true and she denied the rest of the charges in this chapter. . . .

[Response to the Twelfth Accusation]

Chapter 12 . . . She said she refers again to what she has already declared. She confesses that on many holy days she did not attend church or hear Mass, not because she lacked faith—she is a true Christian—but because she was busy cooking and taking care of her household duties, for she was in charge of all of them and could not neglect them.

[Response to the Thirteenth Accusation]

Chapter 13 And to the final accusation, Paula said that justice should be done, and she denied she committed perjury but in everything has told the truth. Then the scribe read her responses to the prosecutor's accusations and she said all of them were correct. . . .

[Attorney Appointed for Paula]

The Lord Inquisitor ordered that Paula be given her written responses so she might discuss them with one of the attorneys who defend these types of cases in the Holy Office, who are *licenciados* Don Pedro de Silva and Don Francisco de Betancur. Paula was to choose one of them as her attorney. She chose Don Francisco de Betancur as her attorney. The Lord Inquisitor then accepted him as nominated and ordered him called. Paula was admonished and sent to her prison. Before me, Luís Blanco de Salcedo secretary.

[Confession: July 15, 1624]

In the morning hearing of the Holy Inquisition of Cartagena on July 15, 1624 . . . the black woman Paula was brought from her prison. . . .

Dijo que ha pedido [*audiencia*] para decir [que] se ha acordado que habrá como un año que habiendo—y luego dijo que habrá más de dos años—que habiéndola castigado su señor por ciertas barras de jabón que faltaban y habiéndola descalabrado, llegaron ciertas personas a él y le dijeron cómo [Paula] estaba descalabrada. A que respondió [Juan de Eguiluz],

—¡Mas que la lleve el diablo el alma!—Y oyéndolo [Paula] dijo con impaciencia,

—¡Mas que me lleven todos los diablos juntos y más!—[Y] se fue a la huerta de la dicha casa. Y estando debajo de un ciruelo oyó una voz que la dijo,

—¡No me llamaste!—[7] Y volviendo [Paula] el rostro a ver de quién era aquella voz, la tornó a decir,

—Prométeme algo y vendré todas las veces que me llamares.—Y luego la pidió que le prometiese el *huelgo,*[8] que entendió [Paula que] quería decir el alma. Y le respondió,

—¡Que el *huelgo* no!—Y la dicha voz la dijo,

—Pues dame y ofréceme las uñas.—Y callando ésta volvió a decir la dicha voz,

—Pues dame de lo que comieres.—Y [Paula] dijo,

—¡Eso sí yo te lo daré!—Entendiendo . . . que estaba hablando con el demonio. Y habiéndose ido a casa y olvidada de lo que había pasado con el demonio, como de allí a una hora, tomó una caña dulce para comer de ella. Y habiendo comenzado a comerla al segundo bocado, al apretar con los dientes la caña doliéndole uno, arrojó la dicha caña. Y dijo,

—¡Ofrézcote al diablo!—Y acordándose entonces de lo que había pasado con el demonio se levantó luego a buscar la caña y no la halló.[9] . . .

[Sigue una larga confesión sobre tratos con el demonio.]

[Y] tornó a decir el demonio:

—Mira, si quieres algo, mejor es que te vayas por ahí conmigo.—Y apareciéndosele luego en figura de mujer con una saya de muy larga que le arrastraba pidió a [Paula] que le diese el alma. [El diablo le dijo] que Aquél no la quería, diciéndolo por Dios, que no se acordaba de ella. Y que lo echase de ver en que cuando le llamaba no venía como él [el diablo] a ver lo que quería y favorecerla. Y engañada [Paula] con los ofrecimientos que le hizo de que la favorecería en todas ocasiones y la llevaría consigo y le daría todo cuanto hubiese menester [Paula] le ofreció el alma y dijo:

—Yo te la doy.—[10] . . .

Y [Paula dijo que] el diablo la andaba persiguiendo a cada paso. Y confiesa que cuando entregó su alma al demonio, [él] la ofreció que la daría todo lo que hubiese menester. Y le hallaría todas las veces que le llamase y tuviese mohína y enojo. [Y Paula] le dio crédito. Y esto fue lo que la movió a condescender con lo que la pedía de que le

[7] In the margin: *Pacto explícito con el demonio.*

[8] Breath.

[9] A long line in the margin marks this section with the notation *Le ofreció la caña dulce.*

[10] In the margin: *Ofrecida el alma al demonio.*

She said she has requested [the hearing] to tell something else she has remembered: that about a year ago—and then she said that it was about two years ago—her master having beaten her because he was missing two bars of soap, and having injured her, certain people told him she was injured, to which he responded,

"May the devil take her soul!" Paula heard him and said, annoyed,

"May all the devils and more take my soul!" Then she went to the garden and sat down under a plum tree. While sitting there she heard a voice saying,

"You did not call me!"[8] Paula turned her head to see who it was and heard the same voice again saying,

"Promise me something, and I will come every time you need me." Then this voice demanded her breath, which [Paula] understood to mean her soul. She responded,

"I will not give you my soul!" And the voice said,

"Well, then give me and offer me your fingernails." And when [Paula] was silent, the voice said again,

"Then, give me the food you eat," to which she said,

"Yes, I will give you that!" She then understood . . . she had been speaking with the devil. And having gone home and forgotten what had happened with the devil, about an hour later, she was eating a piece of sugar cane. And on the second bite, one of her teeth hurt and she threw the sugar cane away. She said,

"May the devil take you!" And then remembering her promise to the devil, she got up and looked for the sugar cane but could not find it.[9]. . .

[There follows a lengthy confession regarding the devil.]

[Paula concludes thus:]

Then, the devil said, "Look if you want something, you had better follow me over there." He appeared to her later in the figure of a woman wearing a red skirt that was so long it dragged. He asked Paula to give him her soul, telling her that God did not even remember or love her because every time she called on Him, he never came as the devil did to see what she wanted and to favor her. And deceived by [the devil's] promise to always help her and to give her everything she needed. Paula offered him her soul saying,

"I will give it to you."[10]. . .

Then Paula said the devil pursued her at every step. She confessed that when she gave her soul to the devil, he offered to give her everything she needed, and that he would find her whenever she called, or when she was upset or angry and she believed him. And this is what moved her to give in to his demand for her soul, which she now

[8] In the margin: "Explicit pact with the devil."

[9] A long line in the margin marks this section with the notation, "She offered him her sugar cane."

[10] In the margin: "Her soul offered to the devil."

ofreciese el alma, de que le pesa de todo corazón y pide [a Nuestro] Señor la perdone tan grandes culpas y yerros. Y a este Santo Oficio que la dé penitencia con misericordia. . . .

[El treinta de noviembre de 1624, el señor inquisidor Agustín de Ugarte Saravia declaró a Paula de Eguiluz hereje apóstata, idólatra, y bruja y le dio la sentencia descrita en la introducción a este capítulo.]

regrets very much and asks Our Lord to forgive her for these dreadful sins and errors, and requests that this Holy Office give her a merciful punishment . . . .

[On November 30, 1624, the Lord Inquisitor Agustín de Ugarte Saravia declared Paula de Eguiluz a heretical apostate, an idolater, and a witch and gave her the sentence described in the introduction to this chapter.]

12

A Spanish Caribbean Captivity Narrative: African Sailors and Puritan Slavers, 1635[1]

David Wheat

Between Iberian and Protestant Worlds: Africans on the Spanish Main

In 1630, English Puritans colonized Providence Island (called Santa Catalina Island in Spanish sources) located slightly more than one hundred miles off the Caribbean coast of Nicaragua. Following unsuccessful efforts to cultivate profitable commodities for export, the colony turned to *privateering* and slave trafficking in the mid-1630s; its location in the western Caribbean gave northern European *privateers* a solid base from which to prey upon Spanish shipping. Less than a decade after the Dutch *privateer* Piet Heyn famously captured Spain's entire silver fleet, authorities in Cartagena de Indias[2] determined to eliminate this new threat.

The Puritan colony resisted attacks by Spanish forces in 1635 and 1640 but finally fell in 1641 (Kupperman). Enslaved Africans—as both profitable commodities and capable laborers who would enable either of the European powers to reinforce their efforts to colonize the Caribbean—were at the heart of the conflict. Each side sought to obtain them, but in notably different fashions: whereas Spanish authorities and would-be slave owners relied on Portuguese slave trade networks to supply enslaved laborers directly from Africa, English and Dutch newcomers sought to obtain Africans by preying on Iberian shipping and slave traffic in the region (Heywood and Thornton, 4–38).

Africans also occupied a central position in this imperial contest in a literal sense, as seen below. The same individual Africans were physically present on both sides of the religious–political frontier. The document presented here highlights the experiences of one extraordinary group of African sailors based in Cartagena who were captured by Dutch pirates in 1634 and resold to the English colonists on Providence Island. After experiencing slavery in two entirely different cultural environments, several of these men evidently preferred the former, and they managed to escape back to the Spanish-American mainland. In addition to indicating contrasts between Africans' position in the colonial Spanish Caribbean, on the one hand, and in the early Anglophone Atlantic, on the other, these testimonies demonstrate enslaved Africans' ability, literally and figuratively, to navigate them both.

[1] See Maps 5 and 13.

[2] Presently a major port and tourist destination in Colombia, in the colonial era Cartagena was the principal port city on the Caribbean coastline of South and Central America, a region known to contemporaries as *Tierra Firme* (or in English, "the Spanish Main"; Sauer, 1–4).

Within the larger structures of Spain's early modern empire, strategically located seaports along the Caribbean Sea and the Gulf of Mexico—the same ports frequented by our African protagonists—played critical roles as maritime hubs and centers of commerce. Heavily fortified during the late sixteenth century, Cartagena de Indias, Havana, Veracruz, and Nombre de Dios/Portobelo represented the principal stops along the *Carrera de Indias,* the ocean route that linked the *metropole* to its American colonies by means of annual convoys of Spanish galleons and merchant ships.

Simultaneously, these circum-Caribbean port cities served as major slave markets and redistribution centers for the transatlantic slave trade. Registered in Seville, Portuguese ships sailed to various African ports—Luanda, *Cabo Verde,* Cacheu, Arda, and *São Tomé*—transporting thousands of African captives to the Americas via the Caribbean. Cartagena de Indias in particular stands out as Spanish America's primary slave trade entrepôt during the late sixteenth and early seventeenth centuries. According to one official report that almost certainly failed to account for additional contraband slave trafficking, one hundred slave ships landed over 17,500 Africans in Cartagena during the years 1615–1623 alone ("Certificaçion").

Too hot and humid for most Spanish emigrants, these low-lying Caribbean seaports and their hinterlands had been populated largely by Africans and people of African descent, both free and enslaved, since the late sixteenth century. Although Amerindian groups maintained a visible presence in the region, disease and conquest had drastically reduced the Caribbean's indigenous populations during the early colonial period. By 1634—one century after the city was founded—urban Cartagena de Indias contained a population of approximately fifteen hundred *vecinos* (i.e., heads of household), including "*mulatas* and freed blacks" (Córdoba Ronquillo).

This estimate did not include the seaport's fluctuating "floating population" of sailors, passengers, slaves, merchants, and others passing through. Nor did it include scattered Iberian *mayordomos* (overseers) living on rural or semirural farms and ranches, nor groups of *encomienda* Indians concentrated in several small villages. By far the most understated segment of Cartagena's population, however, comprised enslaved Africans and *Afrocreoles,* who made up the demographic majority. In 1621, Cartagena's governor estimated that black slaves in Cartagena and its province numbered around twenty thousand (Del Castillo Mathieu, 238–41). Given conflicts of interest, different parties had ample reason to either downplay or exaggerate the size of Cartagena's black slave population; estimates from the mid-1630s range from 12,000 to "over 25,000" (Wheat).

Slave labor in early colonial Latin America is most often associated with sugar mills and silver mines; yet the African sailors discussed below would have been unfamiliar with these forms of slave labor. In Caribbean port cities such as Cartagena, enslaved black populations worked at a wide variety of tasks that ensured the maintenance and defense of the urban seaport and the provision of its populace.

Enslaved men and women were commonly rented out by their masters for wages garnered as cooks, laundresses, street vendors, nurses, domestic servants, porters, oarsmen, and town criers. Clergy, carpenters, caulkers, stonemasons, cobblers, and butchers alike either owned slaves or rented them. Operating fortresses built by royal slaves, local garrisons relied on support personnel consisting of African stable hands, janitors,

cooks, and musicians. Enslaved Africans served in capacities ranging from seamstresses to warehouse guards, from shipwreck salvage crews to button makers.

Outside the urban center, literally thousands of black farm workers raised livestock and food crops, particularly corn, yucca, and plantains. For example, corn grown by slave farmers in the village of Tolú was loaded on boats or rafts and then transported to Cartagena on vessels staffed by enslaved crews.

In addition to connecting Cartagena with these *estancias* (farms or ranches), boats powered by black sailors and oarsmen regularly plied the coastal and riverine passages, which allowed communication and trade between Cartagena and Santa Fé de Bogotá, capital of the New Kingdom of Granada.[3] Originally, Amerindians had been forced to provide labor for an organized system of canoe transportation known as the *boga;* but in the late sixteenth century, indigenous paddlers were replaced almost entirely by enslaved Africans and *Afrocreoles.* Enslaved boatmen and sailors also served on privately owned merchant vessels, as will be seen in these 1635 testimonies.

Though born in West Africa, the two Spanish-speaking *Beafada* men who testified in May 1635 in Portobelo were familiar with the world described above. As slave sailors, they knew the waterways of Cartagena's province and various ports of the southern Caribbean and Central America. In some respects, their Caribbean environment resembled the Guinea-Bissau region they had left behind.[4] On both sides of the Atlantic, they observed local economies oriented toward coastal and riverine commerce heavily reliant on canoes for transportation of food crops and commodities.

Furthermore, Iberian—especially Portuguese—merchants, mariners, exiles, and missionaries had been present on the Upper *Guinea* Coast since the mid-fifteenth century. Interactions between Iberians and West African societies over the following two centuries had created *Luso-African* populations that excelled as intermediaries, interpreters, and slave procurers; *Luso-Africans* often became merchants in their own right.

Like other West African groups in the region, many of the *Beafadas* captured, condemned, or sold into slavery in Spanish America may have already been exposed to Catholic traditions, and they may have already been familiar with Portuguese or with the Afro-Portuguese language, *Crioulo.* As indicated by their testimonies in Portobelo, Francisco *Biáfara* and Juan *Biáfara* spoke Spanish very well, and they knew how to present themselves as devout Catholics. Their high level of acculturation to the Iberian world may be attributed to evangelization efforts conducted in Cartagena, but their African background may have given them significant advantages in the Spanish-American colonial world as well.

The Testimonies of Juan *Biáfara* and Francisco *Biáfara*

The testimonies below are taken from court proceedings initiated when an unusual group of shipwrecked slaves and northern European deserters were delivered to the governor of Portobelo for questioning. In April 1635, Francisco Fernández Fragoso,

[3] The *Nuevo Reino de Granada* roughly corresponds in territory to what is now Colombia.

[4] For more information on *Beafada* communities and their environment in precolonial Africa, see Brooks; Hawthorne; and Rodney. See also Map 13.

a Spanish resident of the city of Granada, Nicaragua, found an Englishman plodding along the shoreline. Unable to speak Spanish, the stranger dropped to his knees, held up his hands, and placed them behind his head. Saying only "*Negro, negro,*" he pointed toward the mouth of the San Juan River, less than one league, or roughly two and a half miles, distant.

During dinner, and throughout the whole evening, Fernández could make out nothing more than "Catalina" and "*negros,*" with the foreigner always pointing in the same direction. The following day, Fernández set out with two companions, each armed with a portable firearm called a harquebus, and with five Indians armed with bows. Arriving in two canoes at the mouth of the San Juan River, they found four Spanish-speaking African men, and a young pock-faced "Englishman." As soon as Fernández arrived, the black men jumped up, saying "Señor, we are peaceful! We are slaves owned by the widow of Amador Pérez, a citizen of Cartagena! We are the ones who were stolen by a Dutchman eight or nine months ago, from our mistress' frigate which was laden with wine, bound for the River Magdalena!"

And thus begins our story. Interviewed by government officials, each member of the motley group offered detailed testimony of their captivity, of collusion and escape, and of sickness, shipwreck, and murder. Along with their African co-workers, Francisco *Biáfara* and Juan *Biáfara* had been on Providence Island for approximately seven months, from October 1634 to April 1635. Questioned closely by Spanish officials, Francisco *Biáfara* and Juan *Biáfara* offered detailed descriptions of the island's location and fortifications. They attempted to recall every ship they had seen visit the island and the goods and passengers carried on board, including a handful of Indians brought from the island of San Andrés. They listed the island's livestock and mention potatoes and corn grown for local consumption and tobacco cultivated for export.

With the possible exception of their assertion that "there were no other blacks on the island" other than their companions, the details they provided corroborate not only each others' accounts but also information gleaned from English sources.[5] "Félix Beles," or rather Philip Bell, served as governor of Providence Island from 1630 to 1636. He had been governor of the Bahamas until 1629 and would take up the same post in Barbados in 1641. The man described below as "Captain Alfero," better known as Daniel Elfrith, admiral of Providence Island, had been a corsair operating in the Caribbean for the previous two decades. He was also Bell's father-in-law, and at one point Elfrith was reprimanded for inviting "Diego el *Mulato,*" a famous Havana-born corsair who sailed under the Dutch flag, to visit the island. Lieutenant William Rous, who appears here as "Captain Rus," was captured by the Spanish and briefly held captive in Cartagena, where he spoke with the itinerant priest Thomas Gage in 1638.

Francisco *Biáfara* and Juan *Biáfara* provided several troubling details without any prompting by Spanish officials. Both men voluntarily reported various "heresies" they had witnessed while on the island, including Bible readings, rosary stomping, and sermons delivered by a married preacher. Likewise, both mentioned that Francisco *Biáfara* was asked to marry an Indian woman who wore a red blanket for a skirt. Employing

[5] See especially Kupperman.

Amerindian and African words commonly used in Caribbean Spanish of the time, both described English houses as *buhíos,* and Francisco *Biáfara* compared the small English forts on Providence Island to *palenques.* Their detailed account given in May 1635 surely helped to instigate the first Spanish assault on Providence Island two months later.

Significantly, these court proceedings constituted the only known account of daily life on Providence Island other than a diary kept by Governor Nathaniel Butler during the final years of the colony's existence. The entire document consists of twenty-six folios and opens with a brief report by Francisco Fernández Fragoso explaining his discovery of four Africans and two northern Europeans camped out at the mouth of the San Juan River.

The following declarations given by deponents Francisco *Biáfara* and Juan *Biáfara* are reproduced below, along with a very brief joint statement by Damián *Carabalí* and Gerónimo *Angola,* both of whom essentially confirm Francisco *Biáfara's* testimony. Two northern European men who had escaped Providence Island alongside the Africans, and who now likewise found themselves questioned by Spanish authorities in Portobelo, gave additional testimonies with the aid of an interpreter. A man identified only as "Herbatons" was a forty-year-old soldier from London, England. A twenty-three-year-old Flemish man, "Juan Yons," claimed to have deserted the English colony because he had grown weary of eating potatoes. Both claimed to be Catholic.

By the early seventeenth century, although Africans' roles in the English Atlantic colonies such as Providence Island were only beginning to materialize, Africans and Iberians had been interacting for over a century in the Americas and for nearly two centuries in Africa and southern Europe. We cannot know the genuine motives that drove these two *Beafada* men, along with several of their colleagues, to escape back to slavery in the Spanish Caribbean, if that was indeed their actual intention. It is clear, however, that their familiarity with Catholicism and their ability to speak Spanish meant that *ladino* Africans such as Francisco *Biáfara* and Juan *Biáfara* were able to maneuver within the Spanish system to a far greater degree than the northern European deserters who accompanied them.

Información hecha cerca de la población que [torn] el enemigo inglés en la Isla Santa Catalina, por el capitán Juan de Ribas, *alcalde mayor.* Portobelo, 9 mayo 1635[1]

[Declaración de Francisco *Biáfara*]

En la ciudad de Portobelo en nueve días del mes de mayo de 1635 años, el señor *capitán* Juan de Ribas, *alcalde mayor* y *capitán a guerra, teniente de capitán general* por Su Majestad para la dicha averiguación e información, hizo parecer ante sí a un *negro* de los que manifestó y trujo Francisco Fernández Fragoso, del cual Su Merced recibió juramento y lo hizo por Dios y la cruz en forma de derecho. Y so cargo de él prometió de decir verdad. Y preguntado cómo se llama, de qué *nación* es, y cuyo esclavo, y qué edad tiene, y en qué ejercicio/oficio servía a su amo, dijo que se llama Francisco, y que es de *casta Biáfara* y esclavo de doña Mariana de Armas Clavijo, viuda del *capitán* Amador Pérez, *vecina* de la ciudad de Cartagena de las Indias, y que la dicha su ama tenía un barco del trato del Río Grande [de la Magdalena], en el cual este declarante andaba por marinero juntamente con Pedro *Folupo,* Gerónimo *Angola,* Damián *Carabalí* y Juan *Biáfara.* Y venían en el barco otros esclavos y por arráez Francisco Rodríguez español, y que yendo a hacer viaje al Río Grande [de la Magdalena] cargado el barco de vino, lo cogió un navío de holandeses, y a todos los esclavos compañeros deste declarante se los llevó a la isla que llaman de Santa Catalina, habiendo dejado en Santa Marta al piloto Francisco Rodríguez a cuyo cargo iba el dicho barco que se llamaba Nuestra Señora del Rosario, habrá ocho meses poco más o menos.

Preguntado qué tamaño tendrá la dicha isla y si es baja o alta y qué tantos días tardó en llegar desde donde le robaron a ella, dijo que la dicha isla es alta y montuosa y que le parece tendrá de bojeo diez u once leguas; y que tardó en llegar a ella siete días desde donde le robaron, que fue en Zanba.[2]

Preguntado cómo se llamaba el *capitán* que los robó, dijo que se llamaba el *capitán* Juan y que era flamenco y que sería hombre de cincuenta años, hombre pequeño de cuerpo, y que no traía más de catorce hombres en un navío y era de dos cubiertas.

Preguntado en qué conformidad los dejó en la dicha isla de Santa Catalina, si fueron o no vendidos y a quién, y si tiene noticia en qué cantidad, dijo que fueron once los esclavos que llevaba del barco de su ama y todos eran suyos. Y como llegó con ellos

[1] Ministerio de Cultura, Archivo General de Indias, Seville, Audiencia de Santa Fe 223, no. 34, fols. 5r–15v.

[2] "Canba" in the original. Possible scrivener error for Çanba, modernized as Zanba.

Inquiry carried out by Captain Juan de Ribas, *Alcalde Mayor*, into the Population that [torn] the English Enemy on the Island of Santa Catalina. Portobelo, May 9, 1635

[Declaration by Francisco *Biáfara*]

In the city of Portobelo on the ninth day of the month of May 1635, Captain Juan de Ribas, *alcalde mayor* and *capitán a guerra, teniente de capitán general* for His Majesty, for this investigation summoned to appear before him a black man from among those presented and brought by Francisco Fernández Fragoso, from whom His Mercy received his oath, which he swore by God and the cross as required by law, and by which he promised to speak the truth. And asked to state his name, his *nation,* and whose slave he was, and his age, and in what office he served his master, he said that his name is Francisco, and that he is of the *Biáfara* caste, and the slave of Doña Mariana de Armas Clavijo, widow of Captain Amador Pérez, *vecina* of the city of Cartagena de Indias. She owned a boat employed in traffic along the Río Grande [de la Magdalena],[1] on which Francisco *Biáfara* worked as a sailor alongside Pedro *Folupo*, Gerónimo *Angola,* Damián *Carabalí,* and Juan *Biáfara.* Other slaves were also on the boat, and its *arráez* [captain] was a Spanish man named Francisco Rodríguez. While making a trip to the Río Grande, with the boat loaded with wine, the boat was seized by a Dutch ship. All the slaves on board, Francisco *Biáfara*'s companions, were carried to the island called Santa Catalina. The pilot Francisco Rodríguez, who had been in charge of the boat named Our Lady of the Rosary, was left in Santa Marta about eight months ago more or less.

Asked what size the island was and whether it is low lying or high and how many days it took to arrive from where he was stolen to the island, he said that the island is high and mountainous, and that it seemed to be about ten or eleven leagues in circumference. It took seven days to reach the island from where he was stolen, which was at Zanba.[2]

Asked the name of the captain who stole them, he said that his name was Captain Juan and that he was Flemish, approximately fifty years old, and small in stature. He brought no more than fourteen men in a ship with two decks.

Asked in what state the captain left them on the island of Santa Catalina, whether they were sold or not, to whom, and for what price, he said that eleven slaves were taken from Mariana de Armas Clavijo's ship, all eleven belonging to her. Upon arriving

[1] Primary commercial artery from Cartagena toward Santa Fe de Bogotá.

[2] According to Francisco *Biáfara,* their boat was captured by Dutch *privateers* at Zanba, a small port located along present-day Colombia's Caribbean coast, just south of Santa Marta. The port of Zanba is mentioned in Francis (51). The boat's Spanish pilot was promptly left ashore in nearby Gaira (Gayra). "Gaira" appears on a map in Navarrete (17). Both locations appear in a travel account dated 1519, published in Urueta (54).

los fue vendiendo el *capitán* Juan Flamenco al gobernador de la isla que llaman *Capitán* Beles. Compró a este declarante y a otros compañeros por 26 libras de tabaco y un puerco cada uno.

Preguntado si hay otros *negros* en la dicha isla, dijo que no hay más de sus compañeros.

Preguntado qué gente de guarnición y vecindad hay hoy en la dicha isla, dijo que habrá como doscientos hombres, diez o quince poco más o menos, y algunos muchachos y cosa de veinte mujeres y que hoy su gobernador que como ha dicho se llama *Capitán* Félix Beles y otros dos capitanes de infantería con su *alférez* y dos banderas que se llaman de *Capitán* Rus hombre mozo robusto y el otro *capitán* Alfero. Y que no traen espadas ni dagas y que todas las armas [son] de arcabuces, mosquetes, y piezas cajas de guerra.

Preguntado qué fuerzas tienen y con qué artillería y qué guardia tienen de día y de noche en las fuerzas, dijo que tienen nueve fuertes pequeños como de *palenques,* algunos en los cuales tienen a dos y a tres y a cuatro y a cinco piezas, todas de hierro colado, algunas dellas en cabalgadas y otras en el suelo atravesadas en maderos; que estos fuertes están a cargo de los dos capitanes y de otras personas; y que el puerto principal es una bahía, y en la bocana della tiene en cada uno de los fuertecillos que ha dicho, y otro de la boca paradentro, y otro junto de la casa del gobernador que tiene una pieza. Y los demás fuertes están de la banda de afuera y que en una parte que estará poco más de una legua está un fuerte en que se hace guardia; que deste es *capitán* el *Capitán* Rus.

Preguntado si los vio meter la guardia ansí en lo poblado como en alguna de las dichas fuerzas, dijo que no, porque todas las armas las tienen en un *buhío.* Y este declarante las vio muy de cerca y están muy mal tratadas.

Preguntado qué labranzas tienen, dijo que siembran tabaco en gran cantidad y pequeñas sementeras de maíz y muy grandes de patatas; que éste es el mayor sustento que tienen; y que crían gallinas y ganado de cerda; y tienen tres vacas y dos toros para hacer *casta;* y que la tierra no tiene ningunos puercos de monte.

Preguntado si la isla tiene muchos ríos y quebradas de aguas, dijo que tiene muchas quebradas y manantiales de muy buenas aguas y que en toda ella se coge mucho pescado y tortugas.

Preguntado qué navíos ha visto llegar a este dicho puerto y de qué *naciones,* dijo que habrá tres meses poco más o menos que llegó a la dicha isla un navío de ingleses de tres cubiertas cargado de ropa, zapatos, *aguardiente* y cerveza, muchas bayetas y listones, y otras cosas; y vendió a trueco de tabaco. Y dejó algunas personas de él y mujeres y se llevó algunos ingleses de la tierra. Y habrá poco más de un mes que se fue de allí. Y que antes deste navío grande vino otro *patache* pequeño cargado de cerveza y otras cosas.

Preguntado si hoy tienen algún navío en el puerto, dijo que no tienen de suyo ninguno; y que antes desean tener uno para que salga de corso, porque esta voluntad la entendió este declarante del suegro del gobernador.

Preguntado qué forma tuvo para huirse de la dicha isla y con quién salió della y en qué embarcación, dijo que este declarante se convocó con Pedro *Folupo* y Gerónimo *Angola* y Damián *Carabalí* y Damián *Biáfara* y con seis ingleses; que estando para

[at Santa Catalina], captain Juan Flamenco sold them. The island's governor, named Captain Beles, bought Francisco *Biáfara* and several other companions for twenty-six pounds of tobacco and one pig each.

Asked if there are other blacks on the island, he said that there are none other than his companions.

Asked what kind of military force and civilian population are currently on the island, he said that there are approximately two hundred men plus or minus ten or fifteen, some boys, and perhaps twenty women. At present, the island is governed by Captain Félix Beles, as mentioned earlier. Two infantry captains with their lieutenant and two regiments are named Captain Rus, a robust young man, and another captain, Alfero. They carry neither swords nor daggers, and their arms consist entirely of harquebuses, muskets, cannon, and war drums.

Asked what forts they have, and what artillery, and what guard they keep by day and night in the forts, he said that they have nine small forts like *palenques,* some of which have two or three or four or five pieces of ordnance all of cast iron, some mounted on supports and others on the ground laid across wooden frames. These forts are under the care of the two captains and other people. The principal port is a bay, and there are several little fortresses along the bay's entrance, and another inside the mouth of the bay, and another next to the governor's house with one cannon. The other forts are on the outer coast, and in one place a little more than one league away is a fort where watch is kept, under the command of Captain Rus.

Asked if he saw them keep watch over the settlement or in some of the forts, he said no because all their arms are kept in one *buhío.* Francisco *Biáfara* saw them from up close, and they are very poorly maintained.

Asked what crops they have, he said that they sow great quantities of tobacco, small plots of maize, and very large plots of potatoes, which are their main sustenance. They raise chickens and swine, and have three cows and two bulls to breed; the land has no wild pigs.

Asked if the island has many rivers and streams, he said that there are many streams and springs with very good water and that all over the island fish and turtles can be caught.

Asked what ships he has seen arrive at the island's port and from what *nations,* he said that about three months ago, an English ship with three decks arrived at the island carrying clothing, shoes, *aguardiente* [liquor] and beer, many fabrics and ribbons, and other things and sold them in exchange for tobacco. The ship left some people and women behind and took some local English people away. The ship left the island about one month ago. Before this big ship, another *patache* had arrived carrying beer and other things.

Asked whether they had a ship in the island's port at present, he said that they had no ship of their own, though they desired to have one in order to embark on corsair raids; Francisco *Biáfara* understood this to be the wish of the governor's father-in-law.

Asked in what manner he escaped from the island and with whom he left and in what type of vessel, he said that he, Francisco *Biáfara,* joined with Pedro *Folupo,* Gerónimo *Angola,* Damián *Carabalí,* and Damián *Biáfara,*[3] and with six Englishmen who were

[3] Error (committed by scrivener?); should read "Juan *Biáfara.*"

partirse en una *chalupa* que era del gobernador, les dijeron,—Si queréis ir a vuestra tierra, que ésta no es para vivir, nos iremos,—Y este declarante los embarcó en su compañía. Y vinieron a parar a la boca de San Juan más de diez días, porque en dos días tomaron la tierra firme. Y después vinieron costeando hasta la boca de San Juan donde en ella habían ya dejado atrás la barca porque se la hizo pedazos la mar.

Preguntado si vinieron con él y los demás *morenos* sus compañeros seis ingleses, cómo no llegaron más de dos, dijo que su compañero Pedro *Folupo* a[l] segundo día de navegación murió en tierra, que era su *capitán* y que en el puerto de San Juan, Juan Inglés que es mozo robusto le dijo a este declarante:—Sabed que quieren caer sobre vosotros estos ingleses y mataros.—Este confesante y sus compañeros estuvieron con cuidado aquella noche. Y que otra noche, viendo que se lo volvió a decir, embistieron con ellos con unos palos y mataron uno y los tres huyeron. Y aunque los buscaron otro día no los hallaron. Y esta noticia dio este declarante y sus compañeros al maestre Francisco Fernández Fragoso a quien hallaron en la boca de San Juan, el cual los halló ranchados. Y que estos dos ingleses siempre se aunaron con este confesante y sus compañeros, y así pudieron salvar las vidas. Y que habrá cosa de veinte días que fueron hallados del dicho Fragoso y los trujo a esta ciudad.

Preguntado si en alguna ocasión le oyó tratar en la isla a los ingleses y holandeses que estaban en ella de alguna armada, dijo que al *capitán* Juan, que es el que los robó, le oyó decir que para el año que viene vendría de su tierra con dos grandes y nuevas, recorriendo esta costa de Portobelo, y a cargar en ella de tabaco. Y así mismo hace saber a Su Merced cómo en la dicha isla no se le consentían traer cruces ni rosarios, antes se las quitaron y pisaron. Y que en ella tienen un *buhío* donde se juntan a la predicación, donde en ella los veía juntar muy de ordinario. Y que en desembarcándose del trabajo, todos toman un libro ansí los hombres como las mujeres y niños. Y esto es lo que vio y alcanzó a ver y entender de toda la dicha isla.

Preguntado si fue o vio ir alguna embarcación de la isla Santa Catalina a la de San Andrés, dijo que él ni ninguno de sus compañeros no salieron de la dicha isla, más de que en el tiempo que él y sus compañeros estuvieron en ella, vieron ir en una *tartana* de vela latina a la isla San Andrés, y otras por tortugas de donde trujeron una india y dos indios; que los indios le decían a este declarante se casase con la india, la cual venia vestida de una manta colorada hecha saya. No tuvo otra noticia de las dichas islas. Y esto es lo que sabe y la verdad, so cargo del juramento hecho, con que se afirmó y ratificó. Y que es de edad de 28 años poco más o menos. No firmó por no saber, el cual yo el *escribano* certifico y doy fe que es persona *ladina* en la lengua española, y que todo lo aquí contenido ha dado por razón capaz y suficiente respuesta a lo que le ha sido preguntado y a otras preguntas que fuera desta materia el señor *alcalde mayor* le hizo, y Su Merced lo firmó.

[Declaraciones de Damián *Carabalí* y Gerónimo *Angola*]

Y Su Merced del señor *alcalde mayor* le preguntó si los demás sus compañeros sabrán declarar y dar razón como él la ha dado, dijo que no los tiene por tan *ladinos* como él.

about to leave in a *chalupa* belonging to the governor. The Englishmen told them, "This place is no way to live; if you want to go back to your land, we're going"; and thus Francisco *Biáfara* embarked in their company. In two days' time, they reached the mainland and then traveled along the coast. After more than ten days, they reached the mouth of the river San Juan,[4] where they stopped and left behind their boat, which had been badly damaged by the sea.

Asked why only two Englishman arrived, because six had originally left the island with him and the other *morenos,* his companions, he said that after their second day at sea, his companion Pedro *Folupo,* who was his captain, died on land. In the port of San Juan, Juan Inglés, a robust young man, told Francisco *Biáfara,* "You must know, these Englishmen plan to attack you all and kill you." Francisco *Biáfara* and his companions took care that night, and on a different night, because they were warned again, they fought the Englishmen with clubs and killed one; three others fled and were nowhere to be found the next day. Francisco *Biáfara* and his companions reported this news to Master Francisco Fernández Fragoso, who found them camped out at the mouth of the San Juan. The remaining two Englishmen were always loyal to Francisco *Biáfara* and his companions, and so their lives were saved. About twenty days ago, they were discovered by Fragoso and brought to this city [Portobelo].

Asked if at any time he overheard the English and Dutch on the island mention a fleet of ships, he said that he overheard Captain Juan, who stole them, say that the following year he would come from his land with two large, new ships, to comb this coast and to load them with tobacco. Also, Francisco *Biáfara* notifies Your Mercy that they did not allow him to wear crosses or rosaries on the island, rather they were confiscated and stomped on. On the island, they had a *buhío* where they gathered to hear sermons and where he saw them gather very regularly. Returning from work, they all held a book, men, women, and children, and this is what he saw, and was able to learn regarding the whole island.

Asked if he undertook or witnessed any voyage from Santa Catalina island to San Andrés [island], he said that neither he nor any of his companions left the island. During the time they were on the island, they saw a *tartana* with lateen sails cross over to San Andrés, and to other islands, for turtles. The ship brought back an Indian woman and two Indian men. The Indians suggested to Francisco *Biáfara* that he should marry the Indian woman, who came dressed in a red blanket worn as a skirt. He had no other news of these islands, and this is what he knows and is the truth, under charge of the oath given, which he affirmed and ratified. He is more or less twenty-eight years of age. He did not sign because he did not know how. I, the scribe, certify and attest that he is a *ladino,* who speaks the Spanish language well, and that he has provided capable, sufficient answers to the questions asked and to other relevant questions posed by the *Señor alcalde mayor,* and His Mercy signed it.

[Declarations by Damián *Carabalí* and Gerónimo *Angola*]

And His Mercy the *Señor alcalde mayor* asked Francisco *Biáfara* if his other companions knew how to declare and give testimony as he had given. Francisco *Biáfara* said

[4] The San Juan River forms the eastern boundary between present-day Nicaragua and Costa Rica.

Y que así Su Merced vea que llamándolos ante sí, y presente este declarante, vean éste su dicho y por él sigan cerca de lo que ha declarado y preguntas que a él se le han hecho, si tienen algo más que declarar. Y luego Su Merced hizo parecer ante sí a Damián *Carabalí* que por su aspecto parece de treinta y cinco años, y a Gerónimo *Angola* que por su aspecto parece de treinta años, y dellos recibió juramento y lo hicieron por Dios y la señal de la cruz en forma de derecho; y prometieron de decir verdad. Y habiéndoles leído las preguntas desta declaración fecha por Francisco *Biáfara,* a cada una dellas dijeron, vista la respuesta y declaración que en cada una dellas hace el dicho Francisco *Biáfara,* dijeron que el susodicho ha satisfecho y declarado toda la verdad, y lo que en cada una dellas pasa. Y ellos lo han *visto* ser y pasar ansí como lo declara, y ellos siendo necesario hacen la misma declaración. Y en algunas cosas en que por no ser tan *ladinos* dudaron, las confirieron sobre el tiempo y vinieron a estar en lo declarado. Y en esta conformidad Su Merced del dicho señor *alcalde mayor* les tomó estas dos declaraciones, y todo lo mandó poner por *auto,* fe, y diligencia que la firmó. Y por ser tarde reservó para mañana diez deste mes tomar la declaración a Juan *Biáfara* por ser muy *ladino.* Juan de Ribas ante mí Juan de Medina Bejarano *escribano* público.

[Declaración de Juan *Biáfara*]

En la ciudad de Portobelo en diez días del mes de mayo de 1635 años, el señor *Capitán* Juan de Ribas, *alcalde mayor* y *capitán a guerra, teniente de capitán general* en ella por Su Majestad, para la dicha información y averiguación fue al hospital de San Sebastián desta ciudad y hizo parecer ante sí a un *negro,* del cual Su Merced recibió juramento por Dios y la cruz; y él lo hizo y prometió de decir verdad.

Preguntado cómo se llama, de qué *nación* es, y qué oficio, y cuyo esclavo, y qué edad tiene, dijo que se llama Juan *Biáfara* y que es esclavo de doña Mariana de Armas Clavijo, viuda del *capitán* Amador Pérez, *vecina* de la ciudad de Cartagena de las Indias, y que él la servía de su marinero en un barco nombrado Nuestra Señora del Rosario del trato del Río Grande de la Magdalena, el cual iba por marinero juntamente con Pedro *Folupo,* Gerónimo *Angola,* Damián *Carabalí,* y Francisco *Biáfara;* que éstos están hoy en esta ciudad, porque los demás a cumplimiento a once esclavos están hoy en la isla de Santa Catalina. Y que iba por arráez Francisco Rodríguez, y que yendo a hacer su viaje los robó un inglés en un navío grande de que venía por *Capitán* Juan Nata, el cual echó en Santa Marta en Gayra al piloto y compañeros españoles. Y de allí los llevó con el barco y la carga, que lo más era vino, a una isla que llaman de Santa Catalina, y tardó en hacer el dicho viaje siete días, y llegaron a ella la nao grande y el barco y que esto habrá poco más de ocho meses.

Preguntado en qué conformidad los dejó el *capitán* inglés que los robó en la isla, dijo que la dicha isla está poblada de holandeses e ingleses, y a ellos los vendió el *capitán* inglés por veinte manojos de tabaco o libras de él y por un puerco, y a este precio los

that he did not take them to be as *ladino* as himself, but that even so, if summoned to appear before His Mercy with Francisco *Biáfara* being present as well, if they were shown his testimony, His Mercy would see whether they offer similar answers to the same questions and whether they have anything else to declare. And then His Mercy summoned to appear before him Damián *Carabalí,* who appears to be thirty-five years old, and Gerónimo *Angola,* who appears to be thirty years old. From them he received an oath sworn by God and the sign of the cross as required by law, and they promised to tell the truth. Having read to each of them the questions asked of Francisco *Biáfara* and his answers, they said that Francisco *Biáfara* had satisfied and declared the full truth of what happened in each question, and that they had seen events unfold exactly as he had declared, and that if necessary they would make the same declaration. And not being as *ladino* [as he], they had doubts about some things, and conferred about the time and finally agreed on what had already been declared [by Francisco *Biáfara*]. And with this agreement, His Mercy the *Señor alcalde mayor* accepted these two declarations from them and ordered that everything be duly recorded and certified, and signed it. And because it was late, he left for tomorrow, the tenth of this month, the declaration of Juan Biáfara, because he is very *ladino.* Signed by Juan de Ribas before me, Juan de Medina Bejarano, public scribe.

[Declaration by Juan *Biáfara*]

In the city of Portobelo on the tenth day of the month of May 1635, the *Señor* Captain Juan de Ribas, *alcalde mayor* and *capitán a guerra, teniente de capitán general* of Portobelo on His Majesty's behalf, for the report and investigation went to the hospital[5] of San Sebastián in this city and summoned to appear before him a black man, from whom His Mercy received an oath, sworn by God and the cross, and Juan *Biáfara* promised to tell the truth.

Asked his name, his *nation,* his profession, and whose slave he was, and his age, he said that his name is Juan *Biáfara* and that he is the slave of Doña Mariana de Armas Clavijo, widow of Captain Amador Pérez, *vecina* of the city of Cartagena de Indias. He served as her sailor on a boat named Our Lady of the Rosary, engaged in river traffic along the Río Grande de la Magdalena. He worked as a sailor alongside Pedro *Folupo,* Gerónimo *Angola,* Damián *Carabalí,* and Francisco *Biáfara,* who are today in this city [Portobelo]; the remainder of the crew of eleven slaves are presently on the island of Santa Catalina. The boat's *arráez* was Francisco Rodríguez. During the course of their journey, they were stolen by an Englishman on a large boat, commanded by Captain Juan Nata, who left the pilot and his Spanish companions in Gayra in Santa Marta. From there, he took them with the boat and the cargo, which was mostly wine, to an island called Santa Catalina. The trip took seven days, and they reached the island in a large ship and the boat, and this happened a little more than eight months ago.

Asked in what manner the English captain who stole them left them on the island, he said that the island is peopled by Dutch and English, to whom the English captain sold them for twenty sheaves, or pounds, of tobacco and for one pig. At this price they

[5] The word "hospital" can refer to either a shelter for the sick or a shelter for the poor.

dejó vendidos al gobernador y capitanes, y que a este declarante lo compró el gobernador de la dicha isla, y a Francisco *Biáfara* y a Gerónimo *Angola* y a Pedro *Folupo.*

Preguntado si hay otros *negros* en la isla, dijo que no halló ningún *negro* en la isla.

Preguntado qué gente de guarnición hay hoy en la dicha isla y si supo o entendió qué tanto tiempo ha que están poblados en ella, dijo que le parece que habrá más de doscientos hombres que toman las armas y algunos muchachos y cosa de veinte mujeres, y hay gobernador que se llama Félix Beles y otros dos capitanes de infantería, y con dos banderas y sus *alférez,* y quel un *capitán* se llama Rus, hombre mozo robusto, y el otro el *capitán* Alfero, y que no traen de ordinario espadas y que todas sus armas que son mosquetes y picas, las tienen con las cajas de guerra, pólvora, y balas en un *buhío* grande junto a la casa del gobernador. Y allí junto della tienen un *buhío* grande donde se juntan muy de ordinario a la prédica, que ésta les hace un inglés mozo casado, y que cuando dejan el trabajo traen sus libros los hombres, niños, y mujeres. Y le quitaron a este declarante y sus compañeros el que no trujesen cruces ni rosarios, porque todos son herejes y que por fuerza los llevaban a su prédica, mas que no la entendían ni la querían saber por ser como este declarante cristiano y sus compañeros.

Preguntado qué fuerzas tiene y con qué artillería y guardia tiene de día y de noche las fuerzas, dijo que no vio más de cinco fuerzas pero que de su compañero Francisco *Biáfara* supo que había nueve, y que las que vio están a la boca del puerto paradentro y una junto de las casas del gobernador. Y que hay una fuerza en una punta donde tienen el atalaya de adonde hacen señal cuando parece vela con una pieza y luego toman las armas. Y que los castillejos que vio son bajos como plataformas de cuatro y de tres piezas cada una, unas en carretones y otras sobre palos.

Preguntado si los vio meter la guardia ansí en lo poblado como en las fuerzas, dijo que no.

Preguntado qué labranzas tienen, y qué tamaño tendrá la isla, y si tiene agua de ríos que corran, y si hay en ella puercos de monte, y si es abundante de pescado y otras plantas diferentes de frutas, dijo que siembran grande sementera de tabaco que lo benefician en rollo, y mucha patata, que es lo más que comen, y que las comen crudas los más. Y que el maíz es poco, y crían gallinas, y tienen tres vacas y dos toros para hacer crianza. Y que no tienen puercos de monte, y que hay algunos plántanos. Y que la isla es alta, montuosa y que tiene de largo más de cuatro leguas y diez de bojeo. Y que el puerto es bahía grande fondable aunque tiene peñascos, y en cada punta tiene su castillo, y mucha agua que corre y la atraviesa, y grandes manantiales, y el agua buena de beber.

Y preguntado que después que está en la isla, qué navíos han llegado a ella, y qué trajeron de mercadurías y gente, y qué llevaron, y de qué *nación,* dijo que vino un navío grande de Inglaterra cargado de cerveza, *aguardiente,* y otras cosas. Y que dejaron gente y cargaron de tabaco a trueco de lo que trujeron. Y que este navío trajo mujeres, y habrá poco más de un mes que se fue. Y antes había venido un *patache* cargado que también dejó gente y cargó de tabaco a trueco de lo mucho que trujo de mercadurías.

were sold to the governor and captains, and Juan *Biáfara* was purchased by the island's governor along with Francisco *Biáfara,* Gerónimo *Angola,* and Pedro *Folupo.*

Asked if there are other blacks on the island, he said that he found no other black on the island.

Asked what military force is currently on the island and if he knew or understood how long the island had been occupied, he said that it seemed to him there were roughly over two hundred men capable of bearing arms, and some boys, and approximately twenty women. There is a governor named Félix Beles and another two infantry captains with two regiments and their lieutenants. One captain is named Rus, a robust young man, and the other captain is named Alfero. They normally do not carry swords, and their arms consist of muskets and pikes, which are stored with the war drums, powder, and ammunition in a large *buhío* next to the governor's house. Nearby they also have a large *buhío* where they gather very regularly to hear sermons given by a young, married Englishman. When they finish their work, the men, children, and women all bring books. And they took away the crosses and rosaries brought by Juan *Biáfara* and his companions because they are all heretics. Juan *Biáfara* and his companions were forced to attend the sermons, but they neither understood nor wanted to know because they are Christians.

Asked what forts they have, with what artillery, and what guard they keep by day and night in the forts, he said that he saw no more than five forts, but that his companion Francisco *Biáfara* found out that there were nine. Those that Juan *Biáfara* saw are inside the mouth of the port, and one next to the governor's houses, and there is one fort on a point where they have a watchtower where they make signals with a cannon when a sail appears, and then they take up arms. The fortifications he saw were low, like platforms, with four or three pieces of ordnance each, some mounted on large wagons and others on wooden frames.

Asked if he saw them keep watch in the settlement as they do in the forts, he said no.

Asked what crops they have, and what size the island is, and if it has running water or rivers, and if there are wild pigs on the island, and if there is an abundance of fish and a variety of fruit-bearing plants, he said that they sow great quantities of tobacco, which they prepare in rolls, and many potatoes, which is what they mainly eat, and they mainly eat them raw. There is little corn, and they raise chickens, and they have three cows and two bulls for breeding. They have no wild pigs, but there are some plantains. The island is high and mountainous, more than four leagues wide and ten leagues in circumference. The port is a great bay with good anchorage, though it has some rocky outcroppings, and at each end there is a castle. There is much running water that crosses the island, and large streams, and the water is good to drink.

And asked what ships arrived on this island while he was there, and what merchandise and people they brought, and what they carried away, and the ships' nationalities, he said that a large ship from England arrived laden with beer, *aguardiente,* and other things. They left people on the island, and loaded tobacco in exchange for what they had brought. This ship brought women and left the island a little more than one month ago. And previously, a *patache* had arrived, which also left people on the island and loaded tobacco in exchange for many goods that it brought.

Preguntado si tienen allí algún navío grande o pequeño para salir en él a hacer mal, dijo que no tienen ninguna embarcación sino *chalupas* con que salen a pescar y con que se sirven en la población de otras cosas. Y que el inglés que los robó allí dijo que había de venir el año que viene con navíos grandes para recorrer estas costas. Y que al suegro del gobernador oyó decir que había enviado a comprar un *patache* para correr las costas de Cartagena y Chagres, el cual es un hombre pequeño y viejo.

Preguntado qué forma tuvo para huirse de la dicha isla él y sus compañeros, y si tiene noticia si hay por allí otras islas pobladas ansí ingleses como indios, dijo que muchas veces oyó decir generalmente a los ingleses que allí cerca estaba una isla la cual llaman San Andrés, y que estaba poblada de indios. Y vio que con un barquillo de vela latina salieron a pescar tortugas, y las trujeron y una india y dos indios. Y que los indios dijeron a Francisco *Biáfara* su compañero se casase con la dicha india, vino vestida con una saya de manta colorada, y quedan en la isla. Y que se corresponden con los ingleses de San Cristóbal según se lo oyó tratar. Y que viéndose que estaban entre infieles acordaron de huirse, y para ello se convocaron este declarante y Francisco *Biáfara* y Gerónimo *Angola* y Damián *Carabalí* y Pedro *Folupo,* que era su *capitán,* de huirse, y no pudieron sacar a los demás compañeros que son Martín *Balanta,* Andrés Jolufo, Francisco *Angola,* Juan *Angola,* Baltasar *Folupo,* Cristóbal *Arará* que estos se quedaron allá. Y hecho el concierto para huirse, bajaron a la playa donde estaba una barca grande de un *alférez,* de la cual se servía el gobernador. Y estando para embarcarse, hallaron en la playa seis ingleses, y todos se convenieron en huirse. Y así se embarcaron, y al cabo de dos días con sus noches reconocieron tierra firme, habiendo navegado con vela. Y de allí vinieron costeando, y su compañero y *capitán* Pedro *Folupo* enfermó y enfureció y murió en tierra. Y viniendo costeando la mar se les rompió la barca. Y salieron a tierra todos, y fueron a dar a la boca de San Juan del desaguadero de Nicaragua junto a la boca de Taure al cabo de días, donde Francisco *Biáfara* entendió de un inglés llamado Juan que está en esta ciudad, que los cuatro ingleses querían matarlos de noche. Y así se velaron y otra noche, por salvar las vidas, dieron en ellos y mataron el uno entre todos a palos, y los tres se huyeron y aunque los buscaron no los pudieron hallar. Y esta noticia dieron al arráez Francisco Fragoso, porque llegó otro día, de cómo había sucedido con su fregata, que hizo diligencia de buscarlos y no los halló. Y como este declarante y sus compañeros viesen gente cristiana y embarcación se agregaron a él, el cual los trajo en su fregata dándoles de comer a esta ciudad con los dos ingleses que siempre fueron con ellos leales.

Fuele preguntado si supo oyó decir en la dicha isla si esperaban alguna armada de Holanda o Inglaterra para estas partes, dijo que nunca supo tal, más de tan solamente en esta razón trató públicamente el *capitán,* que era flamenco, y él que le robó, que para el año que viene como ha dicho vendría con dos naos nuevas a esta costa y dicha isla a vengar el haber cogido un navichuelo de flamencos, que el general don Antonio

Asked if they have any ship on the island, large or small, to go out and do evil, he said that they do not have any vessel except *chalupas,* with which they go out to fish and which serve the settlement for other things. And the Englishman who stole them said that he would return the next year with large ships to scour these coasts. And Juan Biáfara heard the governor's father-in-law, a small and older man, say that he had sent to purchase a *patache* that he would use to travel along the coasts of Cartagena and Chagres.

Asked in what manner he and his companions fled from the island, and whether he knew of other islands in the area peopled by English or Indians, he said that many times he overheard the English say that nearby was an island that they call San Andrés populated by Indians. He saw that they went out in a small boat with a lateen sail to fish for turtles, and they brought back turtles and an Indian woman and two Indian men. And the two Indian men suggested to his companion Francisco *Biáfara* that he marry the Indian woman, who came wearing a red blanket as a skirt. And the English stay on the island [of San Andrés], and from what he has overheard, they communicate with the English on San Cristóbal [Saint Christopher] Island. And seeing that they were among infidels they agreed to flee, and for this purpose Juan *Biáfara* joined with Francisco *Biáfara,* Gerónimo *Angola,* Damián *Carabalí,* and Pedro *Folupo,* who was his captain. They were unable to bring out the other companions, who were Martín *Balanta,* Andrés Jolufo, Francisco *Angola,* Juan *Angola,* Baltasar *Folupo,* and Cristóbal *Arará,* who remained on the island. Having agreed to flee, they went down to the beach where there was the large boat belonging to an officer, which the governor used. Just as they were about to embark, they found six Englishmen on the beach, and they all agreed to escape together. And thus they embarked, and after sailing for two days and nights, they saw the mainland. From there they came along the coast, and his companion and Captain Pedro *Folupo* grew sick and crazed and died on land. And traveling along the coast, the sea broke the boat. They all went ashore, and after several days chanced to arrive at the mouth of the San Juan River, which drains from the [lake] of Nicaragua, near the mouth of the Taure River. Francisco *Biáfara* learned from an Englishman named Juan who is here in this city that the four Englishmen wanted to kill them at night. So they kept guard, and on another night, in order to save their lives, they attacked the English and killed one between them by blows. And the other three fled and could not be found. They reported this news to the *arráez* Francisco Fragoso, who arrived on a different day with his frigate, who looked for them and did not find them. And seeing Christian people in a vessel, Juan *Biáfara* and his companions joined them. And feeding them, Francisco Fragoso took them in his frigate to this city, along with the two Englishmen who always had been loyal to them.

Asked if he knew of, or had heard anyone on the island talk of waiting for a fleet from Holland or England bound for these parts, he said that he never overheard anything regarding this topic, except that the Flemish captain who stole him publicly declared, as mentioned [in the question], that the following year he would return with two new ships to this coast and to the island, to take revenge on general Don Antonio de Oquendo, who had captured a small ship full of Flemish men near the coast of Havana. He had heard nothing more. And that which he said and declared is the truth,

de Oquendo cogió en las costas de la Habana, y no otra cosa. Y que lo que ha dicho y declarado es la verdad, y todo lo que ha sabido *visto* y entendido y ha pasado en esta razón, en la cual so cargo del juramento que fecho tiene, se afirmó y ratificó. Por su aspecto parece ser hombre de más de 35 años. No firmó por no saber. Firmólo el señor *alcalde mayor* Juan de Ribas ante mí, Juan de Medina Bejarano *escribano* público.

and everything that he knew and saw and understood and happened in this case, and this he affirmed and ratified under the oath taken. By his appearance, he seems to be a man over thirty-five years old. He did not sign because he did not know how. The *Señor alcalde mayor* Juan de Ribas signed before me, Juan de Medina Bejarano, public scribe.

13

The Saint's Life of Sister Chicaba, c. 1676–1748: An As-Told-To Slave Narrative[1]

Sue E. Houchins and Baltasar Fra-Molinero

An Early Biography of an African Woman

The *Compendio de la Vida Ejemplar de la Venerable Madre Sor Teresa Juliana de Santo Domingo* (Salamanca, 1752) written by Father Juan Carlos Miguel de Paniagua was one of the earliest, if not the first, biographies of an African woman written in a modern European language. The *Vida* is the hagiography, a saint's life, of Sor Teresa de Santo Domingo (c. 1676–1748), an African *tertiary* nun who lived in a Spanish convent during the first half of the eighteenth century.

Although authored by the priest Paniagua, this text represents collaboration between an African woman and her Spanish biographer. The *Vida* is a hybrid text in which Chicaba, who is the subject of the hagiography, participates in the writing of the narrative by telling her story to the biographer. The *Vida* is a precursor to the African American as-told-to slave narratives of the nineteenth century.

The *Vida* tells the story of a remarkable Black woman who escaped slavery by exhibiting her extraordinary holiness. Sor Teresa attained a reputation for sanctity and healing, exercised some small power within the religious community that never accepted her in the upper ranks of its social hierarchy, and managed to publish her autobiography through the narrative of a priest writing in the third person. Her oral history was transcribed, edited, published, and disseminated to the Americas and throughout the Black Atlantic as a model of religious perfection for other Africans and people of African descent.[2]

Chicaba's Life Story According to Paniagua

Her biographer, Paniagua, claimed that Chicaba, or Sor Teresa, was the youngest daughter of the King of *La Mina Baja del Oro,* somewhere in the coastal area of eastern Ghana,

[1] See Maps 4 and 14. Sue E. Houchins thanks the Woodrow Wilson National Fellowship Foundation for the Career Enhancement Fellowship that supported her research on this project at the Women's Studies in Religion Program at the Harvard Divinity School during 2007–2008.

[2] See Paniagua's prologue to the *Compendio de la Vida* and his *Oración fúnebre* in honor of Sor Teresa, published a few months after her death. In 1757 a heroic poem in Sor Teresa's honor was written in manuscript form in Zaragoza, the *Vida de la venerable negra.* The only known copy is at the Schomburg Center for Research in Black Culture in New York City. The *Vida* itself was published twice, in 1752 and 1764, which is a testimony to its popularity. The excerpts in this anthology correspond to the 1764 edition.

Togo, and Benin.[3] Her captors concluded that she was a member of an important family because of the jewelry she was wearing when kidnapped. Her given name, *Chicaba,* meaning "golden child" or "divine gift," suggests that she was a member of the Ewe people, one of the ethnic groups of the region.[4] Following the Catholic custom with slaves, she was baptized upon capture and given a new, Christian, European name: Teresa.

Enslaved at the age of nine, Teresa/Chicaba was brought to Spain and purchased by the Marchioness of Mancera, Juliana Teresa Portocarrero. During his tenure as viceroy to Mexico, the Marchioness' husband had been a protector of the Mexican writer Sor Juana Inés de la Cruz. As a member of the retinue of this aristocratic household, Teresa developed an unusually intense spiritual life that in time became her key to freedom.

Upon her death in 1703, the Marchioness emancipated Teresa in her will with the request that she enter a convent, for which the mistress had bequeathed her a small but not insignificant annuity. The fact that Teresa was mentioned in the will twice indicates that this was less an imposition than an act of her own will.[5] After being rejected by several other religious communities, Teresa entered the Dominican *tertiary* convent of La Penitencia in Salamanca a year later. Her race and skin color put her at a disadvantage in the highly stratified social hierarchy of Spanish monastic houses. The community accepted her only in a marginal status, as a servant to the other nuns.

Her low status notwithstanding, admission to La Penitencia was an official mark of Chicaba's civil freedom. Although her monastic cell might not have been very different from the quarters she inhabited during her enslavement and monastic life continued to limit her mobility, she was free. The papers she signed attesting to her act of profession as a Dominican *tertiary* also documented her freedom, and the convent was an institution that lived by these papers.

In spite of this inferior status, Teresa/Chicaba's acts of charity, mystical experiences, and fame as a healer or miracle worker moved the Dominican Order soon after her death to initiate the process of beatification for which Paniagua's writings were

[3] What Father Paniagua calls *La Mina Baja del Oro* corresponds to the coastal area east of *Elmina* Castle, which was called *La Mina del Oro* by the Portuguese since 1482.

[4] Spelled both Chicaba and Chicava by the hagiographer, the name is a compound word in Ewe, from *shika* or *sika* (gold) and *va* (to arrive), meaning "the gold has arrived" or the "Golden Child is here."

[5] Testamento de Juliana Teresa Portocarrero, Meneses y Noroña, Marquesa de Mancera, otorgado el 10 de abril de 1703. 13977 fol. 135v. "Iten, después de los días de mi vida quiero y es mi voluntad que Teresa Juliana del Espíritu Santo, mi esclava, quede libre enteramente, y la ruego por lo mucho que la he querido, se entre religiosa en el convento de Santa Ana que antiguamente estuvo sujeto a los Padres Dominicos de la ciudad de Murcia y hoy está sujeto al obispo de dicha ciudad de Murcia. Y para su entrada se le dé de mis bienes todo lo necesario, y también todo lo necesario para su profesión. Iten, mando a Teresa Juliana que hoy es mi *criada* y esclava y la dejo libre en profesando de religiosa se le dé de mis bienes cincuenta *ducados* cada un año, para los gastillos y otras cosas que se le pueden ofrecer durante su vida."

an important step.[6] The text of the *Vida* claims to be making frequent references to Teresa's autobiographical writings, some of which appear in the book as direct quotations.

The *Vida* recorded that Teresa/Chicaba enjoyed special favor with her mistress, who might have educated her as some European women did with their slave companions—especially those who entered the household as children. Therefore, it is entirely possible that this young woman learned to write enough to prepare her to undertake the customary projects of elite religious women: recording her spiritual life and writing religious poetry. Had she been illiterate, Paniagua would surely have noted it and would have chosen a different strategy for conveying her voice in the hagiography.[7]

With the exception of an autographed letter by Sor Teresa preserved in the Convent of Las Dueñas in Salamanca and her signature at the bottom the document certifying her act of profession in June 1704, no other papers written by Sor Teresa Chicaba are known to exist.[8] In both documents, however, one can observe clear and firm handwriting, a sign of someone accustomed to using a quill pen with a certain frequency. The handwriting suggests a person who might well have produced the diary or notes her biographer used to produce the story of her life.

Hagiography and "As-Told-To" Life Stories: Two Related Genres

The *Vida* is an example of a hagiography, which is commonly defined as a life or legend of a saint. The genre "includes accounts of persons regarded as holy or exemplary in their own time, even if they were not formally canonized" (chapters 9 and 10).[9] In the words of Caroline Walker Bynum, saints are "socially constructed," and their legends are "[f]ashioned and authenticated in a complex relationship between clerical authorities and the adherents who spread the holy person's reputation for virtues and miracles" (page x).

[6] Beatification is a formal ecclesiastical process resulting in permission to a local population of faithful to venerate a Christian martyr or someone who in life had a reputation for sanctity and miracles. Two portraits were also commissioned and painted of Sor Teresa with the aim of helping to disseminate her fame as a saint. One of them is displayed in the small museum created in her honor by the nuns of the convent of Las Dueñas of Salamanca, together with other documents and material testimonies of her life. The other remains in a deteriorated state in the Museo Provincial of Salamanca. For a commentary on these two portraits, see Fra Molinero.

[7] The lives of several illiterate black slave nuns were recorded by clergy in Spain (Magdalena de la Cruz), Mexico (Esperanza), and Brazil (Rosa Egipciaca). See Contreras; Gómez de la Parra and Ramos Medina; and Mott.

[8] The Dominican convent of Las Dueñas in Salamanca is where Sor Teresa Chicaba is buried now. During the occupation of Salamanca by Napoleon's troops in 1810, the convent of La Penitencia, where she lived, was demolished. The nuns took Sor Teresa's remains with them as a precious possession together with several objects that belonged to her that had become relics as well as her autographed letter and the document certifying her act of profession. All these items are preserved now in the convent of Las Dueñas, a more aristocratic institution than La Penitencia at the time she lived in Salamanca.

[9] For a view of sainthood outside the Catholic Church, see Wyschogrod.

Hagiographies, therefore, are profoundly political. Paniagua's *Vida* is an example of an even more hybrid genre. Part hagiography—itself a bricolage of forms—and part as-told-to (auto-)biography/spiritual narrative, it is an instance of *pentimento,* or layered narrative, in which Chicaba's unique worldview and sometimes radical intent peeks through the surface of her biographer's prose. As a result, Paniagua's representation of Chicaba's story exhibits its dual origins, African and European.

The priest was not Sor Teresa's confessor. He obtained the materials—both written and oral—for the hagiography through interviews with Sor Teresa Chicaba in the fall of 1748, during the last months of her life. If the manuscripts Paniagua claims to have consulted existed, Sor Teresa would be the first African-born woman known to us to have written in a modern European language.[10]

If read as the oral history of an ex-slave, however, the *Vida* bears a striking resemblance to another genre, the dictated biographies and spiritual narratives of freed African people or ex-slaves in the United States of the late eighteenth and nineteenth century. They are sometimes called "as-told-to slave narratives." The *Vida* would be the first example of this type of slave narrative in the Catholic tradition.

Spiritual narratives, the Protestant first cousin of the Catholic mystical autobiography and its sibling hagiography, were the genre from which the slave narrative evolved. First-person conversion accounts by Blacks of religious justification and sanctification lay "the necessary intellectual groundwork by proving that [Blacks] . . . were as much chosen by God for eternal salvation as whites" (Andrews, 7). Upon the foundation of this theological argument for racial equality, slave narratives made the case for emancipation—legal, political, and economic freedom for Americans of African descent. The first of these narratives, a dictated as-told-to spiritual autobiography, contains an abduction story strikingly similar to Sor Teresa Chicaba's.[11]

Race and Ethnicity in a Holy Woman's Life and *Vida*

Present-day readers may well question why an emancipated Black woman slave would choose a cloistered religious life. However, in Spain and the rest of the Catholic world of Europe and the Americas, female convents were sites of relative spiritual and intellectual freedom and of sexual safety as compared to the alternative of a secular life as a single woman. In France, a slave named Pauline Villeneuve avoided being sent back to the Caribbean by professing as a nun, a decision her Benedictine order successfully defended (Harms, 6–11). In Spanish America, this relative freedom operated both for white and Black women, although the case of women of African descent has received much less attention.

Race was an obstacle to Paniagua's producing a text that would support a case for an African woman's beatification; Blacks were not suitable subjects of Catholic

[10] Úrsula de Jesús is the first woman of African descent known to date to have been credited with writing/dictating her spiritual autobiography. She lived in Lima in the first part of the seventeenth century (see van Deusen).

[11] Joycelyn Moody traces this evolution in a book-length study of African American women's spiritual narratives (see Belinda; Moody).

hagiographies. Sainthood required nobility of lineage and birth from a legitimate marital union. Black slaves, lacking both, were not deemed adequate candidates for sainthood. The ideology of the era made the language of hagiography inadequate in this situation; the *Vida* needed to represent Chicaba's race positively against the contemporary negative discourse that was decidedly anti-Black.

Since the Middle Ages, the devil was represented in Spain as a Black man, and Black men appeared in demonic visions of many Spanish and Spanish-American nuns since the sixteenth century, including Saint Teresa of Avila herself. *Guinea* or Western Africa was seen as a region close to hell (see Olsen). A close reading of the narrative reveals a conflict between the dominant ideology of the day—beliefs sanctioning slavery and racial inequality that Paniagua might have upheld—and an attempt to find textual space for resistance, principles of gender and racial equality that Chicaba might have asserted.

The description of Chicaba's parents and siblings as members of her country's royalty stands in tension with their Blackness and Africanness, but it serves to mitigate Chicaba's abject status as a slave by asserting her exceptional pedigree. However, Teresa/Chicaba's rejection by several convents that would not accept a Black in their community—not even as a lay sister—was testimony to the impossibility of her claims of legitimacy and high lineage to completely displace the negative aspects of the doctrine of *limpieza de sangre,* or blood purity, that prevailed in her time.

In addition, most Spaniards ascribed to the belief in a symbolic relation between skin color and paganism. The eighteenth-century reader of this hagiography/spiritual narrative would have understood that slavery was the fortunate and providential intermediate step through which Africans "transmigrated" on their Christian journey to paradise. That is, the public instinctively justified the capture and bondage of Black people as the means of expunging the moral stain inscribed as color across their bodies.

Thus, the exemplary depiction of Teresa/Chicaba's religious orthodoxy, grasp of Catholic apologetics, sanctity, and compassion in her encounter with a fellow slave simply identified as the "Turkish girl" is an attempt on the part of the priest and the subject of the story to problematize this ideology that demonized Blacks. Allegedly, the Muslim woman became a weapon Satan attempted to wield against the innocent Chicaba.[12] But Teresa's sanctity shielded her from the murderous attacks instigated by the devil.

When the assaults ceased, Chicaba befriended her assailant, who confided that a Catholic priest had seduced and abandoned her, thereby turning her against Christianity. She had adamantly refused to convert despite the efforts of "many spiritual and learned men"; however, "Grace" chose instead a lowly Black slave woman, Teresa/

[12] There is documentary evidence that there were Muslim slaves in the *Mancera* household, as attested by the sale of two Muslim men by the *Marquis of Mancera* a few years before Chicaba's arrival to his home (Archivo Histórico de *Protocolos Notariales* de Madrid, 11.410 fol. 79, February 6, 1677).

Chicaba, as an instrument of salvation (chapter XIII, not anthologized here). A reader in eighteenth-century Spain would have marveled at the unique sanctity that enabled Teresa/Chicaba to prevail where European men had failed. The power of the incident resides in the stark opposition of categories of difference, race and gender: whiteness versus Blackness and men versus women.

Because Teresa/Chicaba was probably the last living witness to this episode in her life, she might have had some part in this representation of her unusual spiritual and intellectual superiority. In addition, occasionally her Blackness is transformed in the narrative into a mark of divine choosing; for instance, during her journey to enter the convent in Salamanca, a blind man recognizes her skin color simply by touching her.

For the most part, slavery and the condition of Blacks under it were not a significant issue in the moral discussions of Paniagua's time. By 1685, the Council of State advised King Carlos II, in response to radical *Capuchin* friars Francisco José de Jaca and Epiphane de Moirans' denunciation of slavery in the Americas, that the enslavement of Blacks was a matter of practical convenience and economic necessity for Spain (Pena González, liii). But the *Vida* betrays a conflicted view of slavery.

The prose exhibits stress when it describes the indignities and mistreatment of the slave Teresa/Chicaba. Yet, it cannot or will not condemn the institution of slavery that was the root cause of it. In other words, Chicaba's race becomes a site of this contradiction at salient points in the narrative. The mistreatment of Teresa/Chicaba by white servants of the *Mancera* household becomes an uncomfortable indictment of white racial violence that goes unpunished, and it becomes deflected in the text. On one occasion, Chicaba was thrown into the pond in Madrid's Retiro Park by some person first recognized as the Marquis but later reidentified as the devil himself.

This narrative revision cautiously absolves members of the Marquis' staff by displacing the crime into the demonic realm. The *Vida*'s narrative has to editorialize on these anecdotes that originate in Chicaba's conversations and papers in an attempt to present racial obstacles as a form of divine trial.

The *Vida* occasionally reveals interventions or narrative resistance to slavery. For example, immediately following the story of Chicaba's "gentle" kidnapping or abduction in Africa by a celestial being clothed like a Spaniard is the harrowing tale of her attempt to throw herself overboard only to be snatched from certain death by the intervention of a Holy White Lady, a syncretism of an African water deity and the Blessed Virgin. Further the protagonist described how, while still in the *Middle Passage,* phantasmal blackbirds followed the slave ship. This vision or hallucination that the text attributes to satanic intervention is similar to the delirium recalled by other captives subjected to unbearable thirst and in a slave ship's hold (see Kiple and Higgins).

A modern audience alert to the double voice of the *Vida*'s narrative might detect Chicaba's voice in the assertion of her Africanness through the recollection of these events. The insistence on remembering her own African name and those of her relatives, as well as the insistence on her royal origins, might indicate an early form of racial consciousness. The framing of her mystical experience as beginning in Africa with the

White Lady also implies an attempt to assert Africa as the place where her Christian spiritual quest originated prior to her abduction.

As evidenced by the anecdotes she must have related to Paniagua, the *Vida* appears to make a constant effort to construct and maintain Teresa/Chicaba's racial identity, her Africanness. Thus, in the aforementioned episode of her near drowning in the pond at the Retiro Park, when she experienced her submersion in the waters of El Retiro's pond as a journey back to her homeland—as *sankofa*—the text asserts that a return to her native land is a voyage to Africa, where she once enjoyed freedom and agency. The submersion/journey represents her as a diasporic African subject. She is someone who is aware of her African origins and ancestry as well as the historicity of her enslavement and social condition once she attains legal freedom.

The preservation of Sor Teresa/Chicaba's memories of Africa and her awareness of racial difference is exemplified with great originality in biblical exegesis in an unusual piece of convent poetry quoted in the *Vida* and attributed to Chicaba. In the poem, Jesus is depicted as a polygamist. The poem in chapter XXXV uses the biblical story of the competition between Mary and Martha to criticize the monastic hierarchy among *choir* nuns, lay sisters, and others. The unusual depiction of Christ as "go[ing] out with other women" seems to attest to the collaboration—oral or written—of Chicaba in the composition of the *Vida.*

One can argue that Paniagua's quotes from her spiritual autobiography, no matter how doctored, are more likely to have originated from her writings than not. Although such quotations cannot be accepted as faithful copies of the original text using today's standards of authenticity, they are marked in italics in the *Vida.* This was a typical practice in religious literature to mark the divine inspiration of the words of the subject of the hagiography. Among all the quoted passages in the narrative, the poem portraying Chicaba's spiritual jealousy of Christ most likely is a faithful representation of her voice.

The poem is striking in its interpretation of the story of Martha and Mary (Luke 10:38–42). In conventional Church exegesis, Martha and Mary are contrasting, hierarchical examples of contemplation and action in the Christian soul, which are translated to the relative status of nuns in a community. Sor Teresa/Chicaba combines the traditional representation of both women and applies their story to her own case.

Catholic theology has been at pains to explain away the idea of a polygamous Christ, the logical consequence of his mystical marriage to many nuns. The feeling of jealousy, which Paniagua rationalizes as a manifestation of Sor Teresa/Chicaba's intense love, might be a reflection of her lived experience in the convent. In the convent, she was relegated to the symbolic status of a "lesser wife," as indicated by the manual labor required of her. In this regard, the recrimination might well be a complaint against some perceived injustice visited upon her by the other sisters. The tension between Martha and Mary in the biblical story might point toward this interpretation.

Sor Teresa/Chicaba's life is worthy of study as an extraordinary woman among other exceptional nuns in Spain and the Americas during the early modern era: Saint Teresa of Ávila, Sor María de Agreda, and Sor Juana Inés de la Cruz. Feminist scholars

have been indispensable in discovering texts and establishing the importance of these early women writers. However, Black women remain invisible in most scholarly essays and monographs in spite of the abundant evidence of their presence as devout Catholics. Chicaba's case makes clear the importance of race in the analysis of the lives of monastic women in Spanish and Spanish-American convents.[13]

[13] Jodi Bilinkoff studies the anti-Jewish racial tension around the Carmelite reformation in sixteenth-century Spain. Racial relations between nuns of Spanish descent and *mestizas* and indigenous nuns are receiving increasing attention (see Bilinkoff; Myers; Rubial; and Sampson Vera Tudela).

[Vida Ejemplar de la Venerable Madre Sor Teresa Juliana de Santo Domingo][1]

Capítulo I

A poca costa y menos trabajo suelen lograr las plumas que se emplean en escribir vidas y acciones de los héroes descubrir los padres, *patria,* deudos y parientes, pero en la del sujeto desta no puede con tanta facilidad correr la pluma porque lo incógnito de la tierra, lo distante de su clima escasea más y más en su distancia las noticias. Y a no haberlas dado la misma Madre Teresa, de todo punto se hubieran escondido a nuestros ojos; porque muertos los que la trajeron en su nave, fallecido los Marqueses de Mancera, todos sus *criados* y familia, *patria* y padres de Teresa se hubieran quedado en la región del olvido, y sólo por su rostro, anduviéramos rastreando su nativo suelo. Éste fue en la *Guinea.* El año, según más ajustada cuenta, de 1676. Ignórase el día en que salió esta feliz criatura a gozar la vida común, pero no el que fue escogida entre millares de la mano poderosa para crédito de su Divina Providencia.

Es la *Guinea* una de las más dilatadas y vastas provincias que en sí contienen los anchurosos términos de la África. Divídese en varios reinos, gobernados cada uno por sí solo. El de la *Mina Baja del Oro* es de los principales. Y aquí fue donde salió a luz esta dichosa niña, de tan ilustre prosapia que sus padres ceñían la corona, teniendo en pacífica posesión el cetro y mando de toda aquella tierra. El nombre de su padre le borró el tiempo de su memoria. Sólo conservó impresas las señales de su cuerpo, facciones y cara: *Era mi padre*—dice en su *relación,* que esta Venerable hizo de su origen—*un hombre corpulento, grueso y de cejas muy pobladas.* Su madre se llamaba Abar, igual al padre en calidad y nobleza. Tuvo la Venerable Madre tres hermanos, mayores que ella; el uno llamado Juachipiter, Ensu el segundo, Joachín el tercero. Estos tres precedieron al nacimiento de esta mujer insigne, a quien luego que nació la pusieron en su lengua el nombre de Chicaba. Para alegría pues de sus padres, gozo de sus hermanos y consuelo del reino todo nació esta infanta, a quien criaron con el cuidado y amor que, ya por niña o ya por última, correspondía a tan querida prenda.

Son los habitadores todos de la *Guinea* de un color atezado y *negro* como advertimos frecuentemente en los que vienen a nuestros países y nos informan historias de mucha autoridad. Siendo color con que a todos los de aquella región matizó sabia la naturaleza, ni a los padres y hermanos de la niña ni a la niña misma podía faltar esta gala. Mas aunque tan obscuros sus aspectos eran mucho más *negros* sus ánimos.

[1] For this anthology, we use Paniagua, *Compendio de la vida.* Spelling and punctuation of the Spanish original have been modernized except in those cases where there is a difference in pronunciation, as in the word *baptizar,* where the original is preserved instead of the modern *bautizar.*

[Exemplary Life of the Venerable Mother Sor Teresa Juliana de Santo Domingo]

Chapter I

Authors of the lives and deeds of heroes exert little effort and face even less difficulty finding out parents, country, family members, and other relatives of their subjects. But in the present case, our pen does not flow so easily. The unknown character of her native land and the remoteness of that region make information about her scarce. Had it not been for Mother Teresa herself, who supplied these details, they would have remained completely concealed from us. After the passing of those who brought her in the ship, as well as the Marquis of Mancera and his wife, all their servants and the rest of their family, Teresa's land of origin and parents would have been forgotten. Only the color of her face would be left to trace her back to her native land. She was born in *Guinea* in 1676, according to the closest estimate. We do not know the day this fortunate creature saw the light of life. We know, though, that she was chosen among thousands by the Powerful Hand and for the glory of Divine Providence.

Guinea is one of the most extensive and vast provinces contained in the huge confines of Africa. It is divided into several kingdoms, each one governing itself independently. The Lower *Mina* off the *Gold Coast* [*La Mina Baja del Oro*] is among the most important ones. That was where this happy girl was born to a most illustrious family. Her parents were reigning princes. Their scepter ruled all that land in peaceful dominion. Time erased her father's name from her memory. She only remembered the shape of his body and the features of his face: *My father was*—she says in the account [*relación*] this venerable woman made of her origins—*a man of large and broad body, and with very thick eyebrows.*[1] Her mother was called Abar and was as important as her father in lineage and nobility. The venerable mother had three brothers, all of them older than she: one was called Juachipiter, Ensú was the second, Joachin, the third one. They all preceded this outstanding woman in birth. When she was born, they called her Chicaba in their language. This princess was born to be a joy to her parents and brothers and a consolation to the entire kingdom. Either because she was a girl or because she was the youngest, all care was lavished on her as if she were a precious jewel.

All the inhabitants of *Guinea* are of a dark, black color, as we frequently observe of those who come to our countries or read from histories of the greatest authority. Because such is the color with which wise nature painted all those from that region, parents and brothers and the girl herself could not help being adorned in the same fashion. However dark was their complexion, even darker was their situation. In their

[1] Father Paniagua uses italics only for quotations that he wants us to accept as being directly taken from Sor Teresa Chicaba's own writings. Otherwise, he represents the imagined speech of Chicaba and all other characters in a variety of typographical forms, and not always consistently.

Adoraban ciegos al lucero de la mañana. Para sus cultos y sacrificios ni usaban ni tenían templos, sino que previniendo la estrella salían muy temprano a adorarla. Vigilia superflua, cuando en el mismo salir a buscar la luz se quedaban con más densas y opacas tinieblas. En sus días festivos salía el *pueblo,* Rey y Reina con toda su familia, según el rito de sus bárbaras ceremonias, epilogadas en doblar la rodilla, y en humilde obsequio hacer a la estrella la salva. Cultos que duraron hasta que el celo de los misioneros *capuchinos,* entrando estos últimos años, lograron plantar la bandera de la fe y desterrar las sombras de la idolatría. [pp. 1–2]

[Sin poder aceptar que el lucero del alba fuera la fuerza creadora de todo, Chicaba emprendió una búsqueda personal que tomó la forma de caminatas contemplativas fuera de su palacio. La gente la reconocía como regalo divino con poder para curar a las personas enfermas.]

Capítulo III

. . . Salió entre otras al campo una mañana con la corta comitiva de algunas *criadas.* Divertidas éstas algún tanto por la campiña, dejaron sola a la Chicaba cuando de repente se vio asaltada de bárbara tropa que, enemiga de su *nación* y de su padre, hicieron presa en la inocente para destrozarla. Exhaladas las *criadas,* que desde lejos vieron el peligro de su señora, entran por la ciudad dando voces. Llegan a Palacio en tropel confuso y en pavorosos ecos publican su peligro. El padre, tan animoso como pronto, salió al campo a tiempo tan oportuno que, animosos con su presencia, los vasallos que a las voces habían concurrido, a valentía de sus brazos destrozan y ahuyentan los bárbaros enemigos, y recuperando su más querida prenda, la restituyen a su padre festivos, dándose el parabién de haber, bien arriesgados, conseguido el triunfo y asegurados todos en la niña su consuelo. . . . [p. 7]

Capítulo IV

. . . Un día pues, bastante distante de ellos [los *criados*], llegó a una fuente cristalina y embelesada, según su costumbre, vio lo que vio, pues ella sola se lo supo. Sucedió lo que dijo, porque no pudo excusarlo; dirélo con las mismas palabras que un *director* suyo lo atestigua.—En una de estas estaciones—habla de lo mucho que andaba Teresa

blindness, they worshipped the morning star.[2] They did not use temples for their worship and sacrifices. Instead, as soon as they saw the star, they came out of their houses very early to adore it. What a superfluous vigil that was, because in the very act of seeking out the light, they remained in thicker and denser darkness. During their feast days, the people accompanied the king and queen and all their family. Following the customary ritual of their barbarous ceremonies, they bent their knees in humble recognition and sang praises to the star. These rites lasted until the zeal of the *Capuchin* missionaries, entering these lands not long ago, succeeded in planting the banner of the True Faith and banishing the shadows of idolatry.[3]

[Unable to accept the morning star as the creator of everything, Chicaba started on a personal search that took the form of contemplative walks in the meadows outside her palace. The people acknowledge her as a divine gift and a healer.]

Chapter III

. . . She went out one morning like any other with a reduced retinue of some female servants. Enjoying themselves for a while across the field, they left Chicaba alone. Suddenly she found herself assaulted by a barbarous army sent by an enemy of her *nation* and her father. They took her prisoner in order to tear her apart. The maids, anguished and seeing from afar the danger into which their lady had fallen, burst into the city shouting. They reached the palace in a confused melee; and with cries of alarm, they announced the peril. The father, as courageous as he was prompt to action, left for the field just in time, and his vassals, who had come at the call of the maids' voices, took courage with his presence. With valiant arms, they shatter and rout the barbarous enemies. After recovering her father's most precious treasure, they brought her back to him in celebration. They congratulated one another for having achieved this triumph because, though they had taken great risks, the girl's life assured their solace. . . .

Chapter IV

. . . One day, distancing herself from them [her retinue] a good while, [Chicaba] arrived at a fountain of crystal waters. Completely taken by it, as was her custom, she saw what she saw, for she alone knew about it. What she said happened, happened; and she could not avoid it. I will tell about it in the very words that one of her *spiritual*

[2] The morning star, or Lucifer (Latin "bringer of light") has been interpreted since Saint Jerome (*To Eustochium* 22.4) as a reference to the devil. Thus, Chicaba's people were worshippers of the devil. Paniagua shows the tension between the moral and the biological discourse on blackness of his time.

[3] This is historically inaccurate. An attempt was made by a *Capuchin* mission in 1658 sent by Spain, which produced a catechism in the Ewe language (see Labouret and Rivet; Law; and Olabiyi). Attempts were made by the bishops of *São Tomé* to send missions to the Kingdom of Benin and Whydah. *Capuchins* were very active in the Christian kingdom of Kongo around the time of its demise in 1688 (see Brásio; Thornton).

para conseguir su ansia—la baptizaron estando al pie de una fuente y pusieron el nombre de Teresa, que después la dieron también cuando la baptizaron en el Puerto de Santo Tomé [*São Tomé*].—Hasta aquí su *director.* Quién fue el ministro, ni lo dice ni lo explica, pero habiendo sido el lance cierto, que fuese un ángel no lo dudará el docto, pues en todo el reino entonces no había quien pudiese administrárselo. Desde este suceso volvió Teresa con algún consuelo, con algunas noticias de quién era el Dios que buscaba; pero como aún niña no parece le quedaron tan impresas que bastasen a sosegarla sus antiguas ansias, con que no omitió repetir sus diligencias. Y así continuó en buscar a quien, aunque ya tenía, aún la parecía ignoraba. Quiso este Dios para ella oculto darla algún claro diseño. Era él por quien en amantes ansias suspiraba. Apareciósela, pues, niño tierno en los brazos de María Santísima. Atónita Teresa con la vista de objeto tan peregrino, se quedó en dulce embeleso, clavados los ojos en Señora y Niño, apacible éste cuanto hermoso para excitarla a que tomase con más atención las señas de su persona. Tenía en las manos pendiente una cinta tan resplandeciente como vistosa. Con ella blandamente tocaba la cabeza de Teresa y al quererla ésta coger retiraba el Niño su mano con gracia, de suerte que ella no podía alcanzarla. Repitió el Niño algunas veces la diligencia, Teresa el afán de poseerla, aunque nunca logró el tocarla, y al cabo de un buen rato que duró este místico prodigioso juego, poniendo Madre e Hijo sus benignos ojos en la niña, se huyeron a su vista quedando Teresa, aunque de edad tan corta, combinando especies en su fantasía. La hermosura de la Señora, la gracia y dulzura del Hijo, lo blanco de sus rostros, siendo todos los que ella había visto tan atezados, fueron a su entendimiento tan perspicaz como agudo, aunque en pueriles años, eficaces incentivos para su ansia y su deseo de acabar de conocer este Dios encubierto y oculto. Finalizado el prodigio se volvió con los suyos, a quienes no descubrió parte alguna del portento. Sólo a su hermano, pasados algunos días, para sosegar su envidia, le dio tal cual, aunque obscura, alguna noticia. [pp. 9–10]

Capítulo VI

. . . Tan confiado como seguro de que se observarían en punto de la custodia de su hija sus órdenes y preceptos caminaba con sus hijos el padre de Teresa a tomar posesión de sus nuevas agregadas provincias. La madre, atenta a cumplir y ejecutar la ley del Monarca en cuya observancia ella tanto interesaba como era la seguridad de su propia hija, hecha vigilante Argos, no la consentía apartarse de su compañía. ¿Pero de qué sirven diligencias humanas contra disposiciones divinas? Cuatro días duró este vigilante amoroso cuidado, ocasionando el mismo amor el descuido que desconsolada su madre lloró por tanto tiempo. Burlado pues el estudio de la madre—el cómo sólo Dios lo

directors used to testify about it.[4] "In one of these pauses"—he talks about how far Teresa walked to reach the object of her burning desire—"they baptized her as she stood by the fountain, and they gave her the name of Teresa, which later on she was given again, when she was baptized in *São Tomé.*" Her *spiritual director* says no more. Who administered the sacrament, he does not say, nor does he explain. Any learned person will have no doubt that this happened indeed. An angel must have done it because, at that time, there was no one in the entire kingdom yet who could have baptized her. After this incident Teresa returned more reassured, with more knowledge of the God for whom she was looking. However, as she was yet a child, this knowledge does not seem to have impressed itself enough on her to quench her long-felt desire. She did not stop going about the same business and continued looking for the One Whom she still did not know, even though she had Him within her. This God, so hidden to her, wished to show some clear sign that He was the one she sighed for with loving pain. He appeared to her as a tender Child in the arms of his Holy Mother. Teresa, stunned by the sight of such an uncanny vision, remained motionless in sweet contemplation, her eyes fixed on the Lady and Her Child, who was as peaceful as He was beautiful. Therefore, Teresa could understand better who He was. He had dangling from His hands a ribbon, as bright as it was pretty. He touched Teresa's head with it softly; and when she tried to take it, the Child withdrew His hand with grace, so that she could not reach it. The Child repeated this action a few times; and Teresa [repeated] her gesture to grab it, but she could never touch it. This mystical and miraculous game lasted for a while, after which, the Lady and Her Son cast their benign eyes on the girl and disappeared from her sight. In spite of her young age, Teresa was left with all sorts of thoughts stirring in her imagination: the beauty of the Lady, the grace and sweetness of Her Son, the whiteness of their faces, when all she had ever seen were dark—these things became powerful incentives for her quick and alert understanding, despite her youth. She wanted to find out once and for all who this God was who was hiding under cover. When the marvel ended, she went back with her people. She did not reveal any part of the wonder to anyone. A few days later, she gave her brother alone some information, although vague, to calm his envy.

Chapter VI

. . . With the confidence and security of knowing that his orders and rules regarding the custody of his daughter would be observed to the letter, Teresa's father went off with his sons to take possession of his newly amassed provinces. Her mother was equally alert to enforce and execute the monarch's decree, because it was of utmost importance to obey it and thus ensure her daughter's security. Like a new Argos,[5] she would not allow Chicaba to leave her company. But what is human purpose in the face of divine decision? This loving vigilance and care lasted four days. The same love was the occasion for a lapse, which her mother would lament for a long time with

[4] A Roman Catholic nun often seeks guidance about her spiritual life from a priest who meets with her outside the sacrament of penance or confession. The director is seldom her confessor.

[5] Argos is a Greek mythological figure that has one hundred eyes.

sabe—frustrada la vigilancia de las guardas, pudo salir Teresa de su casa y ausente de ella se dio priesa a caminar a su amado prado a ver si en él o en la fuente lograba volver a ver aquella Señora con aquel Niño blanco que tan del todo había robado su afecto; y viendo que no hallaba en él el imán de su cariño, embebecida en su ansia, se apartó tanto de su corte y casa que no acertando a volver a ella, ignorando el fin de tan largo camino, tan sofocada del sol cuanto cansada de su trabajo, se sentó a la sombra de un árbol.

Defendida con ella de los ardores del sol, limpió el sudor de su rostro. Aliviada del cansancio, se quedó Teresa, aunque niña y en una soledad desierta, tan sin susto ni pavor alguno que llevada de lo que a su propia edad convenía, quitándose las *manillas* tan preciosas como ricas, empezó a jugar con ellas con tanta quietud y serenidad como pudiera en su propia Casa. . . . [p. 14]

. . . Al pie de un árbol dejamos a Teresa, cuando a la orilla del mar surgió una nave española y entonces, de improviso, la asió de un brazo un joven gallardo, llevándola también todas sus joyuelas. Arrimóla a la orilla del mar y descubriéndola los de la nave, sin ver al que la conducía porque éste se hizo invisible a sus ojos, saltó uno de ellos a tierra y embarcándola en la nave se hizo ésta el mar adentro, sin tratar de más intereses y negocios. Teresa, con el ansia de verse alejar de su tierra, con las lágrimas y fatiga que la ocasionaba verse entre gente extraña, estaba a los umbrales de la muerte ya por la pena y congoja ya por la sed que la ahogaba. Gemía sin consuelo; hacían cuanto podían por acallarla los del navío, pero como las lágrimas procedían más de la sed que la fatigaba que de otra cosa alguna, aunque tantas la afligían, no la acallaban porque ignoraban lo que quería. Acaso vio un vaso de agua y abalanzándose a él presurosa pudo así satisfacer su ansia, hallando en ella la restauración de su vida. Refrigerada y satisfecha la fueron poco a poco acariciando y ella recuperándose algo del susto, pero no sin el ansia de volver a su tierra a la presencia de sus queridos padres. Afligíala el no saber nadar, pues en esta habilidad y destreza, aunque tan niña, la parecía podía libertarse de esclavitud tan penosa. Y viéndose negada a este consuelo hizo, según después aseguró ella propia, este pueril discurso:—la nave, cuanto más se aleja, va más contra la corriente, conque saltando yo en el agua, corriendo como corre hacia mi tierra, sus mismos raudales me han de llevar a ella.—Como lo pensó lo quiso poner por obra pero al tiempo de ejecutarlo se la apareció una Señora que en su majestad y grandeza descubría bien claro era la misma que vio en la fuente dichosa, allá en su *patria.* Enjugó con apacible mansedumbre sus lágrimas, aquietó sus ansias con sus caricias, dejándola libre de todo punto del cariño que a su *patria* abrigaba en su pecho y la llevaba al más lamentable naufragio. [p. 16]

[Es bautizada en Santo Tomé y de allí viaja a España. El demonio ataca el barco en que la transportan en forma de pájaros negros. Desembarca en Cádiz. Vive en Sevilla algún tiempo y finalmente es regalada al rey Carlos II. Éste a su vez se la entrega al Marqués de Mancera y su mujer.]

inconsolable tears. Stealing herself away from her mother's watch—how she did so only God knows—and fooling the vigilance of the guards, Teresa was able to leave the house. Once out, she hurried toward her beloved meadow, where she hoped to see by the fountain the Lady with the white Child who had captured her affection so completely. When she could not find the compass that attracted her love, she was overtaken by her passion and continued walking far away from her household and court. Unable to find her way back and unaware of what was at the end of such a long road, suffering in the heat of the sun and fatigued after such travail, she sat down under the shade of a tree.

Protected by the shadow from the sun's fierce heat, she wiped the perspiration from her face. Finding relief and rest, Teresa, although a child and in such desert solitude, remained unafraid, completely without fear. Doing what was appropriate for her years, she took the beautiful and precious bracelets [*manillas*] off her wrists and started playing with them. She was as calm and serene as if she were in her own house. . . .

. . . We left Teresa resting under a tree, when a Spanish vessel appeared on the shore. Suddenly a gallant young man grabbed her by the arm with the jewels she was wearing. He took her closer to the seashore, and those on the ship noticed her but did not see the man who was leading her. He was invisible to their eyes. One of them jumped overboard and carried her to the ship. The vessel took to the high seas without tending to any other concern or business. Teresa was frightened to see that they were taking her far from her land. With tears in her eyes and frightened to see herself among strange people, she was on the brink of death. Sadness and distress suffocated her, together with thirst. She moaned helplessly, and all the crew tried everything they could to quiet her. But the tears were caused more from her overwhelming thirst than from any other concerns, although so many of these gave her grief. Yet no one could calm her because they did not know what she wanted. By chance, she saw a glass of water, and thrusting herself toward it quickly, she was able finally to quench her thirst. [Chicaba] had restored herself to life, feeling refreshed and more at ease, when [the crew] began to comfort her, and little by little she started to recover from her fright, but not from the anguish of yearning to return to her land and to the company of her dear parents. It distressed her not to know how to swim because she thought that with this ability and skill, even though a small child, she might liberate herself from such painful slavery. Seeing herself denied this remedy, she reasoned childishly to herself, as she later explained: "*The vessel is sailing farther away against the current. If I jump into the water, it will take me to my land, because its waves go in that direction.*" As she finished her thought, she tried to put it into action. But as she was about to execute it, a Lady appeared to her whose majesty and grandeur made it clear that she was the same one she had seen on the happy occasion of the fountain back in her motherland. The Lady dried her tears with peaceful calm, and she also calmed her distress with her caresses. With this she completely freed Teresa from the affection for her motherland that she nurtured in her bosom and that had almost brought her to a most lamentable drowning.

[She is baptized in São Tomé. From there she is taken to Spain. The devil in the form of blackbirds attacks her ship. She arrives in Cadiz and lives in Seville for some time. Finally she is presented to King Carlos II of Spain, who in turn gives her to the Marquis and Marchioness of Mancera.]

Capítulo X

. . . Mandó la marquesa una tarde a las *criadas* saliesen con su *negrita* al lícito desahogo de un decente paseo. Obedeciendo la orden de su ama, se encaminaron al sitio del Buen Retiro, donde en la variedad hermosa de fuentes, jardines y estanques pasasen más divertida la tarde. Al declinar ésta se arrimaron todas al estanque grande y puestas en su repisa, unas en pie, otras sentadas, divertidas todas con el suave bullicio de las aguas, notaron un hombre que en las exteriores señas parecía el *mayordomo* del marqués. Acercóse a ellas, lo que no extrañaron, pues le tenían por de casa, y sin hablar palabra se llegó a Teresa, que bien descuidada estaba en pie a la repisa del estanque; y el fingido *mayordomo* al impulso de un puntapié precipitó a Teresa en las aguas. Asombradas todas de acción tan irregular en sujeto tenido por doméstico, atónitas al ver a Teresa en el peligro, pasmadas sin saber cómo ocurrir al fracaso, se quedaron confusas un grande espacio de tiempo. Bastante a que el agua privase a Teresa de la vida, a no tener consigo el amparo divino, con el cual bajo de las ondas, decía, estaba tan gustosa, como allá en el pradito de su tierra. Recuperadas las compañeras de su asombro y confusión, conferían entre sí propias el *remedio;* y hallándose atajadas por todos caminos para dárselo, se volvían llenas de dolor y llanto, cuando estaba Teresa bañándose debajo de las aguas de placer y contento. A pocos pasos que dieron, antes de salir del Buen Retiro, encontraron a un joven tan gallardo como bien dispuesto, que informado del motivo de sus lágrimas, las obligó cortés a que volviesen con él al puesto. Reconoció el sitio por donde Teresa había caído y sin más diligencia que ponerse a la orilla, reverente el agua, puso en sus manos a Teresa, tan alegre, contenta y festiva, tan sin humedecerse la ropa como si no hubiera caído en el agua. Entrególa a las compañeras, las que preocupadas de gozo de ver restituida a su querida Teresa, tuvieron tan poco cuidado de saber quién era el joven como antes con el susto de saber qué se había hecho y por dónde se había ido el que al arrojarla al agua habían tenido por el *mayordomo.* [pp. 25, 26]

[Después de pasar su juventud en la casa del Marqués y la Marquesa de Mancera, Teresa recibe su libertad y entra en un convento de Salamanca, luego de varios intentos fracasados en otros, por razón del color de su piel.]

Capítulo XIX

. . . Confirieron las religiosas entre sí la materia, y hechas cargo las más de la conveniencia que a su convento tendría joya tan especial, más por su virtud y ajustada vida

Chapter X

. . . One afternoon the marchioness sent all the maidservants, including her little black girl, out for a walk, a decent and licit diversion. They obeyed the mistress' orders, and they went to the site of the Buen Retiro.[6] They planned to entertain themselves among its variety of beautiful fountains, gardens, and pools. As the sun was setting, they all approached the big pool and climbed onto its ledge. Some were standing on it, and others were sitting, and all were distracted by the soft noise of the waters, when they saw a man who looked by all the external signs to be the Marquis' *mayordomo.* He approached them; and they did not think anything of it, because they saw him as a member of the household. Without a word, he went near Teresa, who was standing on the ledge unaware of his presence. The false *mayordomo* kicked Teresa into the water. They were all taken by surprise by such an unusual action in an individual they all considered a fellow member of the household. They were astonished at Teresa's danger and were paralyzed because they did not know how to handle the disaster. They remained confused for a long while. It was long enough for the water to have taken Teresa's life, were she not sheltered by Divine protection. She said that under the waves she was as contented as she had been in the little meadow back in her homeland. Once her companions recovered from the surprise and confusion, they started to discuss among themselves a solution; but they could not find any means to help her and they turned toward home in sorrow and tears. At the same time, Teresa was playing under the water with pleasure and contentment. A few steps away before leaving the Buen Retiro, they found a gallant and well-disposed young man. They informed him of the reason for their tears, and he obliged them to take him to the site. He recognized the place where Teresa had fallen in. The young man made no more effort than to stand by the shore, when the water placed Teresa reverently into his hands. She appeared happy, gay, and joyful as if she had never fallen into the water, and her clothes were not wet. He returned her to her fellow servants. They were so busy with their joy at seeing their dear Teresa restored to them that they neglected to ask who the young man was, just as in their fright, they had forgotten to find out what had happened to the one they believed to have been the *mayordomo* or where he had gone.

[After spending her youth in the house of the Marquis and Marchioness of Mancera, Teresa receives her freedom and enters a convent in Salamanca, after several failed attempts in other places due to her skin color.]

Chapter XIX

. . . The nuns conferred among each other about the matter. Most of them had realized how opportune it would be for the convent to have such a special gem, more for

[6] The Buen Retiro was on the grounds of today's most popular urban park in Madrid. It had been used in the past by the kings of Spain as a place of retreat. It was in Paniagua's time that the park was opened to the public, but not in Chicaba's time in Madrid. It may have happened that the household of *Mancera,* a member of the Council of State, had privileges from the king to use the Buen Retiro.

que por otra circunstancia, estaban casi resueltas a admitirla. Cuando noticiosa de lo que pasaba una señora de la más calificada nobleza de España, que negada a lo esclarecido de su linaje vivía religiosa pobre en el mismo convento, no acertando a negarse a sí propia la que, generosa, lo había dejado todo, impidió la entrada y admisión de Teresa con el vano pretexto de ser *negra* la pretendiente:

—¡Una *negra,* decía, en mi convento! No en mis días; no está fundada esta casa para *negras.* Y así, señoras, pongan fin a la plática, pues para que no tenga efecto pondré todas las diligencias posibles.—Y como señora de tan relevantes prendas, de tan superior y calificada nobleza, hubieron de callar y convenir todas las otras, quedándose Teresa excluida por *negra.* Bien lo sintió después la misma que impidió la entrada, pues a pocos años que sobrevivió al suceso, noticiosa de la virtud heroica que resplandecía en Teresa, arrepentido ya su vano pundonor de no haberla admitido por *negra,* envidiaba en las de la Penitencia su dicha y acierto, según ella se explicó repetidas veces. . . . [p. 51]

[Teresa es admitida como terciaria en el convento de La Penitencia en Salamaca a pesar de la oposición inicial del obispo.]

Capítulo XXII

. . . Concluida la función se retiró el Ilustrísimo, pasmado del fervor que Teresa había mostrado cuando la vistió el hábito, dejando a los concurrentes y familia no menos atónitos de la devoción de la *negra* en su apetecida entrada y dicha conseguida, terminándose así esta plausible función. Ya tenemos a Teresa en el puerto a que tantos años ha dirigió la proa; ya vimos cómo, contentas y alegres, la recibieron a la puerta las religiosas. Pero otra comunidad invisible a los concurrentes, a la *negra* notoria, la recibió a la puerta reglar y con agrado. Notó Teresa al entrar en el convento a cada lado dos *coros* de monjas, que juntos componían cuatro. Mirólos con atención y al principio no dio crédito a sus ojos porque discurrió acaso que turbados le multiplicaban los objetos. Siguieron procesionalmente al *coro* las cuatro filas conformes y ya Teresa notó con más atención las dos que sobresalían pero sin inquietarse su alma. Antes bien, con gran quietud y sosiego advirtió en cada una el rostro y semblante, y que la causaban un júbilo indecible. A todas las veía con la modestia y compostura correspondiente al acto en que estaban y la vida que tenían. Pero en las dos sobresalía mucho más que en las otras la afabilidad sin afectación, la compostura exterior sin átomos de hipocresía, la alegría de sus caras tanto más distinta de las otras cuanto las sobresalientes poseían ya la dicha que no las podía faltar. Las otras, mezclado su gozo con tantas causas cuantas pueden en esta vida interrumpir su dicha. Las dos hileras, en fin, de religiosas que Teresa vio y notó de más eran las religiosas ajustadas que en este mismo convento

her virtue and righteous life than for any other benefits. They were almost resolved to admit her. A lady belonging to the highest nobility in Spain heard the news of what was going on. She had renounced her high birth and lived as a poor nun in the same convent. She had given up everything, yet she could not give up her own pride, so she barred Teresa's admission. Her vain pretext was that the postulant was black.

"A black woman!" she said, "In my convent! Not in my day. This house was not founded for blacks. So, ladies, stop the talking because I will do everything within my power to stop this from happening." And because she was a lady of such high standing and superior nobility, all the others had to be silent and agree. Teresa was excluded for being black. The same person who barred her admission later lamented her mistake. A few years after this event, she heard news of the heroic virtue that shone from Teresa. The lady was remorseful that her vain pride had made her reject Teresa for being black. She envied the nuns in La Penitencia for their fortune and good sense, as she explained repeatedly.[7]. . .

[Teresa gains admission as a tertiary *in the convent of La Penitencia of Salamaca.]*

Chapter XXII

. . . Once the ceremony came to an end, the bishop left. He was astonished at the piety shown by Teresa when he gave her the habit. All present, including his family, were no less astonished by the black woman's devotion. She had achieved her desired admission and gained her happiness, and this felicitous ceremony came to an end. Now we have Teresa in the harbor to which she had directed her sail for so long. Now we have seen how happily and joyfully the nuns received her at the door. But another community, invisible to those present yet noticeable to the black woman, received her with pleasure at the door of enclosure. As she entered the convent, Teresa noticed two *choirs* of nuns on each side. Together with the living ones, they were four. She looked at them carefully. At first, she could not believe her eyes. She thought that maybe her eyes were confused and she was seeing double. The four lines proceeded toward the *choir.* Paying closer attention now, Teresa noticed that two of them were more conspicuous than the others. Her soul was not disturbed; and in the midst of great calm and peace, looking at each of their faces and expressions, she felt an indescribable joy. She saw them behave with the modesty and composure that was appropriate to the ritual they were enacting and the life they led. But in these two rows every detail stood out much more than in the others. She saw cordiality without affectation, external composure devoid of the least atom of hypocrisy, and a joy in their faces that was markedly different from the rest because they were already in possession of that joy that will never disappear. The others' joy was mixed with many other things that could serve as obstacles to true happiness. The two extra lines of nuns that Teresa saw were those who had led virtuous lives in the convent and had found eternal rest in the Lord.

[7] The convent of Santa María Magdalena de la Penitencia of Salamanca, commonly called *La Penitencia,* belonged to the Dominican Order.

habían hallado en el Señor su reposo. Éstas, pues, por especial ordenación divina, en forma y figura visible la recibieron a la puerta y acompañaron a la función sagrada de tomar el hábito. De este suceso debimos el informe a Teresa, que ella misma, dando señas a las que vivían de las facciones y rostro de las que habían fallecido antes que entrase en el monasterio, acreditando lo particular de este suceso, dejan espacioso campo al discurso para venerar, no inquirir, los secretos del Cielo. [pp. 60, 61]

[Teresa ayuda a algunas mujeres pobres a pagar la dote *para entrar en el convento.]*

Capítulo XXXIV

. . . Así sucedió a una religiosa, la que cumplido su año de aprobación, se halló tan sin dinero cuanto abundante y copiosa de deseos de asegurarse por medio de los tres votos en el puerto religioso. Afligíase sobremanera, porque ni ella ni las demás sabían quién la sacaría del aprieto y no hallaban más *remedio* que fiar a la dilación del tiempo que las sacase de su ahogo. Había Teresa corrido desde el principio con todo lo necesario para que la novicia entrase. Y fiada de la Divina Providencia, puestas en Dios sus esperanzas, prosiguió en las prevenciones necesarias a la función de su profesión religiosa. Fuése a matar unas gallinas que habían de servir para la función del día siguiente y añadió con gracejo,

—Estamos ya en la víspera, ¿y vuestra merced se está con esa flema?—

Respondió la religiosa,—¿Y qué haremos con matar las gallinas si no puede ser la función mañana, por faltar lo principal y no sabemos de dónde ha de salir?—

A que Teresa volvió a decir,—Vuestra merced, señora, mate las gallinas, que mañana sin falta ha de profesar la novicia.—

Duro se le hizo a la religiosa el creerlo pero el suceso, arguyendo su falta de fe, acreditó lo mucho que a Dios le agradaba la esperanza de Teresa. A la mañana siguiente, sin falta, acudió a visitar a Teresa una persona de las muchas que la buscaban, quien liberal y piadosa puso en poder del convento cuanta *dote* faltaba a la novicia, conque sin salir del día hubieron de servir las gallinas porque en el mismo hizo su profesión religiosa. Así, a costa de prodigios, acreditó la Divina Omnipotencia lo mucho que se prendaba de la esperanza de esta su querida Esposa. [pp. 97, 98]

Capítulo XXXV

. . . Ansiosa su alma de mantener en sí y las de todas las criaturas racionales la divina gracia, inquirió diligente de su Celestial Divino Dueño el medio para conseguirlo; y oyó se le respondía de este modo:—*Sentía*—dice—*dentro de mi corazón que le amasen mucho mucho.*—Y Teresa con todo su corazón, potencias y sentidos le amó mucho mucho y por eso adelantó tanto.—*Yo que no sé,*—prosigue la Venerable—*qué es amar a Dios ni cómo darle gusto, sólo me parece a mí que le gustará el que en todo trate la verdad un corazón velador y siempre asido sólo a las cosas de su gloria, desterrando cosas terrenas en toda criatura, mirando sólo al Criador y siendo sólo el Señor suyo, alma, vida y*

These nuns, following a special command from God, came to receive her at the door in visible form and shape, and they accompanied her to the sacred ceremony of investiture. We owe this information to Teresa herself. Indeed, she told those still alive about the faces and particular features of those nuns who had already died before she had even entered the convent. Taking this incident into account, we have enough evidence to venerate her and not to question Heaven's secrets.

[Teresa helps poor women pay their dowries.]

Chapter XXXIV

. . . This is what happened to a nun, who after her postulant year found herself as short of money as she was rich and abundant in her desire to secure the harbor of religious life through the three vows.[8] She was very upset because neither she nor the others knew who could get her out of the predicament. Their only remedy would be to hope that the passage of time would play to her advantage. From the beginning, Teresa had covered all the expenses for the novice to be admitted. Trusting Divine Providence and putting all her hope in God, she proceeded with all the preparations necessary for the ceremony of religious profession. She went to kill two hens for next day's feast and said in good humor,

"We are already on the eve, and you are so tepid?"

The nun answered, "And what do we gain by killing the hens if the ceremony will not take place tomorrow because I lack the *dowry.* Where is it going to come from?"

To which Teresa said again, "Madam, you go and kill the hens; tomorrow the novice will profess without fail."

The nun had a hard time believing this. But her lack of faith served to show how much God was pleased by Teresa's hope. The next morning without fail, a person like many others who sought Teresa came to visit her. Liberal and pious, this person gave the convent all that was necessary for the novice's *dowry,* so before the end of the day the hens were served up, because that same day the nun made her profession. In this way and through a miracle, Divine Omnipotence showed how much He cherished the hope of His beloved spouse.

Chapter XXXV

. . . Her soul was eager to keep divine grace within itself as well as within the souls of all rational creatures. With that end, she promptly asked her Celestial Divine Spouse how to achieve this. She heard the following response: "*I felt*—she says—*inside my heart that everyone should love Him very much.*" And Teresa loved Him very, very much indeed, with all her heart, strength, and senses; and that is why she progressed so much in charity. "*I do not know*—the Venerable one goes on—*what it is to love God, or how to please Him; but it seems to me that He likes an attentive heart to be truthful in everything. The heart should be attached only to those things that pertain to His Glory, casting*

[8] All religious women took vows of poverty, chastity, and obedience.

corazón, sin dejar cosa libre fuera de Su Majestad. Bien sé conocerlo, mas el hacer falta.— Así te parecía a ti, Teresa, pero no faltaba en ti la ejecución de lo mismo que sentías y conocías. Y si faltaba, ¿a qué fin aquellas ansias de—te quiero, te quiero, te quiero,— en que, agitado del mismo amor tu pecho, prorrumpiste en ocasión que sin poderte contener te lo llegaron a oír? ¿A qué fin, si no sabías amar, aquellos celos que te ocasionaba la ausencia de tu Esposo?

Tiene el fino amor no sé qué punta de celos que, al paso que son pregoneros fieles de lo activo de su volcán, son exploradores de la afición más intensa. Celoso algún poco de nuestra Venerable vimos en el capítulo XXIX al Amor Divino, cuando la majestad de Cristo la reprendió aquel leve descuido de admitir en su *celda* a los religiosos que fueron a decir misa al convento. Señal clara la amaba, pues así la celaba cuidadoso; y el amor de Teresa para con su Dueño, queriendo acreditarse de encumbrado, tuvo también su poco de celos, que la obligaron en alguna ausencia de su Dueño a prorrumpir en los siguientes versos, en los que la falta de artificio pudo ser industria del amor para representarse sin medida:

Ay, Jesús, dón te has ido,
que un instante no puedo
verme sin tigo.
Ay, Jesús de mi alma,
dónde te has ido,
que parece no vienes,
y te has perdido.
Ay, Jesús ¿qué diré yo?
si os vais con otras,
¿que haré yo?
Clamaré, lloraré
hasta ver a Dios,
y si no, y si no,
morir de amor.
Y ya lo digo,
pues estoy tan sola,
que no has venido
Y si estás con otra,
ya yo lo he visto;
a María y Marta
las has querido.
¡Ay Jesús! dónde te hallaré yo,
pues tan tonta me tiene,
cuando te tengo:
Adiós, adiós, amor,

away from itself all worldly things and creature comforts. The heart should look at the Creator alone, as the Lord is the only thing the heart can call its own. Soul, life, and heart must spare nothing for His Majesty. I am well aware that I know this, but it still needs to be done." That is how it seemed to you, Teresa, but you did not hesitate for a moment to do what you felt and knew. If you think that you did not do enough, what then was all that eagerness of "I love you, I love you, I love you," which on occasion burst from your chest, shaken uncontrollably by that very love? People heard it. If you did not know how to love, why were you so jealous when your spouse was absent?

Fine love has a certain element of jealousy that is both a faithful proclaimer of how active this volcano is and serves as a harbinger of the most intense affection. In chapter XXIX, we saw the Divine Lover a bit jealous of our venerable one when the Majesty of Christ reprimanded her for that slight lapse of admitting to her *cell* the priests who had said Mass at the convent.[9] This was a clear sign that He loved her because He was very jealous. Teresa's love for her Master wanted to take credit for its elevated nature by also being a little jealous. After one of her Master's absences, this jealousy made her exclaim spontaneously the following verses. The lack of artifice in them could well have been the ploy of a love expressing itself without restraint:

> Oh, Jesus, where are you gone?
> I cannot stand a moment
> without seeing you.
> Oh, Jesus of my soul,
> where are you gone?
> It seems you are not coming back
> and you are lost.
> Oh, Jesus, what shall I say?
> If you go out with other women,
> what shall I do?
> I will wail, I will cry
> till I see God,
> and if not, if not,
> I will die of love.
> And because I am so lonely
> I say
> that you have not come.
> And if you are with someone else,
> I have seen it before:
> Martha and Mary,
> you have loved them.
> O Jesus, where shall I find you?
> I feel giddy
> when I have you.
> Good-bye, good-bye, love,

[9] The constitutions of cloistered orders prohibited direct contact between men and women. Only extern sisters and laypersons were allowed to socialize with visiting priests without the barrier of the iron grille between them.

adiós, Señor,
adiós, corazón,
no más, no más,
no más.

De estos versos consta con evidencia lo uno, que el amor hace poco sufrido al amante, cuando el amor de Teresa impaciente se queja de que tarda su Esposo, y de que otra alma se le detiene. Lo otro, lo bien que sabía ejecutar Teresa los actos de amor, cuando ella se lamenta:—bien sé conocerlo, pero hacer, falta.—

Tan fuertes eran los ímpetus del Amor Divino que ardía en el pecho de esta feliz alma que, sin poder contener lo pesado de su cuerpo a lo ágil del espíritu, le arrebató éste más de una vez tras sí, elevándola del suelo. Fueron pocas las veces que así la vieron porque ella se ocultaba y recataba cuanto podía, pero ya hubo vez que sin que ella lo entendiese, lograron verla a impulsos de su amor transportada del todo en su Celestial Divino Dueño, resplandeciente el rostro, bañada de luces la *celda,* gozando a sus solas soberanas dulzuras. Este amor fino labró tanto dentro de su corazón y pecho que a impulsos suyos sentía dentro de él lo que la Majestad Suprema no quiso fiar a otra pluma que la suya, porque ella sola podía dar un rasgo de lo mucho que sentía:—*En este dolor*—habla de un dolor que sentía en su corazón tan extraordinario como explica el suceso—*se me da a entender que está el Señor dentro de él siempre. Por esta razón, si me enojo, o en otra manera de no conformarme, este dolor se me quita. De manera que es dolor grande cuando tengo el corazón sereno y quieto. Es ardor cuando el afecto sube con exceso a desear el cumplir con las obligaciones que debo; y no digo bien, que no es exceso lo que es razón. Me abraso, me quemo, diera voces, pero las doy dentro de mí.*—

Y aún fuera de ti las diste sin poderte contener, alma dichosa. ¿Ésta es la que conocía el amor pero no le practicaba? ¿Ésta la que no ignoraba sus actos pero no los ejercía? ¡Oh mi Dios! y qué suave eres para quien te busca y te ama. Acábelo de explicar concluyendo el suceso Teresa propia:—*Tan grandes son*—dice—*los dolores que tengo en el corazón que por dentro siento se me cubre de sudor. Yo no sé explicarme más que esto; Su Majestad se lo dará a entender a V[uestra] R[everencia], pues quisiera manifestar todo lo que no alcanza mi corta explicación*—. Hasta aquí su pluma y aquí en este punto se abate y encoge la mía, porque recela no la abrase—si bien más feliz entonces—tanto incendio y tanta llama. Haga el docto reflexión sobre esta maravilla, que aunque tiene semejantes en la historia eclesiástica, no por eso deja de ser estupenda. Todas las obra Dios para nuestra enseñanza. [pp. 100–102]

good-bye, Lord,
good-bye, heart,
no more, no more,
no more.

These verses are evidence that love makes the lover intolerant. Teresa's love complains impatiently about her Spouse's tardiness and that another soul detains Him. On the other hand, they express how well Teresa carried out the office of love when she laments, "I am well aware that I know this, but it needs yet to be done."

The impulse of divine love burning in this happy soul's breast was so fierce that the heaviness of her body could not contain the agility of her spirit. Her spirit lifted her up in rapture more than once, raising her off the ground. People saw her in this state only a few times because she hid herself and kept it as secret as she could. Once, however, they were able to see her without her noticing them. Impelled by her love, she was completely transported in her Celestial Divine Master, her face was resplendent, her *cell* was bathed in light, and she enjoyed her royal favors in solitude. She stitched this fine love to her breast and heart so securely that she felt deeply what His Supreme Majesty allowed no other pen but hers to tell.[10] No one but she could express even the slightest trace of what she felt: "*In this pain*—she speaks of an extraordinary pain that she felt in her heart—*I come to understand that the Lord is inside my heart always. Therefore, if I get upset, or I am not in conformity with Him, this pain goes away. So it is very painful when my heart is serene and calm. It becomes burning when my love rises excessively to the point of wishing to fulfill all my duties and obligations. But I am not saying it right, because it is not excessive, because it is reasonable. I am burning, I feel I am searing, I would shout aloud, but I scream inside myself.*"

And you shouted out too, oh fortunate soul, because you could not contain yourself. Is this the same person who knew love but did not practice it? Is this the same woman who accused herself of knowing how to love but not loving enough? Oh my God, and how tender You are with those who seek and love You. Let Teresa finish the explanation of the event: "*The pain I feel in my heart is so great,*" she says, "*that inside I feel as if it is covered in sweat. I do not know how to explain myself except in this manner. His Majesty will help Your Reverence understand everything I would like to say but cannot in this short explanation.*" So her pen wrote, but here is also where mine recoils from the fear of being seared by so much fire and flame, though I would be the happier. Those who are learned may reflect on this marvel, that although Church history records similar cases, hers is nonetheless magnificent. God performs these works to teach us.

[10] This is internal evidence that she must have written about this experience herself.

14

The *Regent*, the Secretary, and the Widow: Power, Ethnicity, and Gender in the Confraternity of Saints Elesbão and Iphigenia, Rio de Janeiro, 1784–1786[1]

Elizabeth W. Kiddy

Black *Nações* and Their Confraternities in Eighteenth-Century Rio de Janeiro

In 1763, Rio de Janeiro became the capital of the colony of Brazil. Rio de Janeiro had risen in prominence during the mining boom in the neighboring captaincy of Minas Gerais, and it had quickly grown to be a bustling port city with a diverse population of Europeans, people of mixed descent, Brazilian-born blacks, and Africans from many different regions, both slave and free (Karasch, *Slave Life*). As in other cities in Spanish and Portuguese America, a wide range of confraternities served to organize this diversity in Rio de Janeiro and shape the religious and social life of the city.

Confraternities were Catholic lay religious associations organized around fidelity to a saint or a particular devotion; they fulfilled both religious and nonreligious functions within society.[2] Confraternity activities were often part of the domain of the street and included collecting alms, taking care of the bodies and souls of the deceased members, and both hosting and participating in feast day celebrations. Many Africans and their descendants, both slave and free, enthusiastically participated in the confraternity system, organizing their own devotions and engaging in the same sorts of activities that all confraternities sponsored.[3]

Black confraternities tended to divide along "ethnic" lines in Rio de Janeiro in the late eighteenth century. Portuguese and African inhabitants recognized these divisions, and they called them *nações* or *nations,* which can be understood to correspond roughly to what today are called "ethnicities" (Karasch, "Minha *nação,*" 128). Different *nations* distinguished themselves with different clothing, hairstyles, and even scarification, and, in many cases, they would retain the language, foods, and devotional practices of their remembered homelands.

The main division among African groups, recognized by the Portuguese and the Africans, was between *Angolans* from West Central Africa and mostly transported from the ports of Luanda and *Benguela,* and *Minas* who left from four main ports west of the Volta River in the Bight of Benin. Both of these terms collapse a wide variety of different ethnicities, some of which are elaborated in the document below (Kiddy,

[1] See Maps 2 and 6.

[2] See also Chapters 6 and 10.

[3] For some works on black brotherhoods in Brazil, see Kiddy, *Blacks of the Rosary;* and Soares, *Devotos.*

Blacks of the Rosary, 43–49). Many Africans from both of these large regions became fervent Christians but practiced a Christianity that mixed, to varying degrees, with African traditions.[4] Much of the devotion of the African Christians, as well as their ethnic rivalries, came to be expressed through the confraternity system.

O Diálogo: The History of a Confraternity Dispute

It was in this context that the *"Diálogo"* was written.[5] Africans who had splintered from the Confraternity of Saints Elesbão and Iphigenia wrote this "Dialogue" in order to tell their side of the story of the conflicts that precipitated the break with the confraternity. Francisco Alves de Souza, the protagonist of the "Dialogue," was a freed black man from the *Maki* Kingdom on the *Mina Coast* (Bight of Benin).[6] Souza moved to Rio de Janeiro from Bahia, the port city for the vast sugar-growing region in the northeast of Brazil, in 1748, and joined the congregation of *Mina Maki*. The "Dialogue" relates the circumstances under which he became the *regent* of that congregation, which was a subgroup within the confraternity of Saints Elesbão and Iphigenia.

Several other main characters appear in the story. Souza's fellow interlocutor, and the foil for his story, is Gonçalo Cordeiro, also a *Maki*, who had been Souza's friend from infancy. The antagonist of the story never speaks, nor is she named—she is referred to only as "the widow."[7] The widow was the wife of the recently deceased king of the congregation Captain Ignacio Gonçalves do Monte.

After his death, the widow surreptitiously had herself crowned queen of the congregation, keeping not only the power, but also the much contested safe with its contents and other belongings of the congregation. The main narrative thrust of the "Dialogue" is the escalating conflict between the two factions, one led by Souza and Cordeiro, the other by the widow. In the selections below, the other characters who speak include the bailiff's secretary, who arrives to compel Souza by law to assume the post of *regent*, and elders of the confraternity, notably Luiz Rodrigues Silva.

The original document, which is more than twice as long as the selections presented here, is excerpted in a way that preserves the action of the story. The entire text is, in fact, primarily in the form of a dialogue, which moves chronologically forward in time from 1784 to 1786. The dialogue format is not uncommon in sixteenth- to eighteenth-century Portuguese literature, especially religious works that used either dialogues or plays to help to convert non-Christians.[8] The dialogue form was also used, at least once, in a pamphlet in Portugal in the eighteenth century to argue for the

[4] On the concept of African Christianity, see Thornton.

[5] The scholar who has worked most thoroughly with this document is Mariza de Carvalho Soares. Her work is an indispensable reference for anyone studying this document.

[6] Soares identifies *Maki* as the Mahi, a people who inhabited the region that neighbored the Kingdom of *Dahomey* in the north ("Can Women Guide and Govern Men?" 81–82).

[7] Soares identifies the widow as a *Coura* woman, from a region far inland from the Bight of Benin, who appears in her husband's will as Victoria Correa da Conceição ("Can Women Guide and Govern Men?" 80–81).

[8] Soares discusses these forms in relation to this "Dialogue" ("Apreço e imitação," 111–15).

abolition of slavery.[9] Perhaps some of these pamphlets also circulated in Brazil. Even with these examples, however, it is unclear where the creators of this "Dialogue" got the idea to tell their side of the story in this format.

Within the text itself, few clues indicate when one day has ended and another begins; in fact, these transitions are indicated only occasionally, by an opening comment asking, "Who is knocking on the door?" At times, it is also difficult to know where the "Dialogue" is taking place, but it seems the two main locations are Souza's home and the meeting room in the Church of Saints Elesbão and Iphigenia. The "Dialogue" is punctuated by two legal documents—the *termo* (entry) written to inaugurate Souza as *regent* and the statutes of the Congregation of the Devotion of the Souls in Purgatory. Both of these represent important legal documents for confraternities and serve as evidence of the legality of the actions of Souza and his compatriots.

Power Relationships in Black Confraternity Life

The "Dialogue" offers a unique look into three important relationships of power in confraternity life. First, the "Dialogue" demonstrates the ties between this congregation of blacks and the civil authorities of the city and the Portuguese state. In order to force Souza to accept the position of *regent,* his compatriots wrote a formal petition. Souza agreed to become *regent* only after he was visited by the bailiff and almost dragged before the magistrate as a result of this petition.[10]

The last part of the "Dialogue" is dominated by the lawsuit that the congregation brought against the widow and the news that Souza had lost the lawsuit. Souza and his group appealed to the *Relação,* or high court, but the court only confirmed the sentence. Finally, Souza was brought before the viceroy, together with the king of the rosary, to defend himself against the widow's claims that he was the leader of an uprising—a serious accusation against a black in eighteenth-century Rio de Janeiro.[11] In a strongly democratic retort, Cordeiro rejected the ruling, saying that Souza was *regent* by the will of the people and only that will had force.

Second, the "Dialogue" exposes power relationships within the confraternities and between different groups of Africans in the city of Rio de Janeiro. The largest conflict appears between the *Angolans* and *Minas.* The *Angolans,* who outnumbered *Minas* in Rio de Janeiro at the time the "Dialogue" was written, are presented in the "Dialogue" as the African "other," barbarians who did not know how to act in a civilized manner and gave all Africans a bad name. This conflict exposes the reality that Africans from vastly different regions did not see each other as a single people but as competing

[9] I refer here to the anonymous mid-eighteenth-century Portuguese pamphlet discovered by Charles R. Boxer that was a dialogue about slaves and slavery between a Portuguese lawyer and a Brazilian miner (see Boxer).

[10] Souza refused to accept the title of king although that was the title used by his predecessor, Captain Ignacio Gonçalves do Monte. Instead, he insisted on adopting the title of regent. His reasoning for this change is elaborated in the "Dialogue" itself.

[11] The black kings and queens of the rosary brotherhoods were important figures in many colonial cities in Brazil (Kiddy, "Kings, Queens, and Judges").

groups interacting within the unequal slave society of colonial Brazil. The "Dialogue" also highlights the story of the division between different groups from the *Mina Coast* and their eventual split into their own congregations. Despite these internal divisions, the *Angolans* remain the true "other."

Third, the document is not as much about ethnic differences as it is about a conflict with a woman who decided to take power and defend her right to that power. The document includes repeated diatribes against women, who were "disturbers of the peace and tellers of tales." Part of this antipathy certainly comes from the particular conflict with "the widow" in which Souza and his compatriots find themselves. In a more general sense, however, the "Dialogue" brings up interesting questions about the role of women and the extent of and limits on their power in the black confraternities to which they contributed significant sums of money (Soares, "Can Women Guide and Govern Men?" 80–81).

The document invites a careful reading between the lines of gender expectations as well as a history of Afro-Brazilian women's agency through the widow's perspective, which is presented here only through the eyes of her antagonists. In the end, the Portuguese state supported the widow's bid for power, and, two years later the congregation of *Mina Maki,* with Souza as their *regent,* began its own confraternity dedicated to Our Lady of Remedies.

[*O diálogo:* Regra ou estatutos que usarão os pretos *minas* com seus nacionais no Estado do Brasil][1]

Entre locutores:

Francisco Alves de Souza, *Regente* da mesma *nação*
O Alferes Gonçalo Cordeiro, secretário da mesma . . .

[Souza resiste ser regente, e a viúva do antigo rei conserva o poder]

CORDEIRO: . . . Ontem me disse *VM* que me não podia na ocasião dar resposta, o que agora espero.

SOUZA: Qual resposta?

CORDEIRO: De ser nosso *regente* e fazer caridade com os vivos e sufragar as almas dos mortos. . . .

SOUZA: Senhor Cordeiro, agora acho-me mais aliviado das minhas paixões, e por essa razão mais desembaraçado para lhe perguntar quem foi a origem ou causa, de meter em cabeça de *VM* e dos mais outros parentes para me quererem eleger por *regente* desta congregação ou *adjunto,*[2] quando entre *VMs* não faltam sujeitos qualificados de capacidades, inteireza, verdade, juizo, e não a mim que não tenho esses predicados?

CORDEIRO: É boa teima do homem, não vi outro igual, estar a maquinar em uma coisa a tanto tempo, que mais parece impertinência que outra coisa. Já disse a *VM* na história do primeiro capítulo o que lhe havia de dizer, e como agora me puxa pela língua sou obrigado a tornar-lhe a dizer que nós não queremos a outro senão a *VM,* porque no tempo do primeiro *regente,* que era o Capitão Ignacio Galvez do Monte, já *VM* governava e além disso, quando o dito esteve doente da moléstia em que faleceu, mandou chamar a *VM* em sua casa, aonde lhe encomendou e entregou essa regência, que não desemparasse esta sociedade e caridades feitas aos nossos nacionais, e *VM* o prometeu assim o havia fazer, sendo testemunhas aqui presentes se achavam Luiz Rodrigues Silva, Antônio da Costa Falcão, e Rosa de Souza de Andrade, e outras pessoas de crédito.

SOUZA: Não há duvida que assim foi, mais agora me dizem que a viúva do dito Monte depois que enterramos o marido que faleceu em 25 de Dezembro de 1783, passados 14 dias a tempo que estive doente de uma erisipela, mandou convocar os nossos nacionais, como é costume quando o marido estava vivo, e os ordenou que ia a Igreja dos gloriosos Santos Elisbão e Efigênia e no seu consistório a tirar esmola pela

[1] Regra ou estatutos, por modo de um diálogo onde se dá notícias das caridades, e sufrágios, das almas, que usam os pretos *Minas,* com seus nacionais no Estado do Brasil, especialmente no Rio de Janeiro por onde se hão de regerem, e governam, fora de todo o abuso gentílico, e supersticioso, composto por Francisco Alves de Souza, preto e natural do Reino de Maki, um dos mais excelente & potentados daquela oriunda Costa da *Mina.* Fundação Biblioteca Nacional, Rio de Janeiro, Seção Manuscritos 9, 3, 11, fols. 1, 12–14, 16–26, 29–36, 38, 41–44.

[2] Throughout the manuscript, *adejunto.*

[The Dialogue: Rules or Statues That Are Practiced by the *Mina* Blacks and Their Kinsmen in the State of Brazil][1]

Between the speakers:

Francisco Alves de Souza, *Regent* of the *Maki nation*
Second Lieutenant Gonçalo Cordeiro, secretary of the same *nation* . . .

[A Reluctant Souza Resists the Regency While the Deceased King's Widow Holds onto Power]

CORDEIRO: . . . Yesterday you said you could not give me a response, so now I am waiting for it.

SOUZA: What response?

CORDEIRO: Whether you will be our *regent* and be charitable toward the living and pray for the souls of the dead. . . .

SOUZA: Senhor Cordeiro, I find myself now less burdened by my passions, and thus more unencumbered to ask you what the reason is that you and the others want to elect me as *regent* of this congregation although among you there is no lack of qualified people with whole, true, and just capabilities, when I do not have these qualities?

CORDEIRO: What obstinacy. I have never seen anything like it. To scheme for so long about one thing, it seems more like impertinence that anything else. I already told you in the first part [of this dialogue] what I have to say, and now you force me to say again that we do not want any other leader than you, because in the time of the first *regent,* Captain Ignacio Gonçalves do Monte, you already governed, and when he was mortally ill he called you to his house and gave the regency to you, so that the association of our kinsmen, and its charity, would not be forsaken—and you promised to do it. Luiz Rodrigues Silva, Antônio da Costa Falcão, and Rosa de Souza de Andrade, and other credible people who are here now witnessed that promise.

SOUZA: I do not doubt that what you say is true, but now they tell me that after Monte's death on December 25, 1783, and during the time I was away for fourteen days when I was sick with a skin infection [*erisipela*], his widow convoked our kinsmen and ordered them to go to the meeting room of the church of the Glorious Saints Elesbão and Iphigenia to ask for alms for the soul of her dead husband. And she had secretly taken measures beforehand with some of her faction, if it is permissible to say

[1] Rules, or statutes, in the form of a dialogue in which the charity and almsgiving of souls is discussed, practiced by the *Mina* blacks and their kinsmen in the state of Brazil, especially in Rio de Janeiro, where they must rule and govern themselves far from any heathen and superstitious abuses, composed by Francisco Alves de Souza, black and from the Kingdom of *Maki,* one of the best and most powerful of the region of the *Mina Coast.*

alma do dito falecido seu marido. E prevenindo-se ocultamente, com alguns de seus parciais, se é lícito assim o dizer, e apanhando a todos incautamente, no dito consistório, fez pôr uma coroa na cabeça dizendo que era rainha com tal sutileza que todos lhe estranharam este modo de proceder e fugiram dela no mesmo dia, porque não eram só ordenação de *maki,* que lá se achavam, senão tudo o que diz ser da Costa da *Mina* e de outras *nações,* que se admiraram de tal tragedia, tudo obra de um *crioulo* bahiano que se acha em sua casa depois da morte de seu marido. E veja *VM* se é ou não abuso e superstição e essa é uma das causas porque tenho teimado que não quero, porque conheço que a viúva não faz gosto que eu o seja sem seu consentimento.

CORDEIRO: Tudo isso são traços do demônio para perverter esta tão boa caridade, assim foi, mais quem consentiu, e aprovou essa eleição?

SOUZA: Eu não sei, pois *VM* bem sabe que estava doente naquela ocasião, mal podia saber dessa tragédia se me não contaram pessoas fidedignas zelosos do bem comum.

CORDEIRO: A viúva o que deve fazer, é cuidar no governo de sua casa, e cuidar em fazer bem à alma de seu marido, cumprindo com o que manda o testamento do dito seu esposo, e não se meter no que lhe não importa. E se ela fez essa coisa não foi por vontade de todos, pois *VM* bem sabe que esse nosso *adjunto* consta de mais de 200 pessoas, entre homens, e mulheres. Não me consta que se fizesse a ela *regenta,* porque havia de ser por eleição e vontade de todos os de *adjuntos,* e nem mulher pode ocupar semelhante cargo maiormente em governar, e reger a homens. . . .

[A congregação obriga a Souza ser *regente,* por meio da justiça]

SOUZA: Olha que batem à porta.

CORDEIRO: Quem é pode entrar que a porta está aberta. Oh, é o Senhor Luiz Antônio Ribeiro de Campos, *escrivão* do meirinho das cadeas que procura a *VM,* não sei para o que.

SOUZA: O que . . . *escrivão* do meirinho que negócio tem comigo? Estou perdido que quererá.

CORDEIRO: Não sei, agora veremos. Entre Senhor, senta-se.

SOUZA: Guarde Deus a *VM.* Quem procura *VM,* meu Senhor?

MEIRINHO: Ao Senhor Francisco Alves de Souza.

SOUZA: Para servir a *VM.* Aqui me tem a sua ordem.

MEIRINHO: Venho aqui notificar a *VM* por requerimentos que fizeram ao Senhor Doctor Juiz de Fora Luiz Rodrigues Silva, Alexandre de Carvalho, e José da Silva e outros pretos *minas* maquinos para *VM* ser seu *regente* e adminstrador dos sufrágios[3] das

[3] There are irregularities in spelling throughout the text. Although many of these can be attributed to nonstandardized spellings in eighteenth-century Portuguese, others jump out as true spelling errors. There are also problems with number agreement and gender agreement in adjectives and nouns. These irregularities may have been, in large part, because the scribe probably was not a native Portuguese speaker and may also have been self-taught. In these cases, the irregularities either have been noted or the correct form has been put in brackets in the text. In the example footnoted here, *sufrágios* is spelled *sufragaçõens* throughout the manuscript.

so, and, taking everyone by surprise, in the meeting room, had them put a crown on her head, announcing that she was queen with such guile that everyone thought her manner of proceeding was strange and ran away from her the same day, because she called not only the *Maki* to go there but people from all over the *Mina Coast* and other *nations.* And everyone was astonished by such a calamity. It was all the work of one *crioulo* from Bahia[2] who was in her house after the death of her husband. And consider yourself whether or not this is abuse and superstition, and this is one of the reasons that I have insisted that I do not want [to be *regent*] because I know that the widow does not want me to be without her consent.

CORDEIRO: All of this is the plotting of the devil to pervert this good charity, but who consented to and approved this election?

SOUZA: I don't know, but as you know I was sick on that occasion, so I would not have even known about this tragedy if worthy and zealous people hadn't told me about it.

CORDEIRO: What the widow should do is to govern her own house and take good care of the soul of her husband, fulfilling what his last will and testament commands and not meddling in other people's business. And if she has done this, it is not by the will of all of the people. As you well know, this congregation consists of more than two hundred people, men and women. I see no proof that she has been made *regent,* because that would have to be by the election and will of all the people, and what is more, no woman can occupy this position, which is to govern and rule over men. . . .

[The Congregation Brings in the Law to Force Souza to be *Regent*]

SOUZA: Someone is knocking on the door.

CORDEIRO: You can come in, the door is open. Oh, it's Senhor Luiz Antônio Ribeiro de Campos, secretary of the bailiff who is looking for you. I don't know why.

SOUZA: What the . . . secretary of the bailiff, what business does he have with me? I am at a loss to know what he might want.

CORDEIRO: I don't know, but we will see—enter, sir, and have a seat.

SOUZA: May God keep you. Who are you looking for, sir?

BAILIFF: Senhor Francisco Alves de Souza.

SOUZA: At your service.

BAILIFF: I have come to notify you of the formal petition that Luiz Rodrigues Silva, Alexandre de Carvalho, and José da Silva, and other *Mina* Makino blacks made to the honorable magistrate,[3] requesting that you be their *regent* and administrator of the

[2] A *crioulo* was a Brazilian-born black. Bahia refers to the city of Salvador in the captaincy of Bahia. It was the first capital of Brazil and the center of the sugar-growing economy in the sixteenth and seventeenth centuries. It had an active slave trade, but after gold was found in Minas Gerais (see Map 6) in the early eighteenth century and the capital of Brazil was moved to Rio de Janeiro in 1763, many slaves, free blacks, and others moved south to find more economic opportunities. Salvador was also home to Souza before he moved to Rio de Janeiro.

[3] Juiz de Fora: a magistrate named by the Portuguese Crown when there was no district court judge available.

almas dos seus nacionais e caridades com os vivos, e que se *VM* não quizer, que venha de baixo de vara a sua presença como se vê do despacho do ministro.

SOUZA: O que tão apertada hora é esta! Passe *VM* a fé e que debaixo de vara não vou falar ao ministro?

MEIRINHO: Sim Senhor, passarei a fé e que é a seguinte:—Certifico que eu citei ao suplicado Francisco Alves de Souza na forma desta petição como nela se contem e manda e declara, e pelo mesmo supplicado me foi dito que não tinha dúvida aceitar o dito cargo. Em fé de que passei a presente. Rio de Janeiro 9 de Março de 1784. O *escrivão* do meirinho das cadeas, Luiz Antônio Ribeiro de Campos.—

SOUZA: Há mais alguma dúvida?

MEIRINHO: Não Senhor da parte de *VM* está concluído, mas faz me fazer outra diligência que vem incluida na mesma petição.

SOUZA: Qual será a diligência que lhe falta?

MEIRINHO: Em notificar a viúva do Capitão Ignacio Galvez do Monte para entregar um cofre com sua caixa, a onde se guarda o[s] dito[s] pertencentes a esta congregação junto com os mais trastes e livros, que dizem os pretos que é da mesma congregação por serem comprados com dinheiro de finta que entre eles deram, e que já lhes tinham pedido, e que a dita viúva a não quer entregar dizendo que ele [Monte] é seu marido. Isto é o que me disseram os pretos.

SOUZA: Enquanto assim pouco me importa isso.

MEIRINHO: Adeus Senhor. Fiquesse em boa paz que isso não há de ser nada.

SOUZA: Adeus Senhor Luiz Antônio. . . .

CORDEIRO: Eu não disse a *VM* que haviam obrigar para ser nosso *regente?* E *VM* entrou a teimar tanto, que deu lugar a chegar as coisas nestes termos.

SOUZA: Em que termos chegou?

CORDEIRO: De ser obrigado; e não se podia passar sem isso.

SOUZA: Eu bem sabia o que havia suceder. . . . Eu lhe prometo que quando me derem a posse de *regente,* de o fazer secretário para também participar do trabalho já que tanto fala.

CORDEIRO: Pois me faz grande *peça* em fazer-me secretário da regência.

SOUZA: Nao lhe pareça *VM* e os mais Senhores que isso será brinquedo.

CORDEIRO: Ponhasse *VM* pronto para no dia treze de março que o havemos de vir buscar para se lhe dar posse na igreja dos gloriosos Santos Elesbão e Efigênia no seu consistório, como é costume e estilo conservado entre nós outros[4] pretos *minas.*

SOUZA: Mais que pronto estou. É necessário um livro para o *termo,* e o mais direi ao depois.

[4] An expression that most likely means "us" or "we."

alms and prayers for the souls of their kinsmen, and of charity for the living, and if you do not want the position I will have to take you under guard to see the minister, as you see in the dispatch.

Souza: Such short notice! You can register that under guard I will not go speak to the minister.

Bailiff: Yes, sir, I will register the following: "I certify that I subpoenaed the supplicant Francisco Alves de Souza with this petition, which contains both an order and declaration, and by the same supplicant it was said that 'I, without a doubt, accept the said post.' In verification of which I enacted the present [document]. In Rio de Janeiro on the ninth of March 1784, the bailiff, Judge Antônio Ribeiro de Campos."[4]

Souza: Is there any more doubt?

Bailiff: No sir, your part is finished; but I have to take care of other business included in the same petition.

Souza: What business is that?

Bailiff: I must notify the widow of Captain Ignacio Gonçalves do Monte to turn in the safe where the money of the congregation is kept, together with other articles and books. The blacks of this congregation told me that these things belong to the congregation because they were bought with their contributions and alms; so they requested the safe be returned, but the widow does not want to return it, saying that he [Monte] is her husband. That's what the blacks told me.

Souza: As far as that goes, it is of little importance to me.

Bailiff: Goodbye, sir. You can feel at ease; this matter will not be a problem.

Souza: Goodbye, Senhor Luiz Antônio. . . .

Cordeiro: Didn't I tell you that we would obligate you to be our *regent,* but you were so stubborn that things had to come to this point.

Souza: What point is that?

Cordeiro: That you would be obligated and that you would have no other option.

Souza: I knew what had to happen . . . I promise you that when I am inaugurated as *regent,* I will make you secretary so that you can participate in the work that you talk so much about.

Cordeiro: You would honor me greatly by making me secretary to the *regent.*

Souza: You [Cordeiro], and all of you present, do not think that this will be a game.

Cordeiro: Be ready on the thirteenth of March, because we will come to get you so that you can be inaugurated in the meeting room of the church of the glorious Saints Elesbão and Iphigenia, as is customary and in the style preserved among us *Mina* blacks.

Souza: I am more than ready. It is also necessary to have a book for the official entry and with a record of what I say thereafter.[5]

[4] This document, as well as the other documents embedded in the dialogue, are copies of historical documents.

[5] Confraternities were supposed to keep books, which were then subject to oversight by state authorities. In order to make them legal, all important acts, as well as minutes of meetings, were

CORDEIRO: Está tudo pronto. Vamos que os pretos estão à espera no consistório. . . .

SOUZA: Deus guarde a *VMs* todos na sua santa paz, assim como disse o Senhor aos seus discípulos quando lhes apareceu depois da sua sagrada ressurreição pondo-se no meio deles, e disse—a paz de Deus esteja convosco: *pax vobis.*—

TODOS: Ele venha em nossa companhia para nos proteger e reger como desejamos. Estamos aqui mais de quarenta pessoas para lhe darmos a posse.

SOUZA: Quais são os irmãos maiores desta congregação?

CORDEIRO: Aqui estão Alexandre de Carvalho, José Antônio dos Santos, Luiz Rodrigues Silva, e José da Silva, todos *forros,* pessoas entre nós de maior gravidade, que estão prontos para dar posse a *VM* com toda a deferência e gravidade.

SOUZA: Tenho tomado a posse e Deus me queira dar saúde e juízo, para os reger, com sossego e quietação para sufragar-mos as almas dos nossos parentes, fazendo caridades aos vivos para maior honra de Deus, e salvação das nossas almas.

CADA UM: Viva! . . .

[A história da irmandade dos *minas* makinos no Rio de Janeiro]

SOUZA: Desde o princípio desta terra em que entraram a conduzir os pretos de África que vêm da Costa da *Mina* e de *Angola,* e pela[s] desumanidades de alguns senhores que os compravam todas as vezes que adoeciam de moléstias incuráveis, e envelheciam, os deitavam fora, a morrerem de fome e frio nus por estas praias sem ter quem os mandassem enterrar, se a Santa Casa da Misericórdia os não mandassem buscar para os enterrar com aquele zelo e caridade que costuma, aí ficariam os cadáveres com o sua invalidez.[5] E por esta razão introduziram os pretos entre si a fazerem este *adjunto* ou corporação a fim de fazerem bem aos seus nacionais, a saber que a *nação* que morrer seus parentes tirar esmolas para o[s] sepultar e mandar-lhe dizer missas por su[a] alma e os que forem pobres acudir-lhe[s] de tempo em tempo com a sua contribuição.

CORDEIRO: Ainda faltam algumas circunstâncias.

SOUZA: Não costume a tomar o recado ao pé da porta porque ainda o não acabei.

CORDEIRO: Perdoe-me que cuidei lhe tinham esquecido e por isso lhe a lembrei.

[5] In the manuscript, *seu inalvidez* or *seu individez.*

Cordeiro: Everything is ready. Let's go because the blacks are already waiting in the meeting room. . . .

Souza: May God watch over all of you in His Holy Peace, just as his son said to His disciples when He appeared to them after His Holy Resurrection, placing himself among them, and saying, "May the peace of God be with you: *pax vobis.*"

All: May He come into our company to protect and rule us, as we desire it. We are here with more than forty people to inaugurate you.

Souza: Who are the elders of this congregation?

Cordeiro: Here are Alexandre de Carvalho, José Antônio dos Santos, Luiz Rodrigues Silva, and José da Silva, all freed blacks and the ones among us with the most authority, who are ready to inaugurate you with deference and gravity.

Souza: I have been inaugurated, and may God grant me health and wisdom to rule you with calm and peace, to pray for the souls of our kinsmen, giving charity to the living for the greatest honor of God and the salvation of our souls.

Everyone: Viva! . . .

[The History of the *Mina Maki* Confraternity in Rio de Janeiro]

Souza: The blacks created this group, or corporation, because ever since the beginning of this land, they [the Portuguese] forcibly brought African blacks from the *Mina Coast* and *Angola,* and some of the masters who bought the Africans were inhumane. When the blacks fell ill with incurable diseases or when they became aged, these masters just threw them away and [left] them to die of hunger and cold, naked on the beaches without having anyone to bury them unless the Santa Casa de Misericórdia sent to bury the bodies with their zeal and charity.[6] Otherwise the abandoned corpses would just lie there. And for this reason the blacks themselves created this group, or corporation, in order to do good for their kinsmen, to let the community know when one of them died, to collect alms in order to bury them, and to order masses for their souls, and so that those who were poor could be assisted from time to time with a contribution.

Cordeiro: We are still missing some details.

Souza: Don't be in such a hurry, as I have not yet finished.

Cordeiro: Excuse me, I thought that you had forgotten and so I reminded you.

---

to be entered into a book that was kept by the organization's secretary. Most confraternities had a book with their statutes (see below), accounting books, a book recording new members, and a book of meeting minutes or books with the certifications of masses celebrated for the souls of the dead.

[6] The Santa Casa de Misericórdia, literally "the Holy House of Mercy," was the confraternity designated by the Portuguese Crown to have the monopoly on burials in the Portuguese Empire. Although other confraternities also had their funeral biers and buried their dead, by law the Santas Casas actually had the right to control burials. They also were in charge of hospitals throughout the empire.

SOUZA: Não me esquecerão por certo.

CORDEIRO: Tenha a bondade de os continuar.

SOUZA: Sim Senhor continuo, e pelo contrário os pretos de *Angola* não só tiram esmolas para enterrar os seus parentes que morrem senão a rojaram com indecência tomar os cadáveres que vão na tumba da Santa Casa da Misericórdia para os pôr nas portas das freguesias a tirar esmolas dos fieies, para os enterrar com cantigas gentílic[a]s e supersticios[a]s[6] como levo dito no primeiro capítulo; porém informando-se disso o meretíssimo Senhor Juiz do Crime desse mau procedimento que os tem mandado prender e castigar. E por esta razão cuidam os senhores brancos que todos os pretos usam do mesmo que praticam esses indivíduos.

Em 1748 que cheguei a esta capital vindo da cidade da Bahia, achei já esta congregação ou corporação de pretos *minas* de várias *nações* daquela costa a saber *dagomé, maki, iano, agolin, sabaru*—todos de lingua geral—com muita união tendo por rei da tal congregação a um Pedro da Costa Mimoxo, também da mesma *nação.* E depois que faleceu êste, nomearam para existir no mesmo cargo o Clemente de Proença, com o mesmo título a que exerceu a muitos anos. E continuando o tempo começaram os pretos elegeram[7] as *nações* umas com as outras, buscando preferências de maiorias, ao que deu ocasião a que as *nações maki, agolin, iano, sabaru* saírem do jugo de *Dagomé* escandalizados e afrontados de alguns ditos picantes que os *dagomés* lhes diziam, procuraram fazer o seu rei e com efeito o fizeram na pessoa do Capitão Ignacio Gonçalves do Monte no ano de 1762 por ser verdadeiro *makino,* e este foi o primeiro que fez *termo* e endireitou e aumentou esta congregação. . . .

CORDEIRO: O que quero é a continuação da história.

SOUZA: Eu a continuo. Com o discurso do tempo se apartaram também as referidas *nações* que estavam com a de *maki, agolin, sabaru* cada um fazendo seu rei à parte até faleceu o dito Ignacio Goncalves em 25 de dezembro de 1783, e como *VMs* me obrigaram judicialmente para tomar posse. E jamais deram a primeira coisa que requero: é de não haver nesta nossa corporação o nome de rei.

TODOS: Pois *VM* nos governa e nos administra, e lhe temos cortesia como a nosso pai, o como o havemos de tratar, se isto já vem dos primeiros fundadores.

SOUZA: O viesse de onde[8] viesse, porque não tenho culpa dos erros dos primeiros fundadores e nem sou culpado nisso, digo que esse distintivo não se use mais porque não; é desonante nos ouvidos de quem os ouve este nome de rei, porque faz pertubar a boa harmonia e *devoção* que temos com os nossos próximos, devendo de dar outro título que condigna com a nossa profissão.

TODOS: Que título poderemos dar?

SOUZA: [O] de *regente*[9] [é] nome próprio para o feito que fazemos.

[6] In the manuscript, *gentílicos e supestertiçiozos.*

[7] In the manuscript, *a lezingarem.*

[8] In the manuscript, *viesse da donde viesse.*

[9] In the manuscript, *A de regente.*

SOUZA: I certainly have not forgotten.

CORDEIRO: Have the kindness to continue.

SOUZA: Yes, Sir. [Our practices are] contrary to those of the blacks from *Angola,* who not only collect alms to bury their deceased kinsmen but have the indecency to drag the cadavers that are going to the tomb of the Santa Casa [through the streets], placing them at the doors of their parishes in order to request alms from the faithful, to bury them with heathen and superstitious songs as I mentioned in the first chapter [of this dialogue]. However, when the most worthy criminal magistrate investigated this bad behavior, he imprisoned and punished them. And this is the reason that whites think that all of the blacks engage in the same practices as these individuals.

In 1748 I arrived in Rio de Janeiro from the city of Bahia, and I found this congregation already in existence, made up of *Mina* blacks from various *nation*s from that coast, such as *Dagome, Maki, Iano, Agolin, Sabaru*—all who used the lingua franca[7]—and they were united under their king, Pedro da Costa Mimoxo, who was also from that *nation.* After he died they named Clemente de Proença to occupy that position, which he held for many years. As time went by, the blacks began to elect leaders of the *nations* among themselves and search for the preferences of the majority. Then there came the time when the *nations* of *Maki, Agolin, Iano,* and *Sabaru* left the rule of *Dagome,* scandalized and affronted by some of the sharp words that the *Dagomes* had said to them, and decided to name their own king, which they did with the person of Captain Ignacio Gonçalves do Monte in 1762, because he was a true *Makino* and he was the first that was entered officially into the book, and who improved and augmented this congregation. . . .

CORDEIRO: What I want is a continuation of the story.

SOUZA: I will continue it. With the passage of time, the other *nations* also distanced themselves—*Maki, Agolin,* and *Sabaru* each named their own king until the death of Ignacio Gonçalves on December 25, 1783, when you obligated me, using the law, to assume this position. And you never gave me the first thing that I requested: that this corporation never use the title of king.

ALL: But you govern and administer us, and we treat you like a father as we should, and moreover, the title comes from the original founders.

SOUZA: It comes from where it comes from, but I am not responsible for the mistakes of the founders, nor am I responsible in this matter. I am saying that this title will not be used anymore because it is dissonant in the ears of those who hear it, because it causes disruption in the harmony and devotion we have with those close to us. We must give a title that is suitable to our devotion.

ALL: What title can we give?

SOUZA: The title of *regent* is the appropriate one for what we are undertaking.

[7] Mariza de Carvalho Soares identifies these names with the West African villages of *Agonli, Dassa,* Za, and *Savalu* ("Can Women Guide and Govern Men?" 85). Because these groups all came from the same region around the Bight of Benin, they had a common trading language, a lingua franca, that was used there and that could also be used in Brazil.

TODOS: Estamos contente[s], mas *VM* nao há de nos tirar o nosso direito, e nem o nosso regalito, que a tantos anos estamos de posse.

SOUZA: Qual é o direito que *VMs* dizem estão de posse?

TODOS: De não tirar os nossos postos, e nomes que a imitação dos *fidalgos* do nosso Reino de *Maki,* se usa entre nos outros a fim de distinguir o maior do menor; do *fidalgo* a mecânico e haver respeito entre uns e outros.

[Souza nomea a nova liderança]

SOUZA: Tudo se há de fazer com boa harmonia e ordem sem ofender pessoa alguma. O que *VMs* querem é que lhe dê os títulos assim como se dá cá na terra dos brancos não é isso?

TODOS: Sim Senhor.

SOUZA: Pois como me deram posse e faculdade para tudo já os nomeio aqueles mais zelosos e caritativos que dão de sim esperança de servirem bem à congregação.

TODOS: Atento estamos com boa vontade a ouvi-lo.

SOUZA: Está aí Luiz Rodrigues Silva?

SILVA: Senhor aqui estou pronto para obedecer ao Senhor *Regente.*

SOUZA: Levante aí a mão do Senhor Gonçalo Cordeiro.

SILVA: Para que posto?

SOUZA: Para secretário desta congregação.

TODOS: Viva o nosso *regente!* Viva o Senhor Secretário que Deus o conserve por muitos anos para fazer bem a sua obrigação.

SOUZA: A José Antônio dos Santos, para *jacobû de atoqquem* que é o mesmo que cá duque, é o primeiro conselheiro com a primeira chave do cofre.

TODOS: Muito bem feito está! Viva e viva!

SOUZA: Alexandre de Carvalho, para *eceçûm valûm,* que é como cá duque, 2° do conselho, com a segunda chave do cofre.

A Marçal Soares, *alolû belppôn lifoto* que é como cá duque, e 3° conselheiro com a 3ª chave do cofre.

A Boaventura Fernandez Braga, *acolû cocoti de daça* que é como cá também duque, 2° secretário e quarto conselheiro com a chave de dentro.

A José Luis, *ajacôto chaûl de zá,* que é como cá marquês de tal parte, e é do conselho o quinto.

ALL: All right, but you should not take from us what is our right and our pleasure, that we have had for so many years.

SOUZA: What is the right that you say you have?

ALL: To not rid ourselves of our positions and titles that are an imitation of the nobles of the Kingdom of *Maki,* that we use among ourselves to distinguish the important from the less important, between the noble and the artisan, so that we maintain respect among ourselves.

[Souza Appoints the New Leadership]

SOUZA: Everything must be done with good harmony and order, without offending anyone. What you want is that I give titles like they do here in the land of the whites, isn't that it?

ALL: Yes, sir.

SOUZA: As you gave me power and faculty to do everything, I now name those who are the most zealous and caring, who foster hope among you and serve well the congregation.

ALL: We are all ready with good will to hear what you have to say.

SOUZA: Is Luiz Rodrigues Silva here?

SILVA: Sir, I am here, ready to obey the lord *regent.*

SOUZA: Raise the hand of Senhor Gonçalo Cordeiro.

SILVA: For what post?

SOUZA: For secretary of this congregation.

ALL: Viva our *regent,* viva Senhor Secretary! May God preserve you for many years to fulfill your obligation.

SOUZA: José Antônio dos Santos will be *jacobû de Atoqquem*[8] which is the same as duke here, and he is the first counselor with the first key to the safe.[9]

ALL: Well done! Viva and viva!

SOUZA: Alexandre de Carvalho will be *eceçûm valûm,* which is also like duke, and he will be the second on the counsel with the second key to the safe.

Marçal Soares will be *alolû belppôn lifoto,* also duke, and third on the counsel with the third key to the safe.

Boaventura Fernandez Braga will be *acolû cocoti de Daça,* duke, second secretary, and the fourth counselor with the key to the inner part of the safe.

José Luis will be *ajacôto chaûl de Zá,* which is like marques here, and fifth on the counsel.

[8] *Jacobû de Atoqquem, eceçûm valûm, alolû belppôn lifoto, acolû cocoti de Daça, ajacôto chaûl de Zá, ledô,* and *aggaû* appear to be terms for positions of authority derived from or in a West African language spoken by the *Mina Makis.*

[9] The safes of the Brazilian confraternities held the most important possessions and the money of the organizations. The safes would often have several locks, each with different keys, to prevent one person from stealing the contents. The most important people in the organizations would keep the keys, but all had to be present to open the safe.

A Luis da Silva com o posto de *ledô,* que é o mesmo que conde é 6° do conselho.

A Luis Rodrigues Silva para *aggaû,* que é o mesmo que General.

A José da Silva para *aggaû* que é o mesmo. E como é já tarde e o tempo será pouco para se fazer o *termo* deixemos para fazermos em outro ocasião o que falta.

TODOS: Viva o nosso *Regente* pelo o acerto com que nos proveu! . . .

[O *termo:* o registro da toma de posse de Souza]

CORDEIRO: *Termo* da obrigação e posse que fizeram os homens pretos *forros* e sujeitos da *nação maki* em que elegeram a Francisco Alves de Souza para seu *regente* administrador como se declaram nos assinados, e obrigação que fizeram e juntamente dá posse que lhe dão; cuja posse e obrigação e nomeação é da maneira seguinte:

Ao Capitão Ignacio Gonçalves do Monte tinhamos feito nosso *regente* e [a]dministrador das esmolas que costumamos a dar para se dizerem missas pelas[10] almas dos nossos irmãos falecidos da *nação mina,* e sujeitávamos a tudo que ele dispunha. Elegemos para a dita ocupação e cargo o Francisco Alves de Souza, homem preto *forro,* casado aregado[11] com bens, e nele concorrem todos os requisitos necessários que se faz a bem de ocupar o dito cargo, e justamente por ser imediato ao dito falecido, que supria as suas vezes, com todo o zelo e prontidão, de que lhe damos posse, e lhe entregamos tudo o quanto o falecido estava de posse, e sujeitamo-nos a tudo que ele determinar e tirando todo o poder e domínio que tiver a mulher do falecido e quer ter que por nenhum dos modos pode ser de *regenta* e administradora por ser contra as leis, e nem podemos ser administrada por uma mulher. E como é assim a nossa vontade lhe concedemos todos os nossos poderes que em direito nos são concedidos e sem constrangimento de pessoa alguma. Fazemos este tão somente por nós assinados para em todo o tempo constar desta nossa eleição e posse que lhe damos e reconhecemos por nosso *regente* e [a]dministrador e bem feitor das almas, dos nossos irmãos falecidos de que todos nos assinamos e pedimos o ajudante Antônio Francisco Soares que êste fizesse e como testemunha o assinasse, Rio de Janeiro 20 de Março de 1784. E Eu Gonçalo Cordeiro secretário do *regente* que sob escrevi e assinei.

Como testemunha que êste fiz e assinei
Antônio Francisco Soares
Gonçalo Cordeiro
Em que asinaram todos como se ve. . . .

[Os estatutos das caridades e sufrágios pelas almas do purgatório]

SOUZA: Quem bate aí? Pode entrar, que a porta está aberta.

CORDEIRO: Como passou *VM* a noite?

SOUZA: Muito bem, para servir a *VM* meu Senhor.

[10] In the manuscript, *pelas as almas.*

[11] I have been unable to find a translation for *aregado.*

Luiz da Silva will have the position of *ledô,* which is the same as count, and will be sixth counselor.

Luis Rodrigues Silva will be *aggaû,* which is the same as general.

And José da Silva will also be *aggaû.* Because it is already late and we would have only a short amount of time to finish the entry, we will finish the rest on another occasion.

ALL: Viva our *regent* for the wisdom he bestowed! . . .

[The Legal Record of Souza's Installation]

CORDEIRO: Official entry of obligation and inauguration of the freed blacks and subjects of the *Maki nation,* in which they elected Francisco Alves de Souza to be their *regent* and administrator, as we declare and sign below, and at the same time inaugurate him. The inauguration, obligation, and nomination have been done in the following way:

Captain Ignacio Gonçalves do Monte was our *regent,* and the administrator of the alms that we use to celebrate masses for the souls of our deceased brothers of the *Mina nation,* and we subjected ourselves to all he decided. We elect to that position Francisco Alves de Souza, a freed black, married with possessions, and declare that he has all the necessary requisites to do a good job in the position, and also because he was second in command to the deceased and substituted for him, demonstrating his ability with zeal and promptness, that we name him *regent,* and give to him all that the deceased had, subjecting ourselves to all that he determines and taking away all the power and dominion that the wife of the deceased has or desires, because under no circumstances can she be *regent* and administrator, because it is against the laws. Nor can we ever be ruled over by a woman. It is our wish to concede to [Souza] all of our powers that by law are conceded to us, without coercion from anyone. We do this on our own so that our election and inauguration will be known for all time. We name you [Souza] and recognize you as our *regent* and as the good administrator of the souls of our departed brethren. All of us sign and ask the clerk Antônio Francisco Soares that he sign as witness, Rio de Janeiro, March 20, 1784; and I, Gonçalo Cordeiro, secretary of the *regent,* wrote [the entry] and signed below.

As witness who made this and signed
Antônio Francisco Soares
Gonçalo Cordeiro
Wherein all signed, as can be seen. . . .

[The Official Statues for the Devotion to the Souls of Purgatory][10]

SOUZA: Who is knocking? Come in, the door is open.

CORDEIRO: How did you pass the night?

SOUZA: Very well. At your service.

[10] There is no clear break in the text preceding this section, but the date on the statutes indicates that two years have passed since Souza's installation.

CORDEIRO: Venho com gosto para ver já acabado estes estatutos. . . . Estou muito admirado da sua atividade, e o modo com que faz estas coisas, com tanta prontidão.

SOUZA: Em nome da Santíssima Trindade, Padre Filho, e Espirito Santo, três pessoas distintas e um só Deus verdadeiro, &c.

Nós, o *regente* e os mais grandes do *adjunto* e congregação dos pretos *minas maki,* desejando que êsta se aumente no serviço de Deus, e tenha seus estatutos por onde se governem, sabendo cada um a obrigação que lhe compete, para que assim se sirva aos nossos naçionais com nossas devotas assistências e sufrágios das almas dos mesmos; se edifiquem os mais fieis cristãos vendo que quanto cabe em nossas capacidades saber fazer caridades uns aos outros ordenando os estatutos seguintes:

Capítulo primeiro Haverá neste *adjunto* ou congregação um *regente* e *regenta* feito por voto e vontade de todos, haverá também um vice-*regente* que fará as vezes do *regente.*

Capítulo segundo As pessoas a quem elegerem para *regentes* sejam naturais e oriundos da Costa da *Mina* e do Reino de *Maki* e não poderão eleger de outro *nação.*

Capítulo terceiro Toda a pessoa que quizer entrar neste *adjunto,* ou congregação—exceto pretos de *Angola*—serão examinados pelo secretário deste *adjunto* e *aggaû* que é o mesmo que procurador geral, verem que não sejam pretos ou pretas que usem de abusos e gentilismos ou superstição que achando ou tendo notícias que usam os não poderão receber.

Capítulo quarto Todas as pessoas que estiverem neste *adjunto* serão devotos de Deus e de sua Sagradíssima Mai Maria Santíssima e dos Santos da Corte do Céu, especialmente dos Santos dos seus nomes, e anjos da guarda e das almas do purgatório por quem militemos ouvindo missas todos os dias, se puder ser especialmente as segundas feiras por serem dias dedicados pela igreja das suas comemorações. . . .

Capítulo quinto Este *adjunto* ou congregação foi feito para se fazer caridades aos nossos nacionais, com estes fundamentos: a saber, primeiro que todos os que forem desta *nação* e estivem neste *adjunto,* e morrerem sendo irmão de qualquer irmandade, terão obrigação de o acompanhar até a sepultura.

CORDEIRO: I come with pleasure, knowing that you have already finished the statutes. . . . I admire your energy and the way you get things done with such promptness.

SOUZA: In the name of the Holy Trinity, Father, Son, and Holy Spirit, three distinct persons in one true God, etc.

We, the *regent* and the important men of the congregation of the *Mina Maki* blacks, desiring this [congregation] to increase in the service of God, and have its statutes by which it is governed, knowing each his obligation, in order to serve our fellow kinsmen with our devoted assistance and alms for their souls. The most loyal Christians would receive edifying impressions seeing how much we are able to do, knowing to be charitable to each other as commanded in the following statutes:[11]

Chapter One There will be in this congregation one *regent* and one *regenta*[12] selected by a vote and by the will of all. There will also be a vice-*regent* who will sometimes take the place of the *regent.*

Chapter Two The people who are elected to be *regent* will be from the *Mina Coast* and the Kingdom of *Maki;* no other *nation* can be elected.

Chapter Three Every person who would like to join this congregation—except for blacks from *Angola*—will be examined by the secretary of the group, and by the *aggaû,* which is the same as the general procurator, to make sure that they are not blacks that engage in abuses and heathen or superstitious practices. If it is found that they do engage in these practices they will not be allowed to join.

Chapter Four All of the people in this congregation will be devoted to God and to his Holy Mother Mary and to the Saints of the Court of Heaven, especially the saints of their names, and the guardian angels of the souls in purgatory, for whom will be celebrated masses every day, especially Mondays, if possible, because they are the days dedicated by the church for their commemoration. . . .

Chapter Five This congregation was created to offer charity to our kinsmen and with these foundations: It should be known that, first, we are obligated to accompany the burials of all who are from our *nation* and are members of this congregation, even if they are also members of another brotherhood. . . .

[11] Statutes were legal documents that officially incorporated the brotherhoods. They were a list of rules that after the Pombaline Reforms in the mid-eighteenth century were supposed to be authorized by the *Mesa de Conciência e Ordens* (Board of Conscience and Orders) in Lisbon, which was the branch of the government that oversaw church affairs. Statutes often postdated the actual formation of the organizations, as can be seen in this case, and sometimes brotherhoods never sent them to be reviewed.

[12] Literally a female regent. Souza's wife, Rita Sebastiana, becomes *regenta* in this instance, but the statutes do not require that the *regenta* be the wife of the regent in future elections. In other black confraternities, the head female (often designated the queen) was not related to the king.

Capítulo sexto Todos os que forem congregados sendo *forros* estiverem doentes, serão assistidos dos da congregação sendo o primeiro, o *regente* e a *regenta,* que assistiram com toda a caridade e decência, e depois destes se queiram os mais, e se o doente for muito pobre, e carecer de ajuntorio para o que lhe for necessário, darão parte ao *regente* para lhe dar as providências necessárias mandando ajuntar aos grandes da congregação e tesoureiros dela, para cada um votar o dinheiro que se deve tirar do cofre, para o remédio da que se infirmou nosso nacional, e se estiver em perigo da vida e desenganado dos professores, farão ou irão chamar padres para o confessar e pôr pronto para receber o Santíssimo Sacramento fazendo seu testamento com actos de católicos.

Capítulo sétimo Os congregados que forem cativos querendo libertar-se tendo o seu dinheiro e lhe faltar para o *ajuste* da sua alforria fará saber ao *regente* para este lhe dar as providências, fazendo juntar os congregados participando-lhes a necesidade que tem o dito do dinheiro para se libertar, para o que o secretário fará um *termo,* a que assinará o dito pretendente com obrigação de o pagar.

Capítulo oitavo O procurador geral desta congregação terá cuidado em solicitar notícias dos congregados visitando-os e vendo os que estão doentes, para dar parte ao *regente;* como também os que tiverem entre si discórdias, fazê-los vir perante o *regente,* para os acomodar porque muitas vezes, por um pequeno incêndio se levanta uma grande lavareda; porque desejamos entre nós paz, e união, assim como encomendou Cristo Senhor Nosso, aos seus apóstolos.

Capítulo nono Haverá nesta congregação um cofre com duas gavetas dentro, e para o bom governo dela será feichado com três chaves, que o *regente* fará eleição em os mais autorizados da congregação, entregando cada e um a sua com títulos de tesoureiro, e as chaves das gavetas de dentro pertencem ao *regente* ou quem suas vezes fizer. Quando for necessário de abrir o cofre, convocará o *regente* aos tesoureiros para cada um com a sua chave abrir, e sem isso as não poderão abrir por carecer um de outro.

Capítulo décimo É o lugar do *regente* nesta congregação o de maior respeito, e veneração e por esta razão todos os da congregação lhe devem obediência com todo acatamento, e o que lhe não prestar obediência será castigado conforme o alvedrio do mesmo *regente,* assim mesmo se entenderá com a *regenta* e todos os mais que têm nomes na mesma congregação.

Capítulo décimo primeiro Todos os congregados que faltarem quando falecer seu irmão e o não acompanharem até a sepultura sendo *forros,* que nao tiverem legítima causa para o fazer dará de esmola para o cofre 120 réis em castigo da sua rebeldia, e os que foram cativos que não tiverem também legítima causa darão[12] de esmola 60 réis em castigo também da sua rebeldia e frouxidão. E os que tiverem legítima causa por razão das suas ocupações, bastão só rezar o Padre Nosso e Ave Maria com Gloria Patris

[12] In the manuscript, *dará.*

Chapter Six Members who are freed but become sick will be helped by the congregation, first, by the *regent* and the *regenta* who will help, with charity and decency, and after them others will help. If the sick person is very poor, lacking money for whatever he needs, the *regent* will take necessary measures, calling together all of the important men of the congregation and the treasurer, so that they can vote on how much money to take from the safe to help our sick countryman. If the sick person is near death and the experts have given up, they will call the priests for confession and to prepare [them] to receive the Holy Sacrament, making his testament according to the Catholic Faith.

Chapter Seven Slave members who want to buy their freedom with their own money but are missing part of their payment will tell the *regent* so that he can take measures to gather together the congregation to collect the necessary money to make a loan to buy the freedom. The secretary will make an entry in the book of obligation to pay back the loan.

Chapter Eight The general procurator will be responsible for gathering news of [members of] the congregation, visiting them and seeing if they are sick, in order to tell the *regent,* also noting whether there are discords, making those people go before the *regent* in order to set things straight, because many times a little flare up will become a huge fire and we desire among ourselves peace and unity, as Christ commanded His apostles.

Chapter Nine There will be in this congregation one safe with two inside drawers, and for the good governance of this organization it will be locked with three keys. The *regent* will carry out an election of those most authorized in the congregation, giving a key to each [of those elected] with their titles of treasurer. The keys to the inside drawers belong to the *regent* or whoever substitutes for him. When it is necessary to open the safe, the *regent* will summon the treasurers so that each one can open it with his key, so that no one can open the safe without the others being there.

Chapter Ten The position of *regent* in this congregation is the highest and most venerated, and for this reason we owe him obedience with total respect. Whoever does not demonstrate obedience will be punished according to the will of the *regent,* and the same will go for his wife and all that have titles in the organization.

Chapter Eleven All of the members who miss a funeral of a fellow member will be fined. Those who are freed, who do not have a legitimate reason, will pay a fine of 120 *réis,*[13] which will be put in the safe as a punishment for their contempt and negligence; and those who are slaves who do not have a good reason will pay 60 *réis.* Those who have a legitimate reason because of their occupations will be required to pray an Our Father and a Holy Mary with a Gloria, offering these prayers to the Holy Passion of

[13] Portuguese currency used in Brazil in the eighteenth century.

oferecida à sagrada Paixão do Senhor pela alma daquele falecido nosso nacional. E pelo contrário o *forro* que não puder assistir ou acompanhar ao mesmo falecido tendo justa causa rezará uma coroa à sagrada morte e paixão do Senhor pela alma do mesmo.

Capítulo décimo segundo Quando se souber, e correr notícia que algum que estiver assentado no livro desta congregação, tiver mau procedimento e forem revoltosos, tanto em prejuízo das suas pessoas como em dano de terceiro e dos congregados seus irmãos, logo será chamado e se fará um *adjunto,* aonde será pelo *regente* e os mais autorisados da congregação admoestado honestamente até[13] três vezes e não tendo o dito emenda e nem obedecendo será expulso por *termo* que fará o secretário, e assinarão o *regente,* e os mais grandes, e autorisados da mesma congregação; e isto se entenderá também nas mulheres por serem algumas orgulhosas, amigas de enredos, perturbadoras da paz e sossego.

Capítulo déçimo terceiro Porquanto vemos que a experiência nos tem mostrado que um estado de folias nas irmandades pretas serve de muita utilidade, assim de exercitar os ânimos dos pretos, como para acudirem de novo muitos de fora, assentarem-se na congregação. . . . Queremos que no dia de Nossa Senhora do Rosário, haja um estado de folias desta *nação maki,* que acompanharão ao Rei de Nossa Senhora do Rosário sendo da Costa da *Mina,* e não o sendo o não acompanharão, e somente se permita as suas saídas para o palácio do Ilustrissimo e Excelentissimo Senhor Vice-Rei deste estado, e depois de brincarem recolher-se cada um para sua casa com toda quietação e sossego que se requer em semelhantes funções.

Capítulo décimo o quarto Todas as segundas feiras da quaresma jejuarão exceto os trabalhadores, e os velhos; ouvirão missa, rezando as nove saudações de São Gregório vulgarmente intituladas *Novena* das Almas, para os que souberem ler e os que a não souberem rezarão nove Padres Nossos, e Ave Marias, com outros tantos Gloria Patris, tudo aplicadas pelas almas do purgatório.

Capítulo décimo o quinto Haverá nesta congregação quatro livros a saber: um livro para se fazer o assento dos congregados, um dito para as certidões das missas, um dito para receita e despesa, e um dito para os estatutos que é obrigação que se impõem ao secretário da congregação de os ter bem claro e limpo com toda a clareza e chaneza que se requer.

[13] In the manuscript, *tê.*

Christ for the souls of their deceased kinsman. On the other hand, a freed person who has a good reason for not accompanying the burial will pray the rosary of Christ's sacred death and passion for the soul of the deceased.

Chapter Twelve When it is discovered that members of this congregation have engaged in bad behavior or been rebellious—either harming themselves, a third party, or others in the congregation—they will be called before a group that includes the *regent* and the other important men of the congregation. If they have been honestly warned three times and there have been no signs of improvement or obedience, they will be officially expelled. The expulsion will be entered in the book by the secretary and signed by the *regent* and the most important men and authorized by the entire congregation. This rule also holds true for the women, some of whom are proud, fond of intrigue, and disturbers of peace and quiet.

Chapter Thirteen Because we have seen from experience that a festive royal court in the black brotherhoods is very useful, as much to lift the spirits of the blacks as to bring together again those from afar, we will have [a royal court] in our congregation. . . . We desire that on the day of Our Lady of the Rosary there be a festive royal court composed from this *Maki nation* that will accompany the King of Our Lady of the Rosary if he is from the *Mina Coast,* and if not [from that coast] the *Maki* court will not accompany him, and will only be permitted to go to the palace of the most illustrious Senhor viceroy.[14] After these festivities, everyone will go back to their homes with complete quiet and calm, which is required at these functions.

Chapter Fourteen All of us, except for the workers and the elderly, will fast every Monday during Lent. We will hear a mass, and those who can read will say the nine praises to Saint Gregory, which are commonly called the *Novena* for the Souls, and those who do not know how to read will pray nine Our Fathers and Ave Marias with the Gloria, all of them dedicated to the souls in purgatory.

Chapter Fifteen This congregation will have four books. One book will be to list the membership of the group, one for certifications of the masses, one for accounts, and one for statutes, and it is the secretary's obligation to keep them clean and clear, with all of the clarity and simplicity that is required.

[14] Throughout Brazil, the biggest confraternity feast day celebration of the blacks was that of Our Lady of the Rosary. The rosary confraternities had a king and queen, often designated the King and Queen of *Congo* (although they often came from different African regions). The feast day celebration would include a long procession, often accompanied by different groups of "ambassadors" playing instruments and singing. The king would come accompanied by his court, or in Portuguese, his *estado.* In Rio, according to this testimony, it appears that they would end up at the house of the viceroy, where, if the king were not from the *Mina Coast,* the *Maki* would meet them.

Capítulo décimo o sexto Toda a pessoa que estiverem assentado nesta congregação hão de serem humildes porque a humildade é uma das virtudes que realça muito na vista de Deus, e a que o mesmo Senhor exercitou estando neste mundo e emcomendou aos seus sagrados apóstolos como se vê dos muitos lugares dos livros. . . .

Feitos estes estatutos em o Rio de Janeiro aos 31 de Janeiro de 1786, e eu Gonçalo Cordeiro, Secretário que o assinei.

Gonçalo Cordeiro
O *Regente* Francisco Alves de Souza . . .

[A viúva ganha a disputa contra a facção de Souza e Cordeiro]

CORDEIRO: Havia dois anos que *VM* governava.

SOUZA: Assim foi, mais a viúva do dito falecido pelo que vejo não quer entregar nada que pertence a congregação. . . .

SILVA: Venho muito aflito. . . .

CORDEIRO: O que tem e o que lhe sucedeu?

SILVA: Venho dar parte ao Senhor *Regente* que a demanda que traziamos com a viúva do Capitão Monte saiu a favor dela para não entregar o cofre, e os trastes, que pertence ao nosso *adjunto* ou congregação, que estou sem sangue por ver a falsidade que usou conosco, sabendo muito bem que custou nosso dinheiro. . . .

SOUZA: Pois, como saiu esta sentença?

CORDEIRO: A sua maior cláusula é que ficará sem efeito o *termo* que nós fizemos e que ela, dita viúva, fosse caixa ou guarda daquele depósito, e não lhe dá mais poderes para coisa alguma.

SILVA: Apelou-se para a *Relação* e veremos.

CORDEIRO: Em que *termos* está [a] apelação Senhor Luiz Rodrigues Silva?

SILVA: Foi comfirmada a sentença.

CORDEIRO: Pois a sentença não lhe dá mais poder, que ser uma mera tesoureira, para guardar o dinheiro que lhe derem e não para dizer que é Imperatriz da Costa da *Mina* como *VMs* bem estão ouvindo, e juntamente querer a força que vamos todos a lhe contribuir, com a nossa esmola; prohibindo-nos que não vamos aqui e nem aí ou lá sem sua ordem e determinação, pondo-nos em tão grande aperto, tanto assim que chegou a mandar tirar a cópia da sentença e com ela fez um requerimento ao Ilustríssimo e Excelentíssimo Senhor Vice-Rei dizendo que não queriam cumprir com acórdão do Supremo Tribunal da *Relação,* e que o nosso *regente* impedia a que fôssemos a sua casa para lhe darmos o dinheiro para ela meter no cofre, e que era cabeça de motim, e que todos os da congregação a queriam por *regenta.* Foi servido sua Excelência de mandar chamar ao rei de Nossa Senhora do Rosário, e ao nosso *regente;* o que lá passou ele como está presente o contará melhor.

SOUZA: Admirado estou da grande imprudência desta viúva com a sentença que alcançou contra os seus irmãos, pois não deverá assim obrar, se bem que a mim, me

Chapter Sixteen Everyone who is a member of this congregation must be humble, because humility is one of the virtues that elevates [us] in the eyes of God, and one that our Lord practiced while in this world and commended to his sacred apostles, as you see in various places in the books. . . .

These statutes were written in Rio de Janeiro on January 31, 1786, and I, Gonçalo Cordeiro, Secretary, sign them.

Gonçalo Cordeiro
The *Regent* Francisco Alves de Souza . . .

[The Widow Wins the Case against Souza and Cordeiro's Faction]

Cordeiro: Two years have passed that you have governed us.

Souza: Yes, they have. But the widow of the deceased, as far as I can see, has not returned anything that belongs to the congregation. . . .

[Luiz Rodrigues] Silva: I am very upset. . . .

Cordeiro: What is the matter and what happened to you?

Silva: I have come to give information to the *regent* that the lawsuit that we brought against the widow of Captain Monte came out in her favor. She does not have to return the safe or the other things that belong to our congregation, and I am appalled to see the hypocrisy that she practiced with us, knowing full well that it cost our money. . . .

Souza: How did the sentence come out?

Cordeiro: The most important clause is that the entry we made [in our books] is without effect, and that she, the widow, will be treasurer or keeper of the safe, and you have no more powers at all.

Silva: I appealed to the high court; so we shall see.

Cordeiro: What happened at the high court, Senhor Luiz Rodrigues Silva?

Silva: The sentence was confirmed.

Cordeiro: The sentence does not give her any more power than to be a worthy treasurer, to guard the money that they gave her, and not to say that she is the empress of the *Mina Coast,* as you have been hearing. Nevertheless, she wanted to demand that we all contribute our alms, prohibiting us from going here and there[15] without her consent, which put us in a great bind. In fact, she ordered a copy of the sentence and with it made a formal petition to the illustrious and excellent viceroy, saying that they [we] did not want to fulfill the sentence of the high court and that our *regent* impeded us from going to her house to give her the money to put in the safe. Worse, she claimed that he was the head of an uprising and that the entire congregation wanted her to be *regent.* The petition was sent, and His Highness [the viceroy] sent for the King of Our Lady of the Rosary and our *regent.* He can recount better what happened there because he is here.

Souza: I am astonished by the great imprudence of this widow and the sentence that she won against her brothers, as she should not act thus. As for me, she has done

[15] Probably the text means "going here and there" to collect alms.

tem feito todo o mal que pode, e tem inventado o seu odioso rancor porque me tem mandado noteficar varias vezes, sem eu lhe dar a mínima causa, tanto assim que não queria que fosse a Igreja de Nossa Senhora do Rosário, e à de Santa Efigênia, vestido e com estado. Vejam *VMs* se isto é de pessoa que tem juizo; ao mesmo tempo que esta Senhora sabe muito bem, a criação [e] educação que tive, e o conceito que o defunto seu marido fazia de mim, pois não obrava nada sem o meu conselho e beneplácito. E chegou tanta a sua maldade que procurando todos os modos de perder-me fez ajuntar a sentença da demanda que obteve contra os seus irmãos como acima se diz, fazem do um sinistro requerimento ao Ilustríssimo e Excelentíssimo Senhor Vice Rei, queixando-se que não queriam cumprir o acórdão do Supremo Tribunal da *Relação* acuzando-me que [ilegible] causa que não faziam, dando a entender que era cabeça de motim e que todos os da congregação estavam da sua parte e que eu impedia para não irem lá. Vendo Sua Excelência estas queixas foi servido mandar chamar ao Rei de Nossa Senhora e juntamente a mim para irmos à sala, e depois de estarmos lá me mandou o dito Senhor dizer que se queria sair, que fosse a casa da viúva. Digo se queria sair a função do Rosário que havia ir ter com a viúva, e se saísse sem lá ir havia de ser preso e bem castigado. E essa foi a ordem que recebi da sala, o que foi cumprido sem a menor discrepância e vejam *VMs* que falsidade, e vejam que ódio com que intentou o perder-me, se Sua Excelência por sua inata bondade e clemência me não valesse, dignando-se em despachar o requerimento que—cumpram o acórdão—talvez imaginando a minha pouquidade e inocência como todos bem sabem talvez me mandaria castigar. . . .

CORDEIRO: . . . Porquanto *VM* não é culpado em nada, e nem se lhe pode pôr culpa, bem sabendo é que obrigamos por justiça para ser *regente* da nossa congregação e votando todos em *VM* como se vê do Livro do *Termo,* a que encruzado é argüir-lhe culpas. Esta congregação é uma *devoção* feita por vontade de todos, que não foi obrigatório porque nunca teve estatutos. E para ela ser *regenta* é preciso que seja por vontade de todos e não de quatro somente, porque bem vemos nas Estórias Sagradas, e humanas, e ainda gentílicas que quem faz o rei é a vontade do povo. E assim tenho dito o que [h]ei de dizer a respeito desta congregação ou *adjunto* porque tempo virá em que se conheça melhor a sua mâ conducta e intenção orgulhosa com que pretende destruir esta tão boa *devoção* que seu marido tanto encomendou na pessoa de *VM.*

all of the harm that she can. She has fabricated lies [with] her hateful rancor. She sent me a summons various times without me having given her the least cause, to the extent that she did not want me to go to the church of Our Lady of the Rosary, nor to that of Saint Iphigenia, dressed and with my retinue. Tell me, is this a person who has reason? At the same time this lady knew well the upbringing and education that I have and the respect with which her deceased husband regarded me—and that he did nothing without my counsel and blessing. But her maliciousness reached such a point that she sought any way possible to make me lose. She put together a lawsuit against her brothers and, as I said above, made the sinister formal petition to the Illustrious and Most Excellent Viceroy, complaining that I did not want to fulfill the sentence of the high court, accusing me [illegible] that I did not want to understand and that I was the head of an uprising, and that everyone in the congregation was on her side, and that I impeded them from going there. Seeing these complaints, His Excellency thought it well to call the King of Our Lady[16] and me to come to a meeting. After we arrived that same gentleman ordered me to say that if I wanted to go [to the rosary celebration] that I would have to go to the widow's house, meaning that in order to participate in the feast day celebration of the rosary I would have to go talk with the widow. If I went without talking to the widow, I would be arrested and punished. This is the order that I received in the meeting, which I fulfilled without the least discrepancy. You all can see the falseness and the hatred with which she intended to beat me, [and] if not for the pure kindness and mercy of His Excellency, which I do not deserve, condescending to dispatch the formal petition—that they fulfill the sentence—perhaps imagining my insignificance and innocence, which everyone recognizes, perhaps would have had me punished. . . .

CORDEIRO: . . . Considering that you are not guilty of anything, nor can anyone place guilt on you, knowing full well that you are obligated by law to be *regent* of our congregation, and we all voted for you as you can see in our official record, it is [ridiculous] to accuse you of crimes. This congregation is a devotion made by the will of all, not an obligation, because there were never statutes. For her to be *regent* it would have to be by the will of all and not by only four, because as we all see in the sacred and human stories, and even the heathen ones, whoever is king, is king by the will of the people. And so I have said what needs to be said in regard to this congregation, because the time will come when there is wider recognition of her bad conduct and proud intent and how she intends to destroy this beautiful devotion that her husband willed to you.

[16] The king of the confraternity of Our Lady of the Rosary.

Part IV
Claiming and Defending Rights

As Afro-Latinos gained familiarity with both the European legal system and lettered culture, they engaged with them to claim and defend their rights. In the four chapters of Part IV, Afro-Latino speakers express a sense that their actions and attitudes are morally upstanding according to the standards of European law and Catholic doctrine and that it is their mostly European abusers who have violated these norms. Before the Portuguese Inquisition in Lisbon, Pernambuco slave Luiz da Costa expresses repugnance at his abusive master's forced act of sodomy, and clearly frames the event as one of violent domination (Chapter 15).

In Lima, both María del Carmen Ollague and Manuela *Zamba* position themselves as faithful wives who have fulfilled their duties within the Church-sanctioned institution of marriage (Chapter 16). In Ollague's case, it is her husband who has violated the sanctity of marriage by abusing her and treating her as a slave, whereas Manuela *Zamba* accuses her owner of having imposed divorce on her by selling her husband to an owner who lives forty leagues away, thus impeding her proper marital life. Both women use the ecclesiastical court system to defend their vision and exercise of proper family life.

The case of Javier, *esclavo,* against his master in San Juan de la Frontera (Chapter 17) also revolves around ownership, and demonstrates how slaves engaged the legal system to negotiate improvements in their living situation by obtaining permission to seek their sale to a new owner. In Javier's case, his master frustrates this attempt; Javier flees, and upon returning receives a punishment so cruel that it exceeds the stipulations of the legal system. Javier is able to bring the weight of the law to his side for protection.

The final case shows a quite different type of petition (Chapter 18), as the Puerto Rican father and son Manuel and Antonio Pérez request proper rewards for their military service to the Crown in Spain; their argument stands on a concept of self-worth and honor as well as on legal documentation. In all five cases, individuals of African descent claim a place of belonging and social standing as subjects of the Iberian empires and, as such, demand protection and recognition of their rights.

15

Confessing Sodomy, Accusing a Master: The Lisbon Trial of Pernambuco's Luiz da Costa, 1743[1]

Richard A. Gordon

Luiz da Costa was barely twenty years old when he was transported from Brazil to Portugal in 1743 to stand trial for sodomy before the Tribunal of the Portuguese Inquisition in Lisbon. Yet, this was not Luiz's first forced transatlantic migration. He arrived in the northeastern Brazilian region of Pernambuco by way of the *Middle Passage,* having been taken captive years earlier. His native land was the Costa da *Mina* in the region of present-day Ghana, Togo, and Benin. When Luiz da Costa was brought from Africa to Brazil, he encountered in Pernambuco an old, relatively wealthy, and densely populated colonial territory.

During much of the colonial period, Pernambuco encompassed not only the present-day state of Pernambuco but also what are now the Rio Grande do Norte, Ceará, Paraíba, and Alagoas. It was one of the original *capitanias,* or captaincies, into which the Portuguese King Dom João III had divided Portugal's South American claim in 1534. João III acted in order to establish an official presence in Brazil and thereby forestall French poaching of Brazil's first export product, the coveted *pau-brasil,* a wood from which red dye was extracted for use in the European textile industries. By the time Luiz arrived in Brazil in the 1720s, Pernambuco was no longer a captaincy. In 1654, it had been incorporated by the Portuguese Crown into the so-called *Estado do Brasil.*

Since its founding nearly two hundred years earlier, the region had witnessed substantial economic and political changes starting in 1534 when the captaincy of Pernambuco was under the leadership of Duarte Coelho and from 1630 until 1654 when Pernambuco was occupied by the Dutch. When the Dutch took possession of the territory in 1630, the capital was moved from Olinda to Recife, a few miles away. The sugar industry that was introduced in the region by Duarte Coelho continued to expand during the Dutch occupation.

Just a few years after gaining their emancipation from Spain at the end of sixty years under their neighbor's control, the Portuguese regained Pernambuco from the Dutch in 1654 and began to rebuild Portugal's colonial economy there. Pernambuco's population grew steadily. In 1693, there were an estimated 62,415 people under Portuguese control in the region (this figure excluded nonsubjugated indigenous inhabitants). This number grew to 67,280 by 1700 and escalated to 363,238 by 1777 (Wadsworth, 8). Throughout the colonial era, sugar dominated the physical, social, and economic landscape of this Brazilian state and provoked an enormous influx of African slaves. Luiz da Costa thus lived in a Pernambuco of intense demographic and cultural change.

[1] See Maps 1, 4, and 6.

Luiz da Costa was probably not one of the many slaves who worked in a sugar mill. We can deduce from his Inquisition confession that he was more likely a domestic slave and that he may have lived in the interior of Pernambuco. Even though the population in Pernambuco clustered principally in the *zona da mata,* or costal region, there were also settlements inland within the arid *sertão* (hinterlands) and the transitional morphological region that divides the hinterlands from the coast, called the *agreste.*

Luiz's *processo* (trial proceedings) lists Vila da Boa Vista as his place of residence. It is not clear where exactly that was; there is no surviving population center with that name and the comprehensive four-volume *Diccionario chorographico, historico e estatistico de Pernambuco* does not list any town with that name at the time of the 1743 trial. This might refer to the Recife neighborhood called Boa Vista, which dates back to the seventeenth century (Galvão, 71–97), although the neighborhood was never designated as a *vila* (a small town). In support of this conjecture is the fact that more than 90 percent of denunciations in Pernambuco to the Inquisition came from the coastal regions (Wadsworth, 47). However, it is more likely that he lived in the interior of the captaincy. Consistent with this possibility, Luiz da Costa mentions in his confession that he went hunting with his master, Manoel Alves Cabral, in the *sertão* near what he calls Aldeia de Bode, which likewise does not appear in the *Diccionário* but would seem to be located in a region quite distant from Recife.

It was during the hunting trip on which Luiz accompanied his master that the offense for which he stood trial took place. In his testimony at trial, Luiz accused Manoel Alves Cabral of having sodomized him under threat of death. A priest who was also in the hunting party, Manoel de Lima, did not witness the act but found Luiz fleeing and heard his story. Lima, who brought the case to the attention of the Inquisition, possibly with the cooperation of Luiz da Costa, might have seen an investigation and trial as preferable to the sexual advances that continued after that first incident, especially given the likelihood that he would be transported to Lisbon to stand trial.

Although some cases that fell under the jurisdiction of the Inquisition were adjudicated in Brazil by bishops, many trials took place in the Tribunal of Lisbon, which retained jurisdiction over Brazil, the Atlantic islands, and Africa (see Wadsworth, especially chapters 1–3). In contrast with the Spanish Inquisition, which established tribunals in Mexico City (1571), Lima (1570), and Cartagena (1610; Wadsworth, 24), Brazil never had its own Inquisition tribunal (a distinction between Spanish America and Brazil that parallels the lack of universities and printing presses in Brazil and their long-standing presence in the Spanish-American colonies).

Rather, the Portuguese Inquisition sent representatives to Brazil several times to evaluate cases in the early years while Portugal was under Spanish control (for example, 1591–1595 to Bahia and Pernambuco; 1618–1620 to Bahia). Subsequently, in particular after the turn of the eighteenth century, the Inquisition developed a substantial network of lay and ecclesiastical representatives in Brazil.

In Pernambuco during Lent, the behaviors prohibited by the Inquisition were publicized, and residents were required to denounce transgressions and confess their own, information that would presumably be communicated to the Portuguese Inquisition. It was likely that Luiz da Costa's case was processed initially through these channels

in Brazil and that the initiator of the case was a priest who Luiz states witnessed some of the events that he refers to in his confession. In some cases, the Lisbon tribunal sent back word that certain accused Brazilians were to be shipped to Portugal for trial, an eventuality that befell Luiz da Costa.

Notwithstanding the lack of Inquisition tribunals in Brazil during the period just preceding Luiz's trial (1709–1737), Brazilians represented more than 50 percent of those punished in Lisbon in *autos-da-fé* (Wadsworth, 47). This was the case, although the overall prosecutions of the Portuguese Inquisition had been declining. The Portuguese Inquisition, which lasted almost three centuries, from 1536 to 1821, carried out 22,481 investigations (with 863 executions) in the ninety years from 1584 to 1674; yet there were only 12,142 investigations (with 446 executions) in the same span from 1675 to 1767 (page 45).

The most common accusations in Pernambuco were, in order of frequency, Judaism, bigamy, witchcraft—a common accusation against African slaves, along with blasphemy—and heretical propositions (Wadsworth, 47). Although offenses such as bigamy and sodomy were not technically considered heresy, they were prosecuted by the Inquisition, as such acts were seen to compromise the sacrament of marriage (Vainfas, "Inquisição," 270–71) and thus constituted, by extension, *erros de fé* (crimes against faith). Formal heresy was defined as a baptized Christian voluntarily refusing to believe in some tenet of the Catholic Church and manifesting that conviction either mentally or externally (Mott, "Sodomia," 254).

Sodomy, which became part of the Spanish Inquisition's purview in 1509 (Vainfas, "Inquisição," 269) and the Portuguese Inquisition's in 1553 (Mott, "Sodomia," 254), accounted for around four hundred of the total full Inquisition trials (of around five thousand denunciations). Thirty of these defendants were burned in *autos-da-fé* by the river Tejo in Lisbon, after being *relaxados,* meaning they were turned over for execution to the civil authorities, who alone were allowed to carry out executions (Higgs, 113; for a description of the severe civil penalties for sodomy in Spain and Portugal beginning in 1603, see Lara, *Ordenações,* 91).

The Portuguese Inquisition prosecuted cases of *sodomia perfeita* or *consumada*—sodomy with phallic anal penetration as well as ejaculation—but not what was referred to as *molície*—all other homoerotic acts (see Vainfas, "Inquisição," 275; and Mott, "Sodomia," 255). Luiz da Costa refers to both *sodomia consumada* and *molície* in his confession. Luiz Mott ("Sodomia," 253) argues that after *New Christians,* sodomites were the social group most persecuted by the Portuguese Inquisition. It was not uncommon in colonial Brazil for Inquisition cases of sodomy to derive, as in Luiz da Costa's case, from abuses of disparate power relations, specifically that of slavery (Vainfas, "Inquisição," 277).[2]

Roughly one year passed between the attack on Luiz da Costa and his trial, but, once he reached the Inquisition jail in Lisbon, his prosecution was expeditious. This

[2] For more information about sodomy as part of rape, as in Luiz da Costa's case, as well as extensive research on voluntary homoeroticism in Brazil and Portugal prosecuted by the Inquisition, see Higgs, Mott, Pieroni, and Vainfas.

was not always the case; some trials lasted for months and even years. He was taken into custody in Lisbon on July 23, 1743, tried on July 30, and sentenced on August 16. And his punishment, a reprimand and injunction to not commit such acts again, was extremely light. As his trial proceedings make clear, the tribunal took into consideration the extenuating circumstances of this case.

Inquisitors at the time sought testimony regarding whether or not sodomy was voluntary or forced, the age of the defendants, and the specific circumstances of the acts (Vainfas, "Inquisição," 275). Although a modern reader may abhor the notion that a rape victim would be prosecuted for the sexual act of the rape—or indeed for any offense to a moral *paradigm* (consider, however, that U.S. laws criminalizing sodomy remained in effect until 2003)—Luiz da Costa's treatment was relatively lenient; the 1603 secular law called for the burning of any sodomite under any circumstances. Even notwithstanding the particular circumstance of Luiz's case,[3] its outcome coincided with a general trend toward less severe punishments in cases of sodomy compared to those of the seventeenth century (see, for example, Higgs, 113).

Luiz da Costa's brief trials consisted of several key parts: the assignment of a guardian to him, as he was under the age of twenty-five; his confession; the tribunal's certification of the evidence; the reprimand of the defendant; and the swearing of the defendant to secrecy. All of these procedures were presided over by the inquisitor Manoel Varejão Távora and recorded by a scribe, Manoel Afonso Rebelo. Both the rigid structure of the trial and the relaying of all words and actions by the scribe influenced how Luiz was able to tell his story and how it ultimately was expressed in the document.

There was very little opportunity for the prisoner to speak. For the most part, the trial proceedings show him to be largely a mute variable in a well-established pattern. The scribe narrates how Luiz da Costa was brought before the court a week after arriving in Lisbon and mechanically records the several obligatory components of the trial. In almost every aspect of the trial, he speaks no more than a few words. The one notable exception is the confession. The inquisitorial conventions mediate the manifestation of Luiz's point of view almost exclusively through this part of the trial.

Within the parameters of this section, the prisoner is allowed to tell his story with some degree of rhetorical autonomy. However, he still has to recount the events that led him to this trial in the form of a confession, rather than, say, in the form of a defense. In other words, even within this section of the trial he does not have free reign on what he says or how he says it. The communication of Luiz da Costa's version of the story is further delimited by the fact that it comes to us as indirect discourse paraphrased in the third person by the scribe. The scribe presumably edited not only the form of the prisoner's discourse but also some of the content, perhaps based on what he deemed most relevant or acceptable for recording.

Nonetheless, in his confession, we can perceive something of Luiz da Costa's voice despite the filter of the scribe's own subjectivity and his use of formulaic language. Therein lies the importance of this document. Luiz's testimony allows us to glimpse

[3] Ronaldo Vainfas points out that that the most severely punished sodomites were the ones who caused public scandal ("Inquisição," 275).

something of the story and perspective of a young African slave living in eighteenth-century Brazil. In the confession section, Luiz recalls at some length the events for which he is on trial, prodded initially by the admonition to bring to mind every detail. How exactly he tells his story, the way that he maneuvers rhetorically within the formal confines of the confession, can give us some insight into his point of view.

The order in which Luiz recounts events, for example, and his decisions to include certain details and exclude others reveal something of his individual perspective. At the end of the trial, his testimony, as recorded by the scribe Rebelo, is read to him, and he is made to swear that the version he hears (and that we read in the document below) is accurate and that he would change nothing. By approving the trial proceedings, Luiz would seem to recognize at least some of his own voice in the mediated narration of the scribe. By looking carefully at those moments in which echoes of Luiz da Costa's words emerge from within the delimiting conventions of the trial proceeding, we can gain rare access into this enslaved man's life from his own perspective.

Processo de Luiz da Costa, homem preto, solteiro escravo de Manoel Alves Cabral, natural da Costa da *Mina*, e morador na Vila da Boa Vista, Bispado de Pernambuco[1]

Inquisição de Lisboa
Nº 6, *processo* 45
Tem custódia em 23 de julho de 1743
Termo de *Curador*

Aos 30 dias do mês de julho de 1743 anos em Lisboa nos *Estaos e Casa* terceira das audiências da Santa Inquisição estando aí na [audiência da] manhã o Senhor Inquisidor Manoel Varejão Távora mandou vir perante si o Luiz da Costa, réu preso contendo nestes *autos* e sendo presente. Por dizer [Luiz da Costa] que era menor de vinte e cinco anos foi mandado vir à Mesa o *licenciado* Felipe Néri, capelão dos Cárceres da Penitência, que sendo também presente lhe foi dito, que . . . [por Luiz da Costa] ser de menor idade, o faziam seu *curador* para que lhe prestasse sua autoridade a fim de poder estar em juízo e nele fazer atos válidos. E pelo sobredito *licenciado* foi dito que aceitava ser *curador* [de Luiz], e lhe prestaria sua autoridade para tudo o que fosse necessário a bem de poder estar em juízo. E assim prometeu cumprir sob cargo do juramento dos Santos Evangelhos, que lhe foi dado. . . .

Manoel Afonso Rebelo o escrevi.

Manoel Varejão Távora

Confissão

Aos 30 dias do mês de julho de 1743 anos em Lisboa nos *Estaos e Casa* terceira das audiências da Santa Inquisição estando aí na [audiência da] manhã o Senhor Inquisidor Manoel Varejão Távora mandou vir perante si a um homem que nos vinte e três dias do presente mês e ano veio preso em custódia para os cárceres desta Inquisição . . . [e que pedira] audiência. E sendo presente [e] por . . . [pedir] para confessar suas culpas, lhe foi dado o juramento dos Santos Evangelhos, em que pôs a mão, sob cargo do que lhe foi mandado dizer verdade e ter segredo, o que tudo prometeu cumprir.

E disse chamar-se Luiz da Costa, homem preto, escravo de Manoel Alves Cabral, não sabem quem foram seus pais, natural da Costa da *Mina,* e morador na Vila da Boa Vista, Bispado de Pernambuco, de vinte anos de idade, pouco mais ou menos.

[1] Arquivo Nacional da Torre do Tombo, Lisbon, Processos da Inquisição, Inquisição de Lisboa no. 6, processo 45, microfilm call number M.F. 2592.

Trial of Luiz da Costa, Black Male, Single, Slave of Manoel Alves Cabral, Native of Costa da *Mina*, Resident of Vila da Boa Vista, Diocese of Pernambuco

Inquisition of Lisbon
N° 6, trial 45
In custody on July 23, 1743
Register of Guardianship

On the thirtieth day of July 1743, in Lisbon in the Third Office of Hearings [*Estaos e Casa terceira das audiências*][1] of the Holy Inquisition, the inquisitor Manoel Varejão Távora, being present in the morning session, commanded that Luiz da Costa, imprisoned defendant in these proceedings and also present, appear before him. Because Luiz da Costa said that he was under twenty-five years of age, the *licenciate* Felipe Néri, chaplain of the Penitence Prison and also present, was commanded to appear before the board. He was told that because Luiz da Costa[2] was a minor,[3] they designated him as his guardian so that he might lend Luiz his authority and make is possible for the young man to stand trial, and so that in the trial his actions might be legally valid. And the *licenciate* declared that he accepted the guardianship and that he would lend Luiz his authority in all ways necessary so that he could stand trial. And he swore to perform these duties under the authority of an oath on the Holy Gospels, which he was administered.

I, Manoel Afonso Rebelo, wrote it.

Manoel Varejão Távora

Confession

On the thirtieth day of July 1743, in Lisbon in the Third Office of Hearings of the Holy Inquisition, the inquisitor Manoel Varejão Távora, being there in the morning session, commanded that a man come before him who on the twenty-third day of the current month and year was received into the custody of the prison of this Inquisition, . . . and who had requested a hearing. And being present . . . and having asked to confess his misdeeds, he was administered the oath of the Holy Gospels, on which he placed his hand, and under the authority of which he was commanded to tell the truth and to maintain secrecy, all of which he swore to fulfill.

And he said that he was called Luiz da Costa, black male, slave of Manoel Alves Cabral; no one knows who his parents were; native of Costa da *Mina* and resident of Vila da Boa Vista, Diocese of Pernambuco; more or less twenty years of age.

[1] The name designating the buildings in which the Lisbon Inquisition carried out its court sessions and where prisoners were kept.

[2] To facilitate the reading, from here on I use the name "Luiz da Costa" or "Luiz" where the document repeats designations like "prisoner" or "confessant."

[3] People who were under twenty-five years old.

E logo foi admoestado, que pois tomava tão bom conselho, como o de querer confessar suas culpas, lhe convêm muito trazê-las todas à memória para delas fazer uma inteira e verdadeira confissão, não impondo porém a si, nem a outrem, testemunho falso, porque só o dizer a verdade é que lhe convém para descargo de sua consciência, salvação de sua alma, e bom despacho de sua causa.

. . . [Ao] que respondeu, que só a verdade havia de dizer. A qual era: Que haverá um ano pouco mais ou menos, achando-se . . . na Aldeia de Bode, *sertão* de Pernambuco, com [o] dito seu senhor Manoel Alves Cabral, saíram num dia a caça pelo mato. E estando ambos sós o provocou o dito seu senhor para ter com ele atos de sodomia, valendo-se para esse efeito de o ameaçar e intimidar com a espingarda que trazia dizendo-lhe [que o] havia de matar se não consentisse no que ele pretendia executar. E sem embargo da repugnância que ele consciente fez, obrigado do medo, consentiu na dita torpeza, tendo com . . . o dito seu senhor um ato de sodomia consumado, havendo seminação e penetração no seu vazo prepóstero, sendo . . . [Luiz] paciente,[2] e o dito seu senhor agente.[3] E que em outras muitas ocasiões, e em diversos lugares o provocara para a mesma torpeza, porém que nunca mais o chegara a praticar com ele, por . . . [lhe] repugnar, e não querer consentir nela. E somente para se ver livre do dito seu senhor lhe consentia [que] praticasse com ele alguns pecados de molície que executou em repetidas ocasiões. E declara mais, que na ocasião acima dita, em que foi à caça com o dito senhor ia também na sua companhia um padre chamado Manoel de Lima, o qual não presenciou o referido por andar caçando pelo mato dentro em distância que não pôde ver com individuação o dito fato, e somente reparou em . . . [Luiz] andar fugindo do dito seu senhor a roda de uma morada, por cuja causa lhe . . . [perguntou] depois o que aquilo era, e . . . [Luiz] lhe declarou na forma que acima fica dito.

Disse mais, que . . . [estando] em casa do dito seu senhor com outro preto chamado José, também escravo do mesmo, e dormindo ambos em uma cama, veio por repetidas vezes o dito seu senhor ter com eles de noite em ocasião em que estavam dormindo, e metendo-se no meio deles. [Luiz] percebera . . . clara e distintamente práticas com o dito preto José, atos de sodomia consumados, os quais o dito preto lhe declarou ao depois ser assim como ele entendia.

E que estas são as culpas que tem que confessar nesta mesa, as quais cometera . . . [por lhe] constranger e intimidar o dito senhor, na forma que acima tem declarado e deve haver cometido. Pede perdão e que com ele se use de misericórdia e mais não disse. . . .

Foi-lhe dito que tomou muito conselho em principiar a confessar nesta Mesa as suas culpas, as quais deve trazer todas à memória para delas fazer uma inteira e verdadeira confissão. [Os Senhores Inquisidores lhe] . . . advertem e recomendam muito [que] se aparte e fuja totalmente da companhia de todas aquelas pessoas que o podem

[2] The one who carries out the passive role in the sexual act, in this case the one who is penetrated.

[3] The one who carries out the active role in the sexual act, in this case the one who penetrates.

And then he was advised that, because he had decided to follow such good counsel as to desire to confess his misdeeds, it would very much behoove him to recall all of them so that he might form from them a whole and true confession, not imputing, however, to himself or to others false testimony, for only the telling of the truth is proper for clearing his conscience, saving his soul, and satisfactorily resolving his case. . . . To which he responded that he would tell only the truth, which was that more or less a year ago, while he was . . . in Aldeia de Bode, in the hinterlands of Pernambuco, with his master Manoel Alves Cabral, they went hunting in the woods. And when they were alone his master induced him to commit acts of sodomy, threatening and intimidating him with the musket that he had, saying that he would kill him if he did not consent to what he intended to effectuate. And in spite of the repugnance that he felt, obliged by fear he consented to the turpitude, realizing with . . . his master a consummated act of sodomy, there being ejaculation and penetration in his posterior orifice, . . . performing Luiz the passive role and his master the active. And on many other occasions, and in diverse places [his master] had attempted to induce him into the same turpitude, though he had never again managed to practice it with him, . . . due to Luiz's repugnance, and his disinclination to consent to it. And only to see himself free from his master's harassment did he consent to practice with him other sinful sexual acts,[4] which he made on repeated occasions. And he additionally declares that on the above-mentioned occasion in which he went hunting with his master there was also in the party a priest called Manoel de Lima, who did not witness the referred incident due to the fact that he was hunting deep in the woods, which prevented him from seeing for himself the said fact, and observed only . . . that Luiz was fleeing from his master around a dwelling, because of which he . . . later asked Luiz what that was all about, and . . . Luiz related to him the facts in the manner in which they are articulated above.

He also stated that . . . while in the house of his master with another black called José, also a slave of the same master, and while they were both sleeping in a bed, his master came repeatedly to be with them at night while they were sleeping, and got into the bed between them. Luiz clearly and distinctly perceived . . . deeds with said black José, acts of consummated sodomy, which said black later declared to him to have been exactly what he had comprehended.

And these are the misdeeds that he has to confess to this board, misdeeds that he had committed . . . because his master had coerced him and intimidated him in the way in which he has declared above and must have committed. He asks for forgiveness and that he be shown mercy and said no more.

He was told that he followed good counsel in initiating his confession of his misdeeds before this board, all of which he should recall so that he might form from them a whole and true confession. [The inquisitors] . . . caution him and strongly recommend that he distance himself and flee the company of anyone who might pervert

[4] *Pecados de molície,* a term that referred to all sexual acts besides anal coitus (e.g., masturbation, fellatio).

perverter e induzir, por qualquer modo, . . . [a] tornar a cometer semelhantes culpas, porque não emendando será castigado com todo o rigor de direito.

E por dizer que não tinha mais culpas que confessar, foi outra vez admoestado . . . e mandado ao seu cárcere, sendo-lhe primeiro lida esta sua confissão, que por ele ouvida e entendida em presença de seu *curador* disse que estava escrita na verdade e que nela se afirmava, ratificava, e a tornava a dizer de novo sendo necessário, e que nela não tinha que acrescentar, diminuir, mudar, ou emendar, . . . sob cargo do mesmo juramento dos Santos Evangelhos que outra vez lhe foi dado.

Ao que estiveram presentes por honestas e religiosas pessoas que tudo viram e ouviram, [e] prometeram dizer a verdade no que fosse perguntados sob cargo do juramento dos Santos Evangelhos os *licenciados* Francisco de Souza e Manoel da Silva Diniz e notários desta Inquisição, e assinaram com . . . [Luiz da Costa], seu *curador* e com o dito Senhor Inquisidor.

Manoel Afonso Rebelo o escrevi.

Manoel Varejão Távora
De Luiz [+] da Costa
Felipe Néri
Francisco de Souza
Manoel da Silva Diniz

E ido . . . [Luiz da Costa] para o seu cárcere foram perguntados aos ditos *licenciados* se lhes parecia que falava verdade, e merecia crédito, e por eles foi dito que lhes parecia falava [a] verdade, e merecia crédito, e tornavam [a] assinar com o dito Senhor Inquisidor.

Manoel Afonso Rebelo o escrevi.

Manoel Varejão Távora
Francisco de Souza
Manoel da Silva Diniz

Crédito

Manoel Afonso Rebelo notário do Santo Ofício desta Inquisição de Lisboa que escrevi a confissão retro do réu Luiz da Costa nela contendo, certifico [que] . . . o Senhor Inquisidor Manoel Varejão Távora [me disse que] lhe dava crédito ordinário [à confissão] e o mesmo lhe dou eu, notário, de que passei a presente de mandado do dito Senhor Inquisidor com quem assinei. Lisboa no St° Offº 30 de julho de 1743. Manoel Varejão Távora.

Manoel Afonso Rebelo
Estando este *processo* nestes *termos* de mandado dos Senhores Inquisidores, lhe fiz concluso.
Manoel Afonso Rebelo o escrevi.
[sinal público]

him and induce him in any way . . . to commit again similar misdeeds, because if he does not mend his ways he will be punished with full force of the law.

And because he said that he had no more misdeeds to confess, he was once again advised . . . and sent to his prison after he was read this, his confession, which he heard and understood in the presence of his guardian and said that it was written truly and that he affirmed it, ratified it, and that he would say the same thing over again if necessary, and that he had nothing to add, remove, change, or correct, . . . under the authority of the same oath on the Holy Gospels, which he was again administered.

This was witnessed by the honest and religious people there present who saw and heard everything and swore to respond truly to anything they were asked under the authority of an oath on the Holy Gospels: the *licenciates* Francisco de Souza and Manoel da Silva Diniz, notaries of this Inquisition, who signed with . . . [Luiz da Costa], his guardian, and the inquisitor.

I, Manoel Afonso Rebelo, wrote it.

Manoel Varejão Távora
Of Luiz [+] da Costa[5]
Felipe Néri
Francisco de Souza
Manoel da Silva Diniz

And [Luiz da Costa] having left . . . for his cell, the above said *licenciates* were asked if it seemed to them that he spoke the truth and if his testimony deserved certification, and they said that it seemed to them that he spoke the truth and that his testimony deserved certification, and they once again signed with the inquisitor.

I, Manoel Afonso Rebelo, wrote it.

Manoel Varejão Távora
Francisco de Souza
Manoel da Silva Diniz

Certification of the Evidence

I, Manoel Afonso Rebelo, notary of the Holy Office of the Inquisition of Lisbon, who wrote the preceding confession of defendant Luiz da Costa, certify [that] . . . the inquisitor Manoel Varejão Távora [told me that] he certified [the confession], which I, the notary, also certify, and which I recorded by order of the inquisitor, and which I with him signed. Lisbon in the Holy Office on the thirtieth day of July 1743. Manoel Varejão Távora.

Manoel Afonso Rebelo
Being this trial recorded in these registers by order of the inquisitors, I concluded it.
I, Manoel Afonso Rebelo, wrote it.
[official mark]

[5] The cross, Luiz da Costa's signature, is slightly taller than it is wide and appears in the indicated space between his first and last names as written by the scribe.

Foi *visto* na Mesa do Santo Ofício desta Inquisição de Lisboa o anuário de testemunhas, que a ela remeteu o [Bispado] Ordinário de Pernambuco, ao confitente Luiz da Costa, preto, escravo, solteiro, natural da Costa da *Mina,* e morador na Vila da Boa Vista, Bispado de Pernambuco; e a confissão que o mesmo fez nesta Mesa. E pareceu a todos os votos que vistas as circunstâncias, . . . e sua confissão, [que] fosse o réu admoestado e repreendido nesta Mesa, . . . [e que] pague as culpas. Lisboa em Mesa 13 de agosto de 1743.

Francisco Machado	Silvio Lobo
Simão José	M. Távora
Manoel Varejão	Diogo Lopes [sinal público]
Tiago [sinal público]	Joachim Jansen Moller [sinal público]

Termo de Repreensão

Aos 16 dias do mês de agosto de 1743 anos em Lisboa nos *Estaos e Casa* do despacho da Santa Inquisição estando aí na audiência [da] manhã os Senhores Inquisidores mandaram vir perante si dos cárceres da custódia ao réu Luiz da Costa contendo nestes *autos.* E sendo presente, e pelos ditos senhores asperamente repreendido, lhe foi dito que não torne a cometer, nem consentir nas culpas . . . [pelas quais] veio preso para os cárceres desta Inquisição, nem em outras semelhantes sob pena de ser gravemente castigado, e que por hora se pode ir para onde bem lhe estiver, o que tudo . . . [Luiz da Costa] prometeu cumprir na forma que se lhe ordenava sob cargo do juramento dos Santos Evangelhos que lhe foi dado, de que fiz este *termo* de mandado dos ditos senhores com quem assinou e com seu *curador,* em presença do qual lhe foi lido, e por ele ouvido e entendido. Manoel Afonso Rebelo o escrevi.

Francisco Machado
Simão José
Manoel Varejão Távora
Tiago [sinal público]
Silvio Lobo
D[e] Luiz [+] da Costa
Felipe Néri

Termo de Segredo

Aos 16 dias do mês de agosto de 1743 anos em Lisboa nos *Estaos e Casa* do despacho da Santa Inquisição, estando aí em audiência de manhã os Senhores Inquisidores, mandaram vir perante si dos cárceres da custódia . . . Luiz da Costa r[eu] preso contendo neste *processo.* E sendo presente lhe foi dado juramento dos Santos Evangelhos, em que pôs a mão, e sob cargo dele lhe foi mandado, que tenha muito segredo em tudo o que viu e ouviu nestes cárceres, e com ele se passou acerca de seu *processo,* e nem por palavra, nem escrito o descubra, nem por outra qualquer via que seja, sob pena de ser gravemente castigado, o que tudo ele prometeu cumprir e sob cargo do dito juramento,

The Board of the Holy Office of this Inquisition of Lisbon saw the directory of testimony, sent to it by the Diocese of Pernambuco, regarding the confessor Luiz da Costa, black, slave, single, native of Costa da *Mina,* resident of Vila da Boa Vista, Diocese of Pernambuco; and the confession that said man made to this board. And it seemed to all of the members of the board that taking into consideration the circumstances . . . and the confession, Luiz da Costa should be advised and reprimanded by this board and that he should atone for his misdeeds. Lisbon, meeting of the board, on the thirteenth day of August 1743.

Francisco Machado   Silvio Lobo
Simão José   M. Távora
Manoel Varejão   Diogo Lopes [official mark]
Tiago [official mark]   Joachim Jansen Moller [official mark]

Register of Reprimand

On the sixteenth day of the month of August 1743, in Lisbon in the Office of Sentencing of the Holy Inquisition, being there in the morning session, the inquisitors commanded that Luiz da Costa, imprisoned defendant in these proceedings, be brought from the custody prison and be made to appear before them. And being present and severely reprimanded by said inquisitors, he was told that he not commit again nor consent to these misdeeds . . . [for which] he was received into the custody of the prison of this Inquisition, nor other similar misdeeds under pain of being gravely punished, and that for now he can go wherever he liked, all of which . . . [Luiz da Costa] swore to perform in the manner in which they ordered under the authority of an oath on the Holy Gospels, which he was administered, from which I made this writ of the said inquisitors with whom Luiz da Costa signed with his guardian, in the presence of whom it was read to him, and by whom it was heard and understood. I, Manoel Afonso Rebelo, wrote it.

Francisco Machado
Simão José
Manoel Varejão Távora
Tiago [official mark]
Silvio Lobo
D[e] Luiz [+] da Costa
Felipe Néri

Register of Secrecy

On the sixteenth day of the month August of 1743, in Lisbon in the Office of Sentencing [*Estaos e Casa do despacho*] of the Holy Inquisition, being there in the morning session, the inquisitors commanded that Luiz da Costa, imprisoned defendant in these proceedings, be brought from the custody prison and be made to appear before them. And being present he was administered the oath of the Holy Gospels, on which he placed his hand, and under the authority of which he was ordered to maintain in strict secrecy all that he saw and heard in these prisons, and all that happened with him regarding his trial, and that he not reveal any of it by word or writing, or by any other means, under pain of being gravely punished. He swore to perform all of this

de que se fez este *termo* de mandado dos ditos senhores, que com os mesmos assinou e com seu *curador.* Manoel Afonso Rebelo o escrevi.

Francisco Machado	Silvio Lobo
Simão José	M. Távora
Manoel Varejão	De Luis [+] da Costa
Tiago [sinal público]	Felipe Néri

A. Secreto	240
Alcaide dos Secretos	200
[ilegível]	100
Cta	036
Curador Néri	400
	976

[carimbo] Lima [sinal público]

under the authority of said oath, from which this writ of the said inquisitors was made. He signed with them and with his guardian. I, Manoel Afonso Rebelo, wrote it.

Francisco Machado	Silvio Lobo
Simão José	M. Távora
Manoel Varejão	De Luis [+] da Costa
Tiago [official mark]	Felipe Néri

A. Secret	240
Alcaide of Secrets	200
[illegible]	100
Cta [??]	036
Guardian Néri	400
	976

Lima [official mark]

16

Slavery, Writing, and Female Resistance: Black Women Litigants in Lima's Tribunals of the 1780s[1]

Maribel Arrelucea Barrantes
Document translation by Joseph P. Sánchez, Angelica Sánchez-Clark, and Larry D. Miller

A Historical Problem

Regardless of ethnicity, social status, and gender, everyone in colonial Lima came to court to solve diverse commonplace conflicts.[2] For this reason, it is revealing to analyze how Lima's black women, both slave and freed, used colonial law and in what cases and how they related to written documents. A focus on slave women and freed women as litigants allows us to see them as more than objects or victims. Women participated in their society and their time, learned to employ cultural codes without needing to read or write, and attempted in court to solve conflicts with other people, whether they were their owners, husbands, or patrons.

In short, black female slaves and freed women who used the courts acted openly as historical agents with their own voices, ideas, and objectives. For colonial Quito, Kimberly Gauderman demonstrated that not all women were victims of a social order based on patriarchal relations of power; many took independent actions, used the legal system to protect their social and economic interests, and punished men who abused them (Guaderman, 8). The documents in this chapter also challenge the prevalent view of colonial society as being so hierarchical and patriarchal that it prevented enslaved women from employing legal strategies on their own behalf.

Church and State as Normative Institutions

Both Church and state governed colonial society, dictating rules and punishments and often entirely confusing the lines of jurisdiction over the public and private affairs of clergy and lay people. Acting for Spain, the colonial state dictated the norms and laws, administered justice through the *Real Audiencia* (Lima's royal court), and publicly punished lawbreakers.[3] The Ecclesiastic Tribunal also heard cases brought by

[1] See Maps 6 and 10.

[2] In earlier publications, I noted a strong tendency to litigate especially among subaltern women (Arrelucea, "Esclavitud"; "Poder femenino"; "Poder masculino").

[3] Punishments included whippings and mutilation in the public *plaza,* and prisoners worked in public works and in bakeries, wearing chains and with the doors open, because the colonial system believed that public punishments intimidated the rest of the population and discouraged rebelliousness. See Flores Galindo; Aguirre ("Mujeres delincuentes").

aristocrats and plebeians, men and women, whites and blacks. A large portion of the city's subaltern population appealed more frequently to the Ecclesiastic Tribunal than to the secular courts because the former was considered closer to God and, therefore, more just.

Slaves went to the Ecclesiastic Tribunal because it gave them an advantage. Unlike the secular courts, the ecclesiastic courts offered slaves an unusual equality with the free population: They were all considered children of God with souls. As such, slaves were evangelized and administered the sacraments, and their faith was monitored to prevent a return to idolatry. Consequently, in cases of excessive cruelty, slaves went first to the Church because there they could present themselves as defenseless creatures new to the faith and needing protection.[4]

In a similar fashion, the Church regulated marriage and sexuality for all individuals, including slaves, favoring free choice in marriage. The Church distinguished between the sacrament of marriage given by God and the institution of slavery created by human beings. Thus, in the face of owners' opposition to slaves' marrying, the Church often compelled owners to buy the other spouse in order to protect the marriage (Trujillo Mena, 297–333). Slaves converted this ecclesiastic protection of marriage into a legal weapon.

If an owner decided to sell a slave outside Lima, the spouse appealed to the Ecclesiastic Tribunal and engaged the power of the written word and the ecclesiastic law to block the sale. As María Emma Mannarelli points out, the Church also determined how people should lead their sexual lives—what was licit, under what conditions, and with whom. According to the Church, the principal function of sex was the configuration of the domestic and social order through the regulation of desire and the control of sexual conduct. In each parish, ecclesiastic investigators monitored these affairs ("Vínculos," 347–48). Thus, the Ecclesiastic Tribunal offered the best space to sanction those who broke the Church's own dictates.

Slaves' Rights

Spanish law considered slaves property without rights over their labor, bodies, earnings, or personal time. However, Spanish law also granted slaves two important rights: to seek *manumission* and to protect their personal safety. The first allowed slaves to buy their freedom, and the second prohibited *sevicia,* understood as excessive ill treatment that placed the slave's life in danger because of inadequate nourishment, clothing, or medicine or that prevented the slave from marrying and living a conjugal life.[5]

[4] From an early date, Lima's church insisted that new slaves from Africa receive baptism, attend mass, confess, take communion, and participate in religious processions (*Segundo Concilio Provincial Limense,* 1567, chapters 126 and 127 in Trujillo Mena, 297–333).

[5] These basic principles are found in the most ancient Spanish laws, such as *Las Siete Partidas del rey Alfonso el sabio,* Partida IV, Título 21, Leyes 1–15 (see Alfonso el sabio) and are repeated in the *Recopilación de Leyes de Indias,* Libro VII, Título V, Leyes 1–10 (see *Recopilación Consejo de Indias*).

In addition, Spanish law made similar concessions to indigenous peoples, establishing tribunals and special functionaries such as the *Protector de Naturales* (legal advocate for indigenous people) to make separate laws for each social and ethnic group in colonial society. Native peoples also learned to use the special legislation, the legal maneuvers, written documents, and argumentation and tricks of the judicial system to defend, among other rights, their rights to communal land ownership, the use of irrigation water and pastures and marriage, and to resist tribute payments and the *mita* labor drafts. Both indigenous people and slaves perceived these legal rights as opportunities; for this reason, from a very early moment, they developed a strong tendency to use legislation in the tribunals to defend their rights.

Even though the majority of the cases preserved in the Archivo General de la Nación (*Audiencia* cases) and the Archivo Arzobispal de Lima (ecclesiastical cases) were written and signed by notaries and secretaries, rather than by slaves themselves, this fact alone does not prove that slaves were ignorant of the judicial system. On the contrary, exhaustive analysis of the cases, the legal strategies, the declarations, the evidence, and the accusations themselves show that slaves litigated knowing what they could obtain (Jouve-Martín, 185; Arrelucea, "Poder femenino," 86). The documentary evidence allows an analysis of the legal strategies employed by people who were unable to read or write, because one did not need formal academic skills to enter the judicial terrain. In addition, any literate person with access to ink and paper could write to the Ecclesiastic Tribunal because no expensive sealed paper or rigid formulas were required.

Ethnicity and Gender Difference before the Courts

The 173 cases presented between 1760 and 1820 by male and female slaves in Lima's *Real Audiencia* and the Ecclesiastic Tribunal fell into specific categories; 113 cases corresponded to women, revealing two principal concerns: petitions for freedom (26 female slaves and 19 male slaves) and the prevention of their sale or that of family members outside Lima (25 female slaves and 15 male slaves). The next most important concerns were cruelty by the master (20 female slaves and 11 male slaves) and freedom to marry (18 female slaves and 7 male slaves).

The cases suggest Lima's slaves most vigorously defended the right to buy their freedom, to control their own bodies, and to dispose of their labor and their time. The other issues litigated questioned the exercise of owners' authority by opposing excessive cruelty, sale outside Lima, and interference in conjugal life, any of which threatened the dense webs of social connections, family, and friends woven by Lima's slaves.

Another problem litigated between masters and slaves involved slaves' property. According to the legal norms, a slave's earnings belonged to the slave owner.[6] But in practice, many slaves—especially wage earners—saved and bought with their own money a variety of items such as clothes, shoes, household goods, mules, and poultry.[7] When

[6] Archivo General de la Nación, Lima, Causas Civiles, legajo 204, cuad. 2736, 1793.

[7] Pioneering studies by Harth-Terré and Márquez Abanto ("El artesano negro"; "Historia de la casa") and Hünefeldt show that a relationship existed between slave wage earners, their capacity

Cases	Litigants Men	Litigants Women	Total
Cruelty by the owner	11	20	31
Cruelty by the spouse	—	15	15
Sale outside Lima	15	25	40
Defense of marriage	7	18	25
Freedom	19	26	45
Retention of property	3	10	13
Retention of children	5	9	14
Total	**60**	**113**	**173**

Figure 3. Litigation by black slaves in the *Real Audiencia* and the Ecclesiastic Tribunal 1760–1820. Source: Based on the cases found in the Archivo Arzobispal de Lima (AAL), Causas de negros, and the Archivo General de la Nación (AGN), Real Audiencia, Causas Civiles.

an owner decided to sell a slave, the problem arose of determining to whom these items belonged. Many slaves availed themselves of the courts to keep their personal property (ten female slaves and three male slaves).

Litigating over this issue meant questioning one aspect of slave owner power, and it appeared that female slaves were sometimes successful in keeping their property. For example, the *mulata* Josefa Escalé accused her master of spiritual cruelty and demanded the return of her furniture, jewelry, clothing, mattress, bed frame, and other household items. The slave owned a surprising number of luxury objects such as silk kerchiefs, shawls, and gloves.[8] These cases show that slave women distinguished clearly between the masters' property and their own, which they actively attempted to protect.[9]

By litigating, slave women questioned the norms governing property and a slave's earnings. These cases reveal that, to the extent that urban slavery relaxed the rules of bondage, flexible practices and rights humanized slaves and brought them closer to a semifreedom, which they used to press for more opportunities and to better conditions viewed as harsh and unjust.

Slaves also formed families. They had spouses and children, and they faced the same family problems as a free people, though these manifested certain characteristics imposed by slavery. Consequently, slaves developed strategies to defend familial bonds, such as securing the *manumission* of an enslaved wife before she conceived children, liberating small children before their price rose, looking for new owners closer to the household, and marrying residents of Lima so that attempts to separate the family could be appealed in court.

---

to accumulate savings, and the existence of effective strategies of action within the colonial system.

[8] Archivo Arzobispal de Lima (AAL), Lima, Causas de negros, legajo 32, 1791.

[9] Additional examples can be found in AAL, Lima, Causas de negros, legajo 32, 1792.

Twenty-five female slaves and fifteen male slaves opposed the sale of their spouses outside of Lima in court. Nine female slaves and five male slaves entered into litigation to block the sale of children or their separation from mothers. This documentary evidence reveals the concern of slaves, especially female slaves, for the protection of family, maternity, paternity, and affections. In addition, a gender analysis shows that female slaves turned to the courts with greater frequency than did male slaves, as they used the courts to combat the intrinsic problems of the institution of slavery: cruelty, deficient food, imprisonment in bakeries, excessive work days, and sale outside of Lima.

Women also approached the courts to demand more humane treatment, not to be treated as merchandise, as when they complained of a husband's abuse, abandonment, or infidelity. Female slaves also denounced other slaves or freed blacks with whom they had conflicts including those involving abuse, threats, fights, or insults. The tribunals were public spaces in which the problems between those of different status could be resolved when the parties could not find satisfactory solutions on their own.

A defense of ethnicity constituted another of the recurring arguments in the petitions presented by slaves. Many presented themselves as humble and poor, but when it was necessary to defend their honor or avoid being sold or punished, they claimed honor for their ethnic status: "It is difficult to grasp by what moral standard one can slander the character of a black just because of his [social] condition as a slave, simply because the information suits the *convento*'s purposes, and, because of some persons of status and character, such slander is declared in a public trial. And thus, from where the example should emanate, comes only our decline."[10] This case reveals how slaves could use the concept of black/slave (*negro/esclavo*) in different ways according to the circumstances. In this case, the slave questioned the common colonial stereotype that delinquency derived from race and social class.

Marriage and Abuse: The Voice of Female Litigants

The intermarriage of slaves and free blacks brought to light problems created by the differences of gender and ethnicity and the exercise of male power within marriage. An especially illustrative case (1787), featured in this chapter, involves María del Carmen Ollague, a recently freed black woman (*negra*) married to Manuel Cosío, a black (*negro*) slave.[11] In her complaint, María relates how, during twelve years of marriage, Manuel mistreated her: He beat her and forced her to work in the *pulpería* (shop) that belonged to both of them. Even though they had two slaves who worked for wages (*esclavos de jornal*), he made her do domestic work in front of everyone, humiliating her. Finally he shut her up in a bakery to work in chains.

Her complaint reveals how black women articulated discourses by means of powerful concepts and images. María begins in a complaining tone, "During the prolonged period of our marriage, I have, of course, been nominally his wife, but in reality I have

[10] From the case of Manuela, a slave belonging to Lima's Santo Domingo Convent, who presented a case to the Ecclesiastic Tribunal to block her husband's sale. AAL, Causas de negros, legajo 31, 1784.

[11] AAL, Causas de negros, legajo 32, exp. 3, 1787.

only been treated as a slave, because, far from the happiness owed a legitimate wife, his actions have been the kind that a bad servant deserves." María compares the status of wife and slave for two reasons: first, because a wife was considered subject to the husband as a slave was to the master, and, second, because violence was permitted as part of conjugal relations just as it was in slave-master relations. For these reasons she compares her treatment to that deserved only by bad slaves.

Whether or not her arguments were truthful, María's objective was to stop the mistreatment by her husband. For this reason she requested to be "sent to a convent, where my aforementioned husband shall be obliged to support me with the required food and clothing. Otherwise, my life is uncertain." María was seeking to escape one prison by entering another. Even though the convent was a religious space with social prestige, it was perceived as a place of confinement, although some were in reality spaces of female liberty because they allowed an escape from the exhausting rhythm of work, the pressure of daily labor, and the control of husband, father, or owner.[12]

María then added that she wished the judge to "make the most effective resolution to punish my avowed husband, giving him a harsh warning [and] ordering that he be notified to abstain from mistreating me under penalty of a fine, in conformity with Your Illustriousness' discretion. Or, considering natural law, I will separate from my said husband, and the marriage of so many years is abandoned. As such, I have resisted this, despite the horrible torments I have suffered, knowing and accepting that [matrimony] has been a work of Divine Providence." This paragraph clarifies María's real objective. She did not want separation or confinement in the convent; she wanted the Tribunal to reprimand her husband. So she sought the protection of men who wielded authority over her husband, given that she most likely lacked a father, godfathers, or brothers to do this.[13]

María finally adds, "I ask and plead that Your Illustriousness see fit to order that my said husband give me my letter granting me freedom, which I seek in this Audience before Your Illustriousness. And, similarly, as I have been his day laborer for five years, giving him six *reales* daily, it is only right that I seek compensation." María ends the petition demanding her letter of *manumission.* She demands liberty on two levels: first, as an ex-slave she wants to be able to prove her personal liberty, and, second, as a woman, she wants a relationship without strife and violence.

Although more urban than rural women slaves litigated, some rural cases demonstrate a surprising argumentative capacity by rural black women who, for example, cite recent legal precedents as well as the medieval Spanish laws known as the *Siete Partidas* to argue their position. One such case, featured as the second document in this chapter, is the petition of Manuela, a *zamba* slave (of indigenous and African parentage)

[12] María's petition shows that the discourse of honor was not limited to elite women; subaltern women also used it. On honor, see van Deusen, *Entre lo sagrado.* For convents as places of female liberty, see Arias; Chambers.

[13] Another element of María's discourse is how she describes the years spent in marriage as a personal investment. This proved a common characteristic in women's petitions for divorce during this period.

belonging to Lima's Santo Domingo Convent but living and working on its rural hacienda. In 1784, she went to the Ecclesiastic Tribunal to block her husband's sale.[14]

In her petition she begins by citing the recent case of a slave woman named Juliana in which the Tribunal ordered the same convent to find a local buyer for the woman's husband in order to avoid breaking up the marriage. Manuela next asks to be sold to a Lima resident, citing the danger to her marriage that a separation from her husband has caused. She also astutely attempts to avoid turning over her wages and insists on the control over her own body, both of which are intrinsic rights not of a slave but of her owner. She then insists upon the sacred character of marriage and the protection that marriage should receive from the Church. The petition also cites the *Siete Partidas* to support her request. As it is difficult to say with certainty what access Manuela had to this legal text, the references to the *Siete Partidas* point to the participation of a legal specialist on her behalf.

Many of the petitions presented before the courts are written with the tone of a supplicant, but Manuela's is different: She questions the actions of the Tribunal, reminds the Tribunal of earlier resolutions, and demands compliance with the law at the same time expressing confidence in her rights and the law. Manuela's case reveals nuances that question some generalizations about rural slave women. For example, although they lived at a great distance from the courts and were subjected to tighter control on the haciendas, this did not mean that they were all entirely victims of the system. Several such rural women cited knowledge of laws and made use of argumentation and the legal process just as urban slave women did, though they did so in smaller numbers than their urban counterparts.

The ecclesiastic defense clashed with the rights of slave owners, who frequently intervened in their slaves' marriage choices. Owners tried to select spouses for their slaves from the same hacienda or a nearby street in order to control their slaves. Nevertheless, during the entire colonial period and the early republican period, slaves and freed people resisted and defended their personal decisions, appealing to the Church and creating a dynamic in which the Church became an intermediary between the state, the owners, and the slaves.[15]

[14] AAL, Causas de negros, legajo 31, 1784.

[15] Aguirre (*Agentes,* 190), Flores Galindo (18), Hünefeldt (54), Jouve Martín (186), and Trazegnies (23).

Queja presentada por María del Carmen Ollague, *negra* libre, contra su esposo Manuel Cosío, *negro,* por sevicia[1]

Ilustrísimo Señor Provisor,

María del Carmen Ollague, *negra* libre en la mejor forma que haya lugar en derecho ante Vuestra Ilustrísima parezco y digo, que hace el tiempo de más de doce años contraje matrimonio según orden de Nuestra Santa Iglesia con Mario Cosío, *negro* esclavo de doña Isabel Solís cumpliendo como Dios manda con dicho estado, sin que el expresado mi marido haya experimentado en mi conducta el menor devaneo. Y por el contrario ha llegado con su mal y público manejo a darme mérito para que yo interponga como interpongo ante Su Ilustrísima Señoría este reverente recurso reducido a hacer presente a Vuestra Señoría mis padecimientos cuales son los siguientes:

En el dilatado tiempo de nuestro matrimonio he tenido desde luego el nombre de su esposa, pero en lo formal sólo he merecido el tratamiento de esclava porque sus procedimientos lejos de lo sagrado que corresponde a una legítima mujer han sido no otros que aquellos a que se hace merecedora una mala sierva. Yo, Señor Ilustrísima, he empleado mis años únicamente en llevarle adelante sus intereses sin que de ellos haya podido ser advitra [árbitra] a lo ridículo de pagar una *cofradía.* Pudiera Ilustrísimo Señor dar a Vuestra Señoría Ilustrísima una idea formal de lo que da mérito a que contra mi expresado marido exponga sus desórdenes, pero mirando que de este modo molesto su justificada atención, sólo diré que siendo Vuestra Ilustrísima servido, estoy pronta a que se me reciba información de los hechos retenidos y de cuanto omito hacer presente a Vuestra Ilustrísima por la razón enunciada, con la calidad . . . mandar se me deposite en un monasterio donde se obligue al expresado mi marido a suministrarme los alimentos y el vestuario correspondiente porque de lo contrario mi vida no está segura.

Este, Señor Ilustrísimo, mi dicho marido es hombre sólo porque me manda a la *pulpería* teniendo esclavos y no vengo tan breve o porque no me despachan o porque como dueño de mi libertad me quedo parlando con Alonza, parienta, es bastante este motivo para que me cierre la calle, la puerta de mi habitación dejándome expuesta como se ha verificado, a que tal vez ladrones o algún otro de los muchos malignantes [sic] que hay me hagan un perjuicio. Y así procediendo, como es regular, me franquea las puertas de su morada es únicamente para darme de patadas, golpes, mordiscones, etc.

[1] Archivo Arzobispal de Lima (AAL), Causas de negros, legajo 32, exp. 3, 1787. I appreciate the help of Isabel Palomino and Ernesto Pajares in obtaining the paleographic version of these documents.

Complaint Presented by María del Carmen Ollague, Free Black Woman, against Her Husband Manuel Cosío, Black Man, for Excessive Cruelty [1787][1]

Most Illustrious Lord Ecclesiastical Judge,

I, María del Carmen Ollague, a free black, in accordance with my legal rights, appear and testify to the best of my ability before Your Illustriousness. It has been more than twelve years that, according to the mandate of Our Holy Church, I married Mario Cosío, a black slave of Doña Isabel Solís, [thus] fulfilling, as God commands, the said [marital] status. [In that time], my said husband has never had reason to suspect even the slightest impropriety on my part. On the contrary, his harmful and infamous behavior has given me good cause to bring before Your Illustrious Lordship this reverent appeal, summarized here to make Your Lordship aware of my sufferings, which are as follows:

During the prolonged period of our marriage, I have, of course, been nominally his wife, but in reality I have only been treated as a slave, because, far from the sacred treatment owed a legitimate wife, his actions have been the kind that a bad servant deserves.[2] Most Illustrious Lord, I have spent my years promoting only his interests, during which, absurdly, I found myself without the means to pay [even] a confraternity [fee]. I could, Most Illustrious Lord, give Your Lordship a report that supports [my case] against my said husband, exposing his abuses. However, seeing that it would only serve to distract you from your dutiful obligations, I will only say that if Your Illustriousness is satisfied, I am eager for Your Illustriousness to hear details concerning the aforementioned facts that I do not present now . . . order that I be sent to a convent, where my aforementioned husband shall be obliged to support me with the required food and clothing. Otherwise, my life is uncertain.[3]

[Case in point], Most Illustrious Lord, my said husband thinks himself a man when he makes me go to the tavern even though he has slaves. And when I fail to return home soon, either because I have not been quickly attended to or because, as I am master of my own freedom, I stay to talk with Alonza, a relative, this gives him enough of a reason to lock me outside of my dwelling, leaving me out on the street as is commonly known, where even thieves or any other evil people can harm me. So then, as he usually does, when he opens the doors of his residence, it is just to kick, punch, and bite me, etc.

[1] The document is written in small, neat handwriting with a signature in the same style, which suggests it was written down by a notary or secretary, whom María possessed sufficient economic resources to pay.

[2] María compares the image of "abused wife" with that of "bad servant." This was natural in colonial discourse. Punishment was viewed as corrective, even by subalterns themselves.

[3] According to colonial discourse, women lost sexual honor in the street, in public; therefore, it was important to remain within enclosed spaces like the home or the convent. María's petition shows that subaltern women used this discourse too, even though elites considered them lacking honor.

Ilustrísimo Señor, son tales los insultos que recibo de dicho mi marido que por no ser capaz de huir omito hacerlo patente a su justificación. Pero hay algo más, Ilustrísimo Señor. Cuando le da alguna de estas locuras (que así deben denominarse) ha tenido animosidad y corazón para ponerme en una panadería el tiempo de su voluntad. Y todo esto se le dispensa por sus amos, sólo por sus intereses y porque parece que desea mi muerte para evitar de ello con la libertad que demuestra apetecer. Esto, Señor Ilustrísimo, me avanzo a decir porque las experiencias me lo enseñan últimamente a Vuestra Ilustrísima en ejercicio de sus superiores facultades tome las providencias más eficaces para escarmiento de mi enunciado marido, mandando se le notifique se abstenga de maltratarme, bajo de una multa conforme al arbitrio de Vuestra Ilustrísima y del más severo *apercibimiento.* O usando del derecho natural yo me separo de dicho mi marido y queda abandonado el matrimonio de tantos años y el mismo que aún a costas de los tormentos gravísimos que he padecido he resistido, con sólo la mira y conformidad de haber sido obra de la Divina Providencia.[2] En cuyos términos a Vuestra Ilustrísima pido y suplico que en consideración a los fundamentos que llevo expresados y haciendo el pedimento más conforme se sirva así mandarlo en *justicia* que pido y espero de la que Vuestra Ilustrísima con tanto acierto distribuye.

Otrosí digo que el expresado mi marido me dio la libertad. Y aunque con respecto a ella me hizo le pagase puntualmente el *jornal* de seis *reales,* hasta el presente ignoro si soy libre o esclava, porque con la malicia que encierran sus procedimientos se la tiene guardada sin querérmela entregar. Y cuando acaso llegan los términos de su locura expidiéndome que en efecto de ella de su casa e igualmente me ha sido preciso a causa de mis enfermedades irme a un hospital, no han querido admitirme por no tenerla a la vista. Y en esta vida Vuestra Ilustrísima pido y suplico se sirva mandar que el expresado mi marido, en el acto de la comparecencia a que aspiro ante Vuestra Ilustrísima, me exhiba mi *carta de libertad* y la misma porque en este término de cinco años le fui su *jornalera* dándole seis *reales* diarios. Pues así es *justicia* que pido costas et supra.

María del Carmen Ollague

Queja de Manuela, *zamba* esclava para que la vendan en Lima [noviembre 3 de 1783][3]

Manuela, *zamba,* menor de veinte y cinco años, esclava de la hacienda de Palpa, propia del Convento de Santo Domingo de esta ciudad, mujer legítima de José Justo, esclavo que fue de la misma hacienda y hoy lo es de don Joaquín de Oyague, abastecedor de pan, por venta que de él le hizo el mismo convento, premisa la venia que impetro como más haya lugar en derecho parezco ante Vuestra Señoría y digo que ha más de tres años que el referido mi marido fue extraído de la hacienda y vendido en esta ciudad

[2] The writing in María's case reflects a key notion within colonial discourse related to marriage: marriage was a sacred sacrament and an unbreakable bond. To voluntarily leave this "sweet prison" challenged the foundations of society. For this reason, the petitions for divorce met general disapproval.

[3] AAL, Causas de negros, legajo 31, exp. 19, 1783.

Most Illustrious Lord, such are the insults I receive from my husband that even though I would clearly be justified to leave, I do not do it because I am incapable of leaving [him]. But there is more, Most Illustrious Lord. When he gets crazy like this (and that is what one must call it), he has become hostile and has had the nerve to put me in a bakery for as long as he wishes. All of this is permitted by his masters solely because it serves their interests and because he seems to want me dead, which would [allow his masters] to avoid giving him his freedom, which he clearly desires. Most Illustrious Lord, I dare say this because of what these experiences have taught me lately. Your Illustriousness, in your superior judgment, make the most effective resolution to punish my avowed husband, giving him a harsh warning [and] ordering that he be notified to abstain from mistreating me under penalty of a fine, in conformity with Your Illustriousness' discretion. Or, considering natural law, I will separate from my said husband, and the marriage of so many years is abandoned. As such, I have resisted this, despite the horrible torments I have suffered, knowing and accepting that [matrimony] has been a work of Divine Providence. With these words, I ask and plead of Your Illustriousness that, in consideration of the grievances that I have expressed in making this most proper petition, you see fit to order it in the [name] of justice, which is what I ask and hope from Your Illustriousness who definitively grants it.

One more thing, I must say that my aforementioned husband purchased my freedom; but, regarding this, even though he made me pay him exactly the daily wage of six *reales,* I still do not know if I am a slave or free because, with the maliciousness that drives his behavior, he has kept it [the letter of *manumission*] to himself, without giving it to me. When he goes crazy, he throws me out of the house, thus it has been necessary to go the hospital because of my infirmities. They have not wanted to admit me because they did not have [this letter] before them. In this life, I ask and plead that Your Illustriousness see fit to order that my said husband give me my letter granting me freedom, which I seek in this audience before Your Illustriousness. And, similarly, as I have been his day laborer for five years, giving him six *reales* daily, it is only right that I seek compensation as expressed above.

María del Carmen Ollague

Complaint of Manuela, *Zamba* Slave, That She Be Sold in Lima [November 3, 1783][4]

Manuela, *zamba,* under the age of twenty-five, slave of the hacienda of Palpa, properly of the Convent of Santo Domingo of this city, [and] legitimate wife of José Justo, a slave, formerly of the same hacienda and who today belongs to Don Joaquín de Oyague, supplier of bread, motivated by the action of this convent to sell him, by your leave, as is my legal right, I appear before Your Lordship and testify that more than three years ago my said husband was removed from the hacienda and sold in this city, thus

[4] The document consists of various loose sheets with small, rough lettering plus Manuela's own signature, indicating that she directed and understood the proceedings, the laws, and their reach.

separándose así nuestra unión y conjugio [sic] en que estábamos muy conformes, sin causa legítima de nuestra parte de que yo tenga noticia, y sin solemnidad alguna de las prevenidas por derecho para semejantes separaciones en estos términos. No se acomoda a mi voluntad ni a mi conciencia el divorcio involuntario que se ejecuta conmigo, dejándome en la misma hacienda y a mi marido en esta ciudad, sirviendo a su amo en cuarenta leguas de distancia. Y el anhelo de ver a dicho mi marido a quien amo, como no sólo me lo permiten sino que me lo mandan las leyes divinas y humanas, me resolví a venirme a esta ciudad oculta de los administradores de la hacienda, a fin de ocurrir a Vuestra Señoría, solicitando se dé providencia para que el convento me venda en esta ciudad donde se halla el dicho mi marido, para comunicarlo y vivir en unión como demanda nuestro estado, sirviendo cada cual a su amo, según el destino que nos dio la Providencia, con el que me hallo conforme.

Mi solicitud tiene el apoyo de un ejemplar que hay entre manos, en que Vuestra Señoría ha proveído, a pedimento de Juliana, esclava de la misma hacienda, casada con otro esclavo de ella, a quien vendió la religión al mismo don Joaquín, separando al matrimonio, que el convento proceda a su venta por precio acomodado y buenas condiciones, por no tener culpa alguna, y que la venta se haga en esta ciudad, concediéndosele el tiempo suficiente para buscar amo que la compre. El caso es igual en todas sus circunstancias, esto me confía esperar la equidad de Vuestra Señoría que sea igual la providencia.

Por tanto y haciendo el mejor pedimento ante Vuestra Señoría, pido y suplico que, atendiendo al hecho deducido que juro por Dios, Nuestro Señor, y esta señal de cruz + ser verdad, se sirva mandar que el Padre Prior de dicho convento proceda a venderme en esta ciudad en precio acomodado y justo, y con buenas condiciones, para que cese el divorcio involuntario que por el citado tiempo se me ha hecho sufrir, y poder continuar la vida maridable en la unión del referido José Justo, sirviendo cada quien a su amo. Y a fin de solicitar el que me acomode, se me conceda suficiente término. Y que entre tanto la parte del convento no me inquiete ni persiga, porque tengo entendido me solicitan con ahínco para prenderme y temo alguna extorsión. Pido *justicia* y espero alcanzarla de su equidad de Vuestra Señoría.

Manuela *Zamba*

[Sentencia del tribunal eclesiástico]

En la Ciudad de los Reyes [Lima] en 7 de noviembre de 1783:

El Ilustrísimo Señor Doctor don Francisco de Santiago Concha, Canónigo Doctor de esta Santa Iglesia Metropolitana, Provincial y Vicario General de este arzobispado habiendo visto los *autos* que sigue Juliana, *negra* esclava de la hacienda de Palpa, propia del convento de Santo Domingo, sobre que se le venda en esta ciudad para hacer vida maridable con Valentín, su legítimo marido, esclavo de don Joaquín de Oyague, a quien usa y perteneciente esta presentación: Mando se notifique al reverendo Padre Ilustrísimo Prior del Convento de Predicadores proceda *incontinenti* a vender la *zamba* que se refiere en este pedimento, lo que practicará en esta ciudad poniéndosele precio justo y reglado, dándosele para este efecto a la dicha esclava el término de nueve días

putting asunder our union and our conjugality, in which we were very content, through no fault of our own of which I am aware, and without any formal proceedings for similar separations, under these terms. The involuntary divorce was done against my will and conscience, leaving me in the same hacienda and my husband serving his master forty leagues away in this city. Desiring to see my said husband, whom I love as I am not only permitted but also commanded by divine and human laws, I decided to come to this city unbeknownst to the administrators of the hacienda, with the purpose of appearing before Your Lordship to seek a judgment so that the convent should sell me in this city, where my said husband is located, in order for us to live and fulfill our union as our [marital] state requires. Each will serve his own master, as Providence has destined for us, with which I am in agreement.

My petition is supported by a precedent before you that Your Lordship has ruled on, which has been petitioned by Juliana, a slave of the same hacienda married to another slave [also] from there, whom the Church sold to the same Don Joaquín, thus splitting apart the marriage. [Your Lordship] has ordered that the convent proceed with her sale at a reasonable price and under good terms, as she was not at fault, and that the sale take place in this city, allowing her sufficient time to seek a master who might buy her. The case is identical in all circumstances; this gives me hope in Your Lordship's fairness, that your judgment will be the same.

And, therefore, having made a most suitable petition before Your Lordship, I ask and plead, given the reasoned facts, which I swear are true by God, Our Lord, and by this sign of the cross +, that you see fit to order that the father prior of said convent proceed to sell me in this city at a reasonable and fair price, under good terms, so that this involuntary divorce, which I have been made to suffer during the referenced time period, can come to an end. And thus, I will be able to continue marital life in union with the aforementioned José Justo, with each of us serving our respective masters. Grant me sufficient time in order to petition whoever can accommodate me and [grant that] meanwhile the party of the convent not disturb or pursue me, as I understand they are eagerly trying to find me in order to arrest me, and I am frightened by the threat. I ask for justice and hope to obtain it from Your Lordship's sense of impartiality.

Manuela *Zamba*

[The Ecclesiastical Tribunal's Sentence]

In the Ciudad de los Reyes [Lima] on November 7, 1783:

I, the Illustrious Lord Doctor Don Francisco de Santiago Concha, canonical doctor of this Holy Metropolitan Church, provincial and vicar general of this archbishopric, having reviewed the proceedings pursued by Juliana, a black slave of the Hacienda de Palpa, properly of the Convent of Santo Domingo, concerning her sale in this city, so that she and Valentín, her legitimate husband, a slave of Don Joaquín de Oyague, could live together in marriage, which are pertinent to and used by the present case, order that the most illustrious father prior of the Convent of Predicadores [Dominican convent] be notified to proceed immediately to sell the *zamba* [Manuela] referred to in this petition. This shall be done in this city, setting a fair and customary price

y que en el entretanto no se le infiera el menor prejuicio a la *zamba* que se expresa y lo firmó.

Concha
Ante mí
Manuel del Bado Calderón

En la Ciudad de los Reyes [Lima] en 10 de octubre de 1783, notifiqué e hice saber el *auto* de la vuelta al reverendo padre maestro fray Domingo Ruedas de la Orden de Predicadores Prior actual del convento grande de Santo Domingo en su persona que doy fe.

José de Cárdenas, Notario Público

Lima y febrero 6 de 1784

Manuela, *zamba* menor de veinte y cinco años, esclava de la hacienda de Palpa propia del convento grande de Santo Domingo de esta ciudad, mujer legítima de José Justo, *negro* esclavo que fue de la misma hacienda y hoy de don Joaquín Oyague, por venta que de él hizo el mismo convento, en los *autos* sobre, que se proceda venderme en esta ciudad a precio justo y con buenas calidades, para que no se separe nuestro matrimonio ni su libre uso. Respondiendo al traslado, sin perjuicio que se me dio del escrito en que la parte del convento pide se le dé traslado de mi solicitud, digo que habiendo *justicia* se ha de servir Vuestra Señoría mandar se guarde y cumpla el *auto* de folio 14 proveído en 7 de noviembre del año próximo pasado de 1783, declarando no haber lugar a la solicitud del convento dirigida a enjuiciar este asunto imponerle silencio y condenarle en costas que a mí es *justicia.* Cuando los hechos son notorios, el derecho expreso y la Providencia porque corre peligro en las tardanzas la resolución más breve es la más justa, son los términos del presente caso.

El Padre Prior actual del convento confiesa en su declaración que aceptó sólo en lo favorable cuanto yo expuse en mi escrito de firma, motivando la Providencia de Vuestra Señoría, y conduce a sostenerla a saber ambos éramos esclavos de la hacienda, que casamos a ciencia y consentimiento del administrador a cuyo cargo estaba su gobierno y dirección, y que se nos ha separado a distancia de leguas, los esclavos cónyuges de un amo. Según la moral más sana y aprobada por los juristas afirma que los esclavos cónyuges no pueden ser separados ni vendidos a distancia en que se les prive o impida la comunicación y uso del matrimonio. Y en disposición del derecho que el amo que así enajene al uno sea compelido a enajenar en el mismo lugar al otro, y lo mismo manda la ley 7, título 5, Partida 4, para evitar peligro de la fornicación entre no hay duda corre en la gente joven en cuya edad estamos ambos. Luego la pronta providencia dada por Vuestra Señoría es arreglada al hecho, al derecho y a la instancia y debe sostenerse pues de lo contrario nada se alega que la enerve.

El Padre Prior dice que vendió a mi marido y a Valentín, esclavo de la misma hacienda y casado con la *negra* Juliana, por viciosos y delincuentes, con calidad de que

for her, and giving the said slave the period of nine days to carry this out. In the meantime, [I order that] no harm be done to the *zamba* who has testified here. Signed,

Concha
Before me
Manuel del Bado Calderón

In the Ciudad de los Reyes [Lima] on October 10, 1783, I personally notified and made aware of the preceding decision, to which I attest, the Reverend Father Fray Domingo Ruedas of the Order of the Preachers, current prior of the Convent Grande de Santo Domingo.

José de Cárdenas, Notary Public

Lima, February 6, 1784

Manuela, *zamba,* under the age of twenty-five, slave of the Hacienda de Palpa, property of the large convent of Santo Domingo of this city, legitimate wife of José Justo, a black slave who belonged to the same hacienda and, now, after being sold by the same convent, [belongs] to Don Joaquín Oyague. The decrees provided that I would be sold in this city at a fair price and under good terms, so that there would be no division in or encumbrances to our marriage. In responding, without prejudice, to the copy of the document given to me, in which the party of the convent requests it be provided a copy of my petition, I say that, in the interests of justice, Your Lordship should see fit to order that the decree on folio 14 provided on November 7, of this past year, 1783, be obeyed and fulfilled. [Your Lordship should] declare that the convent's petition to examine this matter does not have merit, and [Your Lordship] should impose silence on them and order them to pay the costs [incurred], which I would consider to be just. Once the facts are known [and] the law and the ruling made clear, the quickest resolution is the most just, as delays cause risk. These are the terms of the present case.

The present father prior of the convent confesses in his statement that he only conceded to what was favorable [to him] from my testimony in my written document, [which] prompted Your Lordship's decision. In order to uphold [the decision], it is necessary to know that we were both slaves of the hacienda, that we [were] married with the knowledge and consent of the administrator in charge of its management. [Although,] separated by a matter of leagues, [we as] married slaves of one master, according to the wisest morality approved by jurists, [such] married slaves cannot be separated nor sold at such a distance that may prohibit or impede the communication and the practice of matrimony, and under disposition of the law, the master who thus alienates his ownership of one must be compelled to transfer the other to the same place. The same is ordered by *Ley* 7, *Título* 5, *Partida* 4 to avoid the danger of fornication, which is, no doubt, common among the young people, in which age group we both belong. Thus, the timely decision pronounced by Your Lordship is based on the facts, the law, and the particular case, and should be upheld, as nothing to the contrary is alleged that will weaken this [decision].

The father prior says he sold my husband and Valentín, a slave of the same hacienda married to the black woman, Juliana, for being depraved criminals, with the

siempre los tuviesen presos. En la boleta de la escritura de venta nada dice de sus vicios ni de la calidad de prisión. Se ha pedido que la parte del convento presente el instrumento de venta en que ha de constar lo que afirma. Mandó así por Vuestra Señoría pero no se ha presentado. Si se viera, se hallara contente a la boleta de firma dada por el *escribano* Alejandro Cueto, cuya exactitud y buena fe es notoria.

Ahora se dice por parte del convento que los esclavos son viciosos para encubrir el exceso que se cometió en la venta, separando a los cónyuges. Si bastara decir que un hombre es facineroso para estimarlo por tal, nadie hubiera inocente sin acusaciones. Para que se crean los vicios es necesario que se pruebe en forma específica, porque el derecho que es ante todo prudencia y equidad ha establecido por regla de juzgar que nadie se presuma malo mientras no se pruebe tal.

No se alcanza con qué moral se infama la persona de un *negro* por ser de la misma condición de esclavo, sólo porque importa la información a los intentos del convento y que por unas personas de estado y carácter se haga en juicio público tal calumnia y que de donde debe venir el ejemplo venga la ruina.

La certificación que se presenta del *escribano* de cámara don Martín Julián Gamarra no viene al caso, ella no comprende a los esclavos que vendió el convento a don Joaquín Oyague, sino sólo los vendidos a don José Pomiano a quienes desde luego se les probaría sus delitos puesto que el Superior Gobierno concedió licencia para su venta que fuesen malos y viciosos aquellos. Que prueba que lo sean éstos es necesario que tuviesen una misma alma todos. Por eso se ve que es un despropósito presenten una tal certificación, por todo lo cual y además favorable que he aquí por expreso.

A Vuestra Señoría pido y suplico se sirva proveer y mandar según y como llevo pedido en el exordio de este escrito que es a mi *justicia* juro lo necesario costas vuestras.

Manuela *Zamba*
Esclava del convento de Santo Domingo

Lima 4 de febrero de 1783

Vistos estos *autos* en atención a la miseria y orfandad de las partes interesadas en este litigio las que carecen de facultades para poder sostener la litis [litigio] pendiente que solicita la parte del convento de Santo Domingo, sin embargo de lo que tenemos mandado por los *autos* del folio 5 y folio 14 los que hasta el presente no han surtido el efecto debido, vista al Promotor Fiscal General de este arzobispado el que haciéndose cargo de todo lo referido la respuesta que sea de derecho.

Firma, Concha

stipulation that they would always be imprisoned. Their bill of sale says nothing about their vices or the condition of imprisonment. The party of the convent has been petitioned to present the document of sale in which is clearly stated what Your Lordship ordered, but it has not been presented. If it were produced, the signature found on the bill of sale would be that of the scribe Alejandro Cueto, whose meticulousness and trustworthiness are well known.

Now the party of the convent says the slaves are depraved in order to cover up the excesses committed in the sale when they separated the spouses. If it is enough to [simply] accuse a man of being a criminal in order to deem him as such, then no one would be innocent and without any accusations. In order for these vices to be credible, it is necessary to prove each one specifically because the law, which is above all prudent and fair, has established that according to judicial practice, no one should be presumed malicious until he is proven to be so.

It is difficult to grasp by what moral standard one can slander the character of a black just because of his [social] condition as a slave, simply because the information suits the convent's purposes, and, because of some persons of status and character, such slander is declared in a public trial. And thus, from where the example should emanate, comes only our decline.

The notarized document presented by the court's scribe Don Martín Julián Gamarra is not relevant [because it] does not include the slaves the convent sold to Don Joaquín Oyague, but only those sold to Don José Pomiano. [Those slaves'] crimes were later proven. Thus, the superior government granted permission for their sale because they were malicious and depraved. [In order] for those to state that these [slaves, Valentín and José Justo,] are [malicious and depraved], it would be necessary for all [slaves] to have the same character. For that reason, one can see that it is absurd for them to present such a notarized document, given all that I have favorably testified about here.

I ask and plead that Your Lordship see fit to provide and order according to my request in the opening statement of my written testimony, which is to me just. I attest to the necessity of your costs.

Manuela *Zamba*
Slave of the Convent of Santo Domingo

Lima, February 4, 1783

These proceedings have been reviewed, taking into consideration the poverty and paucity of the interested parties in this litigation, who lack the wherewithal to sustain the pending dispute argued by the party of the Convent of Santo Domingo. What has been ordered in the decrees of folios 5 and 14 before us, however, has not up to now had the desired effect. In the opinion of the general public prosecutor of this archbishopric, who has undertaken all that is referenced above, the response shall be legally binding.

Signature, Concha

17

The Case of Javier, Esclavo, against His Master for Cruel Punishment, San Juan, Argentina, 1795[1]

Ana Teresa Fanchin
Document translation by Joseph P. Sánchez, Angelica Sánchez-Clark, and Larry D. Miller

A Denunciation in San Juan de la Frontera

On Christmas Eve, 1795, a court in San Juan de la Frontera held hearings on a denunciation of abuse made by an enslaved man named Javier. For four consecutive days, Javier's master Don Juan de Echegaray had kept him imprisoned in stocks, unleashing his rage against him with countless beatings.

The hearings took place in a city located to the east of the Andean range, in the southern territories of the vast Spanish colonial empire, in what is today Argentina, distant from the political centers of colonial domination. The region is characterized by a mountainous landscape and arid plains and valleys irrigated by the rivers born in the Andes. In 1562, Spanish colonizing forces had crossed the Andes from the Kingdom of Chile and founded the city of San Juan, at two thousand feet above sea level, on the southern bank of the San Juan River, one of the largest rivers of the Tulum Valley, which lies between the Andes to the west and the Sierra Pie de Palo to the east, in San Juan Province. The designation of "Frontera," which was added to the city's name, indicates its delimitation with the lands of the indigenous Chalchaquis to the north, a people conquered by the Spanish forces who emanated southward out of Perú.

The city of San Juan together with Mendoza (1561) and San Luis (1594) fell under the administration of the Reino de Chile and comprised one of its eleven *corregimientos,* until the creation of the Viceroyalty of Río de la Plata in 1776, when the district was transferred to the latter's governmental jurisdiction. From its beginnings in the mid-sixteenth century, San Juan represented a colonial outpost and an essential overland link between Río de la Plata and Chile.

It was across the dusty pampa trails and rugged mountainous paths of the San Juan region that *sanjuanino* muleteers drove their mule trains transporting merchandise. They departed the area carrying skins filled with wine, liquor, grape juice, and vinegars, and bags of locally produced dried fruit, together with goods acquired in Chile and other neighboring areas, to return later with products that satisfied local demands or that they resold in other markets.

A good portion of this stock was sold in public *plazas,* stores, and corner shops and came and went as contraband supplied directly by troop captains and wagoners (Fanchín, "Protagonistas," 69). Documentary evidence suggests that it was also through

[1] See Maps 6 and 12.

contraband that most enslaved blacks were introduced into the region, and so it is difficult to quantify the number of people of color transported in this wretched traffic.[2] What is certain is that the inhabitants of the region did not just watch as people of color passed by in their caravans of horror and death but also acquired them, principally as status symbols to employ in domestic tasks.

Enslaved Blacks in San Juan and Their Legal Controls and Protections

In the 1777 census, 16 percent of the inhabitants of San Juan were registered as African born or of African descent.[3] It is likely that the percentage was actually higher because about half the population was either listed as *mestiza,* which might include people with African ancestors, or without a particular ethnic identity.[4] When the 1777 census was carried out, Don Juan de Echegaray declared that he owned four male slaves, one female slave married to an *indio,* and three minor children. Among the named slaves, three are protagonists of the events related here: the same Javier, Manuel, and Cayetano who testified before the judge. Don Juan de Echegaray was a prominent *hacendado* and the son of a man who founded towns and villages in the area, as instituted by action of the *Junta de Poblaciones de Chile* in the mid-eighteenth century. Thus, along with his wealth, Don Juan de Echegaray had inherited prestige and honor.

When he meted out his cruel punishment to Javier, beating him with four quince rods, he did so with the backing of Spanish colonial law. The *Consejo de Indias, reales audiencias, cabildos,* viceroys, and governors were constantly engaged in creating legislation on the most varied aspects of the activities of black slaves in Spanish America. The regulations regarding escaped slaves, which were sanctioned by the king and incorporated into the *Recopilación de leyes de los reinos de las Indias* (1680), constituted the definitive procedures to be employed in combating *marronage.* The number of lashings to be given to an escaped slave varied according to the length of his or her absence, the slave's distance from home, and the place to which the slave had fled. For a weeklong desertion, a slave was to receive one hundred lashings and was to wear an iron shoe on one foot (Mellafe, *La esclavitud,* 83).[5]

Nevertheless, the law also protected slaves. The thirteenth-century *Siete Partidas* Part 7: Title 8: Law 9) set penalties against the owner who inflicted mortal injury on his slave. The *real cédula* (royal decree) of 1789 reiterated in chapter X that in the case of mortal injuries, contusions, wounds, and mutilations, the owner should suffer "the punishment corresponding to the crime committed if the injured were free" ("*la pena correspondiente al delito cometido como si fuese libre el injuriado*"; Goldberg, 5).

[2] The certificates of births, marriages, and deaths of blacks and *mulattoes* are recorded in the parochial records (kept in the city from 1665 on) in the "Libros de 'no españoles'" that mention their origins—principally *Angola, Guinea,* and the Portuguese colonies of Brazil—as well as those born in this jurisdiction with the usual designation of "*criollo.*" The Archivo Histórico de la Provincia also preserves contracts of purchase and sale of slaves carried out between individuals.

[3] See López-Chávez, who examines slavery in the city's Jesuit haciendas.

[4] For more information on the region's population, see Fanchin, "Los habitantes."

[5] See also Lucena Salmoral.

In addition he should lose the slave through a change of ownership. If the cruelty led to a permanent handicap, the slave could claim freedom. In other words, had it been verified that Javier had been rendered "gravely ill and on the verge of dying" ("*gravemente enfermo y en término de fallecer*"), as the doctor stated in his first testimony, his owner would have been obliged to grant him a letter of *manumission.* But this possibility was lost when the doctor certified Javier's physical recovery.

The Case of Slave Javier vs. Don Juan de Echegaray

In his declaration, Javier testified that his master had given him a document of sale that allowed him to seek a new owner. But, as generally occurred in such cases, Don Juan de Echegaray had set the price too high to make the sale possible. Moreover, Don Juan threatened Javier with a beating if he persisted in his request to be sold. Javier must have known that his master would be true to his word, and he chose to flee. But ten days later, he presented himself voluntarily in the same court that had aided him in producing the document of sale. Thus it was the judicial authority who returned Javier to his owner and recommended a "moderate correction of this minor offense" ("*moderada corrección a este corto delito*").

This ambiguous wording does not specify what the appropriate punishment was, nor does it name the exact offense for which Javier was to be punished. Of course, it is important to remember that this wording was recorded by the scribe who took Javier's declaration in the investigation of the circumstances that provoked the master's rage. The only witnesses to the incident were the master's other slaves, and all of them specified the number of lashings. Even Manuel knew what had happened, despite having only witnessed the beatings on the last day, as he had been out working in the fields. Finally, despite making determinations in favor of Javier, the judge was benevolent toward the master, restoring his condition of honorable citizen (*vecino honorable*).

In other colonial territories the *manumission* of slaves was more frequent, at least in particular circumstances, as in Santiago de Cuba after the proclamation of the free entry of slaves in 1789. Where large slave markets existed, owners could accede more readily to grant freedom to slaves because they could more easily purchase replacements (Belmonte Postigo, 8). In contrast, in San Juan de la Frontera, the social sector that had sufficient material wealth to buy this type of merchandise had fewer opportunities to do so and slaves constituted an important investment for commercial development.

The regulation of free trade occasioned very different effects in the interior to those seen in and around large port cities. In the last quarter of the eighteenth century, Buenos Aires saw a significant rise in *manumissions* by purchase as increased urban development corresponded to an increase in the opportunity for slaves to earn income with which to purchase their freedom (Johnson, "La manumisión en el Buenos Aires," 645). San Juan de la Frontera's response to the economic growth in Buenos Aires was an intensification of its viticulture or wine-growing activity. Thus wine producers such as Don Juan de Echegaray would have been motivated to keep their slave labor, even more so if they had already recuperated—through the slave's work—the initial purchase cost.

In reading the testimonies in the case, it is important to keep in mind factors that shape the testimony. I will name just three. First, there is the question of mediation. Although there was no interpreter who translated the slaves' words, as Javier and his fellow slaves spoke Spanish, their testimony was a reelaboration of their words composed by a "lettered" Spanish court official, who would have modified the slaves' language according to his understanding and legal and linguistic training. Second, this episode exposes a strategy commonly adopted by slaves, who used to their benefit a subterfuge offered by the judicial system. This formal system of justice gave slaves the opportunity to solicit their freedom or, as happened concretely in this case, to petition a document of sale for the purpose of being transferred to a new owner and hopefully to an improved living situation. Thus, the testimonies open a window onto a strategy by which enslaved blacks sought to negotiate better circumstances through the court system. Finally, the case reaffirms the meanings that slavery gave and still gives to its human victims in the concept of the enslaved body: It is well-known that the African population and their descendants were perceived as body merchandise. This combination of coordinates is still sustained in our own time in so many renewed forms of slavery.

Testimonio sobre malos tratos de don Juan de Echegaray a su esclavo Javier[1]

[*Auto* de denuncia sobre castigo al *mulato* Javier, esclavo de don Juan de Echegaray]

En la ciudad de San Juan de la Frontera a los 21 días del mes de diciembre de 1795, don Francisco Ortega y Ramos *alcalde ordinario de segundo voto* de esta ciudad y testigos a falta de *escribano* público digo que . . . ayer veinte del corriente han dado parte que don Juan de Echegaray de esta ciudad ha hecho un cruel castigo de un *novenario* de azotes en un *mulato,* su esclavo, nombrado Javier de cuyo castigo se halla el citado esclavo gravemente enfermo y en término de fallecer. Y como esto es en ofensa de Dios y en contra de *reales disposiciones* que tratan de la corrección de *criados,* por tanto debía de mandar y mando que para el esclarecimiento del hecho que queda relacionado de forma en este *auto.* . . se examinen los testigos sabedores del hecho. . . . Sea la primera [declaración] de don José Casamadrid, profesor de medicina. . . .

[Certificación médica extendida por don José Brizuela y Casamadrid, profesor de medicina de la ciudad]

Don José Brizuela y Casamadrid, profesor de medicina en esta ciudad y en cumplimiento del *auto* que antecede:

Certifico en cuanto puedo y el derecho me permite, en cumplimiento del superior *auto* del *Señor alcalde [ordinario] de segundo voto,* [que] pasé a casa de don Juan de Echegaray de esta ciudad, y en ella reconocí a su esclavo que se hallaba enfermo. . . . Según lo que observé se encuentra con calentura inflamatoria, y magulladas las espaldas y asentaderas, efecto de la convulsión atraída por muy grave castigo que por su amo en él se ha hecho.

[Declaración del esclavo Javier, *mulato,* treinta años de edad]

En la ciudad de San Juan de la Frontera a los 21 días del mes de diciembre 1795, para el esclarecimiento del hecho que motiva el *auto cabeza de proceso,* yo don Francisco Antonio de Ortega *alcalde ordinario de segundo voto* hice comparecer en mi *juzgado* a un *mulato* esclavo de don Juan de Echegaray de esta vecindad que se llama Javier, a quien por ante mí y testigos le recibo juramento que celebro en forma, por Dios, Nuestro Señor, y una señal de cruz, bajo del cual ofreció decir verdad. . . .

Preguntado si se halla enfermo de qué procede su enfermedad y por qué lo tiene su amo con lo precaria que se manifiesta,[2] responde que se siente enfermo principalmente de la espalda y las asentaderas y que la causa de esto es el castigo de cuatro días

[1] Archivo General de la Provincia de San Juan, Argentina, Fondo Tribunales, caja 18, carpeta 75, coc. 15, fols. 1–6v.

[2] In this evidently delicate state of health.

Proceedings Concerning the Physical Abuse Inflicted by Don Juan de Echegaray on His Slave Javier

[Denunciation of the Corporal Punishment Given to the *Mulatto* Javier, Slave of Don Juan de Echegaray]

In the city of San Juan de la Frontera on December 21, 1795, Don Francisco Ortega y Ramos, *alcalde ordinario de segundo voto* of this city, and [other] witnesses, as there is not a public scribe available, I say that . . . yesterday, the twentieth of the present [month and year], it has been reported that Don Juan de Echegaray of this city has, with a *novenario* of lashes,[1] cruelly punished his slave named Javier, a *mulatto.* Due to this punishment, the aforementioned slave is gravely ill and on the verge of dying. And, as this is an offense against God and against royal decrees that deal with the punishment of servants, therefore, I should and do order that, for the clarification of the incident recorded in the customary manner in these proceedings . . . that the witnesses knowledgeable about the incident be questioned. . . . Let the first [statement] be that of Don José Casamadrid, doctor of medicine. . . .

[Medical Certification Issued by Don José Brizuela y Casamadrid, Doctor of Medicine of the City]

Don José Brizuela y Casamadrid, doctor of medicine in this city and in fulfillment of the previous decree:

In fulfillment of the above decree of His Lordship, the *alcalde [ordinario] de segundo voto,* I certify to the best of my ability, and as the law permits me, that I went to the house of Don Juan de Echegaray of this city. There, I examined his slave who was ill. . . . According to what I observed, his back and buttocks are battered and bruised and he is suffering from an inflammatory fever caused by the violence brought on by the very serious punishment inflicted on him by his master. . . .

[Statement of the Slave, Javier, *Mulatto,* Thirty Years of Age]

In the city of San Juan de la Frontera on December 21, 1795, for the clarification of the incident that prompts the initial proceedings of criminal investigation, I, Don Francisco Antonio de Ortega, *alcalde ordinario de segundo voto,* ordered to appear in [this] tribunal a *mulatto* named Javier, a slave of Don Juan de Echegaray of this vicinity. From him, before me and the witnesses, I received his oath made in the customary manner, in the name of God, Our Lord, and by the sign of the cross, by which he swore to tell the truth. . . .

Asked if he is ill, what caused his illness, and why his master has him in this evidently precarious state, he answers that he is ill primarily because of his [injured] back and buttocks, caused by the four-day punishment . . . the last one taking place on the

[1] Although the expression *novenario* refers to a series of events over the course of nine days, the witnesses recount that Javier's punishment was carried out over four days.

. . . siendo el último el de antes de ayer diez y nueve del corriente, . . . verificado por la mano propia de su amo. Que la disciplina con que le azotara eran cuatro varillas de membrillo, y que del número de los azotes llevados no se acuerda a punto fijo,[3] pero sólo sí sabe que la primera tarde de la disciplina fue seguida por un largo espacio de tiempo. [Mientras que] las tres restantes, verificadas por la mañana, han sido hechas en cuatro pausas, pues, castigándolo un rato paraba su amo, se pitaba un cigarro y volvía a darle otro *remesón* otro tanto tiempo como el anterior, el que concluido, hacía su pausa de descanso y volvía a continuar el castigo, el que de esta suerte efectuó en cuatro sesiones en cada uno de los tres días que deja dicho . . . que las *prisiones* que tiene se las [puso] su amo antes de emprender el castigo que ha experimentado [y] que por esto se mantiene con ellas hasta ahora.

Preguntado qué delito o injuria hizo contra su amo de que le ha resultado esta corrección y quiénes son sabedores del castigo: responde que el delito que ha cometido para haber sufrido el castigo de que deja hecha *relación* es el de haber estado huido como diez días. Y que la causa de su fuga fue porque en la noche del día de ella supo que su amo lo quería castigar por sólo haberle pedido *papel de venta* y no haber encontrado amo, siendo la causa el exorbitante precio que en él había puesto [y] que todo esto debe constarle al *juzgado.* Que igualmente en el último día de la fuga . . . se presentó al mismo *juzgado* para que éste lo entregase a su amo, lo que inmediatamente verificó diciéndole [que] diese una moderada corrección a este corto delito. Que los que son sabedores del castigo que en él se ha hecho por haberse hallado presentes son los demás esclavos del citado su amo, los cuales se llaman Pascual, Eusebio, Cayetano, Manuel, [y] Damián; que ésta es la verdad de cuanto en este particular tiene sucedido. . . .

[Declaración de Cayetano, cuarenta años, esclavo de don Juan de Echegaray]

En la ciudad de San Juan de la Frontera a los 22 días del mes de diciembre de 1795, para la sumaria información . . . en el esclarecimiento del delito que motiva el *auto de cabeza de proceso,* yo don Francisco Antonio de Ortega, *alcalde ordinario de segundo voto,* hice comparecer en mi *juzgado* a Cayetano, esclavo de don Juan de Echegaray, a quien por testigos, a falta de *escribano,* le recibí el juramento, que lo hizo por Dios, Nuestro Señor, y una señal de la cruz bajo el cual ofreció decir verdad de lo que dijese. . . .

En lo concerniente al mencionado *auto* responde que sabe, por haberlo visto, que su amo don Juan de Echegaray ha castigado a uno de sus esclavos llamado Javier . . . por su mano propia en cuatro días, el primero a la tarde y los demás por la mañana. Y en cada uno de ellos le ha dado cuatro remesones de a veinte y cinco azotes con cuatro varillas de membrillo. Y que ésta es toda la verdad de lo que sabe. . . .

[3] He does not recall exactly the number of lashings.

day before yesterday, the nineteenth of the present [month], . . . carried out by his master's own hand. [He says] that the device used to whip him was a switch made of four quince sticks and that he does not remember exactly how many lashes he was given but only knows that the first afternoon of the punishment was followed by a long period of time, [whereas] the other three, carried out during the morning, were done with four breaks. After punishing him for a while, his master stopped, smoked a cigarette, and again gave him another beating lasting as long as the previous one. Once finished, he took a break and [then] again continued the punishment. He carried it out in this manner in four sessions on each of the three days, as has been stated. . . . His shackles were [put] on him by his master before he began the punishment he experienced. That is why he is still wearing them, today.

Asked what crime or injury he committed against his master that resulted in this punishment and who is knowledgeable about the punishment, he responds that the crime he committed, for which he has suffered the punishment that has been reported, [was that he] had run away for ten days. The reason for his flight was that, on the night that he ran away, he knew that his master wanted to punish him simply because he had asked for a document of sale [but] had not yet found a [new] master, the reason being the exorbitant price [his master] had put on him. All this should be evident to the tribunal.[2] Similarly, on the last day of the flight . . . he turned himself in to the same tribunal so that it would return him to his master, which was immediately carried out. [The tribunal] told [Echegaray] [that] he should impose a moderate punishment for this minor offense. Those who have knowledge about the punishment inflicted on him are the rest of his master's slaves who happened to be present and whose names are Pascual, Eusebio, Cayetano, Manuel, [and] Damián. This is the truth about what has occurred in this matter. . . .

[Statement of Cayetano, Forty Years of Age, Slave of Don Juan de Echegaray]

In the city of San Juan de la Frontera on December 22, 1795, in preparation of the proceedings . . . regarding the clarification of the crime that prompts the initial criminal investigation, I, Don Francisco Antonio de Ortega, *alcalde ordinario de segundo voto,* ordered Cayetano, a slave of Don Juan de Echegaray, to appear in [this] tribunal, from whom, before witnesses, lacking a scribe, I received the oath that he made before God, Our Lord, and a sign of the cross, under which he swore to tell the truth about what he would say and be asked. . . .

As to what concerns the proceedings mentioned, he answers that he knows, because he saw it, that his master Don Juan de Echegaray has punished, with his own hand, one of his slaves named Javier . . . for four days, the first day in the afternoon and the rest in the morning. On each of these days, he has given him four sessions of twenty-five lashes in each one with four quince sticks, and this is all the truth about which he knows. . . .

[2] This is the same court in which Javier entered his petition for his master to grant him the document of sale.

[Declaración de Damián, treinta años, esclavo de don Juan de Echegaray]

En el propio día [continua el sumario] hice comparecer a Damián, esclavo, [quien] responde lo siguiente: que sabe por haberlo visto, que su amo don Juan de Echegaray por su propia mano ha castigado en cuatro días consecutivos a un *mulato,* su esclavo nombrado Javier, al cual lo ha dado en cada uno de los dichos días una porción de azotes crecida hasta que se cansaba, y con unas varillas de membrillos. Que ésta es la verdad que declara en fuerza del juramento . . . en que se afirma y ratifica. . . .

[Declaración de Eusebio, veinte años, esclavo de don Juan de Echegaray]

El propio día, yo el precitado juez, hice comparecer a Eusebio esclavo de don Juan de Echegaray, de quien por ante mí y testigos, le hice tomar juramento . . . ofreció decir verdad de lo que supiese y le fuere preguntado. Y siendo al tenor del *auto cabeza de proceso,* responde lo siguiente: Que sabe por haberlo visto, que su amo don Juan de Echegaray ha castigado por su propia mano a otro mulato también su esclavo nombrado Javier, [a quien] ha azotado en cuatro días, el primero por la tarde en que le dio muchísimos azotes con unas varillas de membrillos y después en tres días por la mañana en que no ha sido el castigo tan cruel como el primero pero siempre con las varillas. Que ésta es la verdad que declara en fuerza del juramento que hecho tiene.

[Declaración de Manuel, veinte años, esclavo de don Juan de Echegaray.]

En la ciudad de San Juan de la Frontera a los 22 días del mes de diciembre de 1795, yo don Francisco Antonio de Ortega y Ramos, *alcalde de segundo voto* de esta ciudad, en continuación de la sumaria que antecede hace comparecer en su *juzgado* a Manuel, esclavo de don Juan de Echegaray, a quien por ante mí y testigos le recibí juramento . . . por el cual ofrecía decir verdad de lo que supiese y se le fuese preguntado. . . .

Responde que le consta por haberlo visto, que su amo castigó un día ante su presencia al dicho esclavo nombrado Javier[4] . . . lo azotó con varillas de membrillo y dándole a su parecer cosa de veinte y cinco azotes. Y que por ser [Manuel] el que cuida la viña de su amo no se hallaba presente al castigo, que igualmente tiene oído decir a los demás esclavos, sus compañeros, hizo su amo en tres días anteriores de que presenció. . . .

[Veredicto del juez, condena al amo]

San Juan, Diciembre 24 de 1795

[*Autos* y *Visto*]

Resultando de la [exposición] sumaria el exceso del castigo hecho por don Juan Echegaray a su esclavo Xaviel [Javier], y estando al propio tiempo informado el *juzgado*

[4] In the manuscript this is Xaviel.

[Statement of Damián, Thirty Years of Age, Slave of Don Juan de Echegaray]

On the same day [the proceedings continue], I had Damián, a slave, appear, [who] responds as follows: that he knows, because he saw it, that his master Don Juan de Echegaray punished his slave named Javier, a *mulatto,* with his own hand for four consecutive days. On each of the said days, he gave him a large number of lashes with some quince sticks until he got tired. He states that this is the truth, under oath . . . in which it is affirmed and ratified. . . .

[Statement of Eusebio, Twenty Years of Age, Slave of Don Juan de Echegaray]

On the same day, I, the presiding judge, had Eusebio, a slave of Don Juan de Echegaray, appear before me and witnesses, [and] had him take an oath . . . he swore to tell the truth about what he might know and be asked. Doing so, in accordance with the proceeding and initial criminal investigation, he answered the following: that he knows, because he saw it, that his master, Don Juan de Echegaray, has punished with his own hand another *mulatto,* also his slave, named Javier, [whom] he beat for four days, the first day in the afternoon on which he gave him a great many lashes with some quince sticks, and then for three days in the morning. The punishment was not as cruel as the first day, but always [inflicted] with the sticks. He states that this is the truth, under the oath he has made. . . .

[Statement of Manuel, Twenty Years of Age, Slave of Don Juan de Echegaray]

In the city of San Juan de la Frontera on December 22, 1795, I, Don Francisco Antonio de Ortega y Ramos, *alcalde de segundo voto* of this city, in continuance of the above proceedings, had Manuel, a slave of Don Juan de Echegaray, appear in [this] tribunal. Before me and witnesses, I received his oath . . . by which he swore to tell the truth about what he might know and be asked. . . .

He responds that it is evident to him, because he had seen his master punish the said slave named Xaviel [Javier], in his presence that one day . . . he beat him with quince sticks, giving him, it seems, twenty-five lashes. As [Manuel] is the one who takes cares of his master's vineyard, he was not present for the punishment that he also heard the other slaves, his companions, say that his master meted out on the three days before the one [day] he witnessed. . . .

[Judge's Verdict, Sentencing of the Master]

San Juan, December 24, 1795

[Judicial Decree and Findings]

Based on the [evidence presented in the] proceedings, the excessive punishment meted out by Don Juan de Echegaray to his slave, Xaviel [Javier], and the tribunal having

por el médico Casamadrid, encargado en la curación del citado *mulato,* . . . se le condena por ahora a don Juan de Echegaray a que en el preciso término de tres días, que él designe al dicho esclavo para que buscase amo con el *papel de venta* que le dio, sea con los que el dicho Echegaray haiga de buscar sujeto a quien venderlo, teniendo entendido que de no verificarse por su morosidad se procederá de oficio y se le dará la corrección que corresponda [a la] inobediencia, sacándole inmediatamente de la notificación de este *auto* las *prisiones* con que tiene al dicho esclavo, como así mismo se le condena a la satisfacción de asistencia y medicina hasta la entera curación. Que por ella se adeude al profesor Casamadrid, y de las costas de este *expediente* y de las que en sus incidencias se hallan originado con *apercibimiento* para en lo sucesivo. De excederse en las correcciones del castigo se le aplicará toda la pena de la ley que ahora por primera ocasión se le dispensa con atención a las circunstancias de ser uno de los principales *vecinos* honrado y de honor. . . .

been properly informed by Doctor Casamadrid, in charge of treating the aforementioned *mulatto,* . . . Don Juan de Echegaray is hereby sentenced to a specific deadline of three days in which to assign the said slave to find a master with the document of sale he gave him, among [the candidates] the said Echegaray must select a person to whom he will sell him.[3] Let it be understood that if this is not carried out because of procrastination on his part, official proceedings will be initiated and he will be given the punishment that corresponds to disobedience. Upon receipt of this order, the shackles will be removed immediately from the said slave. Also, [Echegaray] is sentenced to pay for the slave's care and medicine until he is completely healed, for this he owes Doctor Casamadrid. [He must also pay] the costs of these proceedings and other related consequences that have arisen. He is also warned that if, henceforth, [he] goes too far in his punishments, the full force of the law will be applied against him. At present, it is waived, given that this is the first incident [and] taking into consideration that he is one of the principal citizens, honored and honorable. . . .

[3] The wording in the original is confusing and might also mean that Don Juan de Echegaray is to find the purchaser within the same three-day time limit that he had originally given Javier to do the same.

18

In the Royal Service of Spain: The *Milicianos Morenos* Manuel and Antonio Pérez during the Napoleonic Invasion, 1808–1812[1]

Jorge L. Chinea

Paul Gilroy's *The Black Atlantic* (1993) challenges scholars to look beyond the dominant *paradigm* of the African diaspora that privileges colonial or national particularities isolated from hemispheric and intercontinental events. He advocates a multidimensional approach linking local, regional, and global developments, one that is consonant with the extensive dispersion of Africans across Europe, Asia, and the Americas through the slave trade.

Gilroy also reminds us that Africans circulated both coercively and voluntarily in the flow of people, goods, ideas, and institutions that shaped the early modern Atlantic world: "The history of the black Atlantic since then, continually crisscrossed by the movement of black people—not only as commodities but engaged in various struggles toward emancipation, autonomy, and citizenship—provides a means to reexamine the problems of nationality, location, identity, and historical memory" (16).

The free and enslaved black sailors that navigated across the many cultures, religions, languages, and political struggles of the Atlantic world were at the forefront of these changes. By embracing a flexible, *diasporic identity,* they witnessed and participated in events taking place on the ocean and the many lands it touched (Bolster, 38–41; Pettinger, ix). Mariners figured prominently in these transatlantic exchanges by virtue of their indispensable role in operating or maintaining ships.

But they were certainly not the only ones, nor were they alone in these endeavors. During the age of slavery and in the postemancipation era, their sea vessels transported a wide assortment of Afro-Latinos and other non-Europeans from all walks of life—among them servicemen. Narratives of their experiences overseas and overland may be found buried in the mass of documents housed in governmental, business, and private repositories. Within these archives lie their hidden, frozen voices waiting for the patient researcher to "bring them back into the sun" (Sánchez González, 7).

The submerged voices of the Afro–Puerto Rican soldiers Manuel and Antonio Pérez exemplify this archival entombment. Until recently, Afro-Latinos had been all but overlooked, understudied, or silenced in the canonical scholarship documenting the clashes and encounters involving Iberians, Africans, and "New World" colonials despite ample evidence of their significant participation in many of those historical developments (Andrews; Scott).

The previously unknown or ignored deeds of the Afro-Latino duo highlighted here is a case in point. Though born in Puerto Rico, they sailed through the Atlantic during

[1] See Maps 4 and 15.

a tour of duty in the Spanish military. Eventually, they joined the anti-French opposition in the Andalusian city of Seville when Napoleon invaded Spain in the early 1800s. By doing so, they repositioned themselves to demand better treatment and other tangible gains in order to improve their social and economic conditions.

If one were to judge by the colonial library—or that body of work built by or reflecting the interests of *Eurocreole* colonial elites—their experiences represent a historical anomaly.[2] For much of the past century, this exclusionary scholarship held that Iberians and *Eurocreoles* were the key protagonists of Puerto Rico's history.

Fortunately, research over the past three or four decades has shown that the so-called *clases vulgares,* the poor, racially ostracized groups that comprised the majority of the population in Spanish America, were not the powerless, inert mass that previous writers had once suggested (see Dávila; Sued Badillo, "Theme of the Indigenous"; and Sued Badillo and López Cantos, *Puerto Rico Negro*). Instead, scholars now see them as *subaltern agents* operating under extremely harsh conditions. Thus, the case involving our two militiamen questions the merit of Eurocentric historical analyses while highlighting the malleability of the black Atlantic as a fluid space wherein the idealized neat boundaries separating colonial subject and metropolitan overseer and the oppressed and the oppressor are often blurred, contested, and overturned.

Afro-Latinos in Spanish Colonial Puerto Rico, c. 1650–1800

Following the exodus of Spanish colonists from the Greater Antilles and the virtual cessation of European immigration and trade triggered by the depletion of alluvial mineral deposits after about 1600, the Africans left behind became a greater share of the population. Along with *cimarrones* and *mestizos,* nonwhites retained this demographic edge over the next two centuries. Subsistence farming, cattle ranching, and seafaring—including fishing, whaling, salt racking, salvaging damaged or sunken ships, piracy, *privateering,* and maritime *marronage*—afforded them the chief means of survival (Chinea, "A Quest"; Morales Carrión, *Puerto Rico*).

The Puerto Rican ship carpenter Alonso Ramírez, who journeyed to Havana, Mexico, and the Far East in the late 1670s, touched on this dismal economic reality.[3] According to this native of San Juan, the gold-mining bust and a string of destructive hurricanes wiped out the cacao exporting business that had been a major source of income. As shipwright work began to dry up, he "determined to steal my body from my very homeland in order to secure in [other places] a better way of life" (Sigüenza y Góngora, 17). So did many others, but not always permanently.

Since at least 1650, "ship carpenters, caulkers, blacksmiths, lumberjacks, and sawyers became common trades in San Juan and other coastal areas" (López Cantos, 168). Woodworkers often carved local trees, whose timber had been highly sought after by the Spanish naval industry, into small boats and canoes that serviced a lucrative

[2] The phrase "colonial library" is borrowed from Schmidt and Patterson (5).

[3] Although scholars have long conjectured that Sigüenza might have "invented" the *Infortunios of Alonso Ramírez,* a recent study by López Lázaro offers new evidence about the historical veracity of the late seventeenth-century account.

contraband trade with the nearby non-Hispanic Caribbean (López Cantos, 169). The *mulatto* Miguel Enríquez reaped a fortune from his seafaring exploits, mainly illicit trade, shipbuilding, pillaging nearby Danish, Dutch, French, and British colonies in the Caribbean, and sacking enemy vessels (López Cantos; Morales Carrión, *Puerto Rico,* 69–70).

The clandestine business persisted through the eighteenth century, as documented by the Spanish clergyman-historian Fray Agustín Iñigo Abbad y Lasierra. In the 1770s, he reported that the local inhabitants of the western seaside town of Arecibo built rudimentary watercraft capable of transporting up to twenty-five men to barter in French Saint Domingue, on the western tip of Hispaniola.[4]

Most of these dealings entailed short sailing trips and rarely extended outside the archipelago; therefore, one can only speculate about the circumstances surrounding our two *afroboricuas*' sojourn in Spain in the early 1800s. It is possible that they either sought out work or were impressed into the Spanish armed and naval services to replenish vacancies caused by the shortage, desertion, death, or incapacitation of Iberian personnel destined for the Hispanic Caribbean.

Field Marshall Alexander O'Reilly, whom the Spanish Crown dispatched to the Indies in response to the 1762 British occupation of Havana, was troubled by the large number of Spanish soldiers, stowaways, ship boys, and seamen who jumped ship and remained underground on the island ("Memoria," 387). Some two thousand deserted between 1769 and 1776 alone (Ortiz, 196). In 1786, the Crown offered incentives to anyone who helped in locating and apprehending them.[5] By the end of the century, metropolitan authorities tied desertion to the spread of idleness and criminality in Puerto Rico. Compulsory or voluntary impressment of local men and boys between the ages of fourteen and sixty via the creation of the *gremio de marina* in 1795 was expected to compensate for the large-scale losses of manpower and simultaneously lessen the growing social "problem" of vagrancy.[6]

As part of his overhaul of the island's defense system, O'Reilly assembled nineteen infantry and five cavalry companies. One of the infantry units was composed of *morenos libres* (Martín Rebolo, 96). The origins of the nonwhite detachment date as far back as the 1660s when *Maroons* fleeing to Puerto Rico from the non-Hispanic Caribbean were required to embrace Catholicism and pledge allegiance to Spain before they could be granted sanctuary or set free.

Since then, *Maroon* males were placed in military installations, or conscripted into the Spanish armed forces, or both (Chinea, "A Quest," 61–67). A *moreno* military detachment was in place as early as 1700 (Stark, 557). In 1718 and 1752, elements of the free black corps were successfully deployed against foreign colonists occupying the

[4] See his description of the town of Arecibo in *Diario* (unpaginated).

[5] Archivo General de Puerto Rico, San Juan, Fondo de los Gobernadores Españoles de Puerto Rico, Asuntos de Marina, 1782–1811, caja 272, Circular, Capital [San Juan], December 20, 1800.

[6] Instrucción aprovada por el Rey para el establecimiento y gobierno de un gremio de gente de mar matriculada, en la isla de San Juan de Puerto-Rico y sus aguadas, año 1796, Archivo General de Indias, Santo Domingo 2330.

adjacent island of Vieques (Chinea, "A Quest," 65; Stark, 557). *Mestizos, pardos,* and *morenos libres* may have also served on other units after O'Reilly's 1765 reorganization.

According to his plan, only peninsular and foreign troops loyal to Spain were to be assigned to San Juan's fixed garrison, or *fijo.* This arrangement proved impractical due to difficulties with keeping the garrison manned at full strength. After 1790, it was decided to replace the European forces with local draftees (Martín Rebolo, 207). Given the long history of *racial miscegenation* in Puerto Rico, particularly during the *pre-plantation period,* the soldiery certainly would have included many nonwhites (Chinea, "Fissures," 185–86).

These nonwhite units soon proved their worth on the battlefield. The *milicianos* outmaneuvered a superior British expeditionary force that attempted to take over Puerto Rico in 1797. Although understated in the official accounts of the combat, the active role played by the *morenos libres* in repelling the attack continues to be celebrated by their descendants to this day (Guisti Cordero). The Puerto Rican militia also saw action in Hispaniola, first to keep the slave rebellion that sparked the Haitian Revolution in 1791 from spreading to Santo Domingo and later to expel French occupation forces during the early 1800s (Artola, 451–63; Morales Carrión, "El reflujo," 25).

After Spain reluctantly ceded Santo Domingo to France in the 1795 Treaty of Basle, about 1,500 ex-slaves and free coloreds from Haiti who crossed into the Spanish lines were resettled in Florida, Honduras, Yucatan, Panama, and Cadiz (Geggus, 180–200). Spanish fighting units, including *morenos libres* within their ranks, escorted the Haitians to their new destinations in Central America and Spain, which explains the presence of Manuel and Antonio in Seville in the years leading to the Napoleonic invasion. Or perhaps the father and son were taken to Europe to perform certain specialized jobs within the military that required knowledge of the leather, metal, and woodworking trades, occupations traditionally relegated to slaves and free coloreds. Manuel's employment as a blacksmith in the *maestranza de artillería* (artillery corps) encamped in Seville prior to the French attack seems to support the last scenario.[7]

"In defense of the just rights of Your Majesty"

So states the *memorial* or petition that Manuel and Antonio addressed to His Royal Highness, Ferdinand VII. Likely penned by a trained scribe, the petition followed a well-established format wherein the supplicants explained their grievances and implored the king for redress. Manuel identified himself and his son Antonio as former black officers who had served in an 1808 military mission against the French invaders attempting to permanently unseat the reigning Spanish emperor.

Next, he declared that the *Supreme Junta,* acting in the name of the deposed Spanish king, had endorsed Manuel's request for a job promotion in Puerto Rico and monetary payment in compensation for "his good services." He went on to explain how

[7] Certification issued by Julián Francisco Senesen y Buendía, Capitán del Regimiento de Caballería de Texas y Secretario de la Suprema Junta de esta capital, Seville, November 16, 1808, Ministerio de Cultura, Archivo General de Indias, Ultramar, legajo 446, nos. 1–2.

some ill-intentioned Spaniards refused to honor the aforementioned concessions and, worse still, had him exiled to a remote Spanish *presidio* in Africa, where he worked without pay for two years. The petition concluded by pleading for royal intercession to ensure that the junta's favorable ruling on their behalf be fully carried out.

A cursory reading of this case could lead to the conclusion that this was just a major misunderstanding resulting from the confusing state of wartime affairs or, at worse, another instance of a miscarriage of justice. Even though that may true, the petition also reveals the Afro-Latino pair as active agents who seized an opportunity to counter the socioeconomic barriers stacked against people of color in Spain and the Americas. The standard treatment of the French occupation of Spain in Latin American studies rarely delves deeply into specific Iberian developments.

Rather, it overwhelmingly stresses the breakdown of the colonial bond and the ensuing rise of independence movements across the Indies. Although colonials pledged their lives and material possessions to restore the Spanish Crown to power, few apparently crossed the Atlantic to fight the French.[8] The noticeable silence that surrounds the possible involvement of Amerindians, Africans, or any of the *castas* in the peninsular conflict itself considerably enhances the *memorial*'s historical importance. In an inversion of roles, it tells the story of heroic Afro-Latino soldiers on Spanish soil willingly taking up arms "in defense of the just rights of Your Majesty." And they were not alone. A detachment of twenty-three veteran Haitian auxiliaries who had been relocated to Cadiz around 1796 also volunteered to fight the French, vowing to "spill the last drop of our blood" in defense of Ferdinand VII (Parrilla Ortíz, 195–97).

It is also important to note that Manuel and Antonio Pérez did not act on specific orders from the military chain of command to which they supposedly reported. Instead, they took matters into their own hands by spontaneously organizing a company of armed free colored men that went out to confront the foreign invaders. The fact that Manuel was elected captain and his son second lieutenant of the improvised unit is a strong indication that they possessed vital leadership and fighting skills that perhaps higher-ups in the military had failed to notice, acknowledge, or promote.

Manuel not only decided to join the Spanish resistance movement of his own free will but also did so at no cost to the government. He furnished uniforms to twelve of the soldiers *a su costa,* that is, "at his expense," as opposed to using public or state funding. Moreover, his armed party subsequently engaged the enemy at the Battle of Bailén (July 19–22, 1808) without ever taking salary or remuneration of any kind.

Manuel also played a role in mobilizing the local Sevillean population against the subjects of France in their districts. Manuel confirmed this when he declared that Field Marshall Joachim Murat Loubieré (the Duke of Berg), who oversaw the Napoleonic offensive in Spain, singled him out as the person responsible for drumming up the anti-French backlash in the city. Berg jailed him and sentenced him to death. However,

[8] The Puerto Rican *Creoles* Antonio Valero Bernabé, a leader of the independence movement of Latin America, and Demetrio O'Daly y de la Puente, a liberal who advocated constitutional government under Spanish rule, also fought in Spain against the French. See Quintana (53) and Ribes Tovar (60–61).

after seventeen painful days behind bars, Manuel managed to break free and rejoin the Spanish forces.

Upon learning of Manuel's selfless sacrifice, courage, and determination, Julián Francisco Senesen y Buendía, secretary of the *Junta Suprema* of Seville, praised his "most active fervor and patriotism in the service of the just cause."[9] He also wrote that Manuel had "subsequently distinguished himself in an [unspecified] important service, which made him worthy of this *Supreme Junta*'s recommending him to the governor and captain general of Puerto Rico for an officer position that he has requested in one of the vacant posts of the free colored military regiments."[10] The secretary ordered that Manuel be compensated with one hundred ducats on his departure to Puerto Rico. He directed Manuel to forward his request for medals bearing the bust of Ferdinand VII for himself and his son through Puerto Rico's captain general when he returned to the island.

Despite Manuel's steadfast dedication to the royal cause, unidentified "spiteful and bad Spaniards who have prevailed over the good and loyal ones" deported him to Spanish *presidios* in Ceuta and Alhucema (located in northern Africa), where he toiled without pay for two long years.[11] Despite the setback, Manuel's persistence, sharp powers of observation, excellent memory, and literacy served him well. He had the presence of mind to document or obtain written, legal copies (referred to as numbers 1 and 2 in the *memorial*) of any information that could help clear his name in the future.

His *memorial* tells us that his exile in Ceuta ran from March 29, 1810 through January 6, 1812, and from January 7 through September 2, 1812 at Alhucema. He served gratis as a master blacksmith and locksmith in the artillery and royal arsenal's furnace room in both places, "leaving in one and the other a net benefit to the royal exchequer of a soldier's daily wages and the seven *reales* [illegible] that the master [craftsman] assigned to the post should have drawn, of which he has kept legalized documents to support the truth of his claims."[12]

The episodes narrated by Manuel open a fascinating window to the past in which Africans (as represented by the Haitian auxiliaries exiled in Spain) and Afro-Latinos played major roles. Their actions took place not just in Latin America but also in one of its metropolitan centers. Moreover, their active involvement in the convoluted revolutionary conflicts of the Atlantic world of the late eighteenth century and first decade of the nineteenth, as Bolster has suggested, debunks the pervasive Euroamerican belief that blacks "were acted on, rather than acting [on local, regional, hemispheric, and global affairs]" (2).

[9] Certification issued by Julián Francisco Senesen y Buendía.

[10] Certification.

[11] Archivo General de Indias, Ultramar, legajo 446, Manuel and Antonio Pérez to King, Madrid, November 26, 1814.

[12] Manuel and Antonio Pérez to King, Madrid, November 26, 1814 (see note 11 above).

The *memorial* presented by Manuel and Antonio Pérez supports this view of Afro-Latinos playing important roles in the Atlantic world by revealing the self-actualizing ethos that led them to confront job discrimination, death threats, and differential justice. Future research about the historically neglected contributions of Afro-Latinos in the Iberian peninsula and elsewhere in Europe may well lead to additional insights about this underexplored intercontinental dimension of the African diaspora in the Caribbean.

Memorial de Manuel y Antonio Pérez[1]

Señor,

Manuel Pérez, y a nombre de su hijo Antonio, de color *negros,* oficiales que fueron de milicias de los de su color de la compañía que se formaba en la ciudad de Sevilla en el año de 1808 en defensa de los justos derechos de Vuestra Majestad y recomendado para su colocación en Puerto Rico su *patria* por la Suprema Junta de Sevilla en premio de sus buenos servicios, con la más reverente sumisión a Vuestra Majestad hace presente:

En la ciudad de Sevilla formó una compañía de los de su color de la que fue electo *capitán,* y su hijo subteniente de la misma en el citado año de 1808 habiendo vestido doce soldados a su costa que fueron a lidiar con los enemigos en la Batalla de Baylén, y en todo el tiempo que han servido no han tomado jamás sueldo, ni gratificación alguna; sufrió igualmente 17 días de rigurosa prisión por el duque de Ver, quien mandó se le quitase la vida por autor de la conspiración contra los franceses en Sevilla, y pudo lograr fugarse, la Junta Central penetrada de los sentimientos nobles de este *negro* le concedió (a nombre de Su Majestad) la gracia que manifiesta con las copias número 1 y 2 pero los perniciosos y malos españoles que han tenido facultades sobre los buenos, y leales, hicieron ilusoria aquella gracia, desterrándole a unos de los *presidio*s menores de *África,* con la nota que original pone en las *reales* manos de Vuestra Majestad señalada con el número 3. No cesó de pedir *justicia* con repetidas instancias de las que aún no tuvo la menor noticia; y si la paternal, e incesable piedad de Vuestra Majestad no decreta el indulto de 2 de septiembre próximo, permaneciera aún en su destierro.

Desde 29 de Marzo de 1810, hasta 6 de enero de 1812 ha estado en la *plaza* de Ceuta en calidad de depósito, en cuyo tiempo ha desempeñado el encargo dela fragua de Artillería y Real Maestranza. Y desde 7 del mismo mes y año que fue conducido al de Alhucemas, desempeñó la de maestro de herrero y cerrajero de aquella maestranza, dejando en una y otra, diariamente a beneficio del real erario una ración y siete *reales* [ilegible] doctiva que debía gozar el maestro destinado a este encargo, delo que conserva documentos legalizados para acreditar la verdad de cuanto manifiesta.

Por tanto, a Vuestra Majestad suplican rendidamente que por un efecto de su notoria bondad y *justicia,* se digne presente los servicios de este desgraciado *negro* que no ha omitido el menor esfuerzo en lo posible a favor de la justa causa y en su virtud mandar, se le den nuevos documentos para pasar a su destino (la Isla de Puerto Rico) según está mandado anteriormente, abonándosele igualmente (por mandato de Vuestra Majestad) los cien *ducados* que por vía de gratificación mandó aquella junta se le diesen para emprender su viaje; cuyas ordenes deberán obrar en la Secretaría de Guerra y Marina, y el Gobierno de Cádiz.

[1] Ministerio de Cultura, Archivo General de Indias, Seville, Ultramar 446.

Petition of Manuel and Antonio Pérez

Sir,

Manuel Pérez, and in the name of his son Antonio, free blacks, former officers of the colored militias of the company that was being organized in the city Seville in the year 1808 in defense of the just rights of Your Majesty and recommended for a job in Puerto Rico, his homeland, by the *Supreme Junta* of Seville in recognition of their good services, in reverent submission to Your Majesty states:

In 1808 he organized a colored company in the city of Seville in which he was elected captain, and his son sublieutenant, having furnished uniforms to twelve soldiers who fought at the Battle of Bailén,[1] never drawing salary or any gratification during all the time they have served; he also suffered a rigorous imprisonment for seventeen days at the hands of the Duke of Ver,[2] who ordered his execution for leading a conspiracy against the French in Seville and managed to escape. Moved by the noble sentiments of this black man, the Junta Central granted him (in the name of Your Majesty) the concessions shown in copies numbered 1 and 2, but the spiteful and bad Spaniards who have prevailed over the good and loyal ones have blocked the dispensation, exiling him to one of the minor *presidios* in Africa with the original note indicated in copy 3 that he now places in Your Royal Hands. He did not stop claiming justice through multiple petitions from which he has not yet heard back; had the paternal and tireless mercy of Your Majesty not granted him the reprieve of the past September 2, he would still be in exile.

He has been quartered at the Ceuta fortress from March 29, 1810 to January 6, 1812, during which time he has been assigned to the artillery and royal arsenal's furnace room. From the seventh of the said month and year when he was taken to the Alhucemas one, he worked as a master blacksmith and locksmith of that arsenal, leaving in one and the other a net benefit to the royal exchequer of a soldier's daily wages and the seven *reales* [illegible] per diem that the master [blacksmith and locksmith] assigned to the post should have drawn, of which he has kept legalized documents to support the truth of all he claims.[3]

Therefore, they plead submissively before Your Majesty that on account of your well-known kindness and justice the services of this hapless black man who has not omitted anything possible to support the just cause [of His Majesty] be accredited and on their merits command that he be given new documents to leave for his destiny (the island of Puerto Rico) as previously determined, likewise be paid (by order of Your Majesty) the one hundred *ducados* that the said junta ordered to undertake his voyage, whose instructions should be in the Ministry of War and Navy and the government [office] of Cadiz.

[1] Battle of Bailén (Province of Jaén), where in 1808 Spanish forces first defeated the French army.

[2] Field Marshall Joachim Murat Loubieré (Duke of Berg), who led Napoleon's forces in Spain.

[3] The *presidios* of Ceuta and Alhucemas were located in modern-day Spanish Morocco, northern Africa.

Atendiendo Su Majestad a que los servicios que manifiestan, los han hecho en España, en defensa de la *patria;* piden á Vuestra Majestad les conceda la gracia de las medallas con el Real busto de Vuestra Majestad y que su embarque, sea en un buque de ordenanza por no poder costear un viaje tan dilatado.

Por todo lo que en su destino prometen padre é hijo esforzarse cuanto esté de su parte para mostrar un eterno agradecimiento a su benéfico, y más digno de los monarcas.

Así lo esperan de la paternal clemencia de Vuestra Majestad rogando en todos tiempos al Ente Supremo premie sus desvelos con una feliz y larga vida triunfante siempre de sus enemigos.

Madrid y 26 de Noviembre de 1814
A.L.R.P.D.S.M.
Manuel Pérez
Antonio Pérez

Considering His Majesty that the stated services were carried out in Spain, in defense of the homeland, they ask that His Majesty award them medals bearing the Royal bust of His Majesty and that their passage [to Puerto Rico] be on a military ship due to their inability to defray the costs for such a prolonged trip.

In return for all [entreated], upon arrival at their destiny father and son promise to spare no effort within their reach to demonstrate an eternal appreciation to the beneficent and most dignified of monarchs.

They so expect of the Paternal Clemency of Your Majesty, praying at all times that the Supreme Being reward his efforts with a happy and long life, triumphant always against his enemies.

Madrid, November 26, 1814
A.L.R.P.D.S.M.[4]
Manuel Pérez
Antonio Pérez

[4] *A los reales pies de Su Majestad:* Spanish abbreviation for "at the Royal Feet of Your Majesty."

Glossary

It is with trepidation that we include and define in the Glossary some of the African names used in the documents. **Ethnonyms** used during the Atlantic slave trade era are complex and can be misleading (see "Historical Protagonists and Questions of Identity" in the Introduction). Apparent ethnic designations used to refer to enslaved Africans might designate the port from which they were embarked, a "brand name" that described desirable or undesirable qualities in a slave, or American re-creations of social bonds. Even when they accurately name an origin or language, they do not refer to static cultural identities but often to identities constructed within historically shifting political alliances and oppositions. Without some explanation of these terms, however, it is very difficult to sort out the different general areas from which the identified speakers came and thus the different alliances and conflicts among African-descent groups in the Americas. We recommend the work of Robin Law (see Bibliography) as a starting point to better understand the complexity of how **ethnonyms** were used during the Atlantic slave trade.

Abbreviations used in the Glossary are as follows: E = English; P = Portuguese; Sp = Spanish. These language designations refer to either the language to which the term belongs or the language context in which it is used in this book.

adjunto (P): adjunct; refers to a gathering or collective in the "Dialogue" (Chapter 14).

África (Sp, P): in early colonial times, the northern part of the continent on the Mediterranean coast.

Afroboricua (Sp): a Puerto Rican of African descent; "Boricua" is from Borínquen, the Taíno name for the island before the 1492 Columbian invasion.

Afrocreole (E): an individual of African descent born in the colonial Iberian world, including Africa, identified in documents as "**criollo/criolla**" rather than by African **ethnonym.**

Agolin / Agonli (P): Gbe village west of the Zou River in the Zou province of today's Benin.

agreste (P): transitional morphological region dividing arid hinterlands (**sertão**) from the coast.

aguardiente (Sp): "burning water"; strong rumlike alcohol, usually from sugarcane.

ajuste (Sp): account adjustment.

Akan (E): a people of West Africa primarily in today's Ghana, Ivory Coast, and Togo. The Asante and the Fanti are two groups included in this ethnicity.

albacea (Sp): executor, person charged with implementing a will.

alcalde (Sp): royal municipal authority who executed edicts to maintain order and exercised some police power.

alcalde mayor (Sp): mayor, superior officer, or provincial governor.

alcalde ordinario de segundo voto (Sp): town council authority who administered justice as a trial court judge.

alcance (Sp): the amount outstanding; debt.

alférez (Sp): member of the city council who could preside in the absence of the justice of the peace; also a military rank, something like "second lieutenant"; standard bearer in church or civil ceremonies.

alguacil (Sp): judicial officer of a town or municipality.

almoneda (Sp): auction; in this context a public sale of the property of the testator after his death.

alvara (P): a decree.

amonestada/o (Sp): admonished; admonishment. The inquisitors warned (or admonished) the accused three times over a period of weeks to search their conscience, confess the truth, and trust the mercy of the tribunal.

Anchico (Sp): Also known as Anzicu, Téké, or Bateke: a people who lived north of the Zaire or Congo River, near the Malebo Pool and the Kingdom of Kongo, in the Democratic Republic of Congo, the Republic of Congo, and to a lesser extent in Gabon.

Angola (P, Sp): Portuguese derivation from *ngola,* referring to an object made of iron, which symbolized political authority supported by spiritual forces. Slave traders used the name to refer to people embarked in the Portuguese colony of **Angola,** regardless of their specific ethnic origin.

apercibimiento (Sp): a judge's warning to the accused that his mandate must be carried out and the accused must not repeat the offense or he or she will again be punished.

apoderado (Sp): legal representative with proxy powers.

aquelarre (Sp): from the Basque *akelarre,* meaning "meadow of the male goat"; the witches' assemblies.

Arará (Sp): Allada or Arda; Bight of Benin; powerful Kingdom of Aja-Gbe speakers prior to the rise of Dahomey. A town in the Beninese province of Atlantique now claims the name.

arroba (Sp): a measure of weight equivalent to about thirty-three pounds.

arte de bien querer (Sp): the practice of preparing ointments, concoctions, and charms to bind lovers or unfaithful husbands.

asiento (Sp): royal monopoly granted to export slaves to the Americas.

audiencia (Sp): the hearing at which the prosecution and the defense made their depositions. See also **Real Audienca.**

auditor general (Sp): the principal royal magistrate who heard criminal and civil cases.

auto cabeza de proceso (Sp): order to investigate an alleged crime.

auto (Sp, P): an official act or a legal proceeding; a decree or judge's determination; a dossier detailing the legal actions of a judicial process.

auto-da-fé, pl. autos-da-fé, auto de fe (Sp): a generally public ceremony that concluded some trials of the modern Portuguese and Spanish Inquisitions in which the penitents were read their sentence, renounced their errors, and, in some cases, suffered corporal punishment or execution.

ayudante de la plaza (Sp): subordinate officer of an urban militia who followed the orders of a superior general.

Balanta (P, Sp): ethnic group from the upper Guinea Coast; Guinea-Bissau region.

Bañón (Sp): Also known as Bainuk or Banyun; ethnic group from Senegal and Guinea-Bissau. Their language today is closely related to that of the **Biáfara.**

banza: see **mbanza.**

banzo (P): in West Central Africa, a package of goods exchanged for some other good, used to set standards where there is no shared monetary system.

barrio (Sp): a division of a city, town, or district.

Benguela: a province and a port city in Angola; also a related ethnonym.

Biáfara (Sp): Also known as Beafada or Biafada; a major ethnolinguistic group in West Africa, between the Senegal and Gambia rivers, in the sixteenth and seventeenth centuries.

boga (Sp): literally "paddle"; an organized system of canoe river transportation for a variety of goods and passengers, particularly along the Magdalena River, connecting the New Kingdom of Granada with the Caribbean. It originally relied on involuntary indigenous laborers, but by the close of the sixteenth century they were replaced by enslaved Africans.

bozal, pl. bozales (Sp): a person recently enslaved and brought from Africa to Europe or the Americas who did not speak a European language.

Bran (Sp): Ethnic group from today's Guinea Bissau and Senegal.

buhío (Sp): Also bohío, from Taíno, a type of thatched hut made from wood and mud.

bula (P, Sp): a solemn papal edict or letter. In the 1550 inquiry against Dom Pedro Nkanga a Mvemba (Kongo, Chapter 1), references to the bull show how rooted Christianity was among political classes after only about fifty years. The force of the bull was moral, not political, but could convince the undecided to side with those favored by the Pope.

cabildo (Sp): governing council of a town or city.

Cabo Verde (Sp): the Cape Verde islands, an important center of the slave trade, west of Senegal and Mauritania in Atlantic Africa. By extension, it designates a slave sent from that location independent of his or her ethnic origins.

Camangala (Sp): a present-day Angolan stream in the province of Benguela; **ethnonym** may refer to this area.

Cambunda (P, Sp): place-name associated with the Kimbundu region of what is today Angola; Cambunda **nations** were active in the Río de la Plata region (Argentina and Uruguay). In Brazil, members of colonial confraternities were identied as Cambunda.

candombes (Sp): music and dance style with lively rhythms from the Río de la Plata region, created by African descendants; also refers to celebrations where dances are practiced.

capellán (Sp): chaplain; ecclesiastic charged with performing masses and other liturgical tasks at a chapel.

capellanía (Sp): foundation in which money or goods are given to the Church or a priest to fund the celebration of masses or other pious acts that are beneficial for the salvation of the soul of the grantor.

capitán (Sp): a ranking officer, generally above a first lieutenant and below a major.

capitán a guerra (Sp): a civil authority trained in issues of war; in colonial times these were mayors and governors.

capitania (P): captaincy.

capuchino (Sp) / **capucho** (P): capuchin friar; offshoot of the Catholic Order of Franciscan friars. Capuchin missions were established by the Vatican with Italian personnel in the 1600s in Kongo and Angola and in Brazil, especially Bahia and the Rio São Francisco. There were also missions sent to the Kingdom of Arda, in the Lower Mina coast in the late seventeenth century. They were independent from the Portuguese colonial government and left important historical records, most notably Giovanni Antonio Cavazzi de Montecuccolo's *Istorica Descrizione de tre' regni Congo, Matamba, et Angola* (1687).

Carabalí (Sp): in Spanish colonial documents Carabalí refers to people exported from the ports of the Niger Delta.

cárceles secretas (Sp): the most rigorous of prisons kept by the tribunal of the Inquisition, particularly for the lengthy confinement of prisoners, not detainees, awaiting trial.

carrera de Indias (Sp): trade route used by Spanish fleets to come and go to the Americas.

carta/s de libertad (Sp): deed of **manumission;** written document given to a slave as proof that she or he had been granted freedom.

Casa de Contratación (Sp): the House of Trade; created in Seville in 1503, it supervised commercial affairs, communication, and emigration to the Americas.

casta (Sp): caste; the position of an individual within the hierarchical social system of Spanish-American colonial society, which based rights and obligations on the identification of an individual's ancestry as being of European, African, indigenous, or a combination of them. (See also the Introduction.)

cautivo (Sp): captive, a term used to signal the illegality of forced enslavement.

celda (Sp) / **cell** (E): individual room in convents. Depending on the particular religious order, they were dwellings or simple spaces for prayer and meditation. Sor Teresa's cell (Chapter 13) was outside the cloistered area where other nuns lived.

chalupa (Sp): a small boat or launch, usually with one deck and two masts for sails.

chichería (Sp): a small shop where *chicha* (an alcoholic corn beverage) and other beverages and foods were sold.

cimarrón, pl. cimarrones (Sp): **Maroon** or runaway slave. The word was first used to name livestock that had escaped from its owner to the hilltops and connotes an indomitable or wild nature.

cirio (Sp): tall, thick wax candle used in daily life for its light; also important in Catholic ritual.

clases vulgares (Sp): poor people. In the Latin American context, the term was often applied to **castas,** or racially ostracized groups.

coartación (Sp): a Spanish system of **manumission,** by which a master and slave agreed on a purchase price; after an initial down payment, the slave could purchase his or her freedom in installments over a set period of time.

cobrera/o (Sp): native of the town of El Cobre, Cuba. A term that denotes origin, not slave status.

cocoliste / coliste (Sp): from Náhuatl *cocoliztli,* epidemic disease or typhoid fever.

cofradía (Sp): a confraternity, or religious fraternity that practices pious acts.

compañías de negros libres (Sp): militia made up of African descendants, **mulattoes,** and people of brown complexion.

compatriotas (Sp): local compatriots, fellow villagers.

confesor (Sp): confessor, the priest to whom a Catholic habitually confesses sins and moral transgressions in the Sacrament of Penance. See **director.**

Congo: from Central West Africa, lower Congo River basin, in modern Angola, a general designation rather than specific ethnicity.

Consejo de Indias (Sp): council that dealt with affairs related to the overseas possessions of the Spanish empire.

coro (Sp) / **choir** (E): place in a convent connected to the chapel but divided by a grille from the people, where nuns say their communal prayers. The name also indicates the highest status among nuns, those who perform the daily prayer of the Church. Sor Teresa Chicaba (Chapter 13) was not expected to participate in the coro.

corregimiento (Sp): regional subdivision of a territory presided over by a *corregidor.*

Coura: region far inland of the Bight of Benin; possibly related to the Beninese town of Aledjo-koura in the Donga province where the people speak a Yoruba dialect.

covacha (Sp): hovel or small dwelling; literally "a small cave."

Creole (E) / **Criollo/a** (Sp) / **Crioulo/a** (P): In Central Africa, the mixed culture that had evolved from the interactions between the Portuguese and the Kimbundu, including language, Christianity, naming patterns, and the like. In Spanish America, someone born in the Americas who was not of indigenous ancestry; used to refer to people of both African and European descent.

criada/o (Sp): laborer; servants or slaves who normally lived in the homes of their masters.

cuadrilla (Sp): squad; used to refer to gangs who hunted runaway slaves.

cuarterón (Sp): in theory, someone who was of one-fourth African origin and therefore considered "whiter" than a **mulato.** In practice, **mulato** and **cuarterón** were used interchangeably because the designations did not imply a change in rights and obligations.

curador (P): guardian; one who has legal responsibility to represent another, such as a minor.

Dagome / Dahomey (E, P, Sp): West African kingdom of Fon speakers; now the Republic of Benin, and related ethnonym (Dagome).

Dassa / Za (E): Yoruba village inside Mahi land. Today the name designates a city in the Zou province of Benin.

depositario (Sp): the title of an office of someone who kept slaves or other possessions or goods that were the subject of litigation.

desamparado (Sp): defenseless, unprotected.

deshonestidades (Sp): immoral acts.

devassa (P): a legal inquest.

devoção (P): literally a "devotion" to a saint or a particular religious manifestation, such as to the souls in purgatory. The idea of devotion is not the same as worship, because in Catholicism only God can be worshipped; so the faithful express their devotion to different figures and ideas. A group united in their devoção might organize a confraternity (see Chapter 14).

diasporic identity (E): cultural markers that are reshaped by a person's or group's history of migration or dispersion outside their original homelands.

director (Sp) / **spiritual director** (E): a spiritual advisor—not necessarily a confessor—who is familiar with the experiences a soul commonly encounters in developing a close relationship with God and who can provide counsel in the spiritual process of seeking transcendence.

disposiciones (Sp): royal decrees.

Dominican Order (E): the Order of Preachers, founded in 1216 by Saint Dominic Guzman to promote the conversion and salvation of souls through dynamic and informed preaching that conformed to Catholic doctrine.

dote (Sp) / **dowry** (E): as in traditional marriages, nuns—who will become brides of Christ—donate money, goods, or real estate to the general fund (endowment) of the convent.

ducado (Sp): gold coin of varying monetary value used in Spain and its American colonies.

Elmina (E, P, Sp): port city located in the central coast of today's Ghana. See also **Gold Coast.**

encomendero (Sp): Spaniard who holds the grant of an Indian town or its labor.

encomienda (Sp): literally "assignment"; errand. During colonial times in the Americas, this term was used for the assignment in which indigenous peoples were forced to work as tributaries to the Spanish authorities, who in turn were charged with their evangelization.

escribanía (Sp): notary office. In colonial cities, these offices were frequently situated in or near the town's main square because most colonial administrative institutions occupied this social and symbolic central space.

escribano (Sp) / **escrivão** (P): notary or clerk; a person authorized to document civil, religious, or commercial formalities and legalize documents. *Escribanos de número* were assigned to a specific town or city, and *escribanos reales* had royal permission to work in different parts of the realm. Specific colonial institutions also had notaries assigned to them.

estancia (Sp): a small farm that grew food crops for market, especially to transport to urban areas.

estaos e casa (P): the buildings where the Lisbon Inquisition carried out its court sessions and where prisoners were kept.

ethnonym (E): a name attributing ethnic identity, but in the Black Atlantic often imposed by slave traders based on port of embarkation.

Etiopía (Sp): during the sixteenth and seventeenth centuries, the word **"Etiopía"** (Ethiopia) simultaneously described Africa to the south of the Sahara and what was known in the medieval imagination as the Kingdom of Ethiopia, which embraced Christianity in the fourth century AD. Although in religious and historical literature the term *etíope* (Ethiopian) sometimes describes a person from this kingdom, it was mostly used in the colonial setting as a learned synonym for "negro" (black).

Eurocreole (E): "white" Spanish-Americans belonging to either the **Creole** or Iberian social group.

expediente (Sp): legal dossier.

fidalgo (P): a noble person. In Kongo, as in Portugal, nobility was determined by birth, but position and authority were more generally dependent on royal favor.

Folupo/a: A small ethnicity located in the Guinea Bissau region.

forro (P): blacks who had gained their freedom; literally "freed blacks."

fuero (Sp): jurisdictional codes granted to a religious, military, or political entity.

geração (P): probably the Portuguese translation of the Kikongo word *kanda* (plural *makanda*), which often means "lineage" or "clan." In Kongo, *makanda* were complex sets of alliances including political clients and slaves. It has a secondary meaning of faction; brothers and their followers might form two separate *makanda.*

gobernador intendente (Sp): person in charge of the city council.

Gold Coast or **Mina Coast** (E) / **Mina Baja del Oro** (Sp) / **Costa da Mina** (P): For Paniagua (Chapter 13), the Mina Baja del Oro is the area east of Elmina Castle (São Jorge da Mina) in Ghana roughly to the Volta River, where the Slave Coast begins. In Portuguese, the Mina Coast is the Slave Coast.

gremio (Sp): guild; association of people of the same trade or occupation ruled by norms and statutes, formed to protect mutual interests and maintain standards.

gremio de marina (Sp): naval guild.

grumete (Sp): a Spanish sailor learning the trade, ranked below a full sailor and above the younger *pajes* dedicated to cleaning and serving the officers and crew.

guanajo (Sp): from Taíno; turkey.

Guinea (Sp, P): first used by Portuguese navigators to refer to coastal West Africa; later loosely applied to the general area of sub-Saharan West Africa connected to the slave trade until the late eighteenth century.

hacendado/a (Sp): owner of estates or ranches.

hato (Sp): open cattle ranch.

horro/a (Sp): a manumitted slave.

hueco (Sp): vacant plot of land.

ídem (Sp): the same as something previously mentioned, used to note every new entry in a list.

indio (Sp): label for indigenous people in the Americas; for the Spanish this was a legal category with assigned rights, such as communal land rights, and assigned obligations, such as paying tribute and providing draught labor.

indulgencia (Sp): indulgence. In Roman Catholic theology, an indulgence is the total or partial remission of the spiritual punishment associated with a sin. In the context of a will, testators express their wish to use their remaining earthly possessions after they die to obtain such indulgences and hence they declare their soul universal heir of those possessions.

inquirição (P): inquest, a legal procedure often to determine the culprits of a crime, scandal, or other disruption of public order.

inquisidor fiscal (Sp): prosecuting attorney of the Inquisition.

in solidum (Latin) / **in sólidum** (Sp): legal term referring to a jointly held responsibility in which each party is fully responsible for payments or duties.

inventario (Sp): inventory; in the context of a will, a complete list of items that were the property of the testator.

Jaga (P): first used to describe invaders or rebels of uncertain origin who invaded Kongo in 1568. After about 1600 the term was applied to an entirely different group, the Imbangala, whose roots lay in the central highlands of modern Angola, and who invaded the Ndongo kingdom before being brought into Portuguese service after 1615. They played a role in both sides in the battle of Ndongo that was waged between Portugal, Njinga, and her Mbundu rivals between 1617 and 1657.

Jolofa/o (Sp): also known as Wolof; a confederation of Senegambia states that broke up into several different kingdoms during the mid-sixteenth century.

jornal (Sp): wage.

jornalera/o (Sp): slave allowed to work for wages outside of the owner's home and obligated to pay the owner a daily or monthly fee, keeping some of the money to acquire goods, pay for a room, and even purchase freedom.

juez ordinario (Sp): ecclesiastic judge or person who knows the causes and actions of a dispute.

junta de poblaciones (Sp): board or council whose policy was to attract indigenous populations into nuclear settlements to found towns.

justicia (Sp): judge or public official who represented the king; the word can also be used to mean "justice."

justicia ordinaria (Sp): the administration of justice within a specific geographical jurisdiction.

juzgado (Sp): judicial court.

La Mina Baja Del Oro (Sp): see **Mina Coast.**

ladino (Sp, P): "latinized," person acculturated to Iberian social norms. The term is primarily used to refer to non-Iberians who became conversant in Spanish or Portuguese. The term also implies adherence to the Catholic faith and loyalty to the Iberian monarchies; cf. **bozal.**

lebambo / libambu (P): from Kikongo, a forked stick or a chain that was placed around a prisoner's neck as a restraining device; in general any device used to restrain prisoners or slaves.

letrado (Sp): a person of letters, usually related to the legal profession.

libre albedrío (Sp): free will.

licenciado (Sp) **/ licentiate** (E): title addressing someone who holds a university degree.

limpieza de sangre (Sp): purity of blood, a social and quasilegal concept that excluded people who did not have "old" Christian ancestry. Among those excluded were descendants of Jews, Muslims, indigenous people in the Americas, and people of African descent.

Lucumí (Sp): The term is supposed to have appeared through the Yoruba greeting *oluku mi* ("my friend!"). However, it was used over time to refer to various neighboring peoples of Yoruba. In seventeenth-century Spanish America, it referred to a speaker of Yoruba or suggested noble or elite characteristics associated with the Dahomey or Oyo kingdoms within the interior of the Bight of Benin.

Luso-African (E): African-born and, generally, familiar with Catholic practices and Portuguese language and other cultural attributes such as food and dress. Sometimes used to refer to Portuguese men who had lived for many years in Africa, it especially applied to their mixed-race descendants born of African mothers.

Luso-Brazilian (E): pertaining to Portugal, Brazil, and Lusophone African cultures.

maese de campo (Sp): field commander, chief administrative officer of the province, with the status of commander general of all royal troops within the province.

Maki / Makino (P): people of the Maki Kingdom on the Mina coast (Bight of Benin), neighboring Dahomey to the northeast.

Malemba (Sp): port city of the Kakongo Kingdom, also the area west of the Luando River valley. Enslaved people referred to as Malembas likely came from this area.

manatí (Sp): manatee leather.

Mancera, Marquis of (E): Antonio Sebastián de Toledo (1608–1715). His third wife, Juliana Teresa Portocarrero y Meneses, was the legal owner of Sor Teresa de Santo Domingo (Chicaba). Mancera was a member of the Council of State under Carlos II of Spain and had been viceroy of Mexico (1664–1673), where his second wife was the protector of writer Sor Juana Inés de la Cruz.

mandadores (Sp): appointed officials; also used in some **Maroon** communities to refer to leadership positions.

Mandé (E, Sp): large ethnic group of West Africa.

mani (Kikongo): sixteenth-century spelling of the Kikongo word *mwene,* a person holding authority or a title. It is followed by the name of the territory they are deputed to govern or the office they fulfill.

manillas (Sp): bracelets, normally made of bronze and used as currency in West Africa for the purchase of slaves. They are frequently mentioned in documents as cargo for slave ships en route to West Africa.

manumission (E): the formal act of freeing someone from slavery.

Maroon (E): see **cimarrón.**

marronage (E): flight from enslavement.

mayor (Sp): superior or leader of a community.

mayoral (Sp): foreman or farm manager, person in charge of supervising and enforcing the slaves' labor.

mayordomo (Sp): head servant of a household or member of a confraternity charged with administering funds and overseeing functions.

mbanza: Kimbundu word referring to a communal compound.

memorial (Sp): document in which something is petitioned.

mestizo/a (Sp): a person of mixed European and Amerindian ancestry.

metropole (E): the parent state of a colony.

Middle Passage (E): the journey of captive Africans from their homelands to the Americas.

milicianos (Sp): members of an armed militia.

milicias urbanas (Sp): urban militias.

Mina (E, P, Sp): name used to refer to people brought to the Americas from **Elmina** and the Gold Coast or Slave Coast areas; in Brazil the term refers to Ewe-Fon group from modern Benin.

Mina Coast or **Lower Mina** (E) / **Mina Baja del Oro** (Sp) / **Costa da Mina** (P): see **Gold Coast.**

moço de capela (P): literally "chapel boy." In Kongo, however, they could be adults; King Diogo sent them on diplomatic missions and to evangelize foreign countries.

monterías (Sp): hunting grounds.

morena/o (Sp): in colonial Spanish America, a person of African descent, possibly enslaved, but usually signifying a person who has freed herself or himself.

morenos libres (Sp): free blacks.

morisco (Sp): a Moor who has converted to Christianity and his or her descendants.

muenho (P): Kimbundu word meaning "life," "life soul," or "spirit." Among the Mbundu, the title probably referred to an official spokesperson.

mulato/a (Sp, P) / **mulatto** (E): an individual of mixed European and African origins. *Mulatos* had a social and legal status that was usually more permissive than that assigned to *negros.*

nação, pl. nações (P) / **nación, pl. naciones** (Sp) / **nation** (E): place of origin or linguistic group of a slave or a slave's family. Frequently this term was assigned to the area where the person had been enslaved according to the geographical divisions established by Europeans as part of the slave trade. These identities are not accurate indications of specific African ethnic groups; nevertheless, in the Iberian colonies they played an important role in the cultural and social organization of black communities. For Africans in Brazil, *nações* were more or less constructed identities and reflected alliances specific to certain contexts and not necessarily to a specific geographic territory.

narrative agency (E): the control exercised by a speaker or writer over the content and form of the story he or she tells.

negra/o, negrita/o (Sp): an individual of African descent; often used to refer to black slaves, as distinct from free blacks (*negros horros*). The diminutive *negrito/a* is used to refer to black people with a sense of familiarity—whether welcome or not. Sor Teresa Chicaba (Chapter 13) is still referred to as La Negrita today in the literature published by the Dominican Order.

new Christians (E): descendants of Jews converted to Christianity under duress in 1492 in Spain and shortly thereafter in Portugal and later the target of accusations of Judaism.

novenario / novena (Sp): a liturgical act referring to a nine-day period of worship and sermons dedicated to a saint.

ouvidor (P): magistrate; in the sixteenth century a person responsible for hearing complaints and charges, usually a judicial office in this case.

Oyo (E, P, Sp): Yoruba empire (fifteenth through nineteenth centuries) established in what is now Nigeria, Togo, and Benin.

pacto (Sp): a pact; in the context of Chapter 11, a pact with the devil implies the act of offering or subjugating oneself to the devil.

palenque (Sp): literally "palisade" or defensive fence made of stakes. The term refers to clandestine **Maroon** communities where homes were built and food crops were planted.

papel de venta (Sp): legal recourse by which a slave could request a transfer of ownership.

paradigm (E): interpretation or model.

parda/o (Sp): brown, **mulatto;** can also refer to a **zambo.** In mid-colonial Spanish America, a person of color born or raised as a free person.

patache (Sp): a service boat normally used to ferry passengers or supplies between a larger ship and the shore.

patria (Sp): homeland; literally "fatherland".

peça (P): piece (in Spanish, *pieza de Indias*); the value of a healthy slave between fifteen and twenty-five years old.

peso (Sp): a standard currency in colonial Spanish America worth eight **reales.**

plaza (Sp): garrison, fortress, or town/city square.

pombeiro (P): slave-trading agents who traveled the interior of Angola.

pre-plantation period (E): historical period generally associated with the absence of large landed estates known as *haciendas* or plantations in a particular colony or country.

presidio (Sp): correctional facility; fortress.

prisiones / grillos (Sp): chains and other instruments with which prisoners are secured in a jail.

privateer (E): an armed ship owned by private individuals holding a government commission and authorized for use in war.

processo (P): legal proceedings.

protocolos notariales (Sp): collection of files kept by public notaries where documents and legal transactions among individuals were recorded.

provedor (P): purveyor, a judicial official whose duty was to inform superiors of illegal activity.

pueblo (Sp): a village; legal category for a population settlement constituting a corporate community.

pulpería (Sp): store that sold various goods such as food, liquor, textiles, and tools.

quilombo (P): from the Kimbundu word *kilombo,* referring to a military encampment.

Quisama (Sp): a large district south of the Kwanza River (Angola).

racial miscegenation (E): interracial mixture.

ranchería (Sp): group of ranches that form a community.

real/es (Sp): silver coin and standard currency in colonial Spanish America, with eight *reales* equaling one **peso** in the seventeenth century.

Real Audiencia (Sp): judicial body, high court of appeal, and viceregal council; in the absence of a viceroy, it could govern a territory.

real cédula (Sp): royal decree.

Real Senhoria (P): a Portuguese title of the king of Kongo, drawn from his official title of "King of Kongo and Lord of the Mbundus."

reconciliada/o (Sp): an individual found guilty by the Inquisition who received absolution and was reconciled to the faith under the terms of grace.

regente/a (P) / **regent** (E): a regent; one who rules in place of a king or queen when absent or unable to rule.

Relação (P): the highest court in Brazil; the appellate court.

relación (Sp): a narrative; in the religious context, a document written about one's life and spiritual experiences following the command and under the guidance of a spiritual **director.**

remedio (Sp): remedy, sustenance.

remesón (Sp): a shaking or pulling out a handful of hair.

renda (P): a revenue-bearing property; in Kongo **rendas** could be freely given and withdrawn by the king or other high officials.

royal slaves (E): known as *esclavos del rey* in Spanish; slaves owned by the king or the state.

Sabaru (P): Gbe village inside Mahi land, which is today in the Zou province of Benin.

sankofa (Akan): among the Akan people, literally "go back and take." It represents the need to return to the past and reclaim what was good and worthwhile. Among some people of African descent exiled in the diaspora, it also represented a return to one's ancestral homeland after death.

São Tomé (P): former Portuguese island colony in the Gulf of Guinea that acted as a clearinghouse for slaves coming from Angola, Kongo, and the Lower Mina region.

sargento mayor (Sp): often translated as "sergeant major"; a senior operating officer second in command to the **maese de campo.**

sargento mayor de la plaza (Sp): subordinate officer of an urban militia, superior to a sergeant.

secta de las brujas (Sp): witches' sect, word used in an accusatory manner to refer to a group of men and women who allegedly rejected God and the sacraments and worshipped the devil.

sertão (P): an arid, inland region (hinterlands).

sevicia (Sp): juridical term that refers to physical and psychological cruelty.

subaltern agents (E): phrase used in postmodernist and postcolonial studies to refer to the oppressed, voiceless, or marginal elements of a society.

Supreme Junta (E) / **Junta Suprema** (Sp): regal council that took over the governmental functions of Spain and its overseas colonies during the Napoleonic invasion.

tabelião (P): notary.

tambo (Sp): in Río de la Plata, dance of African descendants or hidden place where they gathered to perform dances.

tambuquado, tambuquara (P): from the Kikongo word *tambuka,* meaning "to remove from office." The verb was conjugated according to Portuguese rules in this text (Chapter 1), as was the custom for all borrowed words.

tartana (Sp): sailing vessel with one mast and a lateen sail.

tenedor de bienes (Sp): person named by a testator to keep and inventory his property after his death.

teniente de capitán general (Sp): military officer appointed to undertake the duties of the field marshall during his absence.

teniente del rey (Sp): governor deputy; cf. **teniente gobernador.**

teniente general (Sp): general deputy; an office of wide colonial power, whose appointment was ratified by the vice regal government; abbreviated as *teniente.*

teniente gobernador (Sp): deputy governor; person appointed to undertake the duties of the governor in his or her absence.

tercera, terciara (Sp) / **tertiary** (E): third-order nun; a tertiary nun, one who belongs to one of the tertiary orders of a religious institute (Dominicans, Franciscans). Sor Teresa de Santo Domingo, Chicaba (Chapter 13), is referred to as a *tercera,* but her status in the convent was more like the black *donadas* of Spanish America, who entered the religious community in service to the ranking members. Tertiaries were laity—the faithful outside the ranks of the clergy—who, influenced by the spiritual practices and piety of a monastic Catholic religious congregation, entered into a formal relationship with that order and lived lives in accordance to the Rule. In 1285, Munio de Zamora united disparate groups of laity who called themselves the Order of Penance under a rule titled the Penance of Saint Dominic. This third order, unlike many others, includes a few cloistered convents of nuns as wells as some active congregations of sisters and laity organized in fraternities. Teresa Chicaba was a member of an enclosed community of nuns; however, her status in that convent was unique. Paniagua refers to her as a tertiary, as if she were a vowed lay person attached to La Penitencia in Salamanca. His description would make her a tertiary of the Tertiary Order of Penitence. His inability to clearly define her status among Dominicans accentuates her marginality among her sisters.

termo (P): an entry; a record of one of the acts of an organization; a written declaration that forms part of a trial.

Terranova (Sp): person who came, usually, to Perú as a slave from the East Guinea coast.

terreiro (P): a public square; in Kikongo *mbazi;* typically a place where public business was conducted. The **terreiro** or *mbazi* in Mbanza Kongo was located between the palace and the church of São Salvador (built in 1549). This church is still standing, and the palace grounds are well known.

transculturated / **transculturation** (E): a term coined by Cuban sociologist Fernando Ortiz in 1940 to describe the process of selective cultural transformation in areas of intercultural contact.

vecina/o (Sp): neighbor, or a long-term inhabitant of a particular town or city; generally refers to property holders or heads of household and signifies a reputable person. When

used as a legal term, *vecino* is akin to the word "citizen" but on a local level. *Vecinos* were entitled to rights and privileges not enjoyed by outsiders, and they had corresponding responsibilities to the community.

vega (Sp): in the Caribbean, a tobacco farm.

villa (Sp): a town; legal category for a large incorporated population settlement.

virrey (Sp): viceroy, the highest political officer in Spanish America; one who represented the power and authority of the king of Spain. There were two viceroyalties originally—Mexico and Perú.

visto (Sp): decree.

VM (P): *Vossa Mercê,* an address of respect that became *você,* the third person, which is now used as the simple "you." In Spanish, *Vuestra Merced.*

zamba/o (Sp, P): individual of mixed indigenous and African descent. From a legal point of view, **zambos** were considered part of the **mulato** caste. Socially, however, they occupied a more difficult position as the offspring of two castes that were considered morally and intellectually inferior to Spaniards. Some **zambos** lived closer to indigenous communities than to European society, which also led them to occupy a unique cultural space.

Zape (Sp): a people from what is modern-day Sierra Leone.

Bibliography

Introduction

Andrews, George Reid. *Afro-Latin America, 1800–2000.* New York: Oxford UP, 2004.

Butler, Judith. *Gender Trouble: Feminism and the Subversion of Identity.* New York: Routledge, 1999.

García Canclini, Néstor. *Hybrid Cultures: Strategies for Entering and Leaving Modernity.* Introduction by Renato Rosaldo. Trans. Christopher L. Chiappari and Silvia L. López. Minneapolis: U of Minnesota P, 2005.

Gilroy, Paul. *The Black Atlantic: Modernity and Double Consciousness.* London: Verso, 1993.

Klein, Herbert S. *The Atlantic Slave Trade.* Cambridge: Cambridge UP, 1999.

Lienhard, Martín. "De mestizajes, heterogeneidades, hibridismos y otras quimeras." In *Asedios a la heterogeneidad cultural: Libro en homenaje a Antonio Cornejo Polar,* 57–80. Edited by José Antonio Mazzotti and Ulises Juan Zevallos Aguilar. Philadelphia: Asociación Internacional de Peruanistas, 1996.

———. "Padrões da cosmologia congo e sua adaptação-recriação na América escravista." *Anais de História de Além-Mar (Lisboa)* 1 (2000): 245–72.

———. "Una tierra sin amos: Lectura de los testimonios legales de algunos esclavos fugitivos (Puerto Rico y Brasil, siglo XIX)." *América Indígena* 54, no. 4 (1994): 209–27.

Lorenzo Cadarso, Pedro Luis. *La documentación judicial en la época de los Austrias: Estudio archivístico y diplomático,* 2nd ed. Caceres, Spain: Plaza, 2004. [The first edition of this book (1998) can be read online at the Web site of the Facultad de Biblioteconomía y Documentación, Departamento de Historia, Universidad de Extremadura (Badajoz), http://alcazaba.unex.es/~plorenzo/publicaciones/libros/docaust.html. Accessed Jan. 7, 2009.

Modern Language Association Ad Hoc Committee on Foreign Language. "Foreign Languages and Higher Education: New Structures for a Changed World." Modern Language Association. 2007. http://www.mla.org/flreport. Accessed Jan. 7, 2009.

Ortiz, Fernando. *Contrapunteo cubano del tabaco y el azúcar.* Caracas, Venezuela: Biblioteca Ayacucho, 1978.

Rama, Ángel. *Transculturación narrativa en América Latina,* 2nd ed. Mexico City: Siglo Veintiuno, 1985.

Restall, Matthew. "A History of the New Philology and the New Philology in History." *Latin American Research Review* 38, no. 1 (2003): 113–34.

White, Hayden. *The Content of the Form: Narrative Discourse and Historical Representation.* Baltimore, MD: Johns Hopkins UP, 1987.

Chapter 1

Balandier, Georges. *Daily Life in the Kingdom of Kongo: Sixteenth to Eighteenth Centuries.* Trans. Helen Weaver. New York: Pantheon, 1968.

Bontinck, François. "Ndoadidiki Ne-Kino a Mubemba, premier évêque Kongo (c. 1495–c. 1531)." *Revue africaine de théologie* 3 (1979): 149–69.

Brásio, António, ed. *Monumenta missionaria africana.* 11 vols. Lisbon: Agência-Geral do Ultramar, 1952–1971.

Cardoso, Mateus. *Historia do Reino de Congo.* First published 1624. Ed. António Brásio. Lisbon: Centro de Estudos Históricos Ultramarinos, 1969.

Cavazzi da Montecuccolo, Giovanni Antonio. *Istorica descrizione de' tre' regni Congo: Matamba et Angola.* Bologna, Italy: Giacomo Monti, 1687.

Heywood, Linda. "Slavery and Its Transformation in the Kingdom of Kongo, 1491–1800." *Journal of African History* 50, no. 1 (2009): 1–22.

Heywood, Linda, and John Thornton. *Central Africans, Atlantic Creoles, and the Foundation of the Americas, 1585–1660.* Cambridge: Cambridge UP, 2007.

Hilton, Ann. *The Kingdom of Kongo.* Oxford: Oxford UP, 1985.

Lopes, Duarte, and Filippo Pigafetta. *Relazione del Reame di Congo et della Circonvince Contrade.* Rome, 1591. Edited by Giorgio Cardonna. Milan: Bompiani, 1978.

Paiva Manso, Levy Maria Jordão, Visconde de. *História do Congo.* Lisbon: Academia Real das Sciencias, 1877.

Thornton, John. *Africa and Africans in the Making of the Atlantic World, 1400–1800,* 2nd ed. Cambridge: Cambridge UP, 1998.

———. "The Development of an African Catholic Church in the Kingdom of Kongo, 1491–1750." *Journal of African History* 25, no 2 (1984): 147–67.

———. "Early Kongo-Portuguese Relations: A New Interpretation." *History in Africa* 8 (1981): 183–204.

———. "Elite Women in the Kingdom of Kongo: Historical Perspectives on Women's Political Power." *Journal of African History* 47, no. 3 (2006): 437–60.

———. *The Kingdom of Kongo: Civil War and Transition, 1641–1718.* Madison: U of Wisconsin P, 1983.

———. "The Origins and Early History of the Kingdom of Kongo, c. 1350–1550." *International Journal of African Historical Studies* 34, no. 1 (2001): 89–120.

Vansina, Jan. *Kingdoms of the Savanna.* Madison: U of Wisconsin P, 1966.

———. *Paths in the Rainforest: Toward a History of Political Traditional in Equatorial Africa.* Madison: U of Wisconsin P, 1990.

———, and Téofile Obenga. "The Kongo Kingdom and Its Neighbors." In *Africa from the Sixteenth to the Eighteenth Century,* 546–87. Edited by B. A. Ogot. Vol. 5 of the *UNESCO General History of Africa.* Berkeley: U of California P, 1992.

Chapter 2

Alcina Franch, José. "Penetración española en Esmeraldas tipología del descubrimiento." *Revista de Indias* 36, nos. 143–244 (1976): 65–121.

Andrien, Kenneth J. *The Kingdom of Quito, 1690–1830: The State and Regional Development.* New York: Cambridge UP, 1995.

Bailyn, Bernard. *Atlantic History: Concept and Contours.* Cambridge, MA: Harvard UP, 2005.

Beatty-Medina, Charles. "Between the Cross and the Sword: Religious Conquest and Maroon Legitimacy in Sixteenth- and Early Seventeenth-Century Esmeraldas." In *Africans to Colonial Spanish America.* Edited by Sherwin K. Bryant, Rachel S. O'Toole, and Ben Vinson III. Urbana-Champaign: U of Illinois P (forthcoming).

———. "Caught between Rivals: The Spanish-African Maroon Competition for Captive Labor in the Region of Esmeraldas during the Late Sixteenth and Early Seventeenth Centuries." *The Americas* 63, no. 1 (2006): 113–36.

———. "Rebels and Conquerors: African Slaves, Spanish Authorities, and the Domination of Esmeraldas, 1563–1621." PhD diss., Brown University, 2002.

Bryant, Sherwin K. "Finding Gold, Forming Slavery: The Creation of a Classic Slave Society, Popayán, 1600–1700." *The Americas* 63, no. 1 (2006): 81–112.

Cabello Balboa, Miguel. "Verdadera descripción y relación larga de la Provincia y tierra de las Esmeraldas" In *Obras,* Vol. 1, 7–76. Edited by Jacinto Jijón y Caamaño. Quito, Ecuador: Ecuatoriana, 1945.

Calero, Luís Fernando. *Chiefdoms under Siege: Spain's Rule and Native Adaptation in the Southern Colombian Andes, 1535–1700.* Albuquerque: U of New Mexico P, 1997.

Elliot, J. H. "The Spanish Conquest." In *Colonial Spanish America,* 1–59. Edited by Leslie Bethell. Cambridge: Cambridge UP, 1987.

Genovese, Eugene D. *From Rebellion to Revolution: Afro-American Slave Revolts in the Making of the Modern World.* New York: Vintage Books, 1981.

Lane, Kris E. *Quito 1599: City and Colony in Transition.* Albuquerque: U of New Mexico P, 2002.

Newson, Linda A. *Life and Death in Early Colonial Ecuador.* Norman: U of Oklahoma P, 1995.

Ortiz de la Tabla Ducasse, Javier. *Los encomenderos de Quito, 1534–1660: Origen y evolución de una élite colonial.* Seville: Escuela de Estudios Hispano-Americanos, 1993.

Parris, Scott V. "Alliance and Competition: Four Case Studies of Maroon-European Relations." *Nieuwe West-Indische Gids* 55 (1981): 174–224.

Phelan, John Leddy. *The Kingdom of Quito in the Seventeenth Century.* Madison: U of Wisconsin P, 1967.

Pike, Ruth. *Aristocrats and Traders: Sevillian Society in the Sixteenth Century.* Ithaca, NY: Cornell UP, 1972.

Powers, Karen Vieira. *Andean Journeys: Migration, Ethnogenesis, and the State in Colonial Quito.* Albuquerque: U of New Mexico P, 1995.

Price, Richard, ed. *Maroon Societies: Rebel Slave Communities in the Americas,* 3rd ed. Baltimore, MD: Johns Hopkins UP, 1996.

Restall, Matthew. "Black Conquistadors: Armed Africans in Early Spanish America." *The Americas* 57, no. 2 (2000): 171–205.

———. *Seven Myths of the Spanish Conquest.* Oxford: Oxford UP, 2003.

———, ed. *Beyond Black and Red: African-Native Relations in Colonial Latin America.* Albuquerque: U of New Mexico P, 2005.

Rueda Novoa, Rocio. *Zambaje y autonomía: Historia de la gente negra de la provincia de Esmeraldas, siglos XVI–XVIII.* Quito, Ecuador: Abya-Yala, 2001.

Savoia, P. Rafael, ed. *El negro en la historia.* Quito, Ecuador: Ediciones Afroamerica, Centro Cultural Afroecuatoriano, 1992.

Szaszdi, Adam. "El Transfondo de un cuadro: 'Los mulatos de Esmeraldas' de Andrés Sánchez Galque." *Cuadernos Prehispánicos* 12 (1986–1987): 93–142.

Williams, Caroline. *Between Resistance and Adaptation: Indigenous Peoples and the Colonisation of the Chocó, 1510–1753.* Liverpool, UK: Liverpool UP, 2005.

Chapter 3

Birmingham, David. "Central Africa from Cameroun to the Zambezi." In *The Cambridge History of Africa,* Vol. 4, 325–83. Edited by J. D. Fage and Roland Anthony Oliver. Cambridge: Cambridge UP, 1986.

Brásio, Padre António, ed. *Monumenta missionaria africana: África Ocidental.* 15 vols. Lisbon: Agência-Geral do Ultramar, 1971.

Cadornega, António de Oliveira de. *História geral das guerras angolanas: 1680.* Annotated and edited by José Matias Delgado. Vol. 2. Lisbon: Agência-Geral do Ultramar, 1972.

Heintze, Beatrix. *Fontes para a história de Angola do século XVII.* Vol. 1. Stuttgart, Germany: Franz Steiner Verlag, 1985.

Heywood, Linda M., ed. *Central Africans and Cultural Transformations in the American Diaspora.* Cambridge: Cambridge UP, 2002.

Heywood, Linda, and John Thornton. *Central Africans, Atlantic Creoles, and the Foundation of the Americas, 1585–1660.* Cambridge: Cambridge UP, 2007.

Miller, Joseph Calder. *Kings and Kinsmen: Early Mbundu States in Angola.* Oxford: Clarendon, 1976.

Montecuccolo, Giovanni Antonio Cavazzi de. *Istorica descrizione de' tre' regni Congo, Matamba, et Angola.* Bologna, Italy: Giacomo Monti, 1687.

Napoli, Antonio Gaeta da. *La maravigliosa conversione alla Santa Fede di Cristo della Regina Singa e del svo Regno di Matamba nell'Africa meridionale.* Naples, Italy: Passaro, 1669.

Njinga of Ndongo, Rainha. Letter to António de Oliveira de Cadornega, June 15, 1660. In *Histórica geral das guerras angolanas,* 172–73. First published 1680. Annotated and edited by José Matias Delgado. Vol. 2. Lisbon: Agência-Geral do Ultramar, 1972.

———. Letter to Bento Banha Cardoso, March 3, 1625. In *Fontes para a história de Angola do século XVII,* Vol. 1, 244–45. Edited by Beatrix Heintze. Stuttgart, Germany: Franz Steiner Verlag, 1985.

———. Letter to Luís Mendes de Sousa Chicorro, Governor General of Angola, December 13, 1655. In *Monumenta missionario africana; África ocidental (1651–1655),* 524–28. Edited by Padre António Brásio. Vol. 11. Lisbon: Agência-Geral do Ultramar, 1971.

———. Letter to Propaganda Fide (The Sacred Congregation for the Propagation of the Faith), August 15, 1651. In *Monumenta missionaria africana: África ocidental (1651–1655),* 70–71. Edited by Padre António Brásio. Vol. 11. Lisbon: Agência-Geral do Ultramar, 1971.

———. Letter to Serafino da Cortona, August 15, 1657. In *Monumenta missionario africana: África ocidental (1651–1655),* 131–32. Edited by Padre António Brásio. Vol. 12. Lisbon: Agência-Geral do Ultramar, 1971.

Chapter 4

Ares Queija, Berta, and Alessandro Stella, eds. *Negros, mulatos, zambaigos: Derroteros africanos en los mundos ibéricos,* Seville: Escuela de Estudios Hispano-Americanos, 2000.

Franco Silva, Alfonso. *La esclavitud en Sevilla y su tierra a fines de la Edad Media.* Seville: Diputación Provincial de Sevilla, 1979.

Garofalo, Leo J. "The Case of Diego Suárez: Defining Empire through Afro-Iberian Incorporation and Movement in the Early Ibero-American World." Unpublished manuscript.

———. "The Shape of a Diaspora: The Movement of Afro-Iberians to and from Colonial Spanish America." In *Africans to Colonial Spanish America.* Edited by Sherwin Bryant, Ben Vinson, III, and Rachel Sarah O'Toole. Champaign: U of Illinois P (forthcoming).

Gerhard, Peter. "A Black Conquistador in Mexico." *Hispanic American Historical Review* 58, no. 3 (Aug. 1968): 451–59.

González Díaz, Antonio Manuel. *La esclavitud en Ayamonte durante el Antiguo Régimen (siglos XVI, XVII y XVIII).* Huelva, Spain: Diputación provincial de Huelva, 1996.

Lobo Cabrera, Manuel. *La esclavitud en las Canarias orientales en el siglo XVI (negros, moros y moriscos).* Las Palmas, Canary Islands: Ediciones del Cabildo Insular de Gran Canaria, 1982.

Martín Casares, Aurelia. *La esclavitud en la Granada del siglo XVI.* Granada, Spain: Universidad de Granada, 2000.

Pike, Ruth. "Sevillian Society in the Sixteenth Century: Slaves and Freedmen," *Hispanic American Historical Review* 47 (1967): 344–59.

Restall, Matthew. *Seven Myths of the Spanish Conquest.* Oxford: Oxford UP, 2003.

Saunders, A. C. de C. M. *A Social History of Black Slaves and Freedmen in Portugal, 1441–1555.* Cambridge: Cambridge UP, 1982.

Stella, Alessandro. *Histoires d'esclaves dans la péninsule ibérique.* Paris: Editions de l'Ecole des Hautes Etudes en Sciences Sociales, 2000.

Sweet, James H. *Recreating Africa: Culture, Kinship, and Religion in the African-Portuguese World, 1441–1770.* Chapel Hill: U of North Carolina P, 2003.

Chapter 5

Aguado, Fray Pedro de. *Recopilación historial de Venezuela.* First published 1581. Chs. 9–13, 599–630. Vol. 2. Caracas, Venezuela: Academia Nacional de la Historia, 1963.

Arrázola, Roberto. *Palenque, primero pueblo libre de América: Historia de las sublevaciones de los esclavos de Cartagena.* Cartagena, Colombia: Hernández, 1970.

Borrego Plá, María del Carmen. *Palenques de negros en Cartagena de Indias a fines del siglo XVII.* Seville: Escuela de Estudios Hispano-Americanos de Sevilla, 1973.

Etnias de Colombia. Fundación Hemera. Colombia. http://www.etniasdecolombia.org. Accessed May 10, 2009.

Friedemann, Nina S. de. *Ma ngombe: Guerreros y ganaderos en Palenque.* Bogota, Colombia: C. Valencia, 1979.

Heywood, Linda, and John Thornton. *Central Africans, Atlantic Creoles, and the Foundation of the Americas, 1585–1660.* Cambridge: Cambridge UP, 2007.

Landers, Jane G. "*Cimarrón* and Citizen: African Ethnicity, Corporate Identity, and the Evolution of Free Black Towns in the Spanish Circum-Caribbean." In *Slaves, Subjects, and Subversives: Blacks in Colonial Latin America,* 111–45. Edited by Jane G. Landers and Barry M. Robinson. Albuquerque: U of New Mexico P, 2006.

Lienhard, Martín. *O mar e o mato: Histórias da escravidão (Congo-Angola, Brasil, Caribe).* Salvador, Brazil: EDUFBA/CEAO, 1998.

———. "Una tierra sin amos: Lectura de los testimonios legales de algunos esclavos fugitivos (Puerto Rico y Brasil, siglo XIX)." *América Indígena* 54, no. 4 (1994): 209–27.

Lovejoy, Paul E. "Identifying Enslaved Africans in the African Diaspora." In *Identity in the Shadow of Slavery,* 1–29. Edited by Paul E. Lovejoy. London: Continuum, 2000.

McKnight, Kathryn Joy. "Confronted Rituals: Spanish Colonial and Angolan 'Maroon' Executions in Cartagena de Indias (1634)." *Journal of Colonialism and Colonial History* 5, no. 3 (2004). Project MUSE. Unpaginated.

———. "Gendered Declarations: Testimonies of Three Captured *Maroon* Women, Cartagena de Indias, 1634." *Colonial Latin American Historical Review* 12, no. 4 (2003): 499–527.

Movimiento Nacional Cimarrón. Colombia. 2007. http://www.cimarronracismo.org. Accessed May 10, 2009.

Navarrete, María Cristina. *Cimarrones y palenques en el siglo XVII.* Cali, Colombia: Universidad del Valle, 2003.

Palenque de San Basilio. Corporación Festival de Tambores de San Basilio de Palenque. Cartagena, Colombia. 2006. http://palenquedesanbasilio.masterimpresores.com. Accessed May 10, 2009.

Price, Richard, ed. *Maroon Societies: Rebel Slave Communities in the Americas.* Garden City, NY: Anchor, 1973.

Renacientes PCN Colombia. Proceso de Comunidades Negras de Colombia. Hosted by galeotas.org. 2009.http://www.renacientes.org. Accessed May 10, 2009.

Rodríguez, Frederick Marshal. *Cimarrón Revolts and Pacification in New Spain, the Isthmus of Panama and Colonial Colombia, 1503–1800.* PhD diss., Loyola University of Chicago, 1979.

Ruiz Rivera, Julián B. "Cimarronaje en Cartagena de Indias: Siglo XVII." *Memoria (Bogotá: Archivo General de la Nación)* 8 (2001): 10–35.

Salgado, Paulino. *Batata y Su Rumba Palenquera.* (compact disc). Network, 2003.

Simón, Fray Pedro. *Noticias historiales de las conquistas de Tierra Firme en las Indias Occidentales.* First published 1625. Vol. 8, Chs. 22–23, 165–74. Edited by Manuel José Forero. Bogota, Colombia: Biblioteca de Autores Colombianos, 1953.

Thornton, John. *Africa and Africans in the Making of the Atlantic World, 1400–1800,* 2nd ed. Cambridge: Cambridge UP, 1998.

Chapter 6

Blackburn, Robin. *The Making of New World Slavery from the Baroque to the Modern, 1492–1800.* London: Verso, 1997.

Bristol, Joan Cameron. *Christians, Blasphemers, and Witches: Afro-Mexican Ritual Practice in the Seventeenth Century.* Albuquerque: U of New Mexico P, 2007.

Eire, Carlos M. N. *From Madrid to Purgatory: The Art and Craft of Dying in Sixteenth-Century Spain.* Cambridge: Cambridge UP, 1995.

Gomez, Michael A. *Exchanging Our Country Marks: The Transformation of African Identities in the Colonial and Antebellum South.* Chapel Hill: U of North Carolina P, 1998.

Larkin, Brian. "Confraternities and Community: The Decline of the Communal Quest for Salvation in Eighteenth-Century México City." In *Local Religion in Colonial Mexico,* 189–214. Edited by Martin Nesvig. Albuquerque: U of New Mexico P, 2006.

Lovejoy, Paul E. *Identity in the Shadow of Slavery.* London: Continuum, 2000.

Lovejoy, Paul E., and David V. Troutman. *Transatlantic Dimensions of Ethnicity in the African Diaspora.* London: Continuum, 2003.

von Germeten, Nicole. *Black Blood Brothers: Confraternities and Social Mobility for Afro-Mexicans.* Gainesville: UP of Florida, 2006.

———. "Death in Black and White: Testaments and Confraternal Devotion in Seventeenth-Century Mexico City." *Colonial Latin American Historical Review* 12, no. 3 (2003): 275–301.

———. "Routes to Respectability: Confraternities and Men of African Descent in New Spain." In *Local Religion in Colonial Mexico,* 215–34. Edited by Martin Nesvig. Albuquerque: U of New Mexico P, 2006.

Chapter 7

Aguirre, Carlos. *Agentes de su propia libertad: Los esclavos de Lima y la desintegración de la esclavitud, 1821–1834.* Lima, Peru: Pontificia Universidad Católica del Perú, 1993.

Alfonso X [King of Castile and Leon, 1221–1284]. *Siete partidas.* Edited by Licentiate Gregorio López. First published 1555. Facsimile edition. 3 vols. Madrid: Boletín Oficial del Estado, 1985.

Bowser, Frederick P. *The African Slave in Colonial Peru, 1524–1650.* Stanford, CA: Stanford UP, 1974.

Brockington, Lolita Gutiérrez. *Blacks, Indians, and Spaniards in the Eastern Andes: Reclaiming the Forgotten in Colonial Mizque, 1550–1782.* Lincoln: U of Nebraska P, 2006.

Charún-Illescas, Lucía. *Malambo.* Trans. Emmanuel Harris, II. Chicago: Swan Isle Press, 2004.

Eire, Carlos M. N. *From Madrid to Purgatory: The Art and Craft of Dying in Sixteenth-Century Spain.* Cambridge: Cambridge UP, 1995.

Gaspar, David Barry, and Darlene Clark Hine, eds. *Beyond Bondage: Free Women of Color in the Americas.* Urbana: U of Illinois P, 2004.

Gauderman, Kimberley. *Women's Lives in Colonial Quito: Gender, Law, and Economy in Spanish America.* Austin: U of Texas P, 2003.

Graubart, Karen B. *With Our Labor and Sweat: Indigenous Women and the Formation of Colonial Society in Peru, 1550–1700.* Stanford, CA: Stanford UP, 2007.

Herzog, Tamar. *Mediación, archivos y ejercicio: Los escribanos de Quito (siglo XVII).* Frankfurt am Main, Germany: Vittorio Klostermann, 1996.

Hünefeldt, Christine. *Paying the Price of Freedom: Family and Labor among Lima's Slaves, 1800–1854.* Berkeley: U of California P, 1994.

Irolo Calar, Nicolás de. *La política de escrituras.* First published 1605. Edited by María del Pilar Martínez López-Cano. Mexico City: Universidad Autónoma de México, 1996.

Jouve-Martín, José Ramón. *Esclavos de la ciudad letrada: Esclavitud, escritura y colonialismo en Lima (1650–1700).* Lima, Peru: Instituto de Estudios Peruanos, 2005.

Kellog, Susan, and Matthew Restall, eds. *Dead Giveaways: Indigenous Testaments of Colonial Mesoamerican and the Andes.* Salt Lake City: U of Utah P, 1998.

Le Goff, Jacques. *The Birth of Purgatory.* Chicago: U of Chicago P, 1984.

Portocarrero Lazo de la Vega, Melchor Antonio, and Conde de la Monclova. *Numeración general de todas las personas de ambos sexos, edades y calidades que se ha hecho en esta ciudad de Lima.* First published 1700. Edited by Noble D. Cook. Lima, Peru: Comide, 1985.

Powers, Karen Viera. *Women in the Crucible of Conquest: The Gendered Genesis of Spanish American Society, 1500–1600.* Albuquerque: U of New Mexico P, 2005.

Socolow, Susan Migden. *The Women of Colonial America.* Cambridge: Cambridge UP, 2000.

Torres, Carmen. "Los asientos como sistema del comercio negrearo en América: El Real Asiento inglés de 1713." *Boletín de la Academia Nacional de la Historia de Venezuela* 77, no. 307 (1994): 117–22.

van Deusen, Nancy E., ed. and trans. *The Souls of Purgatory: The Spiritual Diary of a Seventeenth-Century Afro-Peruvian Mystic, Ursula de Jesús.* Albuquerque: U of New Mexico P, 2004.

Vila Vilar, Enriqueta. "Los asientos portugueses y el contrabando de negros." *Anuario de Estudios Americanos* 30 (1973): 557–609.

Chapter 8

Aguirre, Carlos. *Agentes de su propia libertad: Los esclavos de Lima y la desintegración de la esclavitud,* 181–210. Lima, Peru: Pontificia Universidad Católica del Perú, Fondo Editorial. 1993.

Andrews, George Reid. *Afro-Latin America, 1800–2000.* Ch. 1, 11–52. Oxford: Oxford UP, 2004.

Cáceres, Rina. *Negros, mulatos, esclavos y libertos en la Costa Rica del siglo XVII.* Mexico City: Instituto Panamericano de Geografía e Historia, 2000.

Chaves, María Eugenia. "Slave Women's Strategies for Freedom and the Late Spanish Colonial State." In *Hidden Histories of Gender and the State in Latin America,* 108–26. Edited by Elizabeth Dore and Maxine Molyneux. Durham, NC: Duke UP, 2000.

Deschamps Chapeaux, Pedro. *Los batallones de pardos y morenos libres.* Havana, Cuba: Editorial Arte y Literatura, Instituto Cubano del Libro, 1976.

Díaz, María Elena. "Conjuring Identities: Race, Nativeness, Local Citizenship and Royal Slavery in a Frontier Location (Revisiting El Cobre, Cuba)." In *Imperial Subjects: Race and Identity in Colonial Latin America,* 197–224. Edited by Andrew B. Fisher and Matthew D. O'Hara. Durham, NC: Duke UP, 2009.

———. *El Cobre, Cuba: Images, Voices, Histories.* Department of History, University of California, Santa Cruz. http://humweb.ucsc.edu/elccobre. Accessed Jan. 1, 2009.

———. "Of Life and Freedom in the (Tropical) Hearth: El Cobre, 1709–1773." In *Beyond Bondage: Free Women of Color in the Americas,* 19–36. Edited by D. B. Gaspar and D. Clark. Chicago: U of Illinois P, 2004.

———. "Mining Women, Royal Slaves: Copper Mining in Colonial Cuba, 1670–1780." In *Mining Women: Gender in the Development of a Global Industry, 1700–2000,* 21–39. Edited by Laurie Mercier and Jaclyn Viskovatoff. New York: Palgrave MacMillan Press, 2006.

———. "Rethinking Tradition and Identity: The Virgin of Charity of El Cobre." In *Cuba, the Elusive Nation,* 43–59. Edited by D. J. Fernández and M. Cámara Betancourt. Gainesville: UP of Florida, 2000.

———. *The Virgin, the King, and the Royal Slaves of El Cobre: Negotiating Freedom in Colonial Cuba, 1670–1780.* Stanford, CA: Stanford UP, 2000.

Granda, Germán de. "Orígen, función y estructura de un pueblo de negros y mulattos libres en el Paraguay del siglo XVIII (San Agustín de la Emboscada)." *Revista de Indias* 43 (1983): 229–64.

Klein, Herbert. "The Colored Militia of Cuba: 1568–1868." *Caribbean Studies* 6, no. 2 (1966): 17–27.

Landers, Jane. "Gracia Real de Santa Teresa de Mose: A Free Black Town in Spanish Colonial Florida." *American Historical Review* 95 (1990): 9–30.

Patterson, Orlando. *Slavery and Social Death: A Comparative Study.* Introduction, 1–14. Cambridge, MA: Harvard UP, 1982.

Pérez, Louis. *Cuba: Between Reform and Revolution.* Chs. 2–3, 34–70. New York: Oxford UP, 1988.

Salas, Esteban, composer. *Esteban Salas: Un barroco cubano.* Performed by Coro Exaudi de La Habana. Conducted by Maria Felicia Perez. Milan Records, 2003. (compact disc). [Period music by the Cuban baroque composer Esteban Salas (1725–1803) who was choirmaster of the Cathedral of Santiago de Cuba from 1764 to 1803. His music may have even been heard in the Marian Sanctuary of El Cobre, barely ten miles away from Santiago.]

Taylor, William B. "The Foundation of Nuestra Señora de Guadalupe de los Morenos de Ampa." *The Americas* 26 (1970): 442–46.

Vinson, Ben, III. *Bearing Arms for His Majesty: The Free-Colored Militia in Colonial Mexico.* Stanford, CA: Stanford UP, 2000.

Chapter 9

Afro-Peru. (compact disc). London: World Music Network, 2002.

Anguiano, Mateo de. *Vida, y virtudes del Capuchino español, el Venerable Siervo de Dios Fray Francisco de Pamplona.* Madrid: Lorenzo García, 1685.

Burns, Kathryn. "Notaries, Truth, and Consequences." *American Historical Review* 110, no. 2 (2005): 350–79.

Charún-Illescas, Lucía. *Malambo.* Trans. Emmanuel Harris II. Chicago: Swan Isle, 2004.

Chaves, María Eugenia. "Slave Women's Strategies for Freedom and the Late Spanish Colonial State." In *Hidden Histories of Gender and the State in Latin America,* 108–26. Edited by Elizabeth Dore and Maxine Molyneux. Durham, NC: Duke UP, 2000.

Cimarrón. "El Quinto Suyo: Afrodescendientes en el Perú," http://www.cimarrones-peru.org/reel.htm. Accessed Sept. 12, 2008.

"Demanda del Capitán don Gerónimo de González, vecino de Trujillo, contra Martín Ximenez, maestro de carpintería; sobre redhibitoria de la venta de una negra Mariana de casta *mina.*" (1685). Ms. Leg. 206. Exp. 1489. Archivo Departamental de La Libertad. Trujillo, Peru.

Estenssoro, Juan Carlos. *Los cuadros de mestizaje del virrey Amat: La representación etnográfica en el Perú colonial.* Lima, Peru: Museo de Arte de Lima, 1999.

Graham, Sandra Lauderdale. "Honor among Slaves." In *The Faces of Honor: Sex, Shame, and Violence in Colonial Latin America,* 201–28. Edited by Lyman L. Johnson and Sonya Lipsett-Rivera. Albuquerque: U of New Mexico P, 1998.

Hanger, Kimberly S. *Bounded Lives, Bounded Places: Free Black Society in Colonial New Orleans, 1769–1803.* Durham, NC: Duke UP, 1997.

———. "Landlords, Shopkeepers, Farmers, and Slave-Owners: Free Black Female Property Holders in Colonial New Orleans." In *Beyond Bondage: Free Women of Color in the Americas,* 219–36. Edited by David Barry Gaspar and Darlene Clark Hine. Urbana: U of Illinois P, 2004.

———. "'The Most Vile Atrocities': Accusations of Slander against Maria Cofignie, *Parda* Libre (Louisiana, 1795)." In *Colonial Lives: Documents on Latin American History, 1550–*

1850, 269–78. Edited by Richard Boyer and Geoffrey Spurling. New York: Oxford UP, 2000.

Higgins, Kathleen J. *"Licentious liberty" in a Brazilian Gold-Mining Region: Slavery, Gender, and Social Control in Eighteenth-Century Sabará, Minas Gerais.* University Park, PA: Penn State UP, 1999.

Hünefeldt, Christine. *Paying the Price of Freedom: Family and Labor among Lima's Slaves, 1800–1854.* Berkeley: U of California P, 1994.

Karasch, Mary. *Slave Life in Rio de Janeiro 1808–1850.* Princeton, NJ: Princeton UP, 1987.

Law, Robin. *The Kingdom of Allada.* Leiden, Netherlands: Research School CNWS. School of Asian, African, and Amerindian Studies, 1997.

———. *The Slave Coast of West Africa, 1550–1750: The Impact of the Atlantic Slave Trade on an African Society.* Oxford: Clarendon, 1991.

Littlefield, Daniel. *Rice and Slaves: Ethnicity and the Slave Trade in Colonial South Carolina.* Baton Rouge: Louisiana State UP, 1981.

Mills, Kenneth, William B. Taylor, and Sandra Lauderdale Graham, eds. "Two Brazilian Wills (1793 and 1823)." In *Colonial Latin America: A Documentary History,* 375–83. Lanham, MD: SR Books, 2002.

Morgan, Jennifer L. *Laboring Women: Reproduction and Gender in New World Slavery.* Philadelphia: U of Pennsylvania P, 2004.

Obregón, Julio Luna. *Efigenia, la negra santa: Culto religioso de los descendientes africanos en el valle de Cañete. Sabino Canas, gestor de la tradición afroandina.* Lima, Peru: Centro de Articulación y Desarrollo Juvenil "Mundo de Ébano," Centro de Desarrollo de la Mujer Negra Peruana (CEDEMUNEP), 2005.

Olwell, Robert. "'Loose, Idle and Disorderly': Slave Women in the Eighteenth-Century Charleston Marketplace." In *More Than Chattel: Black Women and Slavery in the Americas,* 97–125. Edited by David Barry Gaspar and Darlene Clark Hine. Bloomington: Indiana UP, 1996.

O'Toole, Rachel Sarah. "Gender, Slavery, and the Claims of *Casta* in Colonial Coastal Peru." In *Expanding the Diaspora: Africans to Colonial Latin America.* Edited by Sherwin Bryant, Rachel O'Toole, and Ben Vinson III. Urbana: U of Illinois P (forthcoming).

Peru Negro. 2006. http://perunegro.net/. Accessed Sept. 12, 2008.

Reis, João José. *Death Is a Festival: Funeral Rites and Rebellion in Nineteenth-Century Brazil.* First published 1991. Chapel Hill: U of North Carolina P, 2003.

Schafer, Daniel L. *Anna Madgigine, Jai Kingsley: African Princess, Florida Slave, Plantation Slaveowner.* Gainesville: UP of Florida, 2003.

Thornton, John K. *The Kongolese Saint Anthony: Dona Beatriz Kimpa Vita and the Antonian Movement, 1684–1706.* Cambridge: Cambridge UP, 1998.

van Deusen, Nancy E., ed. and trans. *The Souls of Purgatory: The Spiritual Diary of a Seventeenth-Century Afro-Peruvian Mystic, Ursula de Jesús.* Albuquerque: U of New Mexico P, 2004.

von Germeten, Nicole. *Black Blood Brothers: Confraternities and Social Mobility for Afro-Mexicans.* Gainesville: UP of Florida, 2006.

Chapter 10

Andrews, George Reid. *Los afroargentinos de Buenos Aires.* Trans. Antonio Bonanno. Buenos Aires, Argentina: La Flor, 1980.

Bernand, Carmen. "Un sargento contra un rey, ambos a dos negros." In *Negros, mulatos, zambaigos: Derroteros africanos en los mundos ibéricos,* 149–73. Edited by Berta Ares Queija and Alessandro Stella. Seville: Escuela de Estudios Hispano-Americanos, 2000.

Cirio, Norberto P. "Antecedentes históricos del culto a San Baltasar en la Argentina: La Cofradía de San Baltasar y Ánimas (1772–1856)." *Latin American Music Review (Austin)* 21, no. 2 (2000): 190–214.

———. "¿Rezan o bailan? Disputas en torno a la devoción a San Baltazar por los negros en el Buenos Aires colonial." In *Actas de la IV Reunión Científica: Mujeres, negros y niños en la música y sociedad colonial iberoamericana,* 88–100. Edited by Víctor Rondón. Santa Cruz de la Sierra, Bolivia: Asociación Pro Arte y Cultura, 2002.

Díaz, Marisa. "Las migraciones internas a la ciudad de Buenos Aires, 1744–1810." *Boletín del Instituto de Historia Argentina y Americana "Dr. Emilio Ravignani." (Buenos Aires)* 3, nos. 16–17 (1997): 7–31.

Fogelman, Patricia. "Coordenadas marianas: Tiempos y espacios de devoción a la Virgen a través de las cofradías porteñas coloniales." *Trabajos y Comunicaciones (La Plata)* 2, nos. 30/31 (2004–2005): 118–38.

———. "Élite local y participación religiosa en Luján a fines del período colonial: La Cofradía de Nuestra Señora del Santísimo Rosario." *Cuadernos de Historia Regional (Luján)* 20–21 (2000): 103–24.

———. "La población de color en la frontera bonaerense: Los negros y pardos de la Villa de Luján." *Revista Signos Históricos (México)* 2 (1999): 9–33.

———. "Una cofradía mariana urbana y otra rural en Buenos Aires a fines del período colonial." *Andes: Antropología e Historia (Salta)* 11 (2000): 179–207.

———. "Una 'economía espiritual de la salvación': Culpabilidad, Purgatorio y acumulación de indulgencias en la era colonial." *Andes: Antropología e Historia (Salta)* 15 (2004): 55–86.

Goldberg, Marta. "La población negra y mulata en la ciudad de Buenos Aires." *Desarrollo Económico (Buenos Aires)* 61, no. 1 (1976): 66–84.

———. "Las afroargentinas." In *Historia de las mujeres en la Argentina,* Vol. 1, 68–85. Edited by Fernanda Gil Lozano. Buenos Aires, Argentina: Taurus, 2000.

———. "Los africanos de Buenos Aires, 1750–1880." In *Rutas de la esclavitud en África y América,* 269–88. Edited by Rina Cáceres. San Jose: Editorial de La Universidad de Costa Rica, 2001.

———. "Los estudios sobre castas en la demografía histórica argentina." In *Cambios Demográficos en América Latina: La experiencia de cinco siglos,* 715–23. Córdoba, Argentina: Universidad Nacional de Córdoba, 2000.

———. "Los negros de Buenos Aires." In *Presencia africana en Sudamérica,* 529–607. Edited by Luz María Martínez Montiel. Mexico: Consejo Nacional para la Cultura y las Artes (CONACULTA), 1995.

———. "Presencia africana en la historia y cultura argentina." *Con eñe: Revista de Cultura Hispanoamericana (Badajoz)* 11 (2000): 19–24.

———. "Vida cotidiana de los negros en Hispanoamérica." *Tres grandes cuestiones de la historia de Iberoamérica.* Edited by José Andrés-Gallego. (CD-ROM). Madrid: Fundación Ignacio Larramendi, Tavera, 2005.

González, Ricardo. *Imágenes de la Ciudad Capital. Arte en Buenos Aires en el siglo XVIII.* Buenos Aires, Argentina: Minerva, 1998.

Mallo, Silvia. "El color del delito en Buenos Aires." *Revista Memoria y Sociedad: Diásporas Afroamericanas (Bogotá)* 7 (2003): 111–124.

———. "Negros y mulatos rioplatenses viviendo en libertad." *Rutas de la esclavitud en África y América Latina,* 305–22. Edited by Rina Cáceres. San Jose: Editorial de la Universidad de Costa Rica, 2001.

Rodríguez Molas, Ricardo. "La música y la danza de los negros en el Buenos Aires de los siglos XVIII y XIX." *Historia* 2, no. 7 (1957): 103–26.

Rosal, Miguel Ángel. "Algunas consideraciones sobre las creencias religiosas de los africanos porteños (1750–1820)." *Investigaciones y Ensayos (Buenos Aires)* 31 (1981): 369–83.

Chapter 11

Behar, Ruth. "Sex and Sin: Witchcraft and the Devil in Late-Colonial Mexico." *American Ethnologist* 14, no. 1 (1987): 34–54.

Blázquez, Juan. *La Inquisición en América (1569–1820).* Santo Domingo, Dominican Republic: Editora Corripio, 1994.

Ceballos Gómez, Diana Luz. *"Quyen tal haze que tal pague": Sociedad y prácticas mágicas en el Nuevo Reino de Granada.* Bogota, Colombia: Ministerio de Cultura, 2002.

Díaz, María Elena. *The Virgin, the King, and the Royal Slaves of El Cobre: Negotiating Freedom in Colonial Cuba, 1670–1780.* Stanford, CA: Stanford UP, 2000.

Franco, José Luciano. *Las minas de Santiago del Prado y la rebelión de los cobreros, 1530–1800.* Havana, Cuba: Editorial de Ciencias Sociales, 1957.

Henningsen, Gustav. *The Witches' Advocate.* Reno: U of Nevada P, 1980.

Kamen, Henry. *The Spanish Inquisition.* New York: New American Library, 1965.

Marrero, Levi. *Los esclavos y la virgen del cobre: Dos siglos de lucha por la libertad.* Miami, FL: Universal, 1980.

Maya Restrepo, Luz Adriana. "Paula de Eguiluz y el arte del bien querer: Apuntes para el estudio de la sensualidad y el cimarronaje femenino en el Caribe, siglo XVIII." *Historia Crítica* 24 (2002): 101–24.

Medina, Toribio. *La Inquisición en Cartagena de Indias.* Bogota, Colombia: Carlos Valencia Editores, 1978.

Monter, William. "The New Social History and the Spanish Inquisition." *Journal of Social History* 17, no. 4 (1984): 705–13.

Navarrete, María Cristina. *Prácticas religiosas de los negros en la colonia.* Cali, Colombia: Universidad del Valle, 1995.

Splendiani, Anna María, José Enrique Sánchez Bohórquez, and Emma Cecilia Luque de Salazar. *Cincuenta años de inquisición en el Tribunal de Cartagena de Indias, 1610–1660.* Santa Fe de Bogotá, Colombia: Pontificia Universidad Javeriana, Instituto Colombiano de Cultura Hispánica, 1997.

Sweet, James H. *Recreating Africa: Culture, Kinship, and Religion in the African-Portuguese World, 1441–1770.* Chapel Hill: U of North Carolina P, 2003.

Tejado Fernández, Manuel. *Aspectos de la vida social en Cartagena de Indias durante el seiscientos.* Seville: Escuela de Estudios Hispano-Americanos, 1954.

Vidal Ortega, Antonio. "Entre la necesidad y el temor: Negros y mulatos en Cartagena de Indias a comienzos del siglo XVII." In *Negros, mulatos, zambaigos: Derroteros africanos en los mundos ibéricos,* 89–104. Edited by Berta Ares Queija and Alessandro Stella. Seville: Escuela de Estudios Hispano-Americanos, 2000.

Chapter 12

Andrews, Kenneth R. *The Spanish Caribbean: Trade and Plunder, 1530–1630.* New Haven, CT: Yale UP, 1978.

Borrego Plá, María del Carmen. *Cartagena de Indias en el siglo XVI.* Seville: Escuela de Estudios Hispano-Americanos, 1983.

Brooks, George E. *Landlords and Strangers: Ecology, Society, and Trade in Western Africa, 1000–1630.* Boulder, CO: Westview Press, 1993.

Carreira, António. *Os Portuguêses nos Rios de Guiné (1500–1900).* Lisbon: Litografia Tejo, 1984.

"Certificaçion de los negros que han entrado en Cartaxena desde Primero de mayo de 1615 hasta 20 de marzo deste presente año de 1623. Cartagena, 28 marzo 1623." Archivo General de Indias, Seville. Santa Fe 74, no. 6.

Córdoba Ronquillo, Obispo fray Luis de. "Obispo fray Luis de Córdoba Ronquillo a S. M. Cartagena, 10 agosto 1634." Archivo General de Indias, Seville, Santa Fe 228, no. 97.

Del Castillo Mathieu, Nicolás. *La llave de las Indias.* Bogota, Colombia: El Tiempo, 1981.

Francis, J. Michael. *Invading Colombia: Spanish Accounts of the Gonzalo Jiménez de Quesada Expedition of Conquest.* University Park, PA: Penn State UP, 2007.

Games, Alison. "'The Sanctuarye of our rebell negroes': The Atlantic Context of Local Resistance on Providence Island, 1630–1641." *Slavery and Abolition* 19, no. 3 (1998): 1–21.

Hawthorne, Walter. *Planting Rice and Harvesting Slaves: Transformations along the Guinea-Bissau Coast, 1400–1900.* Portsmouth, NH: Heinemann, 2003.

Heywood, Linda, and John K. Thornton. *Central Africans, Atlantic Creoles, and the Foundation of the Americas, 1585–1660.* Cambridge: Cambridge UP, 2007.

Kupperman, Karen Ordahl. *Providence Island, 1630–1641: The Other Puritan Colony.* Cambridge: Cambridge UP, 1993.

Landers, Jane. *Black Society in Spanish Florida.* Urbana: U of Illinois P, 1999.

Navarrete, María Cristina. *Historia social del negro en la colonia: Cartagena, siglo XVII.* Santiago de Cali, Colombia: Universidad del Valle, 1995.

Newson, Linda A., and Susie Minchin. *From Capture to Sale: The Portuguese Slave Trade to Spanish South America in the Early Seventeenth Century.* Leiden, Netherlands: Brill, 2007.

Pargellis, Stanley, and Ruth Lapham Butler, eds. "Daniell Ellffryth's Guide to the Caribbean, 1631." *The William and Mary Quarterly* 1, no. 3 (1944): 273–316.

Phillips, Carla Rahn. *Six Galleons for the King of Spain: Imperial Defense in the Early Seventeenth Century.* Baltimore, MD: Johns Hopkins UP, 1986.

Rodney, Walter. *A History of the Upper Guinea Coast, 1545 to 1800.* New York: Monthly Review Press, 1970.

Sandoval, Alonso de. *Un tratado sobre la esclavitud.* First published in Seville, 1627. Edited by Enriqueta Vila Vilar. Madrid: Alianza Editorial, 1987.

Sauer, Carl O. *The Early Spanish Main.* Berkeley: U of California P, 1966.

Urueta, José P. *Documentos para la historia de Cartagena.* Cartagena, Colombia: Araújo, 1887.

Vidal Ortega, Antonino. *Cartagena de Indias y la región histórica del Caribe, 1580–1640.* Seville: Escuela de Estudios Hispano-Americanos, 2002.

Vila Vilar, Enriqueta. *Hispanoamérica y el comercio de esclavos.* Seville: Escuela de Estudios Hispano-Americanos, 1977.

Wheat, David. "África no desenvolvimento da terceira cidade das Índias." Paper presented at the conference "Cortes, cidades, memórias." Universidade Federal de Minas Gerais, Belo Horizonte, Brazil, Nov. 13, 2007.

Chapter 13

Andrews, Williams L. *To Tell a Free Story: The First Century of Afro-American Autobiography, 1760–1863.* Urbana: U of Illinois P, 1986.

Belinda. "Petition of an African Slave, to the Legislature of Massachusetts." First published 1787 *American Women Writers to 1800,* 253–55. Edited by Sharon M. Harris. New York: Oxford UP, 1996.

Bilinkoff, Jodi. *The Avila of St. Teresa: Religious Reform in a Sixteenth-Century City.* Ithaca, NY: Cornell UP, 1989.

Brásio, Antonio. *Monumenta missionaria africana: Africa Ocidental.* Vols. 13–14. Lisbon: Agência Geral do Ultrmar, Divisão de Publicações e Biblioteca, 1958.

Bynum, Caroline Walker. Foreword. In *Gendered Voices: Medieval Saints and Their Interpreters*, ix–xii. Edited by Catherine M. Mooney. Philadelphia: U of Pennsylvania P, 1999.

Contreras, Pedro de. *Sermón fúnebre en las honras de la Venerable Magdalena de la Cruz, negra de nación.* Seville: Imprenta de los Gómez, 1735.

Fra Molinero, Baltasar. "Baltasar Fra Molinero: Su blog." Wordpress.com. http://bframoli.wordpress.com/chicaba-en-imagenes. Accessed Jan. 1, 2009.

Gómez de la Parra, José, and Manuel Ramos Medina. *Fundación y primero siglo: Crónica del primer convento de carmelitas descalzas en Puebla, 1604–1794.* Puebla, Mexico: Universidad Iberoamericana. Comisión Puebla V Centenario, 1992.

Harms, Robert. *The Diligent: A Voyage through the Worlds of the Slave Trade.* New York: Basic Books, 2002.

Kiple, Kenneth F., and Brian T. Higgins. "Mortality Caused by Dehydration during the Middle Passage." *Social Science History* 13, no. 4 (Winter 1989): 421–37.

Labouret, Henri, and Paul Rivet. *Le Royaume d'Arda et son évangélisation au XVIIe siècle.* Paris: Institut d'ethnologie, 1929.

Law, Robin. "Religion, Trade and Politics on the 'Slave Coast': Roman Catholic Missions in Allada and Whydah in the Seventeenth Century." *Journal of Religion in Africa* 21, no. 1 (1991): 42–77.

Moody, Joycelyn. *Sentimental Confessions: Spiritual Narratives of Nineteenth-Century African-American Women.* Athens: U of Georgia P, 2001.

Mott, Luiz. *Rosa Egipcíaca: Uma santa africana no Brasil.* Rio de Janeiro, Brazil: Bertrand Brasil, 1993.

Myers, Kathleen A. "Testimony for Canonization or Proof of Blasphemy? The New Spanish Inquisition and the Hagiographic Biography of Catarina de San Juan." In *Women in the Inquisition: Spain and the New World,* 270–95. Edited by Mary E. Giles. Baltimore, MD: Johns Hopkins UP, 1999.

Olsen, Margaret M. *Slavery and Salvation in Colonial Cartagena de Indias.* Gainesville: UP of Florida, 2004.

Paniagua, R. P. don Juan Carlos Miguel de. *Compendio de la vida ejemplar de la Venerable Madre Sor Teresa Juliana de Santo Domingo, tercera profesa en el convento de Santa María Magdalena, vulgo de la Penitencia, Orden de Santo Domingo, de la ciudad de Salamanca,* 2nd ed. Salamanca, Spain: Eugenio García de Honorato y San Miguel, impresor de dicha ciudad y Real Universidad, 1764.

———. *Oración fúnebre en las exequias de la Madre Sor Teresa Juliana de Santo Domingo, de feliz memoria, celebradas en el día nueve de enero en el Convento de Religiosas Dominicas, vulgo de la Penitencia.* Salamanca, Spain, 1749.

Pena González, Miguel Anxo. *Francisco José de Jaca: La primera propuesta abolicionista de la esclavitud en el pensamiento hispano.* Salamanca, Spain: Publicaciones de la Universidad Pontificia de Salamanca, 2003.

Rubial, Antonio. *La santidad controvertida.* Mexico City: Fondo de Cultura Económica, 1999.

Sampson Vera Tudela, Elisa. "Fashioning a Cacique Nun: From Saints' Lives to Indian Lives in the Spanish Americas." *Gender and History* 9 (1997): 191–206.

Soler y las Balsas, Luis. *Vida de la venerable negra, la madre sor Theresa Juliana de Santo Domingo, de feliz memoria.* Zaragoza, Spain: Schomburg Center for Research in Black Culture. Ms. Sc Rare F 81–6, 1757.

Tardieu, Jean-Pierre. "Du bon usage de la monstruosité: La vision de l'Afrique chez Alonso de Sandoval (1627)." *Bulletin Hispanique* 86, no. 1 (1984): 164–78.

Thornton, John. *The Kongolese Saint Anthony: Dona Beatriz Kimpa Vita and the Antonian Movement, 1684–1706.* Cambridge: Cambridge UP, 1998.

van Deusen, Nancy E., ed. and trans. *The Souls of Purgatory: The Spiritual Diary of a Seventeenth-Century Afro-Peruvian Mystic, Ursula de Jesús.* Albuquerque: U of New Mexico P, 2004.

Vauchez, Andre. *Sainthood in the Later Middle Ages.* Trans. Jean Birrell. Cambridge: Cambridge UP, 1997.

"Venta de dos esclavos moros, otorgada por Sebastián Antonio de Toledo y Molina, Marqués de Mancera, a favor de Juan de Artieda. 6 de febrero de 1677." Archivo Histórico de Protocolos Notariales de Madrid. Libro 11.410, fol. 79.

Wyschogrod, Edith. *Saints and Postmodernism: Revisioning Moral Philosophy.* Chicago: U of Chicago P, 1990.

Yai, Olabiyi Babalola. "From Vodun to Mawu: Monotheism and History in the Fon Cultural Area." In *L'invention religieuse en Afrique: Histoire et Religion en Afrique Noire,* 241–65. Edited by Jean-Pierre Chrétien. Paris: Karthala, 1993.

Chapter 14

Boxer, Charles R. "*Nova e Curiosa Relação:* Negro Slavery in Brazil: A Portuguese Pamphlet (1764)." *Race* 5 (1964): 38–47.

Conrad, Robert Edgar. *Children of God's Fire: A Documentary History of Black Slavery in Brazil.* State College, PA: Penn State UP, 1994.

Curto, José, and Paul E. Lovejoy, eds. *Enslaving Connections: Changing Cultures of Africa and Brazil during the Era of Slavery.* Amherst, NY: Prometheus/Humanity Books, 2004.

Heywood, Linda M., ed. *Central Africans and Cultural Transformations in the American Diaspora.* New York: Cambridge UP, 2001.

Karasch, Mary C. "Minha *nação:* Identidades escravas no fim do Brasil colonial." Trans. Angela Domingues. In *Brasil: Colonização e escravidão,* 127–41. Edited by Maria Beatriz Nizza da Silva. Rio de Janeiro, Brazil: Nova Fronteira, 2000.

———. *Slave Life in Rio de Janeiro, 1808–1850.* Princeton, NJ: Princeton UP, 1987.

Kiddy, Elizabeth W. *Blacks of the Rosary: Memory and History in Minas Gerais, Brazil.* State College, PA: Penn State UP, 2005.

———. "Kings, Queens, and Judges: Hierarchy in Lay Religious Brotherhoods of Blacks, 1750–1830." In *Africa and the Americas: Interconnections during the Slave Trade,* 95–125. Edited by Renée Soulodre-LaFrance and José Curto. New Brunswick, NJ: Africa World Press, 2005.

Reis, João José. "Identidade e diversidade étnicas nas irmandades negras no tempo da escravidão." *Tempo* 2, no. 3 (1997): 7–33.

Russell-Wood, A. J. R. *The Black Man in Slavery and Freedom in Colonial Brazil.* New York: St. Martin's, 1982.

Schwartz, Stuart B. "Magistracy and Society in Colonial Brazil." *Hispanic American Historical Review* 50 (1970): 715–30.

Soares, Mariza de Carvalho. "A 'nação' que se tem e a 'terra' de onde se vem: Categorias de inserção social de africanos no Império português, século XVIII." *Estudos Afro-Asiáticos* 26, no. 2 (2004): 303–30.

———. "Apreço e imitação no diálogo do gentio convertido." *Ipotesi: Revista de Estudos literários Juiz de Fora* 4, no. 1 (2000): 111–23.

———. "Can Women Guide and Govern Men? Gendering Politics among African Catholics in Colonial Brazil." *Women and Slavery, Vol. 2: The Modern Atlantic,* 79–99. Edited by Gwyn Campbell, Suzanne Miers, and Joseph Calder Miller. Athens: Ohio UP, 2007.

———. *Devotos da cor, Identidade étnica, religiosidade e escravidão no Rio de Janeiro, século XVIII.* Rio de Janeiro, Brazil: Civilização Brasileira, 2000.

———. "O Império de Santo Elesbão na cidade do Rio de Janeiro, no século XVIII." *Topoi* 4 (March 2002): 59–83.

Thornton, John K. *Africa and Africans in the Making of the Atlantic World, 1400–1680,* 235–71. Cambridge: Cambridge UP, 1992.

Chapter 15

Azulay, Jom Tob, producer-director. *O Judeu.* A&B Producoes, 1996.[Film about the Brazilian *converso* António José da Silva, who was burned at the stake in 1739.]

Bethencourt, Francisco. *História das Inquisições: Portugal, Espanha e Itália—Séculos XV–XIX.* São Paulo, Brazil: Companhia das Letras, 2000.

Boxer, C. R. *Race Relations in the Portuguese Colonial Empire, 1415–1825.* Oxford: Clarendon, 1963.

Buarque, Chico, and Ruy Guerra. *Calabar: O elogio da traição.* Rio de Janeiro, Brazil: Civilização Brasileira, 1975. [Play about a seventeenth-century Dutch/Portuguese conflict in which the black soldier Henrique Dias fights on the Portuguese side.]

Diegues, Carlos, director. *Quilombo.* CDK, 1984. [Film about Afro-Brazilian slave resistance in seventeenth-century Pernambuco.]

Ferlini, Vera Lúcia Amaral. "Pobres do açucar: Estrutura produtiva e relações de poder no Nordeste colonial." In *História Econômica do Período Colonial,* 2nd ed., 21–34. Edited by Tamás Szmrecsányi. São Paulo, Brazil: Hucitex/Associação Brasileira de Pesquisadores em História Econômica/Editora da Universidade de São Paulo/Imprensa Oficial, 2002.

Freyre, Gilberto. *The Masters and the Slaves (Casa-Grande & Senzala): A Study in the Development of Brazilian Civilization.* Berkeley: U of California P, 1986.

Galvão, Sebastião de Vasconcello. *Diccionario chorographico, historico e estatistico de Pernambuco.* 4 vols. Rio de Janeiro, Brazil: Imprensa Nacional, 1908.

Higgs, David. "Lisbon." In *Queer Sites: Gay Urban Histories since 1600,* 112–37. Edited by David Higgs. London: Routledge, 1999.

Images of Seventeenth-Century Pernambuco by the Dutch Painter Franz Post (c. 1612–1680). Instituto Ricardo Brennand, Recife. http://www.institutoricardobrennand.org.br/fpost/fpost.htm. Accessed May 10, 2009.

Jones, Gayl. *Song for Anninho.* Detroit, MI: Lotus, 1981. [North American poetic evocation of the destruction of Palmares, a large community of escaped slaves in Pernambuco, from a woman's point of view.]

Julião, Carlos, and Lygia da Fonseca Fernandes da Cunha. *Riscos illuminados de figurinhos de brancos e negros dos uzos do Rio de Janeiro e Serro do Frio (c. 1740–1811 or 1814).* 1960. [Paintings representing African slaves in eighteenth-century Brazil. Some images available online: http://hitchcock.itc.virginia.edu/Slavery/returnKeyword.php?keyword=Juliao.] Accessed Jan. 1, 2009.

Klein, Herbert. *The Atlantic Slave Trade.* Cambridge: Cambridge UP, 1999.

Lara, Sílvia Hunold. *Campos da violência.* Rio de Janeiro, Brazil: Paz e Terra, 1988.

———, ed. *Ordenações Filipinas: Livro V.* São Paulo, Brazil: Companhia das Letras, 1999.

Lima, Walter, Jr., director. *Chico Rei.* Brazil: Embrafilme, 1985. [Film about the Portuguese slave trade, and slavery in eighteenth-century Brazil. The film lacks subtitles and is hard to obtain but provides the best available evocation of eighteenth-century Brazilian slavery.]

Mattoso, Kátia M. de Queirós. *To Be a Slave in Brazil, 1550–1888.* New Brunswick, NJ: Rutgers UP, 1986.

Menard, Russel R., and Stuart B. Schwartz. "Por que a escravidão africana? A transição da força de trabalho no Brasil, no México e na Carolina do Sul." In *História Econômica do Período Colonial,* 2nd ed., 3–19. Edited by Tamás Szmrecsányi. São Paulo, Brazil: Hucitex/Associação Brasileira de Pesquisadores em História Econômica/Editora da Universidade de São Paulo/Imprensa Oficial, 2002.

Mott, Luiz. *O sexo proibido: Virgins, gays e escravos nas garras da Inquisição.* Campinas, Brazil: Papirus, 1988.

———. "Sodomia não é heresia: Dissidência moral e contracultura." In *A Inquisição em xeque: Temas, controvérsias, estudos de caso,* 253–66. Edited by Ronaldo Vainfas, Bruno Feitler, and Lana Lage da Gama Lima. Rio de Janeiro, Brazil: EdUERJ, 2006.

Palacios, Guillermo. *Campesinato e escravidão no Brasil: Agricultores livres e pobres na capitania geral de Pernambuco (1700–1871).* Brasilia, Brazil: Editora Universidade de Brasília, 2004.

Pieroni, Geraldo. *Os excluídos do Reino: A Inquisição portuguesa e o degredo para o Brasil Colônia.* Brasilia, Brazil: Editora Universidade de Brasília; São Paulo, Brazil: Imprensa Oficial do Estado, 2000.

Souza, Laura Mello e. *The Devil and the Land of the Holy Cross: Witchcraft, Slavery, and Popular Religion in Colonial Brazil.* First published 1986. Trans. Diane Grosklaus Whitty. Austin: U of Texas P, 2003.

Sweet, J. H. *Recreating Africa: Culture, Kinships, and Religion in the African-Portuguese World, 1441–1770.* Chapel Hill: U of North Carolina P, 2003. [Award-winning history of the cultural lives of African slaves in Portugal and Brazil.]

Vainfas, Ronaldo. "Inquisição como fábrica de hereges: Os sodomitas foram exceção?" In *A Inquisição em xeque: Temas, controvérsias, estudos de caso,* 267–80. Edited by Ronaldo Vainfas, Bruno Feitler, and Lana Lage da Gama Lima. Rio de Janeiro, Brazil: EdUERJ, 2006.

———. *Trópico dos pecados: Moral, sexualidade e Inquisição no Brasil.* Rio de Janeiro, Brazil: Editora Campus, 1989.

Wadsworth, James E. *Agents of Orthodoxy: Honor, Status, and the Inquisition in Colonial Pernambuco, Brazil.* Lanham, MD: Rowman & Littlefield, 2007.

Chapter 16

Aguirre, Carlos. *Agentes de su propia libertad: Los esclavos de Lima y la desintegración de la esclavitud. 1821–1854.* Lima, Peru: Pontificia Universidad Católica del Perú, 1993.

———. "Mujeres delincuentes, prácticas penales y servidumbre doméstica en Lima (1862–1930)." In *Familia y vida cotidiana en América Latina, siglos XVIII–XIX,* 203–31. Edited by Scarlett O'Phelan, Fanni Muñoz, Gabriel Ramón, and Mónica Ricketts. Lima, Peru: Pontificia Universidad Católica del Perú, Instituto Riva Agüero, Instituto Francés de Estudios Andinos, 2003.

Alfonso X. *Las Siete Partidas del rey don Alfonso el sabio.* Paris: Lecointe y Lasserre, 1843.

Aránguiz, Horacio, ed. *Lo público y lo privado en la historia americana.* Santiago, Chile: Fundación Mario Góngora, 2000.

Archivo Arzobispal de Lima (AAL). Lima, Peru.

Arias, Ybeth. "Economía y sociedad de los monasterios limeños durante la época borbónica: La Encarnación y la Concepción (1750–1821)." Licentiate Thesis, Lima, Peru: Universidad Nacional Mayor de San Marcos, 2008.

Arrelucea, Maribel. "Esclavitud, sexo y seducción en Lima, 1760–1820." *Revista del Archivo General de la Nación* 26 (2006): 167–92.

———. "Poder femenino, sexo y seducción: Esclavas en el recinto doméstico. Lima, 1760–1820." *Diálogos en Historia (Lima)* 4 (2006): 73–105.

———. "Poder masculino, esclavitud femenina y violencia doméstica en Lima, 1760–1820." In *Mujeres, familia y sociedad en la historia de América Latina, siglos XVIII – XXI,* 147–70. Edited by Scarlett O'Phelan and Margarita Zegarra. Lima, Peru: Pontificia Universidad Católica del Perú, Instituto Riva Agüero, 2006.

Chambers, Sara. *De súbditos a ciudadanos: Honor, género, y política en Arequipa, 1780–1854.* Lima, Peru: Red para el Desarrollo de las Ciencias Sociales, 2003.

Cosamalón, Jesús. *Indios detrás de la muralla: Matrimonios indígenas y convivencia interracial en Santa Ana (Lima, 1795–1820).* Lima, Peru: Fondo Editorial de la Pontificia Universidad Católica, 1999.

Flores Galindo, Alberto. *Aristocracia y plebe: Lima 1760–1820.* Lima, Peru: Mosca Azul, 1984.

Gauderman, Kimberly. *Women's Lives in Colonial Quito: Gender, Law, and Economy in Spanish America.* Austin: U of Texas P, 2003.

Gonzalbo, Pilar, and Cecilia Rabell, eds. *La familia en el mundo Iberoamericano.* Mexico City: Instituto de Investigaciones Sociales de la Universidad Autónoma de México, 1994.

Harth-Terré, Emilio, and Alberto Márquez Abanto. "El artesano negro en la arquitectura virreinal limeña." *Revista del Archivo Nacional (Lima)* 25 (1961): 360–430.

———. "Historia de la casa urbana virreinal de Lima." *Revista del Archivo Nacional (Lima)* 26, no. 4 (1962).

Hünefeldt, Christine. *Mujeres, esclavitud, emociones y libertad: Lima 1800–1854.* Lima, Peru: IEP, 1987.

Jouve-Martín, José Ramón. *Esclavos de la ciudad letrada: Esclavitud, escritura y colonialismo en Lima (1650–1700).* Lima, Peru: Instituto de Estudios Peruanos, 2005.

Lauderdale Graham, Sandra. *House and Street: The Domestic World of Servants and Masters in Nineteenth-Century Rio de Janeiro.* Austin: U of Texas P, 1992.

Lavrin, Asunción. *Sexualidad y matrimonio en la América hispánica, siglos XVI–XVIII.* Mexico: Grijalbo, 1991.

———, ed. *Las mujeres latinoamericanas: Perspectivas históricas.* Mexico City: Fondo de Cultura Económica, 1985.

Macera, Pablo. "Sexo y coloniaje." In *Trabajos de historia,* Vol. III, 297–352. Lima, Peru: Instituto Nacional de Cultura, 1977.

Mannarelli, María Emma. *Pecados públicos: La ilegitimidad en Lima, siglo XVII.* Lima, Peru: Flora Tristán, 1993.

———. "Vínculos familiares y fronteras de lo público y privado en Perú." In *La familia en Iberoamérica, 1550–1980,* 327–67. Edited by Pablo Rodríguez. Bogota, Colombia: Convenio Andrés Bello, Universidad Externado de Colombia, 2004.

O'Phelan, Scarlett, ed. *Etnicidad y discriminación en el Perú.* Lima, Peru: Instituto Riva Agüero, Banco Mundial, 2003.

———, Fanni Muñoz, Gabriel Ramón, and Mónica Ricketts, eds. *Familia y vida cotidiana en América Latina, siglos XVIII–XX.* Lima, Peru: PUCP, Instituto Riva Agüero, IFEA, 2003.

O'Phelan Godoy, Scarlett. "Entre el afecto y la mala conciencia: La paternidad responsable en el Perú borbónico." In *Mujeres, familia y sociedad en la historia de América Latina, siglos XVIII–XXI,* 37–56. Edited by Scarlett O'Phelan Godoy and Margarita Zegarra Flórez. Lima, Peru: Pontificia Universidad Católica del Perú, Instituto Riva Agüero, 2006.

Price, Richard, ed. *Sociedades cimarronas: Comunidades esclavas rebeldes en las Américas.* Mexico City: Siglo XXI, 1981.

Real Consejo de Indias. *Recopilación de Leyes de los Reynos de las Indias, mandadas imprimir y publicar por la Magestad Católica del Rey Don Carlos II, nuestro señor.* Madrid: Gráficas Ultra, 1943.

Reyes Flores, Alejandro. *La esclavitud en Lima.* Lima, Peru: Universidad Nacional Mayor de San Marcos, 1985.

Stern, Steve. *The Secret History of Gender.* Chapel Hill: U of North Carolina P, 1995.

Trazegnies, Fernando de. *Ciriaco de Urtecho, litigante por amor.* Lima, Peru: Pontificia Universidad Católica del Perú, 1982.

Trujillo Mena, Valentín. *La legislación eclesiástica en el virreynato del Perú durante el siglo XVI.* Lima, Peru: Lumen, 1980.

van Deusen, Nancy E. "Determinando los límites de la virtud: El discurso en torno al recogimiento entre las mujeres de Lima durante el siglo XVII." In *Mujeres y género en la historia del Perú*, 39–58. Edited by Margarita Zegarra. Lima, Peru: CENDOC-Mujer, 1999.

———. *Entre lo sagrado y lo mundano: La práctica institucional y cultural del recogimiento en la Lima virreinal.* Lima, Peru: Instituto de Estudios Peruanos, Instituto Francés de Estudios Andinos, 2007.

Wiesner-Hanks, Merry. *Cristianismo y sexualidad en la Edad Moderna: La regulación del deseo, la reforma de la práctica.* Madrid: Siglo XXI, 2001.

Chapter 17

Alfonso X, King of Castile and Leon, 1221–1284. *Siete partidas del rey don Alfonso, el sabio, cotejadas con varios códices antiguos por la Real Academia de la Historia.* Madrid: Imprenta Real, 1807. http://www.archive.org/details/lassietepartidas01castuoft. Accessed May 10, 2009.

Ansaldi, Waldo. "Cuestión de piel: Racialismo y legitimidad política." In *Calidoscopio latinoamericano.* Buenos Aires, Argentina: Ariel Historia, 2004.

Belmonte Postigo, José Luis. "Con la plata ganada y su propio esfuerzo: Los mecanismos de manumisión en Santiago de Cuba, 1780–1803." *Revista del Grupo de Estudios Afroamericanos (Universidad de Barcelona) EAVirtual* 3 (2005): 1–33.

Fanchin, Ana. "Los habitantes: Una visión estática." In *Espacio y población: Los Valles Cuyanos en 1777*, 47–89. San Juan, Argentina: UNSJ-Academia Nacional de la Historia, 2004.

———. "Protagonistas de un intercambio cotidiano, desde y hacia Chile por San Juan (Siglo XVIII)." *Estudios Trasandinos* 6 (2001): 67–79.

Goldberg, Marta B. "Negras y mulatas de Buenos Aires 1750–1850." Paper presented at the Forty-ninth Congreso Internacional de Americanistas (ICA). Quito, Ecuador, July 7–11, 1997. http://www.naya.org.ar/congresos/contenido/49CAI/Goldberg.htm. Accessed Nov. 21, 2008.

González Undurraga, Carolina. "Los usos del honor por esclavos y esclavas: Del cuerpo injuriado al cuerpo liberado (Chile, 1750–1823)." *Nuevo Mundo Mundos Nuevos* 6 (Nov. 19, 2006). http://nuevomundo.revues.org/document2869.html. Accessed Nov. 21, 2008.

Johnson, Lyman L. "La manumisión de esclavos en Buenos Aires durante el Virreinato." *Desarrollo Económico* 16, no. 63 (1976): 331–48.

———. "La manumisión en el Buenos Aires colonial: Un análisis ampliado." *Desarrollo Económico* 17, no. 68 (1978): 637–46.

López-Chávez, Celia. "Microhistoria de la esclavitud negra en el siglo XVIII: El caso de la residencia jesuita de San Juan de la Frontera." *Colonial Latin American Historical Review* 5, no. 4 (1996): 441–74.

Lucena Salmoral, Manuel. *Los códigos negros de la América española.* Alcala, Spain: Unesco-Universidad de Alcalá, 1996.

Mellafe, Rolando. *La esclavitud en Hispanoamérica.* Buenos Aires, Argentina: Editorial Universitaria de Buenos Aires, 1984.

———. *La introducción de la esclavitud negra en Chile: Tráfico y rutas.* Santiago, Chile: Universidad de Chile, 1959.

Recopilación de leyes de los reinos de las Indias: Mandadas imprimir y publicar por la magestad católica del rey Don Carlos II, Nuestro Señor. First published 1681. 4 vols. [5th ed. published Madrid, 1841.] [The *Título Quinto*, "De los mulatos, negros, berberiscos, é hijos de indios," is found in Vol. 3, available on Google Books.]

Rodríguez Molas, Ricardo. "El negro en el Río de la Plata." [First published in *Historia integral Argentina, T. I: De la independencia a la anarquía.* Buenos Aires, Argentina: Centro Editor de América Latina, 1970.] Bibliopress: Boletín Digital de la Biblioteca del Congreso de

la Nación. http://www.bcnbib.gov.ar/bibliopress/bibliopress9-3.htm. Accessed Nov. 21, 2008.

Zuluaga, Rosa María. "La trata de negros en la región cuyana durante el siglo XVIII." *Revista de la Junta de Estudios Históricos de Mendoza* 2, no. 1 (1970): 39–66.

Chapter 18

Abbad y Lasierra, Fray Agustín Iñigo. *Diario del viaje a la América.* Caracas, Venezuela: Banco Nacional de Ahorro y Préstamo, 1974.

Andrews, George Reid. *Afro-Latin America, 1800–2000.* New York: Oxford UP, 2004.

Artola, Miguel. "La guerra de reconquista de Santo Domingo (1808–1809)." *Revista de Indias* 21, no. 45 (1951): 447–84.

Bolster, W. Jeffrey. *Black Jacks: African American Seamen in the Age of Sail.* Cambridge, MA: Harvard UP, 1997.

Chinea, Jorge L. "Fissures in *El Primer Piso:* Racial Politics in Spanish Colonial Puerto Rico during Its Pre-plantation Era, c. 1700–1800." *Caribbean Studies* 30, no. 1 (2002): 169–204.

———. "A Quest for Freedom: The Immigration of Maritime Maroons into Puerto Rico, 1656–1800." *Journal of Caribbean History* 31, nos. 1–2 (1997): 51–87.

———. *Race and Labor in the Hispanic Caribbean: The West Indian Worker Experience in Puerto Rico, 1800–1850.* Gainesville: UP of Florida, 2005.

Dávila, Arlene. "Local/Diasporic Taínos: Towards a Cultural Politics of Memory, Reality and Imagery." In *Taino Revival: Critical Perspectives on Puerto Rican Identity and Cultural Politics,* 11–29. Edited by Gabriel Haslip-Viera. New York: Centro de Estudios Puertorriqueños, Hunter College, CUNY, 1999.

Dungy, Kathryn R. "Live and Let Live: Native and Immigrant Free People of Color in Early Nineteenth Century Puerto Rico." *Caribbean Studies* 33, no. 1 (2005): 79–111.

Geggus, David Patrick. *Haitian Revolutionary Studies.* Bloomington: Indiana UP, 2002.

Gilroy, Paul. *The Black Atlantic: Modernity and Double Consciousness.* Cambridge, MA: Harvard UP, 1993.

Giusti Cordero, Juan A. "Piñones sí se acuerda: 200 años de la participación negra en la victoria sobre la invasión inglesa (1797–1997)." *Revista de Genealogía Puertorriqueña* 1, no. 2 (2000): 33–41.

González, José Luis. *Puerto Rico: The Four-Storeyed Country and Other Essays.* New York: Markus Wiener Publishing, 1993.

Kinsbruner, Jay. *Not of Pure Blood: The Free People of Color and Racial Prejudice in Nineteenth-Century Puerto Rico.* Durham, NC: Duke UP, 1996.

Landers, Jane G., and Barry M. Robinson, eds. *Slaves, Subjects, and Subversives: Blacks in Colonial Latin America.* Albuquerque: U of New Mexico P, 2006.

López Cantos, Ángel. *Miguel Enríquez: Corsario boricua del siglo XVIII.* San Juan, Puerto Rico: Puerto, 1994.

López Lázaro, Fabio. "La mentira histórica de un pirata caribeño: El descubrimiento del trasfondo histórico de los *Infortunios de Alonso Ramírez* (1690)." *Anuario de Estudios Americanos* 64, no. 2 (2007): 87–104.

Martín Rebolo, J. F. Isabelo. *Ejército y sociedad en las Antillas en el siglo XVIII.* Seville: Ministerio de Defensa, 1988.

Morales Carrión, Arturo. "El reflujo en Puerto Rico de la crisis dominico-haitiana, 1791–1805." *Revista Eme-Eme: Estudios Dominicanos* 27 (1976): 19–39.

———. *Puerto Rico and the Non-Hispanic Caribbean: A Study in the Decline of Spanish Exclusivism.* Río Piedras: U of Puerto Rico P, 1952.

Moreno, Isodoro. “Festive Rituals, Religious Associations, and Ethnic Reaffirmation of Black Andalusians: Antecedents of the Black Confraternities and Cabildos in the Americas.” In *Representations of Blackness and the Performance of Identities,* 3–17. Edited by Jean Muteba Rahier. Westport, CT: Bergin & Garvey, 1999.

Olsen, Margaret M. “Negros Horros and Cimarrones on the Legal Frontier of the Caribbean: Accessing the African Voice in Colonial Spanish American Texts.” *Research in African Literatures* 29, no. 4 (1998): 52–72.

O’Reilly, Alexander. “Memoria de D Alexandro O’Reylly sobre la isla de Puerto Rico.” First published 1765. In *Antología de lecturas de historia de Puerto Rico (siglos xvi–xviii),* 387–88. Edited by Aida R. Caro Costas. San Juan, Puerto Rico: M. Pareja, 1972 (unpublished).

Ortiz, Altagracia. *Eighteenth-Century Reforms in the Caribbean: Miguel de Muesas, Governor of Puerto Rico, 1769–76.* Rutherford, NJ: Farleigh Dickinson UP, 1983.

Parrilla Ortíz, Pedro. *La esclavitud en Cádiz durante el siglo XVIII.* Cadiz, Spain: Diputación de Cádiz, 2001.

Pettinger, Alasdair. *Always Elsewhere: Travels of the Black Atlantic.* London: Cassell, 1998.

Picó, Fernando. “Esclavos, cimarrones, libertos y negros libres en Río Piedras, P.R., 1774–1873.” *Anuario de Estudios Americanos* 43 (1986): 25–33.

Quintana, Jorge. “La biografía del general Valero escrita por Vicente Dávila.” *Revista del Instituto de Cultura Puertorriqueña* 7, no. 25 (1964): 52–57.

Ribes Tovar, Federico. *100 Outstanding Puerto Ricans.* New York: Plus Ultra Educational Publishers, 1976.

Sánchez González, Lisa. *Boricua Literature: A Literary History of the Puerto Rican Diaspora.* New York: New York UP, 2001.

Schmidt, Peter R., and Thomas C. Patterson, eds. *Making Alternative Histories: The Practice of Archaeology in Non-Western Settings.* Santa Fe, NM: School of American Research, 1995.

Scott, Julius S. “The Common Wind: Currents of Afro-American Communication in the Era of the Haitian Revolution.” PhD diss., Duke University, 1986.

Sigüenza y Góngora, Carlos de. *Infortunios de Alonso Ramírez,* 3rd ed. First published 1690. Puebla, Mexico: Premiá, 1989.

Stark, David M. “Rescued from Their Invisibility: The Afro-Puerto Ricans of Seventeenth- and Eighteenth-Century San Mateo de Cangrejos.” *The Americas* 63, no. 4 (2007): 551–86.

Sued Badillo, Jalil. “The Theme of the Indigenous in the National Projects of the Hispanic Caribbean.” In *Making Alternative Histories: The Practice of Archaeology in Non-Western Settings,* 25–46. Edited by Peter R. Schmidt and Thomas C. Patterson. Santa Fe, NM: School of American Research Press, 1995.

Sued Badillo, Jalil, and Angel López Cantos. *Puerto Rico Negro.* Rio Piedras, Puerto Rico: Editorial Cultural, 1986.

Torres, Arlene. “La gran familia puertorriqueña ‘ej prieta de beldá’ (The Great Puerto Rican Family Is Really Black).” In *Blackness in Latin America and the Caribbean: Social Dynamics and Cultural Transformations,* Vol. 2, 285–306. Edited by Arlene Torres and Norman E. Whitten, Jr. Bloomington: Indiana UP, 1998.

Zenón Cruz, Isabelo. *Narciso descubre su trasero: El negro en la cultura puertorriqueña.* 2 vols. Humacao, Puerto Rico: Furidi, 1975.

Glossary

Law, Robin. “Ethnicities of Enslaved Africans in the Diaspora: On the Meanings of ‘Mina’ (Again).” *History in Africa* 32 (2005): 247–67.

———. “Ethnicity and the Slave Trade: ‘Lucumí’ and ‘Nago’ as Ethnonyms in West Africa.” *History in Africa* 24 (1997): 205–19.

Resources for Teaching Early Modern Afro-Latino Experiences and Their Legacies

Additional Publications of Afro-Latino Voices

Baquaqua, Mahommah Gardo. *The Biography of Mahommah Gardo Baquaqua: His Passage from Slavery to Freedom in Africa and America.* Edited by Robin Law and Paul E. Lovejoy. Princeton, NJ: Markus Wiener, 2001. [Biography based on Baquaqua's (b. 1820s; last documented 1857) own words. Baquaqua was born in what is today Benin and lived in slavery in Brazil, escaping when in the United States and then traveling to freedom in Haiti.]

Barnet, Miguel. *Biografía de un cimarrón.* Havana, Cuba: Academia de Ciencias de Cuba, Instituto de Etnología y Folklore, 1966. [Writing from interviews, anthropologist Miguel Barnet composed as autobiography the life story of the ex-slave Esteban Montejo, whose life spanned the late nineteenth and early twentieth centuries.]

Boyer, Richard, and Geoffrey Spurling. *Colonial Lives: Documents on Latin American History, 1550–1850.* New York: Oxford UP, 2000. [Six chapters present, in English translation, documents in which Afro-Latinos speak.]

Brásio, Padre António, ed. *Monumenta Missionaria Africana: África Ocidental.* 15 vols. Lisbon: Agência-Geral do Ultramar, 1971. [All but one of Njinga's known surviving letters are published in Brásio's works.]

Conrad, Robert Edgar. *Children of God's Fire: A Documentary History of Black Slavery in Brazil.* University Park, PA: Penn State UP, 1994. [Includes a few nineteenth-century narratives by black slaves.]

"Digest of Documents in the Archives of the Indies, Seville, Spain, Bearing on the Negroes of Cuba and Especially Those Employed in the Minas de Cobre." *Journal of Negro History* 12, no. 1 (1927): 60–99.

Equiano, Olaudah. *The Interesting Narrative of the Life of Olaudah Equiano, or Gustavus Vassa, The African, Written by Himself.* New York: Norton, 2000. [In his abolitionist account of his life, Equiano (c. 1745–1797) tells of being born in "Eboe" (in what is now Nigeria) and being enslaved at about age eleven and taken to the West Indies. Although he moved mostly in the Anglophone world, he did spend time in the Spanish Caribbean.]

Jopling, Carol F., ed. *Indios y negros en Panamá en los siglos XVI y XVII: Selecciones de los documentos del Archivo General de Indias.* Trans. Margarita Cruz de Drake. Antigua, Guatemala: Centro de Investigaciones Regionales de Mesoamérica, 1994. [Includes a few testimonies by Afro-Latinos.]

Latino, Juan. *La Austriada de Juan Latino: Introducción, traducción inédita y texto.* Edited by José A. Sánchez Marín. Granada, Spain: Instituto de Historia del Derecho, Universidad de Granada, 1981. [Writings by a black Spanish Renaissance humanist and ex-slave.]

Manzano, Juan Francisco (1797–1854). *The Autobiography of a Slave.* Introduction and modernized Spanish version by Ivan A. Schulman. Trans. Evelyn Picon Garfield. Detroit, MI: Wayne State UP, 1996.

McKnight, Kathryn Joy. "Gendered Declarations: Testimonies of Three Captured Maroon Women, Cartagena de Indias, 1634." *Colonial Latin American Historical Review* 12, no. 4 (2003): 499–527.

Peabody, Sue, and Kelia Grinberg. *Slavery, Freedom, and the Law in the Atlantic World: A Brief History with Documents.* Boston: Bedford/St. Martin's, 2007. [Includes some slave petitions for freedom in nineteenth-century Ibero-America.]

Redworth, Glyn. "Mythology with Attitude? A Black Christian's Defence of Negritude in Early Modern Europe." *Social History* 28, no. 1 (2003): 49–66. ["Carta a unas monjas"—which is housed in Biblioteca Nacional, Madrid (Ms. 6149, item 83, fols. 236r–237v)—is reproduced in this article.]

Schwartz, Stuart B. "Resistance and Accommodation in Eighteenth-Century Brazil: The Slaves' View of Slavery." *Hispanic American Historical Review* 57, no. 1 (Feb. 1977): 69–81. [Includes a translation and the original Portuguese of a remarkable late-eighteenth-century peace treaty, which escaped slaves from the Engenho Santana in the captaincy of Bahia proposed to their master.]

Splendiani, Anna María, and Tulio Aristizábal, eds. *Proceso de beatificación y canonización de San Pedro Claver.* Trans. Anna María Splendiani and Tulio Aristizabal. Bogota, Colombia: Centro Editorial Javeriano, 2002. [Some of the witnesses quoted in this work were Africans or Afro-Latinos. Their testimony was translated into Latin during the beatification and canonization process and was translated back into Spanish by the editors.]

Splendiani, Anna María, José Enrique Sánchez Bohórquez, and Emma Cecilia Luque de Salazar. *Cincuenta años de Inquisición en el Tribunal de Cartagena de Indias, 1610–1660.* Bogota, Colombia: Pontificia Universidad Javeriana, Instituto Colombiano de Cultura Hispánica, 1997. [Includes a few summaries of testimonies by Afro-Latinos.]

van Deusen, Nancy E., ed. and trans. *The Souls of Purgatory: The Spiritual Diary of a Seventeenth-Century Afro-Peruvian Mystic, Ursula de Jesús.* Albuquerque: U New Mexico P, 2004.

Films

[These films are listed by title. Abbreviations for languages listed: E (English), Sp (Spanish), P (Portuguese).]

A Dios Momo [*Goodbye Momo*]. Director Leonardo Ricagni. Mojo Films, 2005. [Feature film. Story of a young Afro-Uruguayan boy's magical encounters with the Murgas during the Montevideo carnival. Sp with E subtitles.]

Bahia, Africa in the Americas. Director Michael Brewer. Berkeley: University of California, Extension, Media Center, 1988. [Documentary film. P with E translations.]

Candombe. Director Rafael Deugenio. ArtMattan Productions, 1993. [Documentary about the preservation of Afro-Uruguayan music and dance traditions brought by slaves. Sp with E subtitles.]

Candombe: Tambores en Libertad. Directors Carlos Paez Vilaró, Hassen Balut, and Silvestre Jacobi. Mistika Films, 2006. [Documentary about the Afro-Uruguayan music and dance traditions brought by slaves. Sp with E subtitles.]

Chico Rei. Director Walter Lima, Jr. Embrafilme, 1985. [Portrays the legendary Galanga, king of Kongo, who was enslaved and taken to Minas Gerais, Brazil, in the eighteenth century, where he found gold, bought his freedom, and became a landowner. P]

Garifuna Journey. Directors Andrea E. Leland and Kathy L. Berger. New Day Films, 1998. [Documentary. Present-day Garifunas tell of their people's history of resistance and their culture. E and Garifuna with E subtitles.]

Gorée: Door of No Return. Directors Ann E. Jonson and Robin Klein. Même Chase Production,1992. [History of the slave trade. E]

Hands of God. Director Delia Ackerman. ArtMattan Productions, 2004. [Documentary about Afro-Peruvian percussionist Julio "Cholote" Algendones (1937–2004), who played a mix of traditional and contemporary styles. Sp with E subtitles.]

Îlé Aiyé [*The House of Life*]. Director David Byrne. Little Magic Films, 2004. [Documentary and poetic evocation of Afro-Brazilian Candomblé. E]

La raíz olvidada [*The Forgotten Root*]. Director Rafael Rebollar. Writers Antonio Noyola and Beatriz García. Producciones Trabuco, 2001. [Documentary on the history and cultural traditions of Afro-Mexicans. Sp with E subtitles.]

La última cena [*The Last Supper*]. Director Tomás Gutiérrez Alea. Writers Moreno Fraginal and Constante Diego. Instituto Cubano de Arte e Industrias Cinematográficos (ICAIC), 1977. [Feature film recreating an eighteenth-century slave uprising following a master's reenactment of the Last Supper with twelve slaves. Sp with E subtitles.]

Maluala. Director Sergio Giral. Instituto Cubano de Arte e Industrias Cinematográficos (ICAIC), 1979. [Feature film portraying nineteenth-century Cuban *Maroon* communities in negotiations and armed confrontations with Spanish colonial government. Sp with E subtitles.]

Negro che, los primeros desaparecidos. Director Alberto Masliah. 2006. [Documentary about the official erasure of Afro-Argentine culture and the struggle of Afro-Argentineans to preserve their cultural heritage. Sp]

Quilombo. Director Carlos Diegues. New Yorker Films, 1984. [Feature film depicting the autonomous *Maroon* republic in seventeenth-century Brazil in conflict with the Portuguese landowners and military under its legendary leaders Ganga Zumba and Zumbi. P with E subtitles.]

Quilombo Country. Director Leonard Abrams. Moving Eye Productions, 2006. [Documentary on the history and traditions of Brazil's Quilombo communities, who descended from *Maroon* communities. P with E subtitles.]

The Slave Kingdoms. From *Wonders of the African World.* Director Henry Louis Gates, Jr. PBS, 1999. [Documentary in which Gates visits Elmina, Abomey, and Asante to interview descendants of slave traders and explore the history of the slave trade. E]

Sons of Benkos. Director Silva Lucas. Palenque Records & Les Films Du Village, 2003. [Documentary on Colombia's African musical culture, particularly in the rural town of *Palenque* de San Basilio, which was formerly a *Maroon* settlement. Sp with E subtitles.]

Susana Baca: Memoria Viva. Director Marc Dixon. 24 Images, Karma Productions, 2003. [Documentary on Susana Baca, cofounder of the Instituto Negrocontinuo, which supports research and performance of Black Peruvian musical culture. Sp with E subtitles.]

Voices of the Orishas. Director Alvaro Pérez Betancourt. University of California, Extension, Center for Media and Independent Learning, 1993. [Docudrama of Yoruba cultural and religious heritage in Cuba. Sp and Yoruba with E subtitles.]

Music

Andy Palacio & the Garífuna Collective. *Watina.* Cumbancha, 2007. (compact disc). [Garífuna music from Belize with indigenous Arawak and Carib as well as West African roots.]

Antología del candombe Vol. II. Bizarro, 1995. (compact disc). [Afro-Uruguayan drum-based processional music.]

Baca, Susana. *Espíritu vivo.* Luaka Bop, 2002. (compact disc). [Baca is an Afro-Peruvian singer and the founder of the Instituto Negrocontinuo.]

Cáceres. *Murga Argentina.* Mañana, 2005. (compact disc). [Afro-Argentine Candombe-carnival-style music.]

Capoeira Angola from Salvador, Brazil. Smithsonian Folkways, 1996. (compact disc).

Ecuador & Colombia: Marimba Masters and Sacred Songs. Music of the Earth, 1998. (compact disc).

Fariñas. *Cajón al muerto.* Camaján, 2002. (compact disc). [Afro-Cuban rumba music in honor of the spirits.]

Grupo Afro Boriqua. *Bombazo.* Blue Jackel Entertainment, 1998. (compact disc). [Afro-Puerto Rican call-and-response music in the bomba tradition.]

Grupo Siquisirí. *En Vivo desde el Rialto Center for the Arts.* Grupo Siquisirí, 2007. (compact disc). [Son Jarocho music from Veracruz, Mexico.]

Ilê Aiyê. *Canto Negro.* Warner Music Brazil, 2003. (compact disc). [Afro-Brazilian ritual music.]

Les joyeuses ambulances, musique funéraire afro-colombienne. Buda, 2004. (compact disc). [Funeral music from the Palenque de San Basilio, Colombia.]

Los Gaiteros de San Jacinto. *Un fuego de sangre pura.* Smithsonian Folkways, 2006. (compact disc). [Colombian gaitero music.]

Millan, Angelica, & Grupo Costa y Sierra. *African Influences in Mexico.* Agave records, 1998. (compact disc).

Perú negro. *Jolgorio.* Times Square, 2004. (compact disc).

Ros, Lázaro. [All his many albums are recommended. Afro-Cuban Regla de Ocho music rooted in Yoruba culture.]

Soul of Angola Anthology: 1965–1975. Lusafrica, 2001. (compact disc set).

The Soul of Black Perú: AfroPeruvian Classics. Luaka Bop, 2000. (compact disc)

Spiro, Michael, and Mark Lamson. *Batá Ketú: A Musical Interplay of Cuba & Brasil.* Bembe, 1996. (compact disc).

Totó la Momposina y Sus Tambores. *La candela viva.* Real World Records, 1993. (compact disc). [Colombian singer of music of Afro-Latino and indigenous roots.]

Valdés, Merceditas & Yoruba Andabo. *Aché IV.* Egrem, 1995. (compact disc). [Afro-Cuban spiritual music.]

Wemba, Papa. *Papa Wemba.* Stern's, 1994. (compact disc). [Congolese rumba or soukous musician.]

AFRO-LATINO LEGACIES IN ART

Araújo, Emanoel, curator. *A divina inspiração, sagrada e religiosa. Sincretismos.* Exhibit curators Carlos A. C. Lemos and Vagner Gonçalves da Silva. São Paulo, Brazil: Museu Afro-Brasil, 2008.

———, curator. *Para nunca esquecer. Negras memórias. Memórias de negros.* Rio de Janeiro, Brazil: Museu Histórico Nacional, 2002.

Assunção, Matthias Röhrig. *Capoeira: A History of Afro-Brazilian Martial Art.* London: Routledge, 2005.

Beumers, Erna, and Hans-Joachim Koloss, eds. *Kings of Africa: Art and Authority in Central Africa. Collection Museum für Völkerkunde Berlin.* Utrecht, Netherlands: Foundation Kings of Africa, 1992.

Centro Cultural de España. *Aportaciones culturales haitianas: VIII Festival Antropológico de Culturas Afroamericanas.* Santo Domingo, Dominican Republic: Centro Cultural de España, 2002.

Grimaldi Forum. *Arts of Africa: 7000 Years of African Art.* Monaco: Grimaldi Forum, 2005.

Herreman, Frank, ed. *In the Presence of Spirits: African Art from the National Museum of Ethnology, Lisbon.* New York: Museum for African Art, 2000.

Hurst, Norman. *Ngola. The Weapon as Authority, Identity, and Ritual Object in Sub-Saharan Africa.* Cambridge, MA: Hurst Gallery, 1997.

Lam, Wifredo. *Wifredo Lam.* Introduction by Graziella Pogolotti. Havana, Cuba: José Martí, 1997.

Mexican Fine Arts Center Museum. *The African Presence in México: From Yanga to the Present.* Chicago: Mexican Fine Arts Center Museum, 2006.

National Museum of African Art. *Selected Works from the Collection of the National Museum of African Art.* Washington, DC: Smithsonian National Museum of African Art, 1999.

Price, Sally, and Richard Price. *Maroon Arts: Cultural Vitality in the African Diaspora.* Boston: Beacon, 1999.

Visonà, Monica Blackmun. *A History of Art in Africa.* New York: Harry N. Abrams, 2001.

Notes on Contributors

Maribel Arrelucea Barrantes is a researcher and teacher at the Universidad Nacional Mayor de San Marcos and the Universidad de San Ignacio de Loyola, in Lima, Peru. She has published on slavery and marronage in Peru, with a focus on gender, in the *Revista del Archivo General de la Nación, Visión Histórica, Perspectivas, Diálogos en Historia,* and *Summa Historiae.* She also contributed to several books, including *Mujeres, familia y sociedad en la historia de América Latina, siglos XVIII–XXI.*

Charles Beatty-Medina is Assistant Professor of Latin American History at the University of Toledo. He specializes in the history of colonial Latin America, the African diaspora, and the southern Atlantic and circum-Caribbean region. His dissertation examines the Maroon communities of Esmeraldas, Ecuador in the sixteenth and early seventeenth centuries. His articles include "Caught Between Rivals: The Spanish-African Maroon Competition for Captive Indian Labor in the Region of Esmeraldas during the Late Sixteenth and Early Seventeenth Centuries" in *Americas: A Quarterly Review of Inter-American Cultural History.*

Jorge L. Chinea specializes in colonial Latin American history. His book, *Race and Labor in the Hispanic Caribbean: The West Indian Immigrant Worker Experience in Puerto Rico, 1800–1850,* received Wayne State University's Board of Governors Faculty Recognition Award in 2006. A past contributing editor for the *Handbook of Latin American Studies,* he is currently Associate Professor and Director of the Center for Chicano-Boricua Studies at Wayne State University.

María Elena Díaz is Associate Professor of History at the University of California, Santa Cruz. Her research on the Atlantic world, colonial Latin America, the colonial Caribbean, and Cuba is interdisciplinary and focuses on slavery and freedom, colonialism, and legal, political, popular, and religious cultures. She is the author of *The Virgin, the King, and the Royal Slaves of El Cobre: Negotiating Freedom in Colonial Cuba, 1670–1780.*

Ana Teresa Fanchin is Professor of History at the Universidad Nacional de San Juan (Argentina), where she directs research at the Instituto de Geografía Aplicada and teaches colonial history, history of demographics, and Latin American women's history in the Department of History and the Department of Graduate Studies. She is Academic Advisor for International Publications and Corresponding Foreign Member of the Academia de Estudios Hispanoamericanos in Cadiz, Spain.

Patricia Fogelman is a historian and researcher at CONICET (Argentina). She earned her doctorate in history at the EHESS (France) and the Facultad de Filosofía y Letras at the Universidad de Buenos Aires. Her research is on religiosity, culture, and power in the colonial Americas. She is completing a post-doctorate at the UFES

(Brazil) on representations of the Virgin and heaven in the colonial Christian imaginary in Minas Gerais. She coordinates the Grupo de Estudios sobre Religiosidad y Evangelización, and she teaches history at the Universidad de Buenos Aires and the Universidad Nacional de Luján (Argentina).

Baltasar Fra-Molinero is Associate Professor of Spanish at Bates College. He is the author of *La imágen de los negros en el teatro del Siglo de Oro* as well as a number of essays on the representation of Blacks in Spain and Latin America from the Renaissance to today. He is working on a critical edition and English translation of the *Vida ejemplar* of Sor Teresa Chicaba in collaboration with Sue E. Houchins.

Leo J. Garofalo is Assistant Professor of History at Connecticut College, where he teaches Latin American and Caribbean history and the history of race and gender in colonial Latin America. He co-edited *Más allá de la dominación y la resistencia: Estudios de historia peruana, siglos XVI–XX,* and an issue of the *Journal of Colonialism and Colonial History* devoted to constructing difference in colonial Latin America, and has published articles and chapters on colonial Peru and the African diaspora in the Atlantic world. He is working on a book, *Making the Markers of Race in Colonial Peru: Taverns, Witches, and Marketplaces in Lima and Cuzco.*

Marta Goldberg is a historian, researcher, and full professor at the Universidad Nacional de Luján (Argentina), where she directs the masters program in social sciences, with a specialization in social history. Her research is on the social history of blacks and mulattoes in Río de la Plata from the late colonial period through the early decades of independence. She is a member of the ALADAA and the Comité Científico Internacional del Programa de la UNESCO "La Ruta del Esclavo."

Richard A. Gordon is Assistant Professor in the Department of Spanish and Portuguese and associated faculty of film studies and comparative studies at Ohio State University. He researches primarily Brazilian- and Spanish-American historical cinema and eighteenth-century Luso-Brazilian culture. His book, *Cannibalizing the Colony: Cinematic Adaptations of Colonial Literature in Mexico and Brazil,* is forthcoming from Purdue University Press. He is working on a book that discusses Brazilian and Cuban films about slavery.

Sara Vicuña Guengerich is Assistant Professor of Spanish at Texas Tech University. She completed her dissertation, "Indigenous Andean Women in Colonial Textual Discourses," at the University of New Mexico. Her research interests include colonial Spanish American literature and history, particularly gender issues.

Linda Heywood is Professor of History at Boston University, where she teaches African, African-American, and women's history. She is the author of *Contested Power in Angola, 1840s to the Present,* editor of *Central Africans and Cultural Transformations in the American Diaspora,* and co-author, with John K. Thornton, of *Central Africans, Atlantic Creoles, and the Foundation of America,* which was awarded the Herskovits prize by the

African Studies Association. She has consulted for museum exhibitions, including African Voices at the Smithsonian Institution and Against Human Dignity sponsored by the Maritime Museum.

Sue E. Houchins is Associate Professor at Bates College, where she teaches African-American and women and gender studies. Her research focuses on the intersection of race, gender, and sexuality among women of the Black Atlantic. She edited *Spiritual Narratives,* a collection of African-American women's writings, and is completing a book on representations of Black lesbians in women's literatures of Africa and the Americas, co-editing a collection of essays on W. E. B. Du Bois, and co-editing a translation of the eighteenth-century hagiography of Sor Teresa Chicaba.

José R. Jouve-Martín is Associate Professor in the Department of Hispanic Studies at McGill University. His research focuses on seventeenth-century colonial lettered culture, the intersection between writing and religious practices, and the use of written documents by slaves and their descendants in Spanish America. He has authored *Esclavos de la ciudad letrada: Esclavitud, escritura y colonialismo en Lima (1650–1700)* as well as articles in journals such as *Colonial Latin American Review, Canadian Review of Hispanic Studies, Theatralia,* and *Hispanófila.*

Larry D. Miller is a research historian at the Spanish Colonial Research Center, University of New Mexico (UNM), and is on the editorial staff of the *Colonial Latin American Historical Review.* He interprets the history and demonstrates the art of blacksmithing at Rancho de las Golondrinas and Bent's Old Fort National Historic Site. He earned his B.A. and M.A. in Spanish at UNM. For eighteen years he worked as a compiler, paleographer, and translator on the Vargas Project's publication of the journals of Don Diego de Vargas. He is co-author of *Martineztown 1823–1950: Hispanics, Italians, Jesuits & Land Investors in New Town Albuquerque.*

Elizabeth W. Kiddy is Associate Professor of History and Director of Latin American and Caribbean studies at Albright College. She is the author of *Blacks of the Rosary: Memory and History in Minas Gerais, Brazil,* and several articles and book chapters on Africans in confraternities in Brazil.

Luis Madureira holds a degree in comparative literature and is Professor in the Department of Spanish and Portuguese at the University of Wisconsin–Madison. He has published two books, *Imaginary Geographies in Portuguese and Lusophone-African Literature: Narratives of Discovery and Empire* and *Cannibal Modernities: Postcoloniality and the Avant-Garde in Caribbean and Brazilian Literature,* and several articles on Luso-Brazilian literature and postcolonial theory. His current research focuses on Mozambican theater and the politics of time in contemporary Lusophone fiction.

Kathryn Joy McKnight is Associate Professor of Spanish and Associate Director for Academic Programs at the Latin American and Iberian Institute at the University of New Mexico. Her book, *The Mystic of Tunja: The Writings of Madre Castillo, 1671–1742,* won

the Modern Language Association's Kovacs prize in 1998. She has published on Afro-Latino documentary narratives in the *Colonial Latin American Review, Colonial Latin American Historical Review, Revista de Estudios Hispánicos,* and the *Journal of Colonialism and Colonial History.*

Rachel Sarah O'Toole is Assistant Professor of the Early Modern Atlantic World and Colonial Latin America in the Department of History at the University of California, Irvine. Her publications include "From the Rivers of Guinea to the Valleys of Peru: Becoming a *Bran* Diaspora within Spanish Slavery" in *Social Text,* and "Danger in the Convent: Colonial Demons, Idolatrous *Indias,* and Bewitching *Negras* in Santa Clara (Trujillo del Perú)" in the *Journal of Colonialism and Colonial History.*

Joseph P. Sánchez is superintendent of the National Park Service's Petroglyph National Monument and the Spanish Colonial Research Center at the University of New Mexico. He is the founding editor of the *Colonial Latin American Historical Review.* He has published studies on the Spanish colonial frontiers in California, Arizona, New Mexico, Texas, and Alaska, including *Between Two Rivers: The Atrisco Land Grant in Albuquerque's History, 1691–1968.*

Angelica Sánchez-Clark is a National Park Service linguist historian with the Spanish Colonial Research Center at the University of New Mexico (UNM). Since 1995, she has been the managing editor of the *Colonial Latin American Historical Review.* She is a doctoral candidate in the Department of Spanish and Portuguese at UNM, writing her dissertation on the nineteenth-century Mexican indigenous intellectual, Ignacio Altamirano. She is co-editor of *Set in Stone: A Binational Workshop on Petroglyph Management in the United States and Mexico.*

John K. Thornton is Professor of History at Boston University, where he teaches African and Atlantic history. He is the author of *The Kingdom of Kongo: Civil War and Transition, 1641–1718; Africa and Africans in the Making of the Atlantic World, 1400–1680; The Kongolese Saint Anthony: Dona Beatriz Kimpa Vita and the Antonian Movement, 1684–1706; Warfare in Atlantic Africa, 1500–1800;* and coauthor, with Linda Heywood, of *Central Africans, Atlantic Creoles, and the Foundation of the Americas, 1585–1660,* which was awarded the Herskovits prize by the African Studies Association.

Nicole von Germeten holds a Ph.D. in history from the University of California, Berkeley and is Assistant Professor of History at Oregon State University. She has published two books: *Black Blood Brothers: Confraternities and Social Mobility for Afro-Mexicans* and *Treatise on Slavery,* an annotated translation of Alonso de Sandoval's 1627 *De instauranda Aethiopum salute,* the earliest known book-length study of African slavery in the Americas.

David Wheat is Assistant Professor of History at Michigan State University. He completed his dissertation, "The Afro-Portuguese Maritime World and the Foundations of Spanish Caribbean Society, 1570–1640," at Vanderbilt University.

Index

Note: All italicized words are defined in the Glossary. We have also added English-language cross-references in the Index to facilitate its use as a tool for considering themes for further investigation.

through all the heavens, and every particle had an innate gravity towards all the rest, and the whole space throughout which this matter was scattered, was finite, the matter on the outside of this space would by its gravity tend towards all the matter on the inside, and by consequence fall down into the middle of the whole space, and there compose one great spherical mass. But if the matter were evenly disposed throughout an infinite space, it could never convene into one mass; but some of it would convene into one mass and some into another, so as to make an infinite number of great masses, scattered great distances from one to another throughout all that infinite space. And thus might the sun and fixed stars be formed, supposing the matter were of a lucid nature."

Newton envisaged a static universe, but the same qualitative picture occurs in an expanding Friedmann universe, as was shown by the Russian physicist Eugene Lifshitz in 1946.

Because of the atomic nature of matter the early universe could never have been completely smooth. It would obviously be gratifying if the inevitable random irregularities in the initial distribution of atoms sufficed ultimately to produce the bound systems of stars we see throughout the universe today. Unfortunately this type of statistical fluctuation fails by many orders of magnitude to account for the observed degree of structure in the universe. Moreover, it remained a puzzle why agglomerations of a certain mass, notably galaxies, should be so plentiful. It appeared necessary to postulate initial fluctuations in a seemingly *ad hoc* manner, and nothing had really been explained; "things are as they are because they were as they were."

Only in the past two or three years has it been realized that the background radiation acts as a gigantic homogenizer on certain preferred scales. To understand just how this works we must look more closely at Gamow's model of the universe. In the early stages, when the universe consisted of a primordial fireball, no structures such as galaxies or stars could have existed in anything like their present form. All space would have been filled with radiation (photons) and hot gas, consisting of the nuclei of hydrogen and helium and the accompanying electrons. The photons would be repeatedly scattered from the electrons. For at least the first 100,000 years of its history (beginning roughly 10 seconds after its emergence

SPHERICAL GALAXY, classified as type E0 in Hubble's scheme, is a member of the Virgo cluster of galaxies. A representative of the most massive type of galaxy, this system, designated M 87, contains about 30 times as many stars as a spiral system such as our own does.

ELLIPTICAL GALAXY in the constellation of Cassiopeia is a member of the local group of galaxies. Designated NGC 147, it is an E4, or intermediate, type of elliptical galaxy. Because of its comparative proximity to our system it can be resolved into individual stars.

from the initial singularity) the universe can be pictured as a composite gas in which some of the "atoms" are particles and the rest are photons. For the universe as a whole there are now at least 10 million times more photons than particles. From thermodynamic considerations one can conclude that photons must also have greatly outnumbered particles in the fireball. For a gas in equilibrium each species of particle contributes to the total pressure in proportion to its number. This still holds (very nearly) for photons, so that the radiation would make an overwhelmingly dominant contribution to the pressure. (During the first 10 seconds, when the temperature exceeds a few billion degrees, the situation is less simple because pairs of photons can interact to form an electron and a positron.)

As the expansion proceeds and the density decreases, the photons lose energy, the temperature drops and the particles move less rapidly. A key stage is reached after about 10^5 years, when the fireball has cooled to 3,000 degrees. The electrons are then moving so slowly that virtually all are captured by nuclei and retained in bound orbits. In this condition they can no longer scatter photons and the universe becomes transparent. Inasmuch as the background temperature today is only about three degrees absolute, one can conclude that the universe has expanded by a red-shift factor of 1,000 since the scattering stopped. (Wavelength is inversely proportional to temperature.)

The microwave background photons have probably propagated freely since the universe became transparent and therefore they should carry information about a "surface of last scattering" at a red shift of more than 1,000. Compare this with the red-shift factor of about one-half for the most distant galaxy known! Because these photons have been traveling unimpeded since long before galaxies existed, they should provide us with remarkably direct evidence of physical conditions in the early universe.

Let us return now to the epoch of the primordial fireball and ask: How were inhomogeneities in the fireball affected by the presence of the intense radiation field? Radiation would inhibit the process of gravitational collapse. Under radiation pressure nonuniformities in the fireball would take the form of oscillations, pressure waves or turbulence. These disturbances, in turn, will be dissipated by viscosity and the development of shock waves. Some wavelengths will be attenuated more severely than others, so that inhomogeneities of favored size will be preserved whereas those less favored will tend to be destroyed. The aim of recent work has been to determine what scales of perturbation are most likely to survive the various damping processes until the scattering of photons comes to an end. Any perturbation whose survival and growth is specially favored should eventually dominate, almost irrespective of how nonuniformities were initially distributed in the primordial fireball. An encouraging result that has already emerged from these studies is that 10^{12} solar masses, roughly the mass of a large galaxy, is one such preferred scale [*see illustration on page 61*].

After the electrons in the initial plasma have been bound into atoms, radiation no longer affects the distribution of mass. At this point the surviving perturbations are free to amplify gravitationally. (It should be noted, however, that on small scales—less than 10^6 solar masses—the kinetic energy of atoms exerts a pressure of its own that inhibits gravitational collapse.) The first generation of bound systems will therefore condense from whatever scale of fluctuations had the largest amplitude at the time of decoupling, that is, when the fireball ceased to be a plasma of electrons and other particles.

At what stage did protogalaxies stop expanding and separate out from the rest of the universe? We might guess that this happened when the mean density was comparable to the present density in the outlying parts of galaxies. In 1962 Olin J. Eggen, Donald Lynden-Bell and Allan R. Sandage of the Hale Observatories investigated the likely early history of our own galaxy by studying

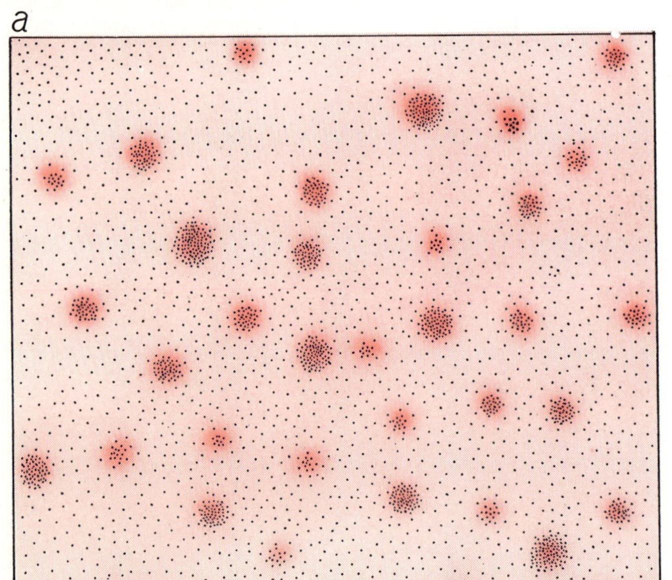

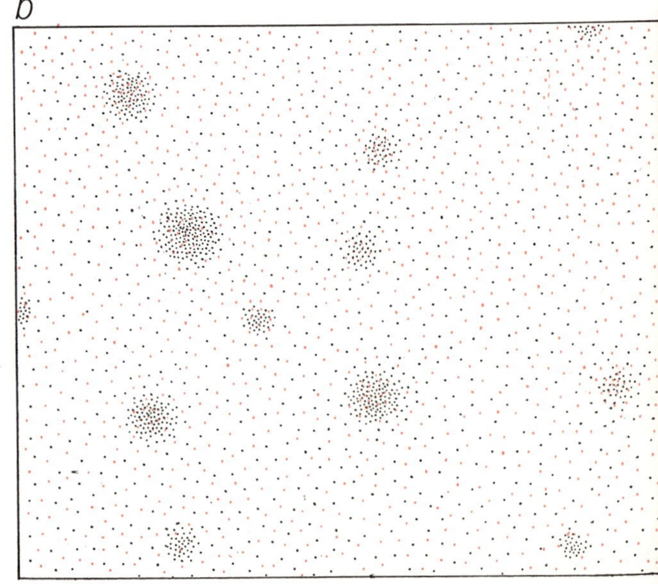

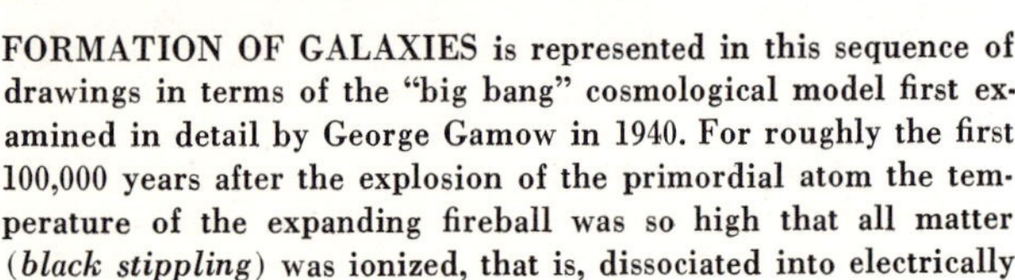
FORMATION OF GALAXIES is represented in this sequence of drawings in terms of the "big bang" cosmological model first examined in detail by George Gamow in 1940. For roughly the first 100,000 years after the explosion of the primordial atom the temperature of the expanding fireball was so high that all matter (*black stippling*) was ionized, that is, dissociated into electrically charged particles (*a*). In this situation photons of radiation could not travel very far without being scattered by the free electrons; as a result the universe during this period was effectively opaque (*light shade of color*). Nevertheless, slight random enhancements in the density of matter above the mean density presumably took place, usually accompanied by corresponding enhancements in the

very old stars in the galactic halo. These stars probably formed while the galaxy was collapsing to its present disklike shape (and before the birth of the stars in the Milky Way), and their orbits indicate that our galaxy attained a maximum radius of about 100,000 light-years. One can then tentatively estimate that galaxies such as our own formed when the universe was 1,000 times denser than it is now, about half a billion years after the expansion began.

Extrapolating backward in time, we find that the protogalaxies would have taken the form of nonuniformities roughly 1 percent denser than the average density of the universe at the decoupling epoch. It is an attractive possibility that these are the dominant surviving irregularities, all smaller scales having been smoothed out during the fireball phase. There are, however, some types of fluctuation that are not eradicated in the fireball, so that smaller gas clouds may have formed first and later collided and agglomerated into galaxies. Robert H. Dicke and P. J. E. Peebles of Princeton have suggested that globular clusters—compact groups of about 10^5 or 10^6 stars that orbit around galaxies—may represent that small fraction of clouds which managed to avoid collisions, fragmented into stars and survived. Clusters of galaxies would have evolved from initial irregularities of smaller amplitude but larger scale than those destined to form single galaxies.

The only contribution of cosmologists to date toward explaining galaxy formation has been to calculate what scales of perturbation are most likely to survive or amplify in the fireball, thereby reducing the need to build these preferred scales into the initial conditions. This removes one element of arbitrariness in the initial conditions prescribed for the universe. There still remains, however, the task of explaining both the origin of the nonuniformity of the universe on all scales except the very largest, and the apparent uniformity encountered on the largest scales.

In fact, the Friedmann models may not provide an adequate description of the fireball when large inhomogeneities are present. It would be conceptually attractive if there were processes that could transform an initially chaotic universe into one that displayed the large-scale uniformity of a Friedmann model. An encouraging step toward this goal has been taken by Charles W. Misner of the University of Maryland, who has considered a "mix master" universe, which expands anisotropically in such a way that all parts of the universe are causally related very early in its history. At the outset matter would be so densely packed that even neutrinos would interact with other particles at a significant rate. Acting like a blender, the neutrinos would destroy the original anisotropy of the fireball by the time it had cooled to about 20 billion degrees. Thereafter the expansion would mimic a homogeneous Friedmann model.

Several types of observation may help to test this general picture of galaxy formation. The fluctuations that develop into galaxies and clusters would give rise to random motions on the surface of last scattering. As a result the microwave background photons would not all have been red-shifted by exactly the same amount; in some directions they might have been scattered off material with a random velocity toward us, whereas in other directions the last-scattering surface may have been receding from us. As a consequence the microwave temperature would be slightly nonuniform over the sky. Edward R. Conklin and R. N. Bracewell of Stanford University, Arno A. Penzias, Johann B. Schraml and Robert W. Wilson at the Kitt Peak National Observatory and Yuri N. Parijsky of the Pulkovo Observatory can detect temperature fluctuations as small as a tenth of a percent on angular scales of a few minutes of arc, but so far they have found no positive effect. This technique, however, has the potentiality of detecting embryonic galaxies or clusters of galaxies when they were merely small enhancements above the mean gas density.

There are reasons to expect galaxies that have just condensed to be brighter than typical galaxies at the present epoch. The energy released by the collapse of the protogalaxy would probably have been radiated away by hot gas be-

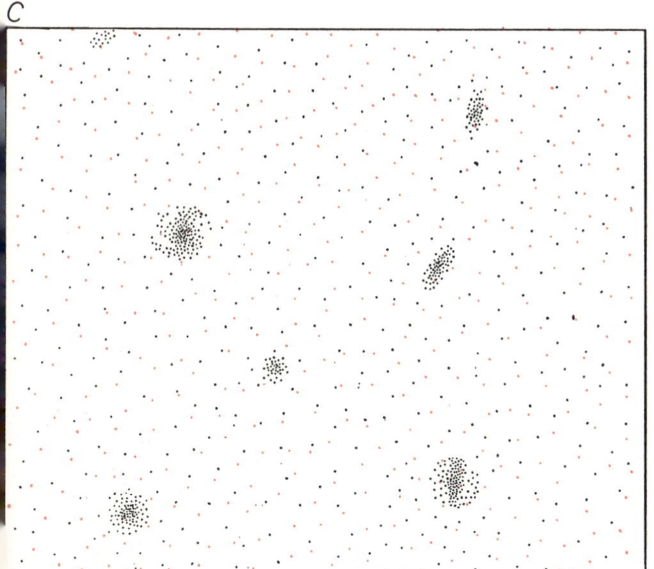

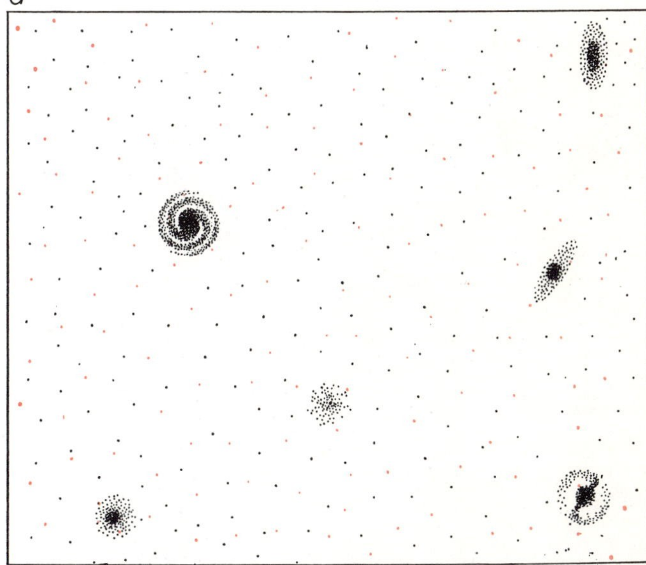

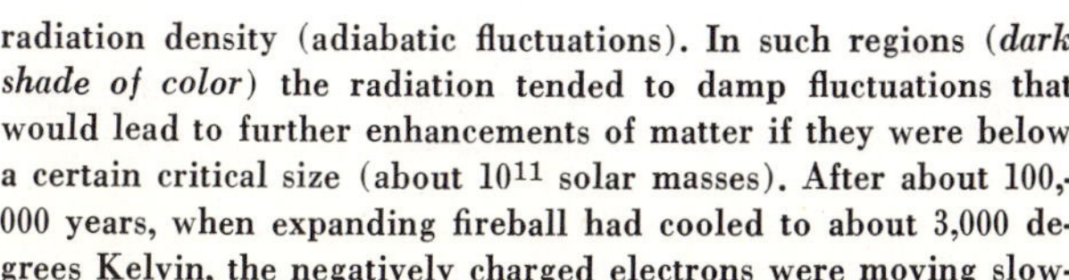

radiation density (adiabatic fluctuations). In such regions (*dark shade of color*) the radiation tended to damp fluctuations that would lead to further enhancements of matter if they were below a certain critical size (about 10^{11} solar masses). After about 100,000 years, when expanding fireball had cooled to about 3,000 degrees Kelvin, the negatively charged electrons were moving slowly enough to be captured by protons and retained in bound orbits, forming hydrogen atoms. In this condition electrons are much less effective in scattering photons and universe thus became transparent (*b*). Expansion and cooling of fireball continued and matter was progressively concentrated by gravitational forces, first into protogalaxies (*c*) and eventually into galactic types seen today (*d*).

SPIRAL GALAXY M 101 in Ursa Major is representative of the Sc type, which is characterized by a relatively inconspicuous nucleus and prominent, loosely wound spiral arms. Our own Milky Way galaxy is either of this type or of the slightly less open Sb type.

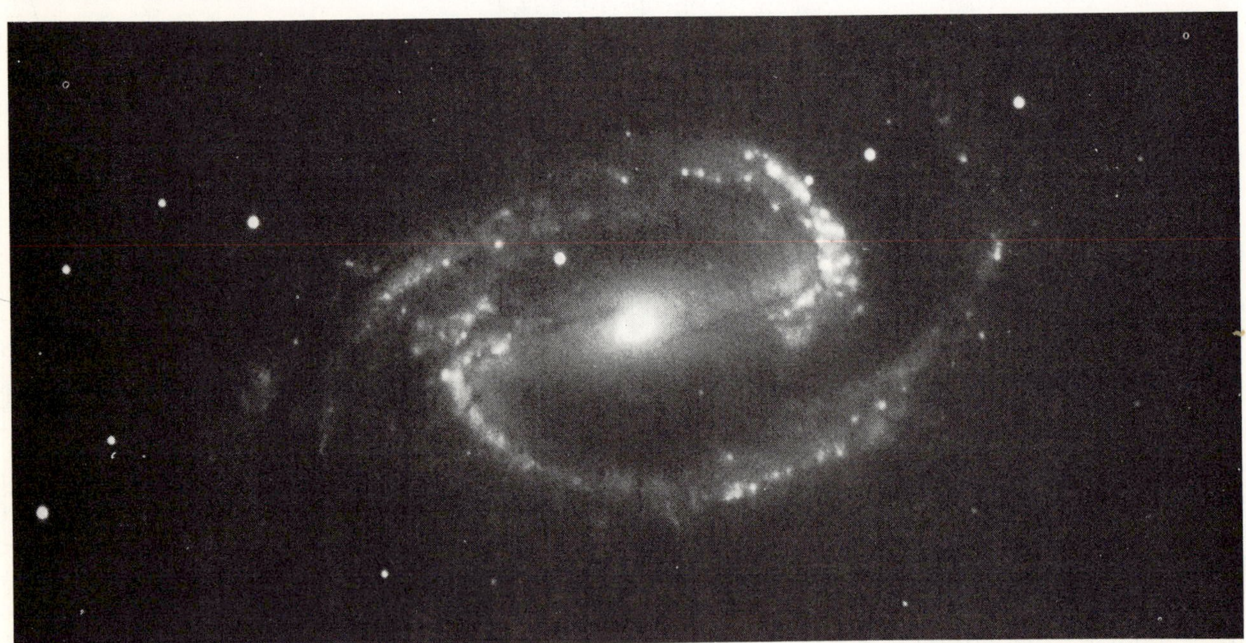

BARRED SPIRAL GALAXY NGC 1300 in Eridanus is classified SBb, which means that it is an intermediate type on the barred-spiral branch of the Hubble sequence. All photographs shown on this page and page 57 were made with the 200-inch Hale telescope.

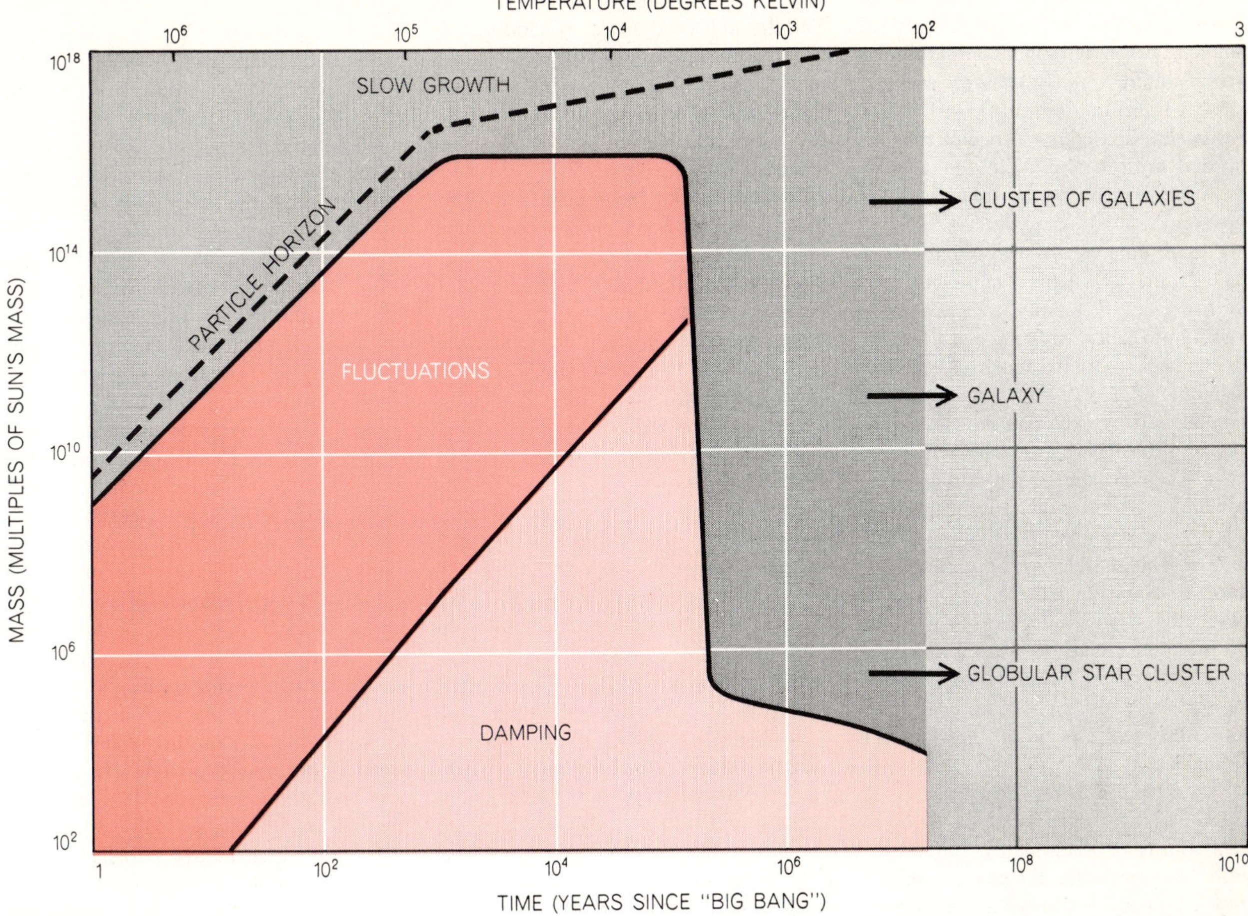

ANOTHER REPRESENTATION of the formation of galaxies is a graph relating the mass of a system to the age and ambient temperature of the universe. Any density enhancement that reaches a minimum value of some 10^{15} solar masses when the universe is about 1,000 years old (the epoch at which the density of matter first equals the mass density of the fireball radiation) has enough gravitational force to overwhelm the effects of radiation pressure. Such an enhancement thereupon enters on a lifetime of slow growth, culminating in a large cluster of galaxies. In an intermediate range (between 10^{11} and 10^{15} solar masses at decoupling) fluctuations in density persist until the decoupling stage is reached and radiation pressure ceases to interact effectively with matter; surviving density enhancements in this range become individual galaxies. Below a certain threshold (10^{11} solar masses at decoupling) radiation pressure damps out most density enhancements. Within this range, however, some density enhancements not accompanied by increases in radiation pressure (isothermal fluctuations) may survive to form globular star clusters, ranging from 10^5 to 10^6 solar masses. "Particle horizon" is boundary of the observable universe, where objects would be receding at speed of light.

fore most of the stars formed. Moreover, the first generation of stars would tend to be heavier and more luminous in relation to their mass than the stellar populations in present-day galaxies. Although most of this energy would be radiated in the ultraviolet, it would be received in the near infrared, owing to the red shift. Robert Bruce Partridge and Peebles at Princeton have suggested that it might be feasible to detect such young galaxies even though these may now have red shifts of about 10.

We are plainly still far from understanding even the broad outlines of the processes whereby the observed aggregations of matter in the universe came into being. We are even further from understanding the detailed morphology of the bewildering variety of different types of galaxies. For example, we have not yet discussed the possible origins of the angular momentum or magnetic fields of galaxies. Peebles has argued that the rotation of galaxies may be induced by tidal interactions soon after formation. Other authors, notably Leonid Ozernoi of the P. N. Lebedev Physical Institute in Moscow, have considered galactic rotation to be of primordial origin. One remarkable feature of the primordial fireball is that it can store rotation in the form of "photon whirls"; subsequently this stored rotation could be transferred to matter whirls.

Galactic magnetic fields may be produced after the formation of the galaxy by a mechanism of the dynamo type. Alternatively, magnetic fields may very well be of primordial origin. Edward R. Harrison of the University of Massachusetts has pointed out that the shear between the photon gas and the matter gas in the fireball could have generated a small magnetic field; if primordial photon whirls are assumed to be present, this mechanism leads to the production of a "seed" magnetic field many orders of magnitude below the value of the magnetic field observed in the spiral arms of our own galaxy. Harrison argues that rapid rotation of the protogalaxy may have subsequently produced sufficient winding of the primordial magnetic field to enhance it by the dynamo mechanism to the field currently observed. Primordial fields alone, he feels, would be insufficient to account for the observed galactic fields. The amount of rotation and the strength of the magnetic field in the protogalaxy probably help to determine whether it will evolve into an elliptical galaxy or into a spiral.

Galaxies are observed to possess random velocities with respect to the cos-

mic expansion. It is a curious coincidence that the rotational velocity of galaxies is of just the same order of magnitude—hundreds of kilometers per second—as these random motions. Perhaps this is simply a consequence of the primordial turbulence, which may have been the source of all structure in the universe.

Present data on the sizes of clusters of galaxies, and on possible "superclusters," are too sparse to enable us to assess the validity of theories that predict the mass spectrum of condensations. Moreover, our knowledge of the masses of galaxies is bedeviled by selection effects. Large and bright galaxies can be seen out to great distances, but small and intrinsically faint ones would only be noticed if they were comparatively close to us. Such objects may therefore occur much more frequently than is believed. A more drastic possibility is that most of the material in the universe may be in some nonluminous form. Evidence for the existence of such material comes from studies of the stability of clusters of galaxies.

This basic problem was first discussed in 1933 by Fritz Zwicky of the California Institute of Technology. For example, if one estimates the mass required to make the Virgo cluster a gravitationally bound system, one finds that the total observed mass in the member galaxies falls short by a factor of 50 or more. One possible way around this paradox is to assume that the Virgo system may be exploding, as the Soviet astrophysicist V. A. Ambartsumian has suggested. Perhaps even more puzzling is the apparent deficiency in mass of the Coma cluster. This system is so spherically symmetric and centrally condensed that astronomers believe it must be a stable system. Yet the observed mass, predominantly in elliptical galaxies, falls short of the mass required for stability by perhaps a factor of five, even if one assumes that the mass-luminosity ratio for ellipticals is around 50.

Similar results have been found for other clusters. Some astronomers have attempted to explain this problem by arguing that nonluminous matter is present in sufficient quantity to stabilize these systems. This material probably cannot all be in gaseous form; neutral hydrogen or ionized hydrogen, whether uniformly distributed or in clouds, ought to be observable either by radio or by X-ray observations.

Alternatively, the "missing mass" may be in the form of "dead," or burned-out, galaxies. An even more intriguing possibility is that concealed within the clusters are many objects that have undergone catastrophic gravitational collapse, as predicted by the general theory of relativity. The gravitational field around such objects would be so strong that no radiation could escape from them; only their gravitational influence could be detected by a distant observer.

Other arguments that indicate the apparent youthfulness of some galaxies stem from observations of clusters of galaxies. To be stable, one such chain of galaxies would require a mass-luminosity ratio of more than 5,000, or 100 times as much mass as the cluster seems to possess. One seems forced to the conclusion that here are newly formed galaxies, born within the past 100 million years. Zwicky has discovered an entire class of compact galaxies whose surface brightness resembles that found only in the nuclei of ordinary galaxies. Even more baffling is the discovery that some quasars emit as much radiation as 1,000 galaxies, the energy apparently coming from a colossal explosive event in a region less than 1 percent the size of the solar system. Seyfert galaxies display the same energetic phenomenon on a somewhat reduced scale.

Ambartsumian has long maintained that galactic nuclei are sources of matter and that indeed the galaxies themselves emerge out of dense primordial nuclei. In recent years Halton C. Arp of the Hale Observatories and Erik B. Holmberg of the University of Uppsala have found evidence that small galaxies may even have been ejected from larger galaxies. These phenomena certainly suggest that violent events, involving perhaps the birth of galaxies, are continually taking place in the nuclei of existing galaxies. One is reminded of Sir James Jeans's prescient conjecture, written in 1929, that "the centers of the nebulae are of the nature of 'singular points,' at which matter is poured into our Universe from some other, and entirely extraneous, spatial dimension, so that, to a denizen of our Universe, they appear as points at which matter is being continually created."

Further progress in this field must await fuller information on the distribution, masses and velocities of galaxies. Moreover, satellite observations in infrared, ultraviolet and X-ray wavelengths may soon reveal completely new and unsuspected types of objects, and should in any case give us confidence that we have a fairly complete inventory of the contents of the universe. We shall then be better able to relate theoretical abstractions to the universe in which we dwell.

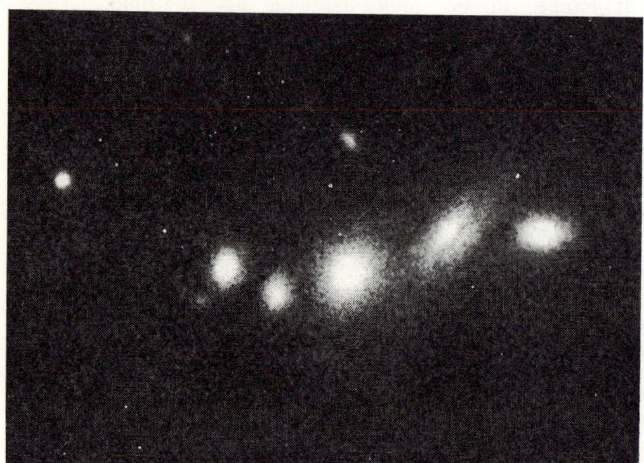

CHAIN OF GALAXIES VV 172 was photographed by Halton C. Arp with the 200-inch Hale telescope. Four of the galaxies are 600 million light-years away; the fifth appears to be twice as distant. Conceivably it has been ejected from the cluster at high velocity.

EXPLODING GALAXY NGC 1275 was recently photographed in red light by C. Roger Lynds with the 84-inch telescope at Kitt Peak. The radiating filaments of gas, reminiscent of the Crab nebula, were not visible in earlier photographs taken in white light.

The Search for Black Holes

8

by Kip S. Thorne
December 1974

Observations at the wavelengths of light, radio waves and X rays indicate that the X-ray source Cygnus X-1 is probably a black hole in orbit around a massive star

Of all the conceptions of the human mind from unicorns to gargoyles to the hydrogen bomb perhaps the most fantastic is the black hole: a hole in space with a definite edge over which anything can fall and nothing can escape; a hole with a gravitational field so strong that even light is caught and held in its grip; a hole that curves space and warps time. Like the unicorn and the gargoyle, the black hole seems much more at home in science fiction or in ancient myth than in the real universe. Nevertheless, the laws of modern physics virtually demand that black holes exist. In our galaxy alone there may be millions of them.

The search for black holes has become a major astronomical enterprise over the past decade. It has yielded dozens of candidates scattered over the sky. At first the task of proving conclusively that any one of them is truly a black hole seemed virtually impossible. In the past two years, however, an impressive amount of circumstantial evidence has been accumulated on one of the candidates: a source of strong X-ray emission in the constellation Cygnus designated Cygnus X-1. The evidence makes me and most other astronomers who have studied it about 90 percent certain that in the center of Cygnus X-1 there is indeed a black hole.

Before I describe the evidence that leads to this conclusion, let me lay some groundwork and indulge my theoretical proclivities by describing some of the predicted properties of black holes [see "Black Holes," by Roger Penrose; SCIENTIFIC AMERICAN, May, 1972]. Physicists educate themselves and their students by means of "thought experiments" whose results are predicted by theory. I shall resort to such an experiment to convey the basic reasoning that underlies the concept of the black hole.

Imagine that at some distant time in the future the human species has migrated throughout the galaxy and is inhabiting millions of planets. Having no further need for the earth, men choose to convert it into a monument: They will squeeze it until it becomes a black hole. To do the squeezing they build a set of giant vises, and to store the necessary energy they fabricate a giant battery. They then scoop out a chunk of the earth and convert its mass into pure energy, the amount of energy obtained being given by Einstein's equation $E = mc^2$, in which E is the energy, m is the mass and c is the speed of light. This energy is stored in the battery. The vises are arrayed around the earth on all sides and, powered by the battery, they squeeze the earth down to a quarter of its original size.

To check their progress the project engineers fabricate from a chunk of the earth a tight-fitting spherical jacket strong enough to hold the planet in its compressed state. They slip the jacket over the earth and open the vises. Then they measure the escape velocity of a rocket placed on the earth, that is, the velocity the rocket must attain in order to be able to coast out of the earth's gravitational field. Before the earth was compressed the escape velocity was the same as it is today: 11 kilometers per second. The compression of the earth, however, brings the earth's surface four times closer to its center, thereby quadrupling the kinetic energy that the rocket must have in order to escape. The escape energy is proportional to the square of the escape velocity; therefore the escape velocity after this first compression is doubled to 22 kilometers per second.

Satisfied that some progress has been made, the engineers repeat the process, compressing the earth still further until its original circumference of 40,000 kilometers is only 10 kilometers. I give the measurement of circumference in-

→

MODEL FOR A BLACK HOLE IN CYGNUS X-1 is a likely explanation for the observations made in the visible and X-ray regions of the spectrum. Gas is being pulled off the supergiant primary star HDE 226868 (*a*) by the gravitational attraction of the black hole. As the gas falls toward the black hole, the hole moves in its orbit out of the way, causing the gas to miss it. The gas nearest the black hole is whipped around it into a tight circular orbit, forming a thin accretion disk. The second illustration (*b*), at a scale of about 20 times smaller than the first, shows the expected shape of the accretion disk. The gravitational pull of the black hole compresses the disk, making it thin. At the same time thermal pressures in the gas react against the compression and try to thicken the disk. Only in the central bulge (*c*) are the pressures sufficient actually to thicken the disk. The large pressures in the bulge are caused by heat from X rays emitted near the black hole. In the core of the accretion disk (*d*) the thermal pressures are even higher than they are in the bulge; the gravity is so enormously strong, however, that it prevents the disk from thickening. The X rays observed from the earth are generated only in the innermost 200 kilometers of the core (*e*), which has the black hole itself at its center. In the innermost 50 or 100 kilometers the disk becomes translucent, violently turbulent and much hotter than it is elsewhere. The disk terminates near the black hole, where the gravitational field becomes so strong that gas can no longer move in an orbit but is sucked directly in. The termination point and the structure of the inner disk are sensitive to the black hole's speed of rotation (*see illustration, page 68*]. Here it is assumed that the black hole is rotating very rapidly; if the rotation is slow, the X-ray-emitting region may be 400 kilometers in radius rather than 200.

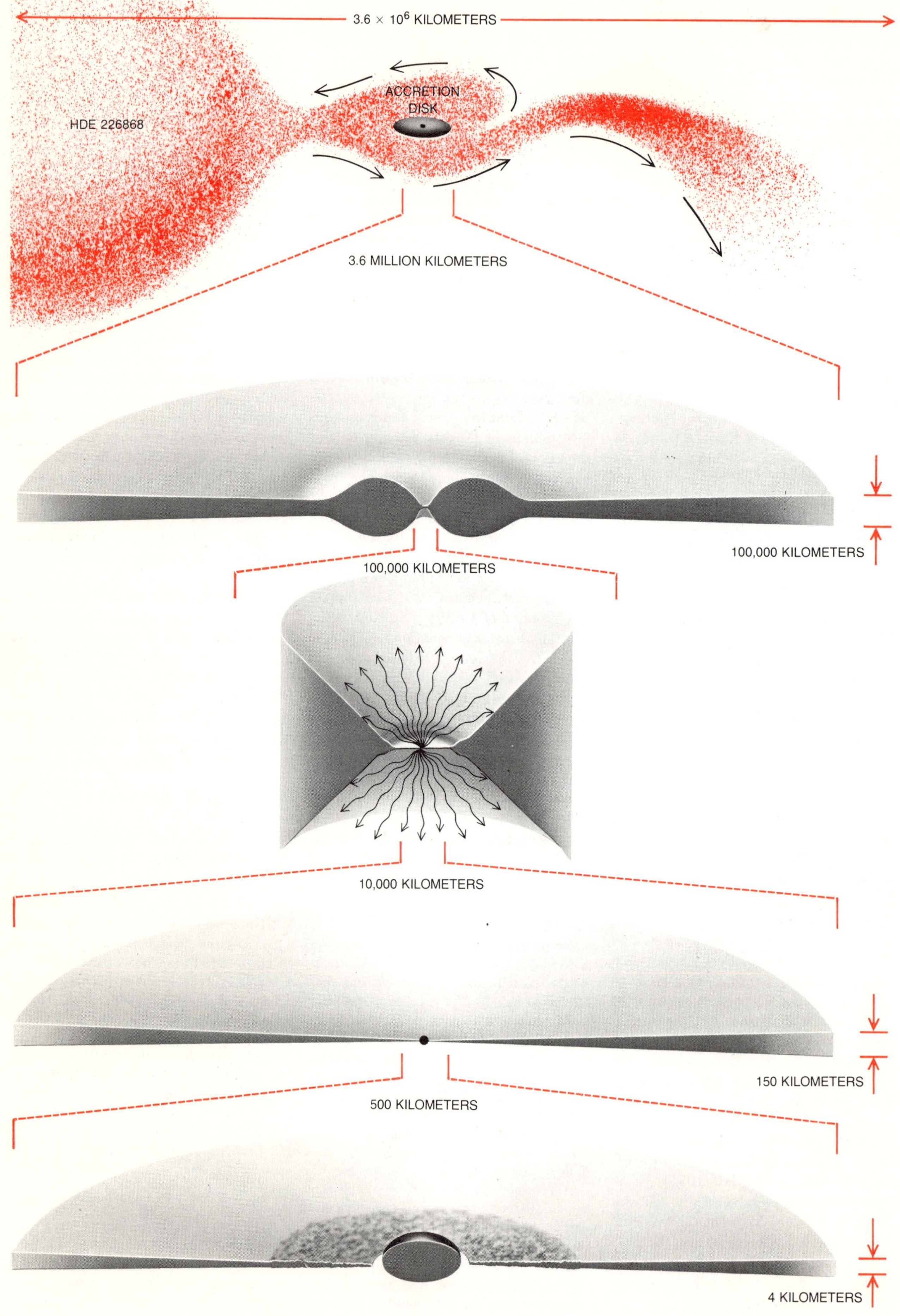
3.6 × 10^6 KILOMETERS
ACCRETION DISK
HDE 226868
3.6 MILLION KILOMETERS
100,000 KILOMETERS
100,000 KILOMETERS
10,000 KILOMETERS
150 KILOMETERS
500 KILOMETERS
4 KILOMETERS

stead of diameter because in the presence of strong gravitational fields space is so highly curved that the object's diameter (d) is no longer related to its circumference (C) by the Euclidean formula $C = \pi d$; moreover, in the case of a black hole the diameter cannot be measured or calculated. This time the rocket needs an escape velocity of 708 kilometers per second in order to coast away from the earth.

After several more compression stages the earth has been reduced to a circumference of 5.58 centimeters. The escape velocity is now 300,000 kilometers per second—the speed of light. One last little squeeze, and the escape velocity exceeds the speed of light. Now light itself cannot escape from the earth's surface, nor can anything else. Communication between the earth and the rest of the universe is permanently ruptured. In this sense the earth is no longer part of the universe. It is gone, leaving behind it a hole in space with a circumference of 5.58 centimeters. Outside the horizon, or edge, of the hole the escape velocity is less than the speed of light, and exceedingly powerful rockets can still get away. Inside the horizon the escape velocity exceeds the speed of light and nothing can escape. The interior of the hole, like the earth that gave rise to it, is cut off from the rest of the universe.

Let us return to the present and use the thought experiment to aid in understanding what happens in a star. There is a key difference between the earth and a massive star. For the earth to become a black hole external forces must be applied; for a star to become a black hole the necessary forces are provided by the star's own internal gravity. When a star of, say, 10 times the mass of the sun has consumed nuclear fuel through its internal thermonuclear reactions for a period longer than a few tens of millions of years, its fuel supply runs out. With its fires quenched the star can no longer exert the enormous thermal pressures that normally counterbalance the inward pull of its gravity. Gravity wins the tug-of-war, and the star collapses.

Unless the star sheds most of its mass during the collapse, gravity crushes it all the way down to a black hole. If, however, the star can eject enough material to reduce its mass to about twice the mass of the sun or less, then it is saved: nonthermal pressures, such as the electron pressures that make it difficult to compress rock, build up and halt the collapse. The star becomes either a white dwarf about the size of the earth or a neutron star with a circumference of some 60 kilometers. (A neutron star is a star where matter is so dense that its electrons have been squeezed onto its protons, converting them into neutrons.) In either case, as with the earth, to convert the object into a black hole one must apply external forces—forces that do not exist in nature [see "Gravitational Collapse," by Kip S. Thorne; SCIENTIFIC AMERICAN, November, 1967].

These predictions, which follow from the standard laws of physics, tell us that there is a critical mass for compact stars (stars with a circumference smaller than the earth's) of about two times the mass of the sun. Below the critical mass a compact star can be a white dwarf or a neutron star. Above the critical mass it can only be a black hole. The magnitude of the critical mass is a key link in the arguments that Cygnus X-1 is a black hole.

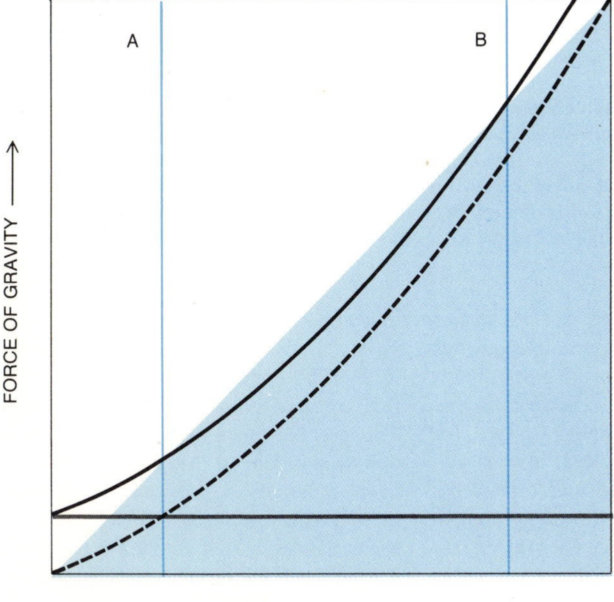

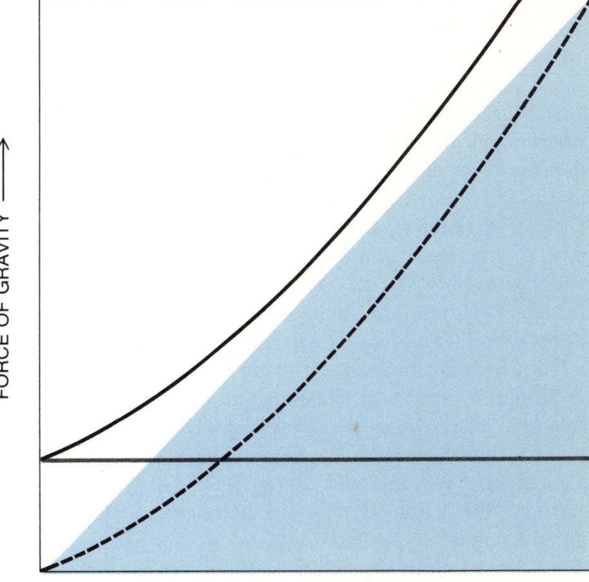

ONLY MASSIVE STARS BECOME BLACK HOLES, as is shown by these diagrams for a star with twice the mass of the sun (*left*) and a star with four times the mass of the sun (*right*). For a star to be stable the total force of gravity (*solid black line*) pulling a star's surface inward must be balanced by the star's internal pressures (*region in light color*) pushing the surface outward. If the force of gravity is stronger, the star collapses; if the internal pressure is stronger, the star explodes. For a compact star (a star smaller than the earth) the internal pressure is large enough to counterbalance gravity if the star's mass is less than three times the mass of the sun. The result is a stable white-dwarf star or a neutron star (a star in which matter is so dense that its electrons have been squeezed onto its protons, converting them into neutrons). If the star is more massive than three times the mass of the sun, however, and has a density greater than the density of the atomic nucleus, the internal pressure actually works against it. According to the general theory of relativity, gravity is produced not only by mass (*gray line*) but also by pressure (*broken black line*). At high pressures the force of gravity generated by the pressure is proportional to the square of the pressure. Thus if the star's internal pressure is very high, it gives rise to gravitational forces that overwhelm the internal pressure and the star collapses. For a compact star with a mass of less than three times the mass of the sun (*left*) there are intermediate pressures that can be counterbalanced by gravity (*vertical lines in color*). For stars more massive (*right*), however, force of gravity always wins and crushes star into a black hole in less than a second.

Therefore one would like to know the critical mass precisely. Precision is not possible, however, because we do not know enough about the properties of matter at the "supernuclear" densities of a white dwarf or a neutron star, that is, at densities above the density of the atomic nucleus: 2×10^{14} grams per cubic centimeter. Nevertheless, an upper limit on the critical mass is known: Remo Ruffini of Princeton University and others have shown that it cannot exceed three times the mass of the sun. In other words, no white dwarf or neutron star can have a mass greater than three times the mass of the sun.

From a physical and mathematical standpoint a black hole is a marvelously simple object, far simpler than the earth or a human being. When a physicist is analyzing a black hole, he need not face the complexities of matter, with its molecular, atomic and nuclear structure. The matter that collapsed in the making of the black hole has simply disappeared. It exerts no influence on the hole's surface or exterior. It makes no difference whether the collapsing matter was hydrogen, uranium or the antimatter equivalents of those elements. All the properties of the black hole are determined completely by Einstein's laws for the structure of empty space.

Exactly how simple black holes must be has been discovered by three physicists: Werner Israel of the University of Alberta and Brandon Carter and Stephen Hawking of the University of Cambridge. They have shown that when a black hole first forms, its horizon may have a grotesque shape and may be wildly vibrating. Within a fraction of a second, however, the horizon should settle down into a unique smooth shape. If the hole is not rotating, its shape will be absolutely spherical. Rotation, however, will flatten it at the poles just as rotation slightly flattens the earth. The amount of flattening and the precise shape of the flattened hole are determined completely by its mass and its angular momentum (speed of rotation). The mass and angular momentum not only determine the hole's shape; they also determine all the other properties of the hole. It is as though one could deduce every characteristic of a woman from her weight and hair color.

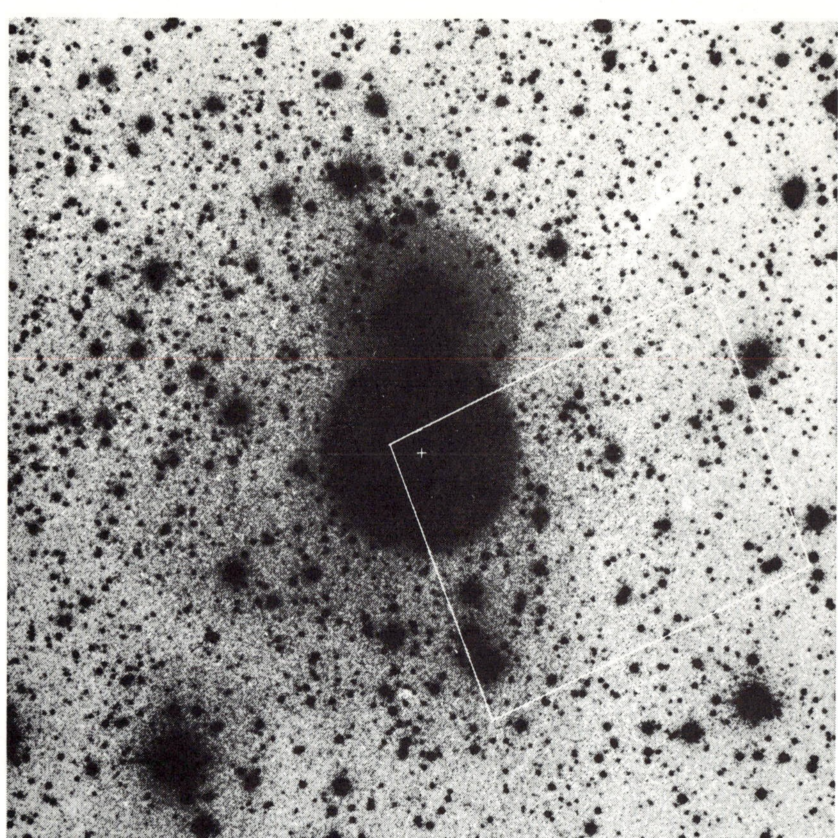

CYGNUS X-1 is believed to be associated with the star HDE 226868, the darkest and largest object in the center of this negative print of a small region of the sky. The photograph was made by Jerome Kristian with the 200-inch reflecting telescope on Palomar Mountain. The photographic plate was exposed so long that exceedingly faint stars (down to the 22nd magnitude) are visible. Superimposed on photograph are location of sources of radio emission (*small cross*) and of X-ray radiation (*white outline*). Position of Cygnus X-1 is not known very well from X-ray observations alone because X-ray telescopes have low resolution. During last week of March and first week of April in 1971, however, Cygnus X-1 underwent a cataclysmic and so far permanent change that caused it to begin emitting radio waves and to double the average energy of its X rays. Because the positions of radio sources can be measured accurately, the change in Cygnus X-1 assisted astronomers in identifying its location.

In calculations the angular momentum is replaced by a more convenient quantity: the rotation parameter. The rotation parameter (a) is equal to the speed of light (c) multiplied by the angular momentum (J), divided by the Newtonian gravitational constant (G) times the square of the hole's mass (m^2): ($a = c\,J/G\,m^2$). The rotation parameter always has a value between zero and one. For a rotation parameter of zero ($a = 0$) the hole is spherical and does not rotate; for a rotation parameter of 1 ($a = 1$) the hole is highly flattened and rotates extremely rapidly. There is no way to make a hole rotate any faster than $a = 1$; in fact, a hole with a rotation parameter very close to 1 should actually slow down until its rotation parameter is about .998 because of friction with the matter and radiation falling into it.

What are the most important properties that can be deduced from a hole's mass and rotation parameter? First, the gravitational field of the hole obeys the standard laws of Newton and Einstein: the hole's attraction for an object is proportional to its mass and inversely proportional to the square of the distance between it and the object if the distance is somewhat greater than the size of the hole. Second, a rotating hole creates a vortex in the empty space surrounding it, thereby swirling all particles or gas that approach it into whirlpool orbits. The greater the hole's rotation parameter, the stronger the vortex. Third, a black hole curves space and warps time in its vicinity. Fourth, a black hole has a clearly delineated horizon into which anything can fall but from which nothing can emerge. Fifth, the circumference of a black hole's equator is 19 kilometers multiplied by the mass of the hole and divided by the mass of the sun. Typical black holes should have masses between three and 50 suns, and circumferences between about 60 and 1,000 kilometers.

Such are the predicted properties of black holes from the viewpoint of the theorist. To the observational astronomer these properties present an exciting challenge: find a black hole and verify the predictions! Until the mid-1960's no one took the challenge seriously. Black

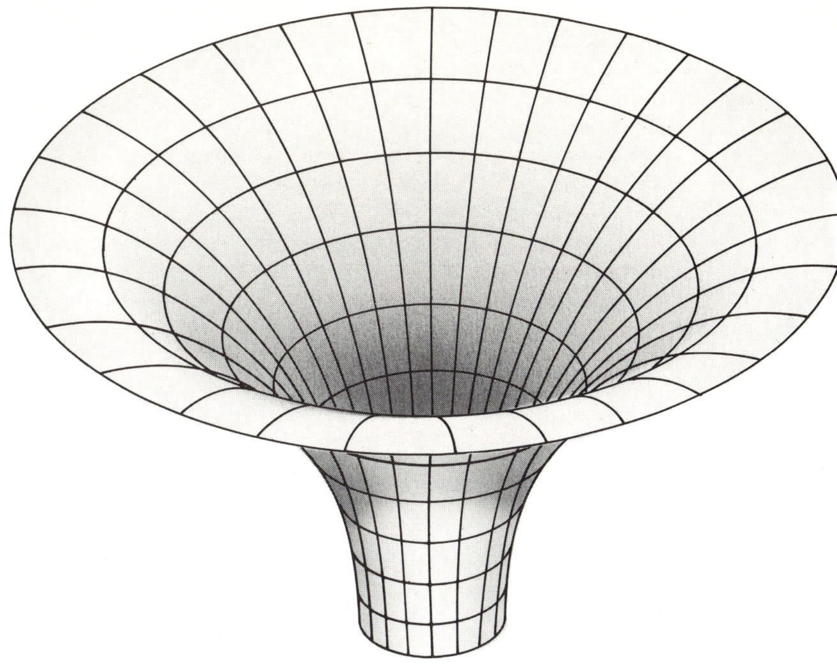

SPACE IS CURVED in the presence of a strong gravitational field. The curvature is depicted in what is known as an embedding diagram, in which three-dimensional space is represented by a flat plane that is warped by the presence of a star or any other kind of massive object. The amount of curvature is related to the strength of the object's gravitational field, and it affects the direction and travel time of rays of light and the measurement of distances.

holes were regarded as being strictly theoretical objects: objects that could be formed by the death of a star but probably never were formed. Even if they were, they could probably never be found observationally. Objects such as black holes and neutron stars were too bizarre to fit naturally into our tranquil universe. Somehow all massive stars would eject most of their mass before they died, thereby saving themselves the fate of becoming neutron stars or black holes. This climate of opinion was rarely verbalized explicitly, but it set the tenor of the times. I do not know of a single proposal to search for black holes before 1963.

In the 1960's, however, our view of the universe began to change radically. Exploding galaxies, rapidly varying radio galaxies, quasars, cosmic microwave radiation from the "big bang" explosion that formed the universe, flaring X-ray stars—all these and other observational discoveries taught us how violent and strange the universe can be. Gradually neutron stars and black holes began to seem more plausible. Then, in 1967, pulsars were discovered, and by late 1968 they were shown to be rotating neutron stars beaming radiation out into space. Since neutron stars really existed, then surely black holes must exist as well.

How could one go about searching for a black hole? If black holes are formed by dying massive stars, the nearest black hole should be no closer to the solar system than the nearest massive star: some 10 light-years away. Since most black holes would have a circumference of less than 1,000 kilometers, their resulting angular diameter in the sky would be a millionth of a second of arc. One could certainly not hope to find a black hole as a black spot in the sky.

Could one take advantage of the fact that a black hole's gravitational field can act as a lens and bend and focus light from a more distant star, thereby making the star look temporarily bigger and brighter? This is not a good way to search for black holes. If the hole were close to the star, the amount of focusing would be too small to be noticeable. If the hole and the star were widely separated, the amount of focusing would be large, but interstellar distances are so vast, that the necessary lining up of the earth, the hole and the star would be an exceedingly rare event—so rare that to search for one would be a waste of time. Moreover, even if such an event were observed, it would be impossible to tell whether the gravitational lens was a black hole or merely an ordinary but dim star.

Suppose the black hole had a companion star that could be seen and studied. Perhaps the presence of the hole could be deduced by its influence on the companion. With this idea in mind two Russian astrophysicists began the first search for black holes in 1964. Ya. B. Zel'dovich and O. Kh. Guseynov looked through catalogues of spectroscopic binary stars for systems that might be a black hole and a normal star revolving around each other. A spectroscopic binary system can look like a single star when it is viewed through even the most powerful telescope. The lines in its spectrum, however, shift periodically from the blue toward the red and back again as the observed star revolves around its darker companion. The periodic shift is produced by the Doppler effect: it is toward the blue as the star moves toward us in its orbit and toward the red as it moves away. The spectral lines of the companion may also be detected, shifting toward the red as the lines from the primary, or brighter, star are shifting toward the blue. In that case the companion is presumably not a black hole. If the companion star cannot be detected, however, it might be a black hole.

Star catalogues are full of binary systems for which the spectral lines of only one star are detected. Several hundred are known, and probably thousands more could be discovered if there were strong reasons to search for them. To shorten the list Zel'dovich and Guseynov investigated the mass of each dark companion. They could estimate the mass roughly from the amount the spectral lines were Doppler-shifted. The more massive the companion, the stronger its pull on the primary star and hence the greater the Doppler shift of the spectral lines. By requiring firm evidence from measurements of the Doppler shift that the mass of the dark companion is three times greater than the mass of the sun (and is therefore not a neutron star or a white dwarf), Zel'dovich and Guseynov brought their list down to a handful of spectroscopic binaries. In some of those systems the primary star was so bright that its dark secondary companion could very well be a normal star masked by the glare of the primary. After discarding those cases Zel'dovich and Guseynov were left with five good candidates for systems incorporating a black hole.

In 1968 Virginia Trimble, who was then working at the California Institute of Technology, and I revised and extended the Zel'dovich-Guseynov list. Unfortunately for us none of the eight good candidates on the new list we prepared presented a truly convincing case for a

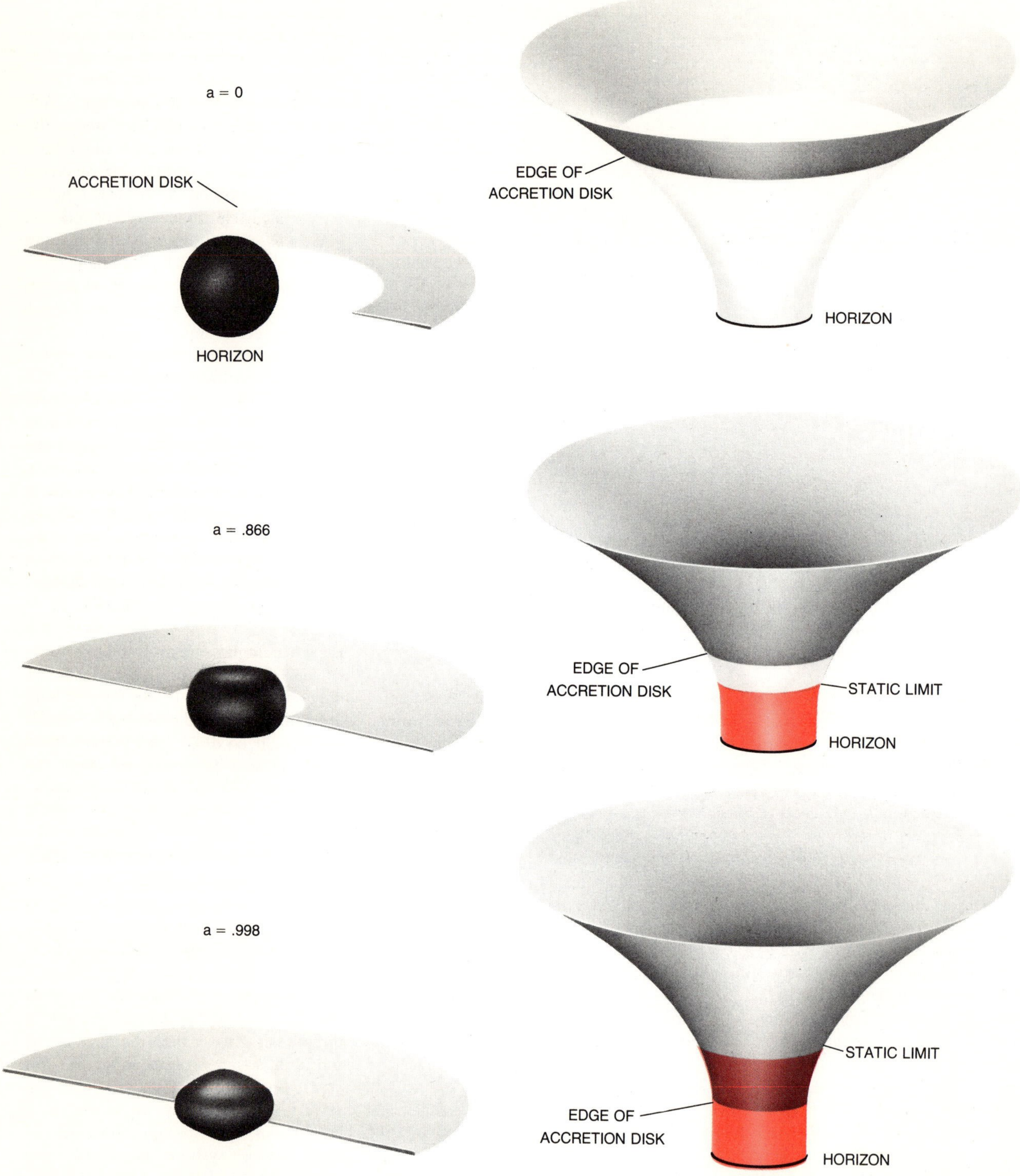

THREE BLACK HOLES, their accretion disks and the curved space that surrounds them are compared to show how they are affected by their speed of rotation. A hole that is not rotating (*top*) has a horizon, or edge, that is spherical. Its rotation parameter *a* is zero, where the rotation parameter is defined as being equal to the speed of light times the black hole's angular momentum, divided by the Newtonian gravitational constant times the square of the black hole's mass. A hole rotating at a moderate speed (*middle*) with a rotation parameter of .866 will be perfectly flat at the poles but will still be rounded at the equator. Rotation does not affect the size of the equatorial circumference. For a black hole rotating at high speed (*bottom*) with a rotation parameter of .998, the horizon has a shape that cannot exist in the flat Euclidean space of everyday experience. In all three black holes the hot, gaseous accretion disk that is believed to surround the black hole in Cygnus X-1 is shown. Gas spirals inward through the disk toward the horizon, heating up by friction and emitting X rays along the way. At the inner edge of the disk the hot gas plunges into the hole. A whirlpool motion in space, created by the black hole's rotation, swirls the disk inward so that its inner edge is close to the horizon if the hole is rotating rapidly. The curved space around the hole and the relative positions of the hole and the accretion disk in the curved space are shown by means of an embedding diagram [*see illustration on the preceding page*]. The static limit is the point where the whirlpool motion of space becomes irresistible. For a rapidly rotating black hole the accretion disk extends far below the static limit. X rays emitted from such a disk may have specific characteristics that would reveal whether black-hole theory is correct.

black hole. In all eight cases Trimble was able to conjure up a semireasonable explanation for why the dark companion was invisible without resorting to the hypothesis that it was a black hole. For example, the dim star might itself be a multiple-star system and thus be less luminous than its mass would indicate. Alternatively the primary star might be more luminous than it appeared to be. Or complexities in the spectrum of the primary star might mask the spectral lines of the secondary star. At that point the search for black holes in binary systems seemed to be stymied.

There was one major hope. As early as 1964 it had been realized that a black hole in a close binary system might pull gas off its companion star. As the liberated gas fell into the hole, it might heat up so much that it would emit X rays. Thus if any of the eight good candidates were found to emit X rays, the supposition that the dark companion was a black hole would become much more convincing.

A search for X rays emitted by binary systems could not be conducted with instruments on the ground because the X rays would be absorbed by the earth's atmosphere. One could use instruments aboard sounding rockets. Such a rocket, however, gets only a short peek at the sky before it falls back to the earth, so that its instruments can detect only the brightest of X-ray stars and can examine them only sketchily. Instruments carried aloft by balloons also get only short glimpses, and atmospheric absorption confines these views to the most penetrating of the X rays. For a definitive search an X-ray telescope aboard an artificial satellite would be needed.

The first such telescope was launched jointly by the U.S. and Italy aboard the *Uhuru* satellite on December 12, 1970. By the spring of 1972 *Uhuru* had gathered enough data to compile a detailed catalogue of 125 X-ray sources. To the astronomer searching for black holes the results from *Uhuru* were simultaneously disappointing and encouraging. They were disappointing because none of the X-ray sources coincided with any of the eight black-hole candidates. They were encouraging because at least six of the X-ray sources appeared to lie in other binary systems, typically systems that had not previously been recognized to be binary and had therefore been overlooked in the earlier searches.

Two of the six definite X-ray binary sources, Centaurus X-3 and Hercules X-1, clearly did not harbor a black hole. One could be certain of that because their X rays arrive in precisely timed periodic pulses: 4.84239 seconds between pulses for Centaurus X-3 and 1.23782 seconds for Hercules X-1. Nothing associated with a black hole can give rise to such regular behavior. Presumably each of these two binaries incorporates a rotating neutron star with its magnetic field inclined to its axis of rotation. Gas that is pulled off the companion star is funneled down the magnetic lines of force onto the magnetic poles of the neutron star, where heat from its impact generates a beam of X rays that sweeps across the sky as the star rotates. Each time the beam sweeps past the earth, the *Uhuru* satellite sees a burst of X rays. A black hole cannot produce such a beam because no off-axis structure such as a magnetic field can ever be anchored in a black hole. The hole would quickly destroy any such structure according to Einstein's laws of gravity.

The four remaining binary X-ray sources are designated 2U 1700-37, 2U 0900-40, SMC X-1 and Cygnus X-1; 2U refers to the second *Uhuru* catalogue and SMC stands for Small Magellanic Cloud, a companion galaxy of our own. Studies at visual wavelengths of each of these sources reveal a supergiant primary star with a telltale periodically varying Doppler shift. There is no sign of spectral lines from the secondary star. In all four cases, however, the visible spectrum shows lines emitted by gas flowing from the primary toward the unseen secondary. The X rays from the three systems 2U 1700-37, 2U 0900-40 and SMC X-1 are eclipsed each time the primary star passes between the earth and the unseen secondary. Therefore the secondary is almost certainly the source of the X rays. The X rays are most likely

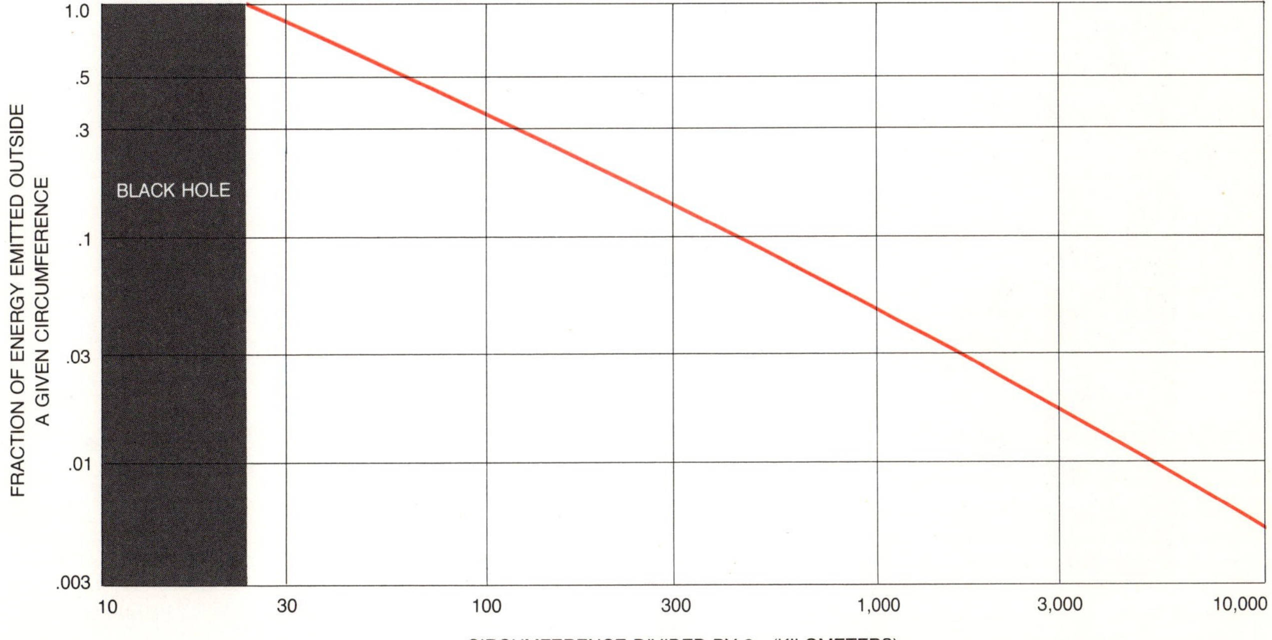

ENERGY EMITTED by various regions of the core of the accretion disk around the black hole in Cygnus X-1 is expressed as a fraction of the total energy. Location on the disk is described in units of circumference divided by 2π, which is not equal to radius because space is highly curved in neighborhood of black hole. Half of energy is emitted from innermost 56 kilometers of disk, where temperature is higher than 30 million degrees Kelvin and energy of a typical X-ray photon exceeds 5,000 electron volts.

generated when the flowing gas is heated by falling into the secondary, just as they are when the gas falls on a neutron star; at least astronomers have not been able to invent any other quantitative explanation for the X rays.

To heat the falling gas to the temperatures necessary for the emission of X rays requires huge amounts of energy, energy that can be supplied only by a drop through a very strong gravitational field. The gravitational field surrounding a normal star or planet is not strong enough. Only three types of object have sufficiently strong fields: white dwarfs, neutron stars and black holes. And the only definitive way to distinguish among these three possibilities is to somehow measure the mass of the secondary star. If the mass exceeds 1.4 times the mass of the sun, the object cannot be a white dwarf. If the mass exceeds three times the mass of the sun, the object cannot be a neutron star. In the latter case it must be a black hole.

Obtaining a rough estimate of the mass of the secondary is not too difficult. One needs only a moderate amount of data from observations of the Doppler shift and fairly good information about the spectrum of the primary. On the basis of such data the mass of the unseen companion of 2U 1700-37 is 2.5 times the mass of the sun, the mass of the companion for 2U 0900-40 is three times the mass of the sun, the mass of the companion for SMC X-1 is twice the mass of the sun and the mass of the companion for Cygnus X-1 is about eight times the mass of the sun.

These figures suggest that at least one and perhaps all four of the X-ray binaries include a black hole. The estimates, however, are quite rough. Individual astronomers interpreting the data in various ways can differ by a factor of two or more in their estimates of masses. And any astronomer who wants to play the devil's advocate can reduce the estimates still further by introducing peculiar interpretations of the data.

Only in the case of Cygnus X-1 do the devil's advocates face difficulties. Even a "worst-case" analysis of these data reveals that the unseen companion has a mass of no less than four times the mass of the sun. Therefore one can conclude that Cygnus X-1 does comprise a black hole. At least this conclusion is the most reasonable one.

Teams of devil's advocates led by John N. Bahcall of Princeton University and James Pringle of the University of Cambridge have invented viable, although less plausible, alternative models to explain the observations. The models assume that the massive secondary around which the bright primary travels is a normal but dim star. In one model the X rays come from a satellite neutron star in orbit around a massive normal secondary. In another model a neutron star emitting X rays circles in a wide orbit around an entire normal binary system. In a third model the X rays do not come from a neutron star or any other compact object at all. Instead between two normal stars stretch strong magnetic fields that are continually being twisted, tied into knots and broken as the two stars rotate. The knotting and breaking of the fields heats gas that is attached to them, and the hot gas emits the X rays. A fourth model assumes that the secondary emitting the X rays is not a black hole but is something even more exciting and bizarre: a massive "naked singularity" in the structure of space-time. Einstein's laws of gravity probably forbid the formation of naked singularities, but all attempts to prove that this is the case have failed.

We now face a situation that is common in astronomy. One model, that a black hole is in orbit around a normal star, can readily explain the observations: the light and the X rays from Cygnus X-1. The other leading models, proposing a secondary that is either a white dwarf or a neutron star, have been killed by the observations. Alternative contrived explanations, however, can still be made to fit the data. Such a situation leads astronomers into the final stage of the search for black holes: the attempt to accumulate more data of higher quality and of new types, data that (I hope!) will gradually kill the contrived models and clinch the case for a

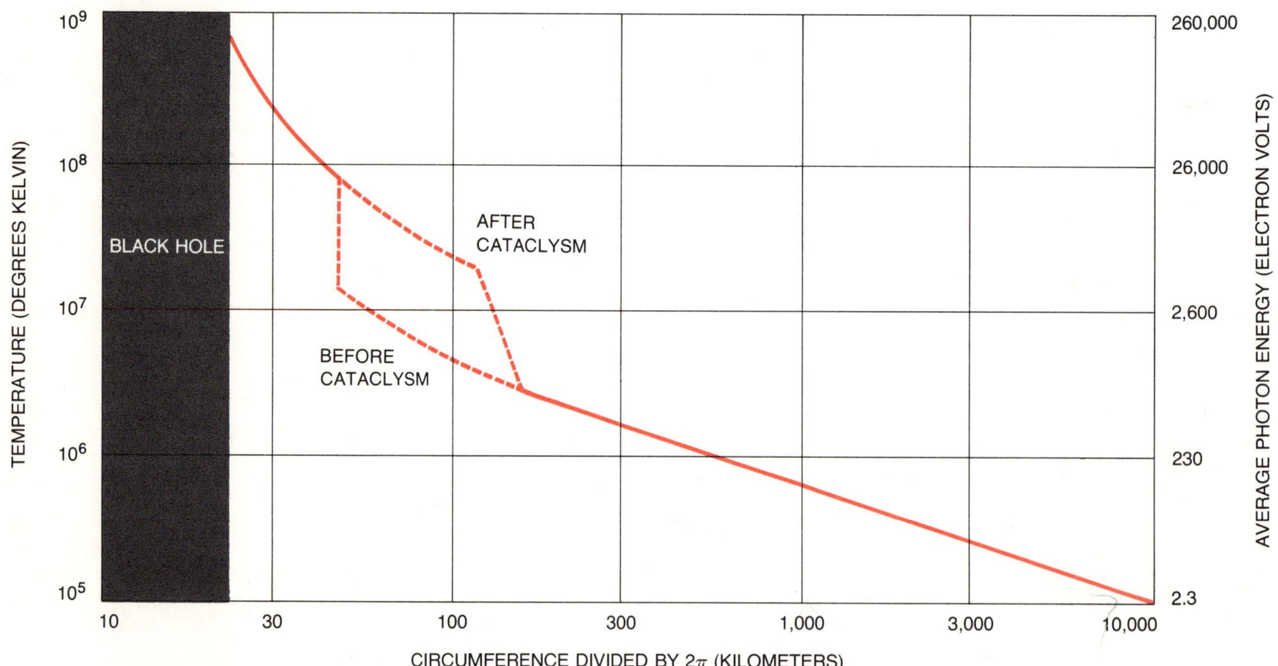

TEMPERATURE OF GAS AND ENERGY OF PHOTONS emitted by core of the accretion disk is shown for various locations. Only X rays more energetic than 2,000 electron volts have been detected with X-ray telescopes available until recently; thus the curve for the less energetic photons is calculated from theory. Future X-ray telescopes will test theory by examining photons between 400 and 2,000 electron volts. Cataclysmic change in Cygnus X-1 may have been a change of state in the region between 50 and 100 kilometers.

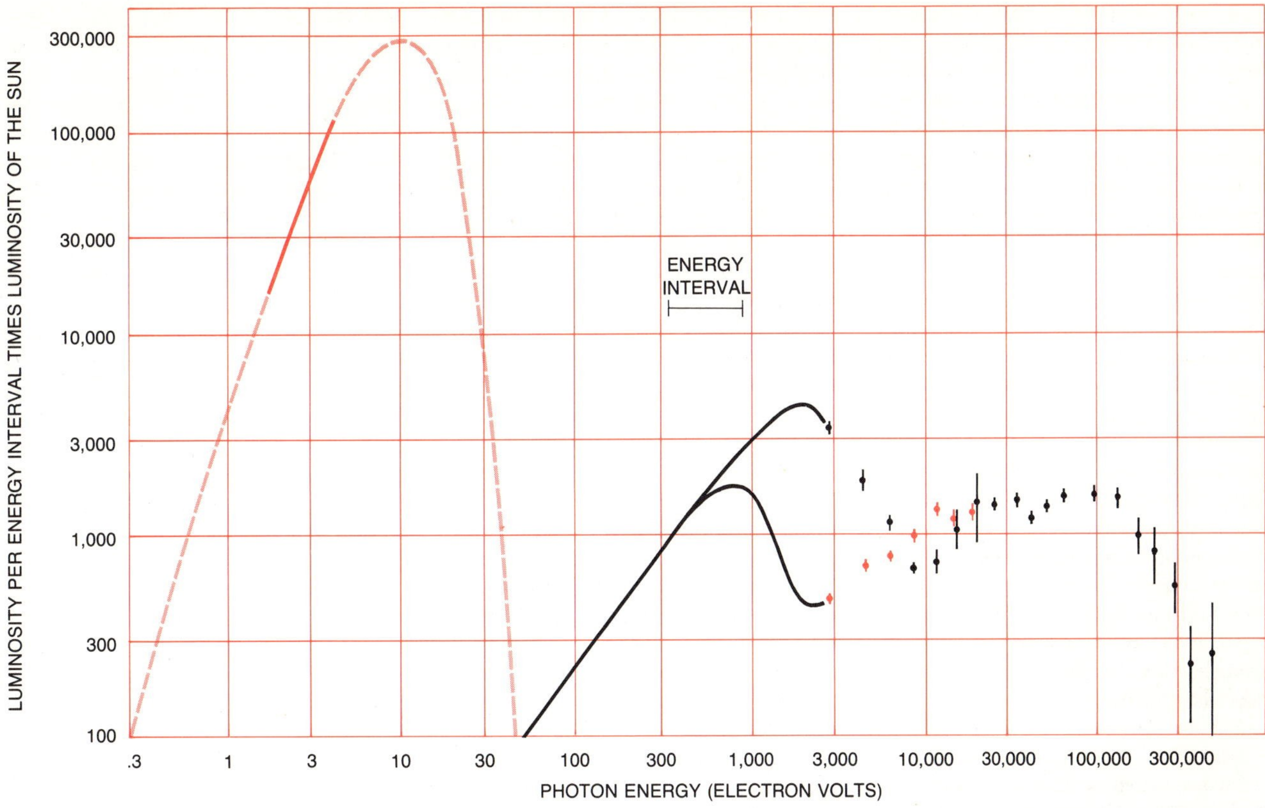

SPECTRUM OF HDE 226868 AND CYGNUS X-1 is shown in terms of the absolute luminosity of the sun. The unit energy interval is the interval over which the energy increases by a factor of the base of natural logarithms, *e*, or about 2.718, for example at an energy between 1,000 electron volts and 2,718 electron volts. The curve in color shows the spectrum of HDE 226868; the solid portion of the curve is known from visual observations and the broken portion is extrapolated into the infrared and ultraviolet regions of the spectrum. The calculated emission from the core of the accretion disk of Cygnus X-1 is shown in gray. The points at energies above 2,700 electron volts are X-ray observations of Cygnus X-1 averaged over short fluctuations ranging from milliseconds to minutes; the vertical error bar on each point shows the statistical uncertainty due to the fact that the observations consisted of only a finite number of photons. Black dots are observations made before the cataclysmic change; colored dots show how the spectrum was altered.

black hole. In this final stage of the search it will be helpful to know what to look for. What kind of signatures should characterize the X rays and the light generated by a binary system whose secondary is a black hole accreting gas from a primary star?

Detailed theoretical studies of such binary systems were begun in 1971 before the observations from *Uhuru* had confirmed the fact that some binaries do emit X rays. The studies were initiated independently on the basis of Newtonian gravitation theory by Nikolai Shakura and Rashid Sunyaev of the Institute of Applied Mathematics in Moscow and by Pringle and Martin J. Rees at the University of Cambridge. Later analyses based on Einstein's general theory of relativity were undertaken by Donald Page and me at the California Institute of Technology, by Igor Novikov and Andrei Polnarev of the Institute of Applied Mathematics in Moscow and by Christopher Cunningham at the University of Washington. All of these studies reveal the same gross structure for the binary system and the flow of gas within it [*see illustration on page 64*].

The gravitational field of the black hole is continually pulling gas off of the supergiant star or out of its immediate vicinity and funneling it into orbits around the black hole. Centrifugal and gravitational forces flatten the orbiting gas into a thin disk around the black hole that is analogous to the rings around Saturn but is far larger. Once a gas filament is sucked into the disk, it would stay in orbit around the hole forever if there were no friction. Friction between adjacent gas filaments, however, forces the gas to spiral slowly inward. The inward velocity is much less than 1 percent of the orbital velocity. A few weeks or months after a filament enters the disk it has spiraled inward by several million kilometers and is approaching the disk's inner edge. There the black hole's gravity becomes irresistible. It sucks the gas filament away from the disk and, within a fraction of a second, through the black hole's horizon into the hole itself.

A by-product of the friction is heat. When a filament is first caught in the disk it might have a temperature of 25,000 degrees Kelvin, the same temperature as the surface of the supergiant primary. As the gas drifts inward through the disk friction heats it until in the last 100 kilometers of its spiraling descent it is hotter than 10 million degrees.

The hot gas radiates energy, about 80 percent of which is emitted from the inner 200 kilometers as X rays. Presumably these are the X rays detected by the telescope aboard *Uhuru*. The remaining 20 percent of the radiation, emitted from the comparatively cool outer parts of the disk, should be less energetic X rays that cannot be detected with the instruments currently available, together with ultraviolet radiation and light that would not be detectable against the glare of the supergiant star.

The case for a black hole in Cygnus X-1 would be much strengthened if theorists working with this model could calculate the properties of the X-ray

emission in detail. The chief stumbling block at this point is friction in the disk. We do not know whether the friction is generated by turbulence in the spiraling gas, by magnetic fields embedded in the spiraling gas or by a combination of turbulence and magnetic fields. Even if we did know the source of the friction, we could not calculate its magnitude because we do not yet know enough about the general physical behavior of turbulent magnetized gases.

It is remarkable that in spite of our ignorance we are still able to calculate with confidence some of the important features of the disk. For example, from the laws of the conservation of energy and of angular momentum we can calculate how much energy each region of the disk radiates. We have concluded that most of the radiation must come from the hot inner 200 kilometers, no matter what the source or magnitude of the friction may be. We cannot, however, calculate the temperature in that inner region or the spectrum of the X rays it should emit. Instead we must discover what the spectrum is from observations and from it infer that the temperatures range between five million and 500 million degrees K. We go back to the models and see that such high temperatures are incompatible with a calm disk having little friction or turbulence but are quite reasonable if the inner region of the disk is violently turbulent and is optically thin, that is, translucent to radiation. We then return to the observations and note that the X rays do not arrive at the earth steadily. Their intensity fluctuates by a factor of two or three or even more over any length of time from milliseconds to days. Such fluctuations are also what one might expect from a turbulent disk.

By working back and forth between theory and observations in this way Richard Price of the University of Utah and I have built up a workable description of the structure of the inner disk of Cygnus X-1. Of course, success in building such a model is not much of a positive addition to the explanation that Cygnus X-1 includes a black hole. Too much was inferred from the observations and too little was calculated from the basic assumptions or the first principles of physics. On the other hand, things could be worse. The observations might have been incompatible with any type of model that assumed that the X rays were emitted by gas flowing into a black hole. In a sense, then, the black-hole model has survived a negative test. This type of test is the chief tool by which astrophysicists prove and disprove models. When a model has withstood a variety of negative tests that have destroyed all its competitors, astrophysicists begin to take the model very seriously.

Negative tests may not be the only way to prove or disprove the black-hole explanation of Cygnus X-1. Sunyaev has suggested one positive test and other theorists are searching for more. Sunyaev's test consists in looking for brief flares in the intensity of the X rays. Such X-ray flares would presumably be generated by temporary hot spots in the inner 100 kilometers of the disk [*see top illustration, p. 74*]. We have no reliable theory that accounts for the origin and destruction of such hot spots. Nevertheless it seems likely that once a hot spot is born it would live for more than one circuit in its orbit around the black hole. The X rays from the hot spot would be beamed in a direction that rotates as the hot spot circles the black hole. The beaming might be caused in part by the process by which the radiation is emitted and in part by focusing of the radiation in the gravitational field of the black hole. Moreover, the Doppler shift would make the X rays more intense as the hot spot approached us in its orbit around the hole, and less intense as it receded. Hence the emission from the hot spot would not arrive steadily but should arrive in bursts, with the interval between bursts equal to the orbital period of the hot spot traveling around the black hole. Thus the model predicts that short X-ray flares are likely to show a substructure of pulses with an interval between pulses of a few milliseconds.

If such pulses were perceived and if the black hole's mass were known, then

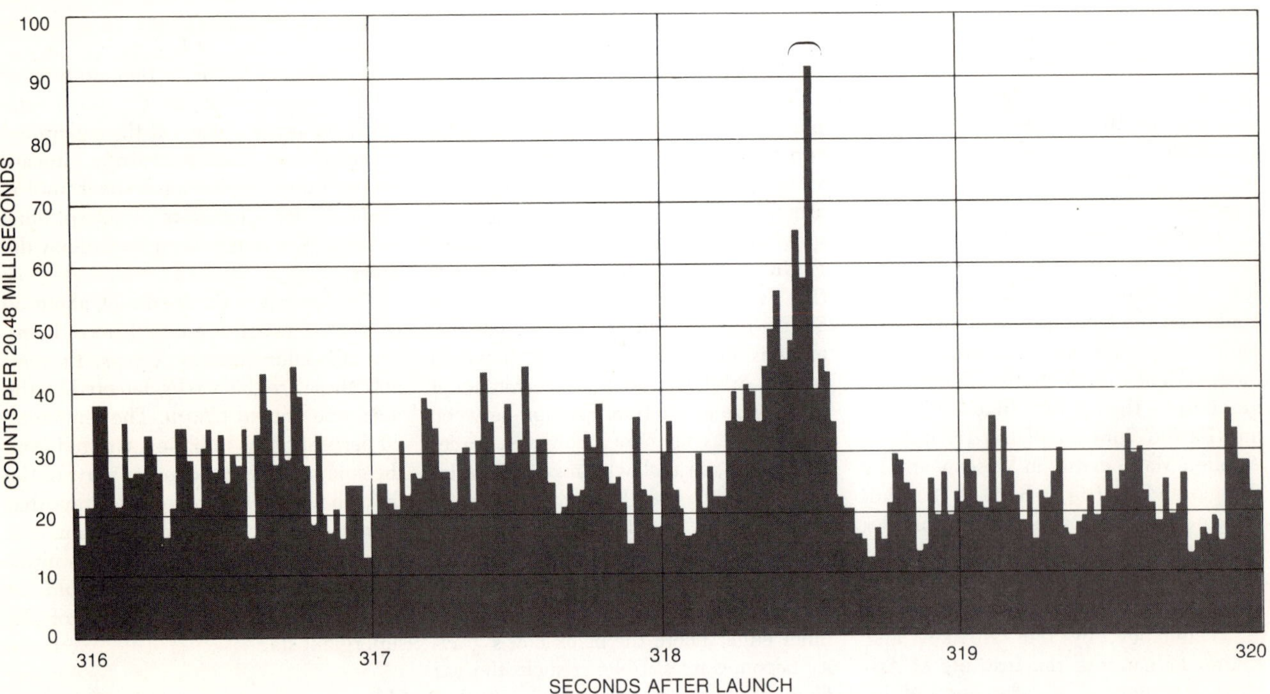

X-RAY FLARE WAS OBSERVED IN CYGNUS X-1 by an X-ray telescope aboard a rocket built by the Goddard Space Flight Center and launched in October, 1973 (*left*). A closer analysis of the flare (*bracket*) itself (*right*) shows that it does appear to have a pulsed substructure (*color*) near the telescope's limit of sensitivity. (Apparent pulses in black are random fluctuations in the X-ray signal.)

the interval between pulses would provide a way of computing the circumference of the hot spot's orbit around the hole. By observing many pulsed X-ray flares and determining the minimum interval between pulses we could learn what the circumference of the inner edge of the disk is, and from that we could infer the speed at which the hole is rotating. For a black hole with a mass eight times the mass of the sun the minimum interval between pulses must be between 3.6 milliseconds for a nonrotating hole (rotation parameter $a = 0$) and .6 millisecond for a rapidly rotating hole (rotation parameter $a = .998$).

Such a pulsed substructure is not, however, obligatory for X-ray flares. Flares without a pulsed substructure could originate in hot spots that are far enough from the black hole (perhaps more than 100 kilometers) so that they are not beamed by the hole's gravitational field and do not vary much because of the Doppler shift. They could also originate in spots that are very large and quickly get strung out into a doughnut around the disk by the orbital motion of the gas. Thus the observation of nonpulsed flares is also quite compatible with the black-hole explanation of Cygnus X-1. If pulsed X-ray flares can be detected, however, they should pulse only in the range predicted by Sunyaev's arguments.

The search for pulsed flares calls for an X-ray telescope that can make an observation in less than one millisecond and that has more than 10,000 square centimeters of area for collecting X-ray photons, so that many photons can be counted in each millisecond. Such a telescope will probably not be put into orbit around the earth until the National Aeronautics and Space Administration launches its first High Energy Astronomical Observatory satellite (HEAO-A), perhaps in 1977. Between now and then we must content ourselves with brief glimpses from the instruments on rockets and balloons.

The first such glimpse, in October, 1973, was promising. X-ray flares lasting about .1 second were observed with a telescope having a time resolution of .32 millisecond and the modest collecting area of 1,360 square centimeters. The largest of the flares does appear to have a pulsed substructure, but not enough photons were counted in the flare to be certain. So here we theorists sit, impatiently awaiting the next generation of X-ray telescopes, those of us in the "establishment" trying with great difficulty to build better black-hole models of Cygnus X-1 and those of us who are devil's advocates trying equally hard to build better non-black-hole models.

While some of us struggle with Cygnus X-1, others search elsewhere for black holes. The possibilities are plentiful, but none has yet yielded strong evidence for a hole. Several other spectroscopic binaries, including Epsilon Aurigae and Beta Lyrae, include a secondary star that has a mass of more than four times the mass of the sun and is surrounded by a huge opaque, or partially opaque, disk. As seen from the earth, the disk periodically blots out the light from the bright primary star. A. G. W. Cameron of the Harvard College Observatory and Edward Devinney of the University of South Florida have suggested that massive objects at the center of these disks might be black holes. Other astronomers find other explanations equally plausible.

The Russian astronomer V. F. Schwartzman is searching for black holes that have no binary companion. He calculates that the interstellar gas being sucked into such an isolated hole should emit light that flickers with a period of several milliseconds. Unfortunately for observers the light would not be very intense; it would have no more than 1 percent of the intensity of the sun's light if the sun were being observed at that distance. Since the nearest such black hole would be many light-years away, it would appear as a faint, rapidly flickering star. To detect the flicker and thereby make a strong case for the existence of an isolated black hole, Schwartzman needs sensitive electronics and a powerful telescope for observing at visible wavelengths. He is working at the Crimean Astrophysical Observatory, where a 240-inch telescope is nearing completion.

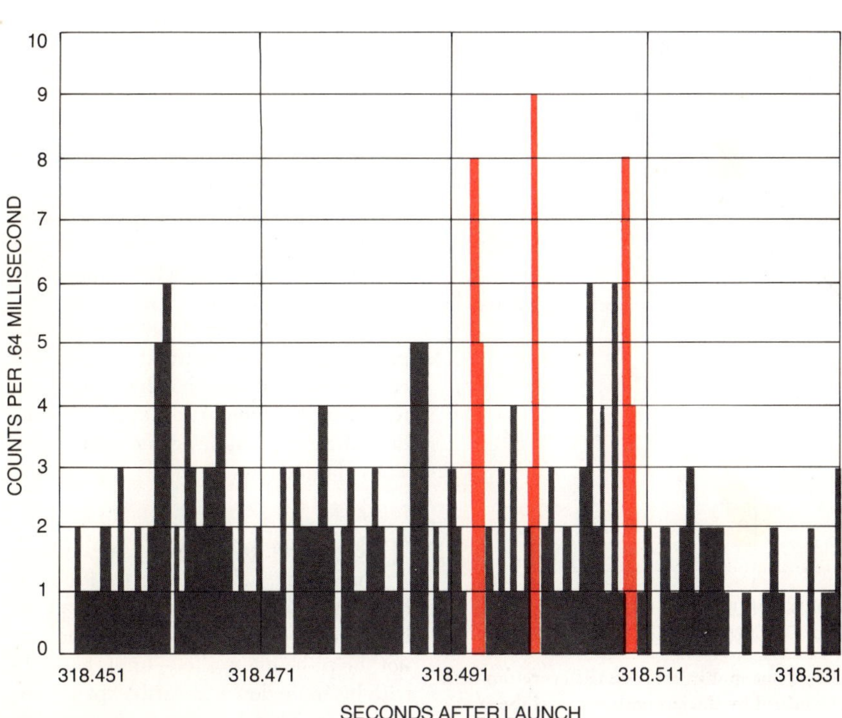

The time interval between pulses was no shorter than .005 second, corresponding to a circumference no smaller than four times the circumference of the black hole. That circumference is not small enough to determine the rotation parameter of the black hole.

The collapse of the star that gives rise to a black hole should also generate a huge burst of gravitational waves. The present first-generation gravitational-wave antennas are only sensitive enough to detect such bursts from our own galaxy, where they would not be expected more than once every few years. Second-generation antennas now under construction at Stanford University, Louisiana State University and the University of Moscow might be able to detect such bursts from the cluster of 2,500 galaxies in the constellation Virgo. Even more sensitive third-generation antennas will surely be able to do so. Theorists expect that in the Virgo cluster there will be several black holes born every year. By detecting and analyzing the gravitational waves from such births one could not only verify the creation of a black hole but also study some intimate details of the newborn hole. It is a project a decade or so in the future.

Thus far I have described only normal black holes created by the collapse of normal stars ranging in mass from three to 60 times the mass of the sun. There are probably supermassive holes and possibly miniholes as well. Donald Lynden-Bell of the University of Cambridge has argued that the dense milieu of gas and stars that fuels grand-scale explosions in the nuclei of some galaxies must ultimately collapse to form a supermassive black hole. If this is true, a galaxy such as our own, which probably had explosions in its nucleus long ago, might possess a huge black hole in its nucleus today. That hole would be a "tomb" from a more violent past. Such a black hole in our own galaxy might be as massive as 100 million times the mass of the sun and have a circumference as large as two billion kilometers. The hole would suck gas from the surrounding galactic nucleus, perhaps forming a gigantic accretion disk analogous to the disks proposed for the spectroscopic-binary systems. Lynden-Bell and Rees calculate that such a disk would emit strong radio and infrared radiation but not X rays. The nucleus of our galaxy does give evidence of several bright infrared and radio "stars." Unfortunately for theorists an accretion disk around a supermassive black hole is not the only possible explanation of the observed objects, and so far no one has invented a definitive test for the hypothesis.

Miniholes far less massive than the sun cannot be created in the universe as it exists today. Nature simply does not supply the necessary compressional forces. The necessary forces were present, however, in the first few moments after the creation of the universe in the "big bang." If the big bang were sufficiently chaotic, then, according to calculations made by Hawking, it should have produced a great number of miniholes. Hawking has shown that miniholes behave quite differently from normal-sized holes. Any hole less massive than 10^{16} grams (the mass of a small iceberg) should gradually destroy itself by an emission of light and particles according to certain laws of quantum mechanics. Those laws, which are not important for the larger black holes, considerably modify the properties of the smaller holes. The result is that all the primordial black holes less massive than 10^{15} grams should be gone by now. Those with a mass between 10^{15} grams and 10^{16} grams are now dying. In its final death throes such a dying black hole would not be black at all. It would be a fireball powerful enough to supply all the energy needs of the earth for several decades yet small enough to fit inside the nucleus of an atom.

Hawking's results are less than a year old, and so their implications have not yet been explored in detail. They may motivate a flood of proposals for searching for miniholes. He and Page are exploring one possibility: that the bursts of cosmic gamma rays that have been detected by instruments on artificial satellites of the Vela series came from explosions of miniholes.

The present list of ways and places that black holes might be found is far from complete. With so many possibilities a theorist such as the author cannot help being excited—until he talks with his more down-to-earth experimenter friends. Then he realizes what a difficult job the search really is. We cannot expect quick results, but the future does not seem unpromising.

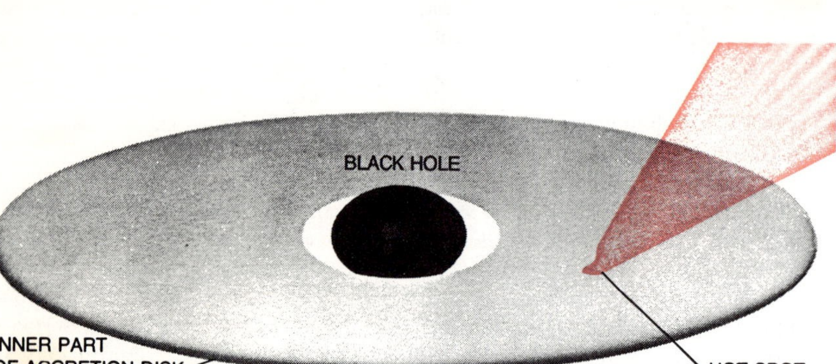

RADIATION FROM A HOT SPOT on the accretion disk of a black hole would be beamed into a wide cone that would sweep out a circle in the sky above the disk each time the spot made an orbit around the hole. As the cone sweeps repetitively past the earth X-ray telescopes would observe pulses of X rays amidst a general increase in the total intensity of the X rays received. The result would be a flare of X rays that would have a pulsed substructure.

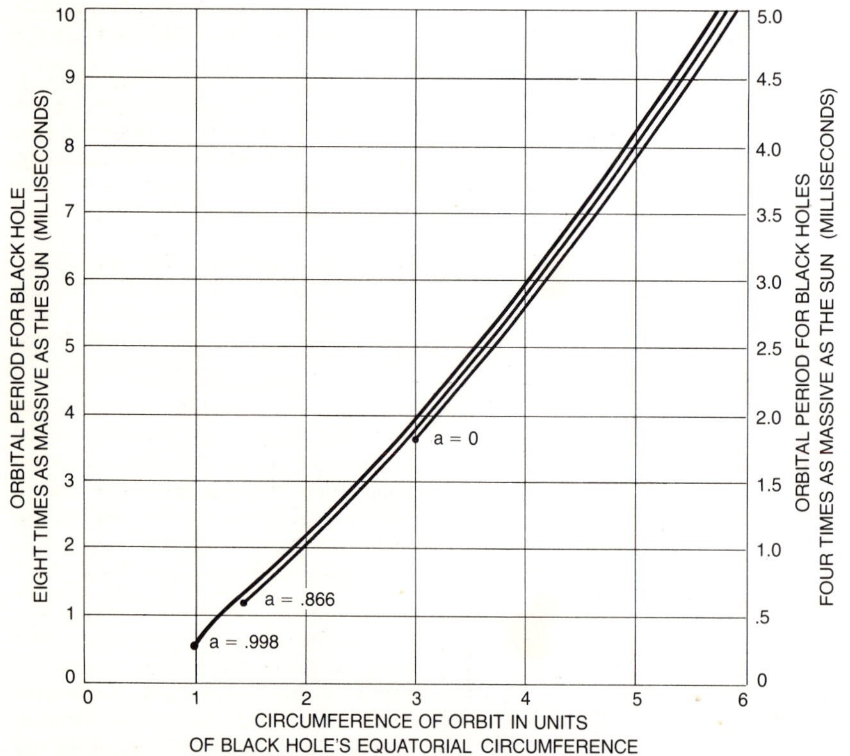

TIME INTERVAL BETWEEN PULSES emitted by a hot spot in orbit on the accretion disk around a black hole is uniquely and precisely determined by the circumference of the spot's orbit and by the mass and rotation parameter *a* of the hole. The more rapidly the hole rotates, the smaller the inner edge of its accretion disk is, and hence the shorter the minimum time would be between pulses in an X-ray flare. Observations of such pulses in X-ray flares can provide a way of measuring the rotation parameter of a black hole in Cygnus X-1.

The Quantum Mechanics of Black Holes

9

by S. W. Hawking
January 1977

Black holes are often defined as areas from which nothing, not even light, can escape. There is good reason to believe, however, that particles can get out of them by "tunneling"

The first 30 years of this century saw the emergence of three theories that radically altered man's view of physics and of reality itself. Physicists are still trying to explore their implications and to fit them together. The three theories were the special theory of relativity (1905), the general theory of relativity (1915) and the theory of quantum mechanics (c. 1926). Albert Einstein was largely responsible for the first, was entirely responsible for the second and played a major role in the development of the third. Yet Einstein never accepted quantum mechanics because of its element of chance and uncertainty. His feelings were summed up in his often-quoted statement "God does not play dice." Most physicists, however, readily accepted both special relativity and quantum mechanics because they described effects that could be directly observed. General relativity, on the other hand, was largely ignored because it seemed too complicated mathematically, was not testable in the laboratory and was a purely classical theory that did not seem compatible with quantum mechanics. Thus general relativity remained in the doldrums for nearly 50 years.

The great extension of astronomical observations that began early in the 1960's brought about a revival of interest in the classical theory of general relativity because it seemed that many of the new phenomena that were being discovered, such as quasars, pulsars and compact X-ray sources, indicated the existence of very strong gravitational fields, fields that could be described only by general relativity. Quasars are star-like objects that must be many times brighter than entire galaxies if they are as distant as the reddening of their spectra indicates; pulsars are the rapidly blinking remnants of supernova explosions, believed to be ultradense neutron stars; compact X-ray sources, revealed by instruments aboard space vehicles, may also be neutron stars or may be hypothetical objects of still higher density, namely black holes.

One of the problems facing physicists who sought to apply general relativity to these newly discovered or hypothetical objects was to make it compatible with quantum mechanics. Within the past few years there have been developments that give rise to the hope that before too long we shall have a fully consistent quantum theory of gravity, one that will agree with general relativity for macroscopic objects and will, one hopes, be free of the mathematical infinities that have long bedeviled other quantum field theories. These developments have to do with certain recently discovered quantum effects associated with black holes, which provide a remarkable connection between black holes and the laws of thermodynamics.

Let me describe briefly how a black hole might be created. Imagine a star with a mass 10 times that of the sun. During most of its lifetime of about a billion years the star will generate heat at its center by converting hydrogen into helium. The energy released will create sufficient pressure to support the star against its own gravity, giving rise to an object with a radius about five times the radius of the sun. The escape velocity from the surface of such a star would be about 1,000 kilometers per second. That is to say, an object fired vertically upward from the surface of the star with a velocity of less than 1,000 kilometers per second would be dragged back by the gravitational field of the star and would return to the surface, whereas an object with a velocity greater than that would escape to infinity.

When the star had exhausted its nuclear fuel, there would be nothing to maintain the outward pressure, and the star would begin to collapse because of its own gravity. As the star shrank, the gravitational field at the surface would become stronger and the escape velocity would increase. By the time the radius had got down to 30 kilometers the escape velocity would have increased to 300,000 kilometers per second, the velocity of light. After that time any light emitted from the star would not be able to escape to infinity but would be dragged back by the gravitational field. According to the special theory of relativity nothing can travel faster than light, so that if light cannot escape, nothing else can either.

The result would be a black hole: a region of space-time from which it is not possible to escape to infinity. The boundary of the black hole is called the event horizon. It corresponds to a wave front of light from the star that just fails to escape to infinity but remains hovering at the Schwarzschild radius: $2GM/c^2$, where G is Newton's constant of gravity, M is the mass of the star and c is the velocity of light. For a star of about 10 solar masses the Schwarzschild radius is about 30 kilometers.

There is now fairly good observational evidence to suggest that black holes of about this size exist in double-star systems such as the X-ray source known as Cygnus X-1 [see the article "The Search for Black Holes," by Kip S. Thorne, beginning on page 63]. There might also be quite a number of very much smaller black holes scattered around the universe, formed not by the collapse of stars but by the collapse of highly compressed regions in the hot, dense medium that is believed to have existed shortly after the "big bang" in which the universe originated. Such "primordial" black holes are of greatest interest for the quantum effects I shall describe here. A black hole weighing a billion tons (about the mass of a mountain) would have a radius of about 10^{-13} centimeter (the size of a neutron or a

proton). It could be in orbit either around the sun or around the center of the galaxy.

The first hint that there might be a connection between black holes and thermodynamics came with the mathematical discovery in 1970 that the surface area of the event horizon, the boundary of a black hole, has the property that it always increases when additional matter or radiation falls into the black hole. Moreover, if two black holes collide and merge to form a single black hole, the area of the event horizon around the resulting black hole is greater than the sum of the areas of the event horizons around the original black holes. These properties suggest that there is a resemblance between the area of the event horizon of a black hole and the concept of entropy in thermodynamics. Entropy can be regarded as a measure of the disorder of a system or, equivalently, as a lack of knowledge of its precise state. The famous second law of thermodynamics says that entropy always increases with time.

The analogy between the properties of black holes and the laws of thermodynamics has been extended by James M.

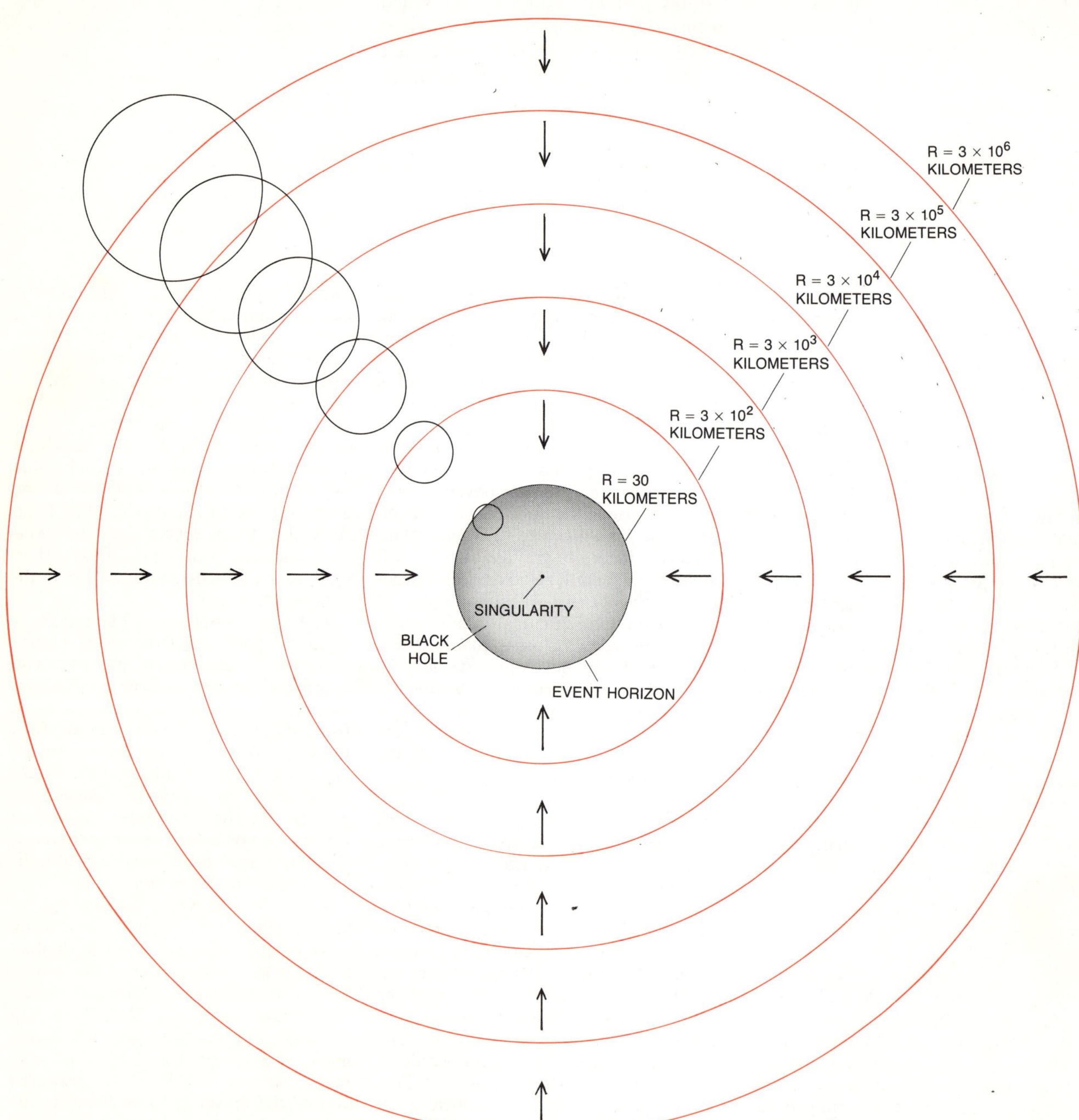

COLLAPSE OF STAR of 10 solar masses is depicted schematically from an original radius of three million kilometers (about five times the radius of the sun) to 30 kilometers, when it disappears within the "event horizon" that defines the outer limits of a black hole. The star continues to collapse to what is called a space-time singularity, about which the laws of physics are silent. The series of six small circles represents the wave fronts of light emitted from the successive surfaces an instant before the star had collapsed to the dimensions shown. Radii of the star and of the wave fronts are on a logarithmic scale. At each stage of collapse more of the wave front falls within the volume of the star as the escape velocity increases from 1,000 kilometers per second to 300,000 kilometers per second, the velocity of light. The final velocity is reached as the star disappears within the event horizon. No light emitted after that can ever reach outside observers.

Bardeen of the University of Washington, Brandon Carter, who is now at the Meudon Observatory, and me. The first law of thermodynamics says that a small change in the entropy of a system is accompanied by a proportional change in the energy of the system. The fact of proportionality is called the temperature of the system. Bardeen, Carter and I found a similar law relating the change in mass of a black hole to a change in the area of the event horizon. Here the factor of proportionality involves a quantity called the surface gravity, which is a measure of the strength of the gravitational field at the event horizon. If one accepts that the area of the event horizon is analogous to entropy, then it would seem that the surface gravity is analogous to temperature. The resemblance is strengthened by the fact that the surface gravity turns out to be the same at all points on the event horizon, just as the temperature is the same everywhere in a body at thermal equilibrium.

Although there is clearly a similarity between entropy and the area of the event horizon, it was not obvious to us how the area could be identified as the entropy of a black hole. What would be meant by the entropy of a black hole? The crucial suggestion was made in 1972 by Jacob D. Bekenstein, who was then a graduate student at Princeton University and is now at the University of the Negev in Israel. It goes like this. When a black hole is created by gravitational collapse, it rapidly settles down to a stationary state that is characterized by only three parameters: the mass, the angular momentum and the electric charge. Apart from these three properties the black hole preserves no other details of the object that collapsed. This conclusion, known as the theorem "A black hole has no hair," was proved by the combined work of Carter, Werner Israel of the University of Alberta, David C. Robinson of King's College, London, and me.

The no-hair theorem implies that a large amount of information is lost in a gravitational collapse. For example, the final black-hole state is independent of whether the body that collapsed was composed of matter or antimatter and whether it was spherical or highly irregular in shape. In other words, a black hole of a given mass, angular momentum and electric charge could have been formed by the collapse of any one of a large number of different configurations of matter. Indeed, if quantum effects are neglected, the number of configurations would be infinite, since the black hole could have been formed by the collapse of a cloud of an indefinitely large number of particles of indefinitely low mass.

The uncertainty principle of quantum

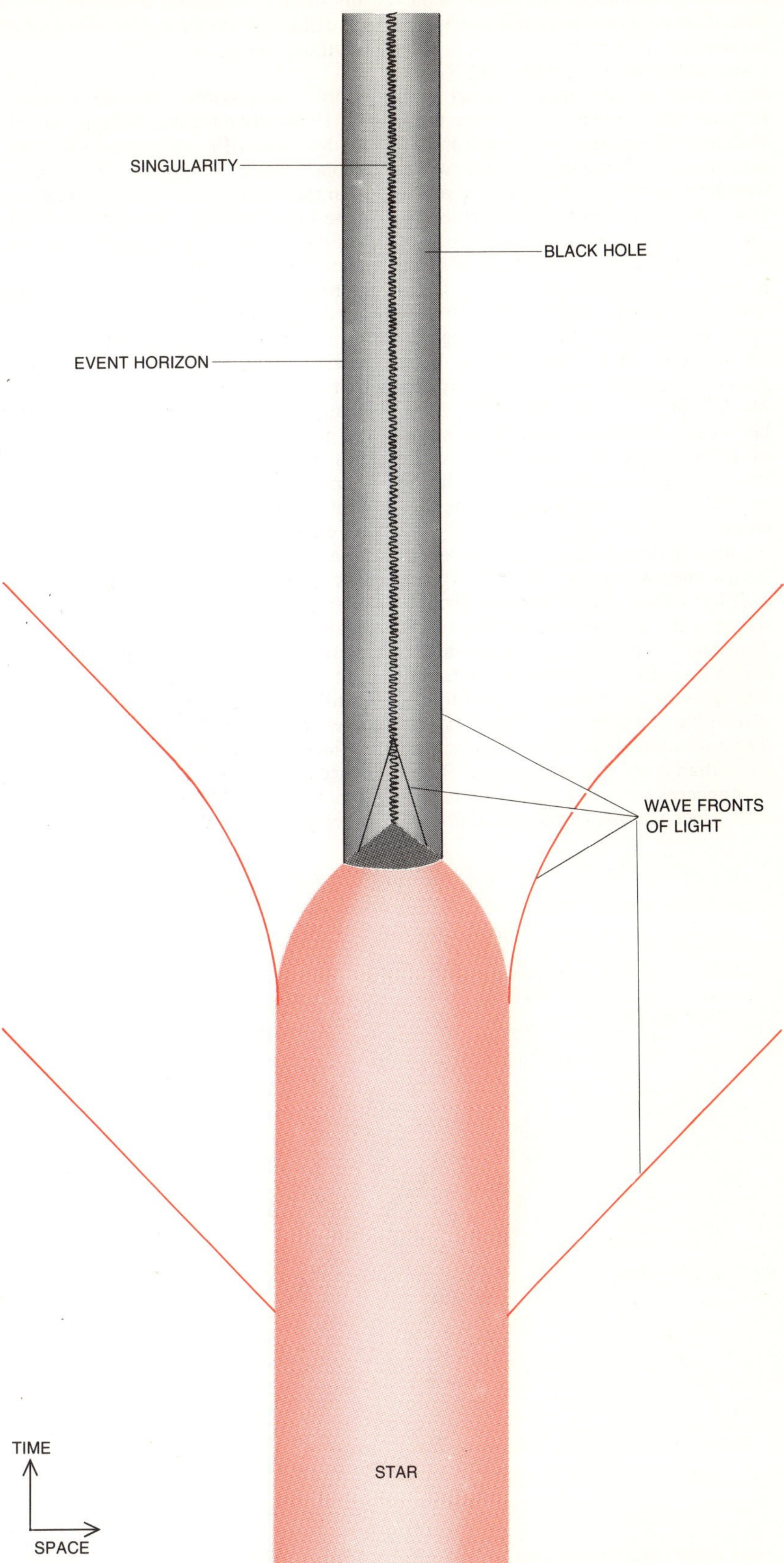

GRAVITATIONAL COLLAPSE OF A STAR is depicted in a space-time diagram in which two of the three dimensions of space have been suppressed. The vertical dimension is time. When the radius of the star reaches a critical value, the Schwarzschild radius, the light emitted by the star can no longer escape but remains hovering at that radius, forming the event horizon, the boundary of the black hole. Inside black hole star continues collapse to a singularity.

mechanics implies, however, that a particle of mass m behaves like a wave of wavelength h/mc, where h is Planck's constant (the small number 6.62×10^{-27} erg-second) and c is the velocity of light. In order for a cloud of particles to be able to collapse to form a black hole it would seem necessary for this wavelength to be smaller than the size of the black hole that would be formed. It therefore appears that the number of configurations that could form a black hole of a given mass, angular momentum and electric charge, although very large, may be finite. Bekenstein suggested that one could interpret the logarithm of this number as the entropy of a black hole. The logarithm of the number would be a measure of the amount of information that was irretrievably lost during the collapse through the event horizon when a black hole was created.

The apparently fatal flaw in Bekenstein's suggestion was that if a black hole has a finite entropy that is proportional to the area of its event horizon, it also ought to have a finite temperature, which would be proportional to its surface gravity. This would imply that a black hole could be in equilibrium with thermal radiation at some temperature other than zero. Yet according to classical concepts no such equilibrium is possible, since the black hole would absorb any thermal radiation that fell on it but by definition would not be able to emit anything in return.

This paradox remained until early in 1974, when I was investigating what the behavior of matter in the vicinity of a black hole would be according to quantum mechanics. To my great surprise I found that the black hole seemed to emit particles at a steady rate. Like everyone else at that time, I accepted the dictum that a black hole could not emit anything. I therefore put quite a lot of effort into trying to get rid of this embarrassing effect. It refused to go away, so that in the end I had to accept it. What finally convinced me it was a real physical process was that the outgoing particles have a spectrum that is precisely thermal: the black hole creates and emits particles and radiation just as if it were an ordinary hot body with a temperature that is proportional to the surface gravity and inversely proportional to the mass. This made Bekenstein's suggestion that a black hole had a finite entropy fully consistent, since it implied that a black hole could be in thermal equilibrium at some finite temperature other than zero.

Since that time the mathematical evidence that black holes can emit thermally has been confirmed by a number of other people with various different approaches. One way to understand the emission is as follows. Quantum mechanics implies that the whole of space is filled with pairs of "virtual" particles and antiparticles that are constantly materializing in pairs, separating and then coming together again and annihilating each other. These particles are called virtual because, unlike "real" particles, they cannot be observed directly with a particle detector. Their indirect effects can nonetheless be measured, and their existence has been confirmed by a small shift (the "Lamb shift") they produce in the spectrum of light from excited hydrogen atoms. Now, in the presence of a black hole one member of a pair of virtual particles may fall into the hole, leaving the other member without a partner with which to annihilate. The forsaken particle or antiparticle may fall into the black hole after its partner, but it may also escape to infinity, where it appears to be radiation emitted by the black hole.

Another way of looking at the process is to regard the member of the pair of particles that falls into the black hole—the antiparticle, say—as being really a particle that is traveling backward in time. Thus the antiparticle falling into the black hole can be regarded as a particle coming out of the black hole but traveling backward in time. When the particle reaches the point at which the

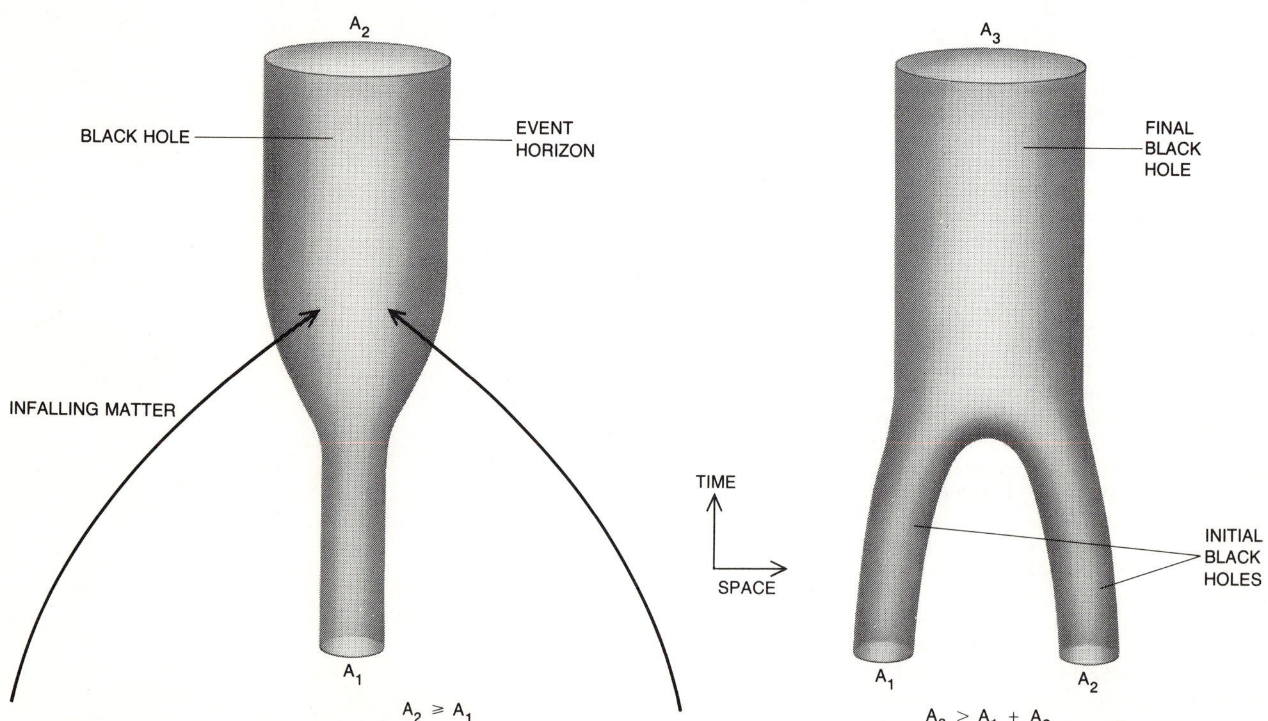

CERTAIN PROPERTIES OF BLACK HOLES suggest that there is a resemblance between the area of the event horizon of a black hole and the concept of entropy in thermodynamics. As matter and radiation continue to fall into a black hole (*space-time configuration at left*) the area of the cross section of the event horizon steadily increases. If two black holes collide and merge (*configuration at right*), the area of the cross section of the event horizon of the resulting black hole is greater than the sum of the areas of the event horizons of the initial black holes. The second law of thermodynamics says that the entropy of an isolated system always increases with passage of time.

particle-antiparticle pair originally materialized, it is scattered by the gravitational field so that it travels forward in time.

Quantum mechanics has therefore allowed a particle to escape from inside a black hole, something that is not allowed in classical mechanics. There are, however, many other situations in atomic and nuclear physics where there is some kind of barrier that particles should not be able to penetrate on classical principles but that they are able to tunnel through on quantum-mechanical principles.

The thickness of the barrier around a black hole is proportional to the size of the black hole. This means that very few particles can escape from a black hole as large as the one hypothesized to exist in Cygnus X-1 but that particles can leak very rapidly out of smaller black holes. Detailed calculations show that the emitted particles have a thermal spectrum corresponding to a temperature that increases rapidly as the mass of the black hole decreases. For a black hole with the mass of the sun the temperature is only about a ten-millionth of a degree above absolute zero. The thermal radiation leaving a black hole with that temperature would be completely swamped by the general background of radiation in the universe. On the other hand, a black hole with a mass of only a billion tons, that is, a primordial black hole roughly the size of a proton, would have a temperature of some 120 billion degrees Kelvin, which corresponds to an energy of some 10 million electron volts. At such a temperature a black hole would be able to create electron-positron pairs and particles of zero mass, such as photons, neutrinos and gravitons (the presumed carriers of gravitational energy). A primordial black hole would release energy at the rate of 6,000 megawatts, equivalent to the output of six large nuclear power plants.

As a black hole emits particles its mass and size steadily decrease. This makes it easier for more particles to tunnel out, and so the emission will continue at an ever increasing rate until eventually the black hole radiates itself out of existence. In the long run every black hole in the universe will evaporate in this way. For large black holes, however, the time it will take is very long indeed: a black hole with the mass of the sun will last for about 10^{66} years. On the other hand, a primordial black hole should have almost completely evaporated in the 10 billion years that have elapsed since the big bang, the beginning of the universe as we know it. Such black holes should now be emitting hard gamma rays with an energy of about 100 million electron volts.

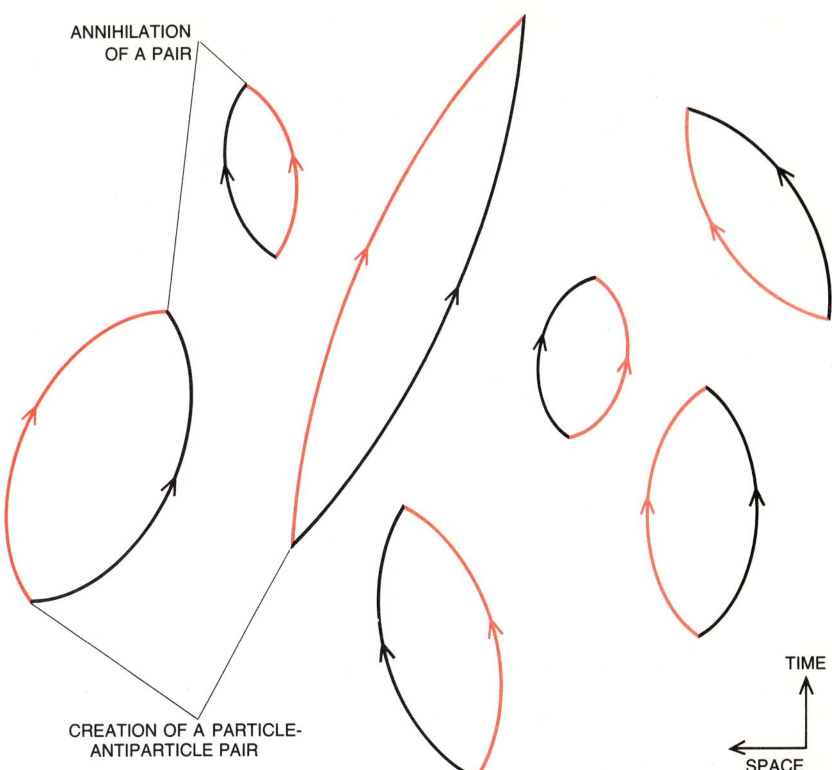

"EMPTY" SPACE-TIME is full of "virtual" pairs of particles (*black*) and antiparticles (*color*). Members of a pair come into existence simultaneously at a point in space-time, move apart and come together again, annihilating each other. They are called virtual because unlike "real" particles they cannot be detected directly. Their indirect effects can nonetheless be measured.

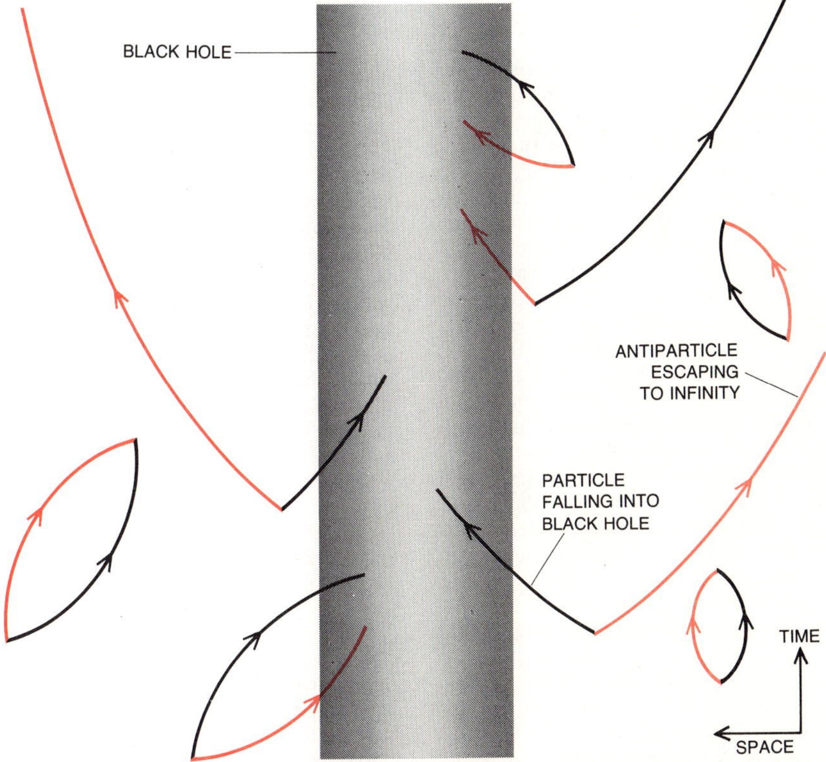

IN THE NEIGHBORHOOD OF A BLACK HOLE one member of a particle-antiparticle pair may fall into the black hole, leaving the other member of the pair without a partner with which to annihilate. If surviving member of pair does not follow its partner into black hole, it may escape to infinity. Thus black hole will appear to be emitting particles and antiparticles.

Calculations made by Don N. Page of the California Institute of Technology and me, based on measurements of the cosmic background of gamma radiation made by the satellite SAS-2, show that the average density of primordial black holes in the universe must be less than about 200 per cubic light-year. The local density in our galaxy could be a million times higher than this figure if primordial black holes were concentrated in the "halo" of galaxies—the thin cloud of rapidly moving stars in which each galaxy is embedded—rather than being uniformly distributed throughout the universe. This would imply that the primordial black hole closest to the earth is probably at least as far away as the planet Pluto.

The final stage of the evaporation of a black hole would proceed so rapidly that it would end in a tremendous explosion. How powerful this explosion would be depends on how many different species of elementary particles there are. If, as is now widely believed, all particles are made up of perhaps six different kinds of quarks, the final explosion would have an energy equivalent to about 10 million one-megaton hydrogen bombs. On the other hand, an alternative theory of elementary particles put forward by R. Hagedorn of the European Organization for Nuclear Research argues that there is an infinite number of elementary particles of higher and higher mass. As a black hole got smaller and hotter, it would emit a larger and larger number of different species of particles and would produce an explosion perhaps 100,000 times more powerful than the one calculated on the quark hypothesis. Hence the observation of a black-hole explosion would provide very important information on elementary particle physics, information that might not be available any other way.

A black-hole explosion would produce a massive outpouring of high-energy gamma rays. Although they might be observed by gamma-ray detectors on satellites or balloons, it would be difficult to fly a detector large enough to have a reasonable chance of intercepting a significant number of gamma-ray photons from one explosion. One possibility would be to employ a space shuttle to build a large gamma-ray detector in orbit. An easier and much cheaper alternative would be to let the earth's upper atmosphere serve as a detector. A high-energy gamma ray plunging into the atmosphere will create a shower of electron-positron pairs, which initially will be traveling through the atmosphere faster than light can. (Light is slowed down by interactions with the air molecules.) Thus the electrons and positrons will set up a kind of sonic boom, or shock wave, in the electromagnetic field. Such a shock wave, called Cerenkov radiation, could be detected from the ground as a flash of visible light.

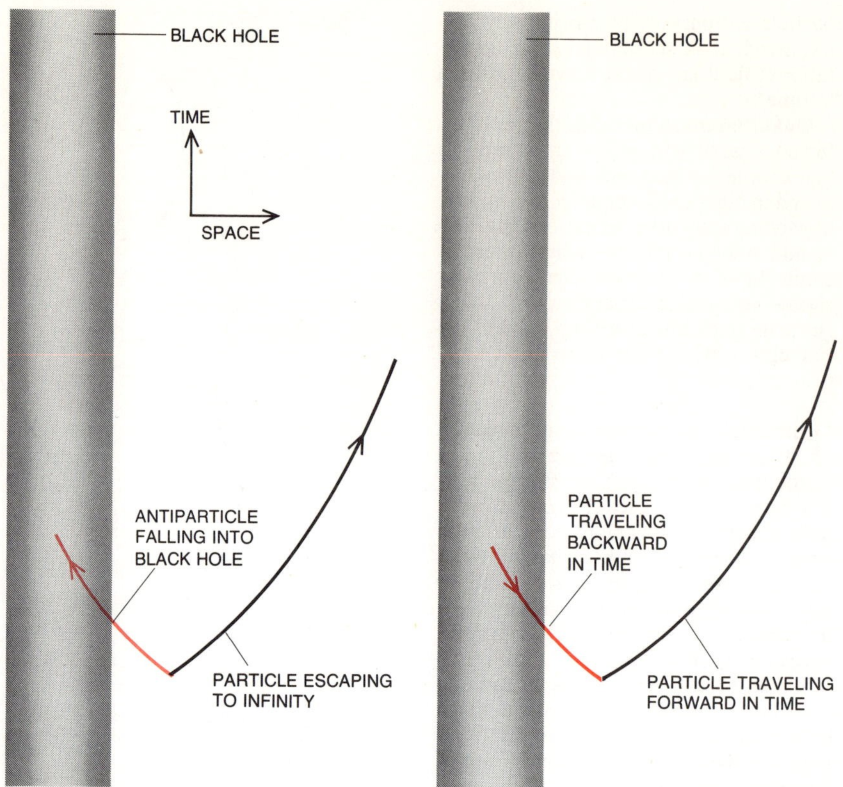

ALTERNATIVE INTERPRETATIONS can explain the emission of particles by a black hole. One explanation (*left*) invokes the formation of a virtual particle-antiparticle pair, one member of which is trapped by the black hole as the other escapes. In another explanation (*right*) one can regard an antiparticle falling into a black hole as being a normal particle that is traveling backward in time out of the black hole. Once outside it is scattered by the gravitational field and converted into a particle traveling forward in time, which escapes to infinity.

A preliminary experiment by Neil A. Porter and Trevor C. Weekes of University College, Dublin, indicates that if black holes explode the way Hagedorn's theory predicts, there are fewer than two black-hole explosions per cubic light-year per century in our region of the galaxy. This would imply that the density of primordial black holes is less than 100 million per cubic light-year. It should be possible to greatly increase the sensitivity of such observations. Even if they do not yield any positive evidence of primordial black holes, they will be very valuable. By placing a low upper limit on the density of such black holes, the observations will indicate that the early universe must have been very smooth and nonturbulent.

The big bang resembles a black-hole explosion but on a vastly larger scale. One therefore hopes that an understanding of how black holes create particles will lead to a similar understanding of how the big bang created everything in the universe. In a black hole matter collapses and is lost forever but new matter is created in its place. It may therefore be that there was an earlier phase of the universe in which matter collapsed, to be re-created in the big bang.

If the matter that collapses to form a black hole has a net electric charge, the resulting black hole will carry the same charge. This means that the black hole will tend to attract those members of the virtual particle-antiparticle pairs that have the opposite charge and repel those that have a like charge. The black hole will therefore preferentially emit particles with charge of the same sign as itself and so will rapidly lose its charge. Similarly, if the collapsing matter has a net angular momentum, the resulting black hole will be rotating and will preferentially emit particles that carry away its angular momentum. The reason a black hole "remembers" the electric charge, angular momentum and mass of the matter that collapsed and "forgets" everything else is that these three quantities are coupled to long-range fields: in the case of charge the electromagnetic field and in the case of angular momentum and mass the gravitational field.

Experiments by Robert H. Dicke of Princeton University and Vladimir Braginsky of Moscow State University have indicated that there is no long-range

field associated with the quantum property designated baryon number. (Baryons are the class of particles including the proton and the neutron.) Hence a black hole formed out of the collapse of a collection of baryons would forget its baryon number and radiate equal quantities of baryons and antibaryons. Therefore when the black hole disappeared, it would violate one of the most cherished laws of particle physics, the law of baryon conservation.

Although Bekenstein's hypothesis that black holes have a finite entropy requires for its consistency that black holes should radiate thermally, at first it seems a complete miracle that the detailed quantum-mechanical calculations of particle creation should give rise to emission with a thermal spectrum. The explanation is that the emitted particles tunnel out of the black hole from a region of which an external observer has no knowledge other than its mass, angular momentum and electric charge. This means that all combinations or configurations of emitted particles that have the same energy, angular momentum and electric charge are equally probable. Indeed, it is possible that the black hole could emit a television set or the works of Proust in 10 leather-bound volumes, but the number of configurations of particles that correspond to these exotic possibilities is vanishingly small. By far the largest number of configurations correspond to emission with a spectrum that is nearly thermal.

The emission from black holes has an added degree of uncertainty, or unpredictability, over and above that normally associated with quantum mechanics. In classical mechanics one can predict the results of measuring both the position and the velocity of a particle. In quantum mechanics the uncertainty principle says that only one of these measurements can be predicted; the observer can predict the result of measuring either the position or the velocity but not both. Alternatively he can predict the result of measuring one combination of position and velocity. Thus the observer's ability to make definite predictions is in effect cut in half. With black holes the situation is even worse. Since the particles emitted by a black hole come from a region of which the observer has very limited knowledge, he cannot definitely predict the position or the velocity of a particle or any combination of the two; all he can predict is the probabilities that certain particles will be emitted. It therefore seems that Einstein was doubly wrong when he said, "God does not play dice." Consideration of particle emission from black holes would seem to suggest that God not only plays dice but also sometimes throws them where they cannot be seen.

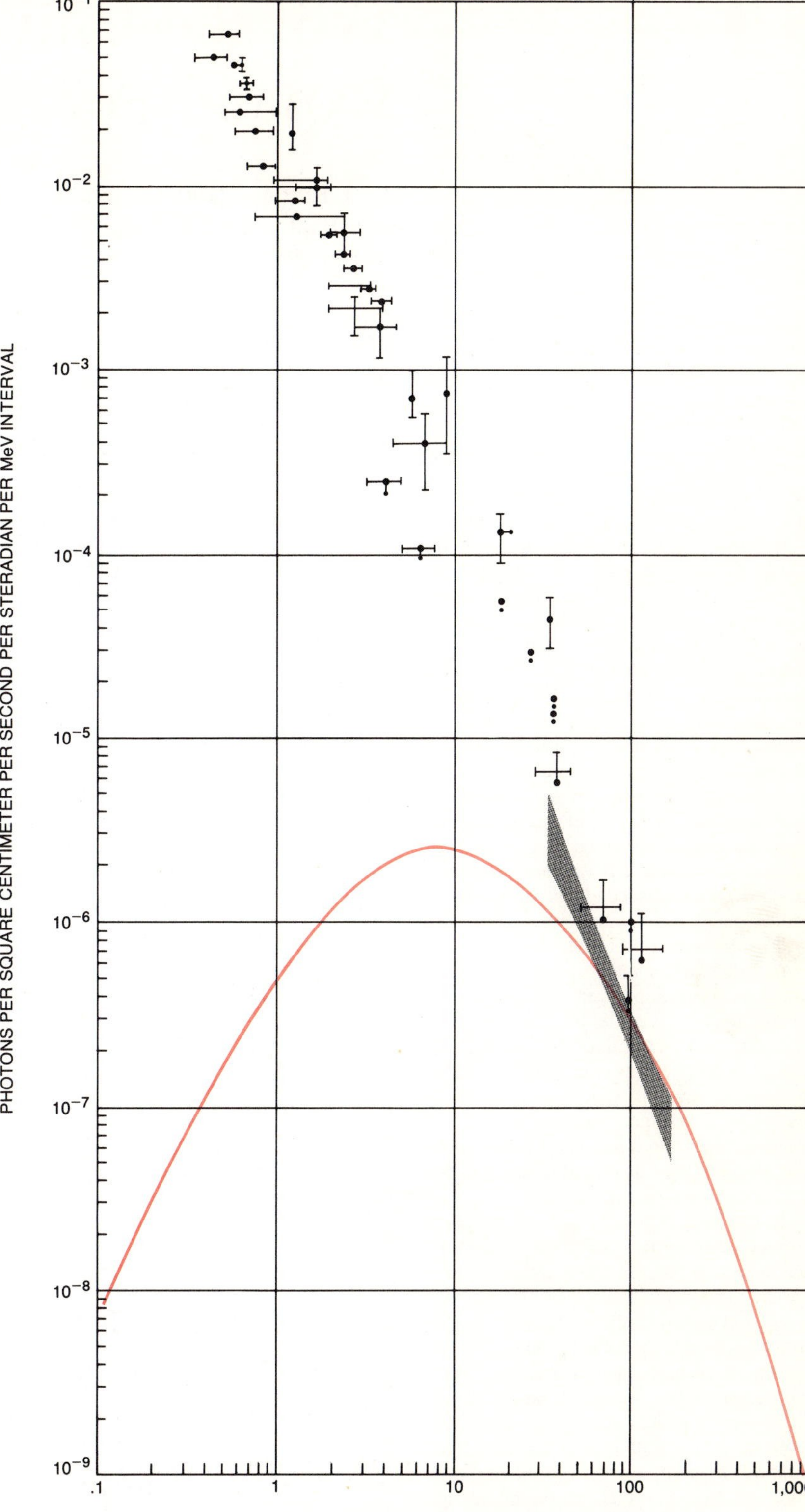

PRIMORDIAL BLACK HOLES, each about the size of an elementary particle and weighing about a billion tons, may have been formed in large numbers shortly after the big bang, the beginning of the universe as we know it. Such black holes would have a temperature of about 70 billion degrees Kelvin, corresponding to an energy of 10 million electron volts (MeV). The particles emitted at that energy would produce a diffuse spectrum of gamma rays detectable by satellites. The data points and the shaded region represent actual measurements of the diffuse gamma-ray spectrum in nearby space. The measurements indicate that the average density of such black holes in the universe must be less than about a million per cubic light-year. Solid curve is predicted spectrum from such a density of primordial black holes, based on plausible assumptions about the density of matter in universe and distribution of black holes.

10

Will the Universe Expand Forever?

by J. Richard Gott III, James E. Gunn, David N. Schramm and Beatrice M. Tinsley
March 1976

The recession of distant galaxies, the average density of matter, the age of the chemical elements and the abundance of deuterium together suggest that the expansion cannot be halted or reversed

Cosmological inquiry is ancient, but only in the past 50 years or so have we begun to understand how the universe began and what its ultimate fate may be. The crucial perception came in the 1920's, when Edwin P. Hubble demonstrated that the spiral nebulas are not local objects but independent systems of stars much like our own, and thereby showed that the universe is a much larger place than had been imagined. Hubble showed further that the entire observable system of galaxies is in orderly motion. As is now well known, the nature of that motion is expansion: all distant galaxies are receding from us.

That the universe is expanding is today considered established. A question that remains unsettled is whether the expansion will continue forever or whether the receding galaxies will someday stop and then reverse their motion, eventually falling together in a great collapse. The answer to this question determines the geometrical character of the universe, that is, it determines the nature of space and time. If the expansion continues perpetually, the universe is "open" and infinite; if it will someday stop and reverse direction, the universe is "closed" and of finite extent.

In order to choose between those possibilities, astronomers construct mathematical models of the universe and then attempt to find observable features of the real universe that would confirm one of the models and exclude all others. So far no single measurement has been made with enough precision to settle the question unambiguously. Several independent tests are possible, however, and pieces of the puzzle have been supplied by many workers employing quite different techniques. It now seems feasible to assemble the pieces. Taken together, the available evidence suggests that the universe is open and that its expansion will never cease.

Isotropic Expansion

Hubble detected the recessional motion of the distant galaxies through measurements of their optical spectra. The spectra of most stars (and hence of galaxies) are interrupted by dark lines representing the absorption of particular wavelengths by atoms in the cooler, outer layers of the stellar atmosphere; each chemical element generates a characteristic pattern of lines whose wavelengths are precisely known from laboratory measurements. When the galaxy is moving away from the observer, the wavelength of each spectral line is increased as a result of the Doppler effect, so that all the lines appear to be displaced toward longer wavelengths and in particular toward the red end of the visible portion of the spectrum. The displacement is called a red shift, and by measuring its magnitude the velocity of recession can be calculated. When an object is moving toward the observer, the wavelengths of the spectral lines are decreased by the Doppler effect and the lines appear to be displaced toward the blue end of the spectrum, an effect called a blue shift. All the distant galaxies whose spectra were measured by Hubble and by later observers show red shifts; they are therefore assumed to be receding from us.

The recessional motion has several remarkable properties. Hubble showed that the velocity with which a galaxy recedes is proportional to its distance from us, so that a constant ratio of distance to velocity can be calculated. The ratio is such that a galaxy 10 million light-years from us recedes with a velocity of 170 kilometers per second; another galaxy twice as far away recedes twice

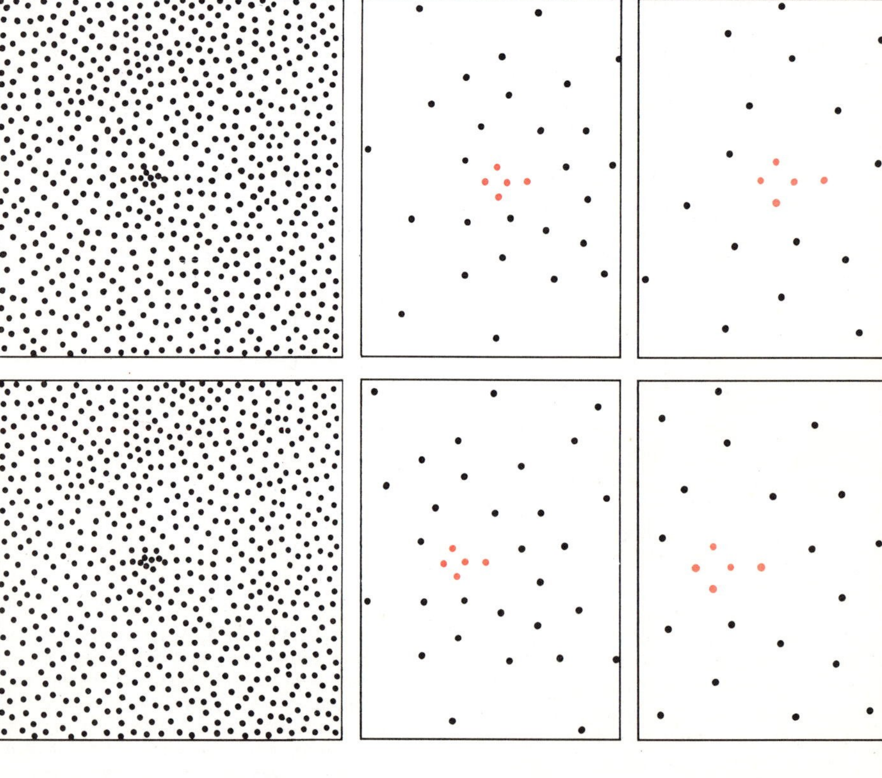

FATE OF THE UNIVERSE is described through mathematical models of its behavior. Two classes of models are generally considered plausible; in both the universe begins in a compact state of infinite density (the big bang). In one class of models the universe expands continuously and indefinitely, albeit at an ever lower rate (*upper series of drawings*). In the other class

as fast, or 340 kilometers per second [*see illustrations on next two pages*]. Small departures from this rule are commonly observed because most galaxies are members of groups or clusters and have orbital motions with a component along the line of sight connecting the earth with the galaxy. Those motions are essentially random, however, so that in any large sample of galaxies they cancel one another. Nonrandom, systematic variations from the ratio have been found only for galaxies at the most extreme distances; as we shall see, these variations do not invalidate the rule but provide important information about the history of the universe.

A second characteristic of the cosmic expansion is its isotropy: it is the same in all directions. No matter where in the sky a galaxy is found, its recessional velocity is related to its distance by the same proportionality. This observation seems to suggest that the universe is remarkably symmetrical and, what is even more extraordinary, that we happen to be at its very center. The crystal spheres of medieval cosmologies were no more geocentric.

There is, of course, another explanation, which can be understood most readily by considering a simple two-dimensional model of an expanding universe. Imagine a spherical balloon with small dots painted on its surface, each dot representing a galaxy. As the balloon is inflated the distance between any two dots (always measured on the surface of the sphere) increases with a speed proportional to the distance between them. No matter which dot is designated the center, all the other dots recede from it uniformly in all directions. Thus each dot observes the same expansion and no one of them has a privileged position. Such an expansion has no center; more precisely, every point is its center.

It follows from this analysis of the expansion that the geometrical configuration of the dots cannot change. A balloon bearing a picture of Mickey Mouse continues to bear the same picture as it is inflated. All distances between points on the balloon are multiplied by the same factor. Similarly, in the real universe eight galaxies that happen to lie at the corners of a cube in one epoch will remain at the corners of a cube, albeit a larger one, as the universe expands.

The Big Bang

Since Hubble's original discovery increasingly precise observations have shown that it is not only the cosmic expansion that is isotropic; all the large-scale features of the universe are indifferent to direction. For example, the distribution of galaxies on the celestial sphere and the distribution of extragalactic radio sources appear to be quite uniform. The most compelling evidence of isotropy was discovered in 1965 by Arno A. Penzias and Robert W. Wilson of the Bell Laboratories; it is the microwave background radiation that seems to bathe the entire universe. The microwave radiation has since been shown to be highly isotropic; it varies by less than one part in 1,000 over the entire area of the sky.

The observation of such remarkable isotropy has led to the adoption of a powerful generalization called the cosmological principle. It states that the universe appears isotropic around all observers participating in the expansion everywhere and at all times. In other words, our galaxy is indeed at the center of the universe, but so is every other galaxy.

The cosmological principle also governs the behavior of the two-dimensional model universe represented by a spherical balloon. If the painted dots are distributed with uniform density over the surface of the balloon, the neighborhood of any chosen point is statistically the same as that of any other point and no direction has any special significance. Indeed, it is not necessary to postulate independently that the dots (or, in the three-dimensional universe, the galaxies) are uniformly distributed. If the universe is isotropic for all observers, then the distribution must be homogeneous; if it were not, an observer at the edge of a density fluctuation would not see a uniform distribution independent of direction.

For the purposes of this discussion we shall adopt the cosmological principle, but it must be remembered that its appeal is mostly philosophical. It has not been ade-

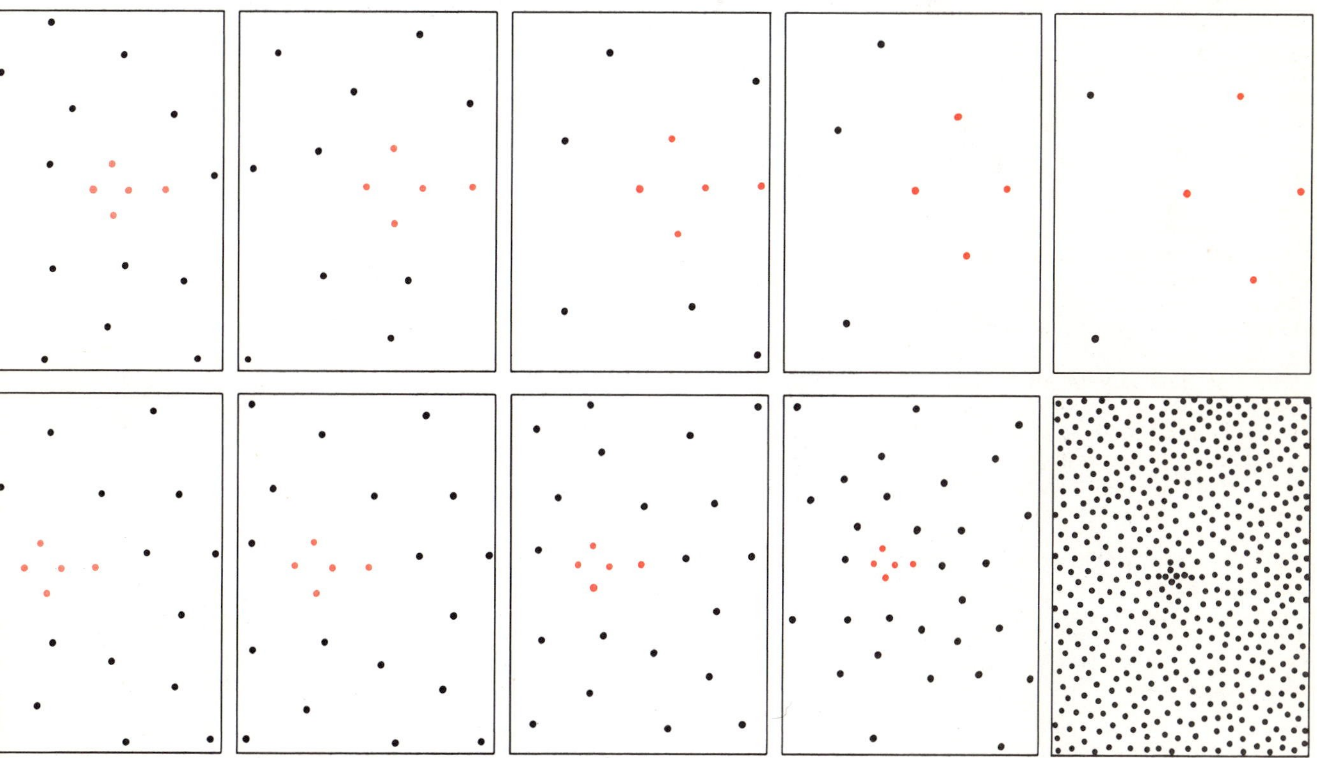

the universe expands to a maximum size, then begins to contract, eventually reaching infinite density again (*lower series of drawings*). The alternatives are illustrated here in an arbitrary region of space in which the cosmic expansion is represented by a decrease in average density. The expansion is isotropic, that is, the same in all directions. As a result an observer at any point perceives himself as being at the center of the expansion, and the shape of any pattern (such as the arbitrary pattern of colored dots) will be preserved in all epochs.

quately tested, and indeed adequate tests may never be possible.

Given our knowledge of the universe as we observe it today, what can we deduce about its history? A simple, hypothetical model with which to begin is one where the recessional velocity of every galaxy has remained unchanged through all time. It is then apparent that any galaxy now receding from us was once arbitrarily close, and that the time that has elapsed since then is equal to the ratio between the galaxy's distance and its velocity. Since the ratio is the same for all galaxies, all of them must have been nearby at the same time; in other words, at some unique time in the past all the matter in the universe was compressed to an arbitrarily great density. The time calculated to have elapsed since that compact state existed, assuming the rate of expansion has not changed, is called the Hubble time. Its reciprocal, by which one multiplies the distance of a galaxy to obtain its recessional velocity, is called the Hubble constant. Measurements of the Hubble time are complicated by uncertainties as to the distance to galaxies, and the measurements have been repeatedly revised since Hubble's first estimate of about two billion years. The Hubble time is now thought to be between 12 and 25 billion years, and the most likely value is about 19 billion years.

If the motions of the galaxies are extrapolated into the past as far as possible, a state is eventually reached in which all the galaxies were crushed together at infinite density. That state represents the big bang, and it marks the origin of the universe and everything in it. By the simple mathematics of

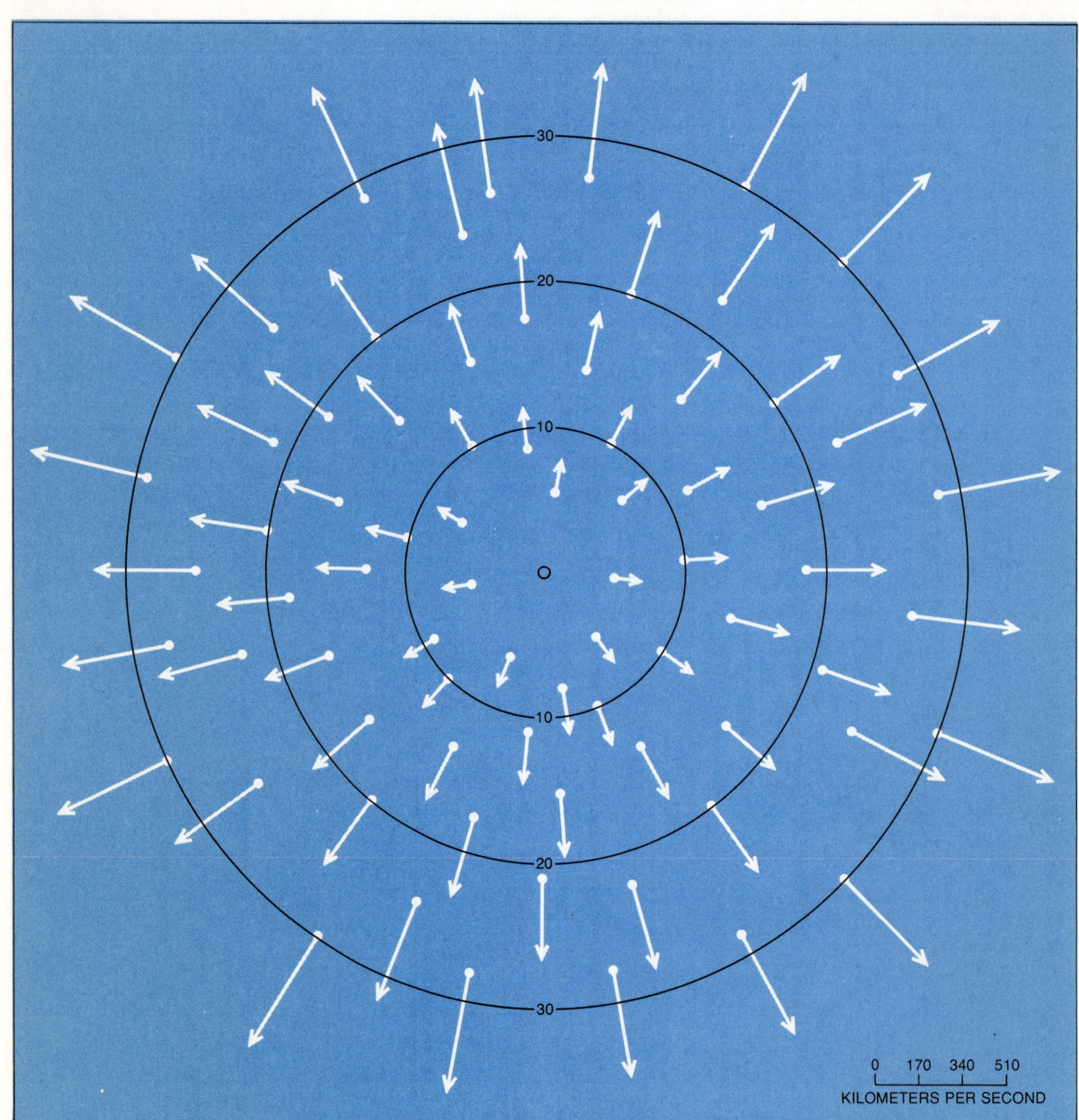

COSMIC EXPANSION seems to place the observer at the center of the universe, from which all distant galaxies are fleeing. The velocity with which a galaxy recedes is proportional to its distance from the observer, a relation first established in the 1920's by Edwin P. Hubble from observations made with the 100-inch telescope at the Mount Wilson Observatory. The principle that the ratio of velocity to distance is constant has since become known as Hubble's law. It can be interpreted most simply as evidence that the expansion of the universe began with the big bang, since the relation implies that in the past all the galaxies were packed together with infinite density. Distances are given here in millions of light-years; velocities are represented by the lengths of arrows, measured on the scale at lower right.

proportionality, if the recessional velocities have not changed, the date of the big bang must be exactly one Hubble time ago. Actually the rate of expansion has almost certainly not been constant, but that does not alter the fact of the big bang; it merely changes the date.

That the universe began with a big bang is an inevitable conclusion if the known laws of physics are assumed to be correct and in some sense complete. It is conceivable, however, that there are laws of nature whose effects are negligible on the scale of the physics laboratory, or even on the scale of the solar system, but that might predominate in determining the behavior of the universe as a whole. One theory requiring new laws of nature was the steady-state cosmology, in which the universe is unchanging and infinitely old. In order to explain the cosmic expansion the steady-state theory postulated the continual creation of matter from the void.

In the steady-state model of the universe it was particularly difficult to account for the microwave background radiation. This radiation field has the spectral characteristics of the thermal radiation emitted by a body at a temperature of 2.7 degrees Kelvin. It seems to be satisfactorily explained only as a relic of an epoch when the universe was very hot and very dense. A steady-state universe cannot have had such conditions, since in that model all conditions, by definition, have not changed.

In big-bang models the background radiation is a natural consequence of conditions in the early universe. The initial state in these models is one of high temperature and density, a state sometimes called the cosmic fireball. At this stage the matter and the electromagnetic energy composing the universe are thought to have been in thermodynamic equilibrium, and as a result the radiation spectrum was that of a very hot body. As the universe has expanded the radiation has cooled, reaching the low-temperature spectrum observed today. The cooling can be understood as an enormous red shift; since all galaxies are constantly receding from the radiation, its spectrum is constantly displaced toward the longer wavelengths associated with lower energies and lower temperatures. In 1946 George Gamow predicted the existence of a thermal background radiation entirely from the theoretical framework of the big-bang model. He estimated its present temperature as being about five degrees K. The general agreement between Gamow's prediction and the observations of Penzias and Wilson is the most compelling evidence for the big bang.

Thus it appears that the universe began from a state of infinite density about one Hubble time ago. Space and time were created in that event and so was all the matter in the universe. It is not meaningful to ask what happened before the big bang; it is somewhat like asking what is north of the North Pole. Similarly, it is not sensible to ask where the big bang took place. The point-universe was not an object isolated in space; it was the entire universe, and so the only answer can be that the big bang happened everywhere.

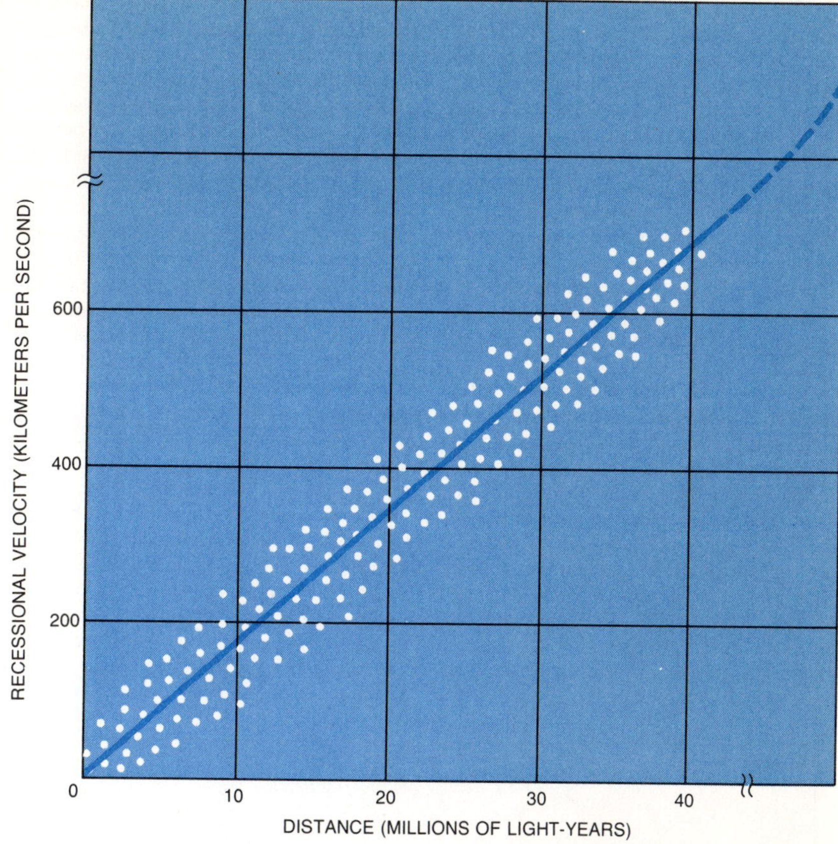

HUBBLE'S LAW is established by measuring the ratio of velocity to distance for many galaxies. The best estimate of the ratio (*solid colored line*) is about 17 kilometers per second per million light-years. Individual galaxies (*white dots*) depart from that value because most are members of clusters and have orbital velocities. The inverse of the ratio is the Hubble time: the time it would have taken for any given galaxy at its present velocity to reach its present position, or in other words the time since the big bang if the velocities have not changed. Actually it is thought that the recessional velocities have declined under the influence of gravitation; as a result the ratio is thought to increase at extreme distances (*broken colored line*).

In most models of the evolving universe the receding galaxies are assumed to follow ballistic trajectories, roughly analogous to those of a thrown ball or an artillery shell. The galaxies were propelled apart by forces acting at the moment of the big bang, but since then they have moved in free flight, without further propulsion. They should therefore continue in uniform motion if no other forces acted on them. Actually the galaxies continue to interact as they fly apart. If only the familiar forces that express the known laws of physics are to be allowed in our models, then only one force can have a significant effect on the expansion: gravitation. We can therefore hope to understand the dynamics of an expanding universe if we can describe the gravitational interactions of all its components.

Gravitational Deceleration

The gravitational force affects all matter, it is always attractive and its range is infinite. Moreover, gravitation has a peculiar geometrical property that significantly aids analysis: A hollow sphere exerts no net gravitational forces on masses in its interior. (Actually, of course, the mass of the hollow shell attracts the masses in the interior, but all the forces exactly cancel, so that at every point in the interior the resultant force is zero.) This proposition was first proved by Newton, but it applies equally well to more recent theories of gravitation, such as the general theory of relativity.

If a spherical region of the universe is selected for examination, the rest of the universe surrounding it can be regarded as a hollow spherical shell, since the cosmological principle requires that the surrounding matter be uniformly distributed in all directions. The selected sphere can then be studied as if it were isolated and not subject to forces from the outside. The cosmological principle also ensures that any selected sphere of galaxies will expand or contract by the same factor as the universe as a whole, regardless of the sphere's location or size. In order to characterize the dynamics of the universe, therefore, we need only examine the dynamics of a representative sphere within it. If the sphere chosen is a small one, the velocities of the galaxies will be much smaller than the speed of light, and their motions can be described in terms of Newtonian mechanics.

A galaxy at the edge of such a small

spherical region feels only the gravitational forces generated by the matter inside the sphere. If that matter is distributed homogeneously, then the resultant force acting on the galaxy attracts it to the center of the sphere. As a consequence the test galaxy does not recede with constant velocity; instead its recessional motion is at all times decelerated. It is thus obvious that in the past the test galaxy and all other galaxies must have been moving faster than they are today. Ignoring the deceleration leads to an overestimate of the age of the universe. That age is one Hubble time only if the rate of expansion has not changed; since the rate has slowed under the influence of gravitation, the big bang must have taken place more recently than one Hubble time ago.

The magnitude of the gravitational deceleration clearly depends on the amount of mass inside the selected sphere. If the sphere contains a great deal of matter, the test galaxy must eventually stop and fall toward the center; the representative spherical region begins to collapse and, on the cosmological principle, so does the entire universe. If there is little matter, the test galaxy will decelerate continuously but never stop. Both the spherical region and the universe as a whole will expand indefinitely. The situation is analogous to that of a projectile shot upward from the surface of the earth: the projectile decelerates but nevertheless will not return to the surface if its velocity exceeds a certain critical value, the escape velocity.

The escape velocity for objects leaving the earth is determined by the mass of the earth; for a test galaxy at the edge of an arbitrary sphere in space the escape velocity is determined by the total mass within the sphere. From the ratio of velocity to distance the actual velocity of the test galaxy with respect to the center of the sphere is known. Its ultimate fate therefore depends on the value of the escape velocity and hence on the mass within the sphere.

Since the universe is assumed to be homogeneous, the determining quantity is the average density of matter in the universe. If the density is smaller than some critical value, the effect of gravitation is too small to halt the cosmic expansion, and all galaxies will recede forever (although ever more slowly). If the density is greater than the critical density, gravitation will prevail, and the expansion will slow to a stop and begin an accelerating contraction ending in a final cataclysm: what might be called the big crunch. The actual value of the critical density depends on the Hubble time, which is not precisely known. If the Hubble time is 19 billion years, the critical density is 5×10^{-30} gram per cubic centimeter, the equivalent of about three hydrogen atoms per cubic meter. That seems to be an exceedingly small density, but it should be remembered that on the average the universe is quite empty.

The effect of gravitation on the cosmic expansion can be incorporated into mathematical models most conveniently by introducing a dimensionless number called the density parameter and denoted by the Greek letter omega (Ω). The density parameter is defined as the ratio of the actual density of the universe to the critical density. If the universe is to expand forever, that ratio must be less than or equal to 1; if Ω equals exactly 1, the universe is expanding everywhere at just the escape velocity, and if Ω is greater than 1, the universe must eventually collapse.

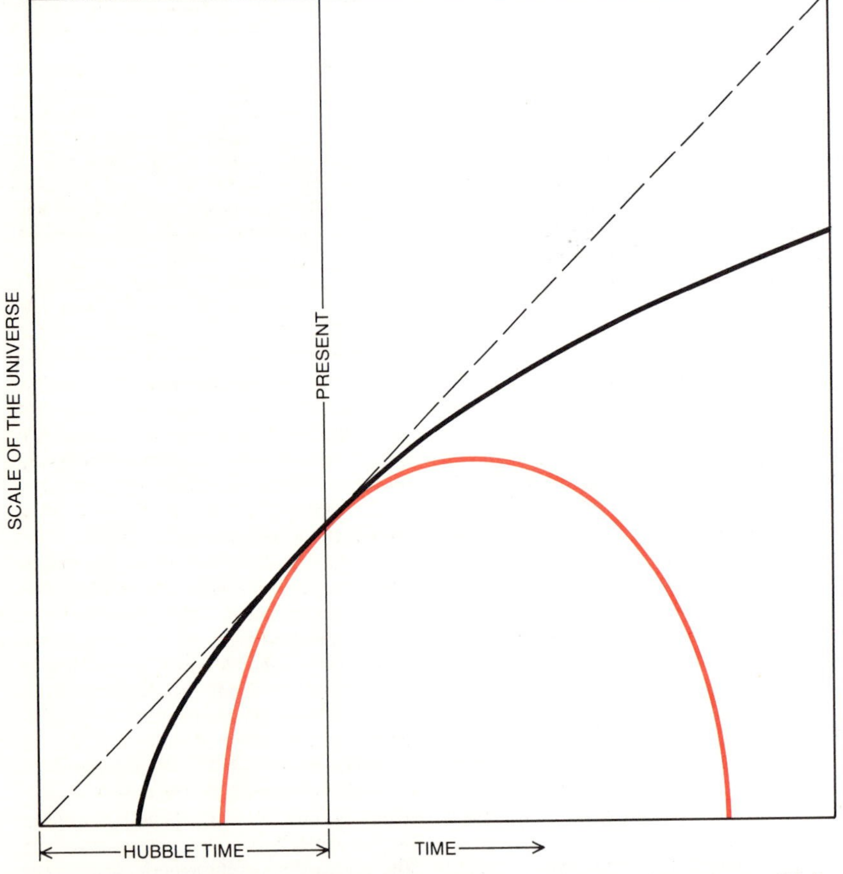

MODELS OF COSMIC EVOLUTION describe changes in the scale of the universe with the passage of time. All models must be consistent with the scale and the rate of expansion observed today, so that all their graphs must be tangent at the present moment. If the rate of expansion is unchanging (*broken black line*), the age of the universe is the Hubble time. Decelerating universes are younger, and both their history and their destiny depend on the magnitude of the deceleration. With modest deceleration the expansion can continue indefinitely, albeit at an ever lower rate (*solid black line*). Greater deceleration implies that the cosmic expansion must stop and then reverse, leading to an eventual collapse (*colored line*). The infinitely expanding universe is said to be "open" and the collapsing universe, which is also the youngest, "closed."

The Geometry of Space

The foregoing discussion could have been derived entirely from the Newtonian theory of gravitation, although it is also valid in the general theory of relativity. In the general theory, however, the value of the density parameter has further consequences; in particular it determines the geometry of space. In the high-density universe fated to collapse, gravitation is sufficiently strong to "close" space. The total volume of the universe is finite at all times, although there is nevertheless no boundary or edge to the universe. A two-dimensional analogue of such a three-dimensional space is the surface of a sphere, which similarly is finite in area although it has no boundary.

If Ω equals 1, so that the universe expands with exactly the escape velocity, the geometry of space is "flat"; it is the familiar Euclidean geometry, and it is represented in two dimensions by an infinite plane.

The geometry of a perpetually expanding universe in which Ω is less than 1 is more difficult to illustrate. The two-dimensional analogue is the surface of a figure called a pseudosphere, and a complete pseudosphere cannot be constructed in three-dimensional space. A saddle-shaped surface has some of the properties of such a space, but it is a defective model in the important respect that it has a center, whereas the real space defines no preferred position [*see illustration on page 88*]. Perhaps the best two-dimensional representation of such a space is a projection of a pseudosphere onto a plane, a device that is employed in several of the works of the Dutch artist M. C. Escher [*see illustration on page 89*].

The three possible kinds of three-dimensional space are distinguished by several ge-

	OPEN	CRITICAL	CLOSED
DENSITY PARAMETER Ω $\dfrac{\text{ACTUAL DENSITY}}{\text{CRITICAL DENSITY}}$	$\Omega < 1$	$\Omega = 1$	$\Omega > 1$
DECELERATION PARAMETER q_0 DECELERATION $\dfrac{\text{DISTANCE}}{(\text{VELOCITY})^2}$	$q_0 < \frac{1}{2}$	$q_0 = \frac{1}{2}$	$q_0 > \frac{1}{2}$
GEOMETRY OF SPACE	HYPERBOLIC (NEGATIVE CURVATURE)	FLAT (ZERO CURVATURE)	SPHERICAL (POSITIVE CURVATURE)
FUTURE OF THE UNIVERSE	PERPETUAL EXPANSION	PERPETUAL EXPANSION	EVENTUAL COLLAPSE

OPEN AND CLOSED MODELS of the universe are distinguished mainly by the average density of matter and by the value of the cosmic deceleration. Density is a crucial factor because in models described by the general theory of relativity it is the sole determinant of the gravitational forces that slow the cosmic expansion. Density is most easily treated as a dimensionless parameter, the ratio of the actual density to the critical density just needed to halt the expansion. Deceleration can also be expressed as a dimensionless number, the deceleration parameter, which in the models considered here is always equal to half the density parameter. These two parameters determine not only the future of the universe but also the geometry of space. The open universe is of infinite size at all times, and in it space has hyperbolic, or negative, curvature. In the universe with critical density, in which the density parameter is exactly 1, space has zero curvature, it is the flat space of Euclidean geometry. The closed universe is of finite size; in it space has spherical, or positive, curvature.

ometric properties, some of which can be represented in the two-dimensional models. A flat plane, of course, is the basis of Euclid's geometry, and on it all the Euclidean axioms and the theorems derived from them are obeyed. On a plane exactly one line can be drawn through a given point parallel to another line; the sum of the included angles in a triangle is always 180 degrees; the circumference of a circle increases in proportion to the radius, and the area of a circle increases in proportion to the square of the radius.

On the surface of a sphere no two lines are parallel, provided that a straight line is defined as one taking the shortest path between two points. Such lines are called geodesics, and on the sphere they are the great circles, any two of which always intersect. Similarly, on a sphere the sum of the included angles in a triangle is always greater than 180 degrees; the circumference of a circle increases more slowly than in proportion to the radius, and the area of a circle increases more slowly than in proportion to the square of the radius.

The surface of a pseudosphere possesses properties opposite to those of a sphere. Through a given point infinitely many lines can be drawn that are parallel to another line, or geodesic. The sum of the angles of a triangle is less than 180 degrees. The circumference of a circle increases faster than in proportion to the radius, and the area of a circle increases faster than in proportion to the square of the radius. The geometry of the three-dimensional space represented by a pseudosphere was first studied in 1826 by Nikolai Lobachevski.

In the simple cosmological models discussed here the geometry of space is uniquely related to the future behavior of the universe. It is notable that in models with Ω greater than 1 the universe is closed in both space and time. The volume of space is finite, and there are definite temporal limits, beginning with the big bang and ending with the big crunch. Models in which Ω is less than or equal to 1 are open in both space and time. Such models have a definite starting point (the big bang), but they are always infinite in extent and they expand indefinitely into the future.

Measurements of Deceleration

There are several possible ways of determining whether the actual universe is open or closed. All of them lead ultimately to an estimate of the rate at which the cosmic expansion is decelerating. One method is simply to measure the deceleration directly, by observing distant galaxies. It is also possible to measure the age of the universe, and by comparing it with the Hubble time (the age if there were no deceleration) to derive an estimate of how much the velocity of expansion has changed. Since the deceleration is a gravitational phenomenon, an equivalent measure is the average density of matter; comparing the actual density with the critical density gives the ratio Ω. Finally, the present abundance of certain chemical elements represents a kind of fossil record of conditions in the very early universe, including the density, and from that information too the value of Ω can be calculated. Evidence from each of these methods has contributed to our present knowledge of the state of the universe.

The deceleration of the cosmic expansion is usually expressed in terms of a dimensionless number called the deceleration parameter and symbolized q_0. Since the deceleration is a gravitational effect, the deceleration parameter is closely related to the average density of matter. In the cosmological models considered here, which are constructed according to the general theory of relativity, q_0 is always equal to exactly half the density parameter Ω. Thus if q_0 is greater than 1/2, the universe is decelerating rapidly enough, because of its high den-

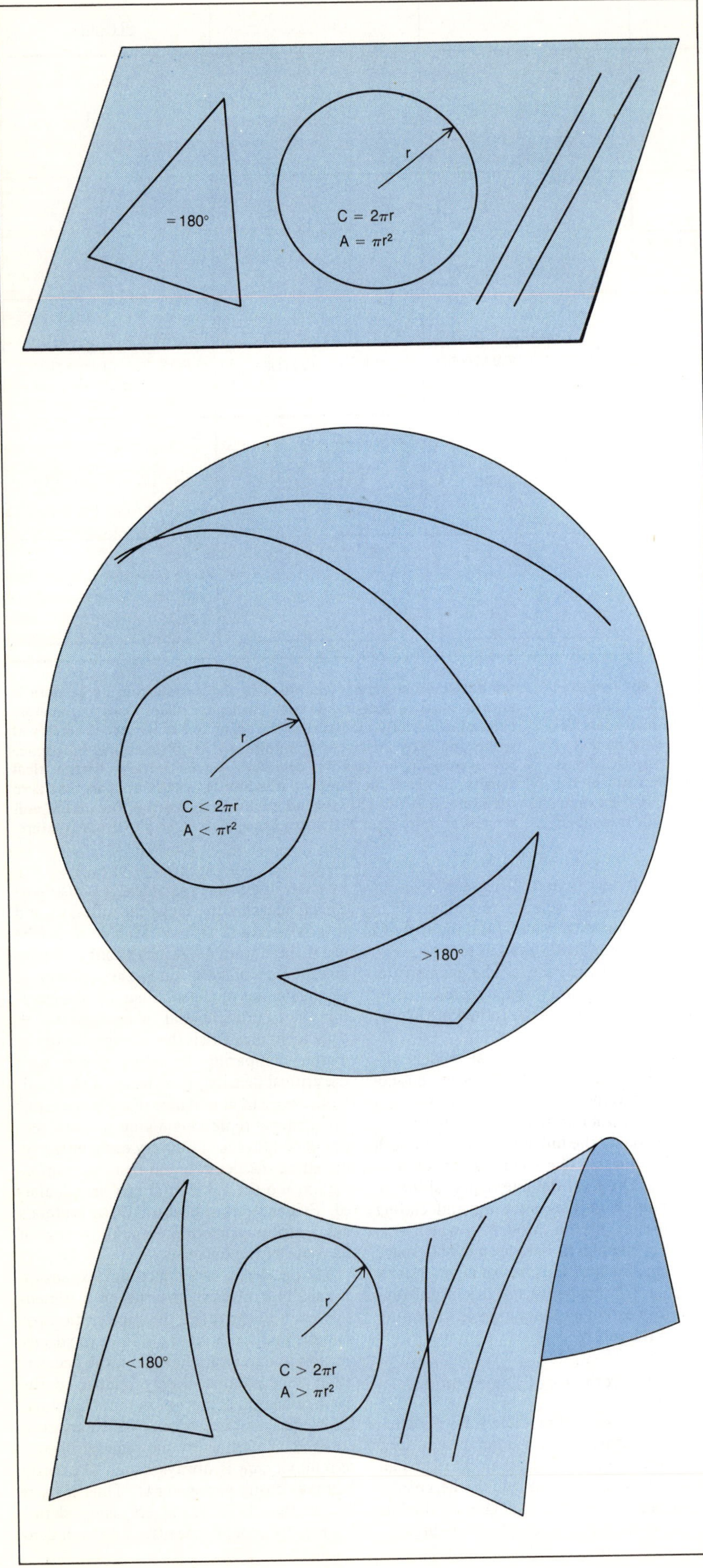

sity, to stop expanding and subsequently collapse. If q_0 is less than 1/2, the expansion cannot stop because the density is too low to halt it.

An obvious approach to determining the rate of deceleration would be to measure the radial velocity of a single galaxy at two times in order to see how much it has slowed down in the interval. Unfortunately the change in velocity expected in a human lifetime is far too small to be detected; indeed, the experimental errors involved in the determination are many orders of magnitude larger. Because of the finite speed of light, however, it is possible to measure the velocities of galaxies in the remote past and to compare them with velocities representing more recent eras. The comparison is possible because as we look at increasingly distant objects in the sky we also see farther and farther into the past. The relation is obvious when distances are measured in light-years: if a galaxy is a billion light-years away, the light we receive from it today was emitted a billion years ago, and the Doppler shift in its spectrum must reflect the distant galaxy's velocity then with respect to our own velocity now. Thus if the cosmic expansion is decelerating, the constant ratio of velocity to distance discovered by Hubble is not expected to hold for the most distant galaxies. At extreme distances the ratio should increase, or in other words the velocities should be greater than those predicted by Hubble's law.

In order to measure the deceleration by this method it is necessary to have an independent measure of the distances of the galaxies. For all but the nearest galaxies the only practical method of estimating the distance to a galaxy is from its apparent luminosity. If all galaxies at all times had the same intrinsic luminosity, then their apparent brightness would vary simply as the inverse of the square of their distance, and the calculation of distance would be a straightforward procedure. Of course, they do not all have the same intrinsic luminosity.

Random variations in brightness (caused, for example, by differences in size) may produce errors in any individual measurement. Because of such variations it is necessary to acquire a large volume of data and to submit it to statistical analysis, but in principle random variations are not a serious con-

GEOMETRY OF SPACE characteristic of each model universe has an analogous surface. The properties of the surfaces are defined by the Euclidean axioms and theorems on parallel lines, on the included angle of a triangle and on the circumference and area of a circle. The flat space of a critical universe is represented by a plane, and the positively curved space of a closed universe corresponds to the surface of a sphere. Some of the properties of the negatively curved space of an open universe can be demonstrated on a saddle-shaped surface, but the saddle is an imperfect analogue because it has a center. The best representation of an open universe is an infinite surface called a pseudosphere, which cannot be constructed in a three-dimensional space.

SURFACE OF A PSEUDOSPHERE is represented in an etching, *Circle Limit IV,* by M. C. Escher. In the etching the surface is projected onto a plane. As in any map projection, the scale is not constant; on the pseudosphere itself the figures of angels and demons would all be the same size. If a single figure is regarded as a unit of measure, it is apparent that the circumference of a circle increases much faster than in proportion to the radius. Similarly, each figure defines a triangle (with the vertexes at the feet and the wing tips); from the number of triangles that meet at each vertex it can be shown that on the pseudosphere the sum of the angles of a triangle is less than 180 degrees. The pseudosphere is an infinite surface of negative curvature, analogous to space in a universe that expands forever. It has no privileged position that could be considered a center, and projection would be unchanged if it were centered on any other point.

cern, since in any large sample they can be expected to cancel out. Systematic variations, however, require explicit correction.

Theories of stellar evolution suggest that the combined light from all the stars in an isolated galaxy probably declines at a rate of a few percent per billion years. Galaxies were therefore probably brighter in the remote past. If the change in brightness were neglected in making measurements of the deceleration, the calculated distances would be too small and as a result the rate of deceleration would be overestimated. The decline in brightness would seem to be quite modest, but it changes the calculated value of the deceleration parameter q_0 by about 1, which is more than enough to decide between an open universe and a closed one. The best current observations, which take into consideration the changes in luminosity resulting from stellar evolution, suggest that q_0 is closer to zero than to 1/2 and therefore that the universe is open and perpetually expanding.

There is a further large uncertainty in the determination of the deceleration. Most of the observed galaxies are situated in relatively dense clusters, and possible interactions between galaxies ought to be taken into account. For example, it has recently been shown that in clusters large galaxies swallow smaller ones, with a consequent change in luminosity and size. It is not yet possible to predict the magnitude of the change, or even to be sure whether it makes the measured luminosity increase or decrease. Adding stars to a galaxy should make it brighter, but in cosmological observations only the luminosity of the central part of the galaxy is measured. If the cannibal galaxy swells significantly, the number of stars in the central region might be reduced and the galaxy would appear fainter.

The Age of the Universe

As a result of statistical uncertainties and our imperfect knowledge of galactic evolution the value of q_0 derived from measurements of recessional velocity is very uncertain. From this test alone one cannot conclude that q_0 is less than 1/2 and that the universe is open; on the other hand, very large values of q_0, such as q_0 equals 2, do seem to be excluded.

The second approach to determining the fate of the universe is to measure its age. If the expansion were not decelerating at all, the age would be equal to the Hubble time. Since it is decelerating it must be somewhat younger than the Hubble time. By finding the difference between the actual age and the Hubble time it is possible in principle to calculate the deceleration parameter q_0.

The age of the universe can be estimated by two methods; both actually yield only lower limits, since they measure the ages of objects in the universe, but those objects were probably formed within the first billion years or so after the big bang. The first method consists in determining the age of the oldest stars that can still be observed today. The oldest stars close enough for detailed observation are thought to be those in the globular clusters associated with our own galaxy. Models of stellar evolution indicate that they are between eight and 16 billion years old.

The age can also be estimated from measurements of the relative abundance of certain heavy elements. All the elements heavier than iron, including several radioactive ones, are thought to have been formed in supernovas, which have probably been exploding in the galaxy since its formation. Because each radioactive element decays at a constant rate, the ratio of the abundance of each radioactive element to the abundance of its decay products can reveal the average age of the heavy elements. The ratios indicate that the age of the galaxy is between six and 20 billion years. The two calculated ages are thus consistent, and they suggest that the big bang took place between eight and 18 billion years ago.

Average Density

Whether a given age within the allowed range corresponds to an open universe or a closed one depends on the value of the Hubble time, and as we have seen that value is not easily determined. Moreover, even if the Hubble time is assumed to equal the recent best estimate of 19 billion years, neither the age limits nor the exclusion of q_0 values greater than 2 is sufficient to decide whether the universe is open or closed [*see illustration on page 91*]. The issue can be decided only by imposing further constraints.

The third test consists in measuring the average density of matter in the universe and thereby deriving the density parameter Ω. A lower limit to the density can be obtained by considering only the mass associated with visible galaxies. The density is found by counting the galaxies in a given volume of space, multiplying by the masses of the galaxies and dividing by the volume.

Weighing a galaxy is not as difficult as it might at first seem. Few galaxies are completely isolated; most are found in small groups or in large clusters, and their mass can be deduced from observations of the gravitational effects they exert on one an-

other. Two galaxies in orbit around each other, for example, must have a gravitational attraction just sufficient to balance the centrifugal force. If their separation and their velocities with respect to each other are known, the determination of their combined mass becomes a simple exercise in Newtonian mechanics. The procedure for clusters of many galaxies is only slightly more complicated. Significantly, the mass calculated in this way includes not only the mass of the galaxies but also the mass of any other matter in the cluster. Constituents that would not be visible, such as black holes or extragalactic dust and gas, are automatically taken into account.

Estimates of the mass of a great many galaxies, combined with counts of the galaxies in large volumes of space, give an indication of the value of the density parameter Ω. If the mass associated with galaxies represents all the mass in the universe, then Ω is only about .04 and the universe must definitely be open and infinitely expanding. This value could be uncertain by a factor of 3, so that a value of Ω as great as .12 would still be consistent with observations, but that is still well below the value of 1 required to close the universe.

The density of the universe can also be estimated by comparing the behavior of distant galaxies with the behavior of those in the local supercluster, the aggregate of galaxies that includes our own local group in addition to many other small groups and the somewhat larger Virgo cluster. Within the local supercluster the mean density of galaxies is two and a half times greater than that in the universe as a whole. If all mass is associated with galaxies, then the average density of matter must also be two and a half times greater in the supercluster than outside it. The difference in density should give rise to a difference in the rate of expansion; because the local density is greater, nearby galaxies should be more strongly decelerated. The magnitude of the difference depends on the value of Ω; if Ω is large, there should be a considerable difference. If Ω is small, then the deceleration everywhere is small, and even a local enhancement in density by a factor of two and a half would cause little change. In fact, the difference is undetectable, being smaller than the probable observational errors. The most straightforward conclusion is that Ω is very small, probably no larger than .1.

Both methods of estimating density are explicitly confined to the matter associated with galaxies, and an obvious objection to them is that there might be substantial amounts of matter elsewhere in the universe. That possibility cannot be excluded, but there is no evidence to substantiate it.

Current theories show that clusters of galaxies could have formed from a universe in which matter was distributed much more smoothly than it is now. Debris left over from the formation of galaxies would also be collected by the clusters. Thus any particles that are not now in the clusters must have preferentially avoided them, that is, the particles must have had the special and unusual initial positions and velocities that would enable them to escape capture. Even if a large amount of matter were distributed uniformly outside the clusters now, it would fall into them in a few billion years.

Alternatively, the necessary mass could consist of some uniformly distributed medium with enough internal pressure to be unaffected by the gravitation of galaxies. It might, for example, be made up of large numbers of neutrinos or of gravitational waves. There is, however, a strong argument against such a pervasive "radiation-like" medium: it would almost certainly have prevented galaxies and clusters of galaxies from ever forming.

The density of all matter in the universe, whether or not it is associated with galaxies, can in principle be determined, but only by extrapolating from conditions in the present universe to those a few minutes after the big bang. The simplest assumptions about that early period suggest that the temperature and density were high enough for some subatomic particles to interact and form sizable amounts of some of the lighter nuclei. In particular a proton and a neutron could fuse to make a nucleus of deuterium, and most of the deuterium nuclei would quickly combine to form helium nuclei, composed of two protons and two neutrons. The proportion of deuterium and helium formed in this way depends on the density of the universe at the time when it was hot enough for the reactions to take place. From the early density and from the present temperature of the microwave background radiation it is possible to deduce the density today.

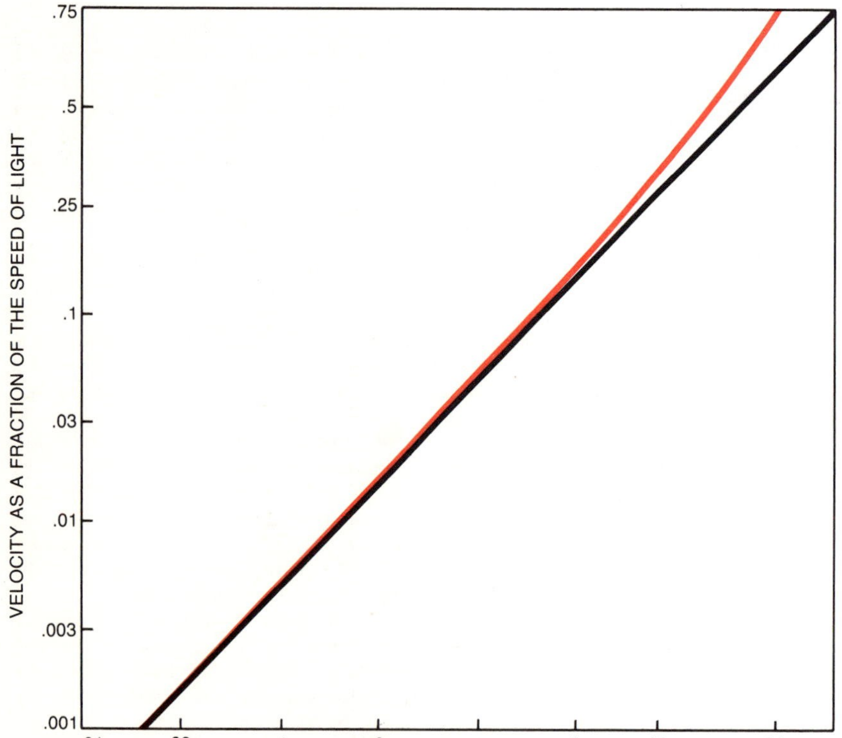

DECELERATION of the cosmic expansion can be detected in the recessional velocities of galaxies in the remote past. It is possible to look into the past by observing the most distant galaxies, since light reaching us now was emitted a length of time ago given by the galaxy's distance in light-years. The deceleration is thus perceived as a departure from Hubble's law; if there were no deceleration, the ratio of velocity to distance would be constant (*black line*); with deceleration the ratio increases at extreme distances (*colored line*). Because of the difficulty of estimating the distance to galaxies it has not been possible to measure the rate of deceleration precisely, but values of the deceleration parameter greater than about 2 have been excluded.

Primeval Density

Mathematical models indicate that for the entire possible range of densities in the early universe between 20 and 30 percent of the matter is converted into helium. The helium abundance measured in a variety of astronomical objects is in this narrow range, which strongly supports the fundamental assumption that the universe went through a period of extreme temperature and density shortly after the big bang. The present abundance of deuterium depends strongly on the early density [*see illustration, page 92*]. The relative abundance of deuterium in nearby interstellar space has been measured by the third Orbiting Astronomical Observatory satellite, named *Copernicus*. After taking account of the deuterium depleted by nuclear reactions in stars, the measured abundance yields an average present density of about 4×10^{-31} gram per cubic centimeter. The measure-

ment is a sensitive indicator of density: if the universe were 10 times denser, the big bang would have made less than a thousandth the observed abundance of deuterium. For this reason uncertainties in the measurement do not result in large uncertainties in the estimated density.

Whether the density determined by the deuterium abundance represents an open universe or a closed one depends on the Hubble time. As we have seen, if the Hubble time is 19 billion years, the critical density is 5×10^{-30} gram per cubic centimeter, so that Ω, the ratio of actual density to critical density, is about .08. For any value of the Hubble time between 13 and 19 billion years, the value of Ω derived from the deuterium abundance is consistent with that derived from the density of galaxies. Conversely, for any plausible value of the Hubble time, a value of Ω as great as 1 is inconsistent with the density required for the manufacture of deuterium.

The abundance of deuterium would seem to provide powerful evidence that the universe is open; unfortunately the arguments supporting that conclusion are somewhat insecure. In extrapolating from the present state of the universe to conditions soon after the big bang the simplest possible model has been employed; other models might allow the observed amounts of helium and deuterium to be made in a much denser, closed universe. Those models are more complicated, even somewhat contrived, but they cannot be excluded. Moreover, the significance of the deuterium abundance depends entirely on the assumption that all the deuterium in the universe was made shortly after the big bang. Other sources, such as supernovas, have been suggested, but so far no mechanism has been found that would

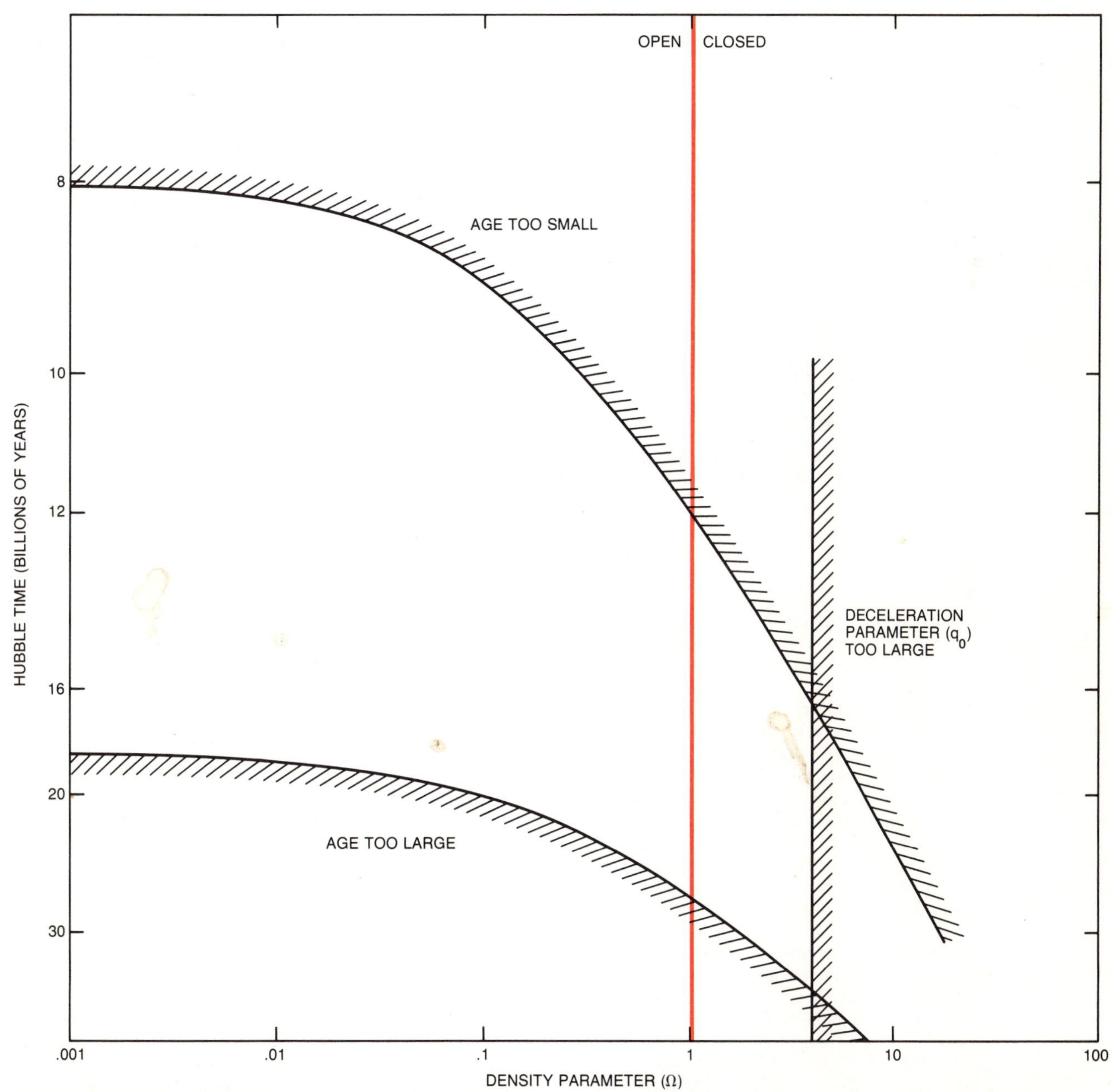

INITIAL CONSTRAINTS on the state of the universe are provided by determinations of its age and of the deceleration parameter. Estimates of the age of the oldest stars and of the average age of heavy elements suggest that the universe is between eight and 18 billion years old; the corresponding limits to the Hubble time depend on the density. Observations of distant galaxies provide an upper limit for the deceleration parameter: it cannot exceed 2, and the density parameter therefore cannot be greater than 4. The constraints derived from these measurements alone do not determine whether the universe is open or closed, since they encompass both kinds of model.

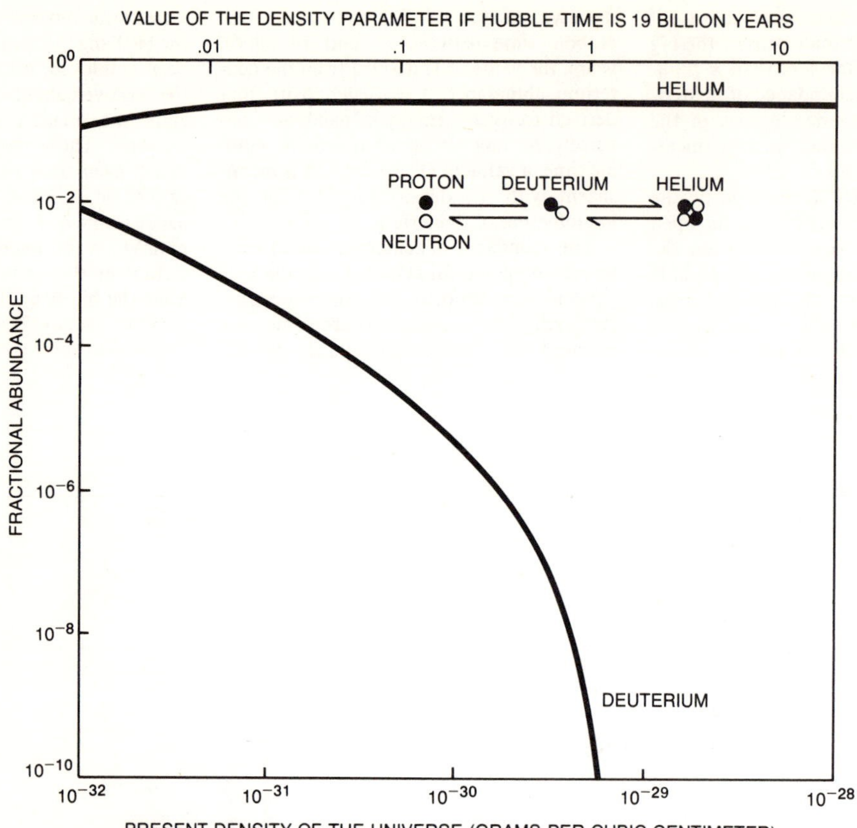

DENSITY OF THE EARLY UNIVERSE influenced the synthesis of deuterium and helium, and from the relative abundances of those elements the present density can be inferred. Deuterium is thought to have been formed by the fusion of protons and neutrons in the first few minutes after the big bang, but if the density then was too great, most or all of the deuterium would have been converted into helium. The abundances of both elements are shown as fractions (by mass) of all the matter in the universe. If the simplest models of the early universe are correct, and if deuterium has not been formed in more recent events, the observed abundance suggests that the density of the universe cannot be greater than about 4×10^{-31} gram per cubic centimeter.

create a significant amount of deuterium without violating other constraints.

Plausible Models

The measurements of the deceleration parameter, of the age of the universe, of the density of galaxies and of the abundance of deuterium all impose independent constraints on the state of the universe. If the measurements are consistent, there must be some class of models of the universe that is allowed by all the constraints. Indeed there is, and moreover it is a relatively small class, so that interesting predictions about the future of the universe are possible [*see illustration on page 93*]. If the universe is not too old, and if its density is at least equal to that observed in galaxies but not too great to make deuterium, the value of Ω must be between .04 and .09. That is far below the value required for a closed universe.

Two additional observations are consistent with the allowed values of Ω and the Hubble time. The calculated age of the stars in globular clusters is sensitive to the abundance of helium, and as we have seen that in turn is determined by the density of the universe. It is therefore encouraging to find that the age and the helium abundance allowed by the combined constraints are compatible with what is known of the globular-cluster stars.

The constraints also require that the Hubble time itself be between 13 and 20 billion years. The direct determination of the Hubble time is difficult, but in recent years much effort has been expended on the problem by Allan R. Sandage and Gustav A. Tammann of the Hale Observatories. Their best value is 18 ± 2 billion years. Robert P. Kirshner and John Kwan of the California Institute of Technology have employed a different technique, relying on the properties of exploding stars in distant galaxies, to make an independent measurement of the Hubble time. They place the value between 13 and 22 billion years.

The consistency of the results obtained by such diverse methods is gratifying, and it encourages confidence that the cosmological model is well determined and the fate of the universe is known. Because of uncertainties in the data and in the theory employed to interpret them, however, the apparent agreement may yet prove to be fortuitous.

A firm prediction of the models considered here is that the deceleration parameter equals half the density parameter, and as we have seen this prediction cannot yet be tested. If in the future it is found to be wrong, more complicated cosmological models will be required. For example, one class of models employs a modification of general relativity once suggested by Einstein, in which a parameter called the cosmological constant is introduced. In these models space itself generates an attractive or repulsive gravitational force, and as a result the deceleration is no longer related in a simple way to the density.

Taken one at a time, each of the constraints we have discussed has possible loopholes. In particular, some of our colleagues would disagree with the small density derived from estimates of the mass associated with galaxies, and with the inclusion of a constraint on density derived from the production of deuterium. Our arguments and conclusions, however, derive

their credibility from the fact that a consistent cosmological model can be constructed by the most straightforward interpretation of each piece of evidence. It is remarkable that such diverse factors as the age of stars, the mass of galaxies, the abundance of chemical elements and the observed rate of expansion of the universe can all be interpreted naturally in terms of one of the simplest cosmological models. This model describes a universe that is infinite in extent and that will expand forever. The case for an open universe is by no means closed, but it is strongly supported by the weight of the evidence.

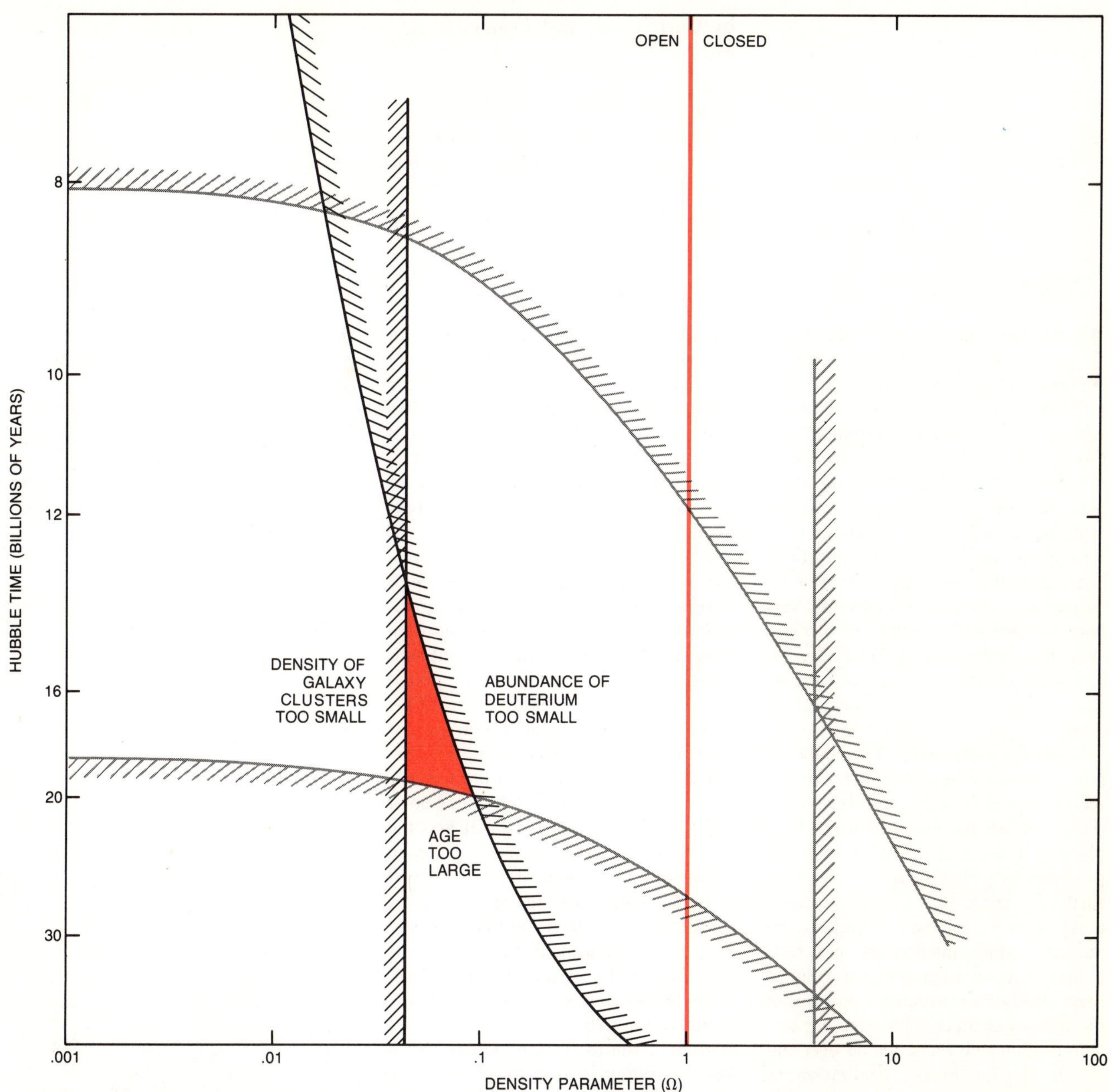

ADDITIONAL CONSTRAINTS combine to suggest that the universe will expand forever. The abundance of deuterium implies an upper limit to the density of all matter in the universe, and therefore also limits the density parameter, although the numerical value of that limit depends on the Hubble time. A maximum value of the Hubble time itself is defined by the estimates of the ages of stars and the heavy elements. Finally, calculations of the mass associated with clusters of galaxies supply a lower limit to the density parameter. Barring seemingly improbable complications, these constraints confine all allowed models to a small range of values of the density parameter and the Hubble time (*colored area*); all models in that range describe a universe that is open, infinite and perpetually expanding.

11 The Search for Extraterrestrial Intelligence

by Carl Sagan and Frank Drake
May 1975

There can be little doubt that civilizations more advanced than the earth's exist elsewhere in the universe. The probabilities involved in locating one of them call for a substantial effort

Is mankind alone in the universe? Or are there somewhere other intelligent beings looking up into their night sky from very different worlds and asking the same kind of question? Are there civilizations more advanced than ours, civilizations that have achieved interstellar communication and have established a network of linked societies throughout our galaxy? Such questions, bearing on the deepest problems of the nature and destiny of mankind, were long the exclusive province of theology and speculative fiction. Today for the first time in human history they have entered into the realm of experimental science.

From the movements of a number of nearby stars we have now detected unseen companion bodies in orbit around them that are about as massive as large planets. From our knowledge of the processes by which life arose here on the earth we know that similar processes must be fairly common throughout the universe. Since intelligence and technology have a high survival value it seems likely that primitive life forms on the planets of other stars, evolving over many billions of years, would occasionally develop intelligence, civilization and a high technology. Moreover, we on the earth now possess all the technology necessary for communicating with other civilizations in the depths of space. Indeed, we may now be standing on a threshold about to take the momentous step a planetary society takes but once: first contact with another civilization.

In our present ignorance of how common extraterrestrial life may actually be, any attempt to estimate the number of technical civilizations in our galaxy is necessarily unreliable. We do, however, have some relevant facts. There is reason to believe that solar systems are formed fairly easily and that they are abundant in the vicinity of the sun. In our own solar system, for example, there are three miniature "solar systems": the satellite systems of the planets Jupiter (with 13 moons), Saturn (with 10) and Uranus (with five). It is plain that however such systems are made, four of them formed in our immediate neighborhood.

The only technique we have at present for detecting the planetary systems of nearby stars is the study of the gravitational perturbations such planets induce in the motion of their parent star. Imagine a nearby star that over a period of decades moves measurably with respect to the background of more distant stars. Suppose it has a nonluminous companion that circles it in an orbit whose plane does not coincide with our line of sight to the star. Both the star and the companion revolve around a common center of mass. The center of mass will trace a straight line against the stellar background and thus the luminous star will trace a sinusoidal path. From the existence of the oscillation we can deduce the existence of the companion. Furthermore, from the period and amplitude of the oscillation we can calculate the period and mass of the companion. The technique is only sensitive enough, however, to detect the perturbations of a massive planet around the nearest stars.

The single star closest to the sun is Barnard's star, a rather dim red dwarf about six light-years away. (Although Alpha Centauri is closer, it is a member of a triple-star system.) Observations made by Peter van de Kamp of the Sproul Observatory at Swarthmore College over a period of 40 years suggest that Barnard's star is accompanied by at least two dark companions, each with about the mass of Jupiter. There is still some controversy over his conclusion, however, because the observations are very difficult to make. Perhaps even more interesting is the fact that of the dozen or so single stars nearest the sun nearly half appear to have dark companions with a mass between one and 10 times the mass of Jupiter. In

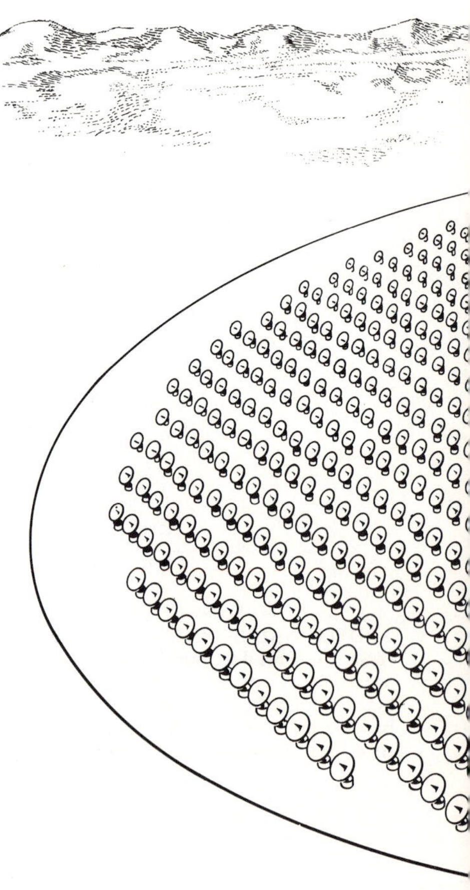

"CYCLOPS," an array of 1,500 radio antennas each 100 meters in diameter, is one system that has been proposed as a tool for detecting signals from extraterrestrial civ-

addition many theoretical studies of the formation of planetary systems out of contracting clouds of interstellar gas and dust imply that the birth of planets frequently if not inevitably accompanies the birth of stars.

We know that the master molecules of living organisms on the earth are the proteins and the nucleic acids. The proteins are built up of amino acids and the nucleic acids are built up of nucleotides. The earth's primordial atmosphere was, like the rest of the universe, rich in hydrogen and in hydrogen compounds. When molecular hydrogen (H_2), methane (CH_4), ammonia (NH_3) and water (H_2O) are mixed together in the presence of virtually any intermittent source of energy capable of breaking chemical bonds, the result is a remarkably high yield of amino acids and the sugars and nitrogenous bases that are the chemical constituents of the nucleotides. For example, from laboratory experiments we can determine the amount of amino acids produced per photon of ultraviolet radiation, and from our knowledge of stellar evolution we can calculate the amount of ultraviolet radiation emitted by the sun over the first billion years of the existence of the earth. Those two rates enable us to compute the total amount of amino acids that were formed on the primitive earth. Amino acids also break down spontaneously at a rate that is dependent on the ambient temperature. Hence we can calculate their steady-state abundance at the time of the origin of life. If amino acids in that abundance were mixed into the oceans of today, the result would be a 1 percent solution of amino acids. That is approximately the concentration of amino acids in the better brands of canned chicken bouillon, a solution that is alleged to be capable of sustaining life.

The origin of life is not the same as the origin of its constituent building blocks, but laboratory studies on the linking of amino acids into molecules resembling proteins and on the linking of nucleotides into molecules resembling nucleic acids are progressing well. Investigations of how short chains of nucleic acids replicate themselves in vitro have even provided clues to primitive genetic codes for translating nucleic acid information into protein information, systems that could have preceded the elaborate machinery of ribosomes and activating enzymes with which cells now manufacture protein.

The laboratory experiments also yield a large amount of a brownish polymer that seems to consist mainly of long hydrocarbon chains. The spectroscopic properties of the polymer are similar to those of the reddish clouds on Jupiter, Saturn and Titan, the largest satellite of Saturn. Since the atmospheres of these objects are rich in hydrogen and are similar to the atmosphere of the primitive earth, the coincidence is not surprising. It is nonetheless remarkable. Jupiter, Saturn and Titan may be vast planetary laboratories engaged in prebiological organic chemistry.

Other evidence on the origin of life comes from the geological record of the earth. Thin sections of sedimentary rocks

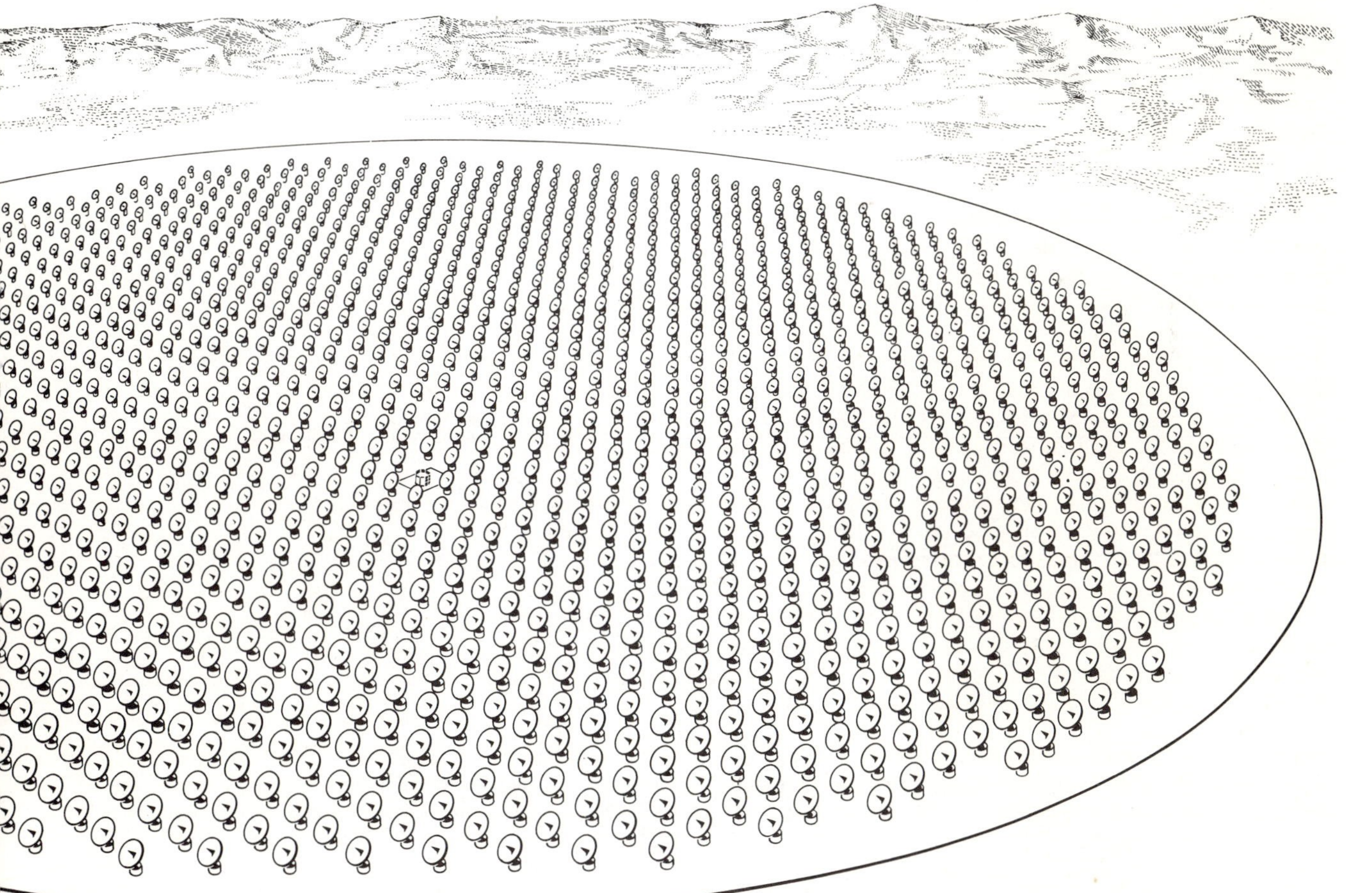

ilizations. The individual antennas would be connected to one another and to a large computer system. The effective signal-collecting area of the system would be hundreds of times greater than that of any existing radio telescope and would be capable of detecting even such relatively weak signals as the internal radio-frequency communications of a civilization as far away as several hundred light-years. Control building shown in center of array includes observatory with telescope operating at visible wavelengths.

between 2.7 and 3.5 billion years old reveal the presence of small inclusions a hundredth of a millimeter in diameter. These inclusions have been identified by Elso S. Barghoorn of Harvard University and J. William Schopf of the University of California at Los Angeles as bacteria and blue-green algae. Bacteria and blue-green algae are evolved organisms and must themselves be the beneficiaries of a long evolutionary history. There are no rocks on the earth or on the moon, however, that are more than four billion years old; before that time the surface of both bodies is believed to have melted in the final stages of their accretion. Thus the time available for the origin of life seems to have been short: a few hundred million years at the most. Since life originated on the earth in a span much shorter than the present age of the earth, we have additional evidence that the origin of life has a high probability, at least on planets with an abundant supply of hydrogen-rich gases, liquid water and sources of energy. Since those conditions are common throughout the universe, life may also be common.

Until we have discovered at least one example of extraterrestrial life, however, that conclusion cannot be considered secure. Such an investigation is one of the objectives of the Viking mission, which is scheduled to land a vehicle on the surface of Mars in the summer of 1976, a vehicle that will conduct the first rigorous search for life on another planet. The *Viking* lander carries three separate experiments on the metabolism of hypothetical Martian microorganisms, one experiment on the organic chemistry of the Martian surface material and a camera system that might just conceivably detect macroscopic organisms if they exist.

Intelligence and technology have developed on the earth about halfway through the stable period in the lifetime of the sun. There are obvious selective advantages to intelligence and technology, at least up to the present evolutionary stage when technology also brings the threats of ecological catastrophes, the exhaustion of natural resources and nuclear war. Barring such disasters, the physical environment of the earth will remain stable for many more billions of years. It is possible that the number of individual steps required for the evolution of intelligence and technology is so large and improbable that not all inhabited planets evolve technical civilizations. It is also possible—some would say likely—that civilizations tend to destroy themselves at about our level of technological development. On the other hand, if there are 100 billion suitable planets in our galaxy, if the origin of life is highly probable, if there are billions of years of evolution available on each such planet and if even a small fraction of technical civilizations pass safely through the early stages of technological adolescence, the number of technological civi-

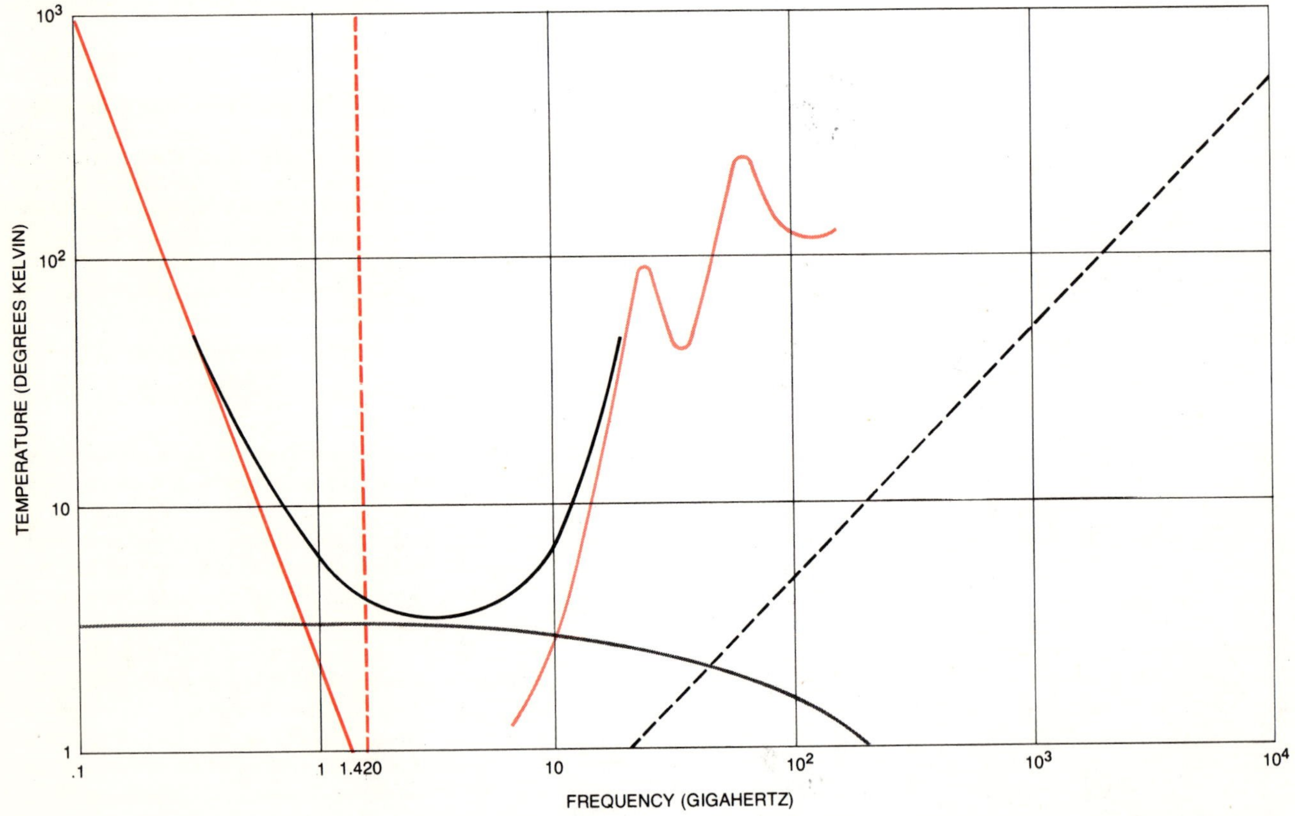

RADIO SPECTRUM of the sky as it is seen from the earth is quite noisy. Any radio telescope picks up the three-degree-Kelvin background radiation (*gray line*), the remnant of the primordial fireball of the "big bang." The background radiation begins to fall off at about 60 gigahertz (billion cycles per second). At that frequency the quantum noise associated with all electromagnetic radiation (*broken black line*) begins to predominate, and the total noise level rises. Noise from within our galaxy (*dark colored line*) is due mainly to synchrotron radiation emitted by particles spiraling in around the lines of force in magnetic fields. Together these three sources of noise define a broad quiet region in the radio spectrum, between about one gigahertz and 100 gigahertz, that would be nearly the same for observers in the neighborhood of the sun and observers in similar regions of the galaxy. The earth's atmosphere is also a source of noise (*light colored line*) because molecules of water and oxygen absorb and reradiate energy at 22 gigahertz and 60 gigahertz. All sources of noise added together yield the curve in black, representing the total sky noise detected on the earth. The broken vertical line in color is frequency of spin-flip of the electron in un-ionized hydrogen atom at frequency of 1.420 gigahertz.

lizations in the galaxy today might be very large.

It is obviously a highly uncertain exercise to attempt to estimate the number of such civilizations. The opinions of those who have considered the problem differ significantly. Our best guess is that there are a million civilizations in our galaxy at or beyond the earth's present level of technological development. If they are distributed randomly through space, the distance between us and the nearest civilization should be about 300 light-years. Hence any information conveyed between the nearest civilization and our own will take a minimum of 300 years for a one-way trip and 600 years for a question and a response.

Electromagnetic radiation is the fastest and also by far the cheapest method of establishing such contact. In terms of the foreseeable technological developments on the earth, the cost per photon and the amount of absorption of radiation by interstellar gas and dust, radio waves seem to be the most efficient and economical method of interstellar communication. Interstellar space vehicles cannot be excluded a priori, but in all cases they would be a slower, more expensive and more difficult means of communication.

Since we have achieved the capability for interstellar radio communication only in the past few decades, there is virtually no chance that any civilization we come in contact with will be as backward as we are. There also seems to be no possibility of dialogue except between very long-lived and patient civilizations. In view of these circumstances, which should be common to and deducible by all the civilizations in our galaxy, it seems to us quite possible that one-way radio messages are being beamed at the earth at this moment by radio transmitters on planets in orbit around other stars.

To intercept such signals we must guess or deduce the frequency at which the signal is being sent, the width of the frequency band, the type of modulation and the star transmitting the message. Although the correct guesses are not easy to make, they are not as hard as they might seem.

Most of the astronomical radio spectrum is quite noisy [*see illustration on opposite page*]. There are contributions from interstellar matter, from the three-degree-Kelvin background radiation left over from the early history of the universe, from noise that is fundamentally associated with the operation of any detector and from the absorption of radiation by the earth's atmosphere. This last source of noise can be avoided by placing a radio telescope in space. The other sources we must live with and so must any other civilization.

INVESTIGATOR	OBSERVATORY	DATE	FREQUENCY OR WAVELENGTH	TARGETS
DRAKE	N.R.A.O.	1960	1,420 MEGAHERTZ	EPSILON ERIDANI TAU CETI
TROITSKY	GORKY	1968	21 AND 30 CENTIMETERS	12 NEARBY SUNLIKE STARS
VERSCHUUR	N.R.A.O.	1972	1,420 MEGAHERTZ	10 NEARBY STARS
TROITSKY	EURASIAN NETWORK, GORKY	1972 TO PRESENT	16, 30 AND 50 CENTIMETERS	PULSED SIGNALS FROM ENTIRE SKY
ZUCKERMAN PALMER	N.R.A.O.	1972 TO PRESENT	1,420 MEGAHERTZ	~600 NEARBY SUNLIKE STARS
KARDASHEV	EURASIAN NETWORK, I.C.R.	1972 TO PRESENT	SEVERAL	PULSED SIGNALS FROM ENTIRE SKY
BRIDLE FELDMAN	A.R.O.	1974 TO PRESENT	22.2 GIGAHERTZ	SEVERAL NEARBY STARS
DRAKE SAGAN	ARECIBO	1975 (IN PROGRESS)	1,420, 1,653 AND 2,380 MEGAHERTZ	SEVERAL NEARBY GALAXIES

ATTEMPTS TO DETECT SIGNALS beamed toward the earth by other civilizations have so far been unsuccessful, but the number of stars that have been examined is less than .1 percent of the number that would have to be investigated if there were to be a reasonable statistical chance of discovering one extraterrestrial civilization. "N.R.A.O." is the National Radio Astronomy Observatory in Green Bank, W.Va.; "Gorky" is the 45-foot antenna at Gorky University in the U.S.S.R.; "Eurasian network" is a network of omnidirectional antennas in the U.S.S.R. that is being operated jointly by V. S. Troitsky of Gorky University and N. S. Kardashev of the Institute for Cosmic Research (I.C.R.) of the Academy of Sciences of the U.S.S.R.; "A.R.O." is the Algonquin Radio Observatory at Algonquin Park in Canada; "Arecibo" is 1,000-foot radio-radar antenna at Arecibo Observatory in Puerto Rico.

There is, however, a pronounced minimum in the radio-noise spectrum. Lying at the minimum or near it are several natural frequencies that should be discernible by all scientifically advanced societies. They are the resonant frequencies emitted by the more abundant molecules and free radicals in interstellar space. Perhaps the most obvious of these resonances is the frequency of 1,420 megahertz (millions of cycles per second). That frequency is emitted when the spinning electron in an atom of hydrogen spontaneously flips over so that its direction of spin is opposite to that of the proton comprising the nucleus of the hydrogen atom. The frequency of the spin-flip transition of hydrogen at 1,420 megahertz was first suggested as a channel for interstellar communication in 1959 by Philip Morrison and Giuseppe Cocconi. Such a channel may be too noisy for communication precisely because hydrogen, the most abundant interstellar gas, absorbs and emits radiation at that frequency. The number of other plausible and available communication channels is not large, so that determining the right one should not be too difficult.

We cannot use a similar logic to guess the bandwidth that might be used in interstellar communication. The narrower the bandwidth is, the farther a signal can be transmitted before it becomes too weak for detection. On the other hand, the narrower the bandwidth is, the less information the signal can carry. A compromise is therefore required between the desire to send a signal the maximum distance and the desire to communicate the maximum amount of information. Perhaps simple signals with narrow bandwidths are sent to enhance the probability of the signals' being received. Perhaps information-rich signals

with broad bandwidths are sent in order to achieve rapid and extensive communication. The broad-bandwidth signals would be intended for those enlightened civilizations that have invested major resources in large receiving systems.

When we actually search for signals, it is not necessary to guess the exact bandwidth, only to guess the minimum bandwidth. It is possible to communicate on many adjacent narrow bands at once. Each such channel can be studied individually, and the data from several adjacent channels can be combined to yield the equivalent of a wider channel without any loss of information or sensitivity. The procedure is relatively easy with the aid of a computer; it is in fact routinely employed in studies of pulsars. In any event we should observe the maximum number of channels because of the possibility that the transmitting civilization is not broadcasting on one of the "natural" frequencies such as 1,420 megahertz.

We do not, of course, know now which star we should listen to. The most conservative approach is to turn our receivers to stars that are rather similar to the sun, beginning with the nearest. Two nearby stars, Epsilon Eridani and Tau Ceti, both about 12 light-years away, were the candidates for Project Ozma, the first search with a radio telescope for extraterrestrial intelligence, conducted by one of us (Drake) in 1960. Project Ozma, named after the ruler of Oz in L. Frank Baum's children's stories, was "on the air" for four weeks at 1,420 megahertz. The results were negative. Since then there have been a number of other studies. In spite of some false alarms to the contrary, none has been successful. The lack of success is not unexpected. If there are a million technical civilizations in a galaxy of some 200 billion stars, we must turn our receivers to 200,000 stars before we have a fair statistical chance of detecting a single extraterrestrial message. So far we have listened to only a few more than 200 stars. In other words, we have mounted only .1 percent of the required effort.

Our present technology is entirely adequate for both transmitting and receiving messages across immense interstellar distances. For example, if the 1,000-foot radio telescope at the Arecibo Observatory in Puerto Rico were to transmit information at the rate of one bit (binary digit) per second with a bandwidth of one hertz, the signal could be received by an identical radio telescope anywhere in the galaxy. By the same token, the Arecibo telescope could detect a similar signal transmitted from a distance hundreds of times greater than our estimate of 300 light-years to the nearest extraterrestrial civilization.

A search of hundreds of thousands of stars in the hope of detecting one message would require remarkable dedication and would probably take several decades. It seems unlikely that any existing major radio telescope would be given over to such an intensive program to the exclusion of its usual work. The construction of one radio telescope or more that would be devoted perhaps half-time to the search seems to be the

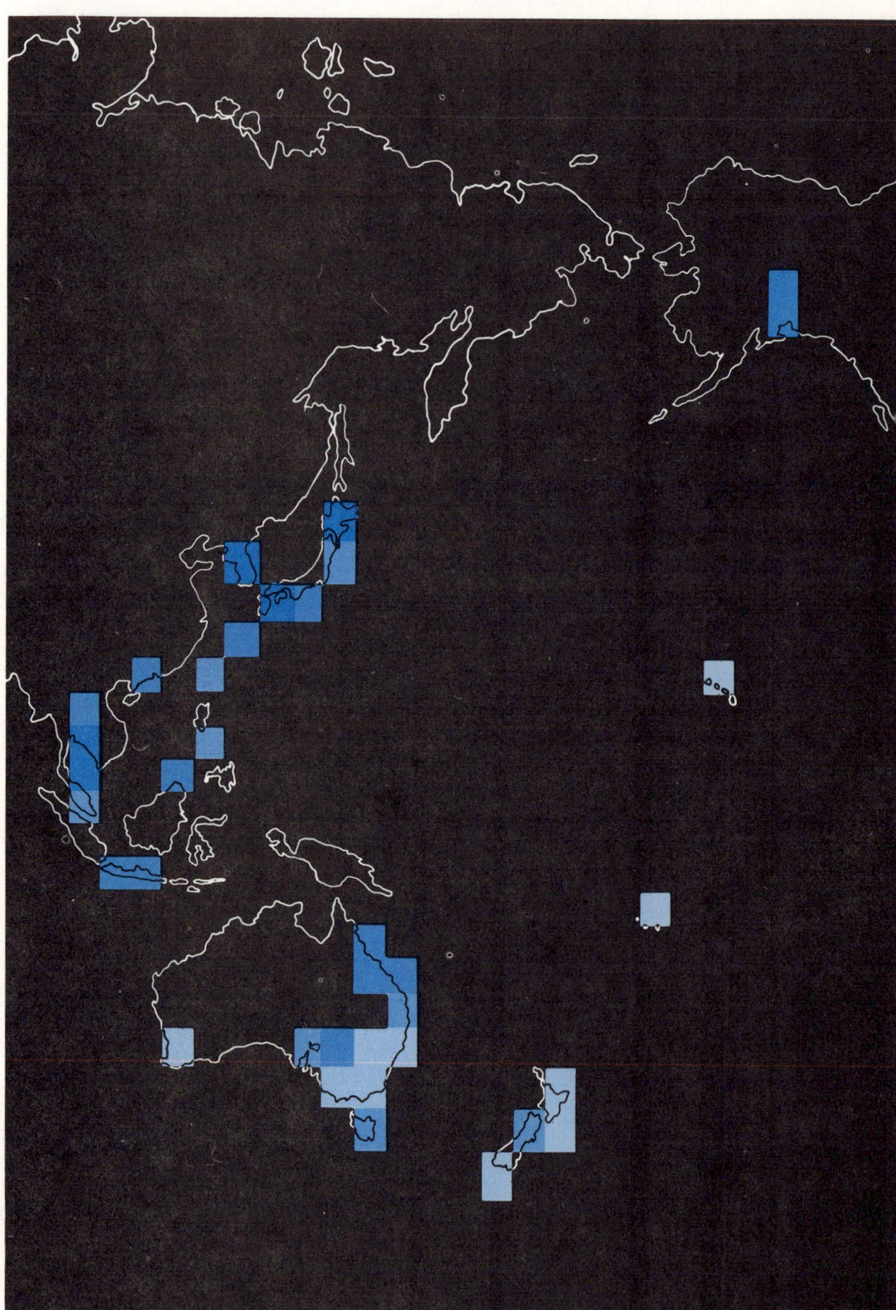

BRIGHTNESS TEMPERATURES
(MILLIONS OF DEGREES K.)

20 300 3,000
90 900 9,000

EARTH IS BRIGHT at the frequencies between 40 and 220 megahertz because of the radiation from FM radio and VHF television broadcasts. The power radiated by the stations is shown averaged over squares five degrees in longitude by five degrees in latitude. The radio brightness is equivalent to

only practical method of seeking out extraterrestrial intelligence in a serious way. The cost would be some tens of millions of dollars.

So far we have been discussing the reception of messages that a civilization would intentionally transmit to the earth. An alternative possibility is that we might try to "eavesdrop" on the radio traffic an extraterrestrial civilization employs for its own purposes. Such radio traffic could be readily apparent. On the earth, for example, a new radar system employed with the telescope at the Arecibo Observatory for planetary studies emits a narrow-bandwidth signal that, if it were detected from another star, would be between a million and 10 billion times brighter than the sun at the same frequency. In addition, because of radio and television transmission, the earth is extremely bright at wavelengths of about a meter [*see illustration on these two pages*]. If the planets of other civilizations have a radio brightness comparable to the earth's

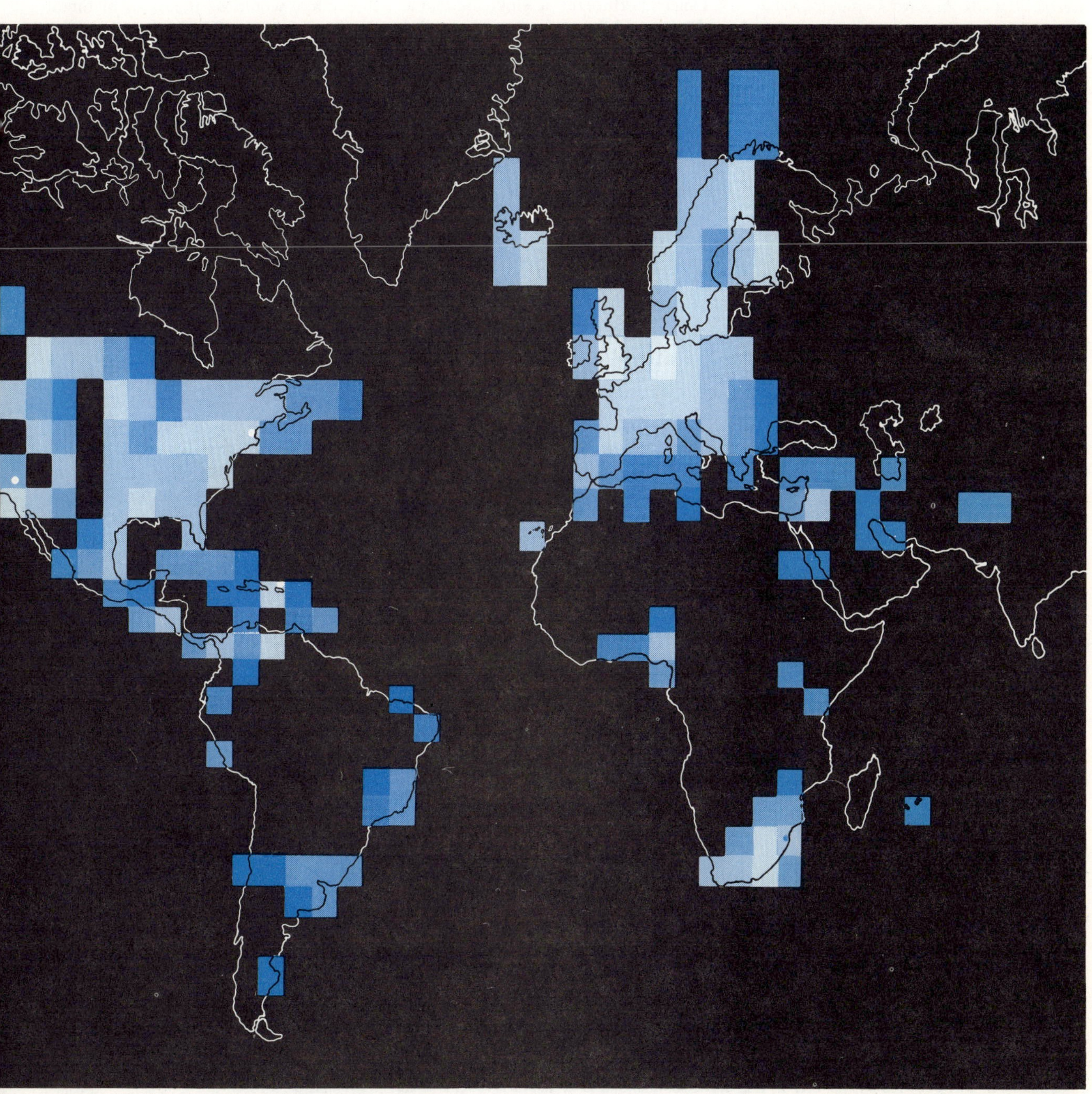

the temperature to which each area on the earth would have to be raised in order to produce the actual radio emission observed. The three brightest areas are the locations of three particularly powerful radar systems: the radio-radar antenna of the Haystack Observatory in Massachusetts, operating at a wavelength of 3.75 centimeters and giving a brightness temperature of 2.3×10^{20} degrees K., the 1,000-foot radio-radar antenna of the Arecibo Observatory, operating at a wavelength of 12.6 centimeters and giving a brightness temperature of 1.4×10^{21} degrees K., and the 210-foot antenna of the Jet Propulsion Laboratory at Goldstone, Calif., operating at a wavelength of 12.6 centimeters and giving a brightness temperature of 6.2×10^{19} degrees. Systems radiate so much power that at those wavelengths and in the direction of their beam they are brighter than the sun and should be detectable over interstellar distances.

from television transmission alone, they should be detectable. Because of the complexity of the signals and the fact that they are not beamed specifically at the earth, however, the receiver we would need in order to eavesdrop would have to be much more elaborate and sensitive than any radio-telescope system we now possess.

One such system has been devised in a preliminary way by Bernard M. Oliver of the Hewlett-Packard Company, who directed a study sponsored by the Ames Research Center of the National Aeronautics and Space Administration. The system, known as Cyclops, would consist of an enormous radio telescope connected to a complex computer system. The computer system would be designed particularly to search through the data from the telescope for signals bearing the mark of intelligence, to combine numerous adjacent channels in order to construct signals of various effective bandwidths and to present the results of the automatic analyses for all conceivable forms of interstellar radio communication in a way that would be intelligible to the project scientists.

To construct a radio telescope of enormous aperture as a single antenna would be prohibitively expensive. The Cyclops system would instead capitalize on our ability to connect many individual antennas to act in unison. This concept is already the basis of the Very Large Array now under construction in New Mexico. The Very Large Array consists of 27 antennas, each 82 feet in diameter, arranged in a Y-shaped pattern whose three arms are each 10 miles long. The Cyclops system would be much larger. Its current design calls for 1,500 antennas each 100 meters in diameter, all electronically connected to one another and to the computer system. The array would be as compact as possible but would cover perhaps 25 square miles.

The effective signal-collecting area of the system would be hundreds of times the area of any existing radio telescope, and it would be capable of detecting even relatively weak signals such as television transmissions from civilizations several hundred light-years away. Moreover, it would be the instrument par excellence for receiving signals specifically directed at the earth. One of the greatest virtues of the Cyclops system is that no technological advances would be required in order to build it. The necessary electronic and computer techniques are already well developed. We would need only to build a vast number of items we already build well. The Cyclops system not only would have enormous power for searching for extraterrestrial intelligence but also would be an extraordinary tool for radar studies of the bodies in the solar system, for traditional radio astronomy outside the solar system and for the tracking of space vehicles to distances beyond the reach of present receivers.

```
0 0 0 0 0 0 1 0 1 0 1 0 1 0 0 0 0 0 0 0 0 0 0 0 0 1 0 1 0 0 0 0 0 1 0 1 0
0 0 0 0 0 0 1 0 0 1 0 0 0 1 0 0 0 1 0 0 0 1 0 0 1 0 1 1 0 0 1 0 1 0 1 0 1
0 1 0 1 0 1 0 1 0 1 0 0 1 0 0 1 0 0 0 0 0 0 0 0 0 0 0 0 0 0 0 0 0 0 0 0 0
0 0 0 0 0 0 0 0 0 0 0 0 0 0 0 0 1 1 0 0 0 0 0 0 0 0 0 0 0 0 0 0 0 0 0 0 0
1 1 0 1 0 0 0 0 0 0 0 0 0 0 0 0 0 0 0 0 0 0 0 1 1 0 1 0 0 0 0 0 0 0 0 0 0
0 0 0 0 0 0 0 0 1 0 1 0 1 0 0 0 0 0 0 0 0 0 0 0 0 0 0 0 0 0 0 1 1 1 1 1 0
0 0 0 0 0 0 0 0 0 0 0 0 0 0 0 0 0 0 0 0 0 0 0 0 0 0 0 0 0 0 0 1 1 0 0 0 0
1 1 1 0 0 0 1 1 0 0 0 0 1 1 0 0 0 1 0 0 0 0 0 0 0 0 0 0 0 0 0 1 1 0 0 1 0
0 0 0 1 1 0 1 0 0 0 1 1 0 0 0 1 1 0 0 0 0 1 1 0 1 0 1 1 1 1 1 0 1 1 1 1 1
0 1 1 1 1 1 0 1 1 1 1 1 0 0 0 0 0 0 0 0 0 0 0 0 0 0 0 0 0 0 0 0 0 0 0 0 0
0 1 0 0 0 0 0 0 0 0 0 0 0 0 0 0 0 0 0 1 0 0 0 0 0 0 0 0 0 0 0 0 0 0 0 0 0
0 0 0 0 0 0 0 0 0 0 0 1 0 0 0 0 0 0 0 0 0 0 0 0 0 0 0 0 0 1 1 1 1 1 1 0 0
0 0 0 0 0 0 0 0 0 0 0 1 1 1 1 1 0 0 0 0 0 0 0 0 0 0 0 0 0 0 0 0 0 0 0 0 0
0 0 1 1 0 0 0 0 1 1 0 0 0 0 1 1 1 0 0 0 1 1 0 0 0 1 0 0 0 0 0 0 0 1 0 0 0
0 0 0 0 0 0 1 0 0 0 0 1 1 0 1 0 0 0 0 1 1 0 0 0 1 1 1 0 0 1 1 0 1 0 1 1 1
1 1 0 1 1 1 1 1 0 1 1 1 1 1 0 1 1 1 1 1 0 0 0 0 0 0 0 0 0 0 0 0 0 0 0 0 0
0 0 0 0 0 0 0 0 0 1 0 0 0 0 0 0 1 1 0 0 0 0 0 0 0 0 0 1 0 0 0 0 0 0 0 0 0
0 0 1 1 0 0 0 0 0 0 0 0 0 0 0 0 0 0 0 1 0 0 0 0 0 1 1 0 0 0 0 0 0 0 0 0 0
1 1 1 1 1 1 0 0 0 0 0 1 1 0 0 0 0 0 0 1 1 1 1 1 0 0 0 0 0 0 0 0 0 0 1 1 0
0 0 0 0 0 0 0 0 0 0 0 1 0 0 0 0 0 0 0 0 0 1 0 0 0 0 0 0 0 0 1 0 0 0 0 0 1
0 0 0 0 0 0 1 1 0 0 0 0 0 0 0 1 0 0 0 0 0 0 0 1 1 0 0 0 0 1 1 0 0 0 0 0 0
1 0 0 0 0 0 0 0 0 0 0 1 1 0 0 0 1 0 0 0 0 1 1 0 0 0 0 0 0 0 0 0 0 0 0 0 0
0 1 1 0 0 1 1 0 0 0 0 0 0 0 0 0 0 0 0 0 1 1 0 0 0 1 0 0 0 0 1 1 0 0 0 0 0
0 0 0 0 1 1 0 0 0 0 1 1 0 0 0 0 0 0 1 0 0 0 0 0 0 0 1 0 0 0 0 0 0 1 0 0 0
0 0 0 0 0 1 0 0 0 0 0 1 0 0 0 0 0 0 0 1 1 0 0 0 0 0 0 0 0 1 0 0 0 1 0 0 0
0 0 0 0 0 1 1 0 0 0 0 0 0 0 0 1 0 0 0 1 0 0 0 0 0 0 0 0 0 1 0 0 0 0 0 0 0
1 0 0 0 0 0 1 0 0 0 0 0 0 0 1 0 0 0 0 0 0 0 1 0 0 0 0 0 0 0 1 0 0 0 0 0 0
0 0 0 0 0 0 1 1 0 0 0 0 0 0 0 0 0 1 1 0 0 0 0 0 0 0 0 1 1 0 0 0 0 0 0 0 0
0 1 0 0 0 1 1 1 0 1 0 1 1 0 0 0 0 0 0 0 0 0 0 0 1 0 0 0 0 0 0 0 1 0 0 0 0
0 0 0 0 0 0 0 0 0 0 1 0 0 0 0 0 1 1 1 1 1 0 0 0 0 0 0 0 0 0 0 0 0 1 0 0 0
0 1 0 1 1 1 0 1 0 0 1 0 1 1 0 1 1 0 0 0 0 0 0 1 0 0 1 1 1 0 0 1 0 0 1 1 1
1 1 1 1 0 1 1 1 0 0 0 0 1 1 1 0 0 0 0 0 1 1 0 1 1 1 0 0 0 0 0 0 0 0 0 1 0
1 0 0 0 0 0 1 1 1 0 1 1 0 0 1 0 0 0 0 0 0 1 0 1 0 0 0 0 0 1 1 1 1 1 1 0 0
1 0 0 0 0 0 0 1 0 1 0 0 0 0 0 1 1 0 0 0 0 0 0 1 0 0 0 0 0 1 1 0 1 1 0 0 0
0 0 0 0 0 0 0 0 0 0 0 0 0 0 0 0 0 0 0 0 0 0 0 0 0 0 0 0 0 0 0 0 1 1 1 0 0
0 0 0 1 0 0 0 0 0 0 0 0 0 0 0 0 0 0 1 1 1 0 1 0 1 0 0 0 1 0 1 0 1 0 1 0 1
0 1 0 0 1 1 1 0 0 0 0 0 0 0 0 0 1 0 1 0 1 0 1 0 0 0 0 0 0 0 0 0 0 0 0 0 0
0 0 1 0 1 0 0 0 0 0 0 0 0 0 0 0 0 0 0 1 1 1 1 1 0 0 0 0 0 0 0 0 0 0 0 0 0
0 0 0 1 1 1 1 1 1 1 1 1 0 0 0 0 0 0 0 0 0 0 0 0 1 1 1 0 0 0 0 0 0 0 1 1 1
0 0 0 0 0 0 0 0 0 1 1 0 0 0 0 0 0 0 0 0 0 0 1 1 0 0 0 0 0 0 0 1 1 0 1 0 0
0 0 0 0 0 0 0 1 0 1 1 0 0 0 0 0 1 1 0 0 1 1 0 0 0 0 0 0 0 0 1 1 0 0 1 1 0
0 0 1 0 0 0 1 0 1 0 0 0 0 0 1 0 1 0 0 0 1 0 0 0 0 1 0 0 0 1 0 0 1 0 0 0 1
0 0 1 0 0 0 1 0 0 0 0 0 0 0 0 1 0 0 0 1 0 1 0 0 0 1 0 0 0 0 0 0 0 0 0 0 0
0 1 0 0 0 0 1 0 0 0 0 1 0 0 0 0 0 0 0 0 0 0 0 0 1 0 0 0 0 0 0 0 0 0 1 0 0
0 0 0 0 0 0 0 0 0 0 0 0 1 0 0 1 0 1 0 0 0 0 0 0 0 0 0 0 0 1 1 1 1 0 0 1 1
1 1 1 0 1 0 0 1 1 1 1 0 0 0
```

ARECIBO MESSAGE IN BINARY CODE was transmitted in 1974 toward the Great Cluster in Hercules from the 1,000-foot antenna at Arecibo. The message is decoded by breaking up the characters into 73 consecutive groups of 23 characters each and arranging the groups in sequence one under the other, reading right to left and then top to bottom. The result is a visual message (*see illustration on opposite page*) that can be more easily interpreted by making each 0 of binary code represent a white square and each 1 a black square.

The estimated cost of the Cyclops system, ranging up to $10 billion, may make it prohibitively expensive for the time being. Moreover, the argument in favor of eavesdropping is not completely persuasive. Half a century ago, before radio transmissions were commonplace, the earth was quiet at radio wavelengths. Half a century from now, because of the development of cable television and communication satellites that relay signals in a narrow beam, the earth may again be quiet. Thus perhaps for only a century out of billions of years do planets such as the earth appear remarkably bright at radio wavelengths. The odds of our discovering a civilization during that short period in its history may not be good enough to justify the construction of a system such as Cyclops. It may well be that throughout the universe beings usually detect evidence of extraterrestrial intelligence with more traditional radio telescopes. It nonetheless seems clear that our own chances of finding extraterrestrial intelligence will improve if we consciously attempt to find it.

How could we be sure that a particu-

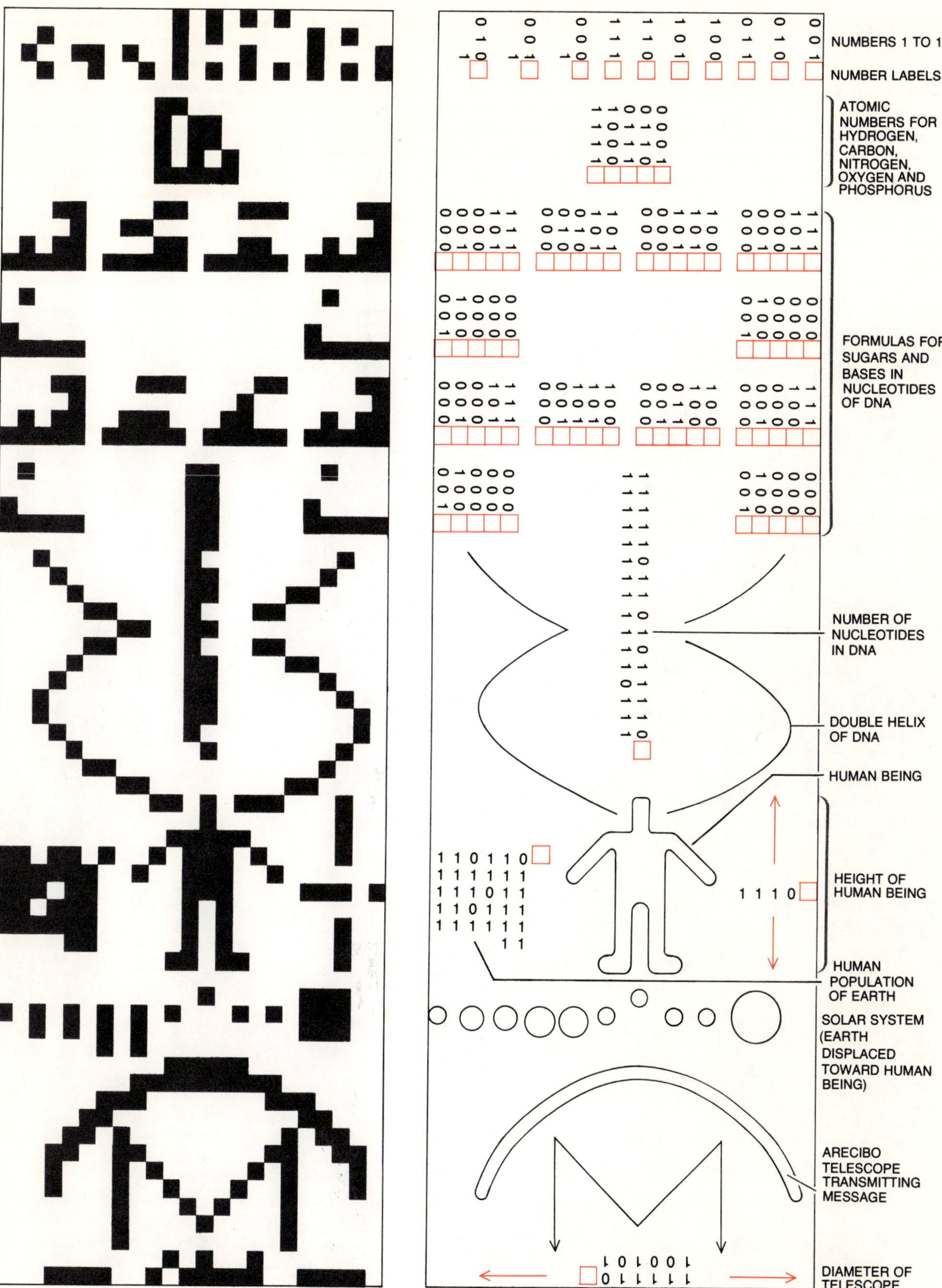

ARECIBO MESSAGE IN PICTURES and accompanying translation shows the binary version of the message decoded. Each number that is used is marked with a label that indicates its start. When all the digits of a number cannot be fitted into one line, the digits for which there is no room are written under the least significant digit. (The message must be oriented in three different ways for all the numbers shown to be read.) The chemical formulas are those for the components of the DNA molecule: the phosphate group, the deoxyribose sugar and the organic bases thymine, adenine, guanine and cytosine. Both the height of the human being and the diameter of the telescope are given in units of the wavelength that is used to transmit the message: 12.6 centimeters.

lar radio signal was deliberately sent by an intelligent being? It is easy to design a message that is unambiguously artificial. The first 30 prime numbers, for example, would be difficult to ascribe to some natural astrophysical phenomenon. A simple message of this kind might be a beacon or announcement signal. A subsequent informative message could have many forms and could consist of an enormous number of bits. One method of transmitting information, beginning simply and progressing to more elaborate concepts, is pictures [*see illustration on preceding page*].

One final approach in the search for extraterrestrial intelligence deserves mention. If there are indeed civilizations thousands or millions of years more advanced than ours, it is entirely possible that they could beam radio communications over immense distances, perhaps even over the distances of intergalactic space. We do not know how many advanced civilizations there might be compared with the number of more primitive earthlike civilizations, but many of these older civilizations are bound to be in galaxies older than our own. For this reason the most readily detectable radio signals from another civilization may come from outside our galaxy. The relatively small number of such extragalactic transmitters might be more than compensated for by the greater strength

THOUSAND-FOOT ANTENNA of the radio-radar system at the Arecibo Observatory is made of perforated aluminum panels whose spherical shape is accurate to within 1/8 inch over the antenna's entire area of 20 acres. The triangular structure suspended above the antenna holds the receiver and the transmitter for the system. Control rooms and office buildings are to lower right of antenna.

of their signals. At the appropriate frequency they could even be the brightest radio signals in the sky. Therefore an alternative to examining the nearest stars of the same spectral type as the sun is to examine the nearest galaxies. Spiral galaxies such as the Great Nebula in Andromeda are obvious candidates, but the elliptical galaxies are much older and more highly evolved and could conceivably harbor a large number of extremely advanced civilizations.

There might be a kind of biological law decreeing that there are many paths to intelligence and high technology, and that every inhabited planet, if it is given enough time and it does not destroy itself, will arrive at a similar result. The biology on other planets is of course expected to be different from our own because of the statistical nature of the evolutionary process and the adaptability of life. The science and engineering, however, may be quite similar to ours, because any civilization engaged in interstellar radio communication, no matter where it exists, must contend with the same laws of physics, astronomy and radio technology that we do.

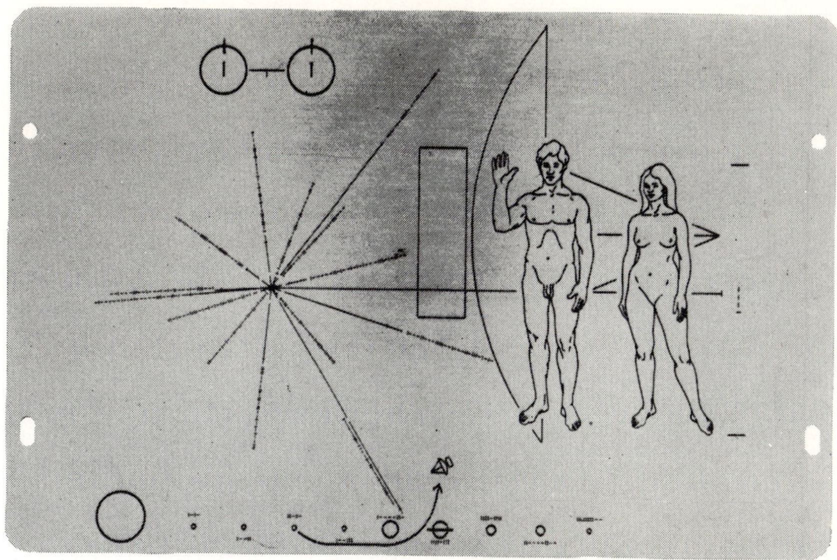

ENGRAVED PLAQUE on the *Pioneer* spacecraft to Jupiter is another message that has been dispatched beyond the solar system. Meaning of symbols is given in text of article.

Should we be sending messages ourselves? It is obvious that we do not yet know where we might best direct them. One message has already been transmitted to the Great Cluster in Hercules by the Arecibo radio telescope, but only as a kind of symbol of the capabilities of our existing radio technology. Any radio signal we send would be detectable over interstellar distances if it is more than about 1 percent as bright as the sun at the same frequency. Actually something close to 1,000 such signals from our everyday internal communications have left the earth every second for the past two decades. This electromagnetic frontier of mankind is now some 20 light-years away, and it is moving outward at the speed of light. Its spherical wave front, expanding like a ripple from a disturbance in a pool of water and inadvertently carrying the news that human beings have achieved the capacity for interstellar discourse, envelops about 20 new stars each year.

We have also sent another kind of message: two engraved plaques that ride aboard *Pioneer 10* and *Pioneer 11*. These spacecraft, the first artifacts of mankind that will escape from the solar system, will voyage forever through our galaxy at a speed of some 10 miles per second. *Pioneer 10* was accelerated to the velocity of escape from the solar system by the gravitational field of Jupiter on December 3, 1973. *Pioneer 11* swung past Jupiter on December 4, 1974, and will travel on to Saturn before it is accelerated on a course to the far side of the galaxy.

Identical plaques for each vehicle were designed by us and Linda Salzman Sagan. Each plaque measures six by nine inches and is made of gold-anodized aluminum. These engraved cosmic greeting cards bear the location of the earth and the time the spacecraft was built and launched. The sun is located with respect to 14 pulsars. The precise periods of the pulsars are specified in binary code to allow them to be identified. Since pulsars are cosmic clocks that are running down at a largely constant rate, the difference in the pulsar periods at the time one of the spacecraft is recovered and the periods indicated on the plaque will enable any technically sophisticated civilization to deduce the year the vehicle was sent on its epic journey. Units of time and distance are specified in terms of the frequency of the hydrogen spin-flip at 1,420 megahertz. In order to identify the exact location of the spacecraft's launch a diagram of the solar system is given. The trajectory of the spacecraft is shown as it leaves the third planet, the earth, and swings by the fifth planet, Jupiter. (The diversion of *Pioneer 11* past Saturn had not been planned when the plaques were prepared.) Last, the plaques show images of a man and a woman of the earth in 1973. An attempt was made to give the images panracial characteristics. Their heights are shown with respect to the spacecraft and are also given by a binary number stated in terms of the wavelength of the spectral line at 1,420 megahertz (21 centimeters).

These plaques are destined to be the longest-lived works of mankind. They will survive virtually unchanged for hundreds of millions, perhaps billions, of years in space. When plate tectonics has completely rearranged the continents, when all the present landforms on the earth have been ground down, when civilization has been profoundly transformed and when human beings may have evolved into some other kind of organism, these plaques will still exist. They will show that in the year we called 1973 there were organisms, portrayed on the plaques, that cared enough about their place in the hierarchy of all intelligent beings to share knowledge about themselves with others.

How much do we care? Enough to devote an appreciable effort with existing telescopes to search for life elsewhere in the universe? Enough to take a major step such as Project Cyclops that offers a greater chance of carrying us across the threshold, to finally communicate with a variety of extraterrestrial beings who, if they exist, would inevitably enrich mankind beyond imagination? The real question is not how, because we know how; the question is when. If enough of the beings of the earth cared, the threshold might be crossed within the lifetime of most of those alive today.

BIOGRAPHICAL NOTES AND BIBLIOGRAPHIES

1. The Red-Shift

The Author

ALLAN R. SANDAGE is astronomer at the Hale (formerly Mount Wilson and Palomar) Observatories. He attended Miami University in Ohio, entered the Navy in 1945, and completed his undergraduate work at the University of Illinois in 1948. He acquired his Ph.D. in astronomy at the California Institute of Technology in 1953, having meanwhile joined the staff of Mount Wilson and Palomar. In 1960 he was awarded the Helen Warner prize of the American Astronomical Society and in 1963 he won the Eddington Medal of the Royal Astronomical Society. In 1960 Sandage and Thomas A. Matthews were the first to isolate the quasars.

Bibliography

COSMOLOGY: A SEARCH FOR TWO NUMBERS. Allan R. Sandage. *Physics Today,* vol. 23, pages 34–41; February 1970.

THE REALM OF THE NEBULAE. Edwin Hubble. Yale University Press, 1936.

RED-SHIFTS AND MAGNITUDES OF EXTRA-GALACTIC NEBULAE. M. L. Humason, N. U. Mayall, and A. R. Sandage. *Astronomical Journal,* vol. 61, pages 97–162; April 1956.

THE TIME SCALE FOR CREATION. Allan R. Sandage. In *Galaxies and the Universe,* edited by Lodewijk Woltjer. Columbia University Press, 1968.

STEPS TOWARD THE HUBBLE CONSTANT, I: CALIBRATION OF THE LINEAR SIZES OF EXTRAGALACTIC H II REGIONS. Allan Sandage and G. A. Tammann. *Astrophysical Journal,* vol. 190, pages 525–538; June 15, 1974.

STEPS TOWARD THE HUBBLE CONSTANT, IV: GALAXIES IN THE GENERAL FIELD LEADING TO A CALIBRATION OF THE GALAXY LUMINOSITY CLASSES AND A FIRST HINT OF THE VALUE OF H_0. Allan Sandage and G. A. Tammann. *Astrophysical Journal,* vol. 194, pages 559–568; December 15, 1974.

2. The Evolutionary Universe

The Author

GEORGE GAMOW was professor of physics at the University of Colorado at the time of his death in 1968; he had just accepted that post in 1956, when this article was first published. Born in Odessa, Russia, in 1904, he studied nuclear physics at the University of Leningrad, where he received his doctoral degree in 1928. He also studied at the University of Copenhagen under Niels Bohr and at the University of Cambridge under Ernest Rutherford. In 1934 Gamow emigrated to the U.S. For over 20 years he was professor of physics at George Washington University. During this period Gamow found his interest turning from the atomic nucleus to astrophysics, the theory of the expanding universe and later to fundamental problems of biology, including molecular genetics and the synthesis of proteins. A quixotic streak, which enlivened his many popular books and articles, sometimes extended to his most serious scientific publications. On one occasion when he and Ralph A. Alpher were preparing a paper, they invited Hans Bethe of Cornell University to collaborate with them. The paper, which happened to concern the beginning of the universe, was therefore most appropriately authored by Alpher, Bethe and Gamow.

Bibliography

THE AGE OF CREATION. Allan R. Sandage. *Science Year 1968*, pages 56–69.

THE CREATION OF THE UNIVERSE. George Gamow. Viking, 1952.

FACT AND THEORY IN COSMOLOGY. G. C. McVittie. Eyre and Spottiswoode, 1961.

THE MYSTERY OF THE EXPANDING UNIVERSE. W. B. Bonner. Macmillan, 1964.

THE PRIMEVAL ATOM. Georges Lemaitre. D. Van Nostrand, 1950.

RELATIVISTIC COSMOLOGY. Wolfgang Rindler. *Physics Today*, vol. 20, pages 23–31; November 1967.

AN UNBOUND UNIVERSE? J. Richard Gott III, James E. Gunn, David N. Schramm, and Beatrice M. Tinsley. *Astrophysical Journal*, vol. 194, pages 543–553; December 15, 1974.

3. The Curvature of Space in a Finite Universe

The Author

J. J. CALLAHAN is associate professor of mathematics at Smith College. A 1962 graduate of Marist College, he went on to obtain his Ph.D. in mathematics from New York University. He was a Benjamin Peirce lecturer at Harvard University for three years before joining the faculty at Smith in 1970. His primary mathematical interests, he notes, are "differential analysis and catastrophe theory and its applications. The themes of this article—geometry and the history of mathematics—are things I am interested in teaching, but I am not a specialist in them." The article developed, he adds, "out of an attempt to explain Einstein's concept of a finite but unbounded space to my nonscientific colleagues at Smith. They found it tough going, and some simply dismissed a finite universe as impossible, because Kant had done so when he studied the question 300 years ago. A sabbatical this past year at the University of Warwick gave me a chance to read what Kant said about space. He does indeed epitomize the commonsense view, which Einstein (and Riemann before him) shattered. I was unable, however, to find any satisfactory explanation of just how the old and the new ideas fit together, so I attempted one myself."

Bibliography

EINSTEIN'S GENERAL THEORY OF RELATIVITY. Max Born in *Einstein's Theory of Relativity*. Dover Publications, Inc., 1962.

PARADISE. Dante Alighieri, translated by Dorothy L. Sayers and Barbara Reynolds in *The Comedy of Dante Alighieri*. Penguin Books, 1962.

MATHEMATICAL THOUGHT FROM ANCIENT TO MODERN TIMES. Morris Kline. Oxford University Press, 1972.

GRAVITATION. Charles W. Misner, Kip S. Thorne and John Archibald Wheeler. W. H. Freeman and Company, 1973.

4. Cosmology before and after Quasars

The Author

DENNIS W. SCIAMA is professor in the Department of Astrophysics at Oxford University. In 1967, when he wrote this review, he held a Peterhouse Fellowship and Lectureship in the Department of Applied Mathematics and Theoretical Physics, Cambridge University. There he built up a group of graduate and post-doctoral students working on general relativity, cosmology, and astrophysics. Born in Manchester, England, in 1926, he was a student of the great theoretical physicist P. A. M. Dirac, and received his Ph.D. degree from Cambridge University in 1952. In that same year he obtained a Research Fellowship at Trinity College, Cambridge, and since then has been a member of the Institute for Advanced Study at Princeton and an Agassiz Fellow at Harvard University.

Bibliography

COSMOLOGY AFTER HALF A CENTURY. William H. McCrea. *Science*, vol. 160, pages 1295–1299; June 21, 1968.

THE COUNTS OF RADIO SOURCES. M. Ryle. *Annual Review of Astronomy and Astrophysics*, vol. 6, pages 249–266; 1968.

THE EVOLUTION OF THE UNIVERSE. Hong-Yee Chiu. *Science Journal*, vol. 4, pages 33–38; August 1968.

THE PHYSICAL FOUNDATIONS OF GENERAL RELATIVITY. D. W. Sciama. Doubleday Anchor, 1969.

THE STRUCTURE OF THE UNIVERSE. E. L. Schatzman. McGraw-Hill, 1968.

COSMOLOGY TODAY. William H. McCrea. *American Scientist*, vol. 58, pages 521–527; Sept.–Oct. 1970.

5. The Cosmic Background Radiation

The Author

ADRIAN WEBSTER is at the Mullard Radio Astronomy Observatory of the University of Cambridge as a research fellow of the Royal Commission of the Exhibition of 1851 and a research fellow of Clare College. He obtained his bachelor's degree in theoretical physics at Cambridge in 1967 and his Ph.D. in radio astronomy there in 1972. For the two academic years beginning in 1971 he

was a research fellow at the Miller Institute for Basic Research in Science at the University of California, Berkeley.

Bibliography

MODERN COSMOLOGY. Dennis W. Sciama. Cambridge University Press, 1971.

OBSERVATIONAL COSMOLOGY. M. S. Longair. *Reports on Progress in Physics,* vol. 34, pages 1125–1248; 1971.

GRAVITATION AND COSMOLOGY: PRINCIPLES AND APPLICATIONS OF THE GENERAL THEORY OF RELATIVITY. Steven Weinberg. Wiley, 1972.

EPPUR SI MUOVE. D. W. Sciama. *Comments on Astrophysics and Space Physics,* vol. 4, pages 35–39; March–April, 1972.

6. The Evolution of Quasars

The Authors

MAARTEN SCHMIDT is professor of astronomy at the California Institute of Technology; FRANCIS BELLO is associate editor of *Scientific American.* Schmidt is also a member of the staff of the Hale (formerly the Mount Wilson and Palomar) Observatories and a staff member of the Owens Valley Radio Observatory. Born in the Netherlands, he took his Ph.D. at the University of Leiden in 1956. In the same year he came to the U.S. as a Carnegie Fellow; in 1959 he moved to Cal Tech.

Bibliography

QUASI-STELLAR OBJECTS. Geoffrey Burbidge and Margaret Burbidge. Freeman, 1967.

SPACE DISTRIBUTION AND LUMINOSITY FUNCTIONS OF QUASI-STELLAR RADIO SOURCES. Maarten Schmidt. *Astrophysical Journal,* vol. 151, pages 393–409; February, 1968.

ON THE NATURE OF FAINT BLUE OBJECTS IN HIGH GALACTIC LATITUDES, II: SUMMARY OF PHOTOMETRIC RESULTS FOR 301 OBJECTS IN SEVEN SURVEY FIELDS. Allan Sandage and Willem J. Luyten. *Astrophysical Journal,* vol. 155, pages 913–918; March, 1969.

SPACE DISTRIBUTION AND THE LUMINOSITY FUNCTIONS OF QUASARS. Maarten Schmidt, *Astrophysical Journal,* vol. 162, pages 371–379; November, 1970.

THE REDSHIFT CONTROVERSY. George B. Field, Halton Arp, and John N. Bahcall. Benjamin, 1973.

7. The Origin of Galaxies

The Authors

MARTIN J. REES is Plumian Professor of Astronomy and Experimental Philosophy at the University of Cambridge. His master's degree in mathematics and Ph.D. in astrophysics are both from Cambridge. His interests include cosmology, diffuse matter in space, and theoretical radio astronomy. JOSEPH SILK is Professor of Astronomy at the University of California, Berkeley. He was a Cambridge undergraduate and obtained his Ph.D. at Harvard University.

Bibliography

THE BLACK-BODY RADIATION CONTENT OF THE UNIVERSE AND THE FORMATION OF GALAXIES. P. J. E. Peebles. *Astrophysical Journal,* vol. 142, No. 4, pages 1317–1326; November 15, 1965.

THE CASE FOR A HIERARCHICAL COSMOLOGY. G. de Vaucouleurs. *Science,* vol. 167, pages 1203–1213; February 27, 1970.

COSMIC BLACK-BODY RADIATION AND GALAXY FORMATION. Joseph Silk. *Astrophysical Journal,* vol. 151, pages 459–471; February 1968.

THE FORMATION AND EARLY DYNAMICAL HISTORY OF GALAXIES. G. B. Field. In *Stars and Stellar Systems, Vol. 9: Galaxies and the Universe,* edited by A. Sandage and M. Sandage. University of Chicago Press, 1976.

THE FORMATION OF STARS AND GALAXIES: UNIFIED HYPOTHESES. David Layzer. In *Annual Review of Astronomy and Astrophysics,* Vol. 2, edited by Leo Goldberg, Armin J. Deutsch, and David Layzer. Annual Review, 1964.

SOME CURRENT PROBLEMS IN GALAXY FORMATION. M. J. Rees. In *Italian Physical Society: Proceedings of the International School of Physics "Enrico Fermi," Course 47: General Relativity and Cosmology,* edited by B. K. Sachs. Academic Press, 1971.

8. The Search for Black Holes

The Author

KIP S. THORNE is professor of theoretical physics at the California Institute of Technology and adjunct professor of physics at the University of Utah. He graduated from Cal Tech in 1962 and received his master's (1963) and Ph.D. (1965) degrees from Princeton University.

Bibliography

BEYOND THE BLACK HOLE. John A. Wheeler. *Science Year 1973,* pages 76–89.

GRAVITATION. Charles W. Misner, Kip S. Thorne, and John Archibald Wheeler. Freeman, 1973.

BLACK HOLE EXPLOSIONS? S. W. Hawking. *Nature,* vol. 248, pages 30–31; March 1, 1974.

9. The Quantum Mechanics of Black Holes

The Author

S. W. HAWKING is a theoretical physicist at the University of Cambridge. He was born in Oxford in 1942 and was graduated from the University of Oxford in 1962. He did his graduate work at Cambridge on general relativity, working under the direction of D. W. Sciama. He is currently a fellow of Gonville and Caius College at Cambridge and reader in gravitational physics in the university's department of applied mathematics and theoretical physics. In 1974–1975 he was Sherman Fairchild Distinguished Scholar at the California Institute of Technology. A Fellow of the Royal Society, he has received a number of honors in the past two years, including the Eddington Medal of the Royal Astronomical Society and the Dannie Heineman Prize for Mathematical Physics of the American Physical Society and the American Institute of Physics. Since 1962, when he began his graduate work at Cambridge, Hawkins has suffered from a progressive nervous disease that has confined him to a wheelchair for the past seven years. "Fortunately," he writes, "theoretical physics is one of the few fields in which this is not a serious handicap."

Bibliography

THE FOUR LAWS OF BLACK HOLE MECHANICS. J. M. Bardeen, B. Carter and S. W. Hawking in *Communications in Mathematical Physics,* vol. 31, no. 2, pages 161–170; 1973.

BLACK HOLES AND ENTROPY. Jacob D. Bekenstein in *Physical Review D,* vol. 7, no. 8, pages 2333–2346; April 15, 1973.

PARTICLE CREATION BY BLACK HOLES. S. W. Hawking in *Communications in Mathematical Physics,* vol. 43, no. 3, pages 199–220; 1975.

BLACK HOLES AND THERMODYNAMICS. S. W. Hawking in *Physical Review D,* vol. 13, no. 2, pages 191–197; January 15, 1976.

10. Will the Universe Expand Forever?

The Authors

J. RICHARD GOTT III, JAMES E. GUNN, DAVID N. SCHRAMM and BEATRICE M. TINSLEY began their collaboration in 1974, while Gott and Gunn were at the California Institute of Technology and Schramm and Tinsley were at the University of Texas at Austin. The key connection came when Gott traveled to Austin to give a talk and the four realized, in Tinsley's words, "that pieces of evidence from our various research specialties could be fitted together into a surprisingly clear case for an open universe. There were several subsequent visits between Texas and California and many long telephone conversations while the work on our joint paper for *The Astrophysical Journal* was in progress, but it was not until the summer of 1975 that all of us actually got together. Then, at the Institute of Astronomy of the University of Cambridge, we used the material from our published paper to write (with the literary assistance of Rosemary W. Gunn) this article for *Scientific American.*" Gott, who was graduated *summa cum laude* from Harvard University in 1969 and obtained his Ph.D. in astrophysics from Princeton University in 1972, was recently appointed to the Princeton faculty. Gunn, a graduate of Rice University, received his Ph.D. from Cal Tech in 1965. He is now professor of astronomy at Cal Tech and a staff member of the Hale Observatories. Schramm acquired his undergraduate degree from the Massachusetts Institute of Technology in 1963 and his doctorate from Cal Tech in 1971. (That same year he won the national Greco-Roman wrestling championship.) He is currently associate professor of astronomy and astrophysics at the Enrico Fermi Institute of the University of Chicago. Tinsley has an M.S. in physics from the University of Canterbury in New Zealand (1963) and a Ph.D. in astronomy from the University of Texas (1967). She is now associate professor of astronomy at Yale University.

Bibliography

MODERN COSMOLOGY. D. W. Sciama. Cambridge University Press, 1971.

THE AGE OF THE ELEMENTS. David N. Schramm in *Scientific American,* vol. 230, no. 1, pages 69–77; January, 1974.

WHAT CAN DEUTERIUM TELL US? David N. Schramm and Robert V. Wagoner in *Physics Today,* vol. 27, no. 12, pages 41–47; December, 1974.

AN UNBOUND UNIVERSE? J. Richard Gott III, James E. Gunn, David N. Schramm and Beatrice M. Tinsley in *The Astrophysical Journal,* vol. 194, pages 543–553; December 15, 1974.

11. The Search for Extraterrestrial Intelligence

The Authors

CARL SAGAN and FRANK DRAKE are professors of astronomy at Cornell University, where Sagan is director of the Laboratory for Planetary Studies and Drake is director of the National Astronomy and Ionosphere Center. "In returning from the International

Astronomical Union meetings in Sydney in 1973," they write, "we spent some days skin-diving in Bora Bora in Tahiti, where our *Scientific American* article was first devised. Since Polynesia had been settled by voyagers crossing thousands of kilometers of ocean, we thought a two-kilometer journey by outrigger canoe would be a modest homage to those intrepid explorers, particularly since we were assured that such canoes are unsinkable. We discovered that this is true; when they are swamped, they only sink as far as the shoulders of the passenger, and the outrigger affords some discouragement to those sharks that are to starboard. The experience confirmed our belief that radio communication is easier than direct contact."

Bibliography

WHAT SHALL WE SAY TO MARS? H. W. Nieman and C. Wells Nieman in *Scientific American*, vol. 122, no. 12, page 298; March 20, 1920.

PROJECT CYCLOPS. B. M. Oliver et al. National Aeronautics and Space Administration, Publication CR-114445; 1972.

COMMUNICATION WITH EXTRATERRESTRIAL INTELLIGENCE. Edited by Carl Sagan. The MIT Press, 1973.

INDEX